HISTORY OF AMERICA:
Challenge and Crisis

VOLUME II

Reconstruction to Present

HISTORY OF AMERICA
Challenge and Crisis

VOLUME II
Reconstruction to Present

CHARLES S. MILLER
DEPARTMENT OF HISTORY
CHAFFEY COLLEGE

NATALIE JOY WARD
LOS ANGELES

JOHN WILEY & SONS, INC.
NEW YORK · LONDON · SYDNEY · TORONTO

Copyright © 1971 by John Wiley and Sons, Inc.

All rights reserved. Published simultaneously in Canada.

No part of this book may be reproduced by any means, nor transmitted, nor translated into a machine language without the written permission of the publisher.

Library of Congress Catalogue Card Number: 73-132853

ISBN 0-471-60518-2

Printed in the United States of America

10 9 8 7 6 5 4 3 2 1

To Mac and Bus

PREFACE

The purpose of this textbook is to stimulate its readers to think, and to this end we have tried to provide a framework, a series of topics, a set of concepts upon which students can hang facts and insights about history, their nation, and themselves. Obviously, no single text can cover all that needs to be taught about United States history; we have therefore selected the elements in each period of time that seem to us to be the most relevant to the world of today. We have followed the story of America's growth in more or less chronological order, however, hopefully violating the sequence of events in no serious way so that the reader may understand the changes wrought through the passage of time. The interrelatedness of past and present and the multiplicity of causes in history have also been stressed. We have been concerned with all aspects of society rather than merely with political events, and we have constantly tried to describe the United States in its world setting.

We recognize that this is a highly personal book and hope that our interest and our concern about the nation both past and present will add a dimension of involvement that will encourage readers to search for their own interpretations of history as a living, breathing part of their lives. If students finish the book with a desire to learn more about American history, we have succeeded.

Many people have helped to make this book possible. We should like to thank our colleagues for their valuable contributions and criticisms. Our editor-in-California, Johns Harrington, Editor of

School Publications, Los Angeles City Schools, corrected our prose and kept us from literary excess. Dr. W. Henry Cooke, Professor Emeritus of the Claremont Graduate School, was our senior adviser. Professors Robert E. Smith and Donald E. Bartell of Chaffey College worked long and hard on illustrations and maps. William R. Simonsen of Chaffey Union High School, Ontario, California, and Gerald E. Martin, Professor of English at Chaffey College, read the manuscript.

Margaret E. Doyle, Phillip Ehrnstein, and Richard Ward assisted with research for various parts of the book, and so too did the staff of the Chaffey College Library and Robert Holcolm, librarian at Van Nuys Junior High School.

Our particular thanks go to the able and perceptive secretaries who worked with us throughout the years—Eva Ochoa, who could read our handwriting, and Ann McCleary, who read, corrected, and typed our material.

Most important of all, we wish to express appreciation to our spouses for their support and encouragement. Without their patience we could never have finished.

1971

CHARLES S. MILLER
NATALIE JOY WARD

CONTENTS

UNIT V   *The Uncertain Resurrection:*
WOULD THE REAL AMERICAN PLEASE STAND UP?   1

CHAPTER 17   Segregation and Immigration   7
     Aftermath of Civil War   9
     The Failure of Radical Reconstruction   11
     Whites Regain Supremacy   21
     The Growth of Cities   24
     Immigrants for a Growing Economy   25
     America—Melting Pot or Mosaic?   31
     Suggested Readings   32

CHAPTER 18   The Second Frontier   35
     The Changing Nature of the Frontier   37
     The Mining Frontier   41
     "The Lagging Rails"   44
     The End of the Indian Nations   46
     The Cattleman and the Cowboy   51

	The Farmer and the West	54
	The Last Farm Frontier	56
	Suggested Readings	59
CHAPTER 19	**The Second Industrial Revolution**	**61**
	Background for an Industrial Economy	63
	The New Industrialism	64
	Industrial Climate	72
	Problems of the Farmer	79
	Prologue to Reform	82
	Suggested Readings	82
CHAPTER 20	**Political Expediency and Self-Interest**	**85**
	Realities of the Post-Civil War Period	87
	Politics and Self-Interest	90
	Revival of the Two-Party System	93
	Presidents and Legislation of the Gilded Age	96
	Suggested Readings	105
CHAPTER 21	**Foreign Affairs at Ebb Tide, 1849–1890**	**107**
	The Last Spasms of Early Expansionism, 1849–1860	109
	First Contacts with Asia	112
	Diplomacy during the Civil War	115
	Era of Fulfillment, 1865–1890	118
	Suggested Readings	121
CHAPTER 22	**Foundations of a New Social Order, 1890–1909**	**123**
	Dissipation and Revival of the Spirit of Reform, 1865–1890	125
	The Agrarian and Industrial Strife of the 1890's	129
	The Progressive Movement	135
	Suggested Readings	144
UNIT VI	*First in War, First in Peace:* BROTHER, CAN YOU SPARE A DIME?	**147**
CHAPTER 23	**Building a Progressive Society, 1909–1920**	153

x   Contents

	Climax of Political Progressivism, 1909–1917	155
	Cultural and Social Changes, 1909–1917	162
	Flaws and Paradoxes of Progressivism	167
	Suggested Readings	172

CHAPTER 24 **The End of Continentalism, 1890–1914**   175
- The "New Expansionism"   177
- The Surge of Internationalism, 1901–1914   187
- Suggested Readings   199

CHAPTER 25 **The Climax and Ebb of Internationalism, 1914–1920**   201
- Outbreak of War in 1914   203
- The Years of American Neutrality   210
- Entry of the United States into the War   214
- Constructing the Peace   218
- Suggested Readings   231

CHAPTER 26 **The Era of Complacency, 1919–1929**   233
- Complacency, Illusion, and Disillusionment   236
- Economics—Catalyst of Change   246
- Politics—The Mirror of the Twenties   249
- Suggested Readings   254

CHAPTER 27 **The Depression Decade, 1929–1939**   257
- Stock Market Crash   259
- The Deepening Depression   261
- The Roosevelt Years   265
- Suggested Readings   278

CHAPTER 28 **Internationalism in Retreat, 1921–1939**   281
- Postwar Withdrawal and Drift   283
- Continued Internationalism   287
- The Emergence of Fascism   289
- The Beginning of the Reckoning   300
- Suggested Readings   304

UNIT VII	*Time of Trial, Time of Hope:* WHAT STEPS ON THE EDGE OF EXTINCTION?		**307**
CHAPTER 29	From Isolation to World Leadership, 1939–1946		313
	Prologue to War in Europe		315
	The Nazi Blitzkrieg		317
	The United States in the Second World War		327
	Final Campaigns, 1943–1945		336
	Suggested Readings		343
CHAPTER 30	Competitive Coexistence, 1946–1961		347
	Postwar Settlements, 1945–1946		349
	The Cold War during the Truman Era		355
	The Cold War during the Eisenhower Years		364
	Suggested Readings		373
CHAPTER 31	The Truman and Eisenhower Years, 1945–1961		375
	Prelude—The Transition from War to Peace		378
	The Truman Years		380
	The Eisenhower Years		392
	Election of 1960		401
	Suggested Readings		405
CHAPTER 32	Due to Circumstances . . .		407
	Camelot and Catastrophe		410
	"All the Way with LBJ"		418
	"Nixon's the One"		426
	Suggested Readings		433
APPENDICES			
	The Declaration of Independence		435
	The Constitution of the United States of America		437
	Admission of the States to the Union		449
	Growth of United States Population and Area		450
	Justices of the United States Supreme Court		451
	Presidents and Vice Presidents		452
	Presidential Elections		453
	Public Debt of the United States, 1855–1969		457
	Employees in Nonagricultural Establishments, 1920–1970		458
INDEX			459

LIST OF MAPS

Reconstructing the South, 1865–1877	16
The Indian Frontier, 1866–1875	48
West to East and South to North	52
The Growth of American Railroads, 1869–1900	66
American Expansion into the Pacific	185
Southward into the Caribbean, 1899–1917	191
Power Alignment during World War I	208
Changes in European Boundaries as a Result of World War I	226
Japanese Expansion, 1931–1940	292
Axis Expansion, 1938–1942	296
Allied Strategy in Europe and Africa, 1942–1945	331
American Strategy in the Pacific, 1942–1945	340
Territorial Changes in Europe as a Result of World War II	351
Territorial Changes in the Pacific as a Result of World War II	354
The Iron Curtain Dividing Europe	357
Southeast Asia, 1970	427

Maps by JOHN V. MORRIS

HISTORY OF AMERICA:
Challenge and Crisis

VOLUME II
Reconstruction to Present

UNIT V

The Uncertain Resurrection:

WOULD THE REAL AMERICAN PLEASE STAND UP?

"Gold Hunter on His Way to California via St. Louis," by H. R. Robinson

CALIFORNIA HISTORICAL SOCIETY

"View of St. Louis, from Lucas Place"

CHICAGO HISTORICAL SOCIETY

THE SMITHSONIAN INSTITUTION

Currier and Ives lithograph, 1868 — NEW YORK PUBLIC LIBRARY PRINTS DIVISION

"The Bosses of the Senate," by Joseph Keppler — LIBRARY OF CONGRESS

"Outward Bound, the Quay of Dublin," lithograph by T. H. Maguire after T. Nichol, 1854

NEW YORK HISTORICAL SOCIETY, NEW YORK CITY

National	International
1868 IMPEACHMENT OF JOHNSON; FOURTEENTH AMENDMENT RATIFIED	**1868** MEIJI RESTORATION IN JAPAN
1869 COMPLETION OF FIRST TRANSCONTINENTAL RAILROAD; BLACK FRIDAY PANIC	**1869** OPENING OF SUEZ CANAL
	1870 FRANCO-PRUSSIAN WAR
1871 EXPOSÉ OF TWEED RING	**1871** GERMAN EMPIRE ESTABLISHED
1872 CREDIT MOBILIER SCANDAL	
1873 PANIC AND DEPRESSION	
1876 DISPUTED ELECTION, TILDEN VERSUS HAYES	**1876** QUEEN VICTORIA PROCLAIMED EMPRESS OF INDIA
1877 END OF RECONSTRUCTION, LAST FEDERAL TROOPS LEAVE THE SOUTH	**1877** RUSSO-TURKISH WAR
1878 BLAND-ALLISON ACT	**1878** CONGRESS OF BERLIN
1879 STANDARD OIL TRUST FORMED	**1879** ZULU WAR IN SOUTH AFRICA
	1882 FORMATION OF THE TRIPLE ALLIANCE; BRITISH OCCUPY EGYPT
1886 AMERICAN FEDERATION OF LABOR FOUNDED	
1887 INTERSTATE COMMERCE ACT	
1890 SHERMAN ANTI-TRUST ACT	**1890** BISMARCK RESIGNS AS GERMAN CHANCELLOR
1892 POPULIST PARTY FORMED	
1893 PANIC AND DEPRESSION	
1894 PULLMAN STRIKE AND COXEY'S ARMY	**1894** FRANCO-RUSSIAN ALLIANCE; OUTBREAK OF WAR BETWEEN CHINA AND JAPAN

CHAPTER 17

Segregation and Immigration

*G**ive me your tired, your poor,*
Your huddled masses yearning to breathe free,
The wretched refuse of your teeming shore,
Send these, the homeless, tempest-tossed, to me:
I lift my lamp beside the golden door.

EMMA LAZARUS, *The New Colossus;*
Inscription for the Statue of Liberty

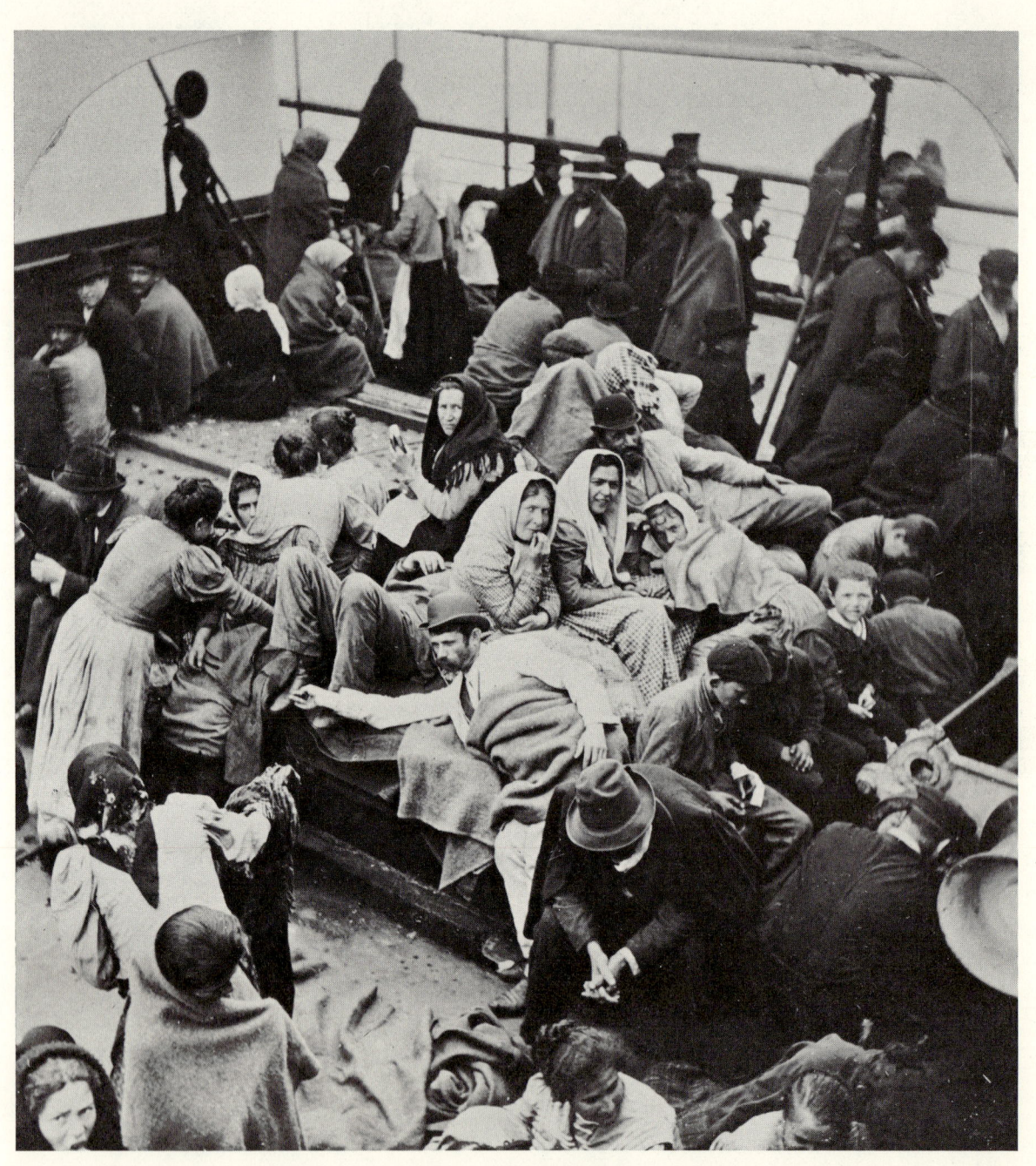

PHOTOGRAPH BY WILLIAM H. ROW, 1902, LIBRARY OF CONGRESS

AFTERMATH OF CIVIL WAR

THE SURRENDER OF THE SOUTH BROUGHT AN END to declared warfare, but peace was illusory. Neither North nor South had escaped the mental and emotional debilitation of Civil War, for the conflict had been too immediate and too close. The energies and hope necessary for rebuilding and new starts would be slow to kindle. Even men who were eager to forgive and forget were confronted with deep and lasting changes in their way of life and their relations with others.

Destruction and Dislocation in the South

The entire society of the South had been fragmented, and its people faced a future haunted by defeat and despair. The returning men in gray, already bitter in vanquishment, found conditions at home even worse than they had feared. It seemed that their whole world had come to an end. In the sections where the war had been fought, the physical destruction was devastating. The labor system was completely disrupted, and only a few whites had any hope that free blacks could be employed to rebuild the collapsed economy. The financial facts were even gloomier. Southern banks and individual investors were ruined, for they had patriotically bought Confederate bonds which had now lost all their value. Confederate money was equally worthless. The real wealth of the South, its fertile land, lay fallow, for there was no money to buy seed, replace tools, or restore farm buildings. The vast acres could not even be sold, for there were no buyers.

Besides the loss in personal property and the disruption of the plantation system, the institutions of social control no longer functioned. Churches and colleges had been destroyed or abandoned, and the school system and agencies of law enforcement had for the most part ceased to exist. Bands of marauders preyed on the helpless population. Factories were largely inoperative because equipment could not be repaired; postal service was two years in returning to normal.

The most abrasive question, however, was

what could be done with four million newly freed blacks. The white Southerner was completely unprepared to change his attitude toward those who had been his slaves. The belief that blacks were properly chattels and would respond only to repression was deeply engrained in most white men. Although there were exceptions, most planters were unwilling to accept the freedman as a potential citizen and attempted to keep the blacks in slavery as long as possible, even though a proclamation had arbitrarily changed their status.

The blacks suffered extreme dislocation and discontent. Many had wandered away from the old plantation, glad to be free but with little thought for the future. Thousands trudged the highways, all their wordly possessions tied in bundles on their heads, looking for land and for food and shelter which they hoped would be provided them, though they knew not by whom. There was talk of "forty acres and a mule" for every freedman. Some blacks believed that all whites would be forced to leave a section of the South and that this area would be divided up for them. These notions encouraged them to go "down country" toward Charleston or other centers where the Union army had camped. Although a fair number of freedmen remained on the home plantation, most took to the roads and woods. Tens of thousands of bewildered and friendless blacks died of starvation and disease during their first two years of freedom.

The presence of this hopeless horde reinforced the old fears of the outnumbered whites, for the balance between the races had not been changed by the war. In many sections of the South the whites were outnumbered three to one. Yet most Southern whites remained in their localities or returned to them and faced the overwhelming task of restoring order to their shattered lives. The more responsible realized that they must dismiss thoughts of their lost patrimony and repair and rebuild their homes and places of business to the degree that they were able. A few even accepted the idea of free blacks and began to work out private arrangements with their former slaves so that agriculture could begin again to a limited extent. But many rebels, stung by defeat, brooded away their days and plotted how to restore their traditional way of life, which seemed even more romantic and desirable now that it had vanished.

Dissension and Divisive Growth in the North

Although the victory belonged to them, Northerners discovered that their lives too had been racked by war. The men in blue returned home tired, sick, and wounded. Many veterans had endured extreme physical suffering and deprivation, especially those who had been confined in the worst of the Southern prison camps. Ex-soldiers often had difficulty finding work, for new immigrants had joined the labor force, and new machines had replaced unskilled workers in certain industries, particularly textile manufacturing. Then too it was obvious that some citizens had benefited from the conflict, including those who had been able to hire replacements and so had avoided military duty themselves. Men whose only contribution to the struggle for the Union had been the blood of others were often the ones who had gained the most. The national emphasis seemed to be shifting. The self-seeking, aggressive posture of business and industrial leaders pervaded the North. This change in spirit was not lost upon the returning troops, who quickly acquired the new "get-rich-quick" attitudes and sought the opportunities offered by the booming economy of the postwar era.

A rage for retribution seemed to still compassion and understanding. The hope tendered by Lincoln that the Union could be generous in victory was soon dispelled, for many Northerners had gone to war to punish the South for its sin of slavery. These men did not attribute their overwhelming military victory to greater economic strength but to God, who obviously had been on their side. Their determination to impose their will on the defeated South, together with their ambitions, prejudice, and high moral purpose, created a climate ripe for harsh and hasty measures.

End of Major Role of Sectionalism

Whatever the immediate emotional climate, it was evident that the states were united once and for all. The idea of "one nation, indivisible" had been clearly established, even though the people of the North and South continued to have separate goals and ambitions and to voice loyalty to their own parts of the country. The South of course had special reason to feel a beleaguered and united separateness, but the Civil War had permanently disposed of the compact theory of the Union. Americans began to identify themselves again as citizens of the United States. Political issues were no longer sectional but concerned problems of the farm, the factory, and the city. In the years following the Civil War, the populations of all parts of the nation became more uniform, for industrialization characterized the era and pervaded all areas of the country. The people of the South slowly began to find their place in the modern industrial world, and as they did so their political interests became more like those of citizens in other sections of the nation.

THE FAILURE OF RADICAL RECONSTRUCTION

Northerners and Southerners alike wanted the nation rebuilt after the destruction of the Civil War, but they could not agree on the way to accomplish the task. Some congressional leaders from each section were willing to compromise, but public opinion and the Radical Republicans with retribution on their minds would not always allow the citizenry a rational approach to "reconstruction" or rebuilding. Since the North was the victor, its leaders determined the methods, but Southern radicals were able to employ delaying tactics which changed the direction of many of the programs initiated.

Problems and Approaches

While the Civil War was still being fought, Union leaders were already planning the steps to be taken when their forces defeated the Confederate armies. Perhaps the major problem considered and one of the first acted upon—because it was to the North's advantage to settle the question—was the status of Negroes. The drive for their emancipation was of course basically humanitarian, but Northerners were well aware of the economic damage—over two billion dollars in property loss alone—that freeing the slaves would inflict on the South. The cause of the Confederacy too would suffer in world opinion if the North could be recognized as a champion of freedom. When President Lincoln signed the Emancipation Proclamation, he understood very well both the moral and expedient values of the document.

Three other important questions had to be answered by the leaders who faced the task of rebuilding the nation. First, should the rebellious states be treated as conquered territory or as integral parts of the nation whose relationship now had to be clarified? Second, should the freed slaves be granted voting privileges? Third, by what means could the economic confusion and social upset created by the war be eliminated?

Lincoln's Position. Never self-righteous, Lincoln made it clear even before the Union victory that retribution was not his purpose and that the South could expect him to help "bind up the nation's wounds." In his second inaugural address he pointed out failures on both sides and pledged to proceed "with charity for all." After the South admitted defeat at Appomattox, Lincoln again urged that it be treated with moderation. Then Booth's bullet ended Lincoln's attempts to enunciate, and put into effect, a mature, rational, and human approach to reconstruction.

The Radicals. Many Republicans had disagreed with Lincoln's moderate position, preferring to treat the South as "vanquished enemy" and to punish Southerners for their "sins." Thaddeus Stevens, a congressman from Pennsylvania, hated the South and believed it had given up its rights by rebelling against the Union. "There are no longer Southern states," he said, but "conquered provinces." Other Republicans, like Senator Charles Sumner of Massachusetts, were idealistically concerned over the welfare of the Negroes but held no animosity for Southerners. Republican party leaders of all persuasions, however, shared the partisan desire to retain control of the federal government, which had been in Republican hands throughout the Civil War. They feared that if Southern legislators were allowed back in Congress, they would use their votes to reinforce the power of the Democratic party, as they had before the conflict.

For all these reasons—to punish the South, to aid the Negro, and to control postwar politics—the radical bloc of Republicans sought to delay the reentry of the Southern states into the Union and advocated a program of reconstruction that would completely change the South's way of life. Stevens wanted to break the aristocratic planters and help the blacks by redistributing land to the freedmen; Sumner urged Congress to grant Negroes the vote. Many Northern interests, including industrial leaders and financiers, supported the Radical Republicans. Ordinary citizens were urged to accept their position by campaigners who "waved the bloody shirt" and continually reminded the public of the "wickedness and bloodthirsty behavior" of Southerners.

Congressional versus Presidential Power. In addition to disagreements about how to treat the South, there was uncertainty about who had the power to deal with the seceded states.

In Lincoln's view, which was diametrically opposed to the congressional position, the President possessed the authority because the Southern states had never left the Union. Southerners could be restored to citizenship through presidential pardon. Lincoln wanted to be generous in granting amnesty; in December 1863 he had declared by proclamation that he stood ready to recognize as legal the Southern state governments that freed slaves within their borders, provided ten per cent of the population pledged loyalty to the Union. Louisiana and Arkansas complied with these conditions in 1864, but their efforts to gain recognition met congressional resistance.

Congress insisted that it and not the President had the authority to prescribe terms and declined to be lenient. On July 4, 1864 it passed the Wade-Davis Bill with the impossible requirement that a *majority* of each state's population must swear both future and *past* loyalty to the Union before establishing a state government. When Lincoln pocket-vetoed this bill, congressmen recognized an opportunity to decry the powers that Lincoln had gained through wartime pressures and attacked him for being too lenient toward the South, too autocratic in his other policies. Their Wade-Davis Manifesto issued in August 1864 clearly indicated their belief that Lincoln's veto had usurped their power to determine whether and how the Southern states should be readmitted. But then the November election was upon the nation, and Congress took no further action until it refused to seat members-elect from Louisiana in February 1865.

Johnson and Lincoln's Program. Lincoln had chosen Andrew Johnson to run with him in 1864 for the vice presidency because he was from a border state, was committed to the Union cause, and had served as an admirable military governor of Tennessee since 1862, when the state fell to Union forces. Johnson was a man of the people, born in desperate poverty like Lincoln and raised with no formal schooling. He was taught to read by his wife. Johnson

The Uncertain Resurrection

was not a member of the Southern aristocracy, but he had become wealthy enough to own some slaves and shared the segregationist views of slaveowners. Although he lacked social polish and had a bad temper, Johnson was scrupulously honest and intelligent. He recognized the nation's many problems, even though he was better able to address the voters of his own Tennessee than he was the Congress. Conditions were so critical, however, that even a president with superhuman tact and skill would have had difficulty in dealing with the crises facing the nation.

To the disappointment of the Radical Republicans, Lincoln's death did not change the plans for reconstruction, for President Johnson sought to carry out the major parts of Lincoln's program. Early in May 1865 he recognized the governments that Lincoln had accepted, those formed by ten per cent of the people in the states of Louisiana, Tennessee, Arkansas, and Virginia. Then at the end of the month he granted amnesty to citizens of the seven remaining states who would take a loyalty oath. Those who had been important Confederate military officers and officials, and Southerners who still retained considerable property, however, had to apply personally to the President for pardon. Johnson appointed local provisional governors to help the newly accepted electorates officially abolish slavery and repudiate secession, establish new state governments, and elect representatives to Congress. By the end of the year most Southern states had qualified. Texas, the one exception, met the requirements by April 1866. Johnson triumphantly announced the restoration of the Union, and Southern representatives were ready to rejoin their Northern counterparts in the Congress of December 1865.

But again the Senate and House of Representatives were unwilling to accept actions of a President. A joint congressional committee met to judge qualification of Southern representatives and, after deliberating from December 1865 to June 1866, recommended that the Southern representatives not be seated. The congressmen reaffirmed their position that Congress, not the President, had the authority to control reconstruction.

Protection of the Negro

The Freedmen's Bureau. The Thirteenth Amendment introduced in Congress early in 1864 to implement Lincoln's Emancipation Proclamation was not ratified by the necessary twenty-seven states until December 18, 1865, but Congress moved in the meantime to establish a temporary agency to deal with the problems of the freedmen. In March 1865 the Freedmen's Bureau was created and soon sent hundreds of agents into the South charged with aiding and educating the Negroes. The agents were also to assign lands abandoned in the South—in parcels of no more than forty acres and for reasonable rents—to refugees and freedmen.

In many ways the status of the freedmen was worse than it had been when they were slaves. They were often hungry and homeless, and after lifetimes of servitude they were also uneducated and unwilling to accept responsibility. Because the Negroes had no money with which to buy land and engage in farming, the only occupation they knew, they usually had little choice but to go back to work for the planters as farm laborers. The blacks were not anxious to perform the same menial tasks they had toiled at as slaves.

The Freedmen's Bureau was therefore extremely important to the Negro in 1865—more important perhaps than his right to vote. The Bureau, with Johnson's qualified support, began a program that promised real help. Daily food, clothing, living quarters, and employment were dispensed to the destitute. Negroes in less desperate straits were taught to read and encouraged to think of themselves as worthy citizens.

In February 1866 Congress attempted to enlarge the powers of the Freedmen's Bureau, which had at first cared only for the newly liberated freedmen. The Bureau was to be empowered to try, under military law, "those who would deprive any freedman of his civil rights." Johnson vetoed this bill—he had come to believe that the future of the blacks should be left to the state legislatures—but it was passed over his veto in July 1866. As the bureau came increasingly under the control of Radical Republicans, it lost favor with Southerners.

Civil Rights Act and the Fourteenth Amendment.
The Southern Negro had, in reality, been deprived of his citizenship under the terms of the Dred Scott decision. Congress moved to reestablish his rights with a Civil Rights Act, passed on April 9, 1866 over Johnson's veto. The act forbade discrimination against native-born Americans (except Indians) because of color or race and more specifically granted Negroes citizenship and upheld their rights to testify in court and own property. Johnson had rejected the bill on the grounds that it invaded an area reserved to the states under the Constitution; many other Americans shared his concern about the constitutionality of the act.

But Congress was not prepared to let constitutional concerns prevent the granting of civil rights to all, so it set about changing the Constitution. On June 13, 1866 Congress passed the Fourteenth Amendment which defined, for the first time, the meaning of national citizenship and specifically included Negroes as citizens. It promised the protection of the federal government to ensure that a citizen's rights would not be infringed on by states. Section II stipulated that a state would lose a portion of its representation in the House of Representatives and the Electoral College if the right to vote was denied or abridged, but this portion was never enforced. The amendment also denied former Confederate leaders the right to participate in state or federal government if they had taken a federal oath of office before the war, and it forbade the federal and state governments to pay any debts incurred by the Confederacy.

Perhaps the most important clauses were those saying that a state could not "deprive any person of life, liberty, or property, without due process of law; nor deny to any person within its jurisdiction the equal protection of the laws." These phrases were to have repercussions for many generations to come.

The Fifteenth Amendment. Congress continued to press for Negro emancipation throughout the period of reconstruction. The Fifteenth Amendment, proposed in 1869 and ratified in 1870, declared that no state might deprive a citizen of the right to vote because of "race, color, or previous condition of servitude" and in effect guaranteed Negroes the suffrage. Although not enforced in the South, it did ensure the rights of Northern Negroes, and it did prove the sincerity of the Congress. The concern of the Radical Republicans was very clear. They honestly felt that without federal legislation the rights of the Negro in the South were in danger, and their fears were justified. Even today the provisions of the Fourteenth and Fifteenth Amendments are disregarded in some sections of the United States.

The Black Codes

Because the majority of the men who became active in the revival of Southern political life had supported slavery before the Civil War, it is not surprising that they refused to accept the actions taken by Congress to grant the rights of full citizenship to the Negro. At first they tolerated the work of the Freedmen's Bureau, but they soon saw that Negroes were not going to be sent back to work as they had hoped, even though the need for labor to rebuild the Southern economy increased daily. The white legislatures organized in the South under Johnson's policies of 1865 determined to solve the problem of the Negro in a way that seemed sensible to them.

On November 24, 1865 Mississippi became the first Southern state to enact a body of laws

The Uncertain Resurrection

to control the Negro. Very soon every former confederate state had passed its own "Black Code," those in the states with large numbers of Negroes being the harshest. The codes generally permitted the blacks to marry, to go to school, to demand protection under the law, to sue, and to give evidence in court, rights previously denied them, but they were not given the right to vote, to serve on juries, and to bear arms. Negroes were required to have steady work and could not leave their jobs except under special conditions; in some states they were obliged to sign written labor contracts and were prohibited from working as artisans. Men without jobs could be arrested as vagrants; if they were convicted, the state contracted their convict labor to employers, perhaps their former owners, for a specified period and for the amount of their fines. These restrictive labor and vagrancy statutes served to control the Negroes and bind them to the land, thus protecting the white community and ensuring it a labor supply. The Black Codes benefited the more helpless Negroes, for they were at least housed and fed for their contracted labor. But whatever value the codes possessed was erased by their obvious intent to treat all blacks as inferiors and to reestablish slavery in another form.

Punitive Plans of the North

Passage of the Black Codes reinforced the fears of the Radical Republicans; and the rejection of the Fourteenth Amendment by all Southern legislatures, except that of Tennessee, during the second half of 1866 and early 1867 provided them additional evidence that these states were not ready for representation in Congress. President Johnson, however, had continued to hope that cooperation was possible and wanted the congressional elections of 1866 to show support for his views and help him prevent punitive action. To preserve his executive power and prevent the legislative branch from overriding his veto, he needed moderates in only one-third plus one of the seats in either house of Congress. The Radical Republicans of course needed twice that number elected to both houses to circumvent the President.

Johnson decided that he could best secure support for his program by inviting all moderates to join a new party which would represent a middle-of-the-road program acceptable to both North and South. But the plan backfired, for the first meeting of the National Union Convention on August 14, 1866 in Philadelphia, attended by delegates from both the North and the South, merely convinced most Northerners that Johnson's only supporters were ex-rebels and Copperheads. Instead of gaining support in the November election, Johnson found himself faced with a Congress that was more than two-thirds Republican. The radicals had gained complete control. Thaddeus Stevens was able to assume leadership of the Committee on Reconstruction and of the Congress. Without fear of presidential veto, he could dictate national policy. The authority to determine the course of reconstruction that Congress had claimed in the Wade-Davis Manifesto, and then exercised by overriding Johnson's vetoes of the Civil Rights Act and the second Freedmen's Bureau Bill, had been reconfirmed by the voters.

The First Reconstruction Act. On March 2, 1867 Congress passed over Johnson's veto an act declaring all Southern state governments illegal and dividing the area into five military districts to be controlled by Congress until these states reconvened constitutional conventions and reestablished their state governments. Tennessee was excepted because its ratification of the Fourteenth Amendment had won it readmission in 1866. In the new elections to be held, Negroes would be able to vote and ex-Confederates (as proscribed by the temporarily defeated Fourteenth Amendment) would not. Congress reserved the right to seat the new representatives and to continue military occupation until the provisions of the act were met. The Southern states refused to hold the elections to choose convention delegates, and as the months dragged on, three additional measures had to be passed to force their compliance.

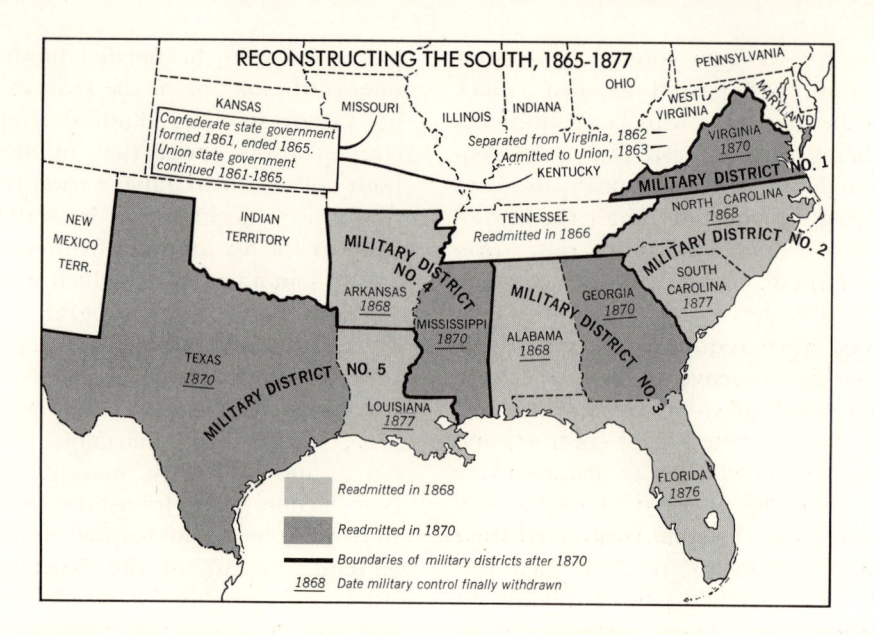

Military Reconstruction. President Johnson did not approve of the first Reconstruction Act and other similar measures, but he faithfully executed the various laws passed by Congress during 1867. The postwar governments of the states were officially dissolved and replaced by the federally sponsored system of five military districts, each with a Union general at its head. Twenty thousand Union troops and some Negro militia were assigned the task of supervising voter registration, through which a completely new Southern power structure was developed. Because so many Southerners had been disfranchised or refused to vote, more than half of the total registered voters were Negroes, although they were a majority of the population in only five states. In other areas majorities consisted of a combination of Negroes and white voters who supported them. Many Negroes participated in the conventions held to draw up new state constitutions; at South Carolina's convention there were more Negro delegates than white. Every new state government eventually established had a Radical Republican majority.

In June and July 1868 Congress readmitted seven Southern states to the Union when their new constitutions were accepted and their new legislatures had ratified the Fourteenth Amendment. The admission of three other states was delayed because of Southern protests over the Fifteenth Amendment, but they too were finally readmitted in early 1870. Georgia, the last state to be accepted, was one of those readmitted in 1868, but it was then expelled for banning Negroes from the legislature. With the return of federal troops, Georgia finally complied with the terms of Congress and became a state again on June 15, 1870.

The Covode Resolution. The relationship between Johnson and Congress continued to deteriorate during this period. After 1866 the Radical Republicans became determined to eliminate the political power of the President because Johnson had failed to support their policies. Between 1866 and 1868, and of course over presidential vetoes, Congress passed acts that prevented the President from appointing new Supreme Court justices, limited his com-

16   *The Uncertain Resurrection*

"The un-making of a president, 1868." The commission to impeach Andrew Johnson.

mand of the army, and forbade him to remove officials whose appointments had been approved by Congress (Tenure of Office Act). Yet the radicals were not satisfied.

On February 24, 1866 the House of Representatives passed the Covode Resolution designed to impeach Johnson. It stated that he had attempted to bring "disgrace and ridicule" on Congress and that he had violated various acts which it had passed. The Senate sat as a court from March 30 through May 16, 1868 to try the President on the impeachment charge of "high crimes and misdemeanors." Chief Justice Salmon P. Chase presided and insisted on holding partisan activities to a minimum, although it was quite clear that the Republicans wanted to replace Johnson with one of their own number. The specific charges of removing Secretary of War Stanton in defiance of the Tenure of Office Act were presented, but, in spite of party pressures, seven Republicans joined twelve Democrats in voting for acquittal. The final vote was thirty-five to nineteen, only one vote short of the two-thirds necessary for conviction and removal from office.

The charges against Johnson were largely political in nature; his retention in office indicated the strength of the system of government established by the Constitution, though proved by a single vote. The legislative branch had not been able to destroy the executive office for its own political ends. Johnson was allowed to reorganize his Cabinet and to serve the remaining months of his term, although he had been badly battered by the impeachment proceedings.

Carpetbaggers and the Negro. Between 1867 and 1877 the new legislatures established in the course of congressional reconstruction passed laws that changed the South drastically. Much to the surprise of the Southerners who were excluded from voting or participating, valuable

Segregation and Immigration   17

Teaching the freedmen: Peace Corps of the 1870's.   THE BETTMANN ARCHIVE

reforms were introduced. Before the Civil War Southern states had lagged behind other parts of the country in social welfare, public education, and public works programs. The new governments, however, cared for the destitute, sponsored schools for Negroes as well as whites and gave the freedmen homesteads, established charitable institutions, built new roads and bridges, repaired and expanded the railroads, and even developed some better systems of taxation.

White men who were elected to the integrated state legislatures were either cooperative Southerners called "scalawags" or newly arrived Northerners, the "carpetbaggers,"[1] who came as federal employees, reformers, and adventurers to assist with Southern reconstruction. Both groups had a variety of purposes, ranging from humanitarianism to personal gain. Although some were irresponsible or unaware of the consequences of their actions, and others were doubtless corrupt and dishonest, they were no more self-seeking than politicians who wrangled enormous sums from public treasuries in the North during this period. Many of these new leaders, especially the carpetbaggers who arrived early, were brave, dedicated, and idealistic men seeking only to help eradicate the vestiges of slavery.

Negroes elected to the new state governments had an even greater range of abilities and motives. Some were completely illiterate, others extremely well educated. Some were immature and dishonest, others temperate. Legislative sessions in a few states were poorly conducted and disorganized, and graft was rampant in many. Some Negro legislators sought to impose confiscatory taxes on others but avoided paying taxes themselves. But the blacks had been given political rights without basic economic assistance and adequate educational opportunities. In view of their immediate past and their complete lack of political training and experience, it was remarkable how many Negroes demonstrated great ability. Negroes held many high offices. In South Carolina Jonathan J. Wright, a qualified attorney trained at the University of Pennsylvania, served on the supreme court. The state treasurer was Francis Cardozo, who had been educated in the British

[1] They were so named because they arrived carrying all their possessions in large carpetbags or suitcases.

The Uncertain Resurrection

Black power at work: South Carolina House of Representatives during reconstruction.

Isles. Florida had the services of Jonathan C. Gibbs as Secretary of State and Superintendent of Public Instruction. Other Negroes were sent as representatives to Congress, sixteen in all between 1869 and 1900. Mississippi sent two Negroes to the United States Senate, Hiram Revels and Blanche K. Bruce.

There is little question that graft, corruption, and unfair practices existed throughout the South during the reconstruction period. Carpetbaggers who were poor when they arrived were wealthy when they returned home. Southern states were often saddled with huge debts for public expenditures they could not afford. Property taxes were so high that many Southern whites had to sell their land. Votes were bought and sold, and politicians used the blacks for selfish purposes. The susceptibility of the Negroes to domination by the unscrupulous carpetbaggers was for years to come considered justification for restricting their franchise. But even though imposed by force and supported by "alien" troops, the reconstruction legislatures did much to rehabilitate the South.

Election of Grant. Despite the strains imposed by governmental infighting, partisan politics were not disrupted during 1868. A few days after President Johnson was acquitted, the Republicans nominated General Ulysses S. Grant for the presidency on the first ballot cast at their convention. They endorsed Radical reconstruction, but not Negro suffrage, and later made the "bloody shirt of the rebellion" the principal focus of their campaign. The Democrats condemned Radical reconstruction and nominated a former governor of New York, Horatio Seymour, on their twenty-second ballot. Grant won handily in the Electoral College, with twenty-six of thirty-four states supporting him. Three Southern states did not participate in the election, and two of the reconstructed states voted Democratic. But even though the Republican

Segregation and Immigration

RUTHERFORD B. HAYES LIBRARY

candidate received an electoral vote of 214 to 80, his popular majority was only 306,000 out of a total of 5,720,000 votes. Over 500,000 Negroes went to the polls for the first time in 1868, and their support decided the election.

White Resistance in the South

Both pride and financial security determined the Southern whites' reactions to the measures passed by integrated legislatures. Because they had been conditioned to believe that Negroes were inferior, they could not visualize them as political leaders. Each act of the legislature was regarded as an attack on the South's traditional way of life, whether it concerned public schools, welfare, or public works. New taxes were regarded as devices to confiscate property. In the minds of white Southerners the pre-Civil War South seemed their lost Garden of Eden, and they continued to seek new ways to regain it.

Action beyond the Law. Since the right to vote was denied many former Confederates and they were not represented in the existing government of their state, they did not consider themselves bound by its laws. White men created extralegal societies, usually secret, to hamstring the reconstruction governments and restore white supremacy. The members of one such group, the Ku Klux Klan—founded in 1866 and led by Nathan Bedford Forrest, a former Confederate general—garbed themselves in white sheets and hoods to frighten superstitious Negroes away from the polls. The organization was formally disbanded in 1869, although its activities continued. Congress took action after Klan members began to use physical violence as well as psychological tactics to arouse terror. The Force Act and the Ku Klux Klan Act in 1870 and 1871 established heavy fines and jail sentences for the activities of Klansmen and gave federal courts original jurisdiction over the cases brought to trial. The federal action proved ineffective, however, for the Klansmen, the Knights of the White Camelia, and other robed ruffians continued to ride through the night in the more isolated areas. The Negroes, fearful for their lives, had already been intimidated and were far less likely to exercise their political rights. Many carpetbaggers also left the South after the Klan and similar vigilante groups began their escapades of intimidation.

Economic Coercion. The activities of terrorist groups were the most obvious symptom of the emergence of a different power structure in the South, but economic changes were far more important. The Black Codes had begun the pattern of economic bondage for the Negro.

20   *The Uncertain Resurrection*

Although the gang labor that the vagrancy laws provided was available only for a short time, when the Negroes were first free and footloose, a new and even more insidious form of enslavement called sharecropping was initiated. Under this plan the landlord (usually white) broke up his plantation into many small units and assigned each to a family (usually black). The planter determined the crops to be grown and arranged for their marketing. In return the laborer (usually black) received one-third of the proceeds. The rest the owner kept for the use of his land (one-third) and for the implements, seeds, and fertilizers (one-third) which he supplied. The laborer might even be refused the right to raise a garden for his own family on the plot of land he worked, although some sort of house was provided. In sharecropping the blacks could achieve a limited amount of personal responsibility, but the degree to which the landlord could control their behavior was quite evident. They could be forced to "remain in their place" with very little effort, for their entire lives were truly dependent on the whim of the landlord. If he wanted his blacks to stop voting, he made his wishes known very quickly and easily, and the number of Negroes participating in each election declined accordingly. In May 1872 a liberal amnesty act reenfranchised most Southern whites who did not already have the vote and allowed them once again to hold office. With few Negroes continuing to go to the polls, white conservatives were elected and the Radicals lost their hold on governments in one after another of the Southern states. By 1876 only Florida, Louisiana, and South Carolina had integrated legislatures, and soon these too were largely white.

WHITES REGAIN SUPREMACY

The Southern whites believed that they must preclude, once and for all, the possibility that Negroes could ever again upset the social and political structure of the South. Radical reconstruction had demonstrated that integrated groups could conduct state governments—even though they had been guilty of the same graft and stupidity that characterized other governments during the period. And once in power the reconstituted white legislatures kept the public school systems and many state functions as they had been structured by the integrated legislatures. They also retained much of the social legislation that had been passed. But the white Southerners were unable to acknowledge this achievement of the Negro and felt impelled to reestablish his inferiority. Terrorism was not the means, because its nature was obvious to all and unacceptable to many Southerners. Yet nearly all seemed willing to evade the law in other ways to lower the status of the Negro.

To maintain white supremacy in a world in which Negroes were now legally "people" presented new problems for the white Southerners. There had been no confusion about the role of the Negro when he was a slave, but now who was he? The federal constitution had been altered, and it said that he was a man—a citizen. But to the white Southerners he was not, and for a hundred years his new status would remain unacknowledged. The whites began to develop a network of legal and nonlegal evasions to enforce their old values—and they were allowed to do so because the champions of the Negro had grown weary of fighting.

Reconstruction Loses Impetus

Opposition in the North. The tensions of war and of reconstruction had spent the energies of Northerners too. The decade had been aptly called an Age of Hate, but hating was now too wearing. Radical leaders were aging, and the moderates were gaining ground. A Liberal Republican movement developed, and its backers nominated Horace Greeley to run for the presidency in the election of 1872. Although their choice of a candidate proved disastrous

(Greeley won only sixty-six electoral votes), even he, a fervent abolitionist and lately a Radical, had spoken out against the vindictiveness of present reconstruction policies. The emergence of such a movement portended the more effective opposition to Republican rule evidenced in the congressional elections of 1874, when the House was won by the Democrats. The Radicals were of course still able to reelect President Ulysses S. Grant in 1872, but thereafter they lost ground as Northerners increasingly downgraded the need for militant changes in the South. The Radicals also lost their zeal for defending the rights of Southern Negroes. Because they wanted the antagonisms between North and South settled and believed that the struggle for Negro rights would prolong them, they accepted second-class citizenship for the blacks. They found this position tenable because very few Northerners believed Negroes to be their equals. Even the leading intellectual magazines of the day caricatured the blacks.

Compromise in 1877. Political maneuvering and compromise in settling the confused and disputed Tilden-Hayes presidential election of 1876 (page 450) spelled the real end of political and military reconstruction. In late 1876 and early 1877 Southern businessmen and congressmen decided to give up their chance to control the presidency in return for the removal of the last federal troops from Southern states and the promise of federal monies for railroads and public works to help revive the still destitute South. And to retain their sixteen-year-old rule of the nation, the Republicans assured the Southerners control of their own state and local governments and of the Negro. The Union had been preserved and the two sections reconciled, but equality for the Negro was in the end brushed aside in a power play. Curtailment of the rights of the blacks would for the most part be unchallenged until the mid-twentieth century when a rising tide of protest would press again for reconstruction of the political machinery and for economic and social reformation as well.

Courts Support Segregation

The Creation of "Jim Crow." In 1875 Congress passed a Civil Rights Act guaranteeing to Negroes equal rights in the use of public facilities, including hotels, trains, and theaters. But 1883 decisions of the Supreme Court held such legislation to be unconstitutional and postponed for eighty years further action by the federal government to assure equal social rights for Negroes. In the 1883 decisions the justices ruled that the Fourteenth Amendment forbade only civil discriminations by public officials, implying that private owners could restrict the use of their facilities with impunity.

This ruling encouraged the state legislatures to go one step further and write the "Jim Crow" laws providing separate public facilities for Negroes. If the blacks were to ride on public carriers, they would not do so with whites. If schools and public places of recreation were to be opened, they too would be separate. The facilities established for "colored" only were purportedly equal to those for whites, but such clauses of the Jim Crow laws were rarely followed or enforced. Eventually, the Supreme Court decision in *Plessy* v. *Ferguson* (1896) gave constitutional sanction to "separate but equal facilities," stating that they did not violate the rights of Negroes. By implication, integration was not necessary to prevent discrimination. An even greater rash of segregation laws were written in the years immediately following the decision, and not all of them by Southern state legislatures.

The only help that the Negroes received from the Supreme Court during these years were the decisions in the Ku Klux Klan cases of 1884; the justices reaffirmed the obligation of the federal government to step in and defend the rights of individual citizens from abuse by others, even when these rights were not spelled out in state law. In practice, however, the federal courts were no better about upholding Negro rights than the state courts. Federal judges were selected on the advice of local officials and were often given these posts in return for political favors. Local courts were of course presided over by locally selected judges who represented the spirit of the community in which they sat. The Negro, now very much alone in his struggle to achieve social equality, made almost no progress. Two societies, separate and unequal, emerged to characterize and demean the United States and its citizenry.

Disfranchisement of the Negro. In many communities in the South, Negroes continued to vote for several decades after reconstruction had ended. Later, during the Populist movement (Chapter 22) in the late 1880's and early 1890's, white conservatives were afraid that the Negroes and poor white farmers might join together and vote them out of power. They passed statutes or amended the state constitutions to disfranchise the Negro, but of course without referring to race. Poll taxes and literacy tests were common ruses. To keep these new laws from disfranchising poor whites as well, many states inserted "grandfather" clauses providing that those unable to pay poll taxes or meet literacy standards might still vote if they had been eligible on January 1, 1867, or if their fathers or grandfathers had been able to vote on that day. The intent of these laws was obvious, for the majority of Negroes had not been granted suffrage until 1868. Mississippi led the way by passing the first of these laws in 1890. The other former Confederate states soon followed. Even though many of these statutes were voided by the courts after 1915, they had served their purpose.

The Solid South. After the Civil War the South declined to support any Republican party candidate. Democratic candidates were often Union veterans, but in the eyes of Southerners they were infinitely better than any member of the party that was related to Lincoln and reconstruction. The new South emerged as an efficient political entity which could wield power for its own ends. For a century it voted solidly Democratic, assuring seniority in Congress for many of its members, who were reelected repeatedly. These men became the chairmen of congressional committees and leaders in party politics. They brought their own ideas on segregation into the national capital and, because of their seniority, they dominated Congress.

There were some signs of change, however, although most of these were economic rather than political. Defeat in the war had proved to a few Southerners that they would have to alter the economy. They recognized the advantages that industry had given to the North, and they wanted to create the same opportunities in the South. During the 1870's the railroads were extended with branches and new lines, and additional cotton mills and iron foundries were built. These moves to expand industry represented the beginning of a new world for the South, even though they were limited by shortages of capital and skilled labor.

The Rural Ghetto. The Negro lived on the margin of society during the remainder of the nineteenth century and in much of the twentieth. His home was in the country, and there he farmed in poverty and hopelessness. Because he had to produce as much cotton as possible and sell every bale to subsist, he overworked the land. Often he did not even save enough soil to grow a few vegetables for himself. He had little opportunity to learn new methods of farming. If he wanted to leave his small plot to seek other work, he was held back by lack of education and segregation policies. As the years passed, his inferior position was increasingly constricted by statutes and tradition. The Negro was as isolated in his rural "ghetto" as were other minorities in their urban slums.

Southern whites had convinced themselves that this way of life was natural. They maintained that the Negro was satisfied with the conditions under which he existed, pointing to the smiling faces, tuneful songs, and gay dances. A happy, humble, affable "Uncle Tom" was the Southern white stereotype of the "good" Negro. Blacks were considered "uppity" if they tried to assert themselves.

Northern Negroes. Negroes began to move out

Segregation and Immigration

of the South during the nineteenth century, but they left in very small numbers. Inertia, ignorance, and lack of skills, as well as the hostility of Northerners, kept the blacks from seeking new opportunities. Although Northerners had supported the abolition of slavery as an abstract principle, many proved as prejudiced as Southerners when faced with personal involvement. Individual free Negroes had been more or less accepted in the North, but it was evident that large numbers of them would not be. The draft riots in New York during the Civil War (page 354) reflected anti-Negro feeling. Moreover, the many Northern workingmen who had feared the competition of slave labor before the Civil War were afterward apprehensive about competing with the cheap labor of freedmen.

The new Northern industries did not recruit Southern Negroes, for they depended on immigrants from Europe for their labor supply. Some of the few Negroes who managed to reach the North found jobs in factories, but most were hired as railroad porters or custodians or were employed in steel mills or on steamships. Negroes also helped build the railroads. In general, they lived in the poorest housing available.

Although segregation and prejudice plagued the Negro in both South and North, complete segregation was not supported by law in the North. Bias might be practiced by individuals or groups, but it was usually not reinforced by government policy. In the North other minority groups shared the economic and social problems of the Negro. With more legal rights and economic opportunities that were at least superior to the tenant farming which prevailed in the South, he could aspire to better things.

THE GROWTH OF CITIES

As the nation grew, so did appreciation for the cities. Urban areas began to rival and then replace the frontier as centers of excitement, of change, and of opportunity. After the Civil War cities were the focus of the new economy and society. Before 1850 there was no urban center in the United States with a population of more than 1,000,000, and in 1860 only 14.7 per cent of all the people lived in towns with populations exceeding 10,000. By 1890, however, New York, Chicago, and Philadelphia had passed the million mark in population and were continuing to grow rapidly.

Migration to the City. Cities offered the challenge and mobility that had attracted settlers to the frontier in early years. In 1850 there were a great many farms, but there were also more men and machines to work them. In addition, farm prices fell during the late nineteenth century, and the new frontier lands suitable for small farms were disappearing. The youth began to leave rural areas to take jobs in factories rather than search for new farmlands as had their predecessors in earlier generations. To young people who had never received money for their labor, city wages often seemed high. The machines of the period required little skill to operate, and almost anyone could run them, including women and children. Thus the young man who wanted to succeed in the new age of business chose to move to the city.

The cities themselves were becoming more appealing too. Water systems were developed, sewers built, and streets paved. Gas was used more extensively to light the streets and then, with Edison's perfection of electric bulbs in 1879, most cities became relatively safe after dark. Electric dynamos were developed to supply power. Streetcars, first drawn by horses and then powered by electricity, provided transportation within the cities. In later decades elevated railroads and subways were constructed in some urban areas. Refrigerated railroad cars transported fresh foods to city dwellers, and the Pullman car made railroad travel to and from the city more comfortable for passengers who could afford its accommodations. The telephone improved communication, and the construction industry flourished. Great bridges were built (Brooklyn, 1883), and the first skyscraper was erected (Jenney's Home Insurance Building, Chicago, 1885).

The Plague of Slums. Fashionable sections of the cities were reasonably clean, quiet, and pleasant, but vast urban areas developed into festering slums. Crowded, dirty, and sordid shacks and tenements were the homes of many newly arrived city dwellers, both native and immigrant. Although some newcomers soon become prosperous and were able to move, there were always thousands more to replace them and to be subjected to the same unhealthy physical and social surroundings. In the slums few public services were provided, and gangs of "toughs" often roamed the streets. Builders contrived to utilize every square foot of property, erecting structures with the maximum number of apartments, each in turn with minimum space, light, and ventilation. What plumbing facilities were provided had to be shared by many families. It is amazing that citizens emerged from these areas, decent and hard-working, many to make important contributions to the nation.

Most well-established residents of the growing cities pointed with pride to the fine new buildings, the parks, and the monuments, but they ignored the slums. Had they been more public-spirited, the corruption of city governments would have frustrated their efforts to eliminate crime and filth. Citizens who attempted to adapt the basic democratic processes to urban life did not succeed. Town meetings were not effective in cities, and people did not know each other. Individual citizens did not accept responsibility for the city because each felt too unimportant to be heard. There seemed no way to unite public opinion and effort.

Offering personal intervention and small favors, unscrupulous politicians gained the votes of newly arrived immigrants and other impoverished citizens who were unable to deal with the complexities of urban life. By the end of the nineteenth century, most urban centers were ruled by political machines or closely knit partisan organizations. Each was no more honest or efficient than its "boss." Because city employees were hired for their political loyalty rather than their competence, the public could expect little from most city administrations. Even cities with good local governments failed to provide many services that are now considered essential. Water supply systems, sewage disposal, police and fire protection, and public transportation had generally been introduced by the 1890's, although some of these services were provided by volunteers or by private industry. Relief and social welfare agencies were almost unknown, and most cities lacked the resources to offer help when the Panics of 1873 and 1893 caused widespread unemployment. Public opinion did not favor dispensing charity, since it was considered morally undesirable for the recipients, but some cities did provide soup kitchens and breadlines when people were starving.

IMMIGRANTS FOR A GROWING ECONOMY

Immigrants had come to the United States each year since the founding of the nation, but they had arrived from different countries and in varying numbers. Most of the newcomers had come from northern and western Europe and, much as those who arrived during the colonial period, were integrated rapidly into society. They moved quickly through the cities into the towns and rural areas. Although they might settle together in certain localities and retain some customs of their homeland, most adopted American ways. Individual immigrants were probably greeted with some disdain, but few problems were created as they were absorbed into the population.

Catholic Advance Guard

There had been some immigration of Germans during colonial days and particularly in the years 1827 to 1838. But during the 1840's and 1850's they began to arrive in great numbers.

The Irish also first came to the United States in these periods. Famine, restrictive legislation, and political unrest had driven these millions of people from their homelands. Because the Irish had very little capital, they settled on the East coast. At first, they were not welcomed by their neighbors and had great difficulty earning enough to survive. Gradually, however, they established themselves and adjusted to the new culture, although they retained elements of their own as well. Politicians were able to appeal to "Irish" prejudices to win "Irish" votes. The immigrants also lived in "Irish" neighborhoods, which became the first "ghettos" in American cities. Not as impoverished as the Irish, the Germans were able to move from East coast cities to other parts of the country. Like the Irish, however, many of them were Catholic and tended to congregate in neighborhoods.

A few Catholics had helped to found the English colonies in America, but through the years their numbers did not increase significantly until the migration during the middle of the nineteenth century. Then Catholicism suddenly became the religious denomination with the largest number of communicants in the United States. Many people feared Catholic domination, and action groups were organized to combat the anticipated changes. Some were secret societies devoted to protecting "native" Americans from foreigners and their customs, and others, such as the Know-Nothing party (page 322), temporarily became political. Candidates nominated for national office by the Know-Nothings in 1854 and 1856 campaigned on a platform urging limitation of immigration and deportation of some aliens. The more violent "nativists" burned churches and published libelous tracts.

The viciousness directed against the Irish and Germans was provoked by economic as well as religious fears. People thought that the large numbers of immigrants could not be provided with jobs and would work for such low wages that the welfare of laborers, who were reasonably well paid in the 1830's, would be seriously damaged. The flood of new unskilled workers arriving during the 1840's and 1850's did indeed prevent wages from rising, for it was difficult for the country to absorb more than a million new residents within a decade without some dislocations. Fifty years later the same fears were aroused when "foreigners" again came in huge numbers to the United States.

Whatever their initial problems, the Irish and Germans adjusted to the new way of life and were accepted by the general population. "Colonies" in parts of New York City, St. Louis, and Milwaukee remained predominantly Irish or German, but the groups were not truly isolated. Since most of the immigrants were literate and many were professional men, skilled craftsmen, and experienced farmers, their opportunities proved almost limitless.

Immigration after the Civil War

Men were on the move everywhere in the world in the last half of the nineteenth century. New industries needed new workers. New means of transportation made travel more feasible, and new communication systems greatly facilitated the exchange of information. In both Europe and the United States cities exerted their magnetism, and millions of people were persuaded to leave peasant villages and farms to work in mills and factories. The immense surge of immigrants crossing the Atlantic Ocean was part of a vast movement of world population from rural to urban areas. Persecution and poverty drove some of the migrants from their homes, but the majority were searching for a better, richer way of life.

Need for Labor. In the closing third of the century, the economy of the United States became particularly attractive to western Europeans. The second industrial revolution was in full swing, and so many jobs were available that fac-

Promises, promises. CARTOON BY JOSEPH KEPPLER, NEW YORK PUBLIC LIBRARY PRINTS DIVISION

tories recruited workers. Businesses were at the same time seeking people to whom they could sell housing, land, railroad and steamship tickets, and the products of the booming factories. Congress passed a Contract Labor Law in 1864, which allowed employers to arrange for immigrants to come to America with expenses paid. For their passage immigrants usually agreed to work for a year without an increase in wages and to repay the cost of transportation. The American Emigrant Company was established to make and execute such contracts for businessmen. Although the Contract Labor Law was repealed in 1868, other organizations continued to recruit labor for the nation's factories.

The work force more than doubled in thirty years. From 10,532,750 employed persons in 1860, the total grew to 23,318,183 in 1890, and the majority were immigrants. Employers and business in general profited from the continuous influx of cheap labor.

Attraction of America. The newcomers, who found jobs almost immediately, gained too. Although wages were low, they were usually higher than those in the "old country." Land could be bought at reasonable prices, or if an immigrant was willing to venture onto the frontier, the land there was his for the taking. New citizens wrote home in glowing terms about the marvelous things that they had done and seen. The "Promised Land" was described in emotion-filled "American letters," which were circulated widely in Europe. The glowing stories of "wealth and comfort" encouraged more and more immigrants to come. After 1880 the flow surged to a flood. In 1882 there were 2,100 newcomers arriving in the United States *each day*. The migration had become one of the greatest mass movements of people in history. By 1914 more than 35,000,000 persons had reached the United States, having left their homelands willingly and without compulsion from any government. They came as individuals, prompted by personal desires, not in groups controlled by organizations or driven by officials. The new citizens were to be strongly influenced by this fact—that they had freely chosen to come to the United States—and so was the nation whose future development would owe so much to them.

Segregation and Immigration

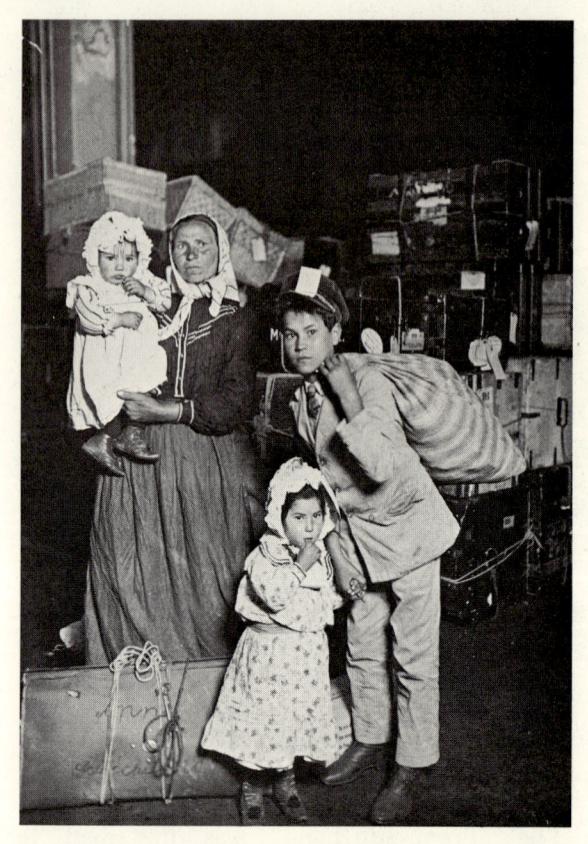

Arrival. PHOTOGRAPH BY LEWIS W. HINE,
GEORGE EASTMAN HOUSE COLLECTION

"New" Immigrants

The term "new" applied to immigrants from eastern and southern Europe distinguished them from the "old" settlers whose homelands were in the northern and western parts of the continent. As the volume of immigration rose, the "old" immigrants—the English, the Swedes, and the Germans—continued to arrive in large numbers. The peak year was 1882 for immigrants from Germany (250,000), Sweden (105,000), Holland (92,000), and Norway and Denmark (64,000). More Englishmen (77,000), surprisingly, migrated in 1888 than in any other year since the founding of the nation.

The "new" immigrants from more distant countries—Italy, Greece, Poland, the Balkan nations, and Russia—began to be attracted to America when news about opportunities in the United States spread during the 1880's. Steamship companies offered cheap rates for travel by steerage from Mediterranean as well as Atlantic ports. After 1880 almost seventeen per cent of the newcomers were from places other than western and northern Europe.

Social Differences. Many "new" aliens in the United States had been peasant farmers in Europe. From stock that had worked close to the soil for centuries, they had never known political or economic freedom. The power of the landlord and the lash of the Cossack had kept them servile. Most were illiterate in their own languages as well as in English, and their ability to understand and deal with modern machinery was limited. Coming to America was the most remarkable single event of their entire lives, and many of them never completely realized the implications of such a move, continuing to identify with the old ways no matter how long they remained in the new land. All these factors combined to make the "new" immigrants particularly vulnerable to exploitation by employers, manipulation by politicians, and the attacks of nativists.

Physical differences distinguished the "new" immigrants from their American neighbors. Many newcomers of Mediterranean or Slavic stock had darker hair and swarthier skins and were shorter in stature than their Teutonic counterparts. They might replace their peasant clothing, learn English, and master a trade and still not lose their "foreign" appearance. Although most of the "new" immigrants were Catholics, increasing numbers of Jews came to the United States, driven from their homelands, especially from Poland, by Russian pogroms during the 1880's. Many progressed no farther than New York City, where they settled in ghettos very similar to those that

The Uncertain Resurrection

they had left. Their treatment by the government and their individual opportunities in the United States, however, were entirely different. But whatever and however grave their weaknesses, the immigrants possessed great strengths—native intelligence, the ability to work and endure hardshops, strong family ties and loyalty, and the comfort and support of their religious convictions.

Ghettos and Slums. Almost all the "new" immigrants huddled together in sections of the cities which they quickly made their own. Their common language encouraged contacts with one another but separated them from outsiders. Lack of money forced them to accept substandard housing. Tenements with inadequate plumbing, monotonous labor in sweat shops, and graft- and crime-ridden neighborhoods were their lot. Some became bitter and returned to their native lands. Others fought against the evils. Struggling for an education, fighting for advancement, competing for every possible opportunity, many immigrants eventually clawed their way out of the smothering slums and made their way into the predominant society. Still others resigned themselves to the limiting, frustrating life of the ghetto, hoping that their children would be able to become real Americans. For some, however, even the most wretched conditions in America were an improvement over those that they had left behind, and they were happy and grateful for the smallest comfort.

The very elderly, clinging to the memories of their youth, remained in the old neighborhoods when their children and the younger, more vigorous immigrants moved from the ghetto into the larger society of the nation. But they did not live there alone, for another minority group always came to fill the gap at the bottom of the social structure. Irish, Poles, Italians, Jews, and in later years Negroes, Mexicans, and Puerto Ricans successively faced the same problems of proverty and segregation. A separate and unequal urban ghetto society developed and persists, whatever its gradually shifting neighborhoods and changing makeup.

Reactions to Later Immigrants

The United States was a land of immigrants; yet it was suddenly plagued by problems of immigration. Aliens, who had been urged to come to the new land, were feared and rejected. Established citizens, alarmed by the huge numbers in which foreigners arrived, turned on them, forgetting for the time being that their families, too, had at one time been immigrants. The newcomers who moved to the rural areas were more easily absorbed, for there were fewer of them and they were forced to establish some communication with their neighbors. For the masses who settled in the cities, however, assimilation was much slower.

Barriers to Assimilation. Mastery of English was particularly difficult for the immigrants in urban areas, for as long as they remained in their own sections, they could communicate easily in their native languages. Signs and announcements began to be printed in German, Italian, Yiddish, and Russian, and foreign language newspapers were published. The newcomers who had to work twelve hours per day, six days per week, had little time to study English. Only the children who attended school were able to learn the new language. Members of the older generation hesitated to abandon their traditional beliefs, especially when they had few opportunities to develop new values. Proud people, with enough ambition to want a better life but not necessarily an entirely different one, they taught their children the folk customs and practices of the lands they had left behind.

Ghetto Stereotypes. The social patterns of the "new" immigrants were so unlike those of the native population, in many ways so contradictory to the Puritan ethic, that criticism was inevitable. The "new" immigrants expressed emo-

Still waiting—in the land of promise.
PHOTOGRAPH BY JACOB A. RIIS, THE JACOB A. RIIS COLLECTION, MUSEUM OF THE CITY OF NEW YORK

tion readily and were warm and "romantic" in their personal relations. Families were large, noisy, and closely knit. As the ethnic and national groups increased in numbers, the foreign-born were superficially stereotyped by the native-born citizenry. The Irish were considered aggressive and belligerent, the Germans stolid and humorless, the Jews stingy and shrewd, and the Italians volatile and noisy. Each ethnic ghetto acquired an image—however falsely it might apply to individuals within the group—which colored the thinking of "the majority" for generations. Only in very recent years have there been organized efforts to dispel these misconceptions.

Restrictions on Immigration. The "new" immigrants, living in poverty, were willing to work for low wages and were accused of disseminating various and dangerous radicalisms. The fears and uncertainties created by cultural differences and economic competition aroused prejudice and hatred. Toward the end of the century Americans gave vent to their antiforeign feelings. Restriction of immigration became a political goal of organized labor. The American Protective Association supported only candidates who were not Catholic. By 1887, the year the association was formed, there was definite support for immigration control in most parts of the nation. Several state legislatures had passed laws limiting immigration during the nineteenth century, but clearly any effective legislation must come from the federal government. Industry still sought workers from other countries, however, and industrial and business leaders exerted pressure on the government not to limit immigration. Certain prophetic steps were taken, nevertheless.

Chinese and Japanese Immigration. Brought to the United States to build the transcontinental railroads, the Chinese settled in the vicinity of San Francisco, where they were not welcomed. Native Americans feared the competition of "coolie labor," and the Workingman's party demanded a halt to their immigration. Federal legislation restricting the entrance of the Chinese was enacted in 1879, vetoed, and then reenacted three years later. More than 160,000 Chinese had been admitted to the United States when the Act of 1882 prohibited any Chinese from entering the country for a decade. Later laws extended the act and then made it permanent until 1943, when finally a token yearly quota (105 immigrants) was authorized.

No significant immigration of Japanese took place before the 1890's, but during that decade and the next, over 150,000 came to America. Repressive measures were taken by Americans, primarily by the Japanese and Korean Exclusion League. In 1906 the San Francisco School Board set up a separate school for the ninety-three Japanese children in the city, an action

30   *The Uncertain Resurrection*

President Theodore Roosevelt finally persuaded the city authorities to rescind. The Japanese government then entered into a "gentlemen's agreement" with the United States to refuse passports to unskilled laborers wishing to emigrate, but a few continued to come. The limitation of Japanese immigration culminated in total exclusion under the Immigration Act of 1924.

Other Attempts at Control. Congress had taken the first step toward limiting immigration and controlling the ethnic composition of the population. The same year that it excluded the Chinese, paupers, the insane, criminals, and other "undesirables" were also barred from the country. But the enforcement of this legislation was sketchy, for records were incomplete and inspections were few.

AMERICA—MELTING POT OR MOSAIC?

When does a foreigner become a United States citizen? Is he an American as soon as he receives citizenship papers or even before? Or does he remain an alien as long as he speaks his native language and retains his ancestral customs? Must he support national values and conform to the culture of the majority of the population, or may he preserve his own heritage?

Two theories have been advanced to explain the process of "americanization." If an immigrant becomes a citizen and retains the distinguishing identity of his homeland, our nation is made up of a population mosaic based on "cultural pluralism." But if an immigrant becomes increasingly assimilated into the national culture, the nation's population is a "melting pot." According to the second theory, an immigrant who moves to the United States is not a real American unless he rejects his background and adopts new traits. The characteristics of American are considered fixed, established very early by the original settlers with only a few customs added by later immigrants. Both theories have found support among scholars.

Contributions of Immigrants and Minorities. Through the years immigrants and freedmen have contributed a great deal to the United States, both as individuals and as representatives of other cultures. Folk dancing, native music and songs, new art forms, handicrafts, exotic clothing and food, social manners and religious beliefs—all have added variety, color, and diversity to American life. The theater, literature, and communications have been enormously enriched. Hundreds of successful businessmen, scholars, artists, and scientists have come from these groups. Some were European-trained, but many were the sons of the poor to whom the New World offered opportunities impossible in their homelands, or the sons and grandsons of slaves who had been denied freedom by the same New World. A list of immigrants and blacks whose great and unique talents have benefited the United States would be almost endless. Every phase of American life has been affected by the accomplishments of such distinguished citizens as

Jacob Riis	Dane	journalism
Louis Brandeis	Jew	law
James J. Hill	Canadian	transportation
Booker T. Washington	Negro	education
Arturo Toscanini	Italian	music
Frederick Weyerhaeuser	German	industry
Amadeo P. Giannini	Italian	banking (Bank of America)
Samuel Gompers	Jew	labor organization
Carl Schurz	German	politics
Joseph Pulitzer	Hungarian	journalism
Alexander G. Bell	Scotch	invention of telephone
Charles Drew	Negro	medicine (blood banks)

Negative Effects of Segregation. During the years segregation of immigrants in the Northern ghetto and of Negroes in the Southern

Segregation and Immigration

fields had serious negative effects, however. For people who might otherwise have been able to contribute much to the nation, opportunities were unnecessarily limited. The political equality of all Americans was challenged by the fact that Northern politicians were able to manipulate foreign votes and the Southern politicians could prevent Negroes from voting.

Those who practiced prejudice also suffered, for they denied themselves and their nation the full talents of great numbers of able citizens. Because politicians could use segregation for their own purposes, graft and corruption grew and the cost of government increased. And by failing to consider the various minorities as their equals, those who were prejudiced projected a distorted picture of themselves, one quite different from what they wanted to present the world. During the twentieth century Americans would be forced to ask themselves, "Who is a full-fledged American?"

SUGGESTED READINGS

Bentley, G. R., *A History of the Freedman's Bureau* (1955).
Berthoff, R. T., *British Immigrants in Industrial America* (1952).
*Billington, R. A., *The Protestant Crusade, 1800–1860* (1938).
Bremner, R. H., *From the Depths: The Discovery of Poverty in the United States* (1956).
Cox, L. and J. H. Cox, *Politics, Principle, and Prejudice, 1865–1866* (1963).
Davis, J., *The Russian Immigrant* (1922).
*Du Bois, W. E. B., *Black Reconstruction* (1935).
Dunning, W. A., *Essays on the Civil War and Reconstruction* (1904).
Erickson, C., *American Industry and the European Immigrant, 1860–1885.* (1957)
Foerster, R. F., *The Italian Emigration of Our Times* (1919).
Franklin, J. H., *From Slavery to Freedom* (1947).
*Handlin, O., *Boston's Immigrants* (1941).
*Handlin, O., *Immigration as a Factor in American History* (1959).
*Handlin, O., *The Uprooted* (1951).
*Hansen, M. L., *The Atlantic Migration, 1607–1860* (1940).
*Hansen, M. L., *The Immigrant in American History* (1940).
*Higham, J., *Strangers in the Land* (1955).
*Hofstadter, R., *The Age of Reform* (1955).
*James. J., *The Framing of the Fourteenth Amendment* (1956).
*Jones, M. A., *American Immigration* (1960).
Milton, G. F., *The Age of Hate* (1930).
Myrdal, G., *An American Dilemma* (1944).
Nugent, W. T. K., *The Tolerant Populists, Kansas, Populism and Nativism* (1963).
Park, R. E. and H. A. Miller, *Old World Traits Transplanted* (1921).
Randall, J. G., *The Civil War and Reconstruction* (1937).
*Riis, J., *How the Other Half Lives* (1957).

*Rischin, M., *The Promised City, New York's Jews, 1870–1914* (1962).
Stephenson, G. M., *History of American Immigration* (1926).
Thomas, M. E., *Nativism in the Old Northwest, 1850–1860* (1936).
Washington, B. T., *Up from Slavery, An Autobiography* (1901).
*Wharton, V. L., *The Negro in Mississippi* (1947).
Wittke, C., *The Irish in America* (1956).
Wittke, C., *We Who Built America* (1939).
*Woodward, C. V., *The Strange Career of Jim Crow* (rev. ed., 1966).

CHAPTER 18

The Second Frontier

*I have fallen in love with American names,
The sharp names that never get fat,
The snakeskin-titles of mining-claims,
The plumed war-bonnet of Medicine Hat,
Tucson and Deadwood and Lost Mule Flat.*
  STEPHEN VINCENT BENET, *American Names*, 1927

From *Ballads and Poems*. Copyright 1931 by Stephen Vincent Benét.
Copyright renewed © 1959 by Rosemary Carr Benét.
Reprinted by permission of Holt, Rinehart and Winston.

LIBRARY OF CONGRESS

THE CHANGING NATURE OF THE FRONTIER

THE PEOPLE OF THE UNITED STATES BEGAN their national life believing that they possessed an infinite amount of land for settlement. They thought of their country as millions of acres of forest, prairies, and mountains stretching endlessly westward. Yet by 1840 the prime farming regions of the Middle West had been settled; and by 1850 the steady flow of farm families had reached areas in the mountain and prairie regions. After 1850 settlers were compelled to establish their homes and farms in less favored areas, to travel into the colder Northern regions, and to undertake the long trek over the trails to California and Oregon. Americans faced the fact that their "infinite land" was far from endless.

Slowing Tempo

The movement toward the Western frontier slowed and almost stopped altogether during the mid-nineteenth century. Prime land was increasingly scarce, and the Indian tribes that had been herded into the new areas from their old hunting grounds resisted more desperately and with greater effect the efforts at settlement, for they had been promised that the Great Plains were theirs forever. The continuing controversy between the North and South over the status of slavery in the new territories also served to retard their settlement. Then as the economic patterns of the United States changed after 1850, a different kind of frontiersman emerged as the scout of civilization.

The Changing Landscape. From the time that the first Puritans moved into the forests along the Atlantic coast, the American pioneer was an independent agent. He and his family moved freely into lands where the challenges were often grave but not so severe that skill, good fortune, and family resources could not overcome them. The soil of the woods was excellent for agriculture, the water sufficient, and the climate familiar and tolerable. The settler could build the same dwelling in Connecticut or in

Indiana; he could grow the same crops and practice the same kind of farming in North Carolina and in east Texas.

But beyond the western edge of the Mississippi River Valley, on the outer rim of this verdant world, existed a different challenge. Past a certain line, which varied with the amount of rainfall, a farmer could not grow the same crops, nor could his family live in the same type of house, for there was no lumber for construction on the Great Plains. Instead of merely leveling dense forests to make room for farmland, the new frontiersman had to worry about inadequate rainfall and what to substitute for wooden fencing, what to build his home of and how to heat it. The climate, the soil, the food, and even the tools needed for farming were all completely different. The way of life that existed from Maine through Iowa was not possible farther west, and to survive the settler had to make many new adjustments.

The Relationship of the Frontier to the Industrial Economy. Many of the first pioneers to explore the arid, windswept Great Plains and the towering Rocky Mountains were not farmers. Minerals and open ranges where cattle could roam freely were the first resources of the new frontier to be exploited, and the valuable ores and beef were sent back East to benefit the new industrial economy. Precious metals helped finance the Civil War and were used for coinage and decoration. Industrial workers had to be supplied with meat, for they lived in the cities and could not produce their own food. A few of the miners and cattlemen who went to the West to seek its wealth made great fortunes. The luck of these few was enough to attract great numbers of men to the last unsettled parts of the nation.

When the surface sources of metals were exhausted, the frontiersmen were forced to develop more efficient methods of mining, such as ore breaking by machines. But because these techniques proved too expensive for individual mineowners, corporations were formed, engineers contracted for, and day laborers hired. Operation of the mines was patterned after the factory system.

Cattle raising, lumbering, and other businesses that flourished on the second frontier were also at first ventures operated by individuals, but the increased demands of industry made expansion and corporate ownership necessary. Big businesses were formed, and developers modernized methods and equipment. The exploitation of the vast spaces in the Far West became essential to the nation's economy and the extensive frontier industries a vital part of its industrial complex.

Sectional Nature of Frontier. The most important aspect of the frontier after 1850 was its changing relationship to the other parts of the nation. Previously, the economic significance of the frontier had been limited to yeilding more of the same crops grown in areas already settled. A Southern cotton farmer, for example, might move west and establish another cotton farm. His new homestead on the frontier was merely an extension of the existing agrarian economy. But the special resources of the Far West made this section unique. The people of the new frontier, like those of the North and the South, found that their area had its own particular problems and concerns, and the entire nation soon recognized its economic and political importance. Far from being merely an extension of older sections, the frontier became a new area of conflict in an already divided nation.

Versatile Frontier Lands. The second frontier was not settled in a continous migration across the continent. Instead, the newcomers arrived in waves, settling where the resource they sought was located. As they mined for metals, raised cattle and sheep, built railroads, or cultivated the land, the migrants created a variety of frontiers. The first was the "mining frontier," and later the "cattle frontier" was established. In certain areas these frontiers encompassed the same land at different times, whereas in others they were geographically separate.

After each wave of exploitation had subsided, only small islands of civilization survived.

Not until almost 1900 did the majority of settlers remain in the Far West, and even today large areas of rangeland and mountains are only sparsely populated. The new pioneers resembled the sixteenth-century explorers of America more than they did the farmers of the seventeenth and eighteenth centuries. They were more interested in returning to civilization with the treasures they had found, or the fortunes they had amassed, than in establishing permanent communities. While the frontiersmen developed mines and cattle ranges, they lived in temporary settlements very unlike those of the East. Although many of these communities later became cities and towns in new Western states, the Far West has many ghost towns, such as Jerome, Arizona, and Bodie, California, settlements abandoned by miners after they had exploited the resources of the surrounding area. Some ghost towns have been immortalized in songs and legends, and a few like Columbia, California, and Virginia City, Nevada, have been restored for tourists as gaudy reminders of frontier days.

The cattle country was also a vast land with few inhabitants. Even during the brief heyday of the cattle barons from 1866 to 1886, there were few cowboys. Today this region, which covers parts of Wyoming, Montana, Colorado, and Kansas, is still largely underpopulated, although some of it has been planted in wheat which seems to stretch to the horizon. It is still not difficult to imagine how the cattle country must have looked during the last frontier days. A few fences, a signboard or two, and an occasional clump of trees are the only additions. The wheat field could easily be buffalo grass, and the cattle grazing could be Texas longhorns or even buffalo.

Transportation to the Frontier

Because of the great increase in facilities for land and water transportation, travel to the second frontier was much different from that utilized in reaching earlier frontiers. Railroads were common in the Eastern half of the nation by 1850 and offered rapid and reliable service to the very edge of the wilderness. Steamboats traveled on the Ohio and Mississippi rivers and parts of the Missouri as well. Emigrant families who were beginning the overland trek to Oregon could ride in style and comfort to Kansas City by steamer and rail. In this city catering to the pioneer, they outfitted themselves before plunging on into the wilds. Perhaps this painfully swift transition from settled ease and comfort to the rigors of traveling in the Far West explains why the Oregon Trail was littered with household treasures, abandoned by their owners as more trouble than they were worth.

Other cities that grew up at the western ends of the railroads were also cosmopolitan, offering migrants more equipment than could be purchased in earlier frontier towns. One such center was St. Louis, and Chicago also mushroomed to answer the same pioneer demands. With the rise of these frontier cities, the new streams of immigrants no longer passed through semisettled regions on their way west. They moved directly from prosperous farm country and youthful industrial and commercial centers into the arid, desolate flatlands of the Great Plains.

And, unlike the earlier frontiersman who often stopped at the first place that looked promising, later wanderers followed one of the great Western trails, marked only by the rutted, dusty tracks of wagon trains, to lands far beyond. Even today traces of the same wheelmarks can still be seen in lands that remain empty and desolate along the route of the Santa Fe Trail where it crosses Raton Pass. Lands of Wyoming, Idaho, and eastern Oregon penetrated by the Oregon Trail have also been scorned by the settler and still look much as they did in frontier days. The great distances traveled through unsettled regions changed the entire tone of the westward movement, for more capital was required, and pioneers found it necessary to travel in larger groups. These later frontiersmen were open to commercial

"*The gold is thar, most anywhar,
And they dig it out with an iron bar.*"
Jesse Hutchinson, Jr.

CALIFORNIA HISTORICAL SOCIETY

exploitation by those who loaned them money and sold them supplies.

West to East and East to West

After 1850 the term "westward movement" no longer accurately described all frontier settlement. Pioneer families continued to move westward, but now there were many who moved back in the direction from which they had come. The special resources sought by the new frontiersman stimulated this two-way traffic. The bankers, barkeepers, and boatmen, enticed to leave their homes and head west by California gold, rarely found it but later journeyed to Colorado, Nevada, Montana, and other destinations in the hope of discovering new bonanzas. The miners who rushed to Cripple Creek (Colorado) or to Virginia City (Nevada) were often the same men who had followed the trails to Angel's Camp or sites on the American River in California without "striking it rich." Many of the empty-handed fortune seekers who returned from the long excursions in the Far West settled on farms in the Great Plains, forming a frontier that moved eastward across land that had been bypassed in the search for instant wealth.

The Uncertain Resurrection

THE MINING FRONTIER

The Gold Rush—A Case Study

The discovery of gold in California in 1848 changed the character of westward migration almost overnight. No longer were all the wagons loaded with women and children, or with farm tools and furniture. The great majority of the new emigrants were men, going west to win their fortunes. The search for gold—viewed as a wild adventure in which great wealth could be gained with little effort—drew the enterprising from all levels of society and every part of the nation. The majority of the many prosperous men who took part in the Gold Rush saved themselves the weary trek across the plains by taking the long voyage around Cape Horn, or by crossing the Isthmus of Panama by rail. The less wealthy adventurers braved the overland trails. All arrived in the sprawling goldfields of California with greed in their eyes and enthusiasm in their hearts.

Gold was reportedly not difficult to find in California. Newspapers and periodicals claimed that the Sierras contained many veins of the ore eroded by rushing mountain streams. As these waters slowed on reaching the sandy soils of the foothills, particles of gold were deposited along the banks. All a man had to do, the stories read, was to pour the sand and water over a box, or pan, built to catch the flakes of gold and let the lighter grains of sand run through. Only a shovel, a pickax, and a pan were needed, and no experience was really required for the shiny flakes of free gold were easily recognized. The greatest challenge was to find the right place on the right stream at the right time—discoveries were made by chance rather than by careful planning.

Few miners actually found their fortunes. Some were discouraged by the hardships of the trail and did not even reach the gold country. Others arrived, unsuccessfully tried their luck, and returned home. Some remained in California to establish farms or to supply the miners.

Yet a sufficient number of prospectors were successful in their quest to attract the fortune seekers of the world. James Marshall made the first big strike on California's American River, and for the next thirty years miners continued to search the western slopes of the Sierras for the precious metal. The Mother Lode Country, as the center of the mining region was called, follows the contour of the Sierra Nevada range and is crisscrossed by many streams. One of these was the Calaveras River, site of the renowned Angel's Camp.

Most of the fortunes, however, were made not from the mines but by the merchants who served the hordes of gold seekers. Prices of food and equipment were so high that the miner had to spend a large percentage of his gold just to keep mining; and to vie for the remainder of the miner's earnings were saloon keepers, gamblers, entertainers, and schemers of all kinds. The famous and the infamous flocked to the gold country and to the camps and mining towns in one of the greatest "get-rich-quick" booms in the nation's history. Towns like Yerba Buena, which was later renamed San Francisco, became cities overnight.

Often the miners were lawless and selfish. Yet the settlers lured by gold to California were able to organize a government that established order and gained the territory's admission to the Union as the thirty-first state by 1850. Before the end of the year 1849 more than 100,000 persons had arrived. Immigration continued at this rate for two more years until the hopes of finding more gold had faded.

By the end of the 1850's the surface and alluvial gold was no longer found in sufficient quantities to sustain the prospectors. The gold that remained was in deposits that had to be blasted from the hillsides, or it was embedded in deep veins of quartz which had to be worked underground. For such undertakings the resources of large companies were required. But the possessed Gold Rush frontiersman seemed likely to continue his quest for minerals to the

Once again:
"Gold! Gold! Gold! Gold!
Bright and yellow, hard and cold."
Thomas Hood
San Francisco, 1851.

CALIFORNIA HISTORICAL SOCIETY

ends of the earth. When he left the California goldfields empty-handed, he wandered elsewhere through the mountains of the West, appearing at each of the strikes that marked the advance of the mining frontier. Sometimes the journey of the "eternal prospector" led him to the south, and then to the east or the north. He was always on the move, forever searching for a wealth that escaped him. Like the fur trappers and forest wanderers of a century earlier, the prospector was in the vanguard of the forces that helped to develop the nation.

Bonanza in Colorado

The second major gold strike led to the settlement of what became the state of Colorado. Several hundred prospectors were working in the Rocky Mountain region, hoping that they could repeat the strikes that had been made earlier in California. In 1858 a few claims were staked on the eastern slopes of the Rockies in an area inhabited by the Arapahoe and Cheyenne tribes. The first discoveries were on Cherry Creek, a tributary of the Platte, more than ninety miles from Pike's Peak. The fortune seekers to come, however, were to think of this best-known landmark in the region as their destination. "Pike's Peak or Bust" was written on the canvas of the covered wagons moving west, and then later the words "Busted by Gosh" were added when the defeated prospectors were forced to retrace their steps eastward.

The trek to Colorado was not as long, hard, or dangerous as that to California, and by 1859 adventurers lined the 700 miles of trail stretching across the plains from Missouri. The men traveled in every type of conveyance, from heavy prairie wagons to light carriages. Others

42   *The Uncertain Resurrection*

rode horseback, and some even pushed handcarts. The number of immigrants was swelled by economic and political catastrophes. The California rush had attracted fortune seekers even in an era of general prosperity. But the Panic of 1857 had caused much unemployment and left many persons desperate to join the search for riches.[1] More than 25,000 migrants headed for the Rocky Mountains before any real evidence of a strike had been made public.

Cherry Creek proved a disappointment to many of the new arrivals, and most of the crowds had started back home by the end of 1859. Unlike the earlier California strike, in Colorado the accessible surface gold was not found in sufficient quantities to make small miners rich. The principal deposits were in the deep veins of solid quartz which required large investments of labor and machinery to extract. Enough of the newcomers remained in the territory, however, that settlers numbered 34,277 by 1860. Often they became farmers, tilling land that the Indians were forced to give up. Because of conflicts with the Indians and the activities of Southern sympathizers who strove to keep the new wealth from benefiting the Union, the entire territory was unsafe for the next twenty years.

The Mountain Territories

During the period from 1860 to 1886 gold and silver were found in a great many widely scattered locations on the high arid plateaus and ragged mountain ranges throughout the West—in areas that were later to become Nevada, Idaho, Montana, Arizona, New Mexico, Wyoming, and South Dakota. There were gold strikes in the Snake River Valley of Idaho in 1861, in Montana in 1863, and on the Colorado River in New Mexico in the same year. From 1869 to 1890, the Comstock Lode in Virginia City, Nevada, yielded more than $300,000,000 in gold and silver. Improvements in equipment made it possible for miners to unearth this rich strike in the midst of a gold camp established during an earlier rush in 1859.

Thousands of miners staked their claims in the Comstock Lode country, but the successful mines were big business ventures and were operated continuously by means of mechanized techniques. These more advanced methods of mining were applied elsewhere to deposits that had not been profitable in previous decades. Leadville, Colorado, which had been bypassed during earlier gold strikes, became a major center of silver production between 1880 and 1893 through investment in the new machinery. Copper and iron were also discovered but were mined only intermittently, for precious metals were what the prospectors sought. In 1885, however, one of the greatest strikes was made at the Bunker Hill and Sullivan mines in Coeur d'Alene, Idaho, where over $250,000,000 in ore was found, most of it lead.

The original camps in many of the mining regions possessed more inhabitants at the time than have lived there since. Towns sprang up wherever the minerals were discovered. Like those of Gold Rush days, communities included first saloons and gambling houses and later schools and churches. Mines were so valuable and the need for control so immediate and great that individual citizens of the towns organized as volunteer vigilante groups to establish order and drive out the lawless. Because miners recognized no outside laws, vigilantes often remained the only authorities in town. Then after each discovery ceased attracting miners, enough settlers remained or eventually arrived to form the usual local and territorial governments and to petition for recognition from Congress. By 1868 all the territories of the Rocky Mountain states had been designated. Dakota, however, was later to be divided into two states. These Western territories be-

---

[1] The agricultural frontier of Kansas was not particularly prosperous, peaceful, or secure in the 1850's, and many settlers had been recruited to the Middle West for political reasons rather than economic reward. These people found the prospect of quick wealth in Colorado especially tempting.

came increasingly important, for their mountain riches helped to pay for the Civil War and persuaded men to build railroads. But once again Indians were driven from lands that the government had promised them.

By 1870 the era of the independent prospector who dreamed of finding a fortune with pickax and pan was fading. Regions in which nuggets and gold dust had been discovered earlier were exhausted of their surface treasures, and the principal remaining sources of ore lay deep underground. But the hillsides, deserts, and mountain valleys of the West are pockmarked with the evidences of the toil of the early adventurers. Names like Hangtown, Hole-in-the Wall, Tombstone, and Eureka help to recall their vigor, their vitality, their violence, and their gaiety. These and the other mining towns that the prospectors established were the first settlements in much of the frontier lands in the continental United States and Alaska. Their efforts had led to the exploration of huge territories. No longer unknown or untamed, the land had been divided into controlled, working units, the outlines of which would be those of future Western states. Moreover, through the prospectors' discoveries of mineral wealth, the West not only strengthened the nation's economy but also attracted and absorbed its restless citizens.

"THE LAGGING RAILS"

The difficulties of transportation to and from the mines of the West varied with their locations. But though the problem of reaching a distant region plagued the immigrant of the second frontier as it had earlier settlers, the steam locomotive offered a better solution than had the rivers, canals, and turnpikes that partially served frontiersmen before 1825. The great distances and widely spaced communities of the West were a grave challenge to railroad builders, however. Early construction, financed privately, offered transportation facilities within single marketing regions. By 1840 these small lines were being connected to serve most of the East and some of the older Western regions. But even by 1849 there was still only one railroad of any consequence in the West. This line, later known as the Chicago and Rock Island, reached the Mississippi River in 1854.

Gaining of Government Support

Lack of Financial Backing. Construction of railroads in the West was not delayed by any lack of interest, for the major political aspiration of leaders in Western territories was the extension of the railroad system. Yet the obstacles were considerable, the greatest being insufficient financial resources. The federal government was still leaving internal improvements to state initiative, but most states resented paying for a railroad that might connect their neighbors with profitable markets without benefiting the state through which it passed and which financed its construction. Indiana's objections to the building of a railroad line to Chicago was a good example. Finally, however, the New Albany and Salem, a chartered local line, was persuaded to build and lease a connecting piece of track for a line that crossed Michigan. By 1852 Chicago had become the western terminus of this railroad system, which had connections to the East coast.

Because of the impasse between federal and state governments, sale of stock was initially the principal source of revenue for financing the projected railroads of the West. But little capital was available for investment on the frontier, for the risks involved did not appeal to investors in Eastern cities. Most entrepreneurs still thought in terms of small businesses and had not yet recognized the need for the huge corporations that were developed in later years.

Eventually, the settlers of the Western regions petitioned Congress for help, pointing out that sale of the remaining public lands could provide a source of revenue for railroad construction. Since Congress had already been using these proceeds to finance road building, it was argued, diversion of funds for investment in railroads would not be a radical change in policy. Canal builders had been granted sections of land located along rights of way, and railroad supporters asked for the same concessions. They reasoned that the lands were necessary to build the railroads and that the value of remaining public lands would be greatly increased by their presence.

Both Senators Thomas Hart Benton of Missouri and Stephen A. Douglas of Illinois were active in gaining government support for railroad construction. Senator Benton, who has been called the political father of Western railroads, was instrumental in backing the explorations of his son-in-law John C Frémont, the renowned "Pathfinder" and eventual presidential candidate. Benton supported plans for a transcontinental railroad as early as 1830. Senator Douglas, who joined the cause later, was responsible for the passage in 1850 of a bill granting alternate sections of land to the states for transfer to the railroads to finance their construction. This law created vast opportunities for political corruption, however, for controls were insufficient and state legislators could release the lands to the railroads when they chose to do so. Yet without the law the building of Western railroads would have been delayed for many years.

Controversy over Routes. Three years after passage of Douglas's Illinois Central Act, five possible routes for the first transcontinental railroad were surveyed. The Northern route was not chosen because it did not serve any population centers, and a central route was rejected because no pass through the Rockies was gradual enough for building a roadbed. Benton supported this route, however, and instructed Frémont to conduct an independent survey of its feasibility. The third route ran beside the Platte River through Nebraska; one Southern route followed the thirty-fifth parallel through Albuquerque, and the other passed through New Orleans, El Paso, and Yuma. Douglas proposed that all three of the latter routes be selected, but Benton refused to back this position. Although it was obvious that not all three were needed at the time, Douglas believed that Congress would be more likely to endorse three than any single route.

Politics immediately became a major factor in the controversy. Because the decade of the 1850's saw the height of the rivalry between North and South for control of unsettled territories through which any railroad line would have to be constructed, none of the series of measures presented to Congress for this purpose had any real chance of passage.

The First Transcontinental Railroad

The California Terminus. Actual work on the building of the railroad that eventually crossed the continent began at the Pacific end. California business leaders, including Governor Leland B. Stanford, Collis P. Huntington, and Charles Crocker, decided to investigate the possibilities in 1861. They arranged for the Central Pacific Railroad Company of California to be chartered. Theodore D. Judah's survey of the Sierras had disclosed great engineering problems, but it also indicated the possibility of constructing a line along the route of the principal trail into the state.

The Californians were quick to submit their plans to Congress, for the outbreak of the Civil War favored the selection of a Northern route. The Southern routes traversed rebel territory and were obviously out of the question. On July 1, 1862 Lincoln signed the Pacific Railway Act, authorizing construction of a transcontinental railway that would lead from Iowa to San Francisco. All building in California would be done by the Central Pacific, but the Union Pacific Railroad was to construct (page 449) the sector of the line to run between the eastern boundary of California and the hundredth meridian. The two companies were granted a free right of way through public lands and were to receive ten sections of public land for

The Second Frontier

each mile of track that was built.[2] These grants were made directly to the railroads rather than to state governments.

Delay Caused by the Civil War. Although the Civil War had led to the selection of a Northern route, the effect of the conflict on the nation's economy and the availability of money for investment delayed the undertaking. Construction of the line was supposed to help the war effort, but the project failed to arouse enthusiasm. The first track was laid in February 1863, but five years later only 136 miles of the railway were in use. Whatever the difficulty of crossing the Sierras, the principal problem continued to be a lack of financial support. In 1864 Congress passed a law that granted the railroad companies twenty sections of land per mile of track, rather than the ten originally authorized, and that enabled them to borrow additional funds. The government would lend the companies $16,000, $32,000, and $48,000 for each mile of track built, depending on whether it crossed plains, plateaus, or mountains. Later there were additional subsidies and incentives to stimulate construction. In 1866, for example, the previous geographic limits were removed. Each company was free to build track as rapidly and as far as it could, and additional prize money was to be awarded to the line that made the most progress.

Race Between East and West. After these new measures were passed, the race to lay track began. During 1868 and 1869 there were months in which gangs of workers laid an average of two and a half miles of track per day. The Union Pacific, whose sector crossed the flatlands of the Great Plains, had few engineering problems and was able to complete 1,086 miles of the line. But the Central Pacific, although the recipient of additional federal funds for construction in mountainous areas, could complete only 689 miles.

---

[2]The sections of land (640 acres) given the railroads alternated with public lands held by the government, creating a checkerboard along the right of way. The railroads were free to sell or dispose of the land as they chose.

Both railroad builders adapted many of the techniques devised on the mining frontier to feed and shelter the great numbers of laborers. Towns grew overnight and were dismantled and moved frequently to keep pace with construction. Whatever was needed to lay the track and to supply the laborers was shipped over the newly built roadway. This task was especially difficult for the Central Pacific because tools and equipment, including locomotives, first had to be shipped by sea to San Francisco. Both companies recruited workers from every available source, the Union Pacific depending primarily on Irish immigrants and the Central Pacific on importation of Chinese laborers.

The difficulties in building the transcontinental railroad made the competition between the Union Pacific and the Central Pacific one of the most colorful and exciting episodes in frontier history. People overlooked the fact that at that time there was little along the entire route but Indians, buffalo, empty plains, and mountains, for they felt that the new railroad was certain to be a great stimulus for further development of the vast lands in the West.

Promontory Point, 1869. It was on May 10, 1869 that the two railroads finally joined the eastern and western sectors of the track at Promontory Point, Utah, and the ceremonies were fittingly gaudy and noisy as the entire nation joined in the celebration. The Governor of California swung a silver hammer to drive a golden spike, and there were champagne and speeches. The phenomenal accomplishments of both companies were praised.

THE END OF THE INDIAN NATIONS

The Indian Frontier

The Indians displaced by earlier pioneers were able to live in new locations much as they had in their previous homes because the topography through much of the Eastern half of the United States has many similar characteristics. There was always additional land to the west to which the Indians could be easily relocated,

The Uncertain Resurrection

The dispossessed. SMITHSONIAN INSTITUTION, NATIONAL ANTHROPOLOGICAL ARCHIVES, BUREAU OF AMERICAN ETHNOLOGY COLLECTION

and the federal government always promised that the next move would be the last. Between 1825 and 1841, however, the Indian frontier was recognized as a barrier to further pioneer movement. A great variety of tribes had settled in an area that was roughly bordered on the east by the Missouri River. Some of the Indians had been moved to what was considered their permanent frontier, but others were native to the Great Plains. The idea that the Indian might have a right to protect these lands and his way of life was hardly considered by most frontiersmen, however, as soon as they became interested in these areas. A major confrontation with the Indians was inevitable.

Penetrating the Frontier. After 1841 the Indian frontier was gradually penetrated. Continual movements through Iowa and Wisconsin forced the Minnesota Indians to yield their lands in exchange for promised compensation which they never received. The Sioux were also cheated of seventy per cent of the compensation offered them in 1851, when they allowed the United States government to build roads and army posts in their area. They agreed to remain north of the Platte River and to permit emigrants to cross their lands at will. The Arapahoe and the Cheyenne accepted the lands lying south to the Arkansas River as their territory. At the time most negotiations were conducted by the government in reasonably good faith, and the tribes and pioneers generally continued to live peacefully with each other.

But, when prospects of a transcontinental railroad grew, the attitude of frontiersmen began to change. Because Indian country was a barrier to the building of the railroad, the settlers who supported its construction began to agitate for the removal of the Indians. Some tribes were persuaded to sign treaties and to move on in 1853. Many others resisted, however, and were forced or bribed to leave their homes. The Kansas-Nebraska Territory was

The Second Frontier

THE INDIAN FRONTIER, 1866-1875

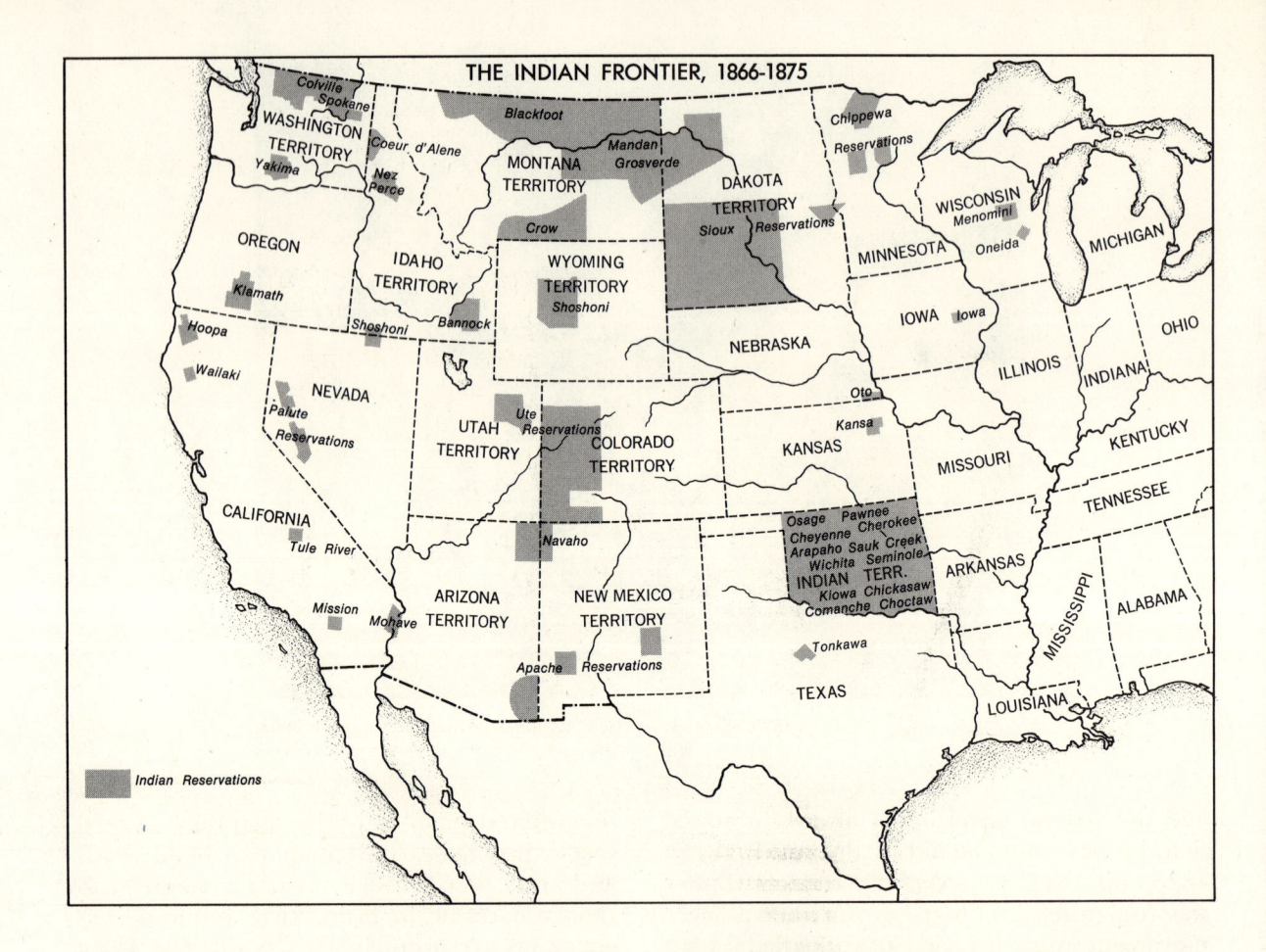

created out of lands acquired by these cessions, although few whites populated the area at the time.

Bureau of Indian Affairs. As the problems relating to relocation increased, the federal government established the Bureau of Indian Affairs in 1849. This agency, which was entrusted with most matters concerning the tribes, was politically staffed like other government agencies during the period. Since bureau personnel were appointed not for their ability but to repay political debts, their morale and standards were low. Many employees were corrupt and systematically cheated their Indian charges. Staff members who were dedicated and sought to safeguard Indian welfare were often accused of disloyalty by the settlers. With such attitudes prevailing and with Congress appropriating inadequate funds, the agency accomplished little.

The Army's Role. Since there were no local governments in Indian territory, the United States Army was assigned the responsibility of maintaining peace and order. Military action was the only means of reprisal; incidents that began only as arrests for drunkenness or petty crimes sometimes led to warfare. Peaceful Indians were punished along with those charged with crimes, and conflict between troopers and Indians was continual throughout the plains region. Matters worsened when the experienced army units were withdrawn from the West for service in the Civil War.

Finally, Congress began an investigation of conditions in 1867, hoping to restore peace in

The Uncertain Resurrection

the territory and to guarantee protection for railroad builders. Councils between government and tribal representatives, which were held in 1867 and 1868, formulated a temporary truce. All the Plains Indians were supposed to move to two small reservations, one in the Black Hills of Dakota Territory and the other in the area which is now Oklahoma. But soon hostilities resumed against those who would not leave their old hunting grounds or refused to remain on the reservations. Peaceful Indians in the Oklahoma area were ordered to assemble at Fort Cobb, and army units undertook to subdue the tribes that were on the warpath. Under the command of Major General George A. Custer, the United States Fifth Cavalry began a systematic series of raids in the territory.

Indian Warfare

The battles waged between the Indians and the army on the Great Plains never constituted an actual war, for the Indians were too few and too poor and had no central leadership. Often their retaliatory raids were led by desperate young chiefs. Between 1869 and 1875 there were over two hundred encounters, but most were small and brief although bloody skirmishes. On a one-to-one basis, Indian braves could often hold their own against cavalrymen, but bows and arrows, no matter how rapidly fired, were eventually no match for increasingly accurate and sophisticated rifles; by the 1870's many cavalrymen were supplied with repeaters. The army posts in Indian territory were expensive to maintain and staff, however. It has been estimated that the government spent a million dollars for each Indian killed.

Continual hostilities led to ever greater savagery and sometimes even to complete annihilation of the weaker force. One such incident was the Chivington Massacre. The Cheyenne and Arapahoe had been on the warpath since 1861 because of the influx of miners heading for the goldfields of Colorado. In 1864 the Indians were able to isolate Denver, and the Colorado militia was sent out to protect the city. On November 28, under Colonel J. M. Chivington, they attacked the main Indian encampment and massacred 450 men, women, and children. A white witness described the slaughter of the Cheyenne: "They were scalped, their brains knocked out; the men used their knives, ripped open women, clubbed little children, knocked them in the head with their guns, beat their brains out, mutilated their bodies in every sense of the word."

Small detachments of United States troops occasionally met with the same fate. In 1875 the Sioux in Dakota were ordered to report to the Indian agency in their territory but they refused, enraged over the invasion of their reserved areas in the Black Hills by prospectors in search of gold. Army troops were dispatched to enforce the order in 1876. During this action Custer, now commanding the United States Seventh Cavalry, recklessly led 264 men against 2,500 Sioux at the Little Big Horn (Montana Territory) on June 25, 1876. The cavalrymen fought bravely against the superior forces, but every one of them was killed. The incident has been referred to often as evidence of the bloodthirsty fighting of the Indians, but it represented only a minor victory in a finally hopeless series of disasters. Sitting Bull and Crazy Horse, chiefs of the Sioux, were defeated on October 3, 1876.

The Red River War (1874), the Nez Percé War (1877), the Apache War (1881–1886), and the Ghost Dance Uprising (1890) were won by white soldiers who overwhelmed the tribes by superior numbers and advanced weaponry.

End of the Buffalo. The destruction of the buffalo was another episode in the downfall of the proud warriors of the Great Plains. These great, shaggy, hunch-backed, wild cows were the only source of livelihood for many of the tribes. The Indians lived near the great herds and relied on the meat for food and skins for clothing and shelter. Dung was utilized as fuel.

To the white man, however, the buffalo

"It is so they die on the plains,
the great, old buffalo . . .
They sink to the earth like mountains, hairy and silent,
And their tongues are cut out by the hunter."
Stephen Vincent Benét, "Ode to Walt Whitman"*

LIBRARY OF CONGRESS

herds were a nuisance, although some animals were killed to feed railroad crews. The huge herds that literally dominated the Great Plains often stopped the trains when they began to cross the prairie. Railroad passengers and crews as well as frontiersmen proceeded to slaughter the animals, even when they had no particular reason for doing so. The hides could be sold for "buffalo robes," and certain portions of the meat were very tasty—especially the tongue and a few choice cuts—but most of the carcass was left to molder on the plains. Many men enjoyed shooting at the herds from railroad cars, and others made a profession of killing the shaggy beasts. The massacre reached fantastic proportions. William F. Cody, known as "Buffalo Bill," was reported to have killed 5,000 animals, during a period of a year and a half, while supplying meat to railroad workers.

Such practices could lead only to the extermination of both the buffalo and the Indians who depended on them. By 1886 the scattered remains of herds and remnants of tribes wandered across the plains. The Indians were persuaded to part with the last of their homelands and with a few of the animals were herded onto reservations where they became wards of the federal government.

Protective Policies. On February 8, 1887 the Dawes Severalty Act, supposedly a reform measure, was passed; it provided that all Indian tribes should be dissolved as legal entities and their lands assigned in plots to individual Indians. But the braves had little inclination to cultivate their 160 acres; often the whites persuaded them to sell their best lands and local authorities charged them excessive taxes. Indian children were separated from their families and brought up in boarding schools where they attended classes taught by white instructors. In 1934 the Indian Reorganization Act reversed

*From *The Selected Works of Stephen Vincent Ben*ét. Published by Holt, Rinehart and Winston. Copyright 1935 by Stephen Vincent Benét. Copyright renewed © 1963 by Thomas C. Benét, Stephanie B. Mahin, and Rachel Benét Lewis.

The Uncertain Resurrection

this destructive policy and again encouraged tribal ownership of Indian lands. Although the government has continued its role as the protector of the Indian, it has accomplished little for his welfare or for his integration into the life of the nation. The first Americans became second-class citizens in their own land.

THE CATTLEMAN AND THE COWBOY

One of the most colorful chapters in American history is that of the "cattle kingdom," created in the late 1860's when a series of events vastly increased the scope and importance of the cattle business. Although the animals had been raised on the frontier since colonial times, demands for beef increased at the middle of the nineteenth century, resulting in a scarcity of cattle in the Middle West and raising the price of the meat. Once again enterprising men on the new frontier used its resources to acquire great wealth. The era of the cattle frontier lasted for only a short time, but its way of life has influenced our history and our folklore.

The Cattle Complex

A Taste for Beef. Early Americans had never suffered a shortage of food, either on the farm or in the city. Their simple, unvaried diets had depended on pork and chicken as staples, although beef was always available. But in the years before and during the Civil War improvements in methods of food processing and distribution created a new market for beef. Chicago and Cincinnati were among the first meat-packing centers of the West (page 427). When the Union Stock Yards were opened in Chicago during 1865, however, the public had little way of knowing how vital to the Western economy this industry would become.

Railroads and the Long Drive. The cattle brought to Mexico by the conquistadors had multiplied rapidly in many regions. Huge herds roamed through southern Texas when Americans first began to settle there at the turn of the century. Many of the animals were unowned, or at least had not been branded by the casual Mexican ranchers. The Americans took over members of this stringy but sturdy stock and interbred them with their English beef cattle to produce the Texas longhorn. For many years only a few animals from these range herds were killed for their hides and none for meat because there was no way to transport beef to market. In the 1850's a few Texan ranchers drove herds north to Illinois and west to Colorado and California, but the route through Indian country was too difficult, and the cattle arrived too thin for these drives to be profitable. After the Civil War, however, cattle commanding only three or four dollars per head in Texas were worth thirty or forty dollars in Chcago, and the railroads were being extended into Kansas. The Texas cattlemen realized that their animals were finally marketable. They need drive them only to the railheads in Kansas, and from there the railroads could transport the cattle to the stockyards of Chicago and on to Eastern markets.

In the spring the cattlemen in southern Texas joined in a roundup during which the animals were sorted, branded, and readied for the "long drive." Herded by cowboys, the cattle were moved slowly but steadily northward to the nearest railroad. All along the route the animals feasted at night on rich grasslands belonging to the government. If conditions were not favorable for an immediate sale when they arrived at the railhead, the cattle were driven still farther to another railroad or were left on the range to graze until market prices had risen. More than 300,000 animals were moved northward each year. The most traveled route, first used in 1866, was the Chisholm Trail, which linked San Antonio to Abilene on the Kansas Pacific Railroad. Then as rail lines were extended farther west, new cow towns sprang up and new trails were developed. The Western Trail led to Dodge City on the Santa Fe and to Ogallala (Nebraska) on the Union Pacific. The Goodnight-Loving Trail, opened in the same period, led to Cheyenne and then Laramie (Wyoming) on the Union Pacific. Later,

The Second Frontier

when the ranges of Wyoming and Montana were used for cattle, the animals were driven south along the Bozeman Trail to the railheads.

The Open Ranges. The sale of cattle was so profitable that other areas of rangeland were soon occupied. During the 1850's and 1860's, the Great Plains had been crossed repeatedly by pioneers with teams of oxen. When any of the animals had to be abandoned on the winter range, they were found to be surprisingly fat and healthy in the spring. The discovery that domestic cattle could prosper as well on the Northern open range as the native bison was important to the economy of the West, particularly since these grassy lands were left unoccupied after the slaughter of the buffalo. In the 1870's cattlemen started bringing young Texas steers to open public ranges in western Kansas, Colorado, Wyoming, Montana, the Dakotas, and Nebraska. There the cattle fed on rich grasses for several years until they were ready for market. The beef improved because the grown steers were no longer subjected to the long drive from Texas. Because the cattleman relied on the grasslands in the public domain to feed his animals, his profits were forty and fifty per cent. To assure his animals sufficient water where it was particularly scarce, the cattleman need buy only a few acres along a watercourse. By controlling a stream, he was certain that only his animals would drink there and graze the surrounding range as far as the divides creating the neighboring streams. The fabulous

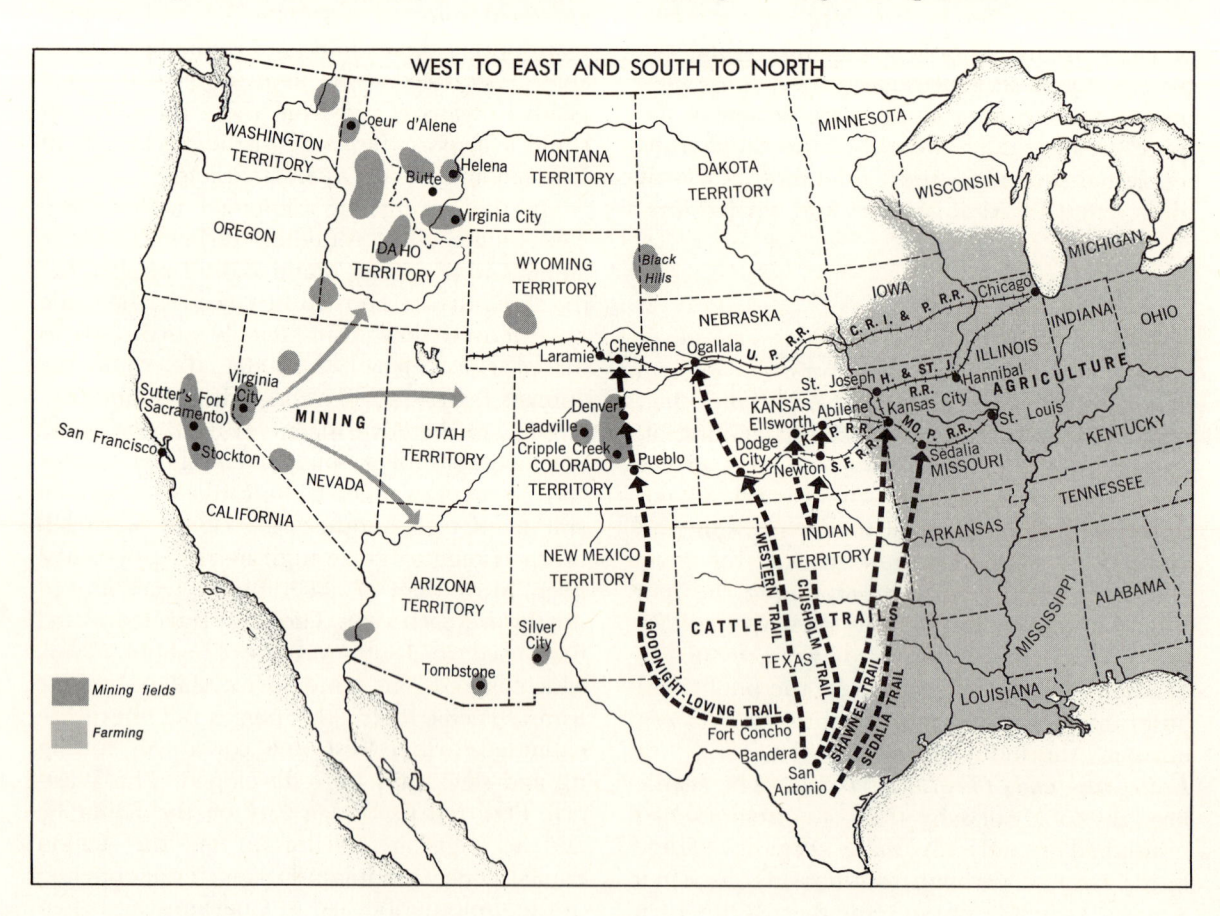

The Uncertain Resurrection

cattle industry grew, attracting Eastern and European investors.

Beef as an Industry. As the demands for beef increased and more and better beef became available, huge new corporations (page 427) that depended on the cattle of the plains were established. Their packing houses, refrigeration cars and plants, and canneries all helped to turn beef into an international business. An increasing number of cattlemen were using the public lands. When the larger cattle companies were formed with capital from the East and Europe, the animals were raised on ranches and sold from them, thus eliminating round-ups. "Barbed wire," an invention which seemed rather insignificant at first, divided the range into separate holdings, making the ranches possible. The wire, spiked with sharp barbs, served to contain cattle, sometimes to their detriment, for when they were free they moved instinctively to protect themselves against the weather. More and more of the public domain was claimed and fenced, and even the cattlemen who still used the open range brought their stock into fenced land for fattening.

End of the Cattle Kingdom. Just as suddenly as it had begun, the boom in the cattle industry ended. During the mid-1880's an oversupply of animals developed at the same time that there was a decline in the demand for beef. In addition, the railroads, which had transported cattle to market, now also carried farmers to the West. Settlers began to establish farms, homes, and towns, thus reducing the amount of land that could be used for grazing and for moving the herds to the north. Although the cattlemen attempted to stop the farmers or "nesters" from taking over the land, the agricultural frontier had finally reached the plains, and there was little they could do to postpone its impact. Then from the autumn of 1885 until the spring of 1887 the elements contributed to the woes of the cattlemen and settlers alike — there were violent blizzards in the winters and a killing drought in the summer.

The Cowboy—Real and Imaginary

The most colorful part of the cow country was the cowboy himself. Although his heyday lasted for less than twenty years, his legend has endured. The cowboy was not a businessman, nor was he an independent frontiersman. He was hired by the cattleowner to do a specific job—to round up and herd cattle to market. Often he was a drifter, uneducated and uncouth. Many former soldiers joined the ranks of the cowboy at the end of the Civil War. Negroes, looking for a new life, were also attracted to the ranges; over 5,000 were employed on them during the principal cattle drives. The plains helped create the myth of the cowboy. The loneliness and the dust and the emptiness of the arid land provided a setting that glamorized the cowboy's strength, manliness, and independence. At a time when the lives of men in the rest of the United States were becoming ever farther removed from the frontier, he was a man's man, still living close to raw and rugged nature. Many saw him as continuing the traditions of the Cavalier gentleman, others those of the Spanish don of the early Southwest. Bred to the saddle and skilled in the use of weapons, the cowboy of the legend was courteous to women, performed a full and arduous day's work, and was ready to enjoy his recreation to the utmost. There was very little of the Puritan in the American cowboy.

For whatever reason, the cowboy became an image for the nation, both at home and abroad. Through the Western-style shows of "Buffalo Bill" Cody and his troupe and of other performers, the cowboy tradition was portrayed in many parts of the world during the 1880's. Cowboy ballads, such as "Oh, Bury Me Not on the Lone Prairie," were sung everywhere, and collections of "Wild West" stories became immensely popular. Today the "Western" is a staple of television as it has long been of radio and motion picture productions. The Western story is considered a typical American art form. The

The Second Frontier

Home, home on the range . . .   LIBRARY OF CONGRESS, ERWIN E. SMITH COLLECTION

era of "good guys" and "bad guys," of dance halls and saloons, planked sidewalks and dusty streets, and bellowing steers and twanging guitars, has lingered on in the hearts and imagination of millions of people.

The End of the Open Range

Although the farmers who followed the railroads into the open Western territory could see no reason to reserve the vast acres for cattle which used them only rarely, there was no way to prevent their intrusion until the invention of barbed wire. Cattlemen put up the first wire fences, but the open range was doomed when the new farm families adopted the practice. The farm families who moved into the grasslands of Kansas and Nebraska were the first to resist the drifting cowboys and their herds with guns and the barbed wire fences. The two types of life could not exist together in peace, and the nomadic herds were compelled to yield.

Beef cattle are still raised on the plains, but the methods have changed; the stock is now bred and raised in the same pasture. Areas in Texas, Montana, the Dakotas, and Wyoming continue to supply beef to the nation, but much of the excitement of the cow country has disappeared. The cowboy, who may now ride the range in a jeep or a helicopter, still wears a "ten-gallon hat" and boots, however, and contends with dust, heat, and loneliness, just as his predecessors did. The present existence of the cowboy is close enough to the legend to keep his tradition alive.

THE FARMER AND THE WEST

Farmers coming West did not present the colorful spectacle created by the gold seekers and cattlemen but, because they remained to de-

54   *The Uncertain Resurrection*

velop the land, they eventually proved to be the more important settlers.

Railroads and Farms

The railroad building that led to the junction of the Central Pacific and Union Pacific at Promontory Point was only the beginning of a vast new transportation network. The Panic of 1873 (a depression which halted most of the activity on the frontier) interrupted, but did not stop, construction of new lines which opened many parts of the unoccupied Western territory to settlement. Between 1879 and 1884 most of the major railroads of the West were completed, except the Great Northern, which did not begin full operation until 1893. Each new line brought sections of the Far West within easy reach of other parts of the nation, for the railroads not only carried passengers and freight but also entered the real estate business as well. As indicated earlier, companies like the Union Pacific and the Central Pacific were financed by the sale of alternate sections of land granted them along their rights of way by the federal government. The railroads provided access to and stimulated the sale of both their own lands and those belonging to the government, primarily by publicizing the real and imaginary virtues of the West.

Land for the Asking

After 1850 a prospective farmer could acquire land on the frontier in several ways. The Distribution-Preemption Act of 1841 permitted squatters to claim up to 160 acres of unsurveyed land in the public domain and then later buy it at the minimum $1.25 per acre (or $2.50 per acre if the plot was part of a grant to a railroad or canal company) without bidding for it at auction when the area was officially opened for settlement. In 1854 the Graduation Act was passed to accelerate Western settlement by reducing the price of land. This legislation specified that all lands left unsold after ten years would be offered for purchase at lower rates, depending on the length of time that they had remained unused. If acreage had been made available on the market for more than thirty years, for example, it might be sold for $12\frac{1}{2}$ cents per acre.

Groups insisting that the government offer free homesteads gained strength from 1840 to 1860, and the Panic of 1857 increased their ranks. After 1860 the Republican party platform endorsed the proposal that public land be granted directly to settlers; on May 20 1862 the famous Homestead Act was finally passed. The best known of all the federal land laws, this measure made it possible for the government to offer a free farm to any head of a family over twenty-one years of age who would pay a small registration fee and live on the land and cultivate it for five years. If a settler had more money than time, he could "prove up" on his land after six months by paying $1.25 an acre.

Between 1862 and 1883 more than 600,000 persons filed for homesteads under the law, but only one-third of these completed the requirements and received final titles. Most of the others bought the land outright or purchased other acreage from railroads or private parties. Equally revealing is the fact that between 1862 and 1904 a total of 147,350,000 acres were acquired free from the public domain (except for filing and other fees), but during that same period 610,760,000 acres were purchased. The impact of the Homestead Act and similar measures seems to have been mostly psychological.

Problems of Land Use. Although the generous land policies of the Homestead Act encouraged settlement and the establishment of many orderly communities, all the lands of the West were treated as though they were suitable for small farms. Yet much of the territory consisted of deserts and mountains, and even the most fertile areas were semiarid plains. Plots of 160 acres were often too small for grazing or for the farmer who had enough money to use the expensive new machinery.

The original Homestead Act was amended many times to meet local demands for increased acreage. Forested areas were opened for timber cutting and the growing of trees. Desert regions were made available in blocks of 640 acres at 25 cents an acre if settlers would irrigate their claims. These larger blocks were also available in stock-raising areas after 1916. Citizens were encouraged to acquire land wherever and whenever possible, for land values were expected to increase and improve the economy. But the geographic limitations, together with lax enforcement of federal policy, proved detrimental. Natural resources were wasted, as were the lives of many men who struggled unsuccessfully to establish farms. Fraud was rampant. A pail of water poured on a desert claim was often accepted as irrigation. Local businessmen encouraged poor neighbors and newly arrived aliens to claim land and then transfer it to them.

Today there is controversy over the proper use of the remaining Western lands. Should they be sold for immediate or future economic gain, or should they be conserved for the recreation of present and future generations? The greater understanding of land use acquired by the public through its interest in environment control and ecology has given hope to those who wish to preserve the wilderness and base our national growth on something other than the exploitation of our dwindling public domain.

Government Grants. During the years from 1810 to 1900, when the federal government was encouraging settlers to occupy the public domain, it used its lands in other ways to support the development of new communities. Grants to railroads were only one phase of this program, for other public and private enterprises also received land. For example, liberal grants were made for the support of schools. The Morrill Act, passed on July 2, 1862, granted to each state 30,000 acres of land for each senator and representative it sent to Congress, the revenue earned from the sale of the land to be used to endow state colleges of agriculture. The sixty-nine "land grant" colleges existing in the United States today were all established under the terms of this act. Among them are many of the leading state colleges and universities, including those in California, Michigan, and Minnesota.

THE LAST FARM FRONTIER

The most promising areas on the remaining frontier were the level, rolling plains east of the Rockies, and these lands were the first to be claimed by homesteaders. Although many of the settlers were attracted by the offers of free land from the government and the advertising appeals of the railroads, some of the newcomers were simply seeking to escape from a society at war. Northerners traveled West to avoid the draft; and, at the end of the war, soldiers from both the North and South decided to seek new opportunities in the West rather than face the ruined economy of the South or return to the routine factory jobs in the North.

Problems of Prairie Life

Immigrants found that the prairies presented unique farming problems. Winters were extremely cold, and summers were blazing hot. Rainfall was scant and uncertain, and much of the water supply lay deep in the earth. There was no wood, and the soil was rough and stubborn and deeply laced with the six-foot-deep roots of prairie grasses. Swarms of grasshoppers ate growing crops. In addition, there were many rattlesnakes, and prairie fires were a common menace. Indians and herds of cattle roamed through the territory, and law enforcement officers were distant, if they were any at all. Thus prospects were bleak, and the hardships discouraged all but the bravest of settlers. Many immigrants who came to western Kansas, Nebraska, and the Dakotas abandoned their

The possessors. NEBRASKA STATE HISTORICAL SOCIETY

land claims and returned to their homes "back East."

New Living Techniques. Yet other settlers remained to find solutions to the problems of prairie life. They built houses of sod and lived below ground level until building materials could be shipped to the prairie by the railroads. In regions among the coldest in the United States, they relied on dried buffalo dung and hay for fuel. To keep out intruders and contain their livestock, the people fenced their lands with the newly invented barbed wire. They dug wells to establish a water supply and erected windmills to harness the constant winds as a source of power. The settlers also devised new agricultural techniques, one of which was "dry farming." In this process farmers plowed deep into the soil so that it would yield moisture and then raked the surface into a fine dust to reduce evaporation.

New Farm Inventions and Crops. New machines coming into use in other parts of the nation were to serve the prairie farms well. The mechanical reaper, first built in 1831, had revolutionized agriculture wherever it was used. By 1860 more than 80,000 of these large machines had been sold; farmers came to depend on them when there was a shortage of laborers during the Civil War. Then mechanical binders were introduced to tie the grain into bundles. In the 1880's the reaper was improved and was combined with other harvesting equipment into giant harvester-threshers. Spring tooth and disk harrows improved the quality and speed of cultivation. With gangplows, seeders, and combines to help him, the farmer could raise twenty bushels of wheat per acre by expending eight to ten hours of work. In 1822, with the tools then available, he had spent fifty to sixty hours to raise the same amount (page 213). Iron plows were in general use by 1850, and John Deere's steel plow later in the decade. By 1877 James Oliver had perfected and was producing an inexpensive, heavy

The Second Frontier

chilled-iron plow which could penetrate the tough sod of the plains even more efficiently. Now wheat could be planted throughout the Great Plains.

New strains and types of grain were introduced on the prairie. The soft-kernel winter wheat grown in Eastern farming regions was killed by rigorous and early winters. A hard spring wheat from Poland and a hard winter wheat from Russia eventually found their way to the plains and proved sturdy enough to flourish there.

The Settlers. Some of the new frontiersmen were of native American stock and had farmed in the Eastern part of the country, but many of the new settlers came directly from Europe, especially from Scandinavia. Between 1868 and 1883 the majority of these hardy Nordic families moved directly into the Western frontier, particularly in Wisconsin and Minnesota. In 1882 alone there were 105,326 of these immigrants.

All faced the same hardships, the same fears. The land itself was disillusioning. For generations people had hoped that better areas could be found to the West, but the settlers on the second frontier recognized that there were no more such opportunities. If the barren, flat, wind-swept prairie was the fulfillment of the American dream, it was a very sobering one. The belief that a young man could always move West to establish a fertile farm was quickly dispelled by the rude realities of dry farming and of living amidst dust and heat and in a sod house. The prospects of what the future might hold were frightening. Yet most of the newcomers remained on the prairie to battle the elements and carry their financial burdens as well.

Closing the Frontier

Colorado, the thirty-eighth state, was admitted to the Union in 1876. For the next thirteen years, however, the remaining areas in the West continued as territories, even though they comprised one-third of the total land mass of the continental United States. By 1880 they also contained nearly two million people, including settlers and Indians. The formation of new states lagged partly because the depression prevented development of the land and partly because there was little political interest. The mining frontier had opened much of the territories to private ownership, but most of the prospectors and mineowners had moved on, leaving behind them many drifters and much lawlessness. The task of creating a basis for statehood was left to the farmers who gradually occupied the West after the departure of the miners and adventurers.

Last States Admitted. As their political awareness increased, the settlers in Western territories petitioned for statehood. Between 1889 and 1907. nine new states were established. Only in the Southwest corner of the nation was there any territory left. In 1912 New Mexico and Arizona were admitted as the forty-seventh and forty-eighth states.

The End of the Frontier. The population of the plains and mountain states soared rapidly. In the Dakotas, for example, it increased from 14,000 to 510,000 in twenty years. Land rushes continued to be common as immigrants raced to establish claims. The settlement of Oklahoma was particularly dramatic. Long considered Indian land, vast acreage in the territory was secured by the government and opened for settlement. On April 22, 1889 a signal was given, and thousands of "boomers" lined up on the boundary line poured across to stake their claims to homestead and town lots. In one year Oklahoma had 60,000 residents, and within ten years the number had increased to 400,000.

The land had all been claimed. There were two persons per square mile (the number regarded as necessary to classify an area as settled) throughout the entire continental United States by 1890. Now that there was no longer a land frontier, citizens came to accept the fact that in no place within our national boundaries could they escape completely from the pressures of the modern world. The hope of adventure may still tempt Americans of today to California and the new states of Alaska and Hawaii, yet the hard fact remains that no longer can men merely push west to better themselves. The second—and last—frontier had offered promises of freedom, probably more imaginary than real. A colorful and romantic era in the development of the United States had finally come to a close.

SUGGESTED READINGS

*Billington, R. A., *Westward Expansion* (1967).
 Bowman, I., *The Frontier Fringe* (1931).
 Caughey, J. C., *History of the Pacific Coast* (1933).
 Chapman, A., *The Pony Express* (1932).
*Clark, T. D., *Frontier America: The Story of the Westward Movement* (1959).
*Collier, J. C., *Indians of the Americas* (1947).
 Debo, A., *And Still the Waters Run* (1940).
 Dick, E., *The Sod-House Frontier, 1854–1890* (1937).
 Frantz, J. B. and J. E. Choate, *The American Cowboy: The Myth and the Reality* (1955).
 Galloway, J. D., *The First Transcontinental Railroad* (1950).
 Gard, W., *Frontier Justice* (1949).
 Gard, W., *The Great Buffalo Hunt* (1959).
*Jackson, H. H., *A Century of Dishonor* (1881).
 Jones, E. L., *The Negro Cowboy* (1965).
 McCracken, H., *George Catlin and the Old Frontier* (1959).
 Mahlin, J. C., *The Grasslands of North America* (1948).
 Nevins, A., *Emergence of Modern America, 1865–1878* (1927).
*Osgood, E. S., *The Day of the Cattleman* (1929).
*Paul, R. W., *Mining Frontiers of the Far West, 1848–1880* (1963).
 Paxson, F. L., *History of the American Frontier* (1924).
 Pelzer, L., *The Cattlemen's Frontier* (1936).
 Pomeroy, E. S., *The Territories and the United States, 1864–1890* (1947).
 Quiett, G. C., *Pay Dirt: A Panorama of American Gold Rushes* (1936).
 Rickard, T. A., *A History of American Mining* (1932).
*Robbins, R. M., *Our Landed Heritage* (1942).
*Rolvaag, O., *Giants in the Earth* (1929).
*Shannon, F. A., *The Farmer's Last Frontier* (1945).
 Sinn, C. H., *Mining Camps: A Study in American Frontier Government* (1885).
*Stegner, W., *Beyond the Hundredth Meridian* (1954).
 Turner, F. J., *The Frontier in American History* (1948).
 Underhill, R., *Red Man's America* (1953).
*Webb, W. P., *The Great Plains* (1931).
 Winther, O. O., *The Great Northwest* (1950).

CHAPTER 19

The Second Industrial Revolution

Your worship is your furnaces.
  Which, like old idols, lost obscenes,
Have molten bowels; your vision is
  Machines for making more machines.
    GORDON BOTTOMLEY, *To Iron Founders and Others*, 1908

THE MANSELL COLLECTION

BACKGROUND FOR AN INDUSTRIAL ECONOMY

Although many of the components necessary for full industrial development existed before 1850, the United States retained a primarily agricultural economy and did not become a major industrial power until the second half of the nineteenth century. Earlier the inventiveness of Americans, the adoption of more complex business techniques, and an increasing population pointed the direction in which the economy was heading. New products, new markets, and new manufacturing methods had combined to create a new way of life for many Americans even before the midcentury mark was reached. The change from an underdeveloped, rural economy to the explosive, dynamic complex of modern times constitutes one of the most important episodes in our history.

During the 1850's industrial development escalated rapidly. Americans were ready for change and were interested in progress and achievement; the basic business structures and industrial processes and machines were all available. Three additional factors were also particularly favorable: continued freedom from government interference, a flow of newly available capital, and, most important, vast natural resources.

Freedom from Governmental Control. During the early years of industrialism in the United States, private enterprise was able to develop without restrictions. The businesses and industries of the nation grew independently and, although they sometimes asked for protection or support, they consistently objected to any form of governmental domination. Even the railroads, which had received direct government aid, were able to expand with few limitations. The principles of laissez faire were always clearly in the minds of both business and government leaders, and few persons even proposed government controls in the United States before 1900. Most citizens would have considered the imposition of controls a form of "internal mercantilism," and they were not willing to accept such economic dictation, which they equated with British policy before 1776. Government controls, it was argued, would return the people to colonial status.

The help and support rendered industry by the federal government began with the Tariff Act of 1816, and thereafter its tariff policies assisted business continually. In the second half of the nineteenth century, even more protection was provided for American industry (Chapter 20). Land policies also favored the growth of business. Private enterprise was encouraged by gifts of land, by the issuance of mineral rights to be developed by private companies, and by outright grants or loans of money.

Capital for Expansion. Businesses, securely established and making large profits by midcentury, were ready to reinvest and expand with their newly available capital. Firms operated by individual owners were replaced by corporations which were to become the basis for modern business and industry. By 1850 all states were chartering such firms. American shipping was also showing profits and doing its share for the nation by producing a large credit balance each year.

Larger amounts of capital were available in many countries other than the United States. The nations of Europe had passed through the first stages of industrial development and were looking for new markets and investment opportunities. With no major war for almost forty years, governments were able to limit defense budgets and taxes, thus freeing capital for private investment. Money from many nations therefore began to flow toward the United States, which showed promise of exceptional growth and productivity. Investors in Great Britain were particularly interested in canal and railroad building.

Natural Resources. The continental United States contained tremendous amounts of varied and valuable natural wealth. In most regions the soil was fertile and supported extensive agriculture. The mountains were rich with coal (Appalachians) and precious metals (Rockies and Sierras). Even the deserts would eventually yield copper, zinc, lead, and phosphates. Seemingly unlimited iron deposits were to be found in the region of the upper Great Lakes. There were undiscovered pools of oil available to be tapped and vast rivers to be harnessed to provide hydroelectric power. The forests still spread over whole states and seemed endless and indestructible. Part of the nation's confidence in the future had come from its Western wilderness, which for most of the century was a place of new opportunities. Until 1891 neither the government nor the public recognized that conservation of resources would ever become necessary.

THE NEW INDUSTRIALISM

Few really new economic ideas originated in the years between 1850 and 1890, yet each element in the economy became larger and more complex. There were more laborers, and there was more need for labor. There were more enterprises, and these became bigger, more complicated, and more powerful. The lives of more people were affected to a greater extent by the new industrialism and the growth of business.

End of Self-sufficiency

The industrial economy reached out to encompass an ever greater number of Americans as the nineteenth century progressed. By the 1870's the factory system had been introduced into all parts of the country, and advances in transportation placed the new products within the reach of nearly everyone. Even farmers became part of the industrial complex, for they produced marketable crops that needed to be processed, transported, and sold. Mines were operated with complicated machinery and large work forces, and cattlemen shipped their animals to the great meat-packing centers. A modern economy, in which men depended on one another for their daily needs, began to develop.

The Economy of War. Although the conditions necessary to encourage growth existed, it was the Civil War that stimulated the tremendous surge of building and expansion—even though the conflict was the most destructive in the history of the nation. Peace in the earlier decades had allowed men to develop the foundations of industry, but the war that followed helped accelerate growth.

As with all conflicts, the nation was not prepared for the Civil War. Even though the North was in a favored position because of its manufacturing strength and technology, it lacked trained troops. The South had the trained military power, but no industrial complex. Both sides attempted to make up for their deficiencies during the war years, but Southerners had the greater difficulty because of their lack of industrial resources. Northerners, on the other hand, engaged in an intensive drive to increase their industrial potential. New factories were opened and new railroads completed; new methods of manufacturing were hurried into use and new manpower resources tapped.

Postwar Expansion. For almost a decade after the Civil War ended, the high rate of industrial development in the North continued. The people of the West—connected to the growing cities of the East by new railroads—produced raw materials and shipped them to factories for processing. The South became the site of new factories because it was forced to modernize during the reconstruction era. The rural population came to depend more on manufactured products for daily needs and on machinery to till the soil. Every area of the nation was becoming a part of the new industrial society during the postwar years.

A Passion for Railroads

By the 1860's railroad building had become a major enterprise. The first transcontinental line was finally completed in 1869 (page 404), but this was only the beginning. There were but 35,000 miles of railroads in the United States by 1865, yet by 1900 there were 192,000 miles. The federal government supported much of this expansion through land grants, especially to the Western railroads, but private interests controlled the construction of the rail network.

Contributions of the Railroads. After 1860 the railroads were a major contributor to the rise in the nation's economy. In addition to shipment of products and transporting farmers to the new lands of the West (page 413), they stimulated the growth of new cities, particularly at railroad junctions, and made it possible for manufacturing plants to be established far from the sources of their raw materials. The railroads themselves provided a tremendous stimulus for industrial expansion, for great quantities of iron, steel, and tools were employed in the construction of their rail lines, locomotives, and railroad cars.

Building New Railroads. Railroads were built even where they were not needed. In the twenty years after the Union Pacific–Central Pacific was completed, four more transcontinental lines were constructed. The Northern Pacific (1883) connected Duluth, Minnesota, with Seattle, Washington, although the population of each city was small and even fewer people lived in the desolate Dakotas which lay between. Two railroads were built across the dry Southwest to California—the Atchison, Topeka, and Santa Fe and the Southern Pacific. In the 1880's so few people used these lines that the owners initiated extensive sales campaigns to recruit passengers. They were offered cheap land and hotel accomodations, but even with these added inducements the lines could not operate at a

The Second Industrial Revolution

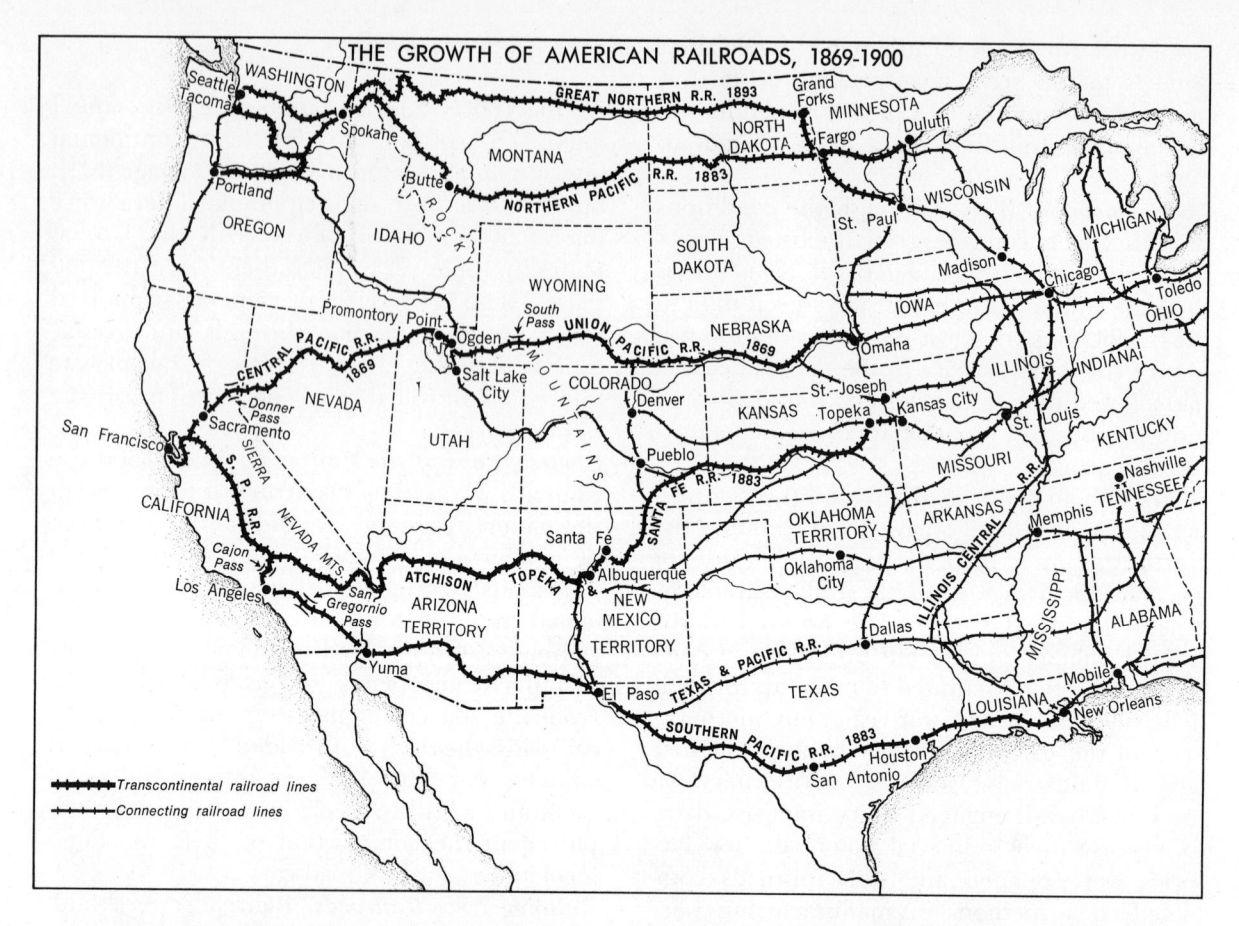

profit. No center of population in the West was large enough to support them.

Although the railroads were extremely important in developing the nation, their lack of business and their weak financial base led to serious difficulties for those who had invested. Unfortunately, the management of the railroads was also poor and indulged in a good deal of chicanery and fraud. During this period the only transcontinental railroad that did not face serious business problems was the Great Northern, built largely through the efforts of James J. Hill, a Canadian, and for the most part without government financing. Because of his sound business practices, Hill was able to weather financial troubles better than his rivals. Yet this line, too, was built through a wilderness and served a limited number of people. Americans soon discovered that there was more to operating a railroad than laying tracks over unsettled wastes.

Reorganizing the Railroads. During the 1860's and 1870's the Eastern lines, constructed to fill local needs, were being reorganized, for they lacked the coordination to operate on a national scale. Gradually, the lines were connected into a network operating on a standard track width and were extended to the entire sprawling nation. One famous consolidation was that masterminded by "Commodore" Cornelius Vanderbilt. Having made his first fortune in steamboats, Vanderbilt turned to railroads in 1869 when he was almost seventy years old. At this time he began to reorganize and revitalize

The Uncertain Resurrection

the lines that were to become the New York Central. He replaced old iron rails with steel, thereby encouraging the rapid growth of another industrial giant in the United States. He offered fast and efficient service to travelers and shippers alike, and in so doing earned more than $100,000,000. Vanderbilt was shrewd and rough in manner, but competent and farseeing. With ruthlessness and courage he built an empire that served the public, even though in his view the railroads were his own property.

Vanderbilt's attitude about his enterprises was typical of the so-called "railroad barons" of the time. They did not feel any responsibility to the nation or to the public, even though much of the early growth of the lines had depended on federal support and on those private stockholders who were bilked so regularly by the railroad men. Vanderbilt and his friends believed that they had earned success through their own efforts, and they felt justified in operating the railroads as they saw fit.

Control of Fares. Inasmuch as railroads completely controlled shipping costs, owners were able to charge exorbitant fares, at least to those customers who were small enough to be victimized. Each line had a virtual transportation monopoly in the area it served and set rates without interference. Because no laws had been passed to control these first large corporate ventures in the United States, the government could offer the hapless consumer no relief. For a time the railroad men were truly "lords of all they surveyed." Only when other industries grew large and powerful were the railroads forced to make some concessions. For example, they granted "rebates," or refunds, to such giant shippers as John D. Rockefeller's Standard Oil Company. The railroad men cooperated with each other by "pooling"; they raised rates by secret agreement and then shared the resulting profits. They very often charged their friends less than they did their enemies. They could even force businesses to fail by refusing service or increasing rates. To justify such acts, the owners claimed that they were merely earning a profit for their stockholders.

Victims of Corruption. Yet stockholders did not benefit from the cutthroat competition because corruption was widespread. Foreigners, who were large investors in railroad stock, often found themselves with worthless paper instead of dividends. Partly because of overconfidence and partly as a result of their unethical practices, the railroads were continually undergoing bankruptcy and reorganization, from which no one profited except the manipulators. Two such freebooters were James Fisk and Jay Gould, who had also been deeply involved in the Crédit Mobilier scandal (page 449).

Steel and More Steel

Other industries paralleled the railroads in growth. Coal mines were developed more fully throughout the Northern states, and iron was found in huge quantities, especially in the Mesabi Range along the shore of Lake Superior. The ore of this vast mineral storehouse was so accessible that it could be mined with steam shovels. Then it was loaded on barges or on the new railroads and sent to the mills and factories where it was transformed into steel, the new miracle alloy.

New Processes. Steel made the United States the world's industrial leader during the nineteenth century. The nation possessed iron and coal in the necessary huge quantities, but the growth of this new industry was delayed until an inexpensive method of manufacturing steel was discovered. Before the Civil War people had used the alloy primarily in the production of cutting tools because it was so expensive, but during the 1850's a new process was discovered that would revolutionize steelmaking. Pig iron was heated until it was red-hot, and then cold air was forced over it. The oxygen ignited the carbon combined with the iron, causing the metal to glow white-hot and burn off the other

The Second Industrial Revolution

Steelmaster: atheist, librarian, pacifist. THE GRANGER COLLECTION

impurities. This was the Bessemer process, discovered independently by both Henry Bessemer, an Englishman, and William Kelly, an American. Although the two men were ridiculed, for their process was believed impractical, the Bessemer system subsequently became the most common method of producing steel until the finer grades produced by the open-hearth method were needed.

Giant Business Complexes. It took more than coal and the Bessemer process to make the United States an industrial giant, however. As late as 1870 Commodore Vanderbilt still had to order steel rails from Great Britain. But within twenty years the nation's industrial capacity had increased so rapidly that the United States was producing more steel than any other nation—one-third of the total world supply. By 1900 it was manufacturing as much as the combined outputs of England and Germany, its two closest rivals.

The advantages of big business were never more evident than in the rapid growth of the steel empire. In Andrew Carnegie, brilliant organizer and manager, the massive power of the efficient business executive was personified. Anticipating the needs of the nation, Carnegie took advantage of the new processes and rallied his assorted companies to market popular products at competitive prices. He could also be ruthless to his competitors, undercut their prices, and drive them out of business. By 1880 the Carnegie Company had consolidated its many properties and companies into an integrated firm—huge, efficient, all-powerful, controlling every step in the production and distribution of steel. This "vertical" control, typical of the structure developed in many other heavy industries, enabled the owners to regulate the entire process of production, from the collection of raw materials to the marketing of a finished product.

The Oil Complex

"Black gold," or petroleum, deposited in many parts of the United States and to become one of its most important natural resources, had in this country been used principally in medicines developed by the Indians. Seepages of oil had been discovered throughout the world for centuries, but its potential as an illuminant was not fully realized until Samuel Kier of Pennsylvania, early in the 1850's, refined it into kerosene and designed a lamp to burn it. This limited use of the resource was enough to launch one of the great success stories of American industry.

Because whale oil, heretofore the world's most important illuminant, was becoming scarce and expensive, kerosene was in immediate demand. But there were no adequate supplies of petroleum. In 1859 the first oil well ever deliberately drilled, near what later became Titusville, Pennsylvania, gushed forth. As the industry boomed, many fortunes were made and lost as speculators rushed to drill wells in expanding fields, especially in western Pennsylvania. Digging a dry hole or a "gusher" meant the difference between ruin and riches. There was little organization or control in the search for oil.

The Standard Oil Company. On another part of the industry order was soon imposed, however. In 1865 John D. Rockefeller, an unprepossessing young man, helped organize a firm in Cleveland to refine petroleum. Renamed the Standard Oil Company in 1867, it became a corporation in 1870 with Rockefeller as its first president. By 1875 Standard Oil had added most of its rivals to its expanding empire, and by 1880 it had established an almost complete monopoly over all operations in the refining and distribution of petroleum products. From controlling thirty-seven per cent of the nation's oil processing industry, Standard Oil had grown to control ninety per cent.

This spectacular achievement was possible because the general business climate favored the rise of large and efficient units unencumbered by competition and the other problems that confronted small firms. Large companies not only manipulated prices to drive out competitors but also received special favors from railroads because their business was so desirable. The giant firms had enough capital to expand when necessary and to survive during periods when business was poor. They were able to gain control of a great number of the plants contributing to their industry.

Rockefeller's companies refined the raw petroleum, shipped the finished product to their distributing stations, and sold it to customers. Each step in the process was wholly owned and controlled, and any competition was driven out by cutting prices. If a rival was unwilling to sell his company, and for the most part the terms offered were generous, he was forced out of business, usually at a loss and often by unfair methods. When Standard Oil had cleared the field, it increased prices again. Without competition and government interference, Rockefeller and others were able to make enormous profits. By controlling the means of processing and distribution, Standard Oil had become master of the oil complex.

The Trust. Such a large enterprise required a new organization. In 1879[1] Rockefeller arranged for Standard Oil—an Ohio corporation prohibited by law from owning companies in other states or investing in their stocks—to join with its out-of-state subsidiaries in a secret agreement. He and nine other "trustees" were given control of all the stock in all the companies and supervision of their operations. The Standard Oil Trust, as this merger was called, became the prototype for the expansion of business beyond corporations. Because they were profitable and efficient, these larger units were able to control and restrain trade.

Other Industrial Giants

Other types of business in the United States also moved toward concentration of management and creation of giant complexes of mines, factories, distribution networks, and even sales outlets.

Meat Packing. During the early part of the eighteenth century, centers in the East had the only meat processing facilities in the nation. To the primitive city stockyards were driven herds of cattle and pigs from local farms. As the population expanded, however, new centers were opened in the West. By 1860 the great beef processing complexes of Chicago and Cincinnati, handling enormous quantities of meat, had been established. In 1870 Swift Packing Company began to ship meat on ice in the new refrigerator cars. Gustavus F. Swift and Philip Armour, another packer, were soon millionaires. By 1880 large national packing plants were pioneering in the "assembly line" butchering of meat and were also expanding into distribution and sales. The eventual size and power of meat-packing companies can be envisioned by their importance in the eyes of reformers like Upton Sinclair. He singled out the Chicago

---

[1] The trust was reorganized again in 1882.

The Second Industrial Revolution

plants as the setting for a muckraking exposé, *The Jungle*, published in 1906 (Chapter 22).

Flour Milling. Although most early mills were simple structures housing primitive machinery, sawmills and gristmills were driven by improved power processes as early as the American Revolution. Even in 1782 grain was being hoisted in elevators. But there were few technological changes in any milling industry between 1815 and 1850, for each mill constituted a local monopoly. Then improvements in transportation led to the development of large specialized milling centers for grain, particularly near Chesapeake Bay. These grain-grinding mills utilized modern industrial methods and soon were producing on a large scale. Suddenly in 1860 the total value of flour and meal production in the United States had grown greater than that of any other manufacturing process—$248,580,365.

Between 1860 and 1900 there were other gradual but important changes. Much of the processing of foods made from grains was transferred from the home to industry. When bread was baked in huge batches by commercial bakeries, flour of a more uniform consistency became essential, and new roller grinders were developed to assure that it would be. Large mills that could serve many farms were built. By 1900 big companies also dominated this industry, and their practices stimulated sharp criticism. In his novel *The Pit* Frank Norris described conditions in the Chicago grain market and attacked the practices of firms in this industrial complex.

The Giants of Industry

The giant industries that developed late in the nineteenth century were clearly the brain children of exceptional men. In fact, the story of industry between 1850 and 1890 is a chronicle of personal triumph. Business leaders became the heroes of the national success story. Without Rockefeller, Carnegie, and J. P. Morgan, trusts and corporations as large as Standard Oil and United States Steel might eventually have been established, but the contributions of these men were prophetic, far reaching, and unique. So powerful that they could act almost independently of government, these leaders often bought or sold legislators, securities, and competitors as well as raw materials and their manufactured products. Yet the great businesses that these men created were to serve as the basis for the modern industrial economy of the United States, and they left their own personal mark on this era of its beginnings.

Andrew Carnegie (1835–1919). The demand for steel produced a vast complex of related industries and factories, but it was Andrew Carnegie, the founder of Pittsburgh's massive steel center, who was responsible for the industry's rapid and successful expansion. Born in Scotland, Carnegie came to America as a child and went to work first as a "bobbin boy." Later he became a private secretary to a railroad executive. He worked hard, succeeded in saving more money, invested shrewdly, and entered the steel business. Eventually, Carnegie established a huge network of mills and factories which were by 1900 producing almost one-fourth of the nation's Bessemer steel. A hard-driving employer, good organizer, and remarkable administrator, Carnegie rejected the corporate structure in favor of an old-fashioned partnership, although at one time he had forty partners. In one year he earned $25,000,000 while his partners shared the remaining profit of $15,000,000. Carnegie finally sold his steel empire to J. P. Morgan for $444,000,000 in cash and spent the rest of life giving away his money, a pattern many other millionaires were to follow in later years.

Carnegie was ruthless in many business dealings and often old-fashioned, but with what were for him sensible motives. He chose ruthlessness because he considered it the most efficient means of dealing with others, and he chose the partnership organization because he did not believe that corporations and monopolies were necessary. His insight into the forces and direction of the growing economy and his long-range planning and far-reaching decisions stimulated the kind of growth that became synonymous with the nation. Carnegie also contended that wealth should be "plowed back" into society. Hundreds of schools and libraries bear Carnegie's name and are evidence of his belief in social responsibility.

John D. Rockefeller (1839–1937). The production of oil was a promising but disorganized industry when John D. Rockefeller became interested in it. At nineteen he was working hard as a bookkeeper for a grocery store, about the time oil was first successfully drilled in Pennsylvania. That same year he established a produce commission firm which flourished during the Civil War. Driven by an ambition to make money, Rockefeller devoted his entire efforts and great ability to amassing capital. In 1865 he joined Samuel Andrews, who had perfected an inexpensive method of refining petroleum, in organizing an oil refinery, the Standard Oil Works at Cleveland.

From this small beginning the company grew spectacularly. As Standard Oil expanded, the fame and fortune of Rockefeller also increased. He became one of the most feared and hated men in the nation. By ruthless price cutting, secret deals with railroad companies, and strict control of all means of shipping, his company was able to place a stranglehold on an entire industry.

Like Carnegie, Rockefeller never doubted his business methods. He improved the efficiency of the industry; he invited rivals to buy into his companies; and he paid high wages and offered fringe benefits long before these became common. In addition, Rockefeller gave vast sums to charity and showed a commitment to the whole society in his contributions to health and education. The University of Chicago, the Institute of Medical Research, the General Education Board, and the Rockefeller Foundation rely on his endowments.

J. P. Morgan (1837–1913). Behind the visible giant industries of steel and oil existed a vast

The first billionaire, seated.   THE BETTMANN ARCHIVE

complex of companies that provided capital for the financing of all kinds of businesses. The "financial wizard" of the era was J. P. Morgan, president of a private investment banking house which had its headquarters on Wall Street in New York City. His companies helped to finance railroads, banks, and industries. When Morgan decided to enter the field of industry, he purchased Carnegie's steel company and merged it with other companies to form the United States Steel Corporation, capitalized in 1901 as the first billion-dollar corporation in the United States.

Even more aloof than most of the other giants of industry, Morgan was born in Connecticut in 1837 and educated in Boston and in Europe. After working in his father's London banking houses, he came to New York in 1860, where he acted as an agent for his family's

The Second Industrial Revolution

firm. By 1869 Morgan had also succeeded in gaining control of the Albany and Susquehanna Railroad, and in 1871 he established his own firm, which was to become one of the world's most important banks.

At his death Morgan bequeathed valuable treasures for public use, as had other business leaders of his time. A wing of the Metropolitan Museum in New York houses much of his art collection, and he contributed to the construction of the Cathedral of St. John the Divine. Despite these gifts, however, Morgan felt only a limited sense of obligation to the public. He believed that what was good for Morgan should be good for everyone.

Robber Barons or Industrial Statesmen? It is very difficult to judge the giants of industry because the entire social climate has changed since their day. They were not bound by current notions of "social responsibility" or by the rights of the public, so these men would not have considered themselves "robber barons." They might have accepted the appellation of "barons," however, for they reveled in their power. Rockefeller was supposed to have said that God gave him his fortune. Vanderbilt was widely quoted as declaring that he did not care about the law because he had the power. His son, carrying on the family tradition, expressed similar disdain for the public and held that the trains ran to suit the owner, not the consumer.

Social Darwinists. The belief that in the struggle for existence only the fittest survive was supported by a theory introduced by Charles Darwin in England during the same era. He held that the various species on earth had evolved from common ancestors through successful adaptation to natural challenges. The Social Darwinists in the United States applied these ideas to society, claiming that the fittest would survive in the business jungle of the time. The aggressiveness of the giants of industry in their elimination of weaker competitors was justified by the laws of nature. The acceptance of this point of view during the nineteenth century enhanced the power and prestige of such men as Carnegie, Rockefeller, and Morgan.

INDUSTRIAL CLIMATE

Until the Civil War there had been little friction between business and the public, for the merchant or manufacturer was a resident of the same community as his customer and felt a personal responsibility to him. Customers could easily complain about poor goods or poor services to the persons who provided them. But many historians have described the latter part of the nineteenth century as an era that "lacked a social conscience." Like the giants of industry, most business leaders came to believe that they owed little to the public or to the nation as a whole.

Tools of Business Expansion

The tremendous increase in size and scope of new business ventures during the 1860's and 1870's caused the personal controls and relationships of earlier years to break down. The bigger, stronger companies destroyed those that were small and weak. The owner of a successful business sought to eliminate competition and establish a monopoly, which would permit him to fix prices as he pleased. If only one company sold oil, people would have to patronize it, whatever the prices, or do without the product. Monopolies sometimes served a useful purpose, however, for they encouraged growth without duplication; seldom did a town need more than one railroad. Special techniques of controlling a particular product or area and of eliminating rival companies were developed.

Pools. The simplest form of control was an agreement between competing businesses to fix prices and regulate production. Each firm would then charge a certain rate for goods or services. Regions were usually divided among companies, so that local monopolies existed. Pooling was a favorite ruse of the railroads, but it was not always successful. The several parties

The Uncertain Resurrection

to the agreement could break it at will and did, for companies were competitive and aggressive.

Trusts. The monopolies that most industries sought to establish during the 1870's were usually informal and flexible. By 1879, however, Rockefeller's Standard Oil Trust made the pattern more formal. A trust consisted of a group of corporations whose stock was controlled by a small board of directors. In effect, this board operated the entire combination of enterprises. By 1882 the Standard Oil Trust directed forty companies and controlled ninety-seven per cent of the oil production in the United States. The trust monopoly became an accepted business structure and was copied by leaders in the sugar, meat, steel, farm machinery, tobacco, and other industries.

Holding Companies. When in the late 1880's the trusts were attacked by both state and federal legislation, not always very effectively, companies resorted to another organization known as the holding company. In this monopoly a separate corporation purchases the manufacturing plants of rival companies and leases them to friendly management. A holding company can also buy controlling stock interests in other businesses and gain control of patent rights. In 1889 New Jersey amended its corporation law to permit the organization of corporations that would not engage in manufacture but would merely own stock of other companies in the state. By 1896 the state permitted a corporation to own securities of other corporations, whether or not they were chartered in New Jersey. The holding company of course attempts to own enough voting stock of each subsidiary corporation to control it. Delaware and West Virginia also allow the incorporation of holding companies, but other states have continued to regard them as an illegal form of monopoly.

The Image of "Big Business"

Public and Government Support. Public opinion supported the frantic and extensive economic growth of the United States after the Civil War. Many citizens were proud of the country's business success and of the financiers whom they believed were responsible for the increasing power of the United States. They looked upon the fortunes of Carnegie and Rockefeller as proof that anyone could become wealthy through hard work. The public considered the country's material gains more important than the suffering and inconvenience inflicted on certain segments of society by the business methods employed. At both the federal and state levels, politicians contended that they should help business to grow but should not attempt to control it. Some officials were bribed, but most honestly believed that "what was good for business was good for the nation." Problems were ignored, for the government shared the general feeling that there should be "no meddling."

The Gilded Age. During this era businessmen were vocal in expressing confidence in their own ability to control the future of the nation. They too were proud of their success and often flaunted material possessions. Millionaires with newly acquired fortunes lived like kings in huge and elaborate mansions and seemed determined to prove that money could buy anything. Marked by gaudiness and frequently by bad taste, the era between the end of reconstruction and 1900 has often been called the "Gilded Age." Whatever the abuses of the period, mass production encouraged the manufacture of quality goods at lower prices. The standard of living in the United States rose as new products became available, and great numbers of citizens shared in the growing prosperity of towns and cities.

The End of Trusting the Trusts. Eventually, however, in spite of the widespread admiration for success and achievement, a real fear of big corporations and trusts developed. Consumers felt at the mercy of these monopolies and accused the corporations of sometimes charging artificially high prices for substandard products. Small businessmen feared that the power of big business would be used to remove all compe-

"God helps them that help themselves" (Benjamin Franklin). THE BETTMANN ARCHIVE

tition. For the first time the laborer began to organize and agitate for a share in the rapidly growing national wealth.

Problems of the Laborer

Before the Civil War most workers looked toward the future with optimism. They could expect to own their own businesses, or acquire land, or move into frontier territory. They were, in general, skilled craftsmen who took pride in their labor and were accepted as productive members of the community. In small businesses and industries, they worked side by side with the owner, who very possibly had in the past been a hired laborer himself. Even the unskilled worker was expected to better himself and eventually join the ranks of the skilled. Employees and employers could communicate and were in contact with each other at work and in the general activities of society.

Lack of Concern for Workers. After 1860, however, the development of large factories created an entirely different atmosphere. Executives or managers rather than owners were frequently in charge, and skilled craftsmen were replaced by masses of unskilled laborers. The new employers had little concern for the personal needs of workers, and as a result the labor force felt little loyalty to the employers. Workers also lost much of their interest in the product, for they performed only a single, unskilled operation and no longer attained a sense of identity by creating an article requiring the application of experience and skill. As the factory became the only important producing unit, the individuals connected with it were demeaned. An employee could no longer hope to have his grievances heard, for he could not compete with the power of capital and management. If the worker was abused or injured or if he lost his job, he had no protection. He did not even have a sympathetic employer to whom he could complain..

Yet in the first decade after the war public sentiment was entirely on the side of the successful owner. The law, the government, and the church treated wealth as "good" and poverty as a necessary "evil." Workers were expected to be humble and to bear their burdens quietly and willingly.

Wages and Working Conditions. Although the worker was treated as a second-class citizen, his income rose throughout the nineteenth century, and the length of his working day decreased. Between 1860 and 1890 wages climbed about fifty per cent. The average pay for a day's labor was about $1.00 in 1860; it had risen to $1.50 by 1890. But never did the wage increases equal the higher productivity of the labor force; the increased profit went to the employer. The workingman's share of the nation's wealth was small, and there was little or no concern about his gaining a fair or reasonable portion. If wage increases were given, they were doled out as gifts, rather than as appropriate rewards for increased productivity and profit.

From 1860 to 1890 the length of the average working day for most skilled and common laborers declined from eleven to ten hours, six days per week. In some industries, however, longer hours persisted. For textile mills a twelve-

The Uncertain Resurrection

. . . except in certain cases—breaker boys in the coal mines. CULVER PICTURES

to fourteen-hour day was common. Steelworkers were employed for twelve hours each day, seven days per week, even in the 1920's.

Yet better wages and hours were not the only considerations. Factories were dark and dangerous. Safety devices were unknown. There was no insurance protection in case of accidents, and workers were not treated when they were injured. Children and women, who worked for extremely low wages and under substandard conditions, were employed in great numbers. In 1910 children between the ages of ten and fifteen still made up over five per cent of the total work force. Fifteen per cent of the workers were women in 1880; by 1900 this figure had risen to more than eighteen per cent. Women were restricted to performing menial and ill-paid tasks in mines and factories. Not until the twentieth century were they considered for office or sales work.

Growing Work Force. Additions to the male labor force came from several sources—from the farm, from the increasing native population, and especially from the ranks of immigrants. This great number of newcomers, together with the unskilled laborers already employed, constituted a large work force which kept wage levels low. The new workers also helped industry by purchasing more goods, by renting housing, and by traveling on ships and railroads. Native-born workers assumed that the constant influx of foreigners was largely responsible for their own poor status, even though immigrants often freed the established labor force to advance to better jobs. Thus the first requests of labor were to restrict immigration.

Power for the Laborer

First Trade Unions. By 1850 the groundwork for unionism had been established, but its benefits were limited primarily to skilled workers. The techniques of collective bargaining,

The Second Industrial Revolution   75

strikes, and boycotts had already been introduced. Individual unions existed, and as early as 1834 a national convention of craft unions was held. The popularity and strength of the movement increased and declined with the economy. Periods of prosperity encouraged the growth of unions, but during depressions they lost members. Craft union membership rolls grew from 200,000 in 1864 to 350,000 in 1873.

But the great majority of workers still had not joined the union movement. The foreign-born did not become vocal union members, for they were even more fearful of losing their jobs than were native-born workers. Public opinion became increasingly anti-union, and employers organized and cooperated to control the labor force more effectively, labeling all union organizers as "rabble rousers."

National Labor Union. Despite the opposition of employers and the passivity of workingmen, unions continued to be formed. The older craft unions weakened as economic conditions changed—only eight survived the Panic of 1873—but obviously labor needed to be organized. The first new attempt to combat the problems created for labor by big business was the founding of the National Labor Union in 1866. This federation of local unions, national unions, and other workers' organizations enlisted about 600,000 members at its peak. Unlike the old craft unions, it sought to represent all labor everywhere, not merely the skilled worker. The union proposed an eight-hour day and favored arbitration of industrial disputes rather than strikes, but since its emphasis was on basic social reform, its principal activities eventually became political. Representatives of the union sought legislative support for cheap money and worker-owned cooperatives. The activities of the group were so politically oriented, however, that it ceased to function after the candidates it supported in the election of 1872 were defeated.

The Knights of Labor. In 1869 the Noble Order of the Knights of Labor was founded by Uriah S. Stephens among the garment workers of Philadelphia. To protect the jobs of those who joined, it began as a secret fraternity. Its organizers preached love and cooperation among members. All workers were eligible to belong —unskilled and skilled, white and Negro, male and female. The Knights of Labor proposed the prohibition of child labor, the establishment of an eight-hour day, and new laws to protect the safety and health of laborers. Moreover, they believed that workers need not resign themselves to being forever wage earners, that by pooling their resources they should be able to own and operate mines, factories, and railroads, to produce and distribute goods on a cooperative basis. After 1881 the society's new leader, Terence V. Powderly, ended the requirement for secrecy. Able to work openly, the Knights helped secure the passage of the Chinese Exclusion Act in 1882 and the 1885 law prohibiting importation of contract labor. Although the Knights were ideologically committed to arbitration, in 1884 and 1885 unions affiliated with their organization won several strikes against the most powerful business combines in the nation, the railroads. These were labor's first major successes. Membership in the Knights of Labor, a mere 20,000 in 1881, rose suddenly to 750,000 by 1885.

Many stresses and strains prevented the Knights from achieving their maximum development, however. The growing organization had difficulty in controlling the activities of local groups. Furthermore, the skilled workers resented being grouped with the unskilled, for they were sometimes called upon to sacrifice their superior bargaining positions for the sake of workers more easily replaced. Then after the Haymaker Riot of 1886 (page 435) the public considered the Knights radicals and turned against them. Skilled workers were the first to leave the association, many to return to their craft unions; by 1890 the membership had dropped to 100,000. Outclassed by a new rival, the American Federation of Labor, the Knights of Labor never regained prominence.

The Uncertain Resurrection

The American Federation of Labor. During the 1870's the craft unions continued to seek a national structure. In 1881 a new Federation of Organized Trades and Labor Unions was formed and soon claimed 50,000 members. In 1886 craft representatives from the weakening Knights of Labor organized the American Federation of Labor. Soon the two new groups merged and selected Samuel Gompers as president. By 1898 more than 250,000 workers belonged to the Federation, and it continued to grow. The old craft unions proved to be the first building blocks in a national labor organization that was to endure. The American Federation of Labor was conservative compared to its predecessors. It concentrated on skilled workers and did not seek sweeping social reforms, accepting the fact that most of its members would remain laborers throughout their lives. It set pragmatic goals for the workingman—shorter hours, higher wages, and better working conditions—and it considered the strike its principal means of winning concessions from employers.

Strikes and Strikebreakers

Although the American Federation of Labor was successfully established during the late nineteenth century, it was not a labor era. The early unions and other labor organizations were unable to achieve their goals, even though they conducted a great wave of strikes, some of the most violent and disruptive in the nation's history. There were, for example, 485 strikes in 1884 and 1,441 in 1886.

Employers maintained that they had the right to break strikes by importing nonunion labor (strikebreakers) and by using coercion if necessary. Fighting both the owners and government, the forces of labor also committed acts of violence but suffered more than their adversaries. An extreme example of violence by laborers, one which received considerable attention, were the activities of the "Molly Maguires," a secret society of coal miners in Pennsylvania who destroyed mine property and killed or injured mineowners who opposed them during the early 1870's. Such tactics and the conduct of other nationally publicized strikes served to deepen public suspicion of the labor movement. Businessmen, government officials, and members of the middle class sometimes feared that the country was on the brink of revolution.

The Railroad Strike of 1877. In 1877 a railroad strike paralyzed much of the transport in the Eastern states and spread as far west as San Francisco. The workers were protesting a series of wage cuts, imposed because of the unsettled financial conditions of the railroads during the depression years of the 1870's. Starting with the Baltimore and Ohio Railroad, workmen struck in fourteen states. Eventually, over 100,000 men were involved. Violence flared along the lines and in the terminal cities, where state militia were called out to control the strikers. Workers were killed and injured by the scores, and in return the strikers destroyed property, over $10,000,000 in Pittsburgh alone.

The most important event of the strike was the use of federal troops, sent to restore order by President Rutherford B. Hayes. The strike was broken, and the men had to accept the reduced wages. With the power of the federal government clearly on the side of business, the public seemed even more convinced that strikes were wrong.

The Haymarket Riot. During 1886, when the influence of the Knights of Labor was at its height, leaders of the group decided to concentrate on the organization of unions in Chicago, where there were already more than 80,000 members. At the same time a number of anarchists who advocated violent overthrow of the government had come to Chicago to arouse radical support. The two groups of agitators were considered almost interchangeable by the public. On May Day of that year members of the Knights of Labor in Chicago joined their brethren and other labor groups throughout the country in a strike to demonstrate support for

The Second Industrial Revolution

"Who ever hears of fat men heading a riot . . . no — no, 'tis your lean and hungry men who are continually worrying society, and setting the whole community by the ears" (Washington Irving).

LIBRARY OF CONGRESS

legislation for the eight-hour day. A striker was killed when police intervened at one of the demonstrations, and on May 4, 1886 the anarchists held a meeting in Haymarket Square to protest treatment of strikers by the authorities. The crowd was orderly, but just as the meeting ended the police arrived and ordered everyone to leave. At this moment a bomb was thrown; one policeman was killed and several persons were fatally injured. A riot broke out, during which seven more policemen and other civilians were killed. No one could identify the person who had thrown the bomb, but the police rounded up eight anarchists and all were charged with murder. Four were executed and three imprisoned. In the public mind the Knights of Labor were identified with the events of May 4 and the anarchists. Sentiment against them was so strong that they never recovered as an organization. When in 1892 the Governor of Illinois, John P. Altgeld, pardoned the three surviving anarchists — because he considered the evidence against them inconclusive — he was subjected to severe criticism and abuse by conservatives, and his political career was ruined.

The Homestead Strike. In 1891 the wages of workers at Carnegie's Homestead steel mill were cut. At the time, the Amalgamated Association of Iron and Steel Workers was trying to

78   *The Uncertain Resurrection*

organize the employees at the plant, but both sides refused to negotiate further after this act. Henry Clay Frick, one of Carnegie's representatives, hired three hundred armed Pinkerton detectives to protect the plant during the crisis. When the men arrived, the strikers attacked them with rifles and dynamite, winning a pitched battle in which ten persons were killed and sixty were injured. The state militia was called to restore order, and the strike was eventually lost, for after five months the workers returned to their jobs on company terms. Once again labor gained the reputation of being an evil force from which the nation had to be protected.

The Pullman Strike. During the 1870's local law enforcement agencies, the state militias, hired forces such as the Pinkerton men, and even federal troops (1877) dealt with the disorders. Not until the Pullman strike (1894), however, was the full weight of the federal government used to end a strike.

During the depression of the 1890's the Pullman Company cut wages drastically without reducing rents for the workers' houses in the company town maintained near Chicago. A committee was sent to protest, and three members of the group were discharged immediately. Shortly thereafter workers at the company went on strike. The action of Pullman Company was supported by the General Managers' Association, representing twenty-four railroads that operated out of Chicago and used Pullman cars (sleepers). The American Railway Union, under the direction of Eugene V. Debs, supported the strike and refused to handle the Pullman cars. Strikers succeeded in stopping rail traffic on all lines west of Chicago; then hoodlums began to loot the halted rolling stock.

At this point Attorney General Olney urged President Cleveland to intervene on the grounds that the United States mail was being interfered with. Governor Altgeld, who had shown impartiality at the time of the Haymarket riots, said no real danger existed, but he was ignored. Federal troops were ordered to Chicago to see that the mail was protected and that the trains went through, and in the process the strike was conclusively crushed.

A federal injunction helped break the Pullman strike. Used in earlier labor disputes, in particular the railroad strike of 1877, this court order forbidding the performance of a certain stated act, or acts, was to become an even more important antilabor device then the deployment of troops. In the Pullman strike Debs and others were ordered to cease obstructing the mails, damaging property, and encouraging laborers to strike. When they refused, they were arrested, tried without a jury, and sentenced to six months in jail. When labor appealed the conviction, it was upheld by the Supreme Court on the grounds that the union had "conspired to hinder and obstruct interstate commerce" under the terms of the Sherman Anti-Trust Act. Because this act had originally been passed with the intended purpose of controlling big business and had failed, its later success in restricting labor was particularly ironic.

PROBLEMS OF THE FARMER

Agriculture in the United States never consisted completely of family farms, on which people were expected to grow all the crops necessary to supply their own needs. In certain sections of the country there had always been one-crop economies, particularly in the colonial and pre-Civil War South. Elsewhere farming became more specialized throughout the early years of the nation. Improvements in transportation and the growth of cities made farm specialization even more profitable during the last half of the nineteenth century, but the average American farmer did not share in the tremendous growth and prosperity that marked the rest of the American economy. In the new era of mechanization, the farmer was faced with debts, transportation problems, and world competition as well as with droughts, floods, and insect pests.

Agrarian Businessmen

Monetary Problems. The new farms were expensive and often had to be financed through bank loans. When a man could cultivate the "back forty" with a wooden or iron plow pulled by a mule, his investment was small and his debts were limited. With the advances in agriculture, however, the farmer had to buy farm machinery and more land and often found himself deep in debt. By the 1870's, with money scarce and the value of the dollar rising, farm debts became more difficult to pay as each year passed.

Then in the 1880's farm prices began to fall. The farmer was continually on the verge of bankruptcy during much of the late nineteenth century. If he had a bad crop, or was ill, the mortgage on his land was foreclosed. His only choices were to become a tenant farmer or to move farther west. By 1890 more than 200,000 farms in Kansas, Nebraska, and Illinois were heavily mortgaged and their owners in danger of losing their livelihood. Farmers, small shopkeepers, and other debtors who had great difficulties in repaying loans because they had borrowed when the dollar was not as valuable demanded that the government resolve their crisis by issuing more money (page 454).

Resentment Against Businessmen. Even though the railroads had made possible the settlement of the second frontier, the farmer regarded the government grants to them as unfair to the people. Since they were usually the only means of transportation available, these carriers had the farmers at their mercy, especially for local, short hauls on the land-locked prairies where there was no competition from other lines. Rejecting the idea that consumers or the government had a right to interfere (page 425), the railroads set their own unreasonable prices and were responsible for the failure of many farms. The farmer feared that railroad companies, as well as banks and other big industries, would drive him into economic slavery as a tenant on lands that he had lost through foreclosure.

As though these pressures were not enough, the farmer also felt exploited by the "middlemen" of agriculture. These were the processors, wholesalers, and commission merchants who marketed and financed raw produce. To the farmer they seemed the nearest and most selfish of his "oppressors." He contended that they paid low wholesale prices for his crops and then sold them at a great profit. Again the farmer was convinced that he needed help in eliminating the injusticies of which he was the victim.

Falling Farm Prices. New equipment increased productivity, but demand for farm products did not keep pace. Despite rising incomes, consumers did not buy more farm products—they merely spent a smaller proportion of their income on food. In addition, farmers in the United States were being compelled to compete, for the first time in the nation's history, with agricultural products from Argentina, Canada, Australia, New Zealand, and other parts of the world. In the same era that more grain reached the market because of additional acreage and better technology, American farmers had to contend with the western European importation of wheat from the pampas of Argentina and the plains of Canada, made possible through improvements in transportation. The price of wheat was determined in Liverpool, England, and world markets were not concerned with the fate of the farmer in the United States. There was also more cotton available on the European markets during this period.

Throughout the last decades of the nineteenth century the farmer sold his farm products in a competitive world market of continually falling prices. His supplies and household goods were purchased in a home market of high prices maintained by monopolies and protective tariffs. And even though the lower prices for farm goods offset gains made in productivity through the use of the new equipment, the farmer still had to purchase the gangplows and combines or his income would become completely inadequate.

Farmers Begin To Organize

With deepening debt and costs of marketing and distribution plaguing all rural sections of the nation, it was only natural that the Western farmer would eventually join with others, especially those in the South, to protest and to try to find solutions to their shared problems. The first groups established were designed to meet the farmer's own occupational and social needs as well as to protect him against the forces that were driving him deeper into debt and despair.

The Grange. Farms were lonely, drab places during the nineteenth century, especially on the barren prairie. Members of farm families felt a real need for some kind of organization to which they could turn for recreation and fellowship. In 1867 the National Grange of the Patrons of Husbandry, a secret fraternal society, was formed to make such fellowship possible and to support agricultural interests. Each local group was called a Grange, and its members were known as Grangers.

Under the energetic leadership of Oliver H. Kelly, who was employed by the New Department of Agriculture (founded 1862), the membership of the Grange had grown to 750,000 by 1874 simply because it met many of the needs of the farm community. The national purposes were "cooperating, control of monopolies, and more instruction in scientific agriculture." The organization was a place to air grievances, especially against creditors, and provided representation at local and national levels. It also agitated for legislation to curb the overwhelming power of the railroads and to prevent other business enterprises and creditors from taking advantage of the farmer. Grangers gained control of some state legislatures in the West and South and in the 1870's were able to pass state laws regulating the freight and passenger rates that railroads charged on local lines. Commissions were also set up to enforce the laws and to keep track of the activities of the lines. The railroads of course objected and took their case to court. In the important *Munn* v. *Illinois* decision (1877) the Supreme Court found that states could control any business serving a public interest by setting the maximum amount that could be charged. If the business found the rates unreasonable, it should take its complaints to the legislatures or the people, not to the courts.

The attempts of the Grange to help the farmer avoid the costs of the expensive middleman and channel overhead revenue back into his own pocket met with disaster, however. The leaders who undertook the operation of cooperative grain elevators, exchanges, and banks lacked the necessary experience. The failure of these experiments in cooperative marketing weakened the farmers' confidence in the entire movement. Although the Grange continued as a social organization in many rural areas, membership declined rapidly after 1875.

Farm Alliances. With the failure of the first cooperative movement of the Grange era, farmers founded other local organizations to voice their grievances. Largely state or regional in nature, the groups merged about 1888 into large bodies, the National Farmers' Alliance of the Northwest and the Southern Alliance. These organizations were influential in many states, particularly in the West and South. The Alliances, like the Granges, held picnics and conventions to relieve the social isolation of farm life. Circulating libraries, study groups, and local newspapers were sponsored to increase the farmers' understanding of current social and political trends. The Alliance also established cooperative stores and elevators and attempted to provide insurance and cooperative purchasing services. With membership numbering in the millions, the Alliances attacked low prices for farm products, the railroads, moneyed interests, and monopolies. But national politics were still beyond their range of influence. Not until the 1890's did the farm bloc begin to have an impact on federal action.

PROLOGUE TO REFORM

The country would never be the same again. The ideas, values, and moral precepts of the aggressive and impersonal society were vastly different from those of the pioneers and Puritans. As the century ended, the public began to question all aspects of the code on which big business was based (Chapter 22), even though its criticism was still tempered by the continuing spirit of optimism and the belief that the amassing of a fortune was every man's true and possible aim. The violence and unrest stirred up by the problems of labor and the destitution of many farmers had set the stage for the reforms of the twentieth century. The age of machines and of big business had arrived; the age of reform and of big government was yet to come.

SUGGESTED READINGS

Burlingame, R., *Engines of Democracy* (1940).

Casson, H., *The Romance of Steel* (1907).

*Chandler, A. D., Jr., *The Railroads* (1965).

*Cochran, T. C. and W. Miller, *The Age of Enterprise* (1942).

Commons, J. R., *History of Labor in the United States* (4 vols., 1918–1935).

Corey, L., *The House of Morgan* (1930).

*David, H., *History of the Haymarket Affair* (1936).

*Diamond, S., ed., *The Nation Transformed: The Creation of Industrial Society* (1963).

*Fine, S., *Laissez Faire and the Welfare State, 1865–1901* (1956).

Fish, C. R., *The Restoration of the Southern Railroads* (1919).

Fogel, R. W., *The Union Pacific Railroad, A Case in Premature Enterprise* (1960).

Ginger, R., *Age of Excess, American Life from the End of Reconstruction to World War I* (1965).

*Ginger, R., *The Bending Cross* (1949).

Gompers, S., *Seventy Years of Life and Labor* (2 vols., 1925).

Grodinsky, J., *Jay Gould: His Business Career, 1867–1892* (1957).

Hacker, L. M., *The Triumph of American Capitalism* (1940).

Hendrick, B. J., *The Age of Big Business* (1920).

*Hofstadter, R., *Social Darwinism in American Thought* (rev. ed., 1955).

Hutchinson, W. T., *Cyrus Hall McCormick* (2 vols., 1935).

Josephson, H., *The Golden Threads* (1949).

Josephson, M., *The Robber Barons* (1935).

Kamepffert. W., *A Popular History of American Invention* (2 vols., 1924).

*Kennedy, G., ed., *Democracy and the Gospel of Wealth* (1949).

*Kirkland, E. C., ed., *The Gospel of Wealth and Other Timely Essays by Andrew Carnegie* (1962).

*Kirkland, E. C., *Industry Comes of Age, Business, Labor and Public Policy, 1860–1897* (1961).

Kouwenhoven, J. A., *Made in America* (1948).

Lane, W. J., *Commodore Vanderbilt* (1942).

Moody, J., *The Masters of Capital* (1921).

Nevins, A., *John D. Rockefeller, Study in Power, Industrialist and Philanthropist* (2 vols., 1953).

Oliver, J. W., *History of American Technology* (1956).

Passer, H. C., *The Electrical Manufacturers, 1875–1900* (1953).

*Pelling, H. M., *American Labor* (1960).

*Riegel, R. R., *The Story of the Western Railroads* (1926).

*Rischin, M., ed., *The American Gospel of Success, Individualism and Beyond* (1965).

Shannon, F. A., *America's Economic Growth* (1951).

Sumner, W. G., *What the Social Classes Owe to Each Other* (1883)

*Tarbell, I. M., *The History of the Standard Oil Company* (one-volume ed., 1950).

*Ware, N. J., *The Industrial Worker, 1840–1860* (1924).

*Ware, N. J., *The Labor Movement in the United States, 1860–1895* (1929).

*Warne, C. E., ed., *The Pullman Boycott of 1894* (1955).

Williamson, H. F. et al., *The American Petroleum Industry, 1899–1959* (1963).

Yellen, S., *American Labor Struggles* (1936).

CHAPTER 20

Political Expediency and Self-interest

No personal considerations should stand in the way of performing a public duty.
  ULYSSES S. GRANT, *Letter*, 1875

"WHO STOLE THE PEOPLE'S MONEY?" — DO TELL. N.Y. TIMES.

'TWAS HIM.

CARTOON BY THOMAS NAST,
THE BETTMANN ARCHIVE

REALITIES OF THE POST-CIVIL WAR PERIOD

CIVIL WAR CHALLENGED THE POLITICAL BELIEFS OF THE people as it did their social and economic patterns, for former methods of dealing with political problems proved no longer adequate. New techniques and a new organization had to be created to cope with governmental change, just as new structures had to be established to accommodate social and economic changes. After the Civil War the nation was faced with three major political problems: the party in power represented only one section of the reunited nation; American values and ethics had been damaged by the war and its aftermath; and the increasingly complex economy would be affected by any course of political action.

Republicans in Power

Republicans as a Sectional Party. The Republican party, established during the pre-Civil War years as a regional party (page 322), was identified with the division of the nation into opposing sections. By 1858 every Northern state, except Indiana and Illinois, was Republican, whereas every Southern state of course remained Democratic. The Republican platform continued to oppose the extension of slavery in the territories, but in 1860 the party began to broaden its base by calling for a protective tariff, a transcontinental railroad, a homestead law, and open immigration. Most of these planks did not appeal to Southerners, nor were they intended to. Republicans were interested in gaining the support of Northern Democrats, and this they accomplished. In 1864 the name of the organization was even changed to the National Union party so that Democrats who could not bring themselves to become Republicans might be willing to support the ticket.

Yet not all Northerners were Republicans. The Democratic party continued to have a strong influence despite its identification with the Southern cause; and throughout the Civil War some Democratic candidates were elected to office in the North, even though the ranks of these officials were thinned. As an indication of Democratic strength in wartime, Lincoln received a majority of only 400,000 out of the 4,000,000 votes cast in the election of 1864. Since even during the Civil War narrow majorities threatened Republican control, party leaders after the war were very doubtful about the wisdom of readmitting Southern states to the Union. Northern interests still determined party aims, and its appeal in the South was not likely to grow.

Republicans as a War Party. Not only were the Republicans identified with the North, but they were also regarded as the "war party." In power throughout the Civil War, most of their actions had been determined by wartime needs. The Republicans had been authors of a series of unpopular measures, such as the Conscription Act (1863) which resulted in draft riots and was criticized for penalizing the poor. Moreover, the Republican Congress had increased taxes. The party had also advocated continuing the conflict until a victory was achieved, whereas the Democrats had supported demands for a negotiated peace. And in its preoccupation with the war effort, the nation failed to notice other legislation initiated by the Republicans. The Homestead and Pacific Railway acts, for example, had been passed in 1862, but their impact on the public was delayed until peace was restored.

Reconstruction as a Political Device. When the Confederacy surrendered, the Republicans, denied the vision and leadership of Lincoln, were not prepared to resolve the complex issues of peace and merely continued the conflict on a political rather than a military basis. Blaming Southerners for the war, the party sought the continued support of the voter by assuring him that the former enemy would be adequately punished.

To prevent white Southerners from being eligible to vote after the Civil War, the Republicans delayed the readmission of Southern states to the Union and took other steps to avoid political opposition. Thus, before the states were readmitted, federal legislation was passed to encourage Negro votes, expected to be Republican, and to discourage white votes, expected to be Democratic. These maneuvers were essential to the continuation of Republican control, as evidenced in 1868 when Grant was elected by the 500,000 Negro votes cast in the territories in the South that were organized into military districts (Chapter 17).

Only through a policy of manipulation and revenge were the Republicans able to sustain their power for twelve years after the end of the Civil War. They did not have overwhelming majority support even in the North, but by appealing to past grievances and hatreds most Republican candidates were able to win elections. And by instituting Radical reconstruction measures, the party received continued backing from Southern Republicans. As late as the mid-1870's, several Republican candidates, including Rutherford B. Hayes, were elected only through the deciding votes of Southerners. With no prospects of offering a program that would appeal to the entire nation, Republicans could hope only to continue the status quo.

Yet the Democrats were unable to overcome the popularity of Republican appeals for revenge, or to cast off accusations of disloyalty. Nor was the Democratic party able to offer programs that would appeal to Southerners without antagonizing their Northern constituents. But before the century ended Democrats were to find ways to create a coalition that would challenge Republican dominance.

Moral Damage Inflicted by Civil War

Reaction Against Wartime Idealism. The Civil War had been a crusade for some citizens, for they had fought not for land, or profit, or status but for principles. Whether abolitionists or devout "states'-righters," they were alike in their unselfishness and devotion and felt the same idealistic concern for a cause. Others, however, had not been so greathearted, being concerned with profit rather than idealism. These were the wartime profiteers, the "get-rich-quick" operators, the clever manipulators of government contracts, the cheats, and the "smart money boys." They flourished during the Civil War, and if the goods and services provided by them were inadequate, they felt no responsibility.

After the war the idealists began to take stock of the results and, finding that the selfish seemed to have thrived while they themselves had suffered for little, if any, gain, questioned their idealism. Northerners complained that Negroes still lived in servitude, despite the war and subsequent reconstruction policies. Southerners, with their way of life almost completely destroyed, resorted to violence and trickery to regain their losses. The "old order" had been changed by war in both the North and South. Traditional virtues had been challenged, and the old rules for success had been broken. Northern profiteers, Southern "night riders," and Western "exploiters" had violated or were violating many of the ethical standards upon which the nation had prided itself. The citizenry suffered a general reaction against the use of "high-sounding" phrases and purposes. Success itself became more important than the method used in achieving it. Americans had always admired a winner, and now they were ready to praise him no matter how he succeeded.

Profiteering. Wars breed a peculiar kind of extravagance because nations spend vast amounts on armaments. When tremendous fortunes can be made, promoters will seize every opportunity to profit from destruction and bloodshed. The Civil War was particularly notorious for profiteering. Both sides were served with selfishness by business and industry; there were more of the new class of millionaires in the North only because their opportunities were greater. Speculators, agents, and manufacturers conspired to cheat the government. Because defective merchandise was sold to the army, soldiers were often ill clothed and without serviceable shoes. Food and drink were inferior or poisonous. The ships that Vanderbilt built for the navy leaked, and the young J. P. Morgan sold the government discarded rifles. The public seemed blind to the situation and its causes. Even though soldiers suffered, there was no widespread criticism of the manufacturers who were defrauding the nation; and public officials were often in league with the swindlers.

Disinclination to Serve. The cost of the conflict was not shared equitably, for few citizens were eager to serve on the battlefield. In the North there was widespread resistance to the draft calls of 1863, largely because the rich could legally avoid military service by paying a substitute three hundred dollars. As the number of able-bodied men declined, bounties for enlistment were offered by states, counties, and cities, encouraging even more undesirable behavior. "Brokers" imported the poor and degenerate of Europe and persuaded newly arrived Irish and Germans to enlist in the army for their bonuses, which could amount to as much as a thousand dollars. Some of these men became "bounty jumpers," increasing the fraud by enlisting several times. After deserting from one unit, they would join another and be paid again. In the South most soldiers were volunteers, but their loyalty and dependability were often limited. Entire companies marched home as soon as their enlistment terms had expired, even on the eve of a battle. Because the South was less populous, it was forced to conscription a year earlier than the North. The Confederate system also allowed the hiring of substitutes, and it exempted plantation owners with twenty or more slaves and many professional and skilled men.

Many soldiers deserted on both sides. Even though deserters were shot when captured, the army rolls were riddled with "absences without leave." More than 200,000 men deserted in the Union army alone, and although records of the Confederate army are not as complete, it clearly had numerous deserters as well.

Widespread Acceptance of "Expediency." Greed, fear, and self-interest undermined the moral standards of soldiers, civilians, and politicians. After the war the materialistic, aggrandizing efforts of self-serving leaders and of swindling speculators did not abate. In fact, they grew worse, and corruption became prevalent. A large number of citizens regarded the lax moral tone of the 1870's as inevitable, and some even approved of corruption. It was considered clever to evade the law and sensible to use influence. Any method was acceptable if wealth might be accumulated or success in other endeavors could be assured.

POLITICS AND SELF-INTEREST

The Grant Administration

The political activities of the 1870's and 1880's were as tainted by sharp practices and self-interest as was the economic and social life of the nation. Public officials were no more moral than the general public who elected them. In 1869 General Grant became President of the United States after a campaign that capitalized on the hatreds and fears of the postwar years. Grant was not an intellectual, nor was he even an experienced politician. His valor and military skill were unquestioned, but understanding and leadership of a nation trying to heal its war wounds and face the new problems of an industrial age were beyond his capacities.

In Grant's judgment loyalty was the most important personal trait. A man loyal to his friends (or to Grant) could do no wrong. Many of Grant's associates were incompetent, misinformed, and even dishonorable, but they never fell from his favor because of these faults. Completely gullible, although personally honest, Grant did not create the lax moral tone of his administration. The officials he appointed and retained, however, directly connected him with some of the most notorious scandals of the era. Most of Grant's Cabinet appointments, made without consulting anyone, went to old friends from the army, politically unknowing and unknown. They in turn dispensed the federal patronage jobs to Grant's and their own relatives and toadies.

The Gold Conspiracy of 1869. Unscrupulous operators were able to influence these inexperienced and unfit federal officials perhaps more than in any other administration in United States history. Soon after Grant assumed office in 1869 two financial adventurers, Jay Gould and James Fisk, Jr., attempted to corner the gold supply of the nation. These financiers planned to make a huge profit by buying all the available gold in the country and then withholding it from the market to force up its price. Their plan would work only if they could keep the United States Treasury from selling gold to bankers and merchants, who needed it to settle international balances and to pay customs duties. Gould and Fisk persuaded Abel R. Corbin, Grant's brother-in-law, to lobby against the federal sale of gold. Despite Grant's refusal to agree to the plan, the necessary orders appeared to have been given and the conspirators spread the word that federal sales had been stopped.

During the week of September 20 the price of gold rose; businessmen sold stocks and bonds and called in debts in an effort to raise the growing amounts of cash needed to purchase the metal. To meet the emergency, Grant ordered federal gold sales of four million dollars, announced on "Black Friday," September 24. The price of gold dropped drastically, and the entire economy of the nation was shaken. Many legitimate businesses were ruined, and many stockholders and speculators were wiped out by the wild fluctuations of the market. Gould, however, managed to sell his gold in time, and Fisk escaped by refusing to accept his obligations and letting those who had acted as his brokers fail. A congressional investigation cleared Grant of any intentional wrongdoing. His associations with Gould and Fisk caused some public concern, however—although not enough to encourage caution and prevent repetition of the same kind of scandal.

Santo Domingo. During these same months in 1869 other speculators approached Grant with

The Uncertain Resurrection

the idea that great profits in minerals, timber, and fruit were possible if the Caribbean island of Santo Domingo (now the Dominican Republic) could be annexed. The treaty of annexation that Grant submitted to his Cabinet was unanimously rejected, as was a similar treaty later sent to the Senate, despite Grant's efforts to force its adoption. The "operators," undaunted, would devise new schemes to use the government for personal gain.

Crédit Mobilier Affair. Promoters took advantage of the federal government's deep involvement in the railroad construction boom during the 1860's. The owners of the Union Pacific created their own construction company, called the Crédit Mobilier, to build their part of the first transcontinental rail line and paid this company a great deal more than the construction cost per mile. The government of course loaned the railroad the money to pay for the construction (page 404). To assure that Congress would not pass legislation calling for the repayment of the loans, the construction company was said to have given shares of its enormously profitable stock to certain politicians, including Schuyler Colfax, Vice President of the United States, and James A. Garfield, a United States congressman who was later to become President. Two other congressmen were officially censured after the investigation that followed (1872), but other people involved were neither cleared nor punished.

Increasing Scandal. The years of Grant's second term were marred by many incidents in which governmental power was manipulated for personal gain. In 1875 the "Whiskey Ring," a conspiracy of revenue officials and distillers which had deprived the United States Treasury of millions of dollars through a system of tax evasion, was uncovered in St. Louis. The chief governmental employee involved was John McDonald, a Grant appointee, although 238 persons and Grant's private secretary, General Orville E. Babcock, were eventually indicted. The President did, however, intervene to save his personal employee from conviction. Another Grant appointee, his third Secretary of War, William W. Belknap, was charged with accepting bribes in the sale of trading posts in Indian territory. When a resolution of impeachment was passed by the House of Representatives on March 2, 1876, Belknap resigned. Later he was acquitted by the Senate, although many senators voted against impeachment only because they believed that they had no jurisdiction over an official who had already left his post.

Nor were members of Congress free from excessive self-interest. On March 3, 1873 they approved a measure increasing their yearly salaries by $2,500—from $5,000 to $7,500—retroactive for two years. By this "salary grab" each congressman would for the next two years have received $5,000 in addition to his past salary. Public indignation was aroused, and a storm of protest forced repeal of the law in 1874.

The Disputed Election of 1876

Political power, as well as wealth, was acquired by strategem in the 1870's and 1880's. When the campaigns for the presidential election of 1876 began, the major parties were almost equal in strength. Republicans were the incumbents and could still warn against "rebel rule" and rely on the support of big business. They were, however, handicapped by the scandalous "good stealings" of Grant's administration and had not nominated James G. Blaine, their strongest and most magnetic candidate, because he had been accused of using his influence to secure a land grant for a Southern railroad. Instead the party selected Rutherford B. Hayes, Governor of Ohio, a man with a successful military record in the Civil War, reputed to be honest and competent but unknown to much of the nation. The Democrats were still suffering from wartime accusations of disloyalty, but they could capitalize on the weaknesses of the Grant administration. Their standard-bearer was Samuel J. Tilden, Governor of New

Political Expediency and Self-interest

York, who was known nationally for his earlier part in breaking up the "Tweed Ring"[1] in New York City and for the reforms he had sought as the state's chief executive.

When the ballots were counted, it appeared that the nation would have its first Democratic president since the Civil War, for Tilden received a 250,000 majority of the popular vote as well as a majority vote in the Electoral College. The Republicans, however, questioned the returns from Oregon and from Florida, Louisiana, and South Carolina, the last three Southern states in which Federal troops were still stationed. They claimed that votes had been cast illegally in these states and that without these faulty ballots Tilden lacked by one vote the majority necessary for election. By December 6 a second set of election returns had been submitted from the three disputed Southern states, for Republicans controlled their election boards and had found enough "irregularities" in votes claimed for Tilden to certify that Hayes had won the election. The problem in Oregon was quite different. The Democratic governor disqualified a Republican delegate to the Electoral College and certified a Democrat in his place, thus violating Oregon law and jeopardizing the validity of the balloting. There was little question that the Republicans had really won that state, however.

For two months the nation faced near chaos, and there was even talk of insurrection. Hostility between parties and sections was still deep, for the Civil War had ended only ten years previously. Congress was divided as well, for the Senate was dominated by Republicans, the House by Democrats. Would a deadlock once again be settled by force? The Constitution does not specify who shall count the electoral ballots when the two houses meet for that purpose and clearly the President of the Senate would choose the Republican returns, the Speaker of the House the Democratic returns.

Finally, Congress acted to resolve the crisis on January 29, 1877 by appointing an Electoral Commission charged with the responsibility of breaking the deadlock. It consisted of five senators, five representatives, and five Supreme Court judges. Each body of Congress was expected to select members to represent its own majority. The Senate sent three Republicans and two Democrats, the House two Republicans and three Democrats. The Supreme Court was instructed to provide two judges from each party. The fifth member of the commission was expected to be an independent, David Davis. He was unable to serve, however, because he had just been elected to the Senate. In his place the Court named a Republican, Joseph P. Bradley.

In its deliberations the commission was influenced by party pressures, and the members voted accordingly. Bradley, who had first gone on record as favoring Tilden, reversed his vote under pressure from Republican politicans. In the end, all eight Republicans supported their party and voted on March 2, two days before the scheduled inauguration, to accept the disputed returns as submitted by Republicans without further investigation.

Although the commission was supposed to be "above politics," it was generally conceded that its decision would be acceptable only if political promises were made. In return for supporting the decision, the Democratic party was able to gain several important concessions from the incoming Republican administration. Federal troops were to be withdrawn from Louisiana, South Carolina, and Florida. In addition, there were to be Southerners in the President's Cabinet, and Congress was to allocate funds for railways and other public works needed in the South.

Although the actions of both political par-

---

[1] During the first five years after the Civil War, this notorious ring of politicians, led by Boss William M. Tweed of Tammany Hall, the Democratic party organization in New York City, robbed the city treasury of nearly $100,000,000. Suppliers, contractors, carpenters, and repairmen were instructed to pad their bills and give Tweed the excess amounts. Thermometers reportedly cost the city $7,500 apiece.

ties before and after the election of 1876 were reprehensible, it had been demonstrated that the government of the United States could survive a major crisis without going to war. Once again compromise was possible.

REVIVAL OF THE TWO-PARTY SYSTEM

Between 1865 and 1900 the number of voters in the United States increased rapidly. The populations of nine new states, immigrants from Europe, and former slaves swelled the ranks of the citizenry. But the control of machine bosses over city politics, the political influence of the leaders of industry, and the dominance of the whites in the communities of the South prevented these citizens from forming powerful voting blocs.

New Democratic Strength

By 1877 both Republicans and Democrats were aware that the dominant issues of Civil War days had lost their appeal. Antagonisms were fading, and people were tired of the old slogans. The reconstruction program in the South had been abandoned for reasons of political expediency. Moreover, the scandals in Grant's administration had weakened the Republican party's image. Voters interested in reform were looking for new party affiliations. Some had supported a Liberal Republican movement in 1872; others backed splinter parties. But still others voted Democratic, for indignant citizens wanted to "throw the rascals out," and the Democrats, as the second major party, offered the best alternative.

The New Solid South. In the 1876 election the resurgent Democrats had nearly elected a President and were able to gain legislative seats in all parts of the nation, but their rise to power centered in the Old Confederacy, the new Solid South. Now that the white Southerners had voted out the carpetbag governments, the South reverted to its sectional support of the Democratic party. From 1887 to 1964 Southerners never wholly supported a Republican candidate for the presidency. The citizens of some Southern states voted for Republicans in 1928 and 1960 in protest against a Catholic candidate, but not until the civil rights issue received vocal Democratic support did white Southerners in greater numbers begin to vote Republican.

A Strong Minority Party. The Democratic party was also strong in some of the Northern cities, where the Irish political bosses, always of great aid to the foreign-tongued immigrants, controlled votes with their powerful machines. The rest of the nation's population supported the two parties about equally from 1872 on. The Democrats were able to elect a president only twice before the end of the century (Cleveland in 1884 and 1892), but the contests were extremely close. Two of the Republican victors attracted fewer popular votes than did their Democratic opponents, and of the twelve Congresses elected, the Democrats controlled the House seven times. Although the Democrats had a majority in the Senate only twice, the upper chamber was three times evenly divided between the two parties during this period.

Platforms Straddle Issues

Although in many parts of the nation voters felt free to choose between the Democrats and Republicans, their platforms were often similar. Trying to include planks that would appeal to all the voters, the conservatives who were in control of both parties straddled issues, evaded extreme positions, and did not concentrate on any single problem. Foreign policy issues and the principal economic enigmas of the day were ignored. Between 1877 and 1901, there was no single dramatic issue in any election, except for the tariff controversy in 1896. Campaigns in this period relied on personalities, on slogans, and on mudslinging, with little real attention to pressing problems. But since holding office meant power, both parties spent immense sums of money and expended much time and energy for their candidates, trying to convince the voters that they had a choice. Rallies drew huge and enthusiastic audiences to hear empty generalities and denigration. Millions thronged to the polls to choose earnestly between indistinguishable candidates.

Economic Complexity and Party Politics

Even if the moral climate had been healthier, political action would still have become increasingly difficult during the 1870's. The United States was facing, for the first time, all the problems attendant to its change from a rural and agrarian country to an urban and industrial power. The social and economic controls necessary to meliorate the inequities of the new industrial system had not yet been devised, nor did most politicians think regulation was necessary (page 431). Until the end of the century the government separated itself from the economic needs of the nation. This neglect was to have profound effects on the politics of the country as well as on the economy. The inaction of Congress during the Panic of 1873 serves as a case in point.

In 1873 overexpansion of industries and speculation caused an economic panic with a five-year-long aftermath of suffering and hard times. Tens of thousands of businesses went bankrupt, and more people were unemployed than ever before in the nation's history. The unskilled, the white-collar workers, and small businessmen alike had to rely on the limited generosity of private charity. Those who held jobs were confronted with slashing wage cuts.

Political leaders of both parties failed to respond adequately. The Republicans did not take emergency measures, nor did they pass legislation to control the speculation that had helped bring on the depression. Congress did pass a bill releasing $26,000,000 in greenbacks to ease the money shortage, and except for Grant's veto of an earlier bill it would have released another $28,000,000, but it rejected the idea of actively attempting to regulate the economy. The Democratic attitude was not much more progressive. Party leaders took the similar position that the economy should be controlled by the rule of the market and that the crisis would correct itself without government action. Democrats were not averse, however, to making political capital of the panics that recurred between 1873 and 1896.

Despite its avowed neutrality, the federal government could not help but influence the economy, even in its lack of policy. Because it did not move to protect labor and the consumer, because it did not investigate business practices, and because it created no effective regulatory commissions or laws, it in effect acted as a friend of business. By ignoring the growing economic and social injustices, it allowed businessmen to conduct their enterprises as they wished. Moreover, even though government remained as passive as possible during the last part of the nineteenth century, the few measures that it did take reflected the wishes of powerful and unscrupulous factions and were not always in the best interests of the nation. In Congress logrolling was the accepted method of operation. One faction would agree to support the special projects of another group with the understanding that it would reciprocate in the future.

Politics and the Tariff. In 1864, to finance the Civil War, tariff rates had been raised to very high levels—nearly fifty per cent of the value of the item imported. These duties were of course prohibitive and provided almost complete protection for domestic industries. Debate about tariff rates was a favorite occupation of legislators during the post-Civil War period. As in the past, manufacturers supported the high rates, and most farmers lobbied for them to be lowered. Many workers feared that their wages would be reduced if goods produced by cheaper labor abroad entered the country without the protective tax. Between 1865 and 1900 the pressure of big business on Congress and on the inner circles of the major political parties prevailed; high tariffs were generally retained and the rates were even increased. Even the legislators who supported the principle of tariff reform demanded the highest rates possible to protect the industries of their constituents. Manufacturers came to feel that they could have duties increased to whatever rate they demanded.

Treasury surpluses also characterized this era. From the end of the Civil War until about 1894, the federal government did not show a single yearly deficit. Since tariffs continued to be the principal source of revenue, they could certainly have been lowered as far as the government's financial needs were concerned—but they seldom were. Clearly the manufacturers were determining important areas of government policy. One of the reasons why the Republicans, who supported big business and its demand for high tariffs during the post-Civil War period, had not wanted Southern representatives seated was the fear that the agricultural South would join with the West to reduce the tariff. The Democrats did not press the issue, however, for high tariffs continued to fill the treasury and satisfy the affluent.

Politics and Money Matters. Despite considerable controversy over the value of the dollar, 1865 to 1895 was a period of "sound" or "hard" money, again reflecting the power of business and banking groups. Yet there was rising dissension over the policy and later, toward the end of the period, Congress was to make some concessions to farmers and other debtor groups. In 1866 Congress had passed a measure providing for the gradual retirement of the greenbacks issued during the Civil War. Because these notes were promises to pay given amounts even though they were not supported by deposits of precious metals, their retirement increased the value of the nation's currency, much to the detriment of debtor groups. If all dollars were again to be supported by gold reserves, debts incurred when there had been "cheaper money" would be more difficult to repay. By 1868 almost $100,000,000 in greenbacks had been withdrawn, and the wartime demand for agricultural products had long subsided; the farmer began to feel the burden of his debt. Democrats proposed reissuing some of the greenbacks to pay off war bonds not specifically requiring redemption in gold. Indeed, the bonds in question had been purchased with greenbacks. The Republicans refused to issue more paper money, but they did agree to stop withdrawing the greenbacks.

Dissension over currency continued until finally in 1875 the "hard money" men, those supporting the system of full gold reserves, won the round with the passage of the Specie Resumption Act. Neither the Republicans nor the Democrats had been willing to support the farmers' need for soft money. The new law obliged the government for the first time since the war to redeem on demand with specie all paper currency, including the greenbacks. The redemption was not to begin until January 1, 1879, however, but by that time the greenbacks, because of the government's promise to honor them, were worth as much as gold-backed paper. Citizens kept their more convenient folding money. By another provision of the Specie Resumption Act, the withdrawal of greenbacks commenced again—on the same date that the paper became redeemable—to continue until $300,000,000 remained in circulation.

The Role of Independent Parties

The two-party system was functioning once again, but because both parties evaded reform, dissatisfied voters turned to independent parties for help on controversial issues. As in the past, such parties seldom won victories at the polls and often disappeared after one or two elections. Yet their positions helped clarify major issues. Very often the most popular planks in their platforms were eventually accepted by one or both of the major parties. For example, the Liberal Republicans supported civil service reform and control of federal land distribution in 1872. The National Labor Reform party, another small activist group established the same year—the outgrowth of the National Labor Union (page 434)—had an equally clear and limited platform, cheap money and worker-owned cooperatives.

In 1876 the new National Greenback party, originated two years earlier by farmers and other debtor groups, nominated a wealthy philanthropist, Peter Cooper, as its first presidential candidate. He pledged to support "all the people" rather than just the wealthy classes. In this and subsequent elections the party presented the only positive platform of its day. It demanded a greater amount of money in circulation, regulation of railroads, better conditions for workers, fewer voting requirements, and an income tax. In the congressional elections of 1878 the Greenback Labor party, with the support of farm and labor discontents, demanded "free silver" (page 455), limitation of the workday, and control of immigration. This group was able to poll more than a million votes and elected fourteen members of Congress. Two years later the party endorsed women's suffrage, a graduated income tax, and control of interstate commerce; but its able presidential candidate, General James B. Weaver, attracted only about 300,000 votes, less than four per cent of the total popular vote. The nation's economy was reviving and corn prices were rising, undeterred by the resumption of specie payments in 1879. The party won even fewer votes in 1884, for by then farmers looked to the free coinage of silver, instead of the issuance of paper money, for the solution of their money problems. Yet the secondary objectives of the Greenbackers—most of them admirable, although they never engendered enough popular support at the time—were a compendium of reforms to come.

PRESIDENTS AND LEGISLATION OF THE GILDED AGE

The post-reconstruction years produced few strong political leaders. The moral climate contributed to the dearth, but the principal reason was that many of the most capable men were attracted by the opportunities in the rapidly growing economy. Men who were leaders of industry during this period are well remembered, yet politicians are not. The period from 1877 to 1895 has been called an era of mediocrity. A few government leaders of merit did emerge, such as Hayes, Arthur, and possibly Cleveland; but they were selected under conditions that did not allow them to act. These men were either at odds with their own political parties or with powerful special-interest groups. Moreover, Congress had damaged the executive branch with its control of reconstruction and its treatment of Johnson; it continued to dominate the government. Presidents were expected to follow when they might have led. The country changed its chief executive every four years during this period.

Hayes Attempts Reform

The maneuvering by which Rutherford B. Hayes was elected President instead of Tilden was not the doing of either candidate, yet Hayes was often treated as though he had perpetrated the frauds. This criticism was difficult for him to accept, for he had strong convictions regarding the nature of democracy. In fact, the new President restored to the White House the qualities of dignity, personal integrity, and a sense of responsibility toward the entire nation.

Several weeks after assuming office, Hayes withdrew the last federal troops from the South, as he had promised, officially ending political and military reconstruction. In addition, he began pressing immediately, but not always successfully, for clean and honest government and for an end to political patronage.

The Uncertain Resurrection

In his inaugural address he spoke of the need for a permanent federal civil service, and he appointed Carl Schurz, a leading civil service reformer, to his Cabinet. One of Hayes's major battles was against the forces of Grantism and the spoils system in the New York Customs House, long controlled by Roscoe Conkling, a United States senator and powerful Republican boss. Some 1,300 people held patronage jobs with the agency. Hayes, against initial senatorial opposition, managed to replace two of Conkling's associates, one of them Chester A. Arthur, Collector of the Port of New York, with his own appointees. He also forbade federal officeholders to manage or contribute to political organizations, but Conkling and other Republicans of his ilk rallied together to defy this order. Hayes himself was forced to reward some unsavory carpetbaggers who had worked to secure him the presidency. Opposed by a hostile Democratic Congress and repudiated by his own party leaders for his ethical standards, Hayes had to abandon his plans for a civil service act.

Hayes and the Silver Controversy. The great public concern over money policies increased during the 1870's, but the cry for "free silver" had replaced that for greenbacks as the rallying slogan of those who supported cheap money. By the phrase "free silver" was meant unlimited coinage of the metal. The Western mine-owners, who first proposed the unlimited purchase of silver by the government, pled their cause with special desperation, for the government was at that time minting no silver dollars whatsoever. In 1873, before the panic and just before silver was discovered in large quantities on the mining frontier, so little of the metal was brought to the mint that Congress passed a law demonetizing silver. The debtor classes joined the mining interests in their campaign to have the coinage of silver resumed, for they believed the additional money would produce the same benefits that they had anticipated from the issuance of greenbacks.

The Democrats and free silver   THE BETTMANN ARCHIVE

The Bland-Allison Act (1878) began as a free-silver measure, but it was amended until it provided for the United States Treasury to purchase and coin two to four million dollars in silver each month. Because bankers warned Hayes, a hard-money man, that they would consider the coinage of silver to be debt repudiation, he vetoed the bill. But Congress, voting after years of depression and responding for once to the farmers' plight, overrode the veto.

"Stalwarts" and "Half-breeds." Several of the problems encountered by the Hayes administration stemmed from a growing division within the Republican party. Two major factions had emerged. The "Stalwarts," who had been in control under Grant, put the party and spoils first. They wrested money from the public treasury and demanded considerable tribute from business leaders for any favors granted them. The "Half-breeds" were hardly reformers, but they

Political Expediency and Self-interest   97

feared public reaction of Stalwart tactics; they themselves were more circumspect in behavior and sought more modest rewards for their cooperation with business interests. The power and patronage of public office, however used, were of course the principal prizes for which the two factions competed. Senator Conkling was the best-known Stalwart leader, John Sherman and Blaine the principal Half-breeds.

The clash of these factions dominated the Republican convention in 1880. The Stalwarts wanted Grant to return to the political arena and run for a third term. Both Sherman and Blaine were also candidates. After a deadlock between the supporters of Grant and Blaine, the delegates nominated James A. Garfield, another unknown from Ohio, on the thirty-sixth ballot. Since he was a Half-breed, an effort was made to maintain party unity by selecting Chester A. Arthur, a leading Stalwart, as the vice-presidential candidate. The slate was elected, despite unsavory incidents in the past of both men. Garfield was alleged to have been involved in the Crédit Mobilier scandal, and Arthur had been removed as Collector of the notorious New York Customs House. In the popular vote the Republicans received a plurality of only 9,464.

The new President found himself besieged by a continuing parade of self-seekers. Garfield was appalled by "the greed for office and the consumption of my time." Every loyal political worker believed that he deserved a good government job or other political favor when his efforts helped elect a candidate, and every political boss considered the dispensing of patronage essential to the maintenance of his political machine. The spoils of office were regarded as the mainstay of a party. Moreover, the federal bureaucracy administering to an industrial society was growing rapidly. Between 1871 and 1884 the number of federal employees rose from 53,000 to 131,000. Garfield broke with the most grasping of the spoilsmen, Senator Conkling, by giving the prime patronage post of the country, Collector of the Port of New York, to one of Conkling's archrivals. During this period of dissension between the President and Conkling, in July 1881, a deranged lawyer, Charles J. Guiteau, who had been denied a consulship, shot Garfield in the Washington railroad station. As the disappointed office seeker was seized, he exclaimed, "I am a Stalwart. Arthur is now President of the United States." The flagrant spoils system had led to the killing of a president.

Arthur, an Unlikely Reformer

How does a man behave when he is placed in the nation's highest office as the result of political maneuvering, patronage, and, finally, murder? In view of the circumstances, little was expected from Chester A. Arthur as President. Wealthy, a widower, and somewhat of a dandy, Arthur's connections with the New York political machine were well known. His educational background and brilliance, however, could not be faulted, for he had been graduated from Union College and elected to Phi Beta Kappa, the scholastic fraternity. He was also personally honest and a good administrator. Confronted with the responsibilities of the presidency, Arthur demonstrated his real stature and conducted himself with great dignity. Even though he had been elected to satisfy the selfish interests of spoilsmen, Arthur undertook the correction of some of the most glaring abuses of the spoils system. He was expected to replace all the Half-breeds who held appointments with Stalwarts, but he resisted the requests of old friends seeking political favors. When a few veteran party hacks were removed, Arthur insisted that the best candidate be selected for each new appointment. Furthermore, the President added many able men to his administration and eliminated much graft and fraud, especially in the post office. Perhaps his greatest contribution was his support of civil service reform, thereby giving the government a system of procuring a staff in an honest and ordered manner. These policies, though in the best interests of the

"*Oh, my name is Charles Guiteau,
My name I'll never deny...*"
Popular song concerning the assassination of Garfield

nation, were politically disastrous for Arthur. Without the support of political machines sustained by patronage, no candidate for office could hope to be renominated during this era.

Beginnings of a Modern Civil Service. Congress had authorized a Civil Service Commission as early as 1871, but many years were to pass before a modern civil service was organized. Grant was President when the first weak law was passed, and he did little to enforce it. In addition, Congress voted no money to operate the Commission; its first president, George William Curtis, resigned in disgust.

In January 1883 Congress, with Arthur's support, passed the first effective legislation to improve the quality of government service. The Pendleton Act was drafted by an outgoing Republican Congress which felt the increasing public pressure for honest, experienced officeholders and did not wish to have Democrats receive credit for reform of the federal bureaucracy. The act established a Civil Service Commission of three men to devise examinations for the selection of civil employees. The names of successful candidates were to be listed publicly, and offices were to be filled from the lists, with some allocation of appointments on the basis of population. The workers were protected too, for the dunning of federal officeholders for campaign contributions was prohibited and so was dismissal for political reasons. The act had many weaknesses, for it applied to only about 14,000 of the lowest offices, and present federal employees were exempted from its statutes. But the president had the power to add other jobs to the classified list, and each suc-

Political Expediency and Self-interest

ceeding chief executive did. In 1886 Grover Cleveland was successful in having the Tenure of Office Act repealed, so that incompetent officeholders could be removed even when they had friends in Congress. At last the nation could expect its government officeholders to qualify for their jobs instead of acquiring them through influence.

Republican "Infighting." The Republican party, no longer a single group but a collection of factions, could usually be counted upon to rally to the party cause. The Democrats also represented a wide range of special and regional interests that usually formed a coalition to support an official candidate. For the sake of being elected, rivals cooperated during campaigns, and even enemies became allies until election day. But often fluctuating and shifting conditions prevented coalitions from surviving through a single administration, for the basic aims of various party segments were very different. Arthur's supporters, the Stalwarts, were greatly disappointed by his sense of political morality and did not nominate him for a second term in 1884. His unexpectedly great achievements earned him the scorn of the political power structure. The Half-breed Blaine was still available as a candidate, still able and charming, but still suffering from a reputed lack of honesty. The Half-breeds backed him despite his reputation, and the Stalwarts eventually decided to support him too, for his chances of victory seemed far surer than those of any other candidate. Many reform-minded Eastern Republicans were not enthusiastic about Blaine, however. Because they took such a strict ethical position, the party faithful labeled the reformers "Mugwumps," a nineteenth-century term meaning self-important persons. The most dedicated of the Mugwumps left their party and openly supported the Democratic candidate.

A Democratic President

Although the Democrats had not been able to elect a President since before the Civil War, they sensed that victory was possible in 1884. The strengths and weaknesses of the perennial candidate Blaine were well known to the voters, and the Democrats hoped that a reformer could defeat him. They therefore nominated Grover Cleveland, Governor of New York, who was known for initiating reform programs in that state. He was not the choice of the political bosses, particularly not those of Tammany Hall, but having these enemies could be counted upon to gain him support elsewhere.

Pure as Cleveland's political reputation was, the opposition was able to find a scandal in his private life. Cleveland, a bachelor, had admitted paternity of and provided support for an illegitimate child. While Blaine's public behavior and suspected dishonesty were the subjects for Democratic gibes, Cleveland's private life and moral behavior were publicly criticized by Republicans. Neither side seemed really concerned with issues in a singularly offensive campaign. Eventually, the stain of public dishonesty seemed to be worse than that of private misbehavior in the eyes of the public, and the voters elected the first Democrat as President since 1858, though by a very narrow margin (4,874,986 to 4,851,981 popular votes). If New York state, which Cleveland carried by only 1,149 votes, had been won by Blaine, the Republicans would have remained in power. The electoral vote was 219 to 182.

Return of the Minority Party. The Democrats had struggled against their Civil War image since 1861. In the eyes of many, they were members of the "rebel party," and even after twenty-four years some citizens expected that after Cleveland's inauguration Washington would fill with unreconstructed Southerners. Moreover, Northerners thought that laws passed to aid the Negro might be repealed and that former Confederates might be repaid for their losses during the Civil War. Cleveland was not, however, a man to act in a rash manner. He was genuinely honest, though abrupt and tactless, and he did not believe his election meant that he had to be subservient to those who had helped him. Furthermore, Cleveland wanted to prove that Democrats, including Southerners, were still respected citizens and could be trusted to act in the best interests of the entire population.

This goal was more easily stated than accomplished, however. After being without federal patronage for twenty-four years, the Democrats badgered Cleveland for offices. He tried to sort the requests and considered only honest and capable applicants, but his efforts earned him considerable criticism. His own party complained that he did not move rapidly enough or far enough in removing entrenched Republicans, though he was eventually to replace two-thirds of all government workers, including most of the postmasters. The ousted party claimed that he failed to uphold his own statement that "A public office is a public trust," but he did add about 12,000 jobs to the civil service lists. Whatever his problems with the spoils system, Cleveland's administration proved conclusively that the choice of a Democratic president would not lead to rebellion and chaos. Never again could Republicans convincingly claim that only their party was capable of governing the nation.

Cleveland's Progress. Although the new President had been elected as a "reform" candidate, the nation was not ready to accept many social and economic controls. Cleveland himself was a conservative, standing for hard money and defense of the public till. With but limited comprehension of the vast economic forces transforming the nation, he believed that government should coddle neither its citizens nor the special-interest groups. Some progress was made, however, between 1884 and 1888. For the first time the federal government began to assume a degree of responsibility for the public welfare. For example, it stopped giving away public lands for the benefit of individual speculators, and it assumed a more protective role toward the Indians by passing the Dawes Severalty Act (page 408). Unfortunately, because the structure of Indian life was little understood, this legislation did more harm than good, for it abolished the tribal nations. The federal government also sought to protect the public from damaging practices of powerful private companies with the Interstate Commerce Act. The tariff, however, emerged as the federal government's most pressing interest.

The Tariff Stumbling Block. Cleveland decided to concentrate his efforts on solving the difficulties created by continually high tariffs. These had produced a huge surplus in the federal treasury, which was not in the nation's best interests. The surplus was simply stored away, reducing the amount of money in circulation at a time when the economy was expanding and needed all possible capital for investment. Several solutions to the problem had been proposed. The federal government could expend the surplus for the benefit of groups that had been loyal and faithful. To do so, bills might be passed to aid these groups and assure their support, or grants and appropriations might be allotted certain areas of the nation whose representatives had been loyal to the administration.

Cleveland, however, rejected these biased alternatives. Since tariffs caused consumers to pay higher prices for manufactured goods, they therefore favored a small sector of the population at the expense of the body of the citizenry. Cleveland was determined to bring the issue to the people, for he believed that they were the victims of a continuing swindle. When he devoted his yearly message in 1887 to an appeal for a lowered tariff, there was a political explosion. Congress was antagonistic because lowering the tariff would jeopardize its support by powerful economic interests. Business leaders rejected the plan because domestic products would be exposed to the open world market. The Republicans claimed that Cleveland wanted free trade, or no tariff at all, which was untrue. The Democrats criticized the proposal as unnecessary, fearing it would affect the upcoming elections. A Democratic House passed a low-tariff measure, but it was rejected by the Republican Senate; protectionism continued.

Demands of the Veterans. The President had already resisted pressures exerted on him to spend the government surplus on other projects. When Civil War soldiers returned to civilian life, many of them maintained close contact with each other. Organizations of veterans were formed soon after the war and held their large memberships throughout the postwar period. Some groups were purely fraternal in nature, but others, like the Grand Army of the Republic, usually known as the G.A.R., were very active in politics. Most G.A.R. members were Republicans, and they exerted great influence on federal pension programs, especially until 1885.

In 1862 a pension law had been enacted to protect the soldier and his immediate family in the event of death or disability. Claims for disability payments were expected to be made immediately, but many veterans neglected to file them. In 1879 President Hayes proposed the Arrears of Pension Bill to help veterans who were suffering because of their own failure to submit earlier claims. This measure, passed by Congress, was expected to correct injustices by paying veterans who had suffered wartime injuries a lump sum for the period between their discharge and the eventual filing of their claims.

This legislation, however, created new problems. The possibility of obtaining large sums of money, paid retroactively, encouraged many abuses by veterans as well as other citizens. Lawyers competed in recruiting persons who would file claims for imaginary disabilities. Veterans suddenly discovered symptoms that had not bothered them previously. If a claim was denied by the Pension Bureau, the applicant could ask his congressman to prepare a special bill. The size of veterans' groups enabled them to exert additional pressure. Moreover, in the 1880's veterans could claim that the benefits granted them would put sums from the large treasury surplus into circulation and thus strengthen the nation's economy.

Only a president as particularly honest and hardheaded as Grover Cleveland was willing to oppose the G.A.R. Although Cleveland approved more private pension bills than any other president, he was the first to veto any of the many fraudulent and otherwise unjustified claims. For his actions he was denounced by veterans' groups and earned their bitter antagonism. The climax came when he vetoed the Dependent Pension Bill, passed by Congress in January 1887, to benefit honorably discharged Union veterans who had served as few as ninety days and were now disabled and unable to support themselves. Cleveland said that the bill "would make the pension list a refuge for frauds rather than a roll of honor."

Complaints Against the Railroads. Considerable resentment against big business was articulated while Cleveland was in office. During the 1860's and 1870's most of the public objections were directed at the practices of the railroads, and most attempts to correct abuses had been made at the local level. As early as 1869, Massachusetts had established a state commission to supervise and regulate the actions of railroad companies. Soon New York and New Hampshire also organized regulatory commissions to which people could bring complaints. In addition, Western states began to fix maximum rates for carriers during the 1870's (page 439). Illinois, Wisconsin, Minnesota, and Iowa all appointed commissions to control railroad rates.

When the railroads appealed to the courts, the Supreme Court verdicts in two important cases, *Munn* v. *Illinois* (1876) (page 439) and *Peik* v. *The Chicago and Northwest Railroad* (1877) indicated that the states did have the right to control railroads within their territories. In 1886, however, this position was seemingly reversed when the Court held in *Wabash, St. Louis, and Pacific Railroad* v. *Illinois* that it was unconstitutional for a state to exercise control over a line passing through it, since Congress had ex-

102 *The Uncertain Resurrection*

clusive power over interstate commerce. This decision ended all effective control of railroads by the states.

Congress was therefore forced to take a position after many years of urging. Committees had investigated the need for control, and a series of bills had been introduced but shelved. In 1887 the first attempt at federal regulation, a largely ineffective Interstate Commerce Act, created a five-man Interstate Commerce Commission. The task of this body was to "look into" the business of the railroads, and it had the authority to hear complaints and order the railroads to stop unlawful practices. The Commission could also request reports from the railroads and was required to submit an annual report of its own to Congress.

Under the terms of the law, rates were to be "reasonable and just" and announced publicly, rebates were prohibited, and pooling of profits was to be stopped. Control of the privately operated railroads by the government for the public good now seemed assured. The hidden strength of the railroads soon limited the Commission's power, however. After 1890 railroad operators were able to circumvent the law to a considerable extent. Because the carriers could ignore the Commission's orders to "cease and desist" from illegal practices until court writs compelled them to obey, their vast resources allowed the railroads to outlast most shippers in protracted litigation. Decisions of the Interstate Commerce Commission were often reversed by the Supreme Court, as in the Alabama Midlands case and the Maximum Freight Rate case, both in 1897. As a result of these decisions, the Commission was allowed only to approve future rates. Apparently, it was assumed that all present rates were "reasonable" and that the chief function of the Commission was the collection and publication of statistics.

Criticism of the Trusts. Other giant ventures were also the targets of criticism during the 1880's. State legislatures were the first to examine the problem of the trusts, as they had the railroad question, but very little was accomplished because of the federal government's protective attitude. Corporations were guarded from state action by the judiciary as well. In the case of *San Mateo County* v. *Southern Pacific Railroad* (1882), counsel presented an interpretation of the Fourteenth Amendment as its argument—that state legislation was invalid if it deprived corporations of "life, liberty or property without due process of law." In 1886 the Supreme Court accepted the argument as the basis for its decision in the *Santa Clara County* v. *Southern Pacific Railroad Company*. The Court ruled that corporations were legal persons and that their property rights were therefore protected against state action. In effect, this ruling invalidated most state legislation that had been passed to control the business community.

By 1890, however, public protests against the behavior of trusts was so widespread that Congress was forced to respond. The Sherman Anti-Trust Act (1890) authorized the federal government to prosecute in cases involving conspiracies in "restraint of trade" in interstate

The Republicans and the trusts.   BROWN BROTHERS

Political Expediency and Self-interest

commerce. The passing of this measure did not guarantee its enforcement, however, for the judicial interpretation of the act sharply limited the scope of the legislation by dividing manufacturing from commerce and stating that the Sherman Act was applicable to commerce only. Chief Justice Melville Fuller decided in the case of *U.S. v. E. C. Knight Company* (1895) that the law did not apply to manufacturers. Most of the combinations and monopolies were able to continue to operate without hindrance under different names. Between 1890 and 1901 only eighteen suits were initiated under the act, and four of these were against labor unions. Despite increasing public pressure, the government was not yet ready to exercise real control over business.

The End of an Era

The Democrats renominated Cleveland in 1888 without much enthusiasm. The Republican factions could not agree to support Blaine as a candidate again, so they finally selected Benjamin Harrison, a pleasant but far from prominent senator from Indiana whose principal claim to fame was the reputation of his grandfather, President William Henry Harrison. Yet the Republican unknown edged out Cleveland in the election almost entirely because the fear of a lowered tariff spurred Republican and some Democratic opposition. Cleveland's achievements were ignored in the appeals of special-interest groups who regarded Cleveland's proposal for a lowered tariff as a threat to private fortunes. Republican money bought many voters in Indiana and New York. Harrison won the Empire State by only 6,500 votes. If these had been Cleveland's, he would have been reelected.

An Even Higher Tariff. Republicans regarded the outcome of the election of 1888 as a mandate from the voters to push the tariff even higher. The McKinley Tariff Act increased most rates to as much as 48.4 per cent, a few percentage points above any previous peacetime levels, and protected more items than ever before. The treasury surplus was to be limited by exempting certain products, notably sugar, from tariff charges. American producers of sugar were to be given a bounty of two cents per pound. The support of Western silver interests, who wanted the government to accept a new agreement for the purchase of silver, helped Congress pass the tariff measure. This faction, which usually opposed a high tariff, was rewarded by passage of the Sherman Silver Purchase Act (1890), obliging the federal government to buy almost all the silver that was being mined. Free silver was finally a reality, but for the farmers and debtors, who had been supported in the past by mining interests, its benefits would be nullified by price rises made possible by the new high tariff rates.

The Republicans, holding the presidency and both houses for the first time since 1875, proceeded to reduce the treasury surplus in other ways. They passed the Dependent Pension Act, a measure very similar to the one vetoed earlier by Cleveland. The outlay to veterans rose from $98,000,000 in 1889 to $157,000,000 in 1893. This "billion-dollar Congress" also increased postal subsidies to steamship lines, passed extravagant river and harbor bills, bought up and canceled government bonds by giving large premiums to bondholders, and returned direct taxes collected from the Northern states during the Civil War. The voters defeated these spendthrifts resoundingly in the congressional elections of 1890.

Public reaction against the new tariff as well as against powerful politicians was also apparent in the 1892 election. Both parties renominated their previous candidates, and once again the incumbent was defeated. Cleveland became the first and only presidential candidate to be returned to office after having been defeated in a previous election.

The Luckless Years. Cleveland's reelection was an endorsement of his honest stand on a major issue, but many conditions had changed during the four years of his absence from the White

House. With such great unrest among the poorer classes (page 435), new political-action groups were gaining power. The Populist candidate received twenty-two electoral votes in 1892. The inability of labor to win in its desperate strikes against industry provoked voters to back any candidate who promised to oppose employers. Although many Democrats represented wealthy and powerful business leaders, the public regarded the Republicans as the party of privilege because of the policies of past Republican administrations. Henry Clay Frick's employment of Pinkerton detectives to suppress the Homestead Strike, for instance, doubtless contributed to the reelection of a Democrat.

Cleveland was able to take little meaningful action during his second term, described as his "luckless years." One of the most tragic events was the Panic of 1893, which staggered the entire economy (page 488). Cleveland was forced to attempt the solution of problems that could not be solved—to deal with the rising protests of debtors, veterans, and laborers at the same time that he was committed to maintaining a climate favorable to business. In an attempt to stop a drastic decline in the United States gold reserve during the panic, he called a special session of Congress to meet on August 7 and requested that the Sherman Silver Purchase Act be repealed. Cleveland won a temporary victory over the free-silver supporters, but the ultimate outcome was disastrous. The gold reserve continued to be depleted, and dissension over repeal split the Democratic party. In addition, Cleveland was unable to fulfill his campaign promise for a lower tariff. The new Wilson-Gorman Tariff Act began as a reform measure, but the bill lost most of its effectiveness by the time Congress had amended it more than 600 times. Its one redeeming feature was a token revenue tax (two per cent on annual incomes in excess of $4,000), but this provision was soon declared unconstitutional. Although Congress was responsible for the failure to lower the tariff, the public blamed Cleveland.

National Politics Without a Clear Majority

As the United States continued its stupendous growth during the nineteenth century and became a world power, new alignments and power structures emerged and old political values changed. The old concern for the good of the republic, based on a personal sense of involvement and commitment, was shunted aside by the acquisitiveness of many special-interest groups. Each sought to advance its own economic, local, or ethnic concerns by means of government action. These special-interest groups multiplied as the United States grew in size and wealth. Gradually, they replaced the old "majority" concept as the controlling force in the federal power structure. The only true majority had become a coalition of minorities. On certain issues the groups joined forces, but often, they were in direct opposition. Compromise or cooperation between the factions was essential to progress, however. When these special-interest groups began to unite and press for action, a new political era came into being.

SUGGESTED READINGS

Barnard, H., *Rutherford B. Hayes and His America* (1954).
*Bentley, G. R., *A History of the Freedmen's Bureau* (1955).
*Buck, P. H., *The Road to Reunion, 1865–1900* (1937).
*Buck, S. J., *The Grange Movement* (1913).
Byars, W. V., *An American Commoner* (1900).
*Cash, W. J., *The Mind of the South* (1941).

Crawford, J. B., *The Crédit Mobilier* (1881).
*Current, R. N., *Reconstruction, 1865–1877* (1965).
Dixon, F. H., *Railroads and Government* (1922).
*Dunning, W. A., *Reconstruction, Political and Economic, 1865–1877* (1907).
*Faulkner, H. U., *Politics, Reform and Expansion, 1890–1900* (1959).
Fish, C. R., *The Civil Service and the Patronage* (1904).
*Franklin, J. H., *Reconstruction after the Civil War* (1961).
*Glad, P. W., *McKinley, Bryan and the People* (1964).
*Glad, P. W., *The Trumpet Soundeth* (1960).
*Goldman, E. F., *Rendezvous with Destiny* (1952).
*Hicks, J. D., *The Populist Revolt* (1955).
*Hoogenboom, A., *Fighting the Spoilsmen* (1961).
Howe, G. F., *Chester A. Arthur* (1934).
*Josephson, M., *The Politicos, 1865–1896* (1938).
*McKitrick, E. L., *Andrew Johnson and Reconstruction* (1960).
*McPherson, J. M., *The Struggle for Equality, Abolitionists and the Negro in the Civil War and Reconstruction* (1964).
Merrill, H., *The Bourbon Democracy of the Middle West* (1953).
Merrill, H., *Grover Cleveland and the Democratic Party* (1957).
Morgan, H. W., *William McKinley and His America* (1963).
Muzzey, W. S., *James G. Blaine* (1934).
Nevins, A., *Grover Cleveland, A Study in Courage* (1932).
Ripley, W. Z., *Railroads, Rates and Regulations* (1915).
Sageser, A. B., *The First Two Decades of the Pendleton Act* (1935).
*Shannon F. A., *The Farmer's Last Frontier, 1860–1897* (1945).
Stampp, K. M., *The Era of Reconstruction, 1865–1877* (1965).
Stanwood, E., *History of the Presidency* (2 vols., 1920).
Tarbell, I. M., *The Tariff in Our Times* (1911).
*Taussig, F. W., *The Tariff History of the United States* (1923).
*Ten Broek, J., *The Antislavery Origins of the Fourteenth Amendment* (1951).
Thorelli, H. B., *The Federal Antitrust Policy* (1955).
*Tindall, G. B., *A Populist Reader* (1966).

CHAPTER 21

Foreign Affairs at Ebb Tide, 1849–1890

In foreign affairs, as in all other relations, a policy has been formed only when commitments and power have been brought into balance.
WALTER LIPPMAN, *William Bolitho—A Memoir*

The United States glances to the east.

LIBRARY OF CONGRESS

The nearly half-century span from 1848 to 1890, though hardly an era of peace and tranquility, was the longest period in American history free of conflict with a foreign nation. In the 1850's the expansionist thrust of earlier years (Manifest Destiny) was extended in various directions, but without much acquired. Then from 1861 to 1865 a dynamic foreign policy became impossible because of the encompassing Civil War. With the conflict ended, the United States government pursued a policy of relatively active expansionism for another dozen years. In the two decades from 1870 to 1890, however, international affairs became a matter of almost complete indifference to the average American citizen, and his interest in territorial expansion reached a low ebb. This chapter traces the shifting course and widening horizons of United States foreign policy during the four decades of a generally diminishing concern with problems abroad. The revival of expansionism around 1890 and the subsequent surge of internationalism will be discussed in Chapter 24.

THE LAST SPASMS OF EARLY EXPANSIONISM, 1849–1860

When the war with Mexico ended in 1848, the spirit of Manifest Destiny was of course not exorcized. Rather, it quickened with the winning of the vast territories ceded to the United States by the treaty signed at Guadalupe Hidalgo (page 268). American citizens believed that, in accordance with the designs of Divine Providence, the nation would eventually acquire lands in Latin America. Regions in northern Mexico, islands in the Caribbean, and lands in Central America were regarded as appropriate areas for national expansion. Some Americans held lingering hopes that Canada would one day be annexed by the United States. These aspirations for adding lands both to the north and to the south led to scattered attempts to acquire new territories, but little was actually accomplished, mostly because of the problems raised by the institution of slavery and the deepening political crisis between the North and the South.

Filibustering Expeditions to Cuba and the Ostend Manifesto

Cuba had long been considered a natural area for future United States expansion. President Thomas Jefferson had declared, "We must have the Floridas and Cuba." Later, he wrote that the "control . . . this island [Cuba] would give us over the Gulf of Mexico, and the countries and isthmus bordering on it . . . would fill up the measure of our political well-being." John Quincy Adams agreed with Jefferson. As he put it, "There are laws of political as well as physical gravitation; and if an apple severed by the tempest from its native tree cannot choose but fall to the ground, Cuba, forcibly disjoined from its own unnatural connection with Spain, and incapable of self-support, can gravitate only towards the North American Union, which by the same law of nature cannot cast her off from its bosom."

By 1849 a great many Cubans and Americans were happily willing to try severing the apple "from its native tree." The two principal means employed were the filibustering expedition and diplomatic pressure. Three of the freebooting expeditions aimed at loosening Spain's control over Cuba were organized by General Narciso López, a Venezuelan adventurer who had already been involved in revolution in the island and had fled to the United States. He was aided by a large number of American volunteers and financed by prominent citizens, some of them Southern planters who saw Cuba with its enormous slave population of 200,000 as a possible slave state. His best-known supporters were Governor John Quitman of Mississippi, an avid expansionist, and John L. O'Sullivan, who had coined the term Manifest Destiny. López landed in Cuba with hundreds of men in 1850 and 1851, but his forces were routed by the Spanish on both occasions. During the third invasion López was captured and executed.

The ambitious Quitman then set about organizing his own large-scale filibustering expedition. He was reported to have assembled in various port cities in the United States 90 pieces of artillery, 12 ships, and 50,000 volunteers. The time seemed especially right for "plucking the ripe apple" in the summer of 1854. The administration of President Franklin Pierce, which was expansion-minded and also supported the Southern cause, was willing to grant at least silent approval. Furthermore, Great Britain and France, two nations that might have aided Spain, were diverted by the Crimean War with Russia. Unfortunately for Quitman, many Northern backers withdrew their support because of the increasing seriousness of the slavery controversy in 1854, evidenced in the debate over the Kansas-Nebraska Bill. The eager Mississippian was forced to abandon his dreams of empire.

What the filibusters could not do by force the United States government sought to achieve by diplomacy. As early as 1848, President Polk had attempted to buy Cuba from Spain for $100,000,000, but his overtures were rudely rejected. Spain's foreign minister declared that the Spanish would rather sink Cuba in the ocean than transfer the island to the United States. In 1854 President Pierce ordered Pierre Soulé, the United States minister in Madrid, to make another offer, but first Soulé was to meet with James Buchanan and John Y. Mason, the United States ministers to Great Britain and France, at Ostend, Belgium, to discuss the problem of acquiring Cuba. Known as the "infamous" Ostend Manifesto, the confidential report issued by the three diplomats recommended that if Spain continued her refusal to sell Cuba, "then by every law, human and divine, we shall be justified in wresting it from Spain."

Details of the agreement leaked out to the newspapers and created an embarrassing situation for the Pierce administration. Enraged Northerners perceived the manifesto as a plot to add another slave state to the Union, and

110   *The Uncertain Resurrection*

Pierce quickly pigeonholed the outrageous proposal. Pierre Soulé was made the scapegoat of the episode and was forced to resign. Although no additional action was taken, the Ostend Manifesto serves as an example of the brass-knuckled attitude of expansionists during this era.

There were no further overt attempts to take possession of Cuba for many years, but Americans continued to covet the "Pearl of the Antilles." As late as 1860, acquisition of the island was advocated as a plank in the platforms of major political parties.

William Walker and Central America

The last and most spectacular of the pre-Civil War filibusters was William Walker of Tennessee. In 1853, in what amounted to a practice session, Walker attempted to detach Baja California (the peninsula of Lower California) from Mexico, but his tiny force was easily scattered by the Mexican authorities. Undaunted, Walker prepared for bigger things. In 1855 "the gray-eyed man of destiny" and his band of "fifty-eight immortals" suddenly descended on strife-torn Nicaragua and conquered it. It was a deed worthy of a Cortez or a Napoleon. Being only five feet, three inches tall and weighing scarcely a hundred pounds, Walker was indeed Napoleonic in size. He established himself as dictator and promptly repealed Nicaraguan laws against slavery.

This exploit was applauded enthusiastically by Southerners and endorsed in the Democratic campaign platform of 1856. President Pierce even granted official diplomatic recognition to the new slave republic, but Walker's attempts to have Nicaragua annexed to the United States failed. As with Cuba, Northerners in Congress had no wish to see another slave state in the Union, or to encourage filibusterism. Walker proved to be a painfully incompetent politician, managing to alienate almost everyone with whom he was associated. In 1857 he barely escaped from Nicaragua with his life. Although he organized another force to invade Central America in 1860, he was captured by the British navy before his plans could mature and turned over to the Honduran government, which promptly executed him.

The Gadsden Purchase

The antagonism of Northern congressmen, alarmed over the possibility of additional slave states, had frustrated the schemes of the Pierce administration to acquire Cuba and portions of Central America. President Pierce did manage, however, during his one term in office, to acquire for the United States a modest addition of territory from Mexico.

This acquisition of land came about by accident when, unluckily for Mexico, Santa Anna was once again in power. The tyrant was toying with the notion of legitimizing his rule by establishing himself as monarch. But his indulgence in profligate luxury and his wasteful spending had emptied the national treasury, and he needed funds to provide himself with the palaces, gaudy uniforms, and other royal trappings that he felt were essential.

The United States minister to Mexico, James Gadsden, promptly took advantage of the situation. An expansionist-minded South Carolinian and a prominent railroad man, Gadsden had been appointed to his post to acquire for the United States a strip of territory south of the Gila River, the boundary between Arizona and Mexico, as the best route for a transcontinental railway from New Orleans to California. In 1854 the Senate gave grudging approval to the treaty drafted by Gadsden and Santa Anna, acquiring the Gila River land for $10,000,000. The Gadsden Purchase, a narrow belt of territory in what later became southern Arizona and New Mexico, was the final addition of land to the continental United States of today. Although a desert area, modest in size compared to other international real estate purchases negotiated by the United States government, the Gadsden territory has proved fertile and productive. The growing and prosperous Tucson, Arizona, is today the region's principal city.

As for Santa Anna, in 1855 the Mexican people drove "His Most Serene Highness" from power for the last time, partly because of their outrage over his unscrupulous sale of land. Gadsden, Pierce, and the subsequent Buchanan administration were to attempt additional intrigues to acquire territory from Mexico, but their schemes were blocked by suspicious Northerners in Congress.

FIRST CONTACTS WITH ASIA

All serious annexation schemes before the Civil War were confined to the Western Hemisphere, but some Americans were already looking farther afield. Commercial contacts in the Pacific and with the Asiatic mainland stimulated thoughts about the possibility of extensive trade with the Orient. In order to secure and protect trade routes to Asia, notions of acquiring strategic islands in various corners of the Pacific Ocean were entertained.

Pacific Islands and Southeast Asia

The Hawaiian Islands were an early object of American interest. The first European to visit them, the English explorer Captain James Cook, lost his life in the islands in 1779. In subsequent decades ships of many nations dropped anchor there, to take on fresh goods and water for their long voyages to and fro across the Pacific and to load sandalwood, valuable in trade with China. Because of its strategic location at the "crossroads of the Pacific," its superb climate, and its lovely and affectionate girls, Hawaii became a favorite stopping place for the increasing number of New England whaling ships which hunted the Pacific from south to north. After 1820 American missionaries exerted strenuous and successful efforts to convert Hawaiians to Christianity. By 1835 other Americans were growing sugar cane and making it the most important industry in the islands.

After the United States acquired frontage on the Pacific in the 1840's, the Hawaiian Archipelago became politically interesting; reports of plots by the British and the French to seize the islands aroused mounting concern. President Pierce, always on the lookout for a juicy morsel of land to grab, submitted a proposal to Congress to annex the Hawaiian Islands. This 1854 project, like so many others of Pierce's schemes, was rejected by an alliance of senators from the North who feared that Hawaii would become a slave state. The South, especially Louisiana, did not want Hawaiian competition in the domestic sugar market. During the next decades, however, an increasing number of American settlers went to the islands and American business interests proliferated, drawing Hawaii ever more securely into the political and economic orbit of the United States. Yet the almost inevitable annexation of the islands by the United States did not take place until after the outbreak of the Spanish-American War in 1898.

Meanwhile, American interest was spreading elsewhere across the Pacific. The first significant contact with the Samoan Islands was made in 1839 through a scientific expedition under the command of Lieutenant Charles Wilkes of the United States navy. Then interest languished until the 1870's when experts came to the conclusion that harbors in the Samoan group would have strategic value as naval bases. By the 1830's enterprising American merchant vessels were touching ports in Southeast Asia, in the Dutch East Indies, and along coasts bordering the Indian Ocean. To make such contacts official, President Jackson in 1832 authorized Edmund Roberts to act as a diplomatic agent and negotiate commercial treaties with some of the exotic states in these distant regions. Roberts, a sea captain with extensive experience in Asia, was successful in making agreements with Thailand (then called Siam) and Muscat, an Arabian sheikdom on the Persian Gulf. But he was unsuccessful in negotiations with Cochin China (central Vietnam), for he refused to kowtow (prostrate himself) before the local ruler. Roberts had also been instructed to open relations with Japan, but he died in 1835 before he could carry out this mission.

First Relations with China

In 1784 a small merchant vessel from New York, *Empress of China*, arrived at Canton with a cargo of furs, cotton, and several tons of ginseng, a root grown in New England that elderly Chinese believed would restore their virility. When the ship returned a year later, the owners realized a twenty-five per cent profit. After this successful venture New England shipping firms maintained extensive commerce with China. By 1800 dozens of American ships were engaged in the China trade.

Although early trade with China was profitable, it was also irksome. The Chinese government allowed foreigners only one port of entry at Canton. Americans chafed under this restriction, viewing China as a vast potential market which could be exploited only by additional commercial contacts. Although rarely harmed, American visitors were subjected to the contempt Chinese officials held for all "foreign devils" and "barbarians."

Exploitations of the British brought about some improvement in the trade with China. In the 1830's they began to transport extensive quantities of opium from India to China. Americans also took advantage of the market, smuggling in quantities of the narcotic from Turkey. The attempts of the Chinese government to repress traffic in this drug led to clashes and finally to open warfare. The so-called Opium War between Great Britain and China broke out in 1839. Small British forces easily defeated the much larger but shockingly inefficient Chinese army. In 1842 China admitted defeat and signed the Treaty of Nanking, ceding Hong Kong to the British and opening five Chinese ports to foreign trade.

The Americans were quick to capitalize on the British breakthrough. In 1843 President Tyler dispatched a capable diplomatic agent, Caleb Cushing of Massachusetts, with four warships to China. Backed by naval power, Cushing negotiated an advantageous agreement with the Chinese, who granted Americans the same commercial privileges that the British had won through war. This agreement was signed by Cushing and the Chinese imperial commissioner in 1844 at Wanghia, a small city between Canton and Macao.

American missionaries first appeared at Canton in 1830. Then, after the treaty of Wanghia, they arrived in increasing numbers to preach the gospel and propagate Western culture among the Chinese people. The work of the missionaries, however, extended much further than the mere search for converts to the Christian faith. As agents of American humanitarianism, they established hospitals, the earliest being an eye clinic founded at Canton by Dr. Peter Parker in 1834. They built schools and translated Western works into Chinese. Reports of the missionaries were relied on by the United States government as the most valuable sources of information available to it about conditions in China. Missionaries sometimes assisted the United States in diplomatic negotiations with China, their activities forging a strong link in the relations between the two countries. Friendship with China was enhanced by the refusal of the United States to participate in the territorial concessions that European powers demanded of China during the latter part of the nineteenth century.

Relations between China and the United States also had their prickly aspects. The Manchu rulers were irked by the occasional participation of American soldiers of fortune in rebellions against the government in the 1860's and by the readiness of American merchants to take advantage of commercial concessions exacted from China by British and French arms. The

ABOVE AND RIGHT BROWN BROTHERS
Two Japanese views of the American landing.

Chinese government was further dismayed by the mistreatment of Chinese immigrants in the Far West, particularly in California during the 1870's, and later by the laws passed in the 1880's and 1890's prohibiting further Chinese immigration. Anti-Oriental bias in the United States helped nurture Chinese nationalism and invited the hatred that the Chinese felt for foreigners in the twentieth century.

The Opening of Japan

The Japanese of the early nineteenth century, like the Chinese, were convinced of the superiority of their culture. Foreigners were considered barbarians and troublemakers. For two centuries the Japanese government had practiced a policy of almost total isolation from the outside world. Early halfhearted attempts to open Japan had been firmly rebuffed.

Two factors contributed to the increasing American interest in Japan at midcentury. American businessmen, having opened China, became aware of Japan as a prospective market. Furthermore, the abuse of American mariners when shipwrecked on the Japanese coasts had angered the United States citizenry.

In response to public demands, President Millard Fillmore decided to make a vigorous effort to establish relations with Japan. Following the example of Cushing's successful expedition to China, the government equipped Commodore Matthew C. Perry with a squadron of four warships, including two new steam frig-

114 *The Uncertain Resurrection*

ates, as a show of force to back up his negotiations. In 1853 Perry's ships steamed into lower Tokyo (then Yedo) Bay.

At first the Japanese were reluctant to meet with the bearded barbarians from across the sea, but they were deeply awed by American technology and the great black ships that belched forth smoke. Perry proved to be as skillful a diplomat as Cushing. Applying a mixture of tact, dignity, and coercion, he managed to cajole and impress the Japanese. Then he discreetly withdrew to the China coast to allow the Japanese time to consider his proposals. When he returned in 1854 with even more warships, the Shogunate government signed a convention with Perry promising proper treatment of shipwrecked sailors and opening two ports to American trade.

Townsend Harris, the first United States consul to Japan, arrived there in 1856 and extended Perry's initial success. Through Harris's diplomatic prodding, the Japanese government made further commercial concessions to the United States and other powers in 1858. Harris warned the Japanese that they must open their land wide to foreign commerce and catch up with the Western world in technology or face possible dismemberment at the hands of aggressive European nations. The Japanese heeded his advice. After 1868 Japan modernized swiftly, replacing its weak feudal system with an efficient centralized government. Almost overnight a backward, self-sufficient agricultural system was transformed into a modern industrial economy. The efforts of Harris and his skilled successors represented one of the brightest pages in the history of American foreign policy. Relations between the United States and Japan remained warm and friendly throughout the remainder of the nineteenth century.

DIPLOMACY DURING THE CIVIL WAR

The outbreak of the long-expected Civil War in 1861 obliged the United States government to abandon for the time being all lingering dreams of expansion. It accepted instead a defensive role, watching with wariness the maneuvers of unfriendly European nations, primarily England and France, as they sought to take advantage of the weakness and internal division of the torn nation. Obviously the North's chances for victory would be seriously diminished if one of the great European powers entered the war alongside the Confederacy. President Lincoln and Secretary of State Seward braced themselves for the inevitable crises with England and France. They did not have long to wait.

The Trent Affair

On November 8, 1861 the United States warship *San Jacinto*, commanded by the same Charles Wilkes of the Samoan expedition, now Captain, halted the British mail steamer *Trent* en route from Cuba to England. A naval boarding party from the *San Jacinto* removed two Confederate agents, John Slidell and James Mason, from the *Trent*, which was then released to proceed to its destination. The two Southern emissaries, who were originally bound for London and Paris to seek help for the Confederate cause, were promptly deposited in a federal prison in Boston. When the incident became public, there was great jubilation in the North. The press generally expressed delight over the seizure of the two "rebs" and "the singe to the fringe" of John Bull. Captain Wilkes, now a hero in the public's eyes, was promoted and awarded a gold medal by Congress.

The incident produced a storm of public indignation in England, however. Prime Minister Lord Palmerston, well known for his anti-Yankee sentiments, reacted drastically and ordered the royal navy alerted for action. A strong contingent of 8,000 troops was hastily dispatched to Canada. In addition, Palmerston drafted a stiff ultimatum, demanding the immediate release of Slidell and Mason and a proper apology for "the insult offered to the British flag."

President Lincoln viewed the affair with consternation. Another Anglo-American war appeared to be a strong possibility. If Great Britain fought on the side of the Confederacy, the nation was ruined. Despite public pressure and an anglophobic press, Lincoln had no choice. After waiting for the clamor to die down, the President gave in gracefully to the British. A suitable note of apology was composed by Secretary Seward, indicating that Captain Wilkes had erred and had acted without instructions. The Confederate envoys were released and the incident was closed.

The Confederate Cruiser Controversy

In the summer of 1862, another major crisis developed over the possibility that the British government might grant diplomatic recognition to the Confederacy. Such a move would facilitate purchases of arms and loans for the Southern states. Already Confederate agents were busy in England and elsewhere in Europe seeking recognition, money, and supplies; sympathy for the Southern cause within the government of Great Britain and that of France, with Napoleon III at its head, was considerable.

Lincoln, Seward, and the capable United States minister in London, Charles Francis Adams, were keenly aware of the gravity of the situation.[1] They had already succeeded in blunting the animosity of the British public by their courteous and dignified apology over the *Trent* incident. The issuance of the preliminary emancipation proclamation in September 1862 was, as discussed in Chapter 16, in part a maneuver to block support for the South and gain sympathy for the Northern cause from the British public, which was strongly opposed to slavery. Although the immediate results were disappointing, British opinion gradually became strongly pro-Union in the later stages of the Civil War, and Adams reported that the Proclamation "has rallied all the sympathies of the working classes." Before this shift in public sentiment took place, however, the British government permitted the construction of cruisers for the Confederate navy. Built in British shipyards, these ships were equipped with armaments and crews in neutral ports, a subterfuge to satisfy technicalities of British naval law. But this device certainly did not satisfy Adams, who protested vigorously, warning the British that such a practice might be used against them in future wars. He stated grimly that the continuance of unwarranted interference in the Civil War would lead to conflict between the United States and Great Britain.

Before the British government acted to halt further construction for the Confederate navy, a few of the ships slipped out to sea. These Confederate commerce raiders did extensive damage to Northern commerce, sending 250 vessels to the bottom. The most famous Confederate cruiser, the *Alabama*, spread destruction from the seas off China to European waters until it was finally sunk by a Union warship off the coast of France in 1864. Another commerce raider, the *Shenandoah*, was still destroying ships after Lee's surrender at Appomattox in 1865. Repercussions from the depredations of the Confederate warships were to engender further controversy between the United States and Great Britain in the years after the Civil War (page 478).

Napoleon III also toyed with the notion of building ships for the Confederates but was reluctant to act independently. When the British stopped supplying raiders, the emperor did likewise, and the French warships earmarked for the Confederacy were sold elsewhere.

Napoleon III and Mexico

The French emperor was a romantic and devious opportunist who dreamed of creating a

---

[1] Adams was the son of John Quincy and grandson of John. His two sons, Henry and Brooks, were later to become renowned historians. Henry was secretary to his father in London during the Civil War.

new French empire as glorious as that of his more famous uncle. He saw great opportunity for expansion in strife-ridden Mexico, still trying to recover from the effects of Santa Anna's corrupt regimes. Since the United States was distracted by its own internal struggle, it would be unable to oppose French schemes in Mexico.

Using the excuse that Mexico had defaulted on loans from European creditors, Napoleon III ordered a French army to invade the country. In spite of considerable Mexican resistance under the leadership of the great national hero, Benito Juárez, French forces captured Mexico City in 1863. Mexico was promptly converted into a French satellite. Napoleon chose an inept but well-intentioned young Hapsburg prince, Maximilian of Austria, to be emperor. Maximilian was clearly a puppet ruler, as he himself fully recognized, with only the French bayonets to sustain him on his slippery throne in the face of the sullen defiance of the great majority of the Mexican people. Seward denounced the French intervention but dared not object too strongly for fear of bringing France into alliance with the Confederacy. Once the Civil War was over, however, he took more vigorous action. In 1866 Seward sent a note to the French emperor strongly hinting that the presence of French troops in Mexico was contrary to the best interests of the United States. And in case Napoleon missed the direction of Seward's note, General Philip Sheridan was dispatched to the Rio Grande with 50,000 battle-hardened veterans of the Union army.

The emperor caught the hint. He had already tired of the costly Mexican adventure. The guerrilla warfare waged by the *Juáristas* made him despair of ever pacifying the Mexicans. Besides, he was becoming increasingly alarmed by the threat of Prussia to France's security in Europe, and all available troops would be needed to protect her Rhine frontier.

In 1867 the French forces withdrew and advised Maximilian to come with them, but the misguided though sincere Austrian refused to

Innocents abroad—Maximilian and Carlota. CULVER PICTURES

abandon his sinking ship of state. The stage was set for the last act of the tragedy. Cordially hated by almost all elements of Mexican society, Maximilian was captured by Juárez. His beautiful wife, the Empress Carlota, dashed hither and yon, appealing for help to save her beloved husband. President Johnson, Queen Victoria, the Pope, and even Napoleon III all heard or received her tearful entreaties, but no help came. On June 19, 1867 Maximilian was shot by a Mexican firing squad, after gallantly forgiving his executioners and, ever true to the romantic tradition, refusing the blindfold.

In the French invasion of Mexico, the United States faced the most direct challenge ever

Foreign Affairs at Ebb Tide, 1849–1890 117

The end of innocence—"Death of the Emperor Maximilian," by Edward Manet, 1868.

offered to the Monroe Doctrine, with the possible exception of the Cuban missile crisis in 1962. Seward never referred to it specifically, but his vigorous action in the affair helped to maintain the doctrine as a fundamental principle of United States foreign policy.

ERA OF FULFILLMENT, 1865–1890

In the years following the Civil War, the American people were vastly preoccupied with internal concerns. The great task of reconstructing the shattered South; the amazing industrial growth and the machinations of financial tycoons; Indian wars, cowboys, and homesteading in the great West; strikes, panics, and "free silver"; colorful political campaigns and hotly contested presidential elections—all kept the nation so engrossed that little thought was devoted to foreign affairs.

During the quarter century after 1865, the United States no longer needed to be a worried spectator of international conflict, partly because of its immense power and partly because of the equilibrium in Europe. Except for a few brief conflicts, European nations were at peace and were also experiencing great industrial growth. Although European imperialists were busily establishing colonial empires in Africa and Asia, they steered clear of the unstable and underdeveloped countries of Latin America. The evident willingness of the United States to enforce the Monroe Doctrine discouraged any territorial expansion in that sector of the globe.

Because of public indifference to foreign relations, the high office of Secretary of State tended to be a political plum awarded to persons without diplomatic experience. It was even suggested that the diplomatic service be disbanded since foreign affairs had become of so little consequence. There were a few highlights, however, and some solid achievements.

Spasms of Expansionism

The era of fulfillment was a poor time for William H. Seward to be Secretary of State, for he was a hot-eyed expansionist, eager to annex almost any scrap of territory on the planet, no matter how remote. At various times he sought to acquire Canada, Hawaii, Cuba, Santo Domingo, Iceland, part of Mexico, and even a chunk of China. Seward persuaded Denmark to sell the Danish West Indies, now the Virgin Islands, but the Senate pigeonholed the treaty. One of the few concrete results of his frantic efforts was the acquisition of the tiny Midway Islands in the Pacific, inhabited only by thousands of gooney birds.

But Seward's great moment was the treaty he negotiated in 1867 to purchase Alaska from Russia. Initially, his proposal was greeted by Congress and the American people with short-sighted indifference or downright hostility. Unfriendly newspapers referred to Alaska as "Seward's Icebox," or "Seward's Polar Bear Gardens." Undaunted, he launched a campaign to convince the nation of the value of Alaskan timber, furs, and fish; a reluctant Congress eventually appropriated the $7,200,000 to purchase the vast piece of real estate. Alaska's wealth and strategic position have subsequently vindicated Seward and demonstrated the accuracy of his predictions.

Like Seward before him, President Grant was interested in expansion but had no luck. When promoters persuaded him in 1869 of the desirability of acquiring Santo Domingo (page 448), he found that the Santo Domingans were willing to accept annexation by the United States and negotiated a treaty, but the Senate did not accept it. Grant also sought to establish American influence in the distant Samoan Islands but was again cold-shouldered by the Senate; however, relations established with Samoa in 1878 led ultimately to annexation of some of the islands at the end of the century. In general, Americans in the 1870's were simply not interested, but their thinking would soon change.

Anglo-American Relations

Relations between the United States and Great Britain were generally placid in the years between 1865 and 1890, with only occasional squalls. But two such great nations with so many relationships and points of contact were bound to have moments of friction. Skilled diplomacy on both sides helped keep tensions to a minimum and achieved reasonable solutions.

Canadian Problems. Most of the disputes between the United States and Great Britain involved Canada. Questions about boundary and fishing rights, which remained unsettled from earlier years, were further complicated by the United States annexation of Alaska in 1867. Although the Canadian people were strongly sympathetic to the North during the Civil War, the government was unable to prevent Confederate agents from using Canadian soil for raids into the United States. The most serious of these was the "shoot-up" of St. Albans, Vermont, in 1864 in which one person was killed and two were wounded. After the Civil War border friction again developed because of hit-and-run raids into Canada conducted by anglophobic Irish-Americans known as the Fenian Brotherhood. The Fenians impractically hoped to win Ireland its independence from Great Britain by capturing Canada and holding it hostage. Quixotic Americans still hopeful of union between Canada and the United States aided the Fenians. In the largest of the incursions, in 1866, twenty persons were killed.

The Fenian raids aroused sentiments opposite to those their American allies had hoped for. Canadians were generally irritated and more determined than ever to resist annexation to the United States. American hopes for union were further dampened by the British North America Act, which granted "dominion" status to Canada. This farsighted law, enacted by the British Parliament in 1867, unified Canada (which had previously been administered as two separate segments) and granted the Canadians a large measure of independence.

The Geneva Award. In the years after the Civil War, Americans frequently raised the question of British payments for the damage inflicted on American commerce by the *Alabama* and other ships built for the Confederacy in British shipyards. At first, the British fumed over the American claims as further evidence of Yankee bombast. After all, Great Britain was the mightiest power on the face of the earth. The British lion was not about to heed the screeching American eagle. But by the end of 1868 Her Majesty's government began to have second thoughts on "the *Alabama* Question." The British had misgivings about the emerging German Empire, and war with Russia loomed. Faced with possible trouble in Europe, the British did not want their hands tied by a quarrel across the Atlantic with their Anglo-Saxon cousins. Moreover, the British were fearful of the precedent established by the building of Confederate raiders, for it might lead to the construction of similar vessels in the United States for Britain's enemies.

Seward had pressed claims of $15,500,000 for the loss of 100,000 tons of American shipping. At the end of Johnson's administration, in January 1879, the British agreed to a convention for arbitrating this and other contested matters. The Senate, however, rejected the treaty fifty-four votes to one because no account had been taken of indirect damages. Senator Charles Sumner calculated that the British owed the United States over two billion dollars. He included in his claims the amount that the Civil War had cost the Union after Gettysburg, on the grounds that the rebellion would have collapsed soon after that battle if the British had not aided the Confederacy. Senator Chandler of Michigan suggested that Great Britain give the United States Canada to square accounts.

Sir John Rose, a skilled Canadian diplomat, later held a series of conversations with Hamilton Fish, President Grant's able Secretary of State, about the troublesome claims. The outcome of these negotiations was the Treaty of Washington of 1871, a complex document covering a number of issues. It was agreed that the *Alabama* question should be submitted to an international tribunal for arbitration. Ownership of the disputed San Juan Islands in Puget Sound was to be determined by the German emperor. (In 1872 the German ruler awarded the islands to the United States.) Other problems relating to fishing rights were satisfactorily resolved by mutual agreement.

In accordance with the treaty, an International Tribunal convened in Geneva, Switzerland, to settle the Confederate raider question. Represented on the Tribunal were jurists from the United States, Great Britain, Brazil, Italy, and Switzerland. After careful study the Tribunal reached its decision in the fall of 1872 and declared that Great Britain, having violated international law, should pay $15,500,000 in reparations to the United States, Seward's original figure. The British willingly accepted the adverse decision, for they did not want other nations to violate the same law. The Treaty of Washington and the Geneva Award were spectacular triumphs in the history of international arbitration. A healthy precedent was established, and in subsequent decades numerous disputes between the two powers were settled by arbitration. From the Geneva Tribunal of 1872 sprang the idea of a permanent world court for arbitration. The present International Court of Justice, one of the principal organs of the United Nations, performs this function today, but unfortunately the court lacks the power and prestige needed to be an effective arbitrator of international disputes.

SUGGESTED READINGS

Adams, E. D., *Great Britain and the American Civil War* (2 vols., 1925).

Bemis, S. F., *A Diplomatic History of the United States* (rev. ed., 1955).

Boykin, E. C., *Ghost Ship of the Confederacy: The Story of the Alabama and Her Captain, Raphael Semnes* (1957).

Bradley, H. W., *American Frontier in Hawaii* (1942).

Callahan, J. M., *Cuba and International Relations* (1899).

Dennett, T., *Americans in Eastern Asia* (1941).

Dulles, F. R., *China and America* (1946).

Dulles, F. R., *The Imperial Years* (1956).

Dulles, F. R., *Prelude to World Power* (1965).

Ettinger, A. A., *The Mission to Spain of Pierre Soule* (1932).

Farrar, V., *The Annexation of Russian America to the United States* (1937).

*LaFeber, W., *The New Empire, An Interpretation of American Expansion, 1860–1898* (1963).

May, E. R., *Imperial Democracy* (1961).

Nevins, A., *Ordeal of the Union* (2 vols., 1947).

Perkins, D., *The Monroe Doctrine, 1826–1867* (1933).

Pratt, J. W., *A History of United States Foreign Policy* (1955).

Rauch, B., *American Interests in Cuba, 1848–1855* (1948).

Scroggs, W. O., *Filibusters and Financiers* (1916).

Shippee, L. B., *Canadian-American Relations, 1847–1874* (1939).

*Sideman, B. B. and L. Freedman, eds., *Europe Looks at the Civil War* (1960).

*Sprout, H. and M. Sprout, *The Rise of American Naval Power, 1776–1918* (1939).

Stevens, S. K., *American Expansion in Hawaii, 1842–1898* (1945).

Tong, T., *United States Diplomacy in China, 1844–1860* (1964).

Treat, P. J., *Diplomatic Relations Between the United States and Japan, 1835–1905* (1932).

Wallace, E. S., *Destiny and Glory* (1957).

Williams, M. W., *Anglo-American Isthmian Diplomacy, 1815–1915* (1916).

*Woldman, A. A., *Lincoln and the Russians* (1952).

CHAPTER 22

Foundations of a New Social Order, 1890–1909

A man who is good enough to shed his blood for his country is good enough to be given a square deal afterward. More than that no man is entitled to, and less than that no man shall have.

THEODORE ROOSEVELT, 1903

THE BETTMANN ARCHIVE

DISSIPATION AND REVIVAL OF THE SPIRIT OF REFORM, 1865–1890

THE HISTORY OF THE UNITED STATES HAS BEEN characterized by reform movements. In fact, although their objectives have varied as the nation has changed, moral crusades have since colonial times been part of the American tradition. Throughout each period the people have been motivated by ideals of perfection. Although the reform spirit may seemingly have dissipated at times and the nation may have appeared about to replace moral values with expediency and self-interest, on each occasion a new wave of conscience has stirred the population, and once again the crusaders have come forward to raise the pertinent issues. As the eminent historian Richard Hofstadter has said, "Americans do not abide very quietly the evils of life." Reformers may not always have proposed wise solutions to all problems, but at least they have called attention to and attacked many of the existing evils in American society.

Reform at Low Ebb

The Civil War was the climax of a reform movement that had had as its goal the abolition of slavery. When this end had been achieved, the impetus to improve the human condition that usually stirred the citizenry subsided. The material destruction of the Civil War was immense, but the psychological damage it inflicted was even greater. The intensification of hatreds by reconstruction measures has been described in Chapter 17. In the postwar letdown even the most dedicated abolitionists found themselves divided and drained. The nation had experienced just about as much crusading as it could cope with for a time.

Passing of the Older Reformers. Moreover, most of the active reformers were elderly by 1865. Those who had been the young rebels of the 1830's and 1840's were rapidly losing touch with the generation that had actually fought the Civil War. The returned veterans were anxious for the agitation to cease and yearned only to go about the ordinary business of living which had been so tragically interrupted by the prolonged conflict.

Reconstruction as Reform. The ranks of those who sought to change society had been decimated but not completely leveled. The most passionate of the undaunted reformers turned their attention to the South. Funds to further Negro education were raised by various religious and humanitarian groups. Many Northern men and women—preachers, teachers, and missionaries—sacrificed their own comfort to live in the South and work with the newly emancipated Negroes. Much of the remaining energy of the abolitionist movement was absorbed in this task. Among these dedicated workers were some who supported the reconstruction policies of the Radical Republicans and urged the most aggressive attacks on the traditional class system. Such efforts produced reactions that undermined the achievements of the reformers. By attempting to pressure the people of the South into accepting Negro equality before they were psychologically prepared, Radical reconstructionists have been blamed for an eighty-year hiatus in progress toward this goal. Other historians claim that lack of effort and energy in the North was responsible for the failure of the Negro to attain full citizenship and social acceptance at this time. W. E. B. Du Bois contended that blacks were the only ones who attempted real reconstruction.

Westward Movement. During the 1860's and 1870's much of the energy of the nation was poured into conquering the Western wilderness. The same dissatisfaction that has moved Americans to reappraise and change their society led many of them into the West, especially during the post-Civil War years. In a period of fewer directions in which to expend the urge for reform, the great surge westward proved a valuable outlet. Many citizens of both North and South avoided the deprivations that they might have suffered in a war-changed society and economy by moving west.

Emphasis on Individualism. In the "get-rich-quick" era following the Civil War, citizens very rapidly developed the point of view that their own personal goals were more important than common objectives. This preoccupation with individual achievement and gain was not stimulating to political and social crusades, however, and was partly responsible for the ebb of reform movements between 1865 and 1890.

Spectrum of Pressures for Change

Changing Social Structure. Although crusading voices seemed for the most part stilled during the 1870's and 1880's, and state and national governments ignored society's ills without compunction, social pressures that would lead to radical change were building. The growing urbanization, the arrival of great numbers of European immigrants, and the expansion of the industrial working classes would all necessitate basic readjustments in American society.

In the early 1870's the farmer had raised the first voice of protest against his many and varied problems (Chapter 19). But almost as damaging as the adversities he faced was his confusion about his role in the economy of the nineteenth century. The farmer tended to see himself as the self-sufficient yeoman of earlier years, who had supposedly fed and clothed himself and his family and owed nothing to anyone. But he had more likely become a rural businessman, confronted with problems of credit, the rise and fall of farm prices, and international competition. Agrarian protests were often made in behalf of the independent husbandman, whereas in reality agriculture had become a business deserving of the same support and protection accorded other major industries.

The plight of the residents of cities was no less grave, however. City administrations were either too small and weak, or, when controlled by the powerful political machines, too corrupt to deal with urban growth. Prosperous and influential citizens, living in country homes or in town houses on well-tended streets, were preoccupied with their own interests and ignored the conditions in poorer sections of the cities (page 383). Because zoning restrictions were practically unknown, factories were erected anyplace businessmen considered it convenient to build, and no space was left for parks and recreation in the areas where tenements for working-class families were constructed. Sewage and water facilities could not be provided nor streets paved at the pace that the real estate developers could raise new sections. In the overcrowded tenements of the ghettos, the newcomers to America were threatened with epidemics, fire, and the destruction of family life. Vice and crime flourished and became endemic to the slums.

Intellectual Critics. Some of the intellectual critics of the late nineteenth century were scientists, some churchmen, and others humanitarians. They protested against the evils of the day long before the general public was ready or willing to accept responsibility for them. The investigations and theories of these intellectual leaders provided insight into a troubled society and set the stage for the public protests of later years.

Philosophers and psychologists challenged the "self-image" of American society, for they wanted to help people understand why they behaved as they did. William James, John Dewey, and G. Stanley Hall were among those who sought to use tools of science in developing new concepts about man and his ideas of reality during the late nineteenth century. James, one of the founders of pragmatism, and Dewey, who espoused this new philosophy, believed that truth does not exist in the abstract, that a concept must be applied and judged by its results. All formal systems of philosophy are unnecessary and irrelevant, they maintained. Dewey wanted intellectuals to disengage themselves from academic trivia and turn to politics, education, and social reform. Human problems should be studied by means of the experimental method of the sciences. The philosophy of pragmatism enhanced the prestige of reformers and encouraged intellectual leaders to work for social change.

The newly emerging academic disciplines of sociology and anthropology challenged established means of looking at society. Another school of philosophers, known as the Reform Darwinists, challenged the fatalism of the earlier Social Darwinists (page 430), who had believed that society changed very slowly if at all, that only evolution could carry mankind beyond misery. The Social Darwinists had considered poverty and slums the just deserts of men outpaced in the economic race. They had opposed poor relief, housing regulations, and public education as interference with natural law. The new dissenters, led by Lester F. Ward, a pioneer in the field of sociology, and the economists Richard T. Ely and Simon Nelson Patten, found the laissez-faire doctrine both unsafe and unsound and stressed the need for social planning to achieve human progress. Ward taught that nature, inefficient and wasteful, must be dominated by man. Reform Darwinists advocated government regulation of the economy and encouraged social scientists to lead movements for political reform.

The most renowned academic rebel was Thorstein Veblen, who regarded the free economy of the nineteenth century as an ineffective system, plagued by constant crises. In *The Theory of the Leisure Class* (1899) he attacked the millionaire as the saboteur of industry. Far from being the most biologically fit and "a product of natural selection," as the Social Darwinists had acclaimed him, the businessman disrupted the industrial process with his concern for money. The millionaire had not created the industrial technology but had merely seized the wealth produced by the skill and labor of others. Veblen contended that production and distribution should instead be managed by technicians.

Although most intellectuals who became concerned with reform advocated solutions that seemed within reason, several nonacademic theorists advanced rather visionary perspectives. Called "utopians," such men believed that a perfect society could be found or created. Their radical new insights attracted considerable attention as citizens became aware of the problems produced by continuing governmental indifference and the uncontrolled aggressiveness of the captains of industry.

One such utopian scheme was a proposed single tax to be levied only on land. Henry George, an economist and journalist, long pondered why progress was accompanied by poverty. After watching the simple frontier society of California in the 1850's and 1860's become class-stratified, he concluded that the only true source of capital is labor, but that this wealth is maldistributed through the private ownership of land. Since the value of land is a social accident and depends on the people who live in the area, speculators who merely hold on to property while population builds should not reap profits. The unearned increment or rent should be returned to society in the form of a single tax on land values. No other taxes or government intervention would be necessary, for the funds collected would be ample to provide all the necessary government services. George's book *Progress and Poverty* (1879) attracted worldwide audiences, and he was nearly elected mayor of New York in 1886.

Other perspectives were even more imaginative. Indeed, they were so revolutionary that they were presented to the public as novels. In Edward Bellamy's romantic *Looking Backward* (1888) a young man of the ugly, strike-torn 1880's awakens in the year 2000 to an ideal socialist Boston, tranquil and beautiful. All the trusts have been nationalized as one great government trust, and industry is efficiently organized by the scientific method. Bellamy's novel was read by millions of Americans, many of whom formed clubs to discuss the author's system of "Nationalism." Ignatius Donnelly, a leader of the Populist party, was concerned with the evils of a planned society. His novel *Caesar's Column* describes the opposite of a utopia; in his New York of 1988, the lower classes, impoverished and brutalized by a small and completely corrupt plutocracy, revolt and civilization is destroyed. Donnelly's future society resembled in many ways the controlled world described by George Orwell in *1984*, a twentieth-century novel satirizing a planned society. The threat or control without consideration for individual freedom continues to be a source of concern in contemporary society.

Challenge to Christian Doctrine. Many of the scientific theories that were advanced in the late nineteenth century directly challenged the religious beliefs of the majority of the population. In particular, Darwin's theory of evolution seemed a complete contradiction of the biblical version of the creation. Many conservative church leaders merely rejected Darwinism as false and continued to preach "fundamental" Christianity. The more liberal churchmen attempted to reconcile religion and evolution. Henry Ward Beecher and Phillips Brooks, among others, contended that the theory of evolution did not destroy Christian faith, but rather helped to establish a more intelligent basis for it. These "theological liberals" were also active in social causes. Beecher was one of the most influential abolitionists before the Civil War and later, as editor of the *Christian Union*, supported the women's suffrage movement and proposals for a civil service system. But his economic and social views were strictly orthodox, for he regarded poverty as a sign of individual sin. He opposed unions and the eight-hour day and urged that strikers be restrained with force if necessary.

The Protestant clergy's lack of sympathy for the workingman's condition in the decades after the Civil War had its effect on his church attendance. Told to accept his lot and hope for a better existence in the hereafter, the workingman found little comfort in religious services. As congregations shrank, churches abandoned their parishes in the blighted slums and moved to the better residential areas of the city. By the 1880's, however, some Protestant clergymen had gained considerable insight into the problems of the slums and began to teach a different "Social Gospel." They considered society itself sinful and believed that Christ had come to establish a better environment as well as to save men's souls. The Social Gospelers sought better housing, wages, and working conditions, civil service reform, regulation of the trusts, and income and inheritance taxes. Washington Gladden, perhaps the most influential of the group, defended the right of labor to organize and strike and advocated "a fixed share" of industry's profits for each worker. Walter Raushenbusch, a radical Social Gospeler, believed that a Christian democracy would emerge only if private property was abolished. Although the clergymen who preached the Social Gospel remained a minority, their movement was eventually to make social service a major agency of modern Protestantism.

The Roman Catholic Church was better prepared in doctrine and experience to deal with the poverty of its urban parishioners, but its activities were limited in the early postwar years to providing for the destitute and maintaining schools and homes for orphans and the aged. It advocated little or no legislation for social and economic reform. In 1886, however, James Gibbon was appointed Archbishop of Baltimore and soon articulated a concern for the betterment of the working classes. He also upheld the separation of church and state, encouraging Catholic immigrants to become patriotic citizens. The Church initiated effective programs to americanize its laity. Then in 1891 Pope Leo XIII issued his famous *De rerum novarium*, criticizing the excesses of capitalism and the attendant poverty of the masses. The encyclical defended the right of workers to organize unions and challenged both church and state to seek social justice.

THE AGRARIAN AND INDUSTRIAL STRIFE OF THE 1890's

Impact of the Depression of 1893

Depressions occurred in the United States at repeated intervals throughout the nineteenth century. Each financial crisis seemed to be worse than the last, probably because a greater portion of the population was employed in factories and therefore directly affected by changes in business conditions. Moreover, the farmer in hard times could still provide his family with shelter and food, but the increasing number of industrial workers in depression-ridden cities had no such recourse. There were panics in 1819, 1837, 1857, and 1873. Each came after a period of growth and expansion, and each was followed by several years of depression. In this rise and fall of economic activity known as the "business cycle," each period of prosperity produced speculation and inflation, which in turn led to an era characterized by deflation, business failures, and human suffering. The Panic of 1893 is a classic example of this cycle, which for many years was thought to be a necessary adjustment of the nation's industrial economy.

Panic of 1893. The nation's economy seemed sound at the beginning of 1893, for there was a great deal of business activity. Construction of a huge railroad network was in progress, and few industrial workers were unemployed, at least by the standards of the time. The newly wealthy industrialists were also spending heavily. Although agricultural income had been declining since 1887, reducing the farmers' purchasing power, and there had been a continual drop in prices, most businessmen still believed that economic conditions were continuing to improve. Early in 1893, however, the failure of the Philadelphia and Reading Railroad indicated that perhaps the economic boom was over. Yet it was not until May 5, when stock prices began to decline rapidly, that the citizenry became aware that their nation was in deep financial trouble. On June 27 the stock market crashed.

Background for Depression. To economists the causes of this catastrophe were evident. The prosperous years of the 1880's had encouraged businessmen to expand the economy beyond its normal limits. Heavy industry, especially railroads, had undergone a tremendous expansion. There had also been extensive speculation on the stock and bond markets. In general, production had increased rapidly, although there had been a gradual cutback when the market appeared to be oversupplied. In addition, for a number of years the American farmer had been able to produce more crops than could be sold on the competitive world market.

The nation's economy was afflicted by other problems as well. European capital was being withdrawn during the 1880's because of financial problems at home and increased opportunities for investment in other emerging areas, such as Africa and Australia. For the first time in many years, the federal government was faced with a Treasury deficit. The rates established by the McKinley Tariff Act were so protectively high that few foreign goods were imported. Tariff revenues decreased, as the framers of the act had intended them to, but at the same time pensions granted to Civil War veterans and other measures passed by Harrison's billion-dollar Congress increased government spending. This outpouring of government funds, plus the issuance of silver certificates through the Silver Purchase Act, weakened the public's faith in its currency and encouraged gold hoarding. A great deal of paper was presented to the Treasury for redemption, seriously reducing the gold reserves. Moreover, when foreign investors sold their American securities, gold had to be sent abroad to complete the transactions.

All these problems combined to create financial chaos in 1893. The farmers had of course already been drastically affected; now railroads fell into receivership, hundreds of banks failed, and thousands of businesses closed. Mass unemployment followed. All economic activities slowed down as prices fell and consumer purchasing power dropped. Vast numbers of the unemployed tramped the streets of factory towns looking for work or wandered aimlessly about the country as hoboes, usually singly but occasionally in large gangs. Cleveland's administration acted quickly to repeal the Sherman Silver Purchase Act (page 462) so that the drain on the gold reserve would be diminished, but this move was of course insufficient to stem economic crisis. The government did little else to ease the situation, for it did not consider the problem of how business was to recover its concern.

Coxey's Army. A group of discontented citizens felt differently, however, and tried to bring their demands and schemes to the attention of the national government by marching on Washington. Led by Jacob S. Coxey, about four hundred jobless marchers arrived in the capital on May 1, 1894. Bedraggled and hungry, they tried to pitch camp on the grounds of the Capitol Building, but they were dispersed by police and their leaders were arrested for walking on the grass. Not even considered by Congress was Coxey's public works relief program. He planned for the treasury to issue $500,000,000 in paper money and hire unemployed men to build roads. Or the funds would be lent to local communities to construct schools and courthouses and make other public improvements. The well-publicized march, however, brought the discontent of the jobless to the attention of many citizens who had previously not recognized the extent of the crisis.

The Populist Movement

Coxey was himself a Populist. Among the most active critics of the government during the Panic of 1893 were the spokesmen of a political

The Uncertain Resurrection

Coxey's army — the first march on Washington.

movement which hoped to preserve the country's rural heritage through "radical" reforms. The simple ideals of Populism were those of an earlier America, when its economy was primarily agricultural. Believing that the federal government had a responsibility to protect this rural way of life, the Populists became the first effective force to challenge the right of industry to control the nation, which it had done without successful opposition for thirty years.

Background and Leadership. The societies formed for the agrarian protests of the 1870's and 1880's provided the impetus for Populism. Feeling the need for action in 1890, after several disastrous years of declining agricultural income, mortgage foreclosures, droughts and crop failures in the West, and overproduction of cotton in the South, various farm groups, most prominent among them the Farmers' Alliances (page 439), determined to enter local politics. Kansas — where in fifteen counties three-fourths of the oversettled arid land would soon belong to mortgage companies — was first with a statewide organization, established in June and called the People's party. Alliancemen of Kansas and the Northwestern states, many of them splendid orators or colorful spellbinders, ran vigorous campaigns for state and congressional offices. They won a substantial number of seats in November. In the South Alliance candidates,

Foundations of a New Social Order, 1890–1909

working within the Democratic party, were perhaps even more successful. Encouraged to try national politics, more than 1,400 delegates attended a convention of protesting groups in May 1891. The Southern opposition to a third party was eventually overcome, and on February 22, 1892 the People's party was formally organized. The first nominating convention was held at Omaha on July 2 of that year.

The leaders of the movement had a unifying cause. They were convinced that there was a great conspiracy in the nation and, in fact, in the world to defraud the common man of his rights[1] and to make farmers and other debtors pay dearly for their lack of capital. The "Anglo-American Gold Trust" profited by the wars, panics, and depressions which their policies caused, the Populists claimed. The nation's only hope was to eliminate gold as the basic medium of exchange and substitute silver or other legal-tender currency.

Populists were also convinced that no stranger could really be trusted. Although they were willing to accept the support of labor organizations, they were afraid of foreign immigrants and of the city in general because of its political intrigues and corruption. Populist policies sought to counteract urban influence as well as to preserve an agrarian society. Support for the movement came almost entirely from the South and the Great Plains, the farm areas where discontent was the greatest.

Populist Platform and Influence. Whatever the many reactionary beliefs of the Populists, the party platform was liberal enough to be considered radical in the 1890's. Populists were called socialists and anarchists for proposing many sweeping changes in government and control of industry. At their convention in July 1892,

[1]There seems to have been an undertone of anti-Semitism in these accusations, for all money lenders were categorized as Jews. Members of the British banking family, the Rothchilds, were involved in extensive money transactions with the federal government at this time, which may have stimulated the animosity. Historians are still discussing and conducting research on this issue.

the Populists established these goals in their bid for power as a third political party: (1) free and unlimited coinage of silver, (2) more money in circulation—at least fifty dollars per person, (3) a postal saving system and federal control and distribution of currency without the interference of banking corporations, (4) a graduated income tax by which persons with high incomes would pay more than did the poor, (5) government ownership of all transportation and communication, including railroads, telephone, and telegraph, and (6) laws prohibiting aliens from owning land and future restriction of immigration. The party also proposed several reforms that would provide more direct contact between the people and the government. These measures included the secret ballot, the initiative and referendum, the direct election of United States senators, and limiting each president to a single term. In addition, the Populists promised the laboring man an eight-hour day. The spirit of reform achieved its strongest expression in thirty years.

Although its strongholds were exclusively rural, the Populist party was an important influence in national politics during the early 1890's. In 1892 James B. Weaver, once nominated by the Greenback Labor party, received 1,027,329 votes as the presidential candidate of the Populists. Almost one-tenth of the nation voted the party's ticket. Grover Cleveland, the Democratic winner, received 5,554,000, and Benjamin Harrison, the Republican candidate, received 5,191,000. But by 1894 the national influence and growth of the Populists had begun to waver. Even though they elected more congressional and local candidates than they had in the 1892 election, they were unable to attract new blocs of voters, such as the urban workers, and they failed to unite the white and Negro farmers of the South.

The loss of Populist momentum can be attributed at least in part to the acceptance of many of the movement's ideals by both major parties. Even though this third party challenged the political dominance of the major

The Uncertain Resurrection

parties for a very short period, it profoundly influenced their thinking and subsequent platforms. Indeed, many of the reforms originally proposed by the small "radical" group were enacted into law during the early twentieth century. Most important was the Populist party's outright rejection of the laissez-faire doctrine, which had kept conservative leaders from attempting control of the industrial economy and moving to alleviate the sufferings of those it victimized.

Crisis and Election of 1896

William Jennings Bryan and the Democratic Platform. The same tensions and dissatisfactions that had caused the residents of rural areas to turn to a new political party were felt within the Democratic party during the 1890's. Both major political parties had, in fact, since early in the decade been torn by factional struggles over fiscal problems and the question of free silver. At least one segment of each party proposed the coining of silver as the solution to farm problems. The Republican national organization, however, rejected this point of view in June 1896, endorsing the single gold standard and nominating William McKinley for President. In the Democratic party the "silver" supporters won out the next month and nominated William Jennings Bryan. Delegates who had supported the gold standard withdrew from the Chicago convention and, as National Democrats, nominated seventy-nine-year-old Senator John M. Palmer of Illinois.

The most persuasive and vocal supporter of bimetallism, William Jennings Bryan had been preaching the gospel of free silver since 1890 as a lecturer and member of Congress. At the Democratic convention he won all silver delegates to his candidacy with the most momentous speech ever delivered before such a body. Its now-famous peroration, "You shall not press down upon the brow of labor this crown of thorns, you shall not crucify mankind upon a cross of gold," evoked half an hour of thrilled and enthusiastic uproar. The big, handsome, thirty-six-year-old candidate seemed the very embodiment of traditional rural America, fighting to preserve itself against the villainy of big business, intrigues with foreign capitalists, and high prices.

The platform adopted at the Democratic convention included many Populist proposals. Most important was a plank advocating the coinage of silver in unlimited amounts and at the ratio of sixteen parts of silver to one of gold, which was the traditional ratio of value established by the government in 1834. In other words, each silver dollar was to contain sixteen times as much silver by weight as there was gold in a gold dollar. In 1896, however, the market value of silver was much less, about thirty-two to one. Owners of silver mines would clearly benefit from the free coinage of silver. Other planks in the Democratic platform condemned trusts, national banks, and high tariffs; recommended stricter regulation of the railroads and a constitutional amendment that would allow the imposition of an income tax; and supported labor by attacking the use of court orders to stop strikes.

The Populist party wanted to continue to function as a separate entity, even though its platform from earlier elections had been largely appropriated by the Democrats. Populists resented the emphasis placed on free silver at the expense of other favored reforms, and they feared that supporting Bryan would lead to their political extinction. Not to nominate him, however, and to wage a separate campaign would assure the election of McKinley. They agreed to endorse Bryan, but they put forward their own candidate for Vice President. The Populists felt certain that Bryan would be elected and declared that "rural America will be saved."

"Battle of the Standards." Bryan, as the nominee of both Democrats and Populists, launched a major campaign to win the presidency. Traveling widely in twenty-one states to tell the nation about the evils of industrialism and the joys of the simple, rural way of life, the vigorous orator made more than 600 appearances and probably talked to some 5,000,000 citizens. In each address he condemned the gold standard as a tool of industrial and business creditors and endorsed free silver as the salvation of the farmers, the silver miners, and others.

Bryan's Republican opponent, William McKinley, had been nominated through the influence of Marcus A. Hanna, a Cleveland businessman who knew how to use his money and position to gain political power. Hanna had earlier supported McKinley for governor of Ohio, and now he again became the king-maker. Turning the administration of his business over to others, he devoted all his time to McKinley's election. Hanna collected more than $3,500,000 from business and industry to pay for the campaign, which had become a full-fledged confrontation between the urban and rural sections of the nation.

Unlike Bryan, McKinley stayed home in Canton, Ohio, and read well-prepared speeches from his front porch to carefully selected visiting delegations. They arrived from all over the nation on cut-rate excursion trains. The huge campaign fund which Hanna had collected was being spent effectively, however. The money went to portray Bryan—by word and picture and well-paid orator; in pamphlet, leaflet, campaign button, and poster; and at rally and parade—as a man who might overthrow the established government of the United States. He was called "radical," "rebel," and "revolutionary" and was condemned as a tool of anarchists. Even important Democratic newspapers opposed Bryan and resorted to similar rhetoric. These accusations frightened the middle-class voter, who was led to believe that Bryan's proposals for limiting business were indeed socialist and that riots and revolution would surely follow if the Democratic nominee was elected. The violent conflicts between employers and laborers in this era of depression and deprivation and Coxey's ragged "army" were still fresh in the minds of many persons. Would the poor turn against those who had property and take over the nation? Would not the stirring words of Bryan encourage debtors to turn on creditors and end the way of life that most citizens cherished?

The Significance of the McKinley Victory. In the election of 1896, McKinley won by a margin of ninety-five electoral votes and defeated Bryan in the popular vote by 7,105,000 to 6,503,000. All the stirring oratory of the silver-voiced Westerner had not overcome the caution of middle-class citizens. Although the farmers of the South and the West voted for the Democratic candidate, they were too few in number to carry the election alone.

The majority of voters lived in urban centers or in the East, where the appeal of Bryan's proposals was very limited. The Democratic campaigns offering free silver as the single remedy for all the nation's problems failed to attract even the indigent city residents, for they, feeling little concern about mortgages and falling farm prices, did not align themselves with the rural poor. Planks in the Democratic platform promised to end the control of big business and prevent the use of court injunctions against strikes, but the factory worker voted solidly with his employer. The dangers of radical change stressed by the Republicans made him fear for his own employment; certainly some industrialists threatened their workers with closed factories if Bryan was elected.

By rejecting the panacea of free silver, the majority of voters appeared opposed to change. Some historians have pointed out that there was actually more support for reform than indicated by the election returns, but at the time McKinley's victory was deemed a triumph for the forces of conservatism. In the first great struggle of the American people against privilege, big business was voted the right to continue its monopolistic practices without government interference. The Populist party was finished as an independent force in national politics, even though it ran candidates in the next three elections. Nevertheless, the campaign had provided an outlet for the very real class tensions of the 1890's. When the voters did not cast their ballots along class lines, the fear of uprising that had haunted the nation during the strikes and violence of the decade finally subsided. In future campaigns reform would not be considered merely an appeal to the masses. Candidates would find it easier to propose improvements in the general standard of living, without being accused of preaching revolution.

THE PROGRESSIVE MOVEMENT

Roots of Progressivism

The Populists had helped to create a climate in which change would be accepted, even though they had not achieved their specific goals. In the more receptive setting for reform that was the aftermath of the Populist-Democratic political defeat of 1896, a new wave known as progressivism gathered momentum almost immediately.

Like the Populists, the progressives rejected the materialism of the Gilded Age and yearned for the ethical values, individual freedom, and democracy of an earlier era. Compassionate and believing in the inevitability of humanitarian progress, they felt obliged to help the underprivileged, whose deprivations must have stemmed from society's mismanagement. The political and economic institutions that had been allowed to grow up in the age of acquisition were to blame for the present corruption and exploitation. The progressives had confidence in the democratic process. If citizens could be aroused from apathy, they would be able to oust the bosses and machines and then force government to control the trusts and to attack social and economic problems. Through active self-government the American heritage could be restored.

As with the Populists, the progressives' concern about society's ills eventually led the likeminded to organize for political action. But the progressives were more practical and factual than the Populists had been in advancing their program of reform. For example, they said that continued disregard of the poor workingman would result in radicalism and revolt and that it was "good sense" to improve working conditions before disaster struck. Before proposing government controls, they made every effort to find out who actually benefited from laissez faire and how government could intervene effectively. In preparing the case to limit women's working hours, lawyers took testimony from doctors, factory inspectors, and social workers to prove that long hours of work were detrimental to women's health. The progressives methodically offered specific and moderate measures to improve a system of democratic government that they believed was basically sound.

Support of Progressivism

The citizenry, having observed the continual impetus for reform in the last decades of the nineteenth century, tended to agree with the progressives that change was inevitable and would be less damaging if it were controlled. Moreover, the new advocacy for reform had greater appeal because it was not restricted to rural areas. Most agrarians and Populists eventually supported the progressive cause, but members of the professions, owners of small businesses, and skilled laborers—urban, middle class, and well educated—consituted the troops in the new army of reform. Their standing in the community as lawyers, educators, and small property owners and their middle-class respectability kept progressives from being scorned as "radicals" and "crackpots." Then too the intellectual currents of the time—pragmatism, the Social Gospel, Reform Darwinism—fostered a climate of opinion considerably more favorable to reform.

The most outspoken group attacking the injustices of the era were professional authors and journalists called "muckrakers."[2] They described the widespread greed and corruption characterizing all phases of national life in articles which appeared in the new mass-circulation magazines then popular, such as *McClure's, Collier's*, the *American*, and *Cosmopolitan*. The editors of these well-illustrated periodicals, which were considerably more lively than the older family magazines, in turn became increasingly eager to publish exposés of business and government malpractices and to urge the public to press for action. The wretched conditions in the slums, crime, governmental corruption and graft, unsafe and unsanitary foods, and big business's unbridled control of the national economy were all attacked. Often the articles and later the muckraking pamphlets and books were written purely for their shock value; sometimes they included sensational accusations. But the muckrakers believed that indignation must be aroused to make the public fight for reform. The more thorough muckrakers, with generous financial backing from their publishers, carried out extensive research and established reportorial standards that have seldom been surpassed.

The first of the famous exposés was written by Thomas W. Lawson in 1902. Called *Frenzied Finance*, it attacked the control of the national financial system by trusts. Ida M. Tarbell wrote her *History of the Standard Oil Company* soon thereafter. This exposure of unethical business practices was serialized in *McClure's*, beginning in 1903. During the next year Lincoln Steffen's *The Shame of the Cities* made its blistering attack on the political machines which controlled governments in most of the nation's urban areas. Charles E. Russell exposed the beef industry in *The Greatest Trust in the World* (1905), and Upton Sinclair used some of the same material in his fictional *The Jungle* (1906), which was even more sensational and compelling.

Although some writers, like Sinclair, criticized the entire American political and economic system, most were moderates who appealed to the middle class and capitalized on its humanitarian concerns and desire for progress. The muckrakers usually had no specific solutions to propose for the problems that they described, but through reading them the public became increasingly involved in the efforts of progressivism. The average American could no longer imagine that his country retained its innocence from an earlier era. Educated middle-class citizens felt more sympathy for the less fortunate and for their fellow consumers with lower incomes than their own. Many of the influential men convinced by the muckrakers to join the progressives were young and of a new generation not likely to tolerate in silence the injustices of the Gilded Age. The corruption and exploitation had occurred in a nation whose government was supposedly representative, so how could any citizen be blameless? On these terms they accepted the responsibility for reform.

During this period the pioneering efforts of such reformers as Jane Addams, who worked in the Chicago slums to create an "island of security and cleanliness," made social service a profession. At her famous community center Hull House, opened in 1889, social workers helped the slum dweller with his many problems and provided encouragement through personal contact. Lillian D. Wald founded a similar "settlement house" on Henry Street in New York City and eventually developed it as a center for the training of nurses. Active in all fields of social work, she originated the concept of municipal school nursing. Evangeline C. Booth stimulated the conscience of Americans when she became national commander of the Salvation Army of the United States in 1904 and labored for thirty years to alleviate the suffering of the poor.

Trade unionists joined the ranks of pro-

---

[2]Theodore Roosevelt was responsible for the name "muckrakers." In a speech condemning such sensational exposés, he compared the authors to a character in John Bunyan's *Pilgrim's Progress* who was so intent on raking the muck at his feet that he could not look up. Roosevelt accused the authors of being unable to see anything but filth.

gressives, at least in their pointed attacks on the evils of child labor and poor working conditions. As early as 1902, the United Mine Workers obtained the rights of government intervention and mediation, as well as a ten per cent wage increase, although they were still refused recognition as an organization. The International Garment Workers' Union was able to improve the sweatshops, where men, women, and children had labored in unsanitary and unsafe conditions. By 1912 Sidney Hillman, leader of the garment workers, had won the right to arbitrate with management about the welfare of the workers.

Progressivism in Cities and States

Western Beginnings. Many of the early political successes of the progressives were scored in the Midwest, the Rocky Mountain region, and the Far West, where agrarians and Populists had pursued similar objectives. Beginning first in the cities, the movement spread quickly to the states and eventually to the federal government. In 1889 Hagen S. Pingree was elected mayor of Detroit. During his seven years in office he exposed councilmen for accepting graft, gained some control over the utility companies, and established a city-owned electric light system. The nation's two largest cities, New York and Chicago, were in the hands of reformers in 1894. Then in 1897 Samuel M. "Golden Rule" Jones, a manufacturer renowned for his liberal approach to employee-management relations, was elected mayor of Toledo, Ohio. An advocate of municipal ownership of public utilities, he aroused citizens to oust the political machine in control of their city. A minimum wage was established for city employees; playgrounds and golf courses were built. In the same state in 1901 Tom Loftin Johnson, a wealthy railway operator and manufacturer, became mayor of Cleveland. A typical progressive leader, he awakened civic consciousness and battled strenuously against political bosses and business interests and for municipal reforms. Property values were reassessed, the city gained control of its streetcars, lowering the fare to three cents, and programs to help the underprivileged were initiated. At the end of the decade Milwaukee elected the nation's first Socialist mayor, Emil Seidel.

The state governments witnessed even more impressive reforms. Robert La Follette, elected governor of Wisconsin in 1900 and twice reelected, was one of the most remarkable men of the era. His administration broke the power of the state's railroad and lumbering interests and forced through the legislature laws to establish direct primaries and limit lobbying and campaign expenditures; to regulate public utilities and railroads; to impose an income tax; and to conserve the state's two important natural resources, forests and waterpower. Appreciating the need for technical knowledge to solve the complex problems of modern government, La Follette enlisted the help of the University of Wisconsin faculty. He pressed the legislature to create commissions of experts to handle railroad and labor regulation, tax assessment, conservation, and highway construction. A reference library was established to assist legislators in drafting bills. In 1905 La Follette was elected to the United States Senate and served there as a national leader of the progressive movement until his death in 1925. In Washington he operated in much the same manner, setting up his own research group to study economic and social problems and to formulate appropriate legislation.

La Follette's "Wisconsin Idea"—to wrest power from business interests and political machines and turn the administration of the state over to popularly elected officials who would seek the advice of experts—set an example for other states. In New York Charles Evans Hughes, serving as counsel for a legislative committee investigating life insurance companies, won fame for his disclosures and was elected governor in 1906. Across the country Hiram W. Johnson obtained the conviction of Abe Ruef, the corrupt municipal boss of San

Francisco in 1908, and went on to become governor in 1910 and to break the hold of the Southern Pacific Railroad on California politics.

In Oregon a private citizen, William S. U'ren, led the crusade for the "Oregon system," which consisted of legislation to assure the public of more direct participation in government. In 1891 the legislature adopted the Australian ballot, in 1899 a registration law, in 1902 the initiative and referendum, in 1904 the direct primary, in 1909 a corrupt practices act, and in 1910 the recall.

Nature of Municipal and State Reform. Because most political abuses in the early twentieth century originated in government's vulnerability to the influence of powerful business interests or to control by political bosses, measures were proposed to return this control to the people and to remove the pressure of outside interests. The reformers pressed for state and city civil service to reduce drastically the number of appointive positions so that political bosses could no longer make appointments in return for contributions or other types of support. In some cities the progressives chose to replace the mayor and city council with a commission of administrators without political connections. The first such city government was appointed by the Texas legislature in 1900 to manage Galveston, after it had been flooded by a tidal wave and the city council showed itself incompetent to deal with the emergency. Many small- and medium-sized cities adopted this plan, with the commissioners, supposedly but not always experts in city government, being elected by the voters. After another disaster, a flood in Dayton, Ohio, in 1913, the city manager plan evolved wherein elected commissioners appoint a single professional manager to conduct city affairs. By 1923 more than three hundred cities had adopted this system of municipal government.

Direct and open primaries were also initiated in most states. Before primaries were adopted, candidates were nominated at conventions by delegates who had themselves been chosen at caucuses. Because a large proportion of those who attended the caucuses were officeholders, aspirants to office, and active party workers, the party machine could usually count on controlling enough delegates to elect its slate. The direct primary allowed all voters to go to the polls and select nominees by secret ballot; many independent men were chosen who would never have been considered by the political bosses. Primaries have not remained completely free of machine control, however.

By 1900 the United State Senate was spoken of as the "millionaire's club," for men of great wealth had been able to pressure trust-dominated state legislatures into electing and reelecting them. These prosperous senators all too often represented the vested interests of the country in the legislation they proposed. The House of Representatives four times—in 1894, 1898, 1900, and 1902—supported a constitutional amendment for the direct election of senators, but the upper chamber defeated these measures. The progressives tried another tactic. Preferential primaries in which voters might express their choices for United States senators were soon established in more than half the states. The legislatures found it politically wise to elect the men who won these primaries. By 1912 enough popularly chosen senators had been seated to pass the Seventeenth Amendment.

Three other major steps were taken to increase the direct involvement of the people in governmental action and to curb the control of bosses and big business. These were the *initiative*, the *referendum*, and the *recall*. The first two give the voters control over unresponsive legislatures. The initiative allows citizens to propose legislation by petition, without the action of any legislative body. The referendum permits the electorate to place on the ballot laws already passed by the legislature and thus abolish them if it so chooses. By means of the recall voters can remove a duly elected official from office by making him stand again in a specially called election. It would seem that democratic government could hardly be more direct, yet the three measures created almost as many problems as they resolved during the following decades, and these reforms have sometimes been abused. The initiative, referendum, and recall have, however, publicized injustices and given public opinion an important means of exerting pressure for improvements.

Other measures were also taken to correct political abuses. The National Short Ballot Organization made the so-called "short ballot" a national issue in 1909, and the next year the organization of the ballot was changed to a certain extent in most cities and states. Woodrow Wilson, president of the group, called this procedure "the key to the whole problem of the restoration of popular government" because "only offices important enough to attract and deserve public examination should be elective, and very few offices should be filled at one time." At the local level this principle was interpreted to favor commissions and city managers rather than mayors and councils. At the state level advocates declared that the short ballot would help to simplify administrative organization and the operation of state legislatures, for fewer jobs would be rotated with each election. The movement was only moderately successful, however.

Progressivism at the National Level

When progressives joined forces at the national level, they widened their objectives. Theodore Roosevelt was the prototype of the new reformer—young, vital, informed, concerned, but still moderate. The son of wealthy and distinguished New York parents, Roosevelt served in the legislature when a very young man and then spent time in the West to recover from personal tragedy. His experiences there made him a vocal champion of the "rugged life." He was unsuccessful in his effort to become mayor of New York City, but he proved an outstanding federal appointee—first as a civil service commissioner and later as Assistant Secretary of the Navy. When the war of 1898 was declared, he resigned this second post to serve as the commander of the Rough Riders, a volunteer unit which made the famous charge up San Juan Hill, one of the heights overlooking Santiago, Cuba. Returning home a hero, Roosevelt was elected Governor of New York and soon began to preach and practice progressivism. Local politicians, fearing the effects of his dynamic leadership, arranged to have him nominated as Vice President on the Republican ticket with McKinley, who was a candidate for reelection in 1900.

Although his critics had hoped to confine Roosevelt to an inactive role, on September 6, 1901 McKinley was shot by Leon Czolgosz, an anarchist, and died eight days later. When Roosevelt became President on September 14, 1901, he was forty-two years old, by far the youngest chief executive to serve the nation up to that time. Energetic, optimistic, and eager and considered a leader of progressivism by his contemporaries, Roosevelt was actually almost conservative by today's standards. He believed that Negroes were naturally inferior, had criticized the labor agitators of the 1890's, and avoided issues such as reducing the tariff and banking reforms. Roosevelt did not wish to discard the existing economic or political system but merely to make a more equitable distribution of wealth and power. The new President sought to accomplish his purposes both through existing executive power and by persuading Congress to pass new legislation.

Progressive Achievements. During the Roosevelt administration the swelling numbers of citizens who wanted injustices eliminated and higher ethical values exercised in business and politics made proposed reforms become political realities. Before 1900 the crusaders had seemed to be crying in the wilderness. Then suddenly the need for change was universally recognized, and the voices urging reevaluation of all phases of national political and economic life were heard and heeded.

The means employed to settle the coal

Theodore Roosevelt, orator, . . . THE BETTMANN ARCHIVE

. . . muckraker . . . THE BETTMANN ARCHIVE

ABOVE
lion tamer . . . CULVER PICTURES

RIGHT
. . . *conservationist* . . . (on the trail with John Muir in Yellowstone National Park).   CULVER PICTURES

strike in 1902 were an excellent example of what could be accomplished in this new emotional climate. Federal legislation to permit arbitration of labor disputes had been enacted as early as 1888, but the statutes had not been effectively utilized. When the United Mine Workers called a strike on May 12, demanding a wage increase, an eight-hour day, and union recognition, the owners refused to allow arbitration. The miners held firm throughout the summer and early fall, avoiding violence and expressing their willingness to arbitrate their claims. Their conduct won much public sympathy. But with winter coming and with coal supplies dwindling, the Eastern cities would soon suffer serious shortages. In October Roosevelt intervened, first inviting the owners and union leaders to the White House and then threatening to take over the mines and have them run by federal troops. The owners finally agreed to arbitrate, but only if no union official served on the commission. Roosevelt appointed a former president of a railroad union to represent the strikers as an "eminent sociologist." The miners went back to work, and the next March the commission granted them a ten per cent wage increase and a nine-hour day, but the union was still refused recognition. For the first time an American president had intervened in a labor dispute in behalf of the public interest

Foundations of a New Social Order, 1890–1909   141

and not just to protect private property. The action of the federal government in this strike was to lead to an entirely new look at organized labor and its role in the national economy. Moreover, Roosevelt's intervention received the support of the public, which had but recently feared all strikes as portending rampant rebellion.

Steps taken by the reform-minded President to control corporations also reflected the new public outlook. The people, no longer condoning the behavior of their old heroes, the robber barons, were ready to salute new heroes, the trust-busters. Corporate interests were consolidating at such a pace that control of all business activity by a few powerful trusts seemed a threatening possibility. In attacking the abuses of the trusts in his first annual message, Roosevelt asked for stronger laws to regulate, but not to disrupt, the huge corporations, for he believed trusts to be the "inevitable development of modern industrialism." He wanted "to do away with any evil in them," to make them "subserve the public good." When Congress did not respond to Roosevelt's request for regulatory laws, he sought, with the help of the courts, to exercise control over the trusts through existing legislation. In 1902 Roosevelt authorized his Attorney General to bring suit under the Sherman Anti-Trust Act against the Northern Securities Corporation, a huge railroad holding company controlled by J. P. Morgan, Kuhn, Loeb and Company, and the railroad operators James J. Hill and Edward H. Harriman. These master planners had merged three important railroads of the Northwest. Wall Street was shocked by Roosevelt's resurrection of the Sherman Act. In 1904 the Supreme Court ruled for the government and ordered the Northern Securities Company to dissolve.

Roosevelt initiated other suits during his administration, forty-four in all, and some were eventually successful, notably those against the meat packers, Standard Oil, and the American Tobacco Company. The President and the courts, realizing that mere size and power did not render a trust illegal, came to distinguish between "good trusts," which traded fairly and passed on the economies of mass production to labor and the consumer, and "bad trusts," which gouged the public to accumulate great wealth. Yet even though many of the suits against the big consolidations were successful in the courts, dissolution was hardly ever complete, for the parts of the trust usually found other means of acting in concert. Roosevelt's "trust-buster" activities did prove, however, that the federal government could at least act to protect the public from the growing power of monopolies. Moreover, the Congress did respond to one of Roosevelt's request for regulatory laws. On February 14, 1903 the Department of Commerce and Labor was created. The Bureau of Corporations in the new department was authorized to investigate interstate corporations and report on their activities.

When in 1904 Roosevelt was President in his own right and by a landside vote, he felt encouraged to push ahead with his "square deal." He determined to find effective measures to control undesirable practices of railroad companies. The Elkins Act (1903), which forced railroads to publish rates and to allow all customers engaged in interstate commerce to pay only those rates, had ended the old rebate system which had penalized the small shipper. But many other abuses remained. The Hepburn Act, enacted in 1906, set the stage for the government's present-day control of transportation. The old and relatively ineffective Interstate Commerce Commission, established in 1887, was expanded from five to seven members and was delegated the power, when complaints were received, of establishing maximum rates. Railroads were also required to accept its recommendations. The Commission need not go to court to enforce its order; if the companies objected to the rates set, they must initiate the court action. The Hepburn Act also extended the jurisdiction of the Commission to express, sleeping car, and pipeline companies and allowed it to prescribe a uniform system of bookkeeping for all railroads so that it might collect reliable comparative statistics.

Roosevelt pressed for the first legislation written to protect the American consumer. The Pure Food and Drug Act, passed by Congress on June 30, 1906, prohibited the production, transportation, and sale of adulterated or mislabeled food and medicine in interstate commerce. On the same date the Meat Inspection Act, allowing federal inspection of plants selling meat in interstate commerce, was enacted. The plants and their products could now be made to conform to standards of safety and cleanliness.

During his terms in the White House, Roosevelt never lost his taste for the "rugged life" and the outdoors, and he became one of the first champions of conservation of the nation's natural resources. Earlier generations had repeatedly destroyed the wealth of the land without thought of the consequences. With characteristic energy and enthusiasm Roosevelt determined to awaken the public to the need to preserve soil, forest, and water. In 1902 Roosevelt secured the passage of the Reclamation Act, which allowed the government to finance the building of dams for irrigation projects with the proceeds from public land sales. The great Roosevelt, Hoover, and Grand Coulee dams, as well as many others, were later built under this act. Administration of the national forests was given to the Department of Agriculture, with power to protect them from looting and devastation by railroads, lumber companies, and ranchers. More than 148,000,000 acres of forests were added to this public reserve, and another 85,000,000 acres were withdrawn from public sale so that the United States Geological Survey could study their mineral and water resources. Although the first national parks had been established before Roosevelt took office, he created five more as well as sixteen national monuments and numerous wildlife preserves.

In 1907 the Inland Waterways Commission was appointed to study the interrelation of soil, forests, and rivers and all conservation problems. On the Commission's recommendation Roosevelt called a national conservation conference, attended by state governors, Cabinet members, Supreme Court justices, members of Congress, businessmen, and conservation experts. This distinguished gathering, which focused the attention of the nation on the conservation movement, recommended the government's retention of all lands bearing coal, oil, phosphate, and natural gas; protection of the water supply of navigable streams; conservation of watersheds; and government regulation of timber cutting on private lands. After this meeting most of the states created their own conservation commissions.

The Progressive Triumph. Reform had become a political reality. Even those who were basically opposed to progressivism dared not resist too openly, for the American conscience was in full possession of the voting booth. The age of privilege was over; social progress and reform won votes. The regulations imposed by government might not yet be extensive enough, eliminating only certain abuses and improving the lot of only certain sections of society. But whatever the failure in actual accomplishment, the temper of public life had changed for the better. The federal government was at last responsive to the needs of the people and was intervening in areas formerly reserved to the states and private interests. The old days of self-interest as the acceptable standard of political action were gone, and gone forever.

SUGGESTED READINGS

*Aaron, D., *Men of Good Hope* (1951).
*Addams, J., *Forty Years at Hull House* (1935).
Barker, C. A., *Henry George* (1955).
*Bellamy, E., *Looking Backward, 2000–1887* (1887).
*Brenner, R. H., *From the Depths: The Discovery of Poverty in the United States* (1956).
*Commager, H. S., *The American Mind* (1963).
*Croly, H., *The Promise of American Life* (1909).
Curti, M., *The Growth of American Thought* (1964).
Destler, C. M., *Henry Demarest Lloyd and the Empire of Reform* (1963).
*DeVoto, B., *Mark Twain's America* (1951).
Dorfman, J., *Thorstein Veblen and His America* (1934).
*Faulkner, H. U., *Politics, Reform, and Expansion, 1890–1900* (1959).
Gabriel, R. H., *The Course of American Democratic Thought* (1956).
*George, H., *Progress and Poverty* (1879).
Ginger, R., *Age of Excess: The United States from 1877 to 1914* (1965).
*Ginger, R., *Altgeld's America* (1958).
*Glad, P. W., *The Trumpet Soundeth* (1960).
*Goldman, E. F., *Rendezvous with Destiny* (1952).
*Green, C. M., *The Rise of Urban America* (1965).
*Hicks, J. D., *The Populist Revolt* (1955).
*Hofstadter, R., *The Age of Reform* (1955).
*Hofstadter, R., *Anti-Intellectualism in American Life* (1963).
*Hofstadter, R., *Social Darwinism in American Thought* (1955).
Hopkins, C. H., *The Rise of the Social Gospel in American Protestantism, 1865–1915* (1940).
Howe, M. D., *The Shaping Years, 1870–1882* (1957).
*Hunter, R., *Poverty* (1904).
Kaplan, J., *Mr. Clemens and Mark Twain* (1966).
*Kazin, A., *On Native Grounds* (1942).
*Kipnis, I., *The American Socialist Movement, 1897–1912* (1952).
Lubove, R. M., *The Progressives and the Slums* (1962).
McKelvey, B. *The Urbanization of America* (1962).
McMarry, D. L., *Coxey's Army* (1929).
*Mann, A., *Yankee Reformers in the Urban Age* (1954).
May, H. F., *The Protestant Churches and Industrial America* (1949).
*Miller, P., *American Thought: Civil War to World War I* (1954).
Morgan, A. E., *Edward Bellamy* (1944).
*Mowry, G. E., *The Era of Theodore Roosevelt, 1900–1912* (1958).
*Mowry, G. E., *Theodore Roosevelt and the Progressive Movement* (1946).
Munro, W. B., *Referendum, Initiative and Recall* (1912).

Patton, C. W., *The Battle for Municipal Reform: Mobilization and Attack, 1875–1900* (1940).

*Pollack, N., *The Populist Response to Industrial America* (1962).

Reigier, C. C., *The Era of the Muckrakers* (1932).

*Riesman, D., *Thorstein Veblen, A Critical Interpretation* (1953).

*Riis, J., *How the Other Half Lives* (1890).

*Steffens, L., *The Shame of the Cities* (1904).

*Veblen, T., *The Theory of the Leisure Class* (1899).

*Warner, S. B., Jr., *Streetcar Suburbs* (1962).

*Weber, M., *The City* (1958).

Weberg, F. B., *The Background of the Panic of 1893* (1929).

*White, M. G., *Social Thought in America* (1949).

*Wilson, E., *The Shock of Recognition* (1955).

UNIT VI

First in War, First in Peace:

BROTHER, CAN YOU SPARE A DIME?

What happens when a nation comes of age? The United States began the twentieth century trying to correct old abuses and to create a better world, only to find that world power can lead to war. World War I commenced in indecision and ended in disillusionment. The nation then turned from global concerns to enjoy the good life of the twenties, but in these years of prosperity and peace the seeds of depression and of even deadlier war were sown. By the thirties the nation and the world had plunged deep into economic and emotional hard times. The New Deal offered some solutions, but another war would start before the crisis at home ended.

CULVER PICTURES

THE BETTMANN ARCHIVE

LIBRARY OF CONGRESS

149

ABOVE: WIDE WORLD PHOTOS

LEFT: CULVER PICTURES

150   THE BETTMANN ARCHIVE

PHOTOWORLD

National		International	
1898	HAWAII ANNEXED; SPANISH-AMERICAN WAR	**1898**	BRITISH RECONQUER SUDAN; FASHODA INCIDENT
1899	HAY PROCLAIMS OPEN DOOR POLICY	**1899**	BOER (SOUTH AFRICA) WAR
		1900	BOXER REBELLION IN CHINA REPRESSED
1901	MCKINLEY ASSASSINATED	**1901**	HAY-PAUNCEFOTE TREATY
1903	PANAMA AFFAIR		
1904	NORTHERN SECURITIES CASE; TR — TRUST-BUSTER	**1904**	ROOSEVELT COROLLARY AND THE "BIG STICK" IN THE CARIBBEAN
		1905	TREATY OF PORTSMOUTH ENDS RUSSO-JAPANESE WAR
1906	PURE FOOD AND DRUG ACT	**1906**	ALGECIRAS CONFERENCE
1907	THE GREAT WHITE FLEET	**1907**	SECOND HAGUE CONFERENCE; FORMATION OF THE TRIPLE ENTENTE
1912	TR SPLITS REPUBLICANS; WILSON ELECTED	**1912**	SINKING OF THE *TITANIC*
1914	CLAYTON ANTI-TRUST ACT	**1914**	WORLD WAR I BEGINS
		1915	SINKING OF THE *LUSITANIA*
1917	UNITED STATES ENTERS THE WAR	**1917**	RUSSIAN REVOLUTION; BOLSHEVIKS SEIZE CONTROL
		1918	ARMISTICE SIGNED ENDING WORLD WAR I
1919	EIGHTEENTH AMENDMENT	**1919**	TREATY OF VERSAILLES
1920	NINETEENTH AMENDMENT		
		1922	WASHINGTON ARMS CONFERENCE; MUSSOLINI DICTATOR OF ITALY
1924	TEAPOT DOME SCANDAL	**1924**	EMERGENCE OF STALIN IN U.S.S.R.
1929	STOCK MARKET CRASH	**1929**	WORLDWIDE DEPRESSION
1930	HAWLEY-SMOOT TARIFF ACT	**1930**	LONDON NAVAL CONFERENCE
		1931	JAPAN SEIZES MANCHURIA
1933	FDR'S NEW DEAL	**1933**	HITLER ELECTED IN GERMANY
1935	SOCIAL SECURITY ACT; WAGNER ACT; CIO ESTABLISHED	**1935**	GERMAN REARMAMENT; ITALY INVADES ETHIOPIA
1936	FDR'S "LANDSLIDE" ELECTION	**1936**	CIVIL WAR IN SPAIN
1937	FDR'S COURT PACKING FAILS; NEUTRALITY ACT	**1937**	JAPAN INVADES CHINA
1938	WAGES AND HOURS LAW	**1938**	GERMANY SEIZES AUSTRIA; CZECH CRISIS; MUNICH CONFERENCE
		1939	WORLD WAR II BEGINS

CHAPTER 23

Building a Progressive Society, 1909–1920

This is the image of America, . . . the fulfillment of what the human race has hoped for, the guarantee that the fund of hope is not expended and exhausted, but that it lies here to bank in our hand from generation to generation as if we were trustees to see that it was handed on unimpaired to those who seek to realize an opportunity.

WOODROW WILSON, 1912

BROWN BROTHERS

CLIMAX OF POLITICAL PROGRESSIVISM, 1909–1917

THEODORE ROOSEVELT WORE THE ROBES OF THE reformer with great style, and he enlisted widespread public support for his various crusades, but many of the abuses that he sought to end were deeply entrenched in American government and business. Lasting and permanent changes could not be made quickly without disrupting the entire society. Because Roosevelt was unwilling to press for immediate and radical solutions, much work remained to be done after he left office. Many of the most far-reaching innovations were yet to be introduced by succeeding presidents who were perhaps less reform-minded than Roosevelt had been.

Taft's Administration

Events of the election campaign of 1908 form an interesting commentary on the increasing strength of the reform movement. Both major parties advanced platforms that pledged to control monopoly and, at last, to consider revision of the exceedingly high tariff, although Democrats were more outspoken in their criticisms of these abuses than were Republicans. Significant too was the fact that antitrust legislation was popular enough to gain widespread political support, for only twelve years earlier this position had been labeled socialistic or worse.

Candidates of the major parties were also closely related to the reform movement. William Jennings Bryan, the stalwart Populist, was once again the Democratic nominee, and Theodore Roosevelt, who had stated publicly that he would not seek another term, had personally selected William H. Taft of Ohio as the Republican standard-bearer. Taft was elected, receiving 7,679,000 votes to Bryan's 6,409,000.

In the election of 1908, both new and old political-action groups attempted to gain public support for more radical changes in society and government, even though the major parties had adopted reform proposals. Eugene V. Debs, the Socialist party candidate, received 421,000 votes. There were five other candidates representing minor groups, among them the Prohibition National, Socialist-Labor, and Independence parties. The few remaining Populists nominated Thomas E. Watson, who polled 28,000 votes.

Continuation of Roosevelt's Policies. William H. Taft had been a noted attorney and public servant for many years before he became President. In addition to serving as a federal judge, he had been dean of the law school at the University of Cincinnati, an able civil governor (1901–1904) of the Philippines just after the islands were acquired by the United States, and Secretary of War in Roosevelt's cabinet.

Taft conscientiously continued the work that Roosevelt had begun, but he did not establish the reputation of a crusader. Perhaps Taft's image as a conservative can be attributed in part to some of his later decisions as Chief Justice of the Supreme Court, or it may have been created by the nature of the man himself. He was ponderous in manner, though he evidenced humor to his friends, and immense in bulk, weighing 300 pounds. But Taft's concept of the presidency was probably the most important single reason for his not being regarded as a champion of reform. Roosevelt had believed that he was elected to represent all the people and continually voiced his concern for their welfare. Taft, on the other hand, believed that as President he should carry out the dictates of Congress and not personally crusade for public reforms.

Taft's Achievements. Efforts by Taft to regulate trusts were markedly successful. He supported the Mann-Elkins Act (1910), which extended the rate-setting authority of the Interstate Commerce Commission to public communications—to the telephone, telegraph, cable, and wireless companies. The act also allowed the Commission itself to suspend railroad rate increases, without waiting for shippers to complain, and set up a special Commerce Court[1] to hear appeals arising from Commission decisions on rates. More than twice as many antitrust proceedings were initiated during the Taft administration as during Roosevelt's terms in office (ninety to forty-four). In 1911 Taft's Attorney General finally won the government's antitrust suits against Standard Oil and the American Tobacco Company, which were instructed by the Supreme Court to dissolve their organizations. That same year Taft's most provocative antitrust suit, prosecution of the United States Steel Corporation, was initiated.

While Taft was in office, Congress passed laws giving the American public a postal savings bank and a parcel post system—services already provided by many European countries—even though these measures were bitterly opposed by bankers and express companies. The Sixteenth, or income tax, Amendment, and the Seventeenth, allowing the people to elect their senators, were also adopted by Congress in 1909 and 1912 and then ratified by the necessary number of states by early 1913. Roosevelt had reserved coal lands without authorization from Congress. Taft obtained that permission and, in addition, withdrew oil lands from public sale. He also set up the Bureau of Mines to protect the nation's mineral resources and safeguard the miners.

Split in Republican Party. The rift that would widen and divide the Republican party, generating enmity between the President and his predecessor, became evident soon after Taft assumed office. The Republican platform had promised the voters a revision of the tariff. During the campaign Taft had interpreted this plank to mean a "substantial revision downward" and pledged himself to call a special session of Congress for this specific purpose—which he promptly did in March 1909. The Payne Bill, written in and passed by the House, made moderate reductions in the schedules. In the Senate, however, Nelson W. Aldrich rewrote the bill to express the protectionist views of his fellow multimillionaire industrialists. Of the 847 changes made in the tariff, some 600

---

[1]This body was, unfortunately, abolished in 1912 because one of its judges had been too friendly to the corporations and had to be impeached.

First in War, First in Peace

were upward. A group of Midwestern Republican senators, led by Robert La Follette and determined that the public should know the true connection between tariffs and trusts, debated the new Payne-Aldrich Bill with all the statistics at their command. During the debates the President, although he had sincerely wanted duties sharply reduced, came to distrust the insurgents as demagogues and drew closer to the Old Guard. The Payne-Aldrich measure passed Congress, with but few concessions to the insurgents, and Taft signed it on August 5, completely betraying his campaign promise. Accustomed to Roosevelt's strong presidential leadership, the public in general and the Midwestern Republican farmers, suffering particularly from high prices, were astounded by Taft's retreat.

An argument concerning the issue of conservation, beginning in the summer of 1909, widened the rift between the progressives and the Old Guard and further weakened the President's position. The Secretary of the Interior, Richard A. Ballinger of Washington, had thrown open to private development certain water power sites that he considered had been rather arbitrarily withdrawn from the public domain by Roosevelt. Gifford Pinchot, Chief of the Forest Service and Roosevelt's good friend, publicly protested Ballinger's actions and was supported by Louis Glavis, an investigator for the Interior Department. Glavis, dismissed by order of the President, then revealed in an article written for *Collier's* that his former boss had agreed not to question the claims of the Guggenheim interests to reserve coal lands in Alaska. Conservationists were outraged by these two reversals of Roosevelt's policies, but Taft, feeling obliged to support the man he had appointed to office, dismissed the still protesting Pinchot the next January. A subsequent congressional investigation of the Interior Department cleared Ballinger of wrongdoing but revealed him to hold the typical wealthy Westerner's predatory attitude toward the public domain. He resigned his post a year and a half later.

In the meantime Roosevelt, who had gone off to Africa after Taft's inauguration, returned from a year-long hunting expedition in the wilds to reestablish communication with the world. He was confronted with a barrage of complaints from progressives. Pinchot delivered his in person, meeting Roosevelt in Italy during the former President's important round of visits to several European capitals. In June 1910 Roosevelt arrived in New York. He made no public criticism of Taft, although privately he expressed his dismay that Taft had not maintained party unity. Then in August in Osawatomie, Kansas, Roosevelt himself widened the breach with an address shocking to the conservatives. He pledged the Republican party to a "New Nationalism," calling for a strong and broadened federal authority and a comprehensive program of national legislation to construct a better society.

That autumn Roosevelt campaigned for progressive and conservative Republicans alike, but the party had already been weakened. The Democrats won the House for the first time since 1892. Although the Republicans continued to claim control of the Senate, it was really in the hands of a coalition of La Follette Republicans and Democrats.

The Progressive Party. Abandoning attempts at party unity altogether and aiming instead for its liberalization, the dissident Republican activists met in La Follette's house in Washington and organized the National Progressive Republican League on January 21, 1911. The progressive movement had finally been solidified as a formal organization, but it was still a part of the Republican party. The League's platform embodied the goals sought on the city and state level for years—direct primaries; the initiative, referendum, and recall; a corrupt practices act; and direct election of United States senators, to be proposed as the Seventeenth Amendment the next year.

Senator La Follette became the League's candidate for President. But on February 2, 1912 the Midwesterner, tired and troubled by family illness, collapsed while delivering a speech. Insurgents who felt that Roosevelt was the stronger candidate used the occasion as an excuse to desert La Follette. Roosevelt had already suggested to seven Republican governors that they urge his candidacy, which they did by open letter on February 10. Eleven days later he declared "My hat is in the ring." Roosevelt campaigned vigorously in the thirteen states that chose convention delegates by presidential primary and won in most, but Taft controlled the party machinery in other states. The former President arrived in Chicago for the June convention a hundred votes short of a majority. His forces challenged the right of 254 Taft delegates to their seats, but the conservative-controlled credentials committee accepted all but a few of them. Taft was renominated on June 22, 1912. Roosevelt's supporters had in the meantime been urging him to organize a

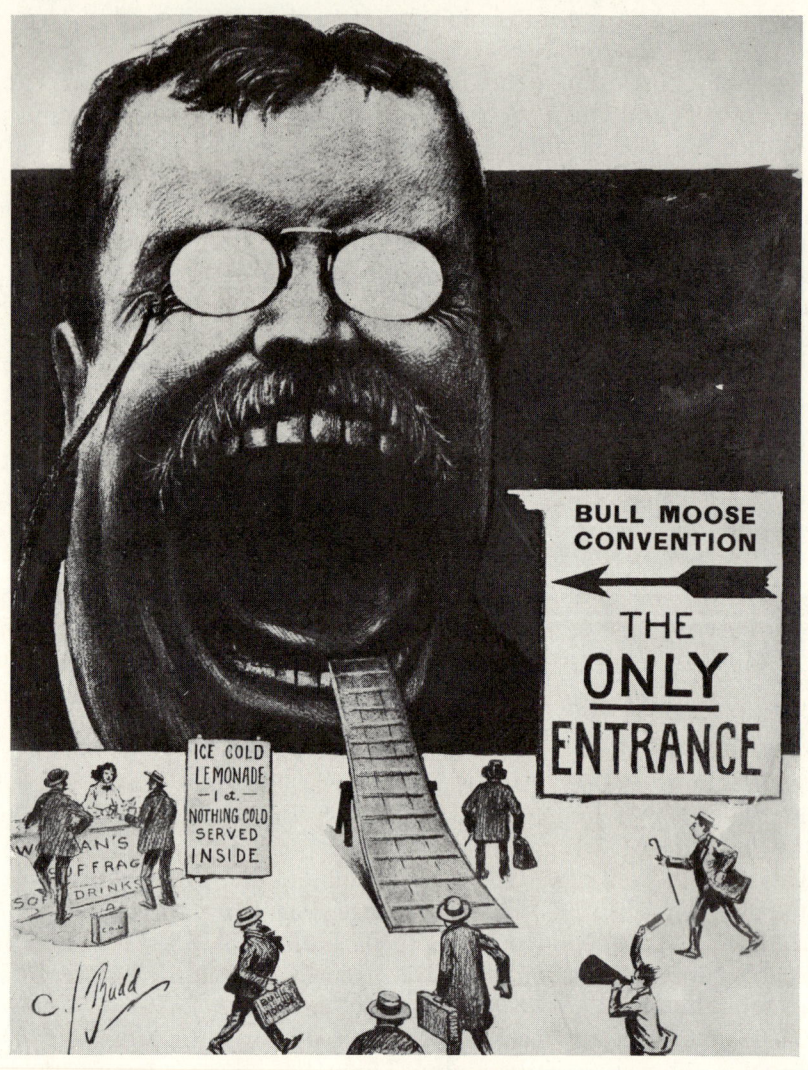

158 *First in War, First in Peace*

new party; the same day that Taft was nominated, the former President told a rump convention of his delegates that he would make the race. On August 5 the progressive group was once again back in Chicago, meeting with the zeal of revivalists to nominate Roosevelt as the candidate of the Progressive, or Bull Moose, party.[2]

Mandate for Continued Progressivism. Once again everyone was for reform in 1912, with some candidates favoring a little more, others a little less. The Democrats, who had also had difficulty in agreeing upon a candidate at their July convention, had finally selected Woodrow Wilson on the forty-sixth ballot. The Democratic party, as well as the Republican and the Bull Moose, pledged continued and even increased governmental action in resolving the nation's problems. Roosevelt had already named his Progressive program the "New Nationalism"; Wilson was to label his the "New Freedom." Roosevelt sought to regulate the monopolies, but Wilson wanted to restore and regulate competition. He advocated that the government break up the great trusts and establish rules ensuring that business would be conducted fairly. Through government regulation free enterprise would have new opportunities to flourish. Taft, the incumbent reformer, found himself forced into the role of a conservative.

The outcome of the campaign proved that the people favored reform of the existing abuses in government and society. Wilson polled forty-two per cent of the popular vote and won overwhelmingly with 435 electoral votes. Roosevelt's percentage of the popular vote was twenty-seven, Taft's twenty-three. Eugene Debs was the choice of 900,000 citizens for whom the policies of Wilson and Roosevelt were not radical enough. Over three-fourths of the voters supported the progressive ideas of Wilson, Roosevelt, and Debs.

---

[2]The party name came from a favorite Roosevelt saying, that he felt "as strong as a bull moose."

Progressivism under Wilson

Character of Woodrow Wilson. The personality and philosophy of another strong president were bound to create new currents of thought. Born in Virginia before the Civil War (December 28, 1856), Wilson was graduated from Princeton and studied law at the University of Virginia. Soon after opening a law office in Atlanta, he decided to return to academic life, earning a doctrate in political science from Johns Hopkins in 1886. He became a teacher of history at Bryn Mawr and Wesleyan and then returned to his alma mater where he taught law and political economics. In 1902 he became president of Princeton University. Although he had never held political office, he was elected Governor of New Jersey in 1910. He quickly began a continuing campaign against political corruption and machines, persuading the very first legislative session of his administration to accept a primary law and a corrupt practices act, as well as a workmen's compensation law and regulation of public utilities. Wilson was the ideal symbol for those reformers who criticized manipulation of the democratic process by professional politicians. Having dealt almost entirely with the philosophy of government and very little with its practical realities, the new President was in a position to advocate corrections in a system he had never been a part of.

An idealist, an intellectual, and a very persuasive and literate speaker, Wilson felt particular sympathy for the small entrepreneur. He deplored the fact that "bigness" was closing the door to individual opportunity. The new President did not wish to change the capitalistic system but merely to enable the small businessmen to compete. The trusts he regarded as barriers to the common man, who would be able to rise in wealth and status if he had opportunities to invest. Wilson hoped that with unfair and illicit competition effectively eliminated by the federal government, virtuous and ener-

The intellectual in the White House. BROWN BROTHERS

getic citizens would continue to invest in small enterprises, which would in turn grow and prosper. The former student of government also had theories about his new role. Impressed by the power of British prime ministers, Wilson believed that the president should provide strong executive leadership for the nation and for Congress. The president should take an active part in the formulation of legislation and work closely with Congress for its passage.

Wilson's Administration. The tide of reform was at its height during Wilson's presidency, and far-reaching changes were to be effected in four areas: tariff reduction, monetary reform, antitrust legislation, and labor legislation. The first problem that Wilson faced was the ongoing controversy over the tariff.[3] Progressives of

---

[3]On April 8 Wilson actually addressed Congress on this topic during a special session, an act which shattered precedent. No president had appeared in person before the Congress since 1800, for it had become customary for the chief executive to send his messages to be read.

First in War, First in Peace

course still opposed the Payne-Aldrich Tariff of 1909, which had lowered duties to about forty per cent of the worth of the products imported, as inadequate. A new Underwood Tariff Bill cutting duties down to twenty-nine per cent passed the House with no trouble. In the Senate, however, the usual monied interests attacked it. Thereupon this President publicly denounced the hordes of lobbyists who had descended on Washington to work for the bill's defeat, pointing out that the masses had no such agents to protect their interests. In September the bill passed, providing the most significant tariff reductions since the Civil War. Important basic commodities—steel rails, raw wool, many foods, boots, and agricultural machinery—were placed on the free list.

To make up for losses in tariff revenue, the Underwood Act provided for a very small graduated tax on personal incomes. The Sixteenth Amendment, allowing Congress to impose direct taxes on individual citizens, had been ratified by the states just seven months earlier. The tax that reformers had long considered the fairest and most equitable, because it places the principal burden on those persons who can afford to pay, was finally operative.

The President was also successful in reforming the currency and banking system, the great faults of which were inelasticity of currency and the concentration of credit in the large banks of the big cities and in J. P. Morgan's Wall Street money trust. In passing the Glass-Owen Federal Reserve Act, in December 1913 after six months of debate, the President and reformers had to overcome the opposition of powerful private banking interests who wanted a great central bank under their own supervision. Instead the new law gave the government control of the reserve system and currency supply, allowing it to intervene in the economy to a degree never before attempted. The Federal Reserve System established by the act divided the country into twelve regions, each with its own Federal Reserve Bank. A Federal Reserve Board, which consists of the Secretary of the Treasury, the Controller of the Currency, and six financial experts appointed by the president, controls the entire system. National banks were compelled to join their district bank, and state banks were eligible to do so. The private member banks actually own the government-controlled regional bank, for each private bank must subscribe six per cent of its capital and surplus to the capital stock of its Federal Reserve Bank. By banking the reserve funds of so many member banks, the regional bank serves them as a stable source of currency and safeguards their deposits.

The new law also provided a new form and a more flexible source of currency. Federal Reserve notes, backed by forty per cent gold reserves, can be issued to member banks in return for commercial paper. That is, a member bank can sell its promissory notes, which it has accepted as security on loans made to businessmen, to the district bank in return for cash (rediscounting). This money is in turn loaned out to additional borrowers. The rate at which the district bank decides to rediscount commercial paper determines the interest a member bank must charge on loans and therefore the amount of additional currency and credit that finds its way into the economy.

Wilson also continued the attack on trusts. In 1914 he successfully supported the creation of a Federal Trade Commission of five members, which was empowered to prevent unfair competition. The Commission was authorized to investigate interstate corporations and to publish its findings, thus disclosing bribery, threats, adulteration, misrepresentation of products to consumers, and price fixing. It could also issue cease and desist orders to any corporation found guilty of engaging in unfair trade practices. Although the Federal Trade Commission Act did not actually define the term "unfair," the Clayton Anti-Trust Act made specific business practices illegal. It forbade price discrimination that might create a monopoly, "tying" agreements that might keep a retailer from buying from a supplier's competitors, and a firm's acquisition of stock in a competing corporation. The rights of directors to serve on the board of more than one large corporation and more than one large bank were restricted. Officers of corporations were made personally liable for violations of these provisions. This measure provided a recourse for the victims of unlawful practices of trusts by authorizing the courts to issue injunctions when offenders failed to comply with the orders of the Federal Trade Commission and other agencies.

Although Roosevelt had been active in the arbitration of labor controversies, no significant changes were made in national labor laws during his tenure. The Clayton Act, by stating that no provisions of antitrust laws could be interpreted as forbidding the existence and operation of farm and labor corporations, implied the right of labor to organize. Through a provision of the earlier Sherman Anti-Trust Act, unions had been declared trusts "in restraint of trade." The court's right to use injunctions against labor was also limited by the Clayton Act; strikes, picketing, and the collection of strike benefits were legalized. The Clayton Act seemed extremely favorable to organized labor at the time it was passed by Congress, but later court decisions interpreted it less liberally than expected.

CULTURAL AND SOCIAL CHANGES, 1909–1917

The ideas and ideals that guided the progressives to political and economic reforms also stirred up a great social and cultural upheaval. Reform characterized every aspect of national life—education, art, music, literature, fashion, and social behavior.

Educational Reform

The Principles of John Dewey. In 1890 James had stated in the *Principles of Psychology* that men could change the world through their own thinking and the practical application of their ideas and that it was "right and necessary" for them to do so. John Dewey, who had been converted to pragmatism (page 485) by reading James, proceeded to do just that by applying the new philosophy to the field of education. Dewey wanted the schools to become instruments of social reform, imbuing children with the spirit of public service and teaching them to become good citizens. Schools should be centers in which young people can learn to live by performing activities that will engage them the remainder of their lives.

Dewey's educational methods were based on the techniques of problem solving, which he believed students needed to learn in order to make decisions effectively. Students must understand why things happen as well as what has occurred. They are not to be treated as receptacles into which the "wisdom of the ages" can be poured without explanation or question. Dewey rejected rote learning as almost useless and opposed the teaching of facts that have little practical value. The emphasis of what was later called progressive education on "life adjustment" engendered a major and continuing debate of the twentieth century.

Vocational education was also basic to Dewey's thinking. He believed that all citizens should receive a general education in the schools, but he recognized the need for trained manpower, which in earlier days had been supplied by the apprentice system or through the immigration of workmen trained abroad. Again, this aspect of Dewey's program grew out of his idea that schools should provide "realistic preludes" or, even better, actual life experiences, rather than serve as ivory towers of learning cut off from the real world.

Expansion of High Schools. The opportunities for youth in the United States to attend school increased greatly during the progressive era. Although in 1900 10.7 per cent of the people were unable to read or write, the figure had dropped to 7.7 per cent by 1910. There was a marked increase in the length of time that young people attended school, even though the average in 1910 was only six years.

In the 1870's the new high schools began to replace the earlier private academies at a faster rate; by 1910 there were 10,000 secondary schools. Acquiring a high school education became the normal expectation of a great many young Americans. Many schools offered a much broader curriculum than they had in the past, allowing students to select their own subjects, which might include history and literature as well as vocational courses. Various new plans, such as the Winnetka proposal (1913), which combined individual and group instruction, and the Dalton system (1920), which featured individual instruction in laboratories, were introduced in the high schools. In the South secondary public school education had lacked the tradition and tax base that supported the institution in other sections, but by 1900 it began to take root. High schools for white young people received more funds, and enrollments increased. There were other changes too. The first junior high school opened in 1896, and the first junior college was established in 1902. By 1915 there were seventy-four junior colleges.

Growth of Higher Education. As the new century began, most of the institutions of higher learning were attacked without mercy by the progressives. The colleges and universities were criticized for being the tools of the wealthy and powerful and for producing graduates who were ill equipped to deal with modern society. It is true that boards of trustees of the privately endowed colleges were sometimes dominated by businessmen, and a few professors were dismissed because their economic views or advocacy of Darwin's theory of evolution offended conservative trustees. Politicians might try to apply the patronage system to professorships at state universities. Many institutions had increased enormously in size, becoming bureaucratized as they grew. But for the most part academic freedom survived serious challenges, and colleges and universities were already offering a vastly expanded curriculum.

The nation's oldest university, Harvard, had led the reform. Charles W. Eliot, its president from 1869 to 1909, made it a model of a new type of higher education—diversified, professional, and broad in its program. He introduced the elective system, gradually decreasing the number of required courses and offering such new subjects as modern languages, laboratory sciences, and economics and other social sciences. A graduate school was created in 1872, and the standards of Harvard's medical and law schools were raised. Three full years of medical courses and laboratory work were required of those taking a degree in medicine. In 1870 C. C. Langdell's students were the first to learn law by studying specific cases rather than textbooks.

Then in 1876 Johns Hopkins was founded by, and named for, a wealthy financier. The university's first president, Daniel Coit Gilman, made graduate work its principal concern. He and many members of the new faculty, scholars of the highest reputation, had studied in Germany, where until 1880 most Americans went for work beyond the master's degree. The teaching at Johns Hopkins emphasized the exacting methods and meticulous research of German scholarship. As graduates of the university became professors at other institutions, advanced work was offered on campuses throughout the United States.

Since the passage of the Morrill Act in 1862 (page 414), federal funds had been available for land-grant colleges in which "agriculture and the mechanical arts" were taught. After 1870 the state universities established through this act began to offer the new varied curricula and professional and graduate schools to students who needed specialized training for an industrial society. James B. Angell, president of the University of Michigan for most of the years that Eliot headed Harvard, made his university one of the leading in the country. Two later acts extended the work begun by the Morrill Act. The Smith-Lever Act (1914) established a program of education for farmers, to be conducted by county agents working through the land-grant colleges. The Smith-Hughes Act (1917) provided funds to encourage the teaching of vocational agriculture and domestic science in secondary schools.

The endowments of many older colleges and universities were increased and new institutions were founded by the private philanthropy of the Gilded Age. Cornell (1868), Stanford (1891), the University of Chicago (1892), and Carnegie Institute (1896) had all been established before the progressive era was well under way.

New fields of study continued to be introduced. By 1910 colleges were offering social psychology and biochemistry. Science, having risen in prestige through the earlier Darwinian revolution, became even more important and specialized. With the new emphasis on research, the role of the teaching scientist was more rewarding. International reputations were established by Josiah Willard Gibbs (Yale) in theoretical physics and physical chemistry, by Albert A. Michelson and Robert A. Millikan (University of Chicago) in physics, and by Thomas Hunt Morgan (Columbia) in genetics.

Education for Women. In the decades after the Civil War, the role of women in society changed as they were employed in businesses and professions. Gradually, the doubts whether women were intellectually and physically capable of benefiting from a college education were dispelled. Some of the Midwestern land-grant universities were coeducational from their inception. Moreover, in the more conservative East Vassar College, founded in 1861, offered work comparable to that taught in any of the better men's colleges. Other first-rate women's colleges that were established in the next decades—Wellesley, Smith, Bryn Mawr, and Radcliffe—provided excellent liberal arts curricula. President Wilson himself had taught at Bryn Mawr.

Expanding Views of Law and History

Legal theory was rudely shaken by pragmatism and the reform spirit. The law was no longer considered semisacred, but subject to the same changes that were affecting other parts of society. Oliver Wendell Holmes and Louis D. Brandeis represented the new type of legal mind. Holmes, as a judge on the Massachusetts Supreme Court and on the United States Supreme Court, interpreted the law as part of the social process and therefore as constantly changing. Judges could not merely apply precedent to the case at hand. "The felt necessities of the time" should determine the rules by which men are governed. Brandeis, a trial attorney before his appointment to the United States Supreme Court in 1916, presented social and economic facts as evidence and repeatedly pressed for court decisions based on economic and social realities instead of on statutes alone.

A "new history" also came into being. Charles A. Beard, whose work emphasized an economic interpretation of history, was one of the most widely read authors in the nation. James H. Robinson, who published his *The New History* in 1912, took the position that the subject, rather than being a descriptive narrative of politics and war, must encompass all of man's experience. Historians must be able to understand social, scientific, intellectual, and artistic progress to be able to reconstruct the past in a way that has meaning for the present.

Progressive Influences on Literature and the Arts

We have already discussed the active role taken by writers in the progressive movement, particularly the muckrakers. Indeed, two of the progressive presidents were themselves authors

First in War, First in Peace

of note. Roosevelt wrote extensively of his adventures, as well as important books of biography and American history. Wilson was a historian of some reputation and more particularly a prominent scholar of comparative government. The works of professional writers also reflected developments during the progressive era.

Literature and Social Protest. The most famous American authors in the 1890's were Mark Twain, who has successfully defied classification to this day, and William Dean Howells and Henry James, who were known as "realists."[4] Twain, considered the great voice of the West, was an ardent democrat who used humorous satire to underscore social injustice, attacking prejudice and snobbery wherever he found it. Howells's masterpiece, *The Rise of Silas Lapham,* one of the first novels to treat a social problem of the times, described the newly rich of the post-Civil War period. Believing that "Art must serve society," he wrote as the years passed novels that protested society's evils in an increasingly liberal tone. James, on the other hand, rejected the role of social reformer, but he presented a penetrating and close examination of complex personalities caught in social and psychological conflicts. He never ceased to be an uninvolved observer, however, usually of the impact of European culture and Europeans on the visiting American's character and mind.

The novels of the "naturalists" Stephen Crane, Frank Norris, and Jack London dealt with the raw, seamy, and violent—fear in battle, seduction and suicide, brutish murder, class war, man's struggle against the wild. Norris's *The Pit* (page 428) and *The Octopus,* about the California wheat farmers' struggle against the railroad, came closest to the propaganda novel which served the progressives so well. Theodore Dreiser, another naturalist, regarded life as a chaos of blind and amoral forces, rejecting the notion so dear to the progressives that man could control his fate. Through the massing of detail he made his novels powerful projections of reality. The literature of the early twentieth century, by its very disclosures, strongly indicted social evils and offered hope that they could be eradicated.

Explosion of the Arts. The arts also underwent a revolution at this time, although it would be inaccurate to claim that progressivism caused the upheaval. The climate in which the changes could be accepted and appreciated, however, was created by progressive thought.

The Armory Show, which opened in New York City in 1913, introduced the American audience to modern European painting. Works of the Postimpressionists Cézanne, Van Gogh, and Seurat and of the abstract painters Picasso, Matisse, and Kandinsky were displayed. Art in the United States has never been the same since. A few painters had previously broken with tradition, most notably the socially conscious men of the "Ash Can School," who chose clerks and slum dwellers, city streets and trash-filled alleys as their subjects. Most American artists, however, were still following the earlier academic tradition and painting only what was beautiful. The Armory Show set the stage for public acceptance of artists who rejected the representational style of the past to paint evocative canvases in which they distorted reality and emphasized form, contrast, and color.

Architecture and interior design also changed radically. In the 1890's and early twentieth century, so many skyscrapers were built that they became the symbol of the nation's cities. At first, the buildings of the period were Romanesque and then for a time classical in design, with considerable emphasis on Greek and Roman columns and porticoes. But architects such as Louis H. Sullivan, with his dictum that "form follows function," and Frank Lloyd

---

[4] American realists, reacting against the romantic and sentimental novels of earlier decades, determined to view the actualities of life dispassionately and to write of the commonplace problems of their new industrial society. Naturalists treated the brutal and ugly aspects of life, emphasizing the primitive emotions of man and his helplessness in determining his fate.

Reform in art: Marcel Duchamp called it "Nude Descending a Staircase, Number 2." Teddy Roosevelt said it could not compare with his bathroom rug.

LOUISE AND WALTER ARENSBERG COLLECTION, PHILADELPHIA MUSEUM OF ART

166   *First in War, First in Peace*

Wright, with his concept that a building should harmonize with its site, were soon preaching utility and fitness rather than ornamentation. These pragmatists in construction design were not able to prevent others from creating many useless and ineffective buildings during this era, but they did introduce in architecture elements of common sense that were to be followed by later generations.

FLAWS AND PARADOXES OF PROGRESSIVISM

The Plight of the Negro

While white American progressives labored to improve their nation, the black man was ignored by government, by industry, and to a considerable extent by the reformer themselves. Without economic power the Negro had only his personal labor to sell, and even in the North he seemed to carry his own personal depression with him. In the early 1890's Negro farmers in the South had been urged to join the Populist movement, but between 1895 and 1907 alarmed white conservative Democrats managed to disfranchise them in every Southern state except Maryland, Tennessee, and Kentucky (page 381). In 1900 the last Negro in the United States Congress, George H. White of North Carolina, did not seek reelection, for he knew he could not win.

The important political progressives did not extend their policies to Negroes. Theodore Roosevelt at first acted as though his "square deal" covered all Americans, but his private letters showed that he never intended to support Negro equality. He wrote that "as a race and in the mass they [Negroes] are altogether inferior to the Whites." Woodrow Wilson was also blind to the needs of the black man. He himself allowed government offices in Washington to institute new regulations segregating federal employees. When a delegation came to protest his action, he said "The only harm that will come will be if you cause them to think it [segregation] is a humiliation." He became annoyed with the delegates and dismissed them, saying "Your manner offends me. . . ."

Those Who Would Wait. The older generation of black leaders who had participated in the abolition movement were dead before progressivism became an important force. By 1895, the same year that Frederick Douglass died, Booker T. Washington was the most prominent Negro in the country and the acknowledged spokesman on black education and black aspirations. Born a slave, Washington grew up in the post-Civil War South and received his education at Hampton Institute, a private school which offered vocational training to aspiring Negroes so that they might escape the deadli-

Booker T. Washington—opportunity for the black man.
TUSKEGEE INSTITUTE, GEORGE WASHINGTON CARVER MUSEUM

George Washington Carver—progress in science.   THE GRANGER COLLECTION

ness of tenant farming. Washington, believing that his people must first become literate and work hard to improve themselves and their economic position, became a teacher himself. In 1881 he opened the Tuskegee Institute in Alabama, and from his school were graduated skilled craftsmen and able farmers. Washington's views—that black men should train for industrial and agricultural jobs and wait patiently through a period of apprenticeship and adjustment before pressing for social and political equality—won him the support of many whites who could envision only a position of inferiority for the Negroes and who regarded segregation as the permanent pattern for American society. Although Washington's acceptance of a lesser role for his race was soon criticized by a group of younger Negroes, he was extremely successful in helping individual blacks. And as an able money-raiser and effective administrator he commanded considerable respect. (Andrew Carnegie donated $600,000 to Tuskegee.)

One of the best known of Washington's protégés was George Washington Carver. Raised by a white farmer for whom his mother had worked, Carver acquired his lifelong interest in agronomy at an early age. He wandered and worked his way through schools and college in Missouri, Kansas, and Iowa, eventually becoming director of agricultural research at Tuskegee. His experiments with worn-out soil proved to him that planting peanuts would restore its fertility. But the poor farmers refused to follow his instructions, and he finally had to convince them by actually growing bumper crops on twenty of the poorest acres in Alabama. Before long so many peanuts were raised that they glutted the market, and Carver had to busy himself developing industrial products that could be made of the surplus peanuts. His work was instrumental in shifting the single-crop agricultural economy of the South to a more diversified and prosperous base. His brilliance helped to dispel the myth of Negro inferiority.

Those Who Would Fight. Not all Negroes were willing to accept a passive role in the face of continued white oppression, however. Washington himself was beaten by a white man for merely entering a building in New York, and more than a hundred blacks were lynched each year. William E. B. Du Bois, the first Negro to receive a doctorate from Howard, was convinced from the first that Washington was leading black men in the wrong direction. Meeting with other college-educated blacks in 1905, Du Bois helped initiate the Niagara Movement for racial equality. The group never openly criticized Washington, but clearly its members wanted to fight more directly for Negro rights. This militancy doubtlessly kept the group terribly poor, so poor that it had to disband by 1910. But from its work came another organization that was to have lasting impact, the National Association for the Advancement of Colored People (NAACP).

Oswald Garrison Villard, grandson of the abolitionist Garrison, called a conference in 1909 and again in 1910 in New York to "renew" the struggle to obtain for Negroes full social, political, and economic equality. Other white progressives attending the conference were social worker Jane Addams, philosopher John Dewey, and novelist William Dean Howells. At the second meeting the NAACP was formally launched, and Du Bois became its first director of publicity and research. He also edited the *Crisis*, which by 1914 was distributed to 35,000 readers each month. Promises to press for Negro rights made by the progressive Wilson before his election proved short-lived, and the NAACP soon found itself hard at work on litigation, sponsoring mass meetings, and circulating petitions.

During these same years another group that has continued to serve the cause of black equality was founded. The National Urban League was organized in New York in 1910 as an interracial association to help Negroes who had moved North into urban ghettos to find homes and jobs. Founded by a white society matron, Ruth Standish Brown, the League flourished and by 1925 was spending $300,000 a year.

These associations, active though they were, were too passive for many blacks who were suffering continued persecution in an era of progress. Marcus Garvey, a native of Jamaica who had come to the United States in 1905 and wanted to lead his black brothers back to Africa, attracted considerable attention. He established himself in Harlem and preached pride in the Negro race, urging his followers to leave "white man's country" and go with him to a new kingdom that he would establish. In the five years that his Universal Negro Improvement Association was in operation, it collected ten million dollars from black supporters. But Garvey's power was temporary, for in 1923 he was convicted of using the mails to defraud. The dynamic leader had given black men self-respect, however. Their acceptance of his faintly ridiculous posturing and of his colorful African Legion dressed in uniforms of black, green, and red was not surprising after generations of suppression.

Prohibition

An interesting but none too successful sidelight of the reform era was the revival of the crusade for prohibition. During the Civil War all states with prohibition laws had repealed them except Maine, but an alarming increase in liquor consumption soon reactivated the temperance movement. The National Prohibition party, which was formed in 1869, is still in existence, having nominated candidates in every election since 1873. The party has been able to elect only one member of Congress, however, and no more than two per cent of the electorate has ever voted for its ticket. Other groups, such as the National Temperance Society and Publication House and the Woman's Christian Temperance Union, founded by Frances E. Willard in 1874, became active in educating the public to the evils of alcohol. But the campaigns in schools and churches did not change the minds of most voters, and prohibition as such continued to be rejected in most states by popular vote. Only five states, all predominantly rural, had "gone dry" before 1890.

The major thrust of the prohibition movement came during the reform era and was di-tion's counties, in some thirty of its states. Despite the countering activities of the United Brewer's Association, a large proportion of the population had come to believe that liquor was dangerous and drinking evil. In 1907 the residents of the Oklahoma Territory, Alabama, and Georgia were the first to vote for statewide prohibition; in 1913, however, a proposed national prohibition amendment failed in Congress. Then during wartime, when saloons were already illegal in about ninety per cent of the nation and more than two-thirds of the population lived in "dry" areas, prohibition was given a clinching argument, the need to conserve grain. The Eighteenth Amendment passed Congress in December 1917, was ratified thirteen months later, and became effective on January 17, 1920. An enforcement bill called the National Prohibition Act, but popularly known as the Volstead Act, was also passed.

Yet the "national consensus" on the sale of alcohol was neither real nor lasting, for support of prohibition had always been greater in rural areas. Workingmen in large cities were the best customers of saloons. The zeal of the progressives who believed society could be reformed by law and the exigencies of war had made the Eighteenth Amendment possible, but neither Congress nor the states were able to establish adequate machinery for its enforcement.

The Feminist Crusade

The crusade for women's rights is another example of a reform from which great good was expected but which actually brought about only limited change. During the late nineteenth century women as well as men were aware of the need for political activism. A National Society for Woman's Suffrage was organized in England as early as 1866, but not until 1890 was its American counterpart, the National American Woman's Suffrage Association, established. The small group of feminists who had begun the fight for women's suffrage in 1848 at last had reinforcements.

Woman with a hatchet—prohibitionist Carrie Nation.
THE BETTMANN ARCHIVE

rected against the places where liquor was sold. The Anti-Saloon League (1893), financed by churches and businessmen, became the most effective organization in the history of the crusade. With an ample budget which allowed it to maintain a widespread and powerful lobby, the League worked effectively for politicians of either major party who favored prohibition and against those who opposed it. By 1906 saloons were banned in more than one-half of the na-

170 *First in War, First in Peace*

Rights for the oppressed "minorities." CULVER PICTURES

Localities were the first to let women vote, usually for school officials. Then in 1869 Wyoming Territory granted women complete suffrage; Colorado, Utah, Idaho, Washington, and California had also extended them the vote by 1911, and other states were letting them participate in certain elections. In the presidential campaign of 1912 Roosevelt and the Progressive party supported women's suffrage. Some women preferred gradual education and persuasion of the public to their cause; others, borrowing from the English suffragettes, chose to rally and demonstrate. Women's active role in World War I was probably their most eloquent effort. In June 1919 the Nineteenth Amendment, forbidding denial of the vote because of sex, passed Congress. It became part of the Constitution in August 1920, in time for a presidential election.

Many of the promises of the amendment were not fulfilled, however. Suffragettes who had carried banners urging men to give women the right to vote were less successful in creating an interest in politics among their own sex. Many women failed to exercise their franchise, and those who did often voted exactly as their husbands or other relatives did. To combat this indifference, the National League of Women Voters was created in 1919 out of the older suffrage organizations. The League stressed the need for education in government and distributed nonpartisan information on political issues, but at most 100,000 women joined.

Feminism took other forms during the 1920's. The General Federation of Women's Clubs grew in size and influence but concentrated on activities in cultural fields. The Woman's Christian Temperance Union and the Young Women's Christian Association also absorbed women's energies. As time passed, the various women's organizations were accused of being too limited in their activities and of popularizing cultural projects that were only of superficial value. Gradually, the groups began to lose momentum. Their membership had come primarily from the leisure classes and in-

Building a Progressive Society, 1909–1920

cluded only a few working women. Those in farming areas had not participated at all. The political activity that might have been expected to follow a real feminist rebellion was never stimulated. The political complexion of the nation changed very little through the addition of millions of women voters.

The Progressive as a Conservative

Progressivism had been responsible for a great resurgence of the American conscience, encouraging the population to take an interest in the correction of many of the abuses of national life. This involvement and activism were healthy, even if the concerns of the reformers and their achievements were often somewhat limited in scope. Perhaps the reason why the movement was not more successful is that many progressives were conservatives at heart. The reforms that they sought were meant to preserve small business as a way of life and to reinstate the democratic heritage of the nation's earlier years. As is often true of those who look to the past, the progressives rejected the future and its insecurities. When their movement led them to less recognizable goals, the progressives became increasingly reactionary. In describing modern outgrowths of progressivism, Hofstadter has said, "Somewhere along the way, the Populist-Progressive tradition has turned sour and become illogical and ill-tempered." The perversity, of course, became evident only later, but the conditions that led to it were always inherent in the backward view of progressivism. The most important progressive years were from 1900 to 1915. But almost before the accomplishments of this period could really be evaluated, circumstances changed drastically. This time World War I brought about the abandonment of reform. By the time the conflict was over, the progressive protest had abated, leaving the nation in the grip of conservatism.

SUGGESTED READINGS

*Berryman, J., *Stephen Crane* (1950).
*Blum, J. M., *Woodrow Wilson and the Politics of Morality* (1956).
Bond, H. M., *The Education of the Negro in the American Social Order* (1934).
Brandeis, L. D., *Other People's Money* (1914).
Carter, E., *Howells and the Age of Realism* (1954).
*Cremin, L. A., *The Transformation of the School: Progressivism in American Education, 1876–1957* (1961).
*Croly, H., *The Promise of American Life* (1909).
*Curti, M., *The Social Ideas of American Educators* (1935).
Dupee, F. W., *Henry James: His Life and Writings* (1956).
Faulkner, H. U., *The Quest for Social Justice, 1898–1914* (1931).
*Flexner, E., *Century of Struggle: The Woman's Rights Movement in the United States* (1959).
Forcey, C., *The Crossroads of Liberalism* (1961).
Ginger, R., *Age of Excess: The United States from 1877 to 1914* (1965).
*Goldham, E., *Rendezvous with Destiny* (1952).
Hechler, K. W., *Insurgency: Personalities and Politics of the Taft Era* (1940).
*Hofstadter, R., *The Age of Reform* (1955).

*Hofstadter, R. and W. P. Metzger, *The Development of Academic Freedom in the United States* (1955).

*Kazin, A. and C. Shapiro, eds., *The Stature of Dreiser* (1955).

Kraditor, A. S., *The Ideas of the Woman Suffrage Movement, 1890–1920* (1965).

*Lerner, M., ed., *The Mind and Faith of Justice Holmes* (1943).

Link, A. S., *The New Freedom* (1956).

Link, A. S., *Wilson* (5 vols., 1947–1965).

*Link, A. S., *Woodrow Wilson and the Progressive Era, 1910–1917* (1954).

*Lippmann, W., *Drift and Mastery* (1914).

Logan, R. W., *The Negro in American Life and Thought* (1954).

*Logan, R. W., *The Negro in the United States* (1957).

Lubove, R. M., *The Progressives and the Slums* (1962).

*Mann, A., *Yankee Reformers in the Urban Age* (1954).

Maxwell, R. S., *La Follette and the Rise of the Progressives in Wisconsin* (1956).

*Mowry, G. E., *The Era of Theodore Roosevelt, 1900–1912* (1958).

Noble, D. W., *The Paradox of Progressive Thought* (1958).

Nye, R., *Midwestern Progressive Politics* (1951).

Odegard, P. H., *Pressure Politics: The Story of the Anti-Saloon League* (1928).

Perry, R. B., *The Thought and Character of William James* (2 vols., 2nd ed., 1948).

Reigier, C. C., *The Era of the Muckrakers* (1932).

Schneider, R. W., *Five Novelists of the Progressive Era* (1962).

Sinclair, A., *The Better Half* (1965).

*Sinclair, A., *The Era of Excess* (1962).

Smith, W., *American Higher Education, A Documentary History* (2 vols., 1961).

Starrett, W. A., *Skyscrapers and the Men Who Built Them* (1928).

Stone, I., *Jack London: Sailor on Horseback* (1938).

Sullivan, M., *Our Times* (vol. 3., 1927).

Szarkowski, J., *The Idea of Louis Sullivan* (1957).

Timberlake, J. H., *Prohibition and the Progressive Movement, 1900–1920* (1963).

*Warner, S. B., Jr., *Streetcar Suburbs* (1962).

Welter, R., *Popular Education and Democratic Thought in America* (1962).

Woody, T., *A History of Women's Education in the United States* (2 vols., 1929).

CHAPTER 24

The End of Continentalism, 1890–1914

Americans must now begin to look outward. The growing production of the country demands it.
ALFRED THAYER MAHAN, 1890

"DESTRUCTION OF THE U.S. BATTLESHIP MAINE," CULVER PICTURES

DURING THE FIRST CENTURY OF THE REPUBLIC the American people had focused their attention primarily on their own continent. They had watched the frontier of the West steadily recede and had been preoccupied with domestic problems and solutions. Rarely and reluctantly had they looked past their shores to the world beyond.

In the last decade of the nineteenth century, an atmosphere of change quickened the American pulse. Altering conditions within the nation and in the world outside provided a new perspective. The continental limits of the United States had been established decades earlier. In the twoscore years following the Civil War, settlers trekked to the empty spaces of the Great Plains; the Indian menace was eliminated; farms and cities sprouted where the wilderness had once existed. By the 1880's the sectional bitterness that had previously agitated the country was dissipating. Then in 1890 many Americans, rather suddenly aware that the frontier had closed, were reluctant to accept the apparent limitations that geography had placed on Western expansion. The end of the era of territorial growth gave the nation "continental claustrophobia."

THE "NEW EXPANSIONISM"

Its Roots

A number of concepts actively entertained by the American mind at the end of the century contributed to the revival of expansionism. Impulses embedded in the American tradition and others derived from European ideas popular at the time combined to produce an explosive spasm that catapulted the United States into the position of a global power.

Economic Impulses. The American business community had always believed that its government should act as an agent to protect trade and open additional commercial opportunities overseas. Partly for these reasons, the United States navy had fought the corsairs along the Barbary Coast in the early 1800's, engaged in war with Great Britain in 1812, and opened Japan to American commerce in the years after 1853.

By 1890 the national economy had arrived

The End of Continentalism, 1890–1914

at what has been called "the takeoff stage." Small and local industries had merged, or were in the process of merging, into large corporations and trusts national in scope. This consolidation brought greater efficiency and increased the profits of shareholders of the great corporations. Many became interested in investing their surplus money abroad, where the risk was great but the possibility of profit was even greater. Manufacturers also sought foreign markets as outlets for the vast quantities of goods pouring forth from the factories. Furthermore, producers became increasingly anxious about ensuring themselves of access to certain raw materials not obtainable within the United States. For example, with the multiplication of rubber products manufacturers required greater amounts of raw rubber from the tropical rainforests of the world. The expanding canning industry needed huge amounts of tin, which could be obtained in sufficient quantities only from abroad. Businessmen gradually came to believe that American economic development, both within and beyond its continental spread, depended on the exercise of United States diplomacy and military power. Without such activity on the part of the government, American business might be excluded from lucrative world markets or cut off from needed raw materials by selfish and powerful foreign nations.

The Sense of Mission. The conviction that Americans had a special destiny was as evident in the 1890's as it had been half a century earlier. They continued to believe that they were creating a "more perfect society," that a prosperous today would be followed by an even better tomorrow. Many citizens were strongly imbued with the concept of the "white man's burden," a phrase aptly borrowed from Rudyard Kipling, who argued that civilized white peoples of European origin had an obligation to share the blessings of their culture with the less fortunate dark-skinned peoples of the earth. This sense of duty to less-developed races and the traditional humanitarianism of Americans compelled them to contribute to the relief of all peoples whenever and wherever they were afflicted by natural disasters, wars, and political oppressions. The government was also expected to intervene politically in world affairs to help peoples abroad overcome natural or man-made misfortunes.

Racism and the Glorification of War. A sinister aspect of the American sense of mission was the growing cult of race superiority. Many citizens came to believe that the Anglo-Saxon race (meaning the peoples of the United States and Great Britain) was ideally suited to lead—and possibly rule—the rest of the world. Josiah Strong, a well-known Congregational minister, wrote in 1885 that "God with infinite wisdom and skill is training the Anglo-Saxon race for an hour sure to come in the world's future.... Then this race of unequaled energy ... having developed peculiarly aggressive traits ... will spread itself over the earth."

There was a strong hint in Dr. Strong's message that America's destiny would have to be achieved by force. Advocacy of war was a dangerous addition to the already heady mixture of mission and racism. Three decades after the terrible Civil War, memories of that conflict were dimming. Forgotten were the horrors and cruelty, the discomforts and the heartaches, and the suffocating boredom and interminable waiting. What was remembered were the moments of glory, the drums and bugles, the serried rows of gleaming bayonets, and "Old Glory" (or was it the "Stars and Bars"?) waving in the breeze. Fathers and grandfathers liked to recount moments of fantastic courage—that heroic third day at Gettysburg atop Cemetery Ridge as "the rebs" swept up the slope, the terrible hour at Cold Harbor, Sheridan's thrilling dash through the Shenandoah Valley, and Sherman's march through Georgia. Youngsters of the day must have sat in awe, wide-eyed, almost smelling the powder and smoke, as they listened to old-timers swap stories of a more glorious and heroic past. Too young to have experienced the Civil War, they envied their more fortunate elders.

Young people also read Stephen Crane's *The Red Badge of Courage*, describing heroics on the Civil War battlefields, and Rudyard Kipling's stories of courageous British soldiers battling ferocious Pathans in India. Still other spokesmen stressed the theme of conflict. William Graham Sumner, a popular Yale sociologist and the foremost of the American Social Darwinists, emphasized the necessity of war to nuture a nation's soul and assure its progress. In 1897 Theodore Roosevelt declared, "No triumph of peace is quite so great as the supreme triumph of war. The courage of the soldier . . . stands higher than any quality called out merely in time of peace." In such an atmosphere the cult of war flourished. Americans came to believe that their "divinely inspired destiny" was to be achieved through expansionism and, if necessary, by war.

Navalism. Alfred Thayer Mahan converted these combative sentiments into precise objectives in his book *The Influence of Sea Power upon History*, published in 1890. A vigorous advocate of territorial expansion and mercantile imperialism, this naval historian argued that a powerful fleet and overseas naval bases were needed to protect American commerce and advance this nation's political and economic interests in other regions of the world. Mahan's book was dull and far from widely read, yet it served to inspire among others two rising young statesmen, Henry Cabot Lodge of Massachusetts and Theodore Roosevelt of New York. These two coming political figures were soon to be in a position to translate Mahan's theories into practice.

The Influence of European Imperialism. In the decades after 1870, there was an extraordinary outburst of overseas colonial expansion by European powers. The British, even though they already had a mighty empire, led the way and set the mood with their widespread imperialism. In the middle 1870's they annexed both Fiji and Cyprus, purchased shares in the Suez Canal, and proclaimed Queen Victoria empress of India. In Africa King Leopold of Belgium, through his agent Henry Stanley, the great British explorer and journalist, seized a vast equatorial region known as the Congo as his own personal domain. Such empire builders as Cecil Rhodes and Sir Frederick Lugard, impelled by their own versions of manifest destiny, acquired control of great tracts of undeveloped but potentially rich African territory for Great Britain. The French did as well for themselves. By 1910 France ruled an area of Africa almost twice the size of the United States. The Germans came to the game of empire making somewhat later, but they were able to acquire extensive portions of Africa. Italy took most of what few crumbs were left by the more powerful European conquerors.

Also busy in Asia and the Pacific, European nations joined Japan in carving up large portions of the Chinese pie into "spheres of influence." By the late 1890's Russia claimed the extensive and rich province of Manchuria and the Liaotung Peninsula as its spheres of special interest; Japan had seized Taiwan (Formosa) and established its authority over Korea; Germany dominated the rich Shantung Peninsula; Great Britain held Weihaiwei in north China and Hong Kong in the south; and the French were in possession of Kwangchow in the south and a large section of the city of Shanghai. In 1907 Persia (Iran) was to suffer a similar fate at the hands of Great Britain and Russia, and the almost numberless islands in the Pacific Ocean were quickly occupied by one or another of the European nations.

Many Americans were frankly envious as they read the yarns of H. Rider Haggard about "darkest Africa," learned the dramatic verses of Rudyard Kipling, or thrilled to the exploits of Stanley in finding Livingstone and of "Chinese" Gordon in confronting the wild dervishes in the depths of the Sudan. They were bedazzled by the distortion of the evolutionary principles of Charles Darwin that declared the "fittest nations" to be the expanding and warlike nations. Empire grabbing appeared both glamorous and essential. Many citizens began to wonder why the United States did not follow the example of European imperialism. As Senator Henry Cabot Lodge expressed it in 1896,

"The tendency of modern times is towards consolidation. . . . Small states are of the past and have no future. The great nations are rapidly absorbing for their future expansion and their present defense all the waste places of the earth. It is a movement which makes for civilization and the advancement of the race. As one of the great nations of the world the United States must not fall out of the line of march."

Imperialistic Frictions. Many Americans did not subscribe to all, or even to any, of the sentiments seeming to justify expansionism. They found imperialism dangerous and inappropriate to the American tradition. But their voices were muffled by the dominant contagion of combativeness during the 1890's. The United States became involved in spats with major European powers as well as with smaller nations over issues far from American shores and of little serious concern to the American people.

In 1889 the United States engaged in a sharp dispute with Germany and Great Britain over control of the remote Samoan Islands. American, German, and British warships were menacingly together in Apia harbor on one of the islands, but in March a typhoon blew up and sank or beached all the vessels, except for the British ship which succeeded in pulling out to sea.

In 1891 an incident in a Valparaiso saloon embroiled Chile and the United States in a threatening situation. Two American sailors on shore leave from the U.S.S. *Baltimore* were killed, and others were seriously injured. President Harrison demanded reparations and even invited Congress to declare war. Eventually, but in time, a humble apology and then an agreement to pay $75,000 to the injured and to the families of the dead arrived from the Chilean government.

Even more serious was the dispute with Great Britain in 1895 over the jungle boundary between British Guiana and Venezuela. For many years the British and the Venezuelans had quarreled about its location and their conflicting claims to a considerable stretch of territory. The discovery of gold in the area had heightened their differences. President Cleveland intervened, announcing that by authority of the Monroe Doctrine the United States would arbitrate the question. When the British government refused the offer, Richard B. Olney, Cleveland's Secretary of State, addressed a bombastic note to Prime Minister Lord Salisbury, declaring that the United States by right of its power was "sovereign on this continent . . . its infinite resources combined with its isolated position render it master of the situation." This twisting of the tail of the British lion made war between the two mighty Anglo-Saxon powers a serious possibility. Fortunately, Great Britain's involvement in a quarrel with Germany over South Africa induced the irritated British government to comply with Cleveland's wishes. Despite the talk of war on both sides of the Atlantic, cooler heads prevailed. Great Britain backed down gracefully, agreed to Cleveland's arbitration proposal, and the incident was closed.

The Climax of New Expansionism—War with Spain

In each of the foregoing incidents, the United States skirted the edge of war over issues that are today recognized as trivial. In a crisis over Cuba, however, the nation was finally plunged into war with Spain. Providing a classic study of the impulses of expansionism and their eventual, inevitable outcome, the Spanish-American War of 1898 and its aftermath illustrated to the

American people the drawbacks and burdens of acquiring an overseas empire.

Origins of the War. The underlying friction that led to the Spanish-American War was the crisis created in 1895 when the Cubans revolted again against Spain. Although Spanish misrule and a natural desire for Cuban independence were the declared reasons for the uprising, the tariff policy of the United States had provided a strong economic motive. The Cuban economy had been greatly stimulated by a provision of the McKinley Tariff Act of 1890 that removed the duty on raw cane sugar, but in 1894 the Wilson-Gorman Act restored a forty per cent tariff on imported sugar. The prosperity that the island had enjoyed for several years dissipated quite suddenly. With purchases of Cuban sugar in the United States declining sharply, thousands of Cubans were thrown out of work, and economic distress was added to the political discontent of the Cuban people.

The Spanish government sought to repress the Cuban revolt in a particularly ruthless manner. By order of General Valeriano Weyler, populations of large sections of the country were driven into barbed-wire concentration camps,[1] where some 200,000 are estimated to have died of disease and starvation. The humanitarian sentiments of the American people, stirred by reports of the camps, were intensified by the sensationalist or so-called "yellow press" newspapers, particularly the *New York World*, published by Joseph Pulitzer, and the *New York Journal*, owned by William Randolph Hearst. Taking advantage of public interest in the disturbing news, the two papers became locked in a circulation duel. Each tried to outdo the other with their often exaggerated or distorted stories of Spanish atrocities.

Such avowed imperialists as Secretary of State John Hay, Captain Mahan, Senator Lodge, and Theodore Roosevelt saw opportunity in the continuing Cuban crisis and by their public statements manipulated American sentiment to achieve their expansionist objectives. If war should come, they surmised, the United States could seize Cuba and strengthen American control over the Caribbean by acquiring the excellent harbors at Havana and Santiago. The expansionists were also keenly aware of the possibilities offered by the Philippines on the other side of the globe. Spain had ruled these Pacific islands since the sixteenth century. By defeating Spain and acquiring control of the Philippines, the United States would have the excellent harbor and naval base at Manila at its disposal. The nation would then become an Asiatic power with opportunity for further expansion in the Far East.

But it usually takes two to make a war. Despite the activities of the expansionists and the sensational articles in newspapers about Spanish atrocities in Cuba, intervention could have been avoided had the Spanish government been more perceptive. Spain completely misjudged the menacing temper of the American people and responded very slowly to President McKinley's kindly suggestions for a more moderate policy toward the Cubans. By the end of 1897, however, Weyler had been replaced by a new general who was ordered to disband the concentration camps, and Spain promised partial self-government for the Cubans. The Spanish also agreed, rather unfortunately, to McKinley's suggestion that navel vessels of the two countries exchange goodwill visits. The United States sent to Havana the pride of the fleet, the splendid new battleship U.S.S. *Maine*, and Spain sent the *Viscaya* to New York. On February 15, 1898 the *Maine* was mysteriously blown up in Havana Harbor, with 260 lives lost; the American public reacted angrily and impetuously, demanding war. The *Viscaya* escaped retaliatory sinking by private citizens through the vigilance of the New York City harbor police.

The public was enraged and Congress angry, but President McKinley, who was a pacifist

---

[1] By twentieth-century standards of war, the Spanish treatment of Cubans in concentration camps was relatively humane.

The End of Continentalism, 1890–1914

"You furnish the pictures and I'll furnish the war." (William Randolph Hearst, allegedly).

CULVER PICTURES

by nature, could still have kept the country from war by demonstrating a little more stubborn courage. The Spanish government hastened to express its regrets and urged a joint Spanish-American inquiry into the circumstances of the *Maine* disaster. An investigation by United States naval officers disclosed that the *Maine* was destroyed by an external explosion, but there was no evidence that Spain was in any way responsible.

During this crucial period most members of the big-business community were opposed to war. J. P. Morgan was especially alarmed over its potentially unsettling effects on the economic stability of the nation. Many other citizens in all walks of life, possibly even a majority, also opposed intervention. But the "hawks of the press" and the noisy war party in Congress were for the moment in control, and McKinley feared to oppose them. Early in April the President prepared a war message. Before it was delivered to Congress on April 11, Spain had ordered its troops to cease hostilities, and McKinley was so informed. He duly included a statement of the capitulation at the end of the presidential message, but without emphasizing it. On April 20, 1898 Congress approved a resolution supporting independence for Cuba, and on April 25 it declared war against Spain.

Shortly after hostilities began, Secretary of State Hay wrote to his friend Senator Lodge that "at last we have our splendid little war." Hearst of the *New York Journal* is said to have claimed that he made the war; McKinley has been accused of causing it through his weakness; Lodge and the other expansionists have also been indicted for their role in encouraging the conflict. In fairness, none of the persons mentioned can claim or should bear the brunt of primary responsibility. The outbreak of war was a result of accumulated frictions, blunders, and, particularly, the prevailing mood of aggressiveness at the time. A study of the events leading up to the Spanish-American War adds meaning to the preamble to the UNESCO Charter, "Since wars begin in the minds of men, it is in the minds of men that the defenses of peace must be constructed."

Course of the War. From the American standpoint it was an ideal war. There was a great deal of shooting and cheering, some moments of glorious heroics, and only 379 American soldiers were killed in action. The whole affair ended after three months. It was a "nice," if not "splendid," little war—except, of course, for those who died from disease, food poisoning, and Spanish bullets.

The first battle took place, surprisingly enough, not in Cuba but in the Philippines. Ten days after the sinking of the *Maine*, Theodore Roosevelt, as Assistant Secretary of the Navy, had taken advantage of Secretary John D. Long's weekend absence to cable secret instructions to Commodore George Dewey. He was to move his naval squadron from San Diego, California, to the British naval base at Hong Kong and await further instructions. On May 1 Commodore Dewey's squadron steamed into Manila Bay and surprised a number of Spanish warships anchored there. Within a few hours 381 Spanish were dead, and their fleet was converted to scrap iron by United States naval artillery—without the loss of a single American life. This exploit made Dewey a war hero of the first rank. Across America the news of the victory at Manila was greeted with wild enthusiasm. Actually, it was no contest. The seven Spanish vessels were rusting old hulks, several of them completely unseaworthy and others with no artillery.

Two days earlier, on April 29, Spain had dispatched a large squadron of naval vessels westward from the Cape Verde Islands. While the Spanish ships were at sea, the sensationalist yellow press newspapers took full advantage of the opportunity. Lurid headlines predicted a naval assault on New York City or an attack on the national capital. Citizens who lived along the Atlantic seaboard were alternately thrilled and frightened by the rumors of an impending Spanish invasion. If the Spaniards had been aware of the existing state of panic, they could have created havoc by bombarding a beach resort and blowing up a few bathhouses along the New Jersey coast. Instead, the Spanish warships sailed predictably into the harbor of Santiago, Cuba, where they were promptly bottled up by the United States navy. The Spanish ships attempted to escape on July 3, when the artillery of American troops threatened them during the siege of the city, but they were easily destroyed by the squadron that was guarding the harbor—at a cost of only three American lives.

The only significant military compaign of the war was the American invasion of Cuba.

"You may fire when you are ready, Gridley." CULVER PICTURES

The End of Continentalism, 1890–1914 183

"Far better it is to dare mighty things, to win glorious triumphs . . ."
(Theodore Roosevelt).

BROWN BROTHERS

On June 20 an incredibly disorganized United States army of 17,000 men landed near Santiago—the First Volunteer Regiment, or Rough Riders, without their horses—and took six days to disembark. They moved against the port a few days later. Lieutenant Colonel Theodore Roosevelt led the gallant charge that would put him into the history books and on the road to the White House, but after two days of fighting the American attack seemed spent. Fortunately, with over 200,000 Spaniards on the island, only 1,200 were mobilized to meet the Americans at Santiago. On July 17 the city surrendered.

Eight days later a second American expeditionary force occupied Puerto Rico. The Spanish troops in the Philippines, after token resistance, yielded to a combined force of American troops and Filipino insurgents on August 13, one day after a peace protocol had been signed in Santiago. On October 1 formal meetings to draw up a peace treaty convened in Paris. By the terms of the treaty, signed in December, Spain gave up most of the remnants of her once-splendid colonial empire, including Cuba, Puerto Rico, Guam, and the Philippines.

Annexation of Hawaii and Samoa. While the Spanish-American War was in progress, Congress passed a joint resolution annexing the Hawaiian Archipelago. The campaign in the Philippines had renewed public interest in Hawaii as an essential steppingstone to the expansion of United States influence in the Far East; Captain Mahan and other advocates of naval power viewed Pearl Harbor as an excellent naval base from which to control the Pacific Ocean.

The nation's interest in the islands, dating from the early nineteenth century when Hawaii became a port of call for American whaling ships and an area of intensive missionary activity, had eventually led, in 1893, to a revolution promoted by American sugar interests. With the last native ruler overthrown, a provisional republic was established, and the government petitioned for admission to the United States. President Cleveland withheld approval, however, partly because of the unethical behavior of United States officials in aiding the organizers of the revolution. But the more compliant President McKinley consented to the annexation of the island republic as a territory on July 7, 1898.

In 1899 the vexing problem of the Samoan Islands, over which the United States, Germany, and Britain had almost battled ten years earlier, was raised again by native civil war. During the spring of the devastating typhoon, representatives of the three powers had met in Berlin. Germany had proposed dividing the islands. The United States, which wanted the archipelago to retain its autonomy, had insisted instead that a tripartite protectorate be estab-

184   *First in War, First in Peace*

AMERICAN EXPANSION INTO THE PACIFIC

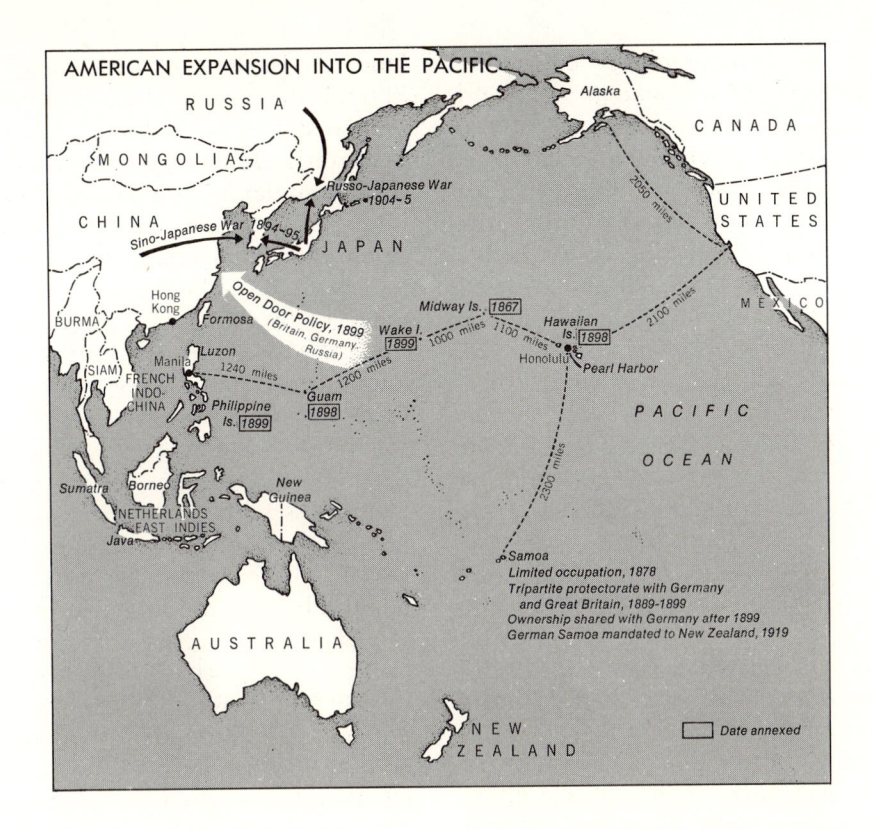

lished. Now in 1899 the United States, newly imperialistic, had no qualms about assuming outright control of Tutuila with its valuable harbor of Pago Pago. Germany took the western islands, and Great Britain was given the Gilbert and the Solomon islands, which had belonged to Germany. Thus even as Spain was dropping an empire into our laps, other distant lands were also being added to the expanding United States.

Aftermath of Expansion. By 1899 the United States had acquired a respectable overseas empire of about 168,000 square miles (an area slightly larger than that of California) and a subject population of approximately 9,000,000. Although this venture was modest compared to the huge European colonial empires of the time, the appetites of the warmongers and imperialists were largely sated. Americans had experienced the glory of war and the exultation of victory over the decrepit Spanish foe at a limited cost in manpower and resources. The nation now possessed strategic naval bases and coaling stations in the Caribbean and at points across the Pacific. Missionary societies had opportunities to convert the heathen on American soil. And commercial interests had new areas of development within the enlarged American union.

Cuba and the Platt Amendment. Even as imperialism was reaching a climax in 1898, doubts were raised about the morality of adding new territories containing large numbers of alien peoples who could not for the most part be assimilated. Just five days before Congress declared war on Spain, Senator Henry Teller of Colorado had introduced an amendment to Congress's war resolution disclaiming any intention of the United States to annex Cuba. The senator and other anti-expansionists, concerned whether the nation's principles were being upheld, wanted some assurance that the

The End of Continentalism, 1890–1914

United States was about to go into battle "for the liberty and freedom of Cuban patriots" and not for "the purpose of increasing our territorial holdings." The Teller Amendment was adopted by the Senate without any open expression of dissent. Momentarily, it appeared that the expansionist faction headed by Senator Lodge and Senator Albert Beveridge of Indiana had been outflanked. The amendment did not mention other Spanish possessions, however, nor did it rule out a United States protectorate over Cuba.

In compliance with the Teller Amendment, the federal government prepared to withdraw the army of occupation from Cuba in 1901. The Cubans were urged to devise a constitution, but the United States demanded that they accept a series of proposals drafted by Senator Orville H. Platt of Connecticut as an appendix to their document. The chief provisions of the so-called Platt Amendment granted the United States a veto over Cuba's foreign and financial policies and the right to intervene with military forces to preserve Cuban "independence." The amendment also required Cuba to lease a naval base at Guantánamo Bay (near Santiago) to the United States.

In 1902 the army of occupation was withdrawn. Cuba achieved nominal independence, but through the Platt Amendment the island had really become a United States protectorate. During succeeding years American presidents invoked the Platt Amendment again and again as justification for military intervention. Even though a treaty signed in 1934 abrogated the intervention provisions of the amendment, the United States still retains a lease on the Guantánamo base.

The Philippine War. While the Treaty of Paris was being drawn up, the Philippines were for a while a quandary to President McKinley. He did not believe that the United States could honorably restore the islands to Spanish misrule, but in establishing some sort of control over them, should he demand Manila, the island of Luzon, or the whole archipelago? Should the islands be annexed or granted immediate independence? After wrestling manfully with his conscience, McKinley claimed divine guidance and stated "that there was nothing left for us to do but take them all, and to educate the Filipinos and uplift and Christianize them." (The President was astoundingly ignorant of the fact that most of the people were already Christians.) He sent word to his Paris negotiators that they must obtain the islands. By the Treaty of Paris Spain ceded the Philippine Islands to the United States for $20,000,000; they were to become a United States possession.

The decision delighted expansionists but horrified other Americans who felt that seizure of the Philippines was a perversion of American ideals. In the two-month-long Senate debate on acceptance of the treaty, annexation of the Philippines was the principal issue; the anti-imperialists mounted formidable opposition, both in the chamber and throughout the country. Ratification was by only two votes more than the required two-thirds. Even more upset were the Filipinos themselves, who had been under the impression that Commodore Dewey and his forces had come to liberate them from Spanish oppression. On the basis of this erroneous assumption, the Philippine insurrectionists, led by Emilio Aguinaldo, who had been encouraged to return from exile by Dewey, had cooperated with the Americans in eliminating Spanish rule from the islands.

When the Filipinos recognized that they were getting only a new set of foreign overlords, they turned on the Americans. On the night of February 4, 1899, with a surprise attack on an American sentry post, the Philippine insurrection began. It was a long, bloody, guerrilla war, the type of conflict that would become familiar in the twentieth century. Because the Filipinos were aware that they did not have the power to engage the Americans in open battles, they resorted to harassment of lines of communication and sudden raids upon isolated outposts. Both sides were guilty of shocking brutalities, the Americans of establishing concentration camps very similar to those that they had protested in Cuba.

In 1901 Aguinaldo was captured. Organized warfare against American rule was broken a year later, although there were sporadic guerrilla raids by Filipinos as late as 1916. At the height of the struggle, 120,000 American troops had to be concentrated in the islands before resistance subsided. Approximately 250,000 people were killed. Unlike the preceding Spanish-American War, there was little glory in this brutal and far more costly encounter.

The Philippine insurrection confronted Americans with the drawbacks of expansionism. Enthusiasm for retaining the islands waned rapidly. By 1904 the Senate was seriously considering independence for the Philippines. Three years later Theodore Roosevelt, in disavowing his own goals of earlier years, recognized the costly burden of ruling the distant Pacific archipelago and wished he could establish a reasonable cause for American withdrawal. But no such course was found. In 1902 the Organic Act had provided for a bicameral legislature, with a popularly elected lower house. The Jones Act of 1916 gave the islands territorial status, and the people were allowed to elect the upper house too; the act also declared that the United States would withdraw as soon as a stable government had been established. The Filipinos made so much progress that President Wilson considered them ready for independence. Later administrations were not so sympathetic, however. In 1934 a bill was passed that would free the Philippines, after ten years of political and economic transition; but the economic terms, imposing on island products the usual tariffs collected on foreign imports, were very ungenerous. The Philippines did not receive complete independence until July 4, 1946, after the Second World War, and even then the United States continued to maintain over thirty bases in the area.

THE SURGE OF INTERNATIONALISM, 1901–1914

The victory over Spain in 1898 and the annexation of its territories converted the United States into a world power with far-flung responsibilities. No longer was the nation able or willing to isolate itself from world affairs. Already an Asiatic and Caribbean power at the turn of the century, the United States was soon to become enmeshed in the affairs of the Far East and Latin America. During these same years the United States would also be involved for the first time in Europe and Africa, two areas that it had traditionally avoided.

This shift from continentalism to internationalism was speeded by the anarchist's bullet that cut down President McKinley in September 1901. Not only did the assassination end the life of the President, but it marked the end of an era. McKinley was wedded philosophically to the nineteenth century. At best a cautious internationalist, McKinley saw the Atlantic and Pacific oceans as gigantic moats which kept America secure from the Old World. Only with hesitation and considerable doubt had he involved the United States in distant international problems.

Theodore Roosevelt's Philosophy on Foreign Policy

The new President did not suffer from his predecessor's doubts. An avowed internationalist anxious to extend his country's influence through participation in world affairs, Theodore Roosevelt for the most part based his actions on a set of clearly defined principles and a keen recognition of the complex conditions of the twentieth century. Roosevelt's primary concern was a traditional one—the security of the nation from possible outside aggression. But, more than his predecessors, the new President was aware of the world's changing power structure. Across the Atlantic was the potential menace of the new and mighty German Empire. Traditionally, the United States had relied on the overwhelming power of the British navy to protect its Atlantic shores. But soon after the turn of the century Germany challenged Britain's supremacy on the high seas by constructing an enormous navy, clearly meaning to match that of the British in gross tonnage. Kaiser Wilhelm II tended to flaunt his nation's great military power in a frightening manner, for he and his advisers talked frequently of Germany's "mailed fist" and its "place in the sun."

In the rising empire across the Pacific, the Japanese had abandoned their hermitlike isolation and had modernized their economy and military establishment with astonishing agility during the last decades of the nineteenth century. In 1895 Japan demonstrated its new strength by soundly thrashing the extensive but decaying Chinese Empire. Then in 1904 and 1905 Japan inflicted a series of defeats on a major European power, tsarist Russia.

In light of these developments, Roosevelt concluded that the United States needed a strong navy to protect its own widespread Pacific interests as well as the Atlantic shoreline. He also regarded the construction of an interoceanic canal in Central America as essential to national defense.

Roosevelt believed that the United States had achieved the status of a great power, and therefore it must behave like one. The United States must be prepared to participate in world councils, using its great physical and moral strength to achieve solutions to world problems, even though these problems might not be of immediate concern to the American people. He sensed that international crises in remote parts of the globe could ultimately affect the national welfare. The new President also firmly supported the Monroe Doctrine, which he regarded as an instrument to shield the weak Latin-American nations from the predatory aims of European powers. In addition, he felt that the United States had a special responsibility for these weak and unstable Latin-American peoples—that it should make certain they behaved themselves and did nothing to invite European aggression. He reasoned that the United States had the right, in fact the duty, to exercise "an international police power" in Latin-American affairs to forestall European intervention. This principle, which is to be described in more detail later in the chapter, is known as the Roosevelt corollary to the Monroe Doctrine.

In foreign policy as in domestic affairs, Roosevelt was unwilling to accept the guidance of Congress. As he put it,

"I should not dream of asking the permission of Congress. . . . It is for the enormous interest of this government to strengthen and give independence to the executive in dealing with foreign powers. . . . Therefore the important thing to do is for a president who is willing to accept responsibility to establish precedents which successors may follow even if they are unwilling to take the initiative themselves."

Roosevelt's philosophy was heavily tainted with self-righteousness, for he operated under the assumption that there were only two ways of doing things—his way and the wrong way. Many of his dramatic pronouncements led to solid achievements, but their long-range consequences were sometimes damaging.

Isthmian Affairs during Roosevelt's Administration

Roosevelt's efforts to arrange for the building of a Central American interoceanic canal illustrated the drawbacks of his foreign policy. There were two stages in the diplomacy, negotiations with the British and Roosevelt's maneuvers to obtain a strip of land across the

Panamanian Isthmus. Both were to have far-reaching implications.

The Hay-Pauncefote Treaty. An important step in the building of a canal had been taken while McKinley was still President. Under the provisions of the earlier Clayton-Bulwer Treaty (1850), the United States and Great Britain had agreed that any canal built in Central America should be unfortified and jointly controlled by the two nations. By the end of the century, however, the United States had decided it should have exclusive control. In 1899 Secretary of State John Hay opened negotiations with Sir Julian Pauncefote, British minister in Washington, to abrogate the Clayton-Bulwer agreement. At first, the British were reluctant to make concessions, but their precarious position in Europe and involvement in the protracted Boer War in South Africa made them more receptive.

The Hay-Pauncefote Treaty was signed in 1901 after Roosevelt had become President. Under its provisions, the United States was given a free hand to build, operate, and fortify an isthmian canal. The specific terms alone were a diplomatic triumph for the United States, but its implications were even more important. In effect, Great Britain surrendered Caribbean leadership to the United States, even though the British had long believed they should have at least an equal role. In the next few years Great Britain gradually reduced her naval and military forces in the West Indies, thus acknowledging that future protection of these possessions would have to come for the most part from the United States. The Hay-Pauncefote Treaty symbolized the nation's emergence as a world power equal to the great Old World nations.

The Panama Revolution. The famous builder of the Suez Canal, Ferdinand de Lesseps, had in 1878 obtained the right from Colombia to dig a canal across Panama. After years of labor on the project, yellow fever, inefficiency, and graft brought ruin to the Frenchman. Vast quantities of machinery were abandoned to rust in the Panama jungle. The New Panama Canal Company bought out the dubious assets of the bankrupt De Lesseps, for the sole purpose of selling them to the United States, and obtained an extension of the concession through Panama until 1904. Then in November 1901 a commission appointed by McKinley reported in favor of the Nicaraguan route for the canal, largely because the French company demanded $109,000,000 for its Panama concession and equipment.[2] Alarmed by the commission's decision, the company quickly lowered its price and sent its agent, the dynamic Philippe Bunau-Varilla, to persuade the American government to choose the Panama route. By the next June Congress had been convinced, but the act the legislative body passed stipulated that Colombia must grant the United States control over the right of way.

John Hay negotiated a treaty with Tomás Herrán, the Colombian representative. Under its terms the United States was to obtain a zone across the Isthmus six miles in width for a cash payment of $10,000,000 and an annual rental fee of $250,000. The United States Senate promptly approved the treaty in March 1903, but the Colombian Congress at Bogotá rejected it, for the Colombians wanted a larger down payment and perhaps they meant to wait until the French company had lost its concession in 1904.

Two men were especially perturbed by this unexpected snag. Roosevelt castigated the Colombians, calling them "dagoes," "contemptible little creatures," "jack rabbits," "cat rabbits," and "homicidal corruptionists." The other concerned person, Philippe Bunau-Varilla, was

---

[2] A third alternative would have been to cross Mexico at the Isthmus of Tehuantepec. In recent years interest in the Nicaragua project has been revived, for the Panama Canal is no longer adequate to handle the increased volume of traffic. At present, ships must wait for days at either entrance before they are allowed to proceed through the canal.

The End of Continentalism, 1890–1914

dismayed at the prospects of his company's losing $40,000,000, the agreed-upon price for its concession. Neither Roosevelt nor Bunau-Varilla was willing to accept the verdict at Bogotá. Both felt that if the United States could not obtain the concession one way, other more drastic means must be considered.

Bunau-Varilla wangled an interview with Roosevelt and Secretary Hay, and the President indicated during this conversation that he would not be unhappy if the people of Panama seceded from Colombia. This was just what Bunau-Varilla needed for encouragement. He was already hatching a plot for such a rebellion, and much of the planning with Panamanian patriots and influential Americans took place in the elegant Waldorf Astoria Hotel in New York City. Money was raised to buy weapons and bribe Colombian officials, and arrangements were made for the assistance of the United States.

On November 3, 1903 a "spontaneous" revolution broke out in Panama; the U.S.S. *Nashville* was on hand and had been ordered to prevent Colombian troops from landing to put down the insurrection. The only casualties in the brief skirmish were a Chinese laundryman and a French poodle. On November 6 the United States, with suspicious promptness, recognized the independence of the new Republic of Panama. Bunau-Varilla, the accredited Panamanian minister in Washington despite his French citizenship, signed a treaty with the United States on November 18, based on President Roosevelt's terms. Under the provisions of the Hay–Bunau-Varilla Treaty, the United States was granted in perpetuity lease of a strip of land ten miles wide across Panama, as well as complete sovereignty within this zone. Payments were the same as those prescribed in the earlier Hay-Herrán Treaty.

Aftermath of the Panama Affair. In 1904 construction of the canal began, and it was opened to commercial traffic in August 1914. With his characteristic vigor Roosevelt had cleared away the diplomatic undergrowth in order to obtain the canal zone. He had refused to submit to the "blackmailers of Bogotá," as he called them, and in later years he was to boast, "I took the Canal." Defending this action as a "mandate from civilization," he never doubted that he should have consented to the conspiracy.

In terms of United States prestige, however, the adventure was costly. It aroused grave suspicions in Latin-American nations regarding their powerful northern neighbor. In Colombia, quite naturally, it produced a deep hostility that has survived to this day. Many people in the United States and in European countries were shocked by Roosevelt's ruthless tactics. Furthermore, the Panama affair eventually cost the nation perhaps as much as Roosevelt had saved, for in 1921 the United States paid Colombia $25,000,000 to ease its conscience.

The Roosevelt Corollary and the Dominican Intervention

In an address to Congress in 1904, Roosevelt declared,

"If a nation shows that it knows how to act with reasonable efficiency, and decency in social and political matters, if it keeps order and pays its obligations, it need fear no interference from the United States. Chronic wrong-doing, or an impotence which results in a general loosening of the ties of civilized society, may, in America, as elsewhere, ultimately require intervention by some civilized nation, and in the Western Hemisphere the adherence of the United States to the Monroe Doctrine may force the United States, however reluctantly, in flagrant cases of such wrong-doing or impotence, to the exercise of an international police power."

The statement was, in short, a broad declaration of principle by Roosevelt that the United States would act as the policeman in the Caribbean. In stating this corollary or extension to the Monroe Doctrine, he had in mind a particular

SOUTHWARD INTO THE CARIBBEAN, 1899-1917

CUBA
Occupation by U.S. troops, 1898-1902
Tied to U.S. by Platt Amendment, 1901
Intervention by U.S., 1906-1909
Short intervention by U.S., 1917

DOMINICAN REPUBLIC
American-Dominican customs receivership, 1905
Occupation by U.S. troops, 1916

VIRGIN ISLANDS
Purchased by treaty from Denmark, 1916

HAITI
Occupation by U.S. troops, 1915

PUERTO RICO
Occupation by U.S. troops, 1898

NICARAGUA
Customs receivership agreement, 1911
Bryan-Chamorro Treaty, 1914

PANAMA
U.S. recognition of independence, 1903
Hay–Bunau-Varilla Treaty, 1903

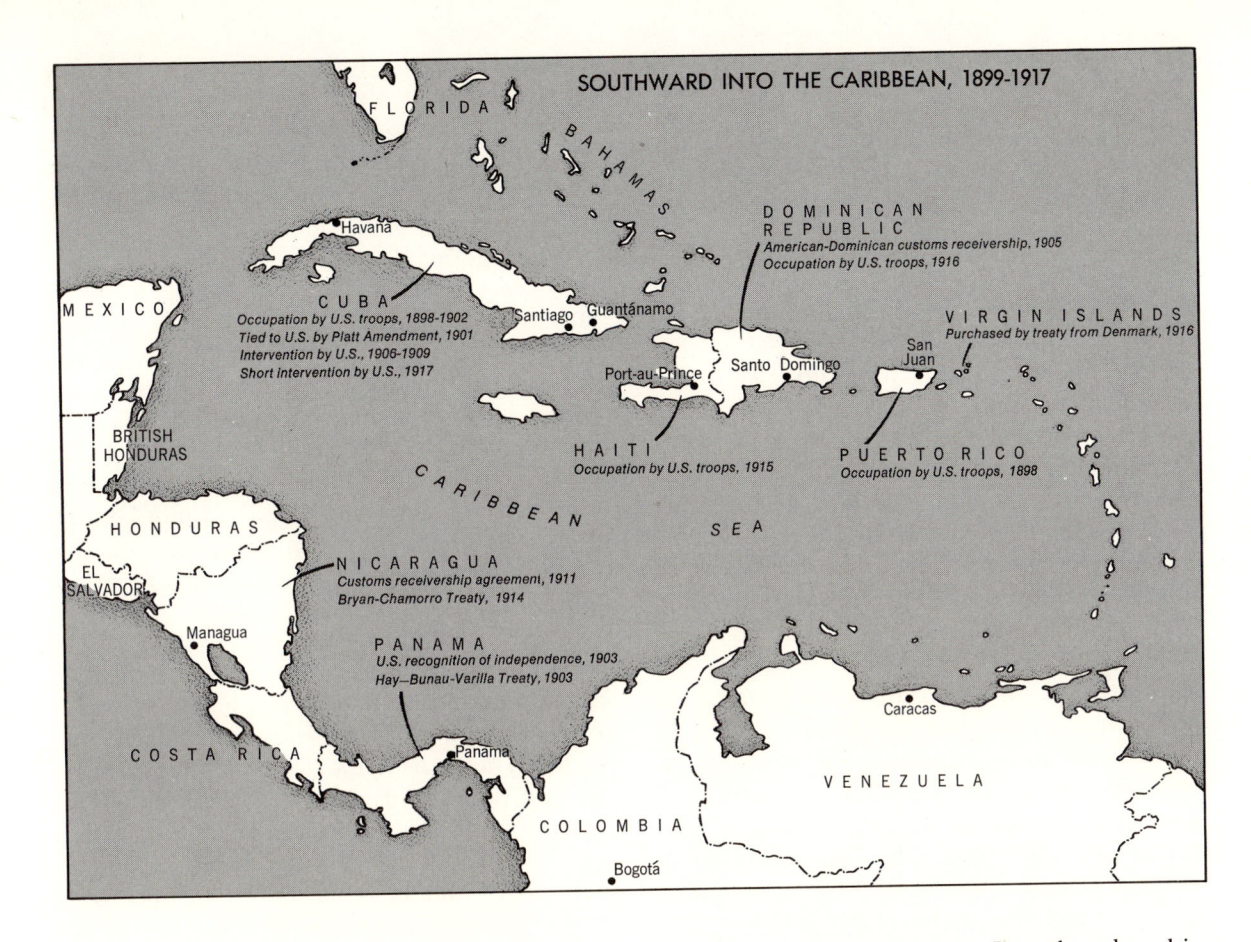

country, the Dominican Republic. The President was becoming alarmed by its increasing internal chaos and the rumors of possible intervention by France and Italy to collect overdue debts.[3] In 1905 he obtained from the Dominican government an agreement allowing the United States to administer its customs and manage its debt payments. It took only a hint of force to convince the Dominicans that they had to accept. Much to Roosevelt's chagrin the Senate failed to approve the arrangements, but for two years he carried them out as an executive agreement. Finally, in 1907, the Senate ratified a permanent treaty incorporating a revised version of the terms. The Dominican affair is yet another instance in which Roosevelt took action before being granted legal authorization.

The Roosevelt corollary was also used by later administrations to justify armed interventions in Central American and Caribbean republics. Although the corollary was formally renounced by the United States in 1930, President Lyndon Johnson's intervention in the

---

[3] Still fresh in the President's mind was the British-German blockade of Venezuela in 1902–1903 for the purpose of collecting defaulted debts. At first, Roosevelt had been inclined to allow European nations to "spank" Venezuela. Roosevelt became concerned, however, over reports of German brutality, the sinking of Venezuelan gunboats, and the destruction of a town by German artillery. Although Venezuela eventually bowed to European naval power and arbitrated its debts, Roosevelt concluded that the United States should be ready with a policy when a similar crisis arose.

The End of Continentalism, 1890–1914

very same Dominican Republic during 1965 raised its specter.

Roosevelt's Relations with Nations in the Far East

Because American trade, particularly with China and Japan, had been increasing steadily over the years, it was inevitable that the United States would become more involved in Far Eastern affairs. In the preceding McKinley administration the United States had begun to formulate national policies to guide the government in its actions.

The "Open Door" and the Boxer Rebellion. During the late 1890's the United States became increasingly alarmed over the "spheres of influence" being established in the decaying Chinese Empire by European nations. Because it seemed likely that soon there would be no independent China left, the United States believed that it was time to protect American markets and other interests there. In 1899, while McKinley was President, Secretary of State Hay addressed the first "Open Door" note to the other powers involved with China. It was merely a request that the commercial rights of persons of all nationalities be respected by the powers within their own spheres of influence. The replies were evasive and qualified, with the exception of the British reply which endorsed Hay's proposal.

Hay took stronger measures in 1900 after the Boxer uprising. A group of Chinese nationalists, misnamed "Boxers," sought to drive the "foreign devils" out of China that summer. Within a short time several hundred missionaries, businessmen, and officials had been murdered, and a group of foreigners who had sought safety within the walls of the British legation in Peking were besieged. Since the Chinese government was both unable and unwilling to stop the Boxers, an international military expedition, including a detachment of United States marines, landed on the coast of China and marched on Peking. Suffering very few casualties, this force rescued the desperate defenders within the British legation, who had survived the siege for fifty-five days. The action was historic, for the troops of the United States had for the first time been engaged on the continent of Asia.

During the Boxer incident Secretary Hay, with President McKinley's approval, addressed another circular note to the great powers that held spheres of influence. This time he declared that the policy of the United States would be to "preserve Chinese territorial and administrative entity" and protect the principle of free trade with all parts of China. Hay's Open Door notes were significant, not because they gave China any real protection but because they were symbolic of the expanding political interests of the United States.

The Russo-Japanese War and Portsmouth. In 1904 the Japanese navy delivered a "sneak" attack on the Russian warships stationed at Port Arthur, a naval base leased by Russia from China. There ensued a bloody conflict between the two powers for control of northern China, with both obviously ignoring Hay's Open Door policy. This struggle presented Theodore Roosevelt with a magnificent opportunity to act as an international statesman, for the adversaries were willing to accept arbitration by a neutral party. Russia was beset by domestic revolution and corruption, and Japan, although having won most of the battles, was at the end of her limited resources. Roosevelt was fearful that the Japanese might lose. As he put it, "Japan is playing our game," for he regarded Japan as a counterpoise to Russia.

In the summer of 1905, Russian and Japanese delegates met with Roosevelt as mediator at Portsmouth, New Hampshire. Partly through the President's efforts, Japan obtained the southern half of the island of Sakhalin and, by taking over Liaotung Peninsula and the South Manchurian Railroad from Russia, became the dominant power in Manchuria—even though both Russia and Japan agreed by terms of the treaty to evacuate that region. At the

"Take up the white man's burden" (Rudyard Kipling). *The United States intervenes in China, 1900.*   THE BETTMANN ARCHIVE

Portsmouth conference Roosevelt became impatient with the persistent Japanese demands for huge indemnities, which the Russians flatly refused to pay. Not many months later, Roosevelt was to become even more alarmed over the growing menace of Japan and regret his earlier partiality to the nation.

In retrospect, Roosevelt has been criticized for his role. Had he not intervened, it has been reasoned, Russia would eventually have crushed Japan. By allowing the Japanese to win the war, Roosevelt unwittingly laid the groundwork for Japan's attack on Pearl Harbor in 1941. At the time, however, the settlement seemed reasonable, and Roosevelt's actions have been described as the crowning achievement of his diplomatic career. Roosevelt attained worldwide recognition when he was awarded the 1906 Nobel peace prize for his efforts in bringing about the end of the Russo-Japanese War.

Japanese-American Relations after Portsmouth. Even as Roosevelt was negotiating on behalf of the Japanese at Portsmouth, Secretary of War William Howard Taft was settling other problems with the Far Eastern nation. In secret meetings held in Tokyo, Taft indicated to Count Taro Katsura, prime minister of Japan, that the United States recognized his country's domination of Korea, which it had seized from

The End of Continentalism, 1890-1914

The Great White Fleet—parading America's sea power.   BROWN BROTHERS

China in 1895. In return, Katsura assured Taft that Japan had no claims to the Philippines. The Taft-Katsura Memorandum illustrates Roosevelt's penchant for secret, personal diplomacy. The understanding on Korea was never approved by the Senate, which, in fact, was not even aware of its existence.

From this high point of friendliness, Japanese-American relations deteriorated rapidly. The Japanese people reacted angrily to Roosevelt's refusal to support its demands for war indemnities from the Russians at Portsmouth, and anti-American riots erupted across the country. Resentment against the United States was heightened by reports of the boycotts and restrictive legislation imposed against Japanese nationals in California, reaching a climax in 1906 when San Francisco's school board placed its Japanese children in a separate school (page 388). Roosevelt's maneuverings to end this segregation and then to extract from the Japanese a "gentlemen's agreement," by which Japanese laborers wishing to come to the mainland of the United States were refused passports, eased tensions at least for the moment.

By now the President's original optimism concerning the energetic Japanese had been considerably dampened. He ordered an impressive naval demonstration to make them, as well as the rest of the world, aware of the armed might of the United States. Sixteen warships, painted white and attended by various auxiliary vessels, weighed anchor at Hampton Roads, Virginia, in December 1907, for a voyage around the world.[4] The first major foreign port of call for the "Great White Fleet" was Yokohama, Japan, where it was greeted with courtesy and enthusiasm. The vessels then continued their voyage without incident through the Indian Ocean and the Suez Canal into the Mediterranean. The awesome display of naval might, which now exceeded the German and was second only to that of the British, decidedly enhanced the prestige of the United States.

In the meantime Roosevelt sought to extend the Taft-Katsura Pact. In November 1908 Secretary of State Elihu Root (who had replaced the ailing John Hay in 1905) concluded an

[4] Critics of the President angrily protested this decision. Some feared that the Japanese might try to "Port Arthur" the navy by another torpedo "sneak attack." Members of Congress, objecting to the cost of such an expedition, threatened to deny the navy the necessary appropriations. Roosevelt, with his customary imperiousness, bluntly indicated that he had enough money in the existing budget for the fleet to reach its destination. It would then be up to Congress to provide the funds to get the ships home again. Congress meekly complied.

First in War, First in Peace

agreement with Baron Kogoro Takahira, Japan's ambassador in Washington, to stabilize relations between the two countries. Under the provisions of the Root-Takahira agreement, they promised to maintain the "existing status quo" in the Pacific, to respect each other's possessions there, and to support the integrity of China. The Japanese, however, interpreted the agreement as recognizing their special interests in Manchuria, and the California legislature was soon to draft a bill debarring them from owning land in that state.

President Roosevelt and the Moroccan "Open Door" Question

Theodore Roosevelt established another precedent by involving the United States for the first time in the internal affairs of Europe. In 1904 France had sought to extend her already gigantic African empire by forcing the weak government of Morocco to accept French control and protection. This move was abruptly interrupted by Kaiser Wilhelm II of Germany, who visited Morocco in 1905 and dramatically declared that Germany desired the continued independence of the sultanate. The kaiser also appealed to Roosevelt to assist in maintaining an "Open Door" for Morocco.

This situation created a "war scare" in Europe. Bitter rivals for many years, Frenchmen still nursed memories of their humiliation at the hands of Germans in the Franco-Prussian War of 1870, and many Germans were not averse to a punitive war against France. Furthermore, both nations were heavily armed, and both had allies. A general European conflict appeared a real possibility.

In the spring of 1905, Roosevelt responded to the kaiser's appeal and convened a general international conference to resolve the Moroccan dispute at Algeciras, a small seaport in Spain. The American diplomats were instrumental in securing German acceptance of the final solution, even though their role in the deliberations was minor. Since neither France nor Germany was really ready for war, they were willing to compromise. Partly because of the support of the United States, France was given a larger measure of control than other powers in an international bank established to stabilize Moroccan finances. In addition, France and Spain were to train and control the police of the country. It was a minor diplomatic victory for the French but one that would allow them to dominate the country in later years. Germany was of course angry over being outvoted. In the long run the Algeciras Conference did little more than delay the showdown between Germany and France until 1914. At the time, however, it appeared that Roosevelt had again served the cause of peace.

The importance of the event to the United States lay in Roosevelt's break with the traditional policy of nonentanglement in European politics. American support of France at the Algeciras Conference foreshadowed closer diplomatic ties with both France and Great Britain in the years to come.

Taft's Foreign Policies

In 1909 William Howard Taft "inherited" the mantle of power from Theodore Roosevelt. Although the new President agreed with many of his friend's principles, Taft's vacillating temperament made it almost impossible for him to pursue his predecessor's policies successfully. Moreover, Taft disagreed with Roosevelt concerning the role of the United States in Europe. When a new quarrel arose between France and Germany over Morocco in 1911, Taft, unlike Roosevelt, remained strictly neutral.

In addition, Taft left foreign affairs largely in the hands of his Secretary of State, Philander C. Knox. As a former corporation lawyer, Knox believed that the government should be the agent for American commercial interests abroad, and he used the nation's power to establish new areas for investment. He also prodded Americans into risking capital in overseas enterprises. Such economic involvement, Knox believed, would develop needed stability in the economic and political affairs of underdeveloped countries as well as provide additional markets.

This policy, which has been called "dollar diplomacy," was experimented with in China and Latin America. To give the United States a stronger voice in China's affairs, Knox induced J. P. Morgan and other bankers to furnish capital for the development of Chinese railroads. The financiers participated reluctantly, withdrawing from the plan as soon as Taft left the White House. About the only tangible result was the hostile reaction of Japan and Russia, who resented the interference in their spheres of influence in China. Dollar diplomacy was pursued with more vigor in the Caribbean. Under pressure from Secretary Knox, bankers invested capital in Honduras, Nicaragua, and Haiti to refund their foreign debts. When the Nicaraguans revolted in 1912 over restrictions imposed on them through the take-over of their finances and custom service by American bankers after their government had defaulted on a loan made by a British syndicate, President Taft applied the Roosevelt corollary and ordered the marines to intervene. In effect, Nicaragua became another satellite of the United States, for the marines were to remain for twenty years. The ruthless pursuit of dollar diplomacy, viewed as Yankee imperialism, caused considerable resentment in Latin America. This policy and Taft's diplomacy in general were notably ineffective.

Wilson's Latin-American Policies

On October 27, 1913 President Woodrow Wilson declared that in the operations of foreign policy "morality must guide us. . . . Human rights, national integrity, and opportunity as against naterial interests . . . is the issue we now have to face. . . . The United States will never again seek one additional foot of territory by conquest."

Although far different from Theodore Roosevelt in temperament, Wilson was a strong supporter of his Latin-American policies. Unlike Taft, Wilson showed no hesitation in pursuit of a goal and never doubted the correctness of his actions. Wilson emphatically endorsed the Roosevelt corollary and used the "big stick" to chastise "wayward" Caribbean nations with a vigor for exceeding that of Roosevelt.[5] Yet Wilson openly denounced the dollar diplomacy of Taft and Knox as catering to "material interests," and he himself took personal charge of foreign affairs. Wilson appointed William Jennings Bryan, the elder statesman of the Democratic party, as Secretary of State but treated him with ill-concealed contempt.

The most distinctive aspects of Wilson's foreign policies were his principles of moral "recognition" and "nonrecognition." Influenced by his Calvinist upbringing, Wilson was convinced that there were "good and bad governments." Good governments were usually democratic, but bad governments were not. Thus, he reasoned, the United States should grant diplomatic recognition only to good governments. Bad governments should be opposed and oppressed peoples encouraged to overthrow their immoral rulers.

Nicaragua. During Wilson's administration the military occupation of Nicaragua initiated by Taft was continued. The position of the United States was strengthened in 1914 with the negotiation of the Bryan-Chamorro Treaty, which was ratified by the Senate in 1916. Under its terms the United States obtained an option to build a canal through Nicaragua and to establish naval bases.

The Dominican Republic. For a few years after President Roosevelt first applied his corollary to the Monroe Doctrine, the Dominican Repub-

---

[5]"Speak softly and carry a big stick" was a favorite adage adopted by Theodore Roosevelt during his presidency to describe his approach to public problems. The phrase was inaccurate, inasmuch as Teddy Roosevelt was incapable of speaking softly. In cartoons, however, Roosevelt was often shown brandishing a "big stick."

lic was relatively stable. But by 1911 repeated assassinations had again created chaos in the island republic. Wilson sent troops to intervene in 1914, and they supervised Dominican elections. Because of continued unrest, however, Wilson ordered a gradual military occupation of the entire nation. By 1916 the United States had established a military government, and troops were not withdrawn until 1924. Although the Americans attempted to improve the country by building roads, schools, and hospitals, their presence was deeply resented. The island republic was later ruled for many years by General Rafael Trujillo, a ruthless dictator who had been trained by the occupation authorities.

Haiti. Conditions in Haiti became even more unstable than those in the Dominican Republic. Haitian presidents were invariably shot, poisoned, or bombed, and a mob literally tore President Guillaume Sam limb from limb. The day after President Sam was murdered (July 28, 1915), United States naval forces seized Port-au-Prince, the capital of Haiti. In succeeding weeks they gradually overcame the resistance of guerrilla fighters and extended their control over the entire country. More than 2,000 Haitians lost their lives before the country was pacified. Haiti became a virtual protectorate ruled by Admiral W. B. Caperton, the United States proconsul. The occupation did produce order and prosperity for a time, and the United States even provided the Haitians with a constitution, but in the long run little was accomplished. As soon as United States troops were withdrawn in 1934, government by tyranny and violence returned. Today Haiti is the most backward nation in the Western Hemisphere, governed by the despotic and corrupt Jean Duvalier, whose father and predecessor, François, died in 1971.

The Mexican Quagmire. Although the story of United States intervention throughout the Caribbean area has been a sorry one, its interference in Mexico was almost catastrophic. The United States became involved after a revolution, begun in 1910, had unseated dictator Porfirio Díaz. Díaz had assumed power in 1877 and had brought much needed stability to the country.

During his lengthy regime Díaz financed the government by inviting large-scale investments of foreign capital, mainly from Germany, Great Britain, and the United States. The price for the internal calm was costly, however, for Indian lands were often expropriated for sale to foreigners and to the new Mexican landowning class. The Indian villagers were reduced to peonage or near slavery.

By 1911 the peons had overthrown the despotic government of Díaz, and Francisco Madero, a liberal educated in the United States, was chosen president. But this visionary reformer without political experience did not hold his position long. In February 1913 he was murdered by the order of his defense minister, General Victoriano Huerta, who had seized control of the government.

President Wilson, outraged by this incident, was almost alone among Western powers in refusing to grant diplomatic recognition to the Huerta regime, despite the entreaties of business and financial interests. Then in 1914 he lifted an earlier arms embargo so that munitions could be supplied to rebels under the command of General Venustiano Carranza, but Huerta drew strength from the resented American interference. Two incidents led to more direct action—the unwarranted arrest of some American sailors on shore leave by the *Huertistas* at Tampico and the report that a large shipment of arms from Germany was being sent to Huerta.

Although the sailors were released with expressions of regret from a superior officer, neither Wilson nor Admiral Henry T. Mayo, in command of United States naval forces off the Mexican coast, was satisfied. In order to block the arrival of the German munitions ship and humiliate the Huerta government, United States marines landed and captured Vera Cruz on April 21, 1914 against spirited resistance.

Nineteen Americans and 126 Mexicans were killed in the assault. The possibility of a second Mexican War appeared imminent, but by July 1914 Huerta had abdicated, and General Carranza was able to enter Mexico City in triumph. On the surface it appeared that Wilson's refusal to recognize Huerta's government and his support of Carranza were a victory for morality and stability. But many Americans were openly critical of the President's actions, and Mexicans were plainly shocked. General Carranza denounced the seizure of Vera Cruz as "a violation of the rights that constitute our existence as a free and independent sovereignty."

Nor did peace then come to Mexico. Other revolutionary factions led by Emilio Zapata and the bandit Francisco Villa resumed fighting. In January 1916 Villa's forces murdered sixteen American engineers aboard a train in northern Mexico. They had been invited by Carranza to return and operate abandoned mines. Then in the spring *Villista* raids were conducted across the frontier into the United States. The town of Columbus, New Mexico, was shot up in Wild West fashion before Villa's forces ducked below the Rio Grande. Nineteen Americans were killed.

President Wilson, compelled to intervene, ordered a force of 6,600 men under the command of General John J. Pershing to pursue Villa and bring him to justice. On March 15, 1916, with the reluctant approval of Carranza, the second invasion of Mexico by United States troops began. Despite Pershing's extraordinary efforts, the daring bandit eluded his grasp. In the course of the campaign, Villa executed another raid into the United States, capturing a village in Texas and killing four more citizens. The exasperated Carranza, frightened by Pershing's ever-increasing forces, demanded that either the United States army leave Mexico or the two countries would face war. Fortunately, developments elsewhere saved the President from further humiliation. The United States was being drawn ever closer to the vortex of the great European war. The army and General Pershing would soon be forced to play a much larger role on the battlefields of France. In early 1917 the American troops were withdrawn, leaving behind them an aftermath of bitterness.

Latin-American Affairs in Retrospect. Although lofty hopes often motivated United States policies in Latin America they were diluted by dollar diplomacy, fears for national security, and insufficient regard for the rights of the other nations. All too often American impatience and lack of understanding proved the nation's undoing. Roosevelt and Wilson readily compared the United States to the unloved policeman who must do his duty, but their analogy was without logic. The action of the policeman in maintaining public order is sanctioned by some higher public authority. He does not make laws to suit himself and then enforce them. The record of achievements in Latin America during the period from McKinley to Wilson is not a proud one.

The Peace Movement after 1900

A minor development in United States foreign relations after 1900 was the revival of the peace movement, which had been dormant since the early reform era of the 1840's. Against the clamor for expansion and conflict, the "peacemongers" worked consistently to lessen the possibilities of war. Societies that were campaigning for peace acquired resources and became respectable. Businessmen, politicians, and intellectuals became members, although in the past only reformers and clergymen had joined the organizations.

One of the early societies for promoting peace was the Anti-Imperialist League, formed in 1899 to fight expansionism and our Philippine policy in particular. Such contrasting personalities as former President Cleveland, Senators George F. Hoar of Massachusetts and "Pitchfork Ben" Tillman of South Carolina, university presidents Charles W. Eliot of Harvard and David Starr Jordan of Stanford, reformers Lincoln Steffens and Jane Addams, writers William Dean Howells and Mark Twain, steel king Andrew Carnegie, and labor leader Samuel Gompers all joined the League.

Especially active in providing funds for the peace movement were Carnegie and Edward Ginn, the Boston publisher. Both men established foundations to study problems of international relations, and Carnegie also financed a magnificent "Peace Palace" at The Hague to house the Permanent Court of International Arbitration. Such varied organizations as the Young Men's Christian Association and the United States Chamber of Commerce became known for their zeal in promoting the abolition of war.

The United States participated in the two Hague peace conferences called by Tsar Nicholas II of Russia in 1899 and 1907. The delegates reached an agreement to lessen the horrors of war by providing for the proper treatment of prisoners and cooperation with the Red Cross and by abolishing such efficiently destructive weapons as the dumdum bullet and poisonous gas. The outlawed weapons were used during the First World War, however, in spite of the agreements. Moreover, the Hague conferences did not achieve their major objective, that of limiting the armaments of major powers.

The various secretaries of state in the early years of the twentieth century—John Hay, Elihu Root, Philander C. Knox, and William Jennings Bryan—all sought to establish means for settling international quarrels by arbitration. Large numbers of arbitration and "cooling off" treaties with other countries were signed by the United States. But the Senate refused to allow any major questions involving the United States to be submitted to a neutral court of arbitration, thereby rendering these treaties less effective.

The prospects for continuing world peace seemed favorable in 1914. Citizens of the United States had come to recognize the cost and disadvantages of expansionism, and the countries of Europe were completing a century of general peace and almost uninterrupted progress. There was a vibrant optimism in the Western world. Whatever serious problems remained, it seemed reasonable to expect that they would be resolved in this era of general prosperity and goodwill. Then a revolver was fired in Sarajevo, shattering the apparently calm and secure world.

SUGGESTED READINGS

Allen, H. C., *Great Britain and the United States* (1955).

Anderson, E. N., *The First Moroccan Crisis, 1904–1906* (1930).

*Beale, H. K., *Theodore Roosevelt and the Rise of America to World Power* (1956).

*Bemis, S. F., *The Latin American Policy of the United States* (1943).

Calkott, W. H., *The Caribbean Policy of the United States, 1890–1920* (1942).

Campbell, C. S., Jr., *Special Business Interests and the Open Door Policy* (1951).

*Cline, H. F., *The United States and Mexico* (2nd ed., 1963).

Curti, M., *Bryan and World Peace* (1931).

Davis, G. T., *A Navy Second to None* (1940).

Dulles, F. R., *The Imperial Years* (1956).

*Freidel, F., *The Splendid Little War* (1958).

Gelber, L. M., *The Rise of Anglo-American Friendship* (1938).

*Greene, T. P., ed., *American Imperialism in 1898* (1955).

*Griswold, A. W., *The Far Eastern Policy of the United States* (1938).
Healy, D. F., *The United States in Cuba, 1898–1902* (1963).
James, H., *Richard Olney and His Public Service* (1923).
Jessup, P. C., *Elihu Root* (2 vols., 1938).
*Kennan, G. F., *American Diplomacy, 1900–1950* (1951).
*LaFeber, W., *The New Empire, An Interpretation of American Expansion, 1860–1898* (1963).
*Link, A. S., *Wilson the Diplomatist* (1957).
*May, E. R., *Imperial Democracy: The Emergence of America as a Great Power* (1961).
*Merk, F., *Manifest Destiny and Mission in American History* (1963).
*Millis, W., *The Martial Spirit* (1931).
Moon, P. T., *Imperialism and World Politics* (1926).
*Morgan, H. W., *America's Road to Empire: The War with Spain and Overseas Expansion* (1965).
Morgan, H. W., *William McKinley and His America* (1963).
Morgenthau, H., *In Defense of the National Interest* (1951).
Munro, D. G., *Intervention and Dollar Diplomacy in the Caribbean, 1900–1921* (1964).
*Osgood, R. E., *Ideals and Self Interest in America's Foreign Relations* (1953).
Padelford, N. J., *The Panama Canal in Peace and War* (1942).
Perkins, D., *The Monroe Doctrine, 1867–1907* (1937).
Pratt, J. W., *America's Colonial Experiment* (1950).
*Pratt, J. W., *Expansionists of 1898* (1936).
*Quirk, R. E., *An Affair of Honor: Woodrow Wilson and the Occupation of Vera Cruz* (1962).
*Roosevelt, T., *The Rough Riders* (1899).
Scott, J. B., *The Hague Peace Conferences of 1899 and 1907* (2 vols., 1909).
*Sprout, M., *The Rise of American Naval Power, 1776–1918* (1939).
Stevens, S. K., *American Expansion in Hawaii, 1842–1898* (1945).
Treat, P. J., *Diplomatic Relations Between the United States and Japan, 1895–1905* (2 vols., 2nd ed., 1938).
*Vevier, C., *The United States and China, 1906–1913* (1955).
*Weinberg, A. K., *Manifest Destiny* (1935).
West, R. S., Jr., *Admirals of the American Empire* (1948).
White, J. A., *The Diplomacy of the Russo-Japanese War* (1964).
*Williams, W. A., *The Tragedy of American Diplomacy* (2nd ed., 1962).
Wisan, J. E., *The Cuban Crisis as Reflected in the New York Press* (1934).
Wolff, L., *Little Brown Brothers* (1961).

CHAPTER 25

The Climax and Ebb of Internationalism, 1914–1920

It must be a peace without victory.

WOODROW WILSON, 1918

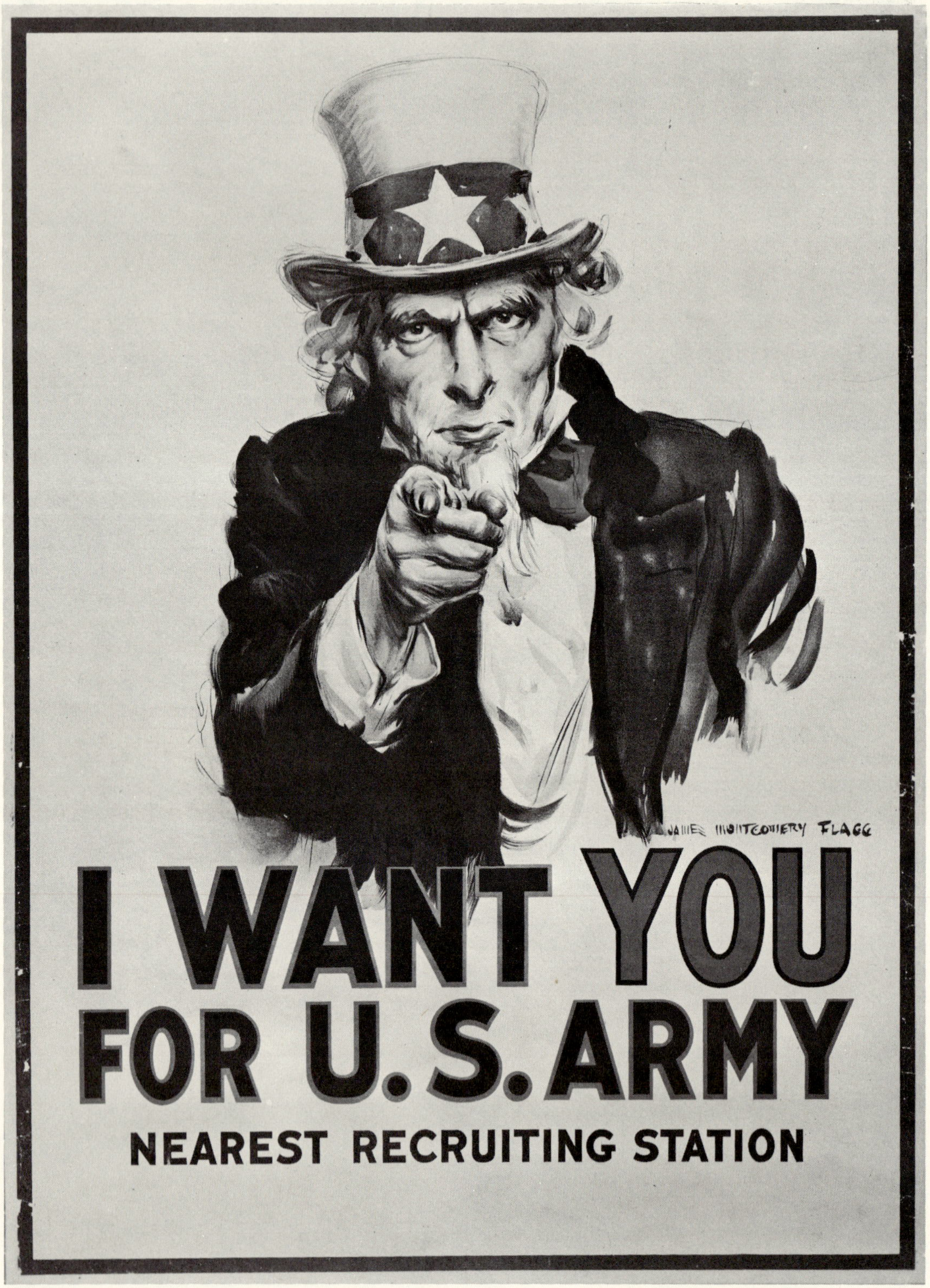

LIBRARY OF CONGRESS

OUTBREAK OF WAR IN 1914

SALIH ALICH, NOW A RESIDENT OF POMONA, California, remembers that on a lovely, warm Sunday morning in early summer, when he was ten years old in his native Bosnia, a province of Austria-Hungary, he had planned as usual to play with his friends in the park. Because His Imperial Highness was expected to visit the city that day, he had thought too of going later to the boulevard along the river bank to watch the parade. But Salih's parents would not allow their son to leave the house that morning, giving him no good reason for their decision. They themselves did not understand exactly what was expected to happen in Sarajevo that Sunday. They knew only that for days rumormongers had spread tales of impending disaster, and they were apprehensive for their son's safety.

A few minutes after eleven o'clock that morning of June 28, 1914, two shots rang out. The Archduke Franz Ferdinand, heir to the Habsburg throne of Austria-Hungary, and his wife, Sophie, had been assassinated in an open touring car in the streets of the city. The murderer, a young Serbian nationalist named Gavrilo Princip, was captured immediately afterward. The rash but seemingly disrelated act was to shatter the fragile peace and stability of Europe, leading summarily to the outbreak of general hostilities a few weeks later. The conflict eventually became the most terrible war in history up to that time; no major world power, including the United States, was to escape the holocaust.

In this crucible of conflict would be forged the new role of world leadership for the United States, with encompassing responsibilities and grave involvements. Woodrow Wilson would at the war's conclusion offer mankind a dream of universal peace and a plan for world order. But the United States would turn its back on the leadership it had won and by refusing participation ensure the failure of Wilson's dream.

Origins of the Conflict

The European Equilibrium, 1870–1890. During the last part of the nineteenth century, most of the European nations had experienced great

The Climax and Ebb of Internationalism, 1914–1920   203

economic growth, paralleling that of the United States. Europeans, busily engaged in making a better material world for themselves, seemed too preoccupied for the moment to concern themselves with other goals and submerged discord. The businessman, the industrial worker, and even the peasant shared in the general progress and economic prosperity. The period was also distinguished by extensive advances in technology and the arts and expansion of learning in the humanities. Europeans and Americans came to believe that war was unthinkable for civilized men, for there had not been a general conflict since the days of Napoleon. Many shared the opinions of Norman Angell, author of *The Great Illusion* (1910), that modern war was economically impossible.

Yet deep psychological tensions, energies, and rivalries existed among Europeans that found no outlet in an industrial society. During the twenty years of peace from 1870 to 1890, these forces were kept in check by three principal factors—the internal prosperity already mentioned, imperialism, and the genius of Otto von Bismarck.

In the European scramble for colonies in Asia and Africa, new markets, raw materials, and investment opportunities were acquired. The prestige won for a nation by its imperialism was also a very powerful motivation, at least for the ruling classes whose own wealth and power made them conscious of status. But even the ordinary European citizen, his energies no longer completely spent by physical toil, was exhilarated, for the acquisition of remote and wonderful lands allowed him the vicarious release of emotion. Aggressiveness, the spirit of adventure, curiosity, and humanitarianism—all were expended as he followed avidly the reports of inevitable victories of European troops in skirmishes with native warriors, of explorations and missions to bring the "blessings of Western Civilization to child-like peoples in the dim, hot, southern regions of the world." For a time the European nations concentrated most of their competitive energies on developing colonies.

The delicate political system arranged by the shrewd statesmanship of Bismarck, chancellor of the German Empire, also helped to preserve peace. As the chief minister of the kaiser, Bismarck erected a complex checking and counterchecking system of alliances and friendly agreements centering around Germany, for he needed peaceful conditions and time to consolidate the empire he had created. The core of Bismarck's system was the Triple Alliance, formed in 1882 and consisting of Germany, Austria-Hungary, and Italy. Bismarck further assured peace by maintaining a powerful army, thus discouraging attempts to upset the balance of power. The only nation hostile to Germany was France, and it was kept in a position of friendless, diplomatic isolation.

The Breakdown of European Equilibrium. In

Bismarck—architect of the Triple Alliance.   CULVER PICTURES

1890 the able but aged chancellor was suddenly forced to resign from office by his brash young ruler, Kaiser Wilhelm II. Almost immediately, the delicately balanced system of Bismarck began to disintegrate. In 1894 France broke out of her diplomatic quarantine and signed an alliance with Russia. By 1900 Great Britain had become increasingly alarmed over Germany's aggressive commercial and diplomatic policies, which were challenging its world interests. The British were particularly concerned about Germany's growing naval strength, interpreted as a direct threat to their security. Consequently, England signed an agreement of friendship with France, known as the "Entente Cordiale," in 1904. Three years later France's two partners, England and Russia, settled their differences. Thus by 1907 Europe was divided into two armed and hostile camps—the Triple Alliance headed by Germany and the Triple Entente in which France, Great Britain, and Russia were partners.

In the meantime, beginning in 1898, the Triple Alliance gradually become unglued as Italy made a number of secret agreements with France. By 1914 Germany was isolated and encircled by increasingly hostile powers. Only the doddering Hapsburg empire of Austria-Hungary remained loyal. A large part of the blame for this decline in Germany's diplomatic prestige must be placed on Kaiser Wilhelm II. Although Germany's achievements were envied, the dynamic but unstable personality, violent speeches, and rampant militarism of its leader created fear of the nation's intentions.

Psychological Origins of World War I. During the first years of the nineteenth century, the European mentality became deeply infected by two corrosive impulses, nationalism and militarism. Nationalism may be defined as a devotion to one's own nation, ethnic group or culture. In this sense the term is interchangeable with patriotism. In the late nineteenth century the feeling of nationalism gradually became exaggerated, until in each nation it verged on a cult, with citizens believing their country to be superior to all other nations. The flag and other national emblems were revered with almost religious fervor, warlike anthems were sung, and national history, with emphasis on past glories and folk heroes, was intensively studied. This adoration of flag and fatherland would permit no slight upon the national honor. Even the smallest insult brought threats of rectification by force of arms. The growing power of public opinion, intensified by the exaggerated sense of nationalism, made the solution of international problems increasingly difficult as the twentieth century began.

Militarism was as much of a cult as nationalism. The European Social Darwinists, like those in America, applied the doctrine of "the survival of the fittest" to society, theorizing that nations, like animal and plant species, are in constant conflict. The most aggressive, strongest, and most intelligent peoples survive and rule; the weak are eliminated or subjugated. The militarists reasoned that war is an essential part of this process and a means of progress. Far from being an evil, war came to be regarded as a "biological necessity." Most nations had universal military training and huge standing armies and navies. Military uniforms were seen everywhere before 1914. The ordinary soldier was no longer looked down upon as a yokel or bumpkin but rather respected as a patriot who represented his nation's glory.

Hostilities Begin

The assassination of the Austrian archduke by Princip provoked a diplomatic crisis between Austria-Hungary and Serbia for reasons that stretched back to 1908 when Austria had annexed the Serbian provinces of Bosnia and Herzegovina. To solve the problem of the continuing disaffection of these two provinces, Franz Ferdinand had more recently proposed changing the dual monarchy of Austria and Hungary to a triple monarchy in which Bosnia and Herzegovina would enjoy autonomy and the Serbians and other Slavs living in the em-

"The shot heard round the world." The assassination of the Archduke Franz Ferdinand (1914). CULVER PICTURES

pire could participate in its affairs on an equal basis with the Austrians and the Magyars (Hungarians). To the Serbian nationalists living in the two provinces, however, the proposal was a threat to their plans for a united and greater Serbia. And so in June 1914 a group of assassins converged on Sarajevo for the widely publicized visit of the archduke. The consternation of the Austrians after the assassination was intensified by their belief that the Serbian government had known of the plot and had made little effort to prevent its execution.

After waiting a few weeks, the Austrian government on July 23 delivered a purposely harsh ten-point ultimatum to Serbia, compliance with which would have meant surrender of independence. An answer was demanded within forty-eight hours. A few minutes before the expiration of this time limit, the Serbian government responded to the Austrian minister at Belgrade, who promptly rejected the reply because Serbia had not fully accepted every point in the ultimatum. On July 28, 1914 Austria-Hungary declared war on Serbia.

Serbia's powerful friend Russia, the leader of the Slavic world, felt it could not stand by while the smaller country was crushed. On the following day Tsar Nicholas II ordered a mobilization of Russian armies on the Austrian frontier. This menacing action brought a response from Germany in support of its friend, Austria-Hungary. When Russia rejected a demand to halt mobilization, Germany declared war on Russia on August 1. Then two days later, because it was unable to obtain a pledge of neutrality from France, Russia's partner in the Triple Entente, Germany also declared war on the French.

Despite its close ties with France, the other member of the Triple Entente, Great Britain hesitated before making a decision regarding its role in the growing conflict. The British Cabinet, with the exception of a minority which included Winston Churchill, was not in favor of war. As early as 1839, however, the Great Powers had signed a treaty pledging to respect the neutrality of Belgium in the event of a conflict. This agreement had been renewed again and again, with both Germany and Great Britain as signers. Germany's invasion of Belgium on August 2, to strike at France, decided the British course of action. On August 4 Great Britain declared war on Germany, rejecting the German chancellor's last-minute pleas that, after all, the treaty protecting Belgium was "nothing but a scrap of paper." Thus within an eight-day period all the members of the Triple Alliance (renamed the Central Powers during the course of the war) and of the Triple Entente

206 *First in War, First in Peace*

(later known as the Allies) were at war, except for Italy, which had decided to maintain neutrality for the time being.

Citizens in every country, from statesmen to laborers, greeted the beginning of hostilities in Europe with great enthusiasm. The scenes were reminiscent of the United States in 1898, when war was declared against Spain. Cheering crowds waved farewell to departing soldiers, and orators made the traditional patriotic speeches about the fatherland, honor, and the glorious flag. As usual, God was claimed to be on both sides. People were generally convinced the war would be brief and would lead to certain victory for their nation. Yet leaders of greater perception recognized the seriousness of the conflict. Sir Edward Grey, the British foreign secretary at the time, remarked prophetically, "The lamps are going out all over Europe. We shall not see them lit again in our lifetime." It is doubtful, however, that any observer could have fully realized how desperate and tragic would be the struggle and destruction that ensued.

Although a quarrel in eastern Europe had begun the war, the first important military operations occurred in western Europe as the Germans undertook to carry out their Schlieffen Plan. Years earlier, General Alfred von Schlieffen had determined the strategy that Germany would adopt in the event it must fight France and Russia simultaneously. To avoid the heavily fortified Franco-German frontier, massive German armies would demand passage through Belgium, and hope to outflank and destroy the French army with a quick, knockout blow. Limited forces would be deployed on the eastern frontier to contain the enormous, but slow-moving, Russian army.

In accordance with this plan, now somewhat altered and weakened, a mighty German army of two million men smashed into Belgium when the small country refused them passage. Within three weeks the valiant Belgians were engulfed and the German wave swept into France. In a crucial battle along the Marne River in early September, the French finally halted the Germans only twenty-five miles short of Paris, their major objective. The Battle of the Marne was decisive. It saved France and stabilized the "western front," putting an end to the Schlieffen Plan and destroying Germany's hope of an early victory. The war of maneuver and movement was over. The struggle now became one of attrition. Leaders on both sides soon realized that the war would be long and costly.

The Long Stalemate

After the Battle of the Marne, German and Allied troops (French, British, and remnants of the Belgian army) hastily erected a series of parallel defensive trenches which stretched more than 300 miles across France, from the Swiss border to the English Channel. In strenuous and unbelievably murderous and maiming assaults throughout a period of almost four years, neither the Germans nor the Allies could penetrate each other's defenses. The cost in manpower during the prolonged trench warfare was staggering. The fine young men of entire nations was squandered in successively futile attempts to crack the lines of the opposing sides. The French and the British suffered 1,400,000 casualties in 1915 without appreciable results. One of their major offenses, at Ypres, was repulsed by the German use of chlorine gas. At Verdun in eastern France, a massive German assault begun in February 1916 was finally checked by the French in July at a cost of more than 300,000 casualties to each side. The British lost 60,000 men in one day in the Battle of the Somme, which began that same July, and more than half a million before the attack was called off in November. Only six square miles of German-held territory had been regained. The next year, during the same five months, the British mounted eight heavy attacks at Passchendaele in Belgium. Fighting most of the time in driving rain, they

The Climax and Ebb of Internationalism, 1914–1920

POWER ALIGNMENT DURING WORLD WAR I

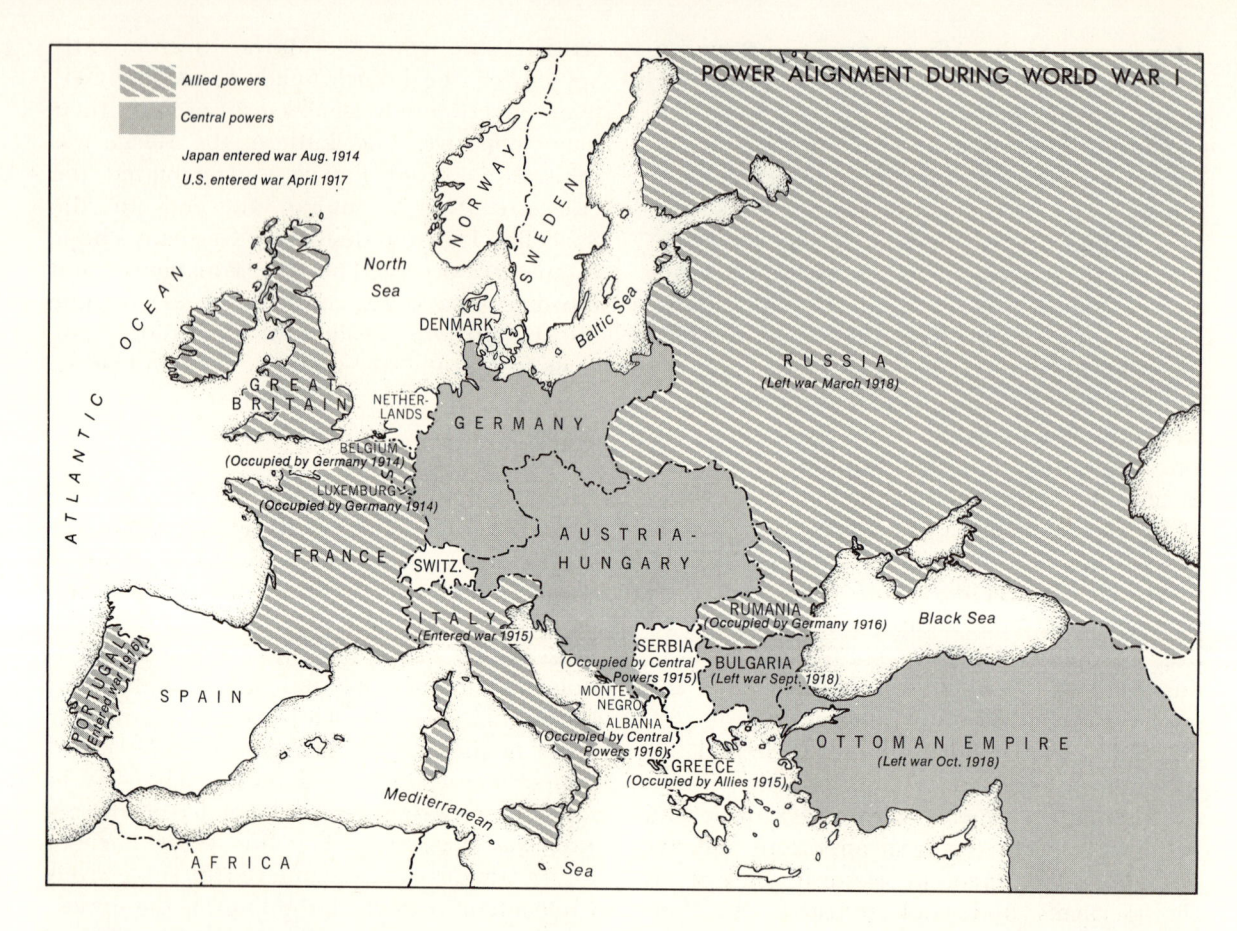

- Allied powers
- Central powers

Japan entered war Aug. 1914
U.S. entered war April 1917

gained five miles of water-logged ground and lost another 450,000 men.

On the eastern front the conflict was equally costly. A Russian invasion of eastern Germany in August and September 1914 was crushed by great German victories at Tannenberg and the Masurian Lakes. During a German offensive in Galicia in May and June 1915, Russia lost more than a million men and came very close to total collapse.

The War Spreads. Although the main arenas continued to be those in France and eastern Europe, other nations entered the war. In the autumn of 1914 Japan seized Germany's possessions in China and the Pacific, and the Ottoman Empire (Turkey) joined the Central Powers later the same year. There was also intensive fighting in the Middle East and in Africa. Each new entrant intensified the war and often added still another bloody front to the titanic conflict. Italy officially deserted the Triple Alliance in favor of the Allies in May 1915. Along the crests of the Alps, the Italians and Austrians battered each other for two years with the great ferocity described by Ernest Hemingway in *Farewell to Arms*. Although the front was only about sixty miles in length, the Italians never succeeded in advancing more than ten or twelve miles. By the end of the war, very few European nations had managed to remain neutral.

The War at Sea. Some of the most crucial struggles of the First World War were those between naval powers. From the outset the tremendous superiority of the combined British and French navies enabled the Allies to close the sea lanes

208   *First in War, First in Peace*

to merchant shipping of the Central Powers. The Allied naval blockade was much more extensive than any in history, for the contraband list was extended to include most commodities, even foodstuffs. The North Sea was declared a military area and mined so heavily that no ship could proceed through it without first receiving specific directions from British officials. Slowly but surely the flow of military supplies and of food for Germany's civilian population was reduced. In the long run this blockade may have been more decisive in the Allied victory than the battles fought on land.

Surprisingly, Germany's powerful surface fleet was rarely used during the conflict, although German surface raiders slipped through the Allied blockade and inflicted heavy damage on Allied merchant shipping before the raiders were swept from the seas. The kaiser's great High Seas Fleet challenged the mighty British navy only once when in 1916, in the Battle of Jutland, it clashed briefly with the British in what has been described as the greatest naval engagement in history. As soon as the main British fleet arrived, however, the Germans avoided a showdown by scuttling back to port, never to emerge again.

The German submarine, better known as the U-boat, became the chief weapon with which to challenge Allied naval supremacy on the high seas. When the Germans launched their "unrestricted submarine campaign," in which Allied vessels were torpedoed without warning, they threatened the very existence of Great Britain. At one point in early 1917, the British, who depended on the importation of food for survival, had barely enough reserves to last a month. If the Germans had concentrated more of their resources on building U-boats, they might have won the war despite the great superiority of Allied manpower and other resources. Instead, the U-boat warfare served to anger the people of the United States to such an extent that the nation joined the Allies in 1917, thus assuring Germany's ultimate defeat.

The "New Warfare." The First World War developed a mode of warfare unlike that of any previous conflict in the history of mankind. This was "total war," in which entire populations were involved in a national effort. Everyone was expected to do his part, man, woman, and child. The economy of each nation was mobilized to create "war socialism." Production of nonessential commodities was limited or prohibited. Private enterprise was controlled by an "economic czar" appointed by the government, and he determined who should produce what and how much. Wages and prices were regulated, and the distribution of food, clothing, and other necessities was rationed.

Along with economic control came "thought control." The mobilization of men's minds was believed essential for victory. Exaggerated patriotism and hatred for the enemy were deliberately fostered. Newspapers were rigorously censored, and items that might weaken the will of the people to conquer were deleted. Official propaganda, often badly misrepresenting the facts, was substituted for truth. The newspaper reader was subjected to a regular diet of stories either magnifying national successes or describing in detail the latest atrocities perpetrated by the foe.

In this atmosphere of superheated patriotism, civil liberties were seriously compromised. Persons suspected of being "slackers" or critical of the war effort were persecuted or punished. Even in Great Britain and France total control gradually replaced the democratic process.

The most shocking aspect of the "new warfare," however, was the savagery with which it was conducted. New methods of destruction were devised—ranging from poison gas, submarines, armored tanks, and air attacks to long-range artillery which killed military personnel and civilians. Especially disturbing was the callous readiness of military commanders to send vast numbers of soldiers to certain death in the meaningless battles on the various fronts. Often the best a combat soldier could hope for was a long period of waiting and despair in the muddy trenches. In the end he was sent "over the top" to die or be mutilated by enemy fire in some hopeless bayonet charge across "no-man's-land." The conquests of Genghis Khan and the slaughter of the American Civil War were made insignificant by the mass murder of the First World War.

THE YEARS OF AMERICAN NEUTRALITY

On August 18, 1914 President Wilson called upon the American people to "be neutral in fact as well as in name during these days that are to try men's souls." Americans were dismayed by the outbreak of war, understanding little of the alliances and rivalries that had drawn in so many nations, but their first and strongest emotion was relief that they were not involved. The average citizen in 1914 hardly suspected that this European war would ever be America's. For nearly three years the United States managed to remain technically neutral, but the long tradition of noninvolvement in Europe's affairs, spelled out in the words of Washington, Jefferson, and the Monroe Doctrine, was to be abandoned at first emotionally then economically, and at last militarily.

Division of American Sentiment

Wilson's admonition to Americans to be "impartial in thought" fell on the ears of millions whose sympathies were almost immediately engaged. In 1914 over a third of a population of 92,000,000 were foreign-born or the children of immigrants. Citizens of direct German or Austro-Hungarian descent, numbering some 11,000,000, tended to be partial to the Central Powers. They were joined by some 4,500,000 Irish-Americans, motivated by their traditional hostility for Great Britain. This large minority sought for the most part to keep the United States from helping either side. Millions of "old-stock" Americans, who were accustomed to being suspicious of Great Britain or who adhered to the Jeffersonian principle of avoiding entanglement in European affairs, also supported the neutralist position.

In 1914 only a small minority believed that the United States should actually join the Allies, but a very large proportion, probably a majority, were favorably enough disposed toward Britain and France to want to give them economic aid. Shocked by Germany's violation of the neutrality of Belgium, these citizens regarded ruthless German militarism, personified by the mustachioed, spike-helmeted kaiser, as a menace to all decent nations. Many believed that Americans owed a debt to the suffering French. After all, France had helped the United States to win its independence. The outbreak of war also reminded other citizens of their sentimental and cultural attachments to England. Intellectuals, including President Wilson, had long held a reverent regard for English literature and for parliamentary institutions as the cradle of the American democratic tradition, a sentiment which had been carefully cultivated by British foreign policy. Since 1896 the British had graciously conceded to the United States on matters of dispute between the two countries. They had also actively supported the United States in international affairs, sometimes in opposition to all other major powers. American regard for Great Britain had never been higher than it was in 1914.

The Growth of Pro-Allied Sentiment

Propaganda Efforts. Both the Allies and Central Powers initiated extensive propaganda campaigns to win the favor of the United States, the British far more successfully than the Germans. With skill and imagination, British sources flooded the press with "news items" on "the rape of Belgium." Americans were told that the savage "Huns" burned libraries, destroyed cathedrals, assaulted women, and skewered babies with their long bayonets. The account of the Belgian child whose hands were chopped off by a maniacal German soldier,

210 *First in War, First in Peace*

"confirmed" by a photograph of a tragically mutilated girl, was particularly shocking. An investigation after the war, however, was unable to yield any evidence of such an atrocity, either in Belgium or in German-occupied France.

American newspaper correspondents with the German army tried to counteract such distortions. They cabled a report declaring that, as far as they could observe, the stories of atrocities were groundless. In fact, some reporters commended the German soldiers on their excellent behavior. Such small voices of protest were drowned, however, in the deluge of British propaganda that poured out of Europe. Americans read that the inhuman Germans collected the dead after each battle and sent the corpses to a factory, where they were boiled to make soap. The public was shocked further by an account of Germany's brutal "execution" of the lovely English nurse, Edith Cavell, as a spy. The fact that the English and the French shot several German women for espionage was ignored.

German counterpropaganda efforts were marred by contradictions, the slowness of transmitting news from Berlin (the British cut the cables linking the United States with Germany), and actual atrocities committed by German commerce raiders on the high seas. In addition, the Germans damaged their cause through espionage and sabotage. To hamper trade and the flow of munitions to the Allies, German and Austrian agents sought to destroy industrial and transportation facilities. The Secret Service of the United States Treasury Department exposed a number of German plots. Dr. Albert, a principal German agent, made their task rather easy one August day in 1915 when he left his briefcase on a New York elevated car. Some of his documents were later published in the newspapers. In July 1916 the public was particularly shocked by the notorious "Black Tom explosion" on the Jersey City waterfront. A munitions factory was blown up; lives were lost, and war materials bound for France were destroyed. The incident was thought to be the work of German agents, although no substantive proof was ever found.

Increasing Economic Ties. Shortly after the outbreak of war, industries in the United States were deluged with Allied contracts for military equipment. By September 1914 Bethlehem Steel was busy filling the largest arms order ever placed by the British government with a foreign firm. In October 1914 the British awarded the Du Pont Company a contract for $100,000,000 to manufacture gunpowder. The United States, remaining technically neutral, acted as the great arsenal for the Allies while the British blockade effectively deprived Germany of access to American productive facilities.

As the months went by, Allied purchases increased in quantity and variety. The ever-growing demand for food and raw materials benefited the American farmer and other producers. Private loans to the belligerents were at first restricted, but in 1915 it became apparent that the Allies would need credit to make additional purchases. To raise the necessary money, the Allied governments appointed J. P. Morgan's bank to sell war bonds to the American people. By 1917, principally through the efforts of the House of Morgan, more than $2,300,000,000 had been loaned to the Allies.

These demands for supplies and credit all helped to strengthen the United States economy. Soon millions of people were employed directly in the production of goods for Germany's enemies. Still thousands more indicated their belief that the Allies would win through their purchases of British bonds. Thus the fate of the nation's economy and the welfare and the hopes of large numbers of citizens became dependent on the success of the Allied war effort.

Volunteer Groups. Sympathy for the Allies also increased as Americans volunteered for service with the British, French, and Italian forces. Many simply enlisted as soldiers in regular units but others joined special volunteer units

OCEAN STEAMSHIPS.
CUNARD

EUROPE VIA LIVERPOOL
LUSITANIA

Fastest and Largest Steamer
now in Atlantic Service Sails
SATURDAY, MAY 1, 10 A. M.
Transylvania, Fri., May 7, 5 P.M.
Orduna, - - Tues., May 18, 10 A.M.
Tuscania, - - Fri., May 21, 5 P.M.
LUSITANIA, Sat., May 29, 10 A.M.
Transylvania, Fri., June 4, 5 P.M.

Gibraltar-Genoa-Naples-Piraeus
S.S. Carpathia, Thur., May 13, Noon

NOTICE!

TRAVELLERS intending to embark on the Atlantic voyage are reminded that a state of war exists between Germany and her allies and Great Britain and her allies; that the zone of war includes the waters adjacent to the British Isles; that, in accordance with formal notice given by the Imperial German Government, vessels flying the flag of Great Britain, or of any of her allies, are liable to destruction in those waters and that travellers sailing in the war zone on ships of Great Britain or her allies do so at their own risk.

IMPERIAL GERMAN EMBASSY
WASHINGTON, D. C., APRIL 22, 1915.

CULVER PICTURES

---

consisting entirely of Americans. The most renowned was the Lafayette Escadrille, a squadron of aviators with an outstanding combat record in the French Air Corps. In 1915 the American Field Service was organized to provide ambulances, drivers, and medical corpsmen to serve with the French. Both groups were made up largely of young men from private colleges who kept their well-to-do families informed of the "heroic" war efforts of the Allies. By contrast, very few, if any, Americans chose to volunteer in any capacity with the German armed forces.

The U-Boat War. During the first few months of the war, diplomatic relations between the United States and Germany were generally tranquil. This situation changed abruptly, however, when the kaiser's government proclaimed a submarine blockade of the British Isles, in protest against the Allied stoppage of food shipments to Germany. In February 1915 German U-boats were instructed to sink all Allied vessels, warships or merchantmen, on sight and without warning. The Germans had found that the newly developed submarine, too vulnerable once surfaced, could not operate effectively under the established rules of war which required a raider to stop the enemy ship, examine its papers and cargo, and allow its crew to remove themselves to lifeboats before their ship was sunk.

President Wilson responded promptly and drastically to this challenge. He warned that the United States would hold the German government to a "strict accountability" for any attacks on American ships and for injury or death to United States citizens. The Germans in turn urged that Americans be warned not to sail on ships of belligerents, but Wilson believed that they were only exercising a traditional right of neutrals to travel. On March 28, 1915 a U-boat sank the British steamer *Falaba*, with the loss of one American life. On May 1 three persons aboard the American oil tanker *Gulflight* were killed in an accidental attack by a German submarine. The climax came when the giant

British Cunard liner *Lusitania* was torpedoed on May 7 with the loss of nearly 1,200 civilians, more than a hundred of them Americans. This incident probably did more to create hostile opinion in the United States against Germany than all the outpourings of the British propaganda machine. The public considered the sinking of an "unarmed passenger ship" carrying women and children the supreme atrocity.

After some hesitation President Wilson sent a stiffly worded message to Berlin, demanding that the German government disavow the sinking of the *Lusitania* and take "steps to prevent the recurrence" of such acts. At first the Germans stalled, but in the succeeding exchange of notes they were faced with the threat of war with the United States. In September, after two more Americans lost their lives in the sinking of the British steamer *Arabic*, the German government backed down, promising that liners would be sunk in the future only after adequate warning and that protection would be provided for passengers and crews.

Despite the pledge, German policy shifted, notably toward ships plying the English channel. With instructions to regard all such vessels as troop ships, a German submarine torpedoed the French channel steamer *Sussex* in March 1916. Several Americans were seriously injured. Wilson delivered another ultimatum, and the Germans pledged again in May that no more neutral or belligerent merchantmen would be sunk without warning—provided the Americans held the Allies accountable for their violations of international law. Wilson rejected the condition, but for nine months the Germans kept their promise.

1916, a Year of Uncertainty

Although Wilson wanted the nation to remain neutral, a rising tide of sentiment called for direct participation in the war on the side of the Allies. Beginning in 1915 an increasing number of books and magazines sensationalized the threat of Germany's policies to the security of the United States. Hollywood producers joined the campaign with films depicting the horrors of a German invasion. Audiences were treated to scenes of goose-stepping Prussians marching up Broadway and spike-helmeted soldiers battering down the doors of the White House with their rifle butts. The kaiser was cast as the "Beast of Berlin," contemplating the conquest of America. Political leaders, among them Theodore Roosevelt and Henry Cabot Lodge, organized a "national preparedness" campaign to arouse the country to the need for a standing army. President Wilson was subjected to violent abuse for not upholding "American honor" more vigorously. Roosevelt became almost pathological in his denunciation of the "spineless mollycoddler" of 1600 Pennsylvania Avenue.

In his efforts to preserve the country's neutrality, Wilson attempted to mediate the war. Twice he sent his friend and unofficial advisor, Colonel Edward M. House, to Europe on peace missions. On the first, in early 1915, House tried unsuccessfully to persuade the English to give up their blockade and the Germans their submarine attacks. During the second mission House met again with Sir Edward Grey, the British foreign secretary, in February 1916. Together they drew up a memorandum calling on President Wilson to summon a peace conference "on hearing from France and England that the moment was opportune." If the Allied proposals for peace were not accepted by the Germans, America would enter the war against Germany. Wilson added the word "probably" to this last statement and endorsed the memorandum. Nothing came of the plan, however, for the British continued to believe that the Allies could win a military victory.

The uncertainties of the war eventually convinced Wilson that unarmed neutrality was not in the best interests of the country. The United States must prepare for war while it continued to seek peace. Moreover, he could not afford to give the Republicans the popular issue of national defense in the upcoming campaign. In December 1915 he presented Congress with a program for strengthening the army and navy, and in January and February he toured the nation to speak for preparedness. Huge parades demonstrated public support. That summer Congress passed a series of acts providing for moderate expansion of the army and rather extensive additions to the navy and merchant marine.

Wilson's attempts to resist the pressure for war were aided by the abatement of the German U-boat campaign, the strong isolationist feelings of many citizens, and American resentment of Great Britain's ruthless suppression of the Irish rebellion during Easter in 1916. The anglophobic Hearst newspapers described the behavior of British soldiers in Dublin as far worse than that of the Germans in Belgium. Anglo-American friction continued to increase during the summer and autumn of 1916, for immediately after the *Sussex* pledge the British had intensified their blockade of Germany. Their arbitrary restrictions on neutral trade became even more annoying. Mail from the United States was subjected to British censorship; American business firms suspected of trading with Germany through neutral nations were blacklisted and British subjects forbidden to trade with them.

In the election campaign of 1916, the Democrats capitalized on the neutralist sentiment with the slogan, "He kept us out of war." Wilson drew strong support for his reelection from Midwestern isolationists and other antiwar minority groups. His Republican opponent was Charles Evans Hughes, who was constantly embarrassed by the noisy prowar elements in his party, foremost among them the bellicose Theodore Roosevelt.[1] Midwestern Republican leaders, such as Senator La Follette of Wisconsin, were even more stubbornly determined to stay out of war than Wilson. Hughes should have been able to add together the Republican and Progressive votes of 1912, but because of the dissension in his party and Wilson's progressive reforms, he was defeated by a narrow margin.

Wilson's policy of neutrality had apparently been approved, even though public feeling increasingly favored intervention. But a number of crucial blunders by Germany in 1917 canceled out American neutralist sentiment and forced Wilson to decide for war.

ENTRY OF THE UNITED STATES INTO THE WAR

Germany's Blunders and the Decision for War

On January 31, 1917 the German government announced that unrestricted submarine warfare would be resumed and ordered U-boats to sink all vessels on sight, Allied and neutral, without warning. The kaiser's generals were convinced that victory could be achieved more quickly if Allied supply lines, particularly those from America, were cut. The Germans recognized that the United States would probably declare war, but they felt certain that United States troops would arrive in Europe too late to make any difference in the outcome. Admiral Alfred von Tirpitz, the kaiser's naval chief, assured His Majesty that German U-boats would prevent any American soldiers from setting foot on French soil.

President Wilson's reaction to Berlin's flagrant challenge was prompt and decisive. First, he broke off diplomatic relations. The staff of the United States embassy in Berlin was ordered home, and Germany's ambassador in Washington was handed his passport. German assets in the United States were frozen, and its shipping in the nation's harbors was con-

---

[1] Roosevelt had wanted the Republican nomination, but the Old Guard still resented his 1912 defection. He refused the designation of the delegates at the last Progressive party convention, meeting concurrently with the Republican, because he feared that dividing the anti-Wilson forces would ensure a Democratic victory.

Opposing leaders, Wilhelm II and Wilson. CULVER PICTURES

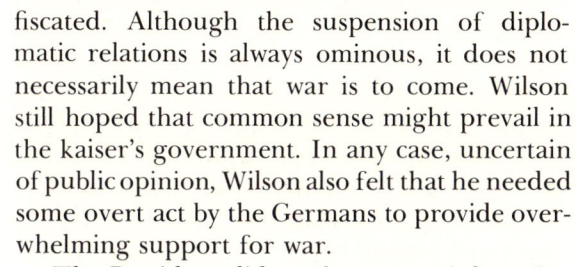

fiscated. Although the suspension of diplomatic relations is always ominous, it does not necessarily mean that war is to come. Wilson still hoped that common sense might prevail in the kaiser's government. In any case, uncertain of public opinion, Wilson also felt that he needed some overt act by the Germans to provide overwhelming support for war.

The President did not have to wait long for this justification. On March 1 newspapers published the story of the sensational Zimmermann note. Anticipating war with the United States, Alfred Zimmermann, the German foreign secretary, had sent a secret message to the German minister in Mexico. If war broke out, he was to urge the Mexican government to join the conflict on Germany's side to recover the "lost territory in Texas, New Mexico, and Arizona." Mexico was also to sound out Japan on the possibility of an attack on the United States. The note was a fantastic blunder, since Mexico was totally unprepared for war. The whole affair might have gone unnoticed, except that the British intelligence service had broken Germany's secret code and informed Wilson of the "stab in the back." The President ordered the contents of the Zimmermann note released to the press. Public anger over the incident was compounded in subsequent weeks by the torpedoing of five American merchant vessels. Now Wilson had the "overt acts" he needed.

Uniqueness of America's Role

On April 2, 1917 President Wilson appeared before Congress and called upon the American

The Climax and Ebb of Internationalism, 1914–1920   215

people to fight a war "for the ultimate peace of the world." In ringing tones he declared that the

"world must be made safe for democracy. Its peace must be planted upon the tested foundations of political liberty. We have no selfish ends to serve. We desire no conquest, no dominion. We seek no indemnities for ourselves, no material compensation for the sacrifices we shall freely make."

This was Wilson's greatest moment. His words expressed the shining idealism that has been a recurrent theme in United States history. In language as moving and fine as that of Jefferson and Lincoln, Wilson proposed that the United States wage war not for material gain but simply for the betterment of mankind. The President was calling upon the people to fight and to die for a purpose without precedent, the majestic principle of everlasting world peace. Four days later both houses overwhelmingly approved a resolution for war.[2]

In response to Wilson's plea, the nation sprang to arms with exhilarating enthusiasm. Although many did not fully comprehend the breadth and implications of Wilson's transcendent idealism, they nevertheless felt its impact. Thousands, if not millions, saw themselves as modern crusaders, marching to the liberation of the oppressed peoples of the Old World. Despite the horror of the already protracted conflict, Americans entered this most terrible war in history in a lighthearted spirit. They were convinced that once the thousands of brave American boys arrived on the western front, the hordes of German soldiers would soon be crushed.

For the first time in its history, the United States was intervening directly and forcibly in the affairs of Europe. The dicta of Washington, Jefferson, and Monroe had been abandoned. In joining Great Britain and France, however, the United States called itself not an "ally" but an "associated power." Thus some tiny semblance of separateness and independence of action was preserved.

The Home Front

Military Mobilization. Recruiting stations were swamped with volunteers the first weeks after war was declared, but military leaders feared that the numbers would eventually prove inadequate. In May 1917 Congress passed the Selective Service Act requiring all males between the ages of twenty-one and thirty-one to register with local draft boards for military service. The measure overcame stiff opposition from members of Congress who believed that enforced conscription was a violation of democratic principles. In previous wars the nation had relied upon volunteers, except for the disastrous Draft Act of 1863 which had been evaded or resisted with violence.

Even though the majority of the population supported the effort, the United States was woefully unprepared for the demands of modern warfare. When it entered the conflict, the nation had a regular army of only 200,000 men, most of whom were scattered throughout the West at Indian outposts. There were no training facilities ready for the multitudes of conscripts, soon to be in uniform—in fact, there were not enough uniforms. The army was in dire need of weapons and ammunition of every kind, from heavy artillery to small arms. The building of enough ships to carry troops and supplies to France was a tremendous task.

Both the government and the people attacked these problems with vigor. Training camps were hastily thrown up. Often there was no time and materials for constructing cantonments and barracks, and trainees had to live in

---

[2]The vote for war was far from unanimous. Six senators and fifty representatives voted against the declaration of war. Jeannette Rankin of Montana, the first woman elected to Congress, was among the fifty. Miss Rankin holds the special distinction of being the only representative to vote against participation in both world wars.

tent cities. Hastily trained soldiers, some of them with only six weeks of service, were hustled aboard transports to Europe. By November 1918 more than four million men had been inducted, and more than two million of them had been shipped "over there." Weapons, uniforms, and equipment that were lacking had to be supplied by the British and French; the British "tin hat" became the standard helmet of the American soldier.

Economic Mobilization. Wilson and his administration recognized that World War I was a "conflict of smokestacks" and that more than raw courage and armies of recruits were needed. With victory to be won as much in the factory as on the battlefield, industry had to be mobilized for war. President Wilson established the War Industries Board, an independent agency, to speed the conversion of factories to war production; to establish materials priorities, fix prices on raw materials, standardize products, and reduce waste; and to coordinate all wartime purchasing for the Allies and the United States. Bernard M. Baruch, a Wall Street financial wizard who served as chairman of the WIB, became virtually an "industrial dictator," answerable only to the President.

Wilson appointed Herbert Hoover to head an agency whose task it was to increase the production and decrease the consumption of food. Hoover had earlier acquired an international reputation as the efficient director of aid to suffering Belgians under German occupation. Preferring a voluntary system to enforced rationing and using propaganda skillfully, he prevailed upon Americans to cut down food consumption by changing their eating habits. Citizens were urged to observe "wheatless Mondays," "meatless Tuesdays," and "porkless Thursdays." From his office poured an unending stream of advice to housewives on how to use leftovers or how to bake "victory bread" without white flour. Homeowners raised vegetables in their own backyard "war gardens." City parks were converted into farms, cultivated by volunteers after their normal working day. "Hooverization" achieved impressive results. Despite the shortage of manpower in agriculture, the amount of food shipped to the Allies tripled in 1918. The mobilization of food resources was the most successful of the conversions of the economy to a wartime basis.

Other portions of the national economy were also placed under "czars" who were responsible to the President. After a monumental tie-up of the railroads in December 1916 and January 1917, the lines were "nationalized" under the direction of the "Czar of Transportation," William Gibbs McAdoo, who also served as Secretary of the Treasury and was, incidentally, Wilson's son-in-law. Fuel resources, principally oil and coal, were carefully regulated by Harry A. Garfield, a son of the former President.

Mobilization of shipbuilding was the least successful of the efforts to convert the economy to wartime production. An Emergency Fleet Corporation had been established as a government agency to build 12,000,000 tons of shipping, but because of the haste with which the program was undertaken, it was grossly inefficient. A total of $2,600,000,000 was spent, but most of the vessels were completed too late to be of much service. In its desperation to acquire the needed merchant marine, the Emergency Fleet Corporation ordered 518 ships made of wood and even experimented with several vessels constructed of reinforced concrete. Only by seizing interned German ships, buying neutral ships, and taking over all private shipping was the Corporation able to increase the available tonnage and reduce the submarine danger.

Expenses of the war were paid for in part by increasing taxes of all sorts—on personal incomes, inheritances, "excess profits," corporations, liquor and tobacco, amusements, and so on. But the principal source of revenue were the government bonds, known as "Liberty Loans," sold directly to the American people. To promote sales the government staged a high-pressure publicity campaign through newspapers, mass meetings, and movies. The task was made easier by the high interest rate that the government offered on Liberty Loans and later, in 1919, on Victory Bonds. From 1917 to 1919, about $11,000,000,000 was collected in taxes and over $20,000,000,000 through the sale of bonds.

Mobilization of Men's Minds. In early 1917 the government created the Committee on Public Information, headed by George Creel, an able and resourceful journalist. It was Creel's job to organize the effort to "sell" the war to the American public. Under his imaginative leadership a vast propaganda campaign was launched. Novelists, actors, opera stars, evangelists, college professors, journalists, and especially historians were called on to explain at mass meetings the nobleness of America's crusade against the Prussian warlords. To add further zest to the news, Creel readily invented stories about the heroism of American soldiers on the battlefield, before any had arrived in France, and about "clouds" of American planes in combat, even though there were no American-made planes in action at any time during the war.

Creel's activities were unnecessary and unfortunate. The nation's citizens, including the Irish-Americans and the German-Americans, were already loyal to the war effort. In later decades the crude propaganda and gross distortions foisted upon Americans by their own government were revealed to an immediately indignant public.

In order to repress criticism of the war effort and halt the activities of pacifists, Congress passed the Espionage and Sedition acts forbidding interference with the draft and virtually depriving Americans of free speech. Violators were severely punished with heavy fines and imprisonment. Union leader "Big Bill" Haywood was sentenced to twenty years for sedition, socialist Eugene V. Debs to ten years for delivering a speech that attacked capitalism. One of the most disturbing aspects of the war effort was the outburst of germanophobia. Persons of German birth or ancestry were subjected to persecution by overly zealous, hysterical neighbors. Those with Germanic surnames often found it advisable to alter their names. Schmidt was changed to Smith, Müller became Miller, and Schneider was anglicized to Taylor. The "hate fever" was carried to absurd extremes. People publicly smashed recordings of Wagner's operas, and orchestras found it unsafe to play the music of Beethoven and Mozart. Instruction in the German language was abolished in high schools and colleges. German textbooks and dictionaries were frequently burned in "patriotic" bonfires while those who watched the flames sang national hymns. Sauerkraut was renamed "liberty cabbage," the hamburger was called a "victory steak sandwich," and the wiener became known as a "hot dog."

CONSTRUCTING THE PEACE

The Military Crisis in Europe, 1917–1918

The United States entered the war none too soon. In the spring of 1917 the long stalemate on the western front was broken when the French suffered a decisive defeat in a major offensive in Champagne. Units of the French army were in a state of near mutiny, and all Allied peoples showed signs of deep weariness. On the eastern front the situation was even more perilous. German and Austrian armies had overrun Serbia. Although Rumania had joined the Allies in August 1916, the initial offensive of the Rumanian army collapsed in less than six weeks, and the capital, Bucharest, was occupied by German troops December 6.[3] In the meantime the Germans were eventually able to check the offensives of their principal eastern antagonist, Russia, with their own sledgehammer attacks. By August 1917 the Russian armies were in full retreat.

[3]In the Treaty of Bucharest (May 7, 1918) Rumania was forced to cede Dobruja to Bulgaria and to turn the Carpathian passes over to Austria-Hungary. The Germans acquired a ninety-year lease on the Rumanian oil wells.

First in War, First in Peace

Russian Surrender. Internally, the Russian nation was in a state of chaos. The transportation system had broken down, and throughout the country people were starving. Bread riots were staged in the major cities. In March 1917 Tsar Nicholas II was overthrown, and the Romanov dynasty, which had ruled the country since the seventeenth century, came to an end. Alexander Kerensky was named prime minister of the provisional government in July and attempted to keep Russia in the war, but the nation's resistance was almost exhausted. In November 1917 he was overthrown, and the Bolsheviks (Communists), headed by N. Lenin, seized power. Lenin's policy was to take Russia out of the war as quickly as possible. In December an armistice was concluded on the eastern front, and in March 1918 negotiations with the Germans were completed at Brest-Litovsk. The conditions of surrender were humiliating, however, for huge areas of Russia were placed under German control.

The Last Offensive. Even before the Russian giant withdrew completely from the war, the Germans were formulating plans for ultimate victory on the western front. They made little effort to hide their intentions. Throughout the winter of 1917 and 1918, troop trains rumbled westward across central Europe, carrying veteran German armies released from the Russian campaign. The German High Command made it clear that a mighty offensive to crush the Allies would be launched in the spring. In the meantime the question uppermost in the minds of Allied statesmen and generals was whether the United States could do the impossible—mobilize an army, equip it, and move it across 3,000 miles of ocean and into the trenches befor the Germans launched their all-out offensive. The leaders were not optimistic.

In spite of the difficulties that had to be overcome, by early 1918 the American Expeditionary Forces (AEF) were arriving in France in large numbers (at the rate of 30,000 a month). Commanded by General John J. Pershing, the United States forces were at first dispersed among the Allied armies as replacements, but later, at Pershing's insistence that they act as a separate army, they took over a large sector of the western front near Verdun.

In March the German offensive began with a powerful attack along the Somme battlefield in the British sector. The British army was sent reeling backward almost forty miles but finally checked the German advance before it reached Amiens, an important rail center. In April a second offensive farther north near Armentières drove the British back seventeen miles before the Germans stopped attacking because they had few reserves. The French felt the fury of the third German thrust along the sector between Noyen and Reims, yielding thirteen miles the first day, May 27. Three days later the Germans again reached the Marne and Paris was threatened, but stubborn Allied resistance, stiffened by units of the AEF at Château-Thierry, broke the force of the German offensive within a week.

On July 15 the weary and depleted German troops attacked once again near Reims. By that time not only were the French and Americans holding their own—the Germans advanced only three miles across the Marne—but three days later they were able to mount a counterattack. In August it was evident that the tide was running with the Allies. Their attacks gradually became a sustained offensive. On September 12 the American First Army, in its first major assignment as an independent force, attacked the Saint Mihiel salient southeast of Verdun. The deep extension of the German line was wiped out in two days of fighting. Then in late September, as part of the last Allied assault all along the western front, the AEF launched a strong offensive in the Meuse-Argonne sector. Lasting forty-seven days, it was one of the fiercest battles in American military history. More than a million Americans participated in the attack, and casualties were severe, about ten per cent. The United States forces reached their objective, the Sedan-Mézières railroad, the first week in November.

The Climax and Ebb of Internationalism, 1914–1920

German shock troops in trenches in France, 1918.

But the Central Powers had already begun to collapse. Bulgaria surrendered on September 30, and the Ottoman Turks signed an armistice on October 30. On November 3 Austria capitulated to the Italians. The kaiser fled to neutral Holland on November 10, and Germany was proclaimed a republic. On November 11 the guns finally fell silent on the western front as the Germans agreed to an armistice with the victorious Allies.

Costs of the War. Military buffs will long debate how decisive was the armed intervention of the United States in World War I. There seems to be no final answer to this question, but undoubtedly the presence of the AEF in France hastened the defeat of beleaguered Germany, already starved by the Allied blockade and weakened by the war of attrition on the western front. Of greater significance is the question how a medium-sized nation such as Germany, with an area comparable to Montana and assisted by three feeble allies, could have survived for four years against so many powerful adversaries.

In any event, the most terrible war in history was over. The cost in human and physical resources is almost impossible to comprehend. Americans felt that the United States had lost heavily. Nearly 50,000 Americans were killed in battle in the second most costly war the country had yet fought. But compared to the American dead were 1,400,000 French soldiers killed in action out of a population of only 40,000,000. Although the proportion may

*"The Yanks are coming, the Yanks are coming . . .
And we won't come back till it's over over there."*
George M. Cohan, "Over There"*

THE BETTMANN ARCHIVE

seem small, these losses represented the flower of French manhood, for it is always the young, the strong, the brave, and the intelligent who are slaughtered on the battlefield. In addition, 3,000,000 Frenchmen were permanently maimed, had limbs shot away, were blinded, or had their lungs scarred by poison gas.

Other nations suffered comparable losses. The British killed in action totaled 950,000, the Germans 1,600,000, and the Russians 1,700,000. Even more shocking is the realization that many of these nations were to lose again and more heavily in the next ordeal of general war twenty years later.

It is difficult to estimate civilian casualties during the First World War. Certainly, millions died in air raids and artillery barrages and through starvation, malnutrition, and disease. A terrible influenza epidemic swept across Europe and the United States in late 1918, taking an additional toll of 10,000,000 lives. The financial cost was also staggering. For France, it was $26,000,000,000, Germany $39,000,000,000, the British Empire $38,000,000,000, and the United States $22,000,000,000. Against such a backdrop of economic and human carnage a peace settlement had to be made.

Negotiating the Peace Settlement

When a coalition of nations has defeated an enemy, there is almost always a squabble among the victors about how the peace settlement should be made. The differences that separated the Allies at the end of the First World War were further complicated by the deep division in American public opinion regarding the role that the United States was to play.

The Fourteen Points. In his 1917 war message President Wilson had stated the broad, visionary purpose of the United States, as he perceived it. Nine months later, on January 8, 1918, he delivered a carefully prepared address to Congress, in which he enumerated in precise terms the nation's war aims. These goals comprised his famous "Fourteen Points,"

---

*Copyright 1917 by Leo Feist Inc., New York, New York. Copyright renewed 1945. Used by permission.

The Climax and Ebb of Internationalism, 1914–1920

which can be summarized briefly as follows.

1. Open covenants or agreements, openly arrived at. (In other words, treaties should be negotiated openly, and the public should be constantly informed of progress. There must be no secret treaties or clauses.)

2. Freedom of navigation on the high seas in peace and in war. (The oceans belong to all peoples who choose to use them. Wilson qualified this principle, however, by recognizing the legality of a naval blockade under international law.)

3. Elimination of tariff barriers among nations.

4. Reduction of armaments and military forces to make the occurrence of another international war unlikely. (The only task of military forces should be to preserve internal peace.)

5. Granting a voice to colonial peoples in determining their own destiny. (This is the famous principle of "self-determination.")

6. Evacuation of all Russian territory by German troops.

7. Restoration of Belgium as an independent state.

8. German evacuation of occupied France and the return of Alsace-Lorraine to France.

9. Readjustment of frontiers in northern Italy "along clearly recognizable lines of nationality" so that Italians would be under Italian rule.

10. Offering the heterogeneous nationalities of Austria-Hungary autonomy or complete independence.

11. Evacuation of German and Austrian troops from Rumania, Serbia, and Montenegro, and granting Serbia free and clear access to the sea.

12. Self-determination for the peoples of the Turkish Empire and the establishment of the Straits (the Dardanelles and the Bosporus) as an international waterway open to all nations.

13. Establishment of an independent Polish state with free and secure access to the Baltic Sea.

14. Formation of a general association of nations to guarantee the political independence of all nations and to preserve international peace.

When Wilson first outlined his Fourteen Points, and indeed even before he sent American troops to France in June 1917, he knew of secret treaties among the Allies that would stand in the way of a reasonable peace settlement. At the end of 1917, the Bolshevik government in Russia released the text of these treaties to the world, and they were published in American newspapers. These secret treaties had been concluded both among the major Allies and with powers such as Japan, Italy, and Rumania to induce them to join the Allied side. France had been promised Alsace-Lorraine and the rich Saar Basin; Great Britain would receive most of Germany's colonies and acquire control over much of the Near East; Italy expected to take from Austria-Hungary the Trentino and the Southern Tyrol, to acquire control of the Adriatic Sea, and to enlarge her African colonies; Japan was to receive the German holdings in Shantung province; Rumania would be given Transylvania. But these provisions had been drawn up by men of position and power. In early 1918 the war-weary common man of Europe read of the Fourteen Points and was heartened by their promise that a better world would emerge after the sacrifices and horror of the conflict. Those who throughout the world struggled for self-determination found new hope. In the last weeks of the war, Wilson encouraged the Germans to surrender on the basis of the Fourteen Points and forced the Allies to accept them, with some modification,[4] as the terms for the armistice by threatening to make a separate peace with Germany.

At home, however, there was evidence that not all Americans shared the President's high

---

[4]Great Britain insisted that the second point guaranteeing freedom of the seas must not restrict its naval supremacy. Invaded territories were to receive full compensation for all damages done "by land, by sea, and from the air."

moral purpose or accepted his specific Fourteen Points. Wilson had not consulted the people before formulating his peace proposals,[5] nor did he ask for congressional approval. He simply assumed that he had the right and the responsibility to formulate the nation's goals. To reinforce his position as spokesman, Wilson called upon the voters in October 1918 to support the Democratic party in the coming congressional elections. A Democratic victory, he declared, would constitute a mandate to construct a just and lasting peace based on his views. The Americans who went to the polls on November 5, however, returned a Republican majority to both houses of Congress. The outcome of the election was not necessarily a repudiation of Wilson, for the choices of many voters were determined largely by local issues and by personalities. But the President had very clearly not received the mandate that he had expected.

Selection of the Peace Commission. Despite the election returns, Wilson still assumed that he had the support of the American people and proceeded to choose peace delegates as he had originally planned. Selected in the belief that they would support him, or at least not oppose his position, were Robert Lansing, the Secretary of State; Tasker H. Bliss, a retired general; Wilson's close friend Colonel House; and, as a slight bow to bipartisanship, Henry L. White, a skilled diplomat and Republican. For experts to advise the United States delegation, Wilson chose James T. Shotwell, professor of history at Columbia; Charles Homer Haskins, renowned medieval scholar from Harvard; and Christian Gauss, professor of literature and humanities from Princeton. David Hunter Miller, an expert on international law, and Walter Lippmann, a brilliant young journalist, were also included.

[5]The Fourteen Points were suggested to Wilson by The Inquiry, a group of scholars and publicists chosen by Colonel House to advise the State Department on the peace settlement.

Notably excluded from the delegation were politicians of any stature. Although the upper chamber would ultimately have to approve the peace treaty, not a single senator was invited, not even one from Wilson's own party. Especially irked were the Republican senators, now a majority, many of whom were in general agreement with the President and were well qualified to advise him on foreign policy. In all likelihood Wilson ignored the Senate because he would have been obliged to appoint Henry Cabot Lodge, who would soon be chairman of the Foreign Relations Committee and whom Wilson disliked.

Wilson's decision to attend the peace conference in person also caused problems, for at that time no president had left American territory while in office. The press criticized him roundly, advising him to stay home and leave the treaty making to the skilled delegates and advisers. By remaining in Washington, Wilson could have exerted control over the general proceedings and yet avoided exhausting his energy and vast prestige in troublesome details and dangerous disputes. Moreover, he could have spared himself personal confrontation with the skilled European statesmen who were to wreck his program.

The Paris Conference—Setting the Stage

The President arrived in Europe on December 13, 1918. Since the conference was not to begin in Paris until January, he spent part of the time visiting cities in western Europe to ascertain for himself European public opinion. Everywhere he was greeted with overwhelming enthusiasm and even adulation. Wilson became the hero of the moment and for some a savior of mankind, for Europeans believed that in him the New World had finally come to liberate the Old. Wilson symbolized the youthful America, a St. George ready to do battle against the "scourge of war." Mayors kissed his hand and children tossed flowers in his path. Candles were lighted for the President in cathedrals, and in homes pictures of him clipped from newspapers were displayed next to the crucifix. Few leaders in history have seemed to personify so completely the hopes of men.

On January 15, 1919 representatives of the twenty-seven victorious Allied nations sat down to the hard business of making the peace. Deliberations of the assembly, known as the Preliminary Peace Conference,[6] were held in the Palais de Justice, a spacious convention hall in Paris. In addition to the large official delegations, there were observers from neutral powers, battalions of news reporters, pleaders of special causes, adventurers, religious fanatics, hangers-on, and pickpockets. Since it was impossible to accomplish very much in the noise and confusion, the delegations of the ten major powers withdrew for private talks away from the convention atmosphere. Even these arrangements proved cumbersome. "The Big Four"—President Wilson, Prime Minister David Lloyd George of Great Britain, Premier Georges Clemenceau of France, and Premier Vittorio Orlando of Italy—eventually found it necessary to meet in comparative isolation, either at Clemenceau's residence or at the United States Embassy. There they conducted the real business of structuring the peace treaty, receiving the advice of their experts and hearing the pleas of the delegations from lesser powers. But the Big Four dwindled to the Big Three for a time after Orlando disagreed with Wilson and angrily returned to Italy. It had become evident to Orlando that Wilson intended to ignore the promises of extensive territorial compensation made to Italy by Britain and France in the secret Treaty of London, negotiated earlier in 1915 when Italy joined the Allies.

Conflicting Aims. Whatever the agreements made in the pressure to obtain an armistice, not all the Allied leaders honored them as the goals of the peace treaty. Wilson was of course still determined to establish a peace with justice, based on his Fourteen Points. Firmly opposed to the traditional territorial rewards for victorious nations, and to the numerous secret wartime treaties by which the Allies had promised one another concessions at its end, he pressed vigorously for the concept of self-determination and the formation of an international league to keep the peace. At first, Lloyd George paid lip service to Wilson's principles, but as the conference progressed he concentrated on obtaining whatever he could for Great Britain. Clemenceau sharply opposed Wilson's program from the beginning. The French premier was principally interested in forging a strong military alliance of Great Britain, the United States, and France to prevent Germany from regaining power. Clemenceau also wanted colonial territory and heavy monetary compensation from Germany. He considered Germany "a guilty nation" which must be humbled and forced to pay for the tremendous costs of the war. Although the Italians supported Wilson's idea of a league of nations, they also wanted to acquire new territory by the terms of the peace treaty. The Japanese were willing to support Wilson only if their country was established as the preeminent power in the Far East. The lesser powers too had conflicting goals and aspirations, ranging from the acquisition of territories and other forms of compensation to the establishment of Wilson's idealistic League of Nations.

As the conference progressed, it became clear that Lloyd George and Clemenceau were determined to "cut Wilson down to size," in spite of the power of the United States and the personal prestige of its very doctrinaire President. When the British prime minister, extremely successful in gaining extensive territory for his nation, was soundly criticized at home for not obtaining more, he is alleged to have exclaimed in sardonic disgust, "How can you people expect me to do any better when I had

---

[6]The formal peace conference convened only briefly, opening May 7 with the presentation of the completed treaty to the German representatives.

First in War, First in Peace

Napoleon sitting on my left hand and Jesus Christ on the right?" Clemenceau expressed his contempt for Wilson's principles in excellent English, often liberally sprinkled with Anglo-Saxon obscenities. As Clemenceau put it, "Mr. Wilson bores me with his Fourteen Points; why, God Almight has only ten." The bitter and sarcastic old Frenchman (he was seventy-eight years of age at the time) proved a tough antagonist to the strong-willed American President. The resulting treaty was to be an unfortunate and unsatisfactory compromise between the lofty idealism of Wilson and the cold, narrow pragmatism of Clemenceau.

The Absentees. German delegates arrived in Paris on April 29, full of optimism because their country had surrendered with the understanding that the peace would follow Wilson's Fourteen Points. They had fully expected to be allowed participation in the conference, but they were quickly shut up in a hotel and treated almost as prisoners. On May 7 the final draft of the treaty was presented to the Germans. At no time had they been consulted or even informed of the progress of the negotiations except through the newspapers. The other Central Powers—Austria-Hungary, Bulgaria, and Ottoman Turkey—were treated with equal disdain.

The Allies had also not invited Russia to participate, even though the losses the Russians had suffered in killed and wounded were greater than those of any other people who had fought in the war. Wilson, Lloyd George, and Clemenceau all considered Bolshevism dangerous and took the position that the Russians had forfeited their right to join the conference by yielding to Germany in the Treaty of Brest-Litovsk. Even if an invitation had been issued, it is unlikely that the Lenin government would have accepted it. The Bolshevik leaders, who were intent on their own plans for world revolution, would not have been willing to compromise by "collusion" with the "imperialists." Thus the principle of a just peace was from the very beginning seriously damaged by the exclusion of two of the great powers as well as of lesser nations.

The Peace of Paris

Actually, a number of separate peace treaties were signed in or around Paris in 1919 and 1920. The particular treaty settling the fate of Austria, and expressly forbidding the country to unite with Germany, was signed at Saint Germain. The Treaty of Neuilly reduced the borders of Bulgaria, the Treaty of Trianon those of Hungary. The rearrangement of the Ottoman Empire (Turkey) was accomplished by the Treaty of Sèvres. By far the most important of the treaties, however, was the one signed at Versailles in June 1919. These agreements for the most complicated peace ever made are all loosely grouped together for convenience and referred to as the Peace of Paris.

Territorial Provisions. By the terms of the Versailles Treaty, Germany was stripped of its extensive colonies. The Pacific islands north of the equator were turned over to Japan, and those south of the equator were awarded to Australia, except for German Samoa which was given to New Zealand. Germany's colonies in West Africa were divided between Great Britain and France. The large German colony in East Africa (now part of the nation of Tanzania) was turned over to Great Britain, and German Southwest Africa went to the Union of South Africa. Both Cameroon and Togo were divided between Britain and France. Germany's suzerainty over the large Chinese province of Shantung was given not to China but to Japan.

In each of these decisions, Wilson's principle of self-determination was clearly violated. To avoid complete repudiation of his fifth point, the lands were given to the Allied countries as "mandates," not as outright possessions. Presumably, the ruling powers would supervise each territory under the authority of the League of Nations and prepare its population for independence. Although this tactic was

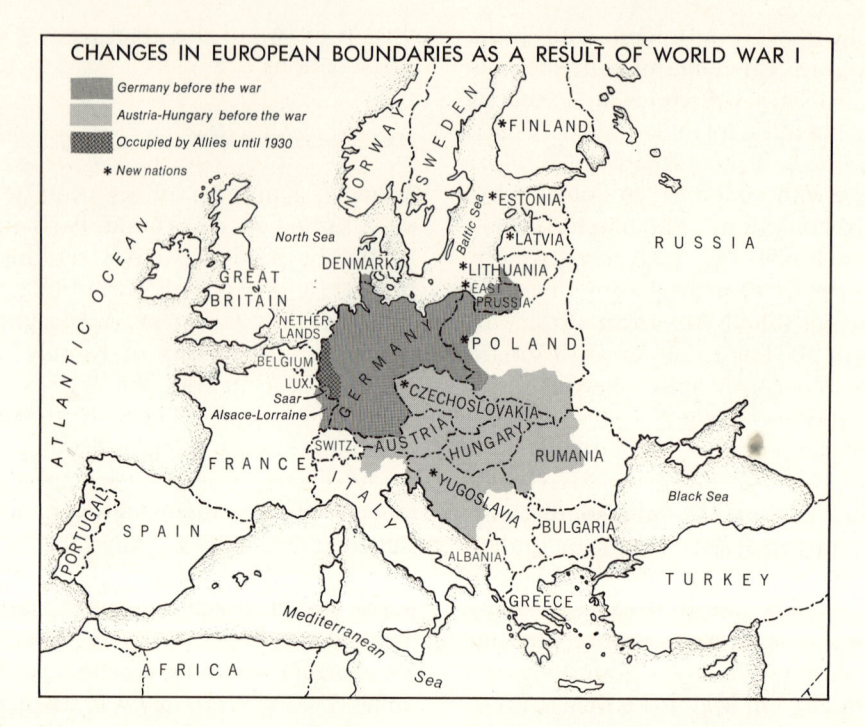

CHANGES IN EUROPEAN BOUNDARIES AS A RESULT OF WORLD WAR I

- Germany before the war
- Austria-Hungary before the war
- Occupied by Allies until 1930
- * New nations

somewhat of a fiction to satisfy the sensibilities of the Wilsonian idealists, many of the nations did at least make a show of preparing their new subjects for eventual freedom.

Germany also lost heavily in Europe. The province of Alsace-Lorraine was returned to France, without offering its people an opportunity to vote whether they preferred to belong to France or Germany. Again the Wilsonian principle of self-determination was violated, although the population would probably have selected France if a vote had been taken. Other scraps of German territory were awarded to Belgium and to neutral Denmark. The small but coal-rich Saar Basin in western Germany was placed under the direct authority of the League of Nations, but for fifteen years France would be allowed the output of its mines. Then its future status was to be determined by plebiscite.

In accordance with Wilson's wishes, a Polish state was re-created in eastern Europe. The earlier independent Poland had in the eighteenth century been ruthlessly parceled out to her aggressive neighbors—Russia, Austria, and Prussia. In order to provide the new Poland with access to the Baltic Sea, the conferees took additional territory from Germany, dividing the defeated nation into two parts, the main section and a rump area known as East Prussia, separated by the so-called Polish Corridor. Yet there were millions of German-speaking people in this strip, particularly in urban areas, who did not want to be under Poland's rule. At the northern end of the Polish Corridor, the port of Danzig, whose population consisted almost entirely of Germans, was established as a "free city" under the supervision of the League of Nations; both Germany and Poland were granted free use of its harbor facilities. Little did the participants in the Paris Conference of 1919 realize that twenty years later the Second World War would begin over the problems caused by the creation of Danzig and the Polish Corridor.

Although the reduction of Germany was sizable and severe, it was mild by comparison to the treatment accorded Austria-Hungary, the

First in War, First in Peace

former Hapsburg dual monarchy, which was eliminated altogether. In its place an independent, land-locked Austria, with a population of almost seven million German-speaking people, and a small, also land-locked, Hungary was established. The eastern hub of Hungary, called Transylvania, inhabited by millions of Magyars, was transferred to Rumania as a reward for her support of the Allies during the war. Serbia, Montenegro, and other larger areas of the former Austria-Hungary were joined to form the new nation Yugoslavia, with the Serbian monarch its designated king.

The most interesting readjustment was made in the northern parts of the former Austria-Hungary. Czech (Bohemian) nationalists had long campaigned for independence under the leadership of Thomas Masaryk, and during the war Czechs had abandoned their Hapsburg rulers by the thousands to fight valiantly with the Allies. The Slovaks, formerly ruled by Hungary, also desired their independence. At first, the Big Three considered creating two independent states of Czechia and Slovakia. Then they decided that the two peoples should be welded into the single state of Czechoslovakia, even though a deep cultural chasm separated the Czechs from the Slovaks. To provide Czechoslovakia with a "natural geographic frontier," the Big Three spliced to it a fringe area in the west called the Sudetenland. The crest of the Erzgebirge Mountains gave Czechoslovakia a natural and defensible boundary. The fact that three million Germans lived in the Sudetenland was ignored, but in later years Hitler would destroy Czechoslovakian independence for the sake of this population.

The treaty makers at Paris also recognized the independence of Finland, Lithuania, Latvia, and Estonia, four nations on the Baltic Sea which had formerly been part of Russia. Bessarabia, a strip of Russian land north of the Danube River, was awarded to Rumania. Tiny Bulgaria paid a heavy price for being on the losing side. The one wedge of Bulgar territory bordering on the Aegean Sea, part of the area known as Thrace, was handed to Greece, and a small enclave of land on the Black Sea, called Dobruja, was turned back to Rumania.

The Ottoman Empire (Turkey), in an extensive reduction in territory, was confined to the Anatolian Peninsula and shorn of almost all its non-Turkish-speaking peoples in the Middle East. Arab chieftains, all members of the Hashemite family, were awarded rule of these former Turkish lands because they had collaborated with the glamorous British desert leader, Colonel T. E. Lawrence, who during the war had helped organize the Arab revolt against the Turks. The patriarch of the Hashemites, Sharif Hussein, was in 1916 proclaimed king of Hejaz, a long strip of land on the Red Sea coast of the Arabian Peninsula, and Hussein's firstborn son, Emir Faisal, received Mesopotamia (Iraq) as his domain in 1921. That same year Trans-Jordan, carved out of the desert by British mapmakers, was given to Faisal's brother Abdullah. His grandson Hussein rules this artificially created nation today.

Iraq and Trans-Jordan were both mandates of Great Britain. Palestine was also mandated to the British, who intended to establish in at least part of the sacred soil of Abraham and Moses a future homeland for the Jews. The ancient biblical land of Syria, from which Lebanon would soon be detached and made a separate country, was turned over to France as a mandate.

No international settlement in history has made more extensive changes in boundaries than did the Peace of Paris. Whole nations were submerged or reorganized with new and unfamiliar names; countries unknown before 1914 were formed. As the delegates at the Paris Peace Conference redrew the maps of Europe and Asia, and established new governments, entire populations were transferred, often without their approval, to other nations. The names invented for the new countries were sometimes in contradiction to political, social, and economic realities. Conflicting claims and prior agreements made the task of the political

The Climax and Ebb of Internationalism, 1914–1920

engineers at Paris complicated, if not impossible. Many of the political oddities that were products of the conference table still exist today. Amazingly enough, a few of the countries, such as Yugoslavia and Iraq, have emerged as viable nations with hopeful futures.

Economic and Military Settlements. One of the most vicious and controversial clauses written into the treaty signed at Versailles was Article 231, the "war guilt clause," which compelled Germany to accept complete responsibility for the war. It is difficult to understand why Wilson, with his sense of justice, was willing to agree to this provision. The German people would not forget in years to come this deeply unjust, unrealistic, and completely arbitrary act. Clemenceau was particularly insistent about including Article 231 in the Versailles Treaty to justify his plan to levy heavy enough reparations on Germany to pay the total cost of the war; figures exceeding $100,000,000,000 were casually discussed. Wilson refused to demand any reparations for the United States. Moreover, he exacted a compromise whereby Germany was to pay the total cost of the war to Belgium but to the other Allies only amounts that would cover damages to civilians and their property and future pensions to Allied soldiers. The total reparation bill, which was set in May 1921 by the Reparations Commission, was $33,000,000,000, well beyond Germany's capacity to pay. The German debt, most of which was in fact never met, was to become a source of serious political controversy in later decades, contributing to the increasing estrangement of the United States from its wartime allies. Only Bulgaria of the other Central Powers was assessed reparations.

Added humiliations to the new German republic were the decisions that the Rhineland should be occupied by the Allies for fifteen years and that this area plus a belt thirty miles wide on the right bank of the Rhine was to be demilitarized. Conscription was forbidden. The German army must be limited to 100,000 men and the navy to six warships and small surface vessels. Germany was to have no submarines and the warships could weigh no more than 10,000 tons. Despite Wilson's plea, the victorious powers refused to accept similar reductions in their own military and naval forces.

The League of Nations. Of Wilson's Fourteen Points the closest to his heart and the most important was his proposal for a general association, or league, of nations empowered to maintain world peace. The President himself helped draw up the Covenant (charter) of the League of Nations, structuring it somewhat in the Western parliamentary tradition. Its legislative functions were to be performed by an Assembly, or lower house, in which each member state had one vote; and by a Council, or upper house, consisting of one representative from each of the great powers—France, Great Britain, Italy, Japan, and the United States—as permanent members and four (later more) from smaller nations holding seats on a nonpermanent basis. A Secretariat, established to perform what may be loosely described as the executive function, was charged with keeping records, arranging for meetings, supervising mandated territories, and enforcing League statutes within its very limited power. According to the plan, member nations were to be assessed dues in accordance with their ability to pay.

Geneva, Switzerland, was designated as the permanent headquarters of the League, The Hague, in the Netherlands, as the location for the judicial branch or Permanent Court of International Justice. Nations were permitted to apply for membership, but they could also withdraw from the League at any time after giving two years' notice.

The most controversial clause in the League Covenant was Article X, which stated that member nations would "undertake to respect and preserve as against external aggression the territorial integrity and existing political independence of all Members of the League." This provision seemed to indicate that the League could call upon any member nation to supply military forces to do its bidding, and it was this clause that was to draw the principal criticism of Wilson's opponents and of isolationist groups in the United States. The only other physical weapons at the disposal of the League were "economic sanctions," whereby the League could call upon member states to establish an economic boycott of any offending power. It was Wilson's hope that the League would act as a great forum of world opinion and that members would rely primarily on moral suasion rather than physical force. The French had proposed an international police force under League direction, but this idea was rejected. At best, the League was a feeble political organism, possessing even less real authority than the United States when it was governed by the Articles of Confederation.

Signing the Treaty. The Treaty of Versailles was signed on June 28, 1919, five years to the day after the assassination of Archduke Franz Ferdinand, in a ceremony held in the mirrored ballroom of the magnificent palace built by King Louis XIV. This was a special humiliation imposed upon the Germans by Premier Clemenceau. Forty-eight years earlier the German Empire had been proclaimed in the same Hall of Mirrors. When the German delegates were first shown the draft of the treaty in May, they had denounced it bitterly as a violation of the armistice terms and a betrayal of Wilson's Fourteen Points, the basis on which the Central Powers had laid down their arms. Count von Brockdorff-Rantzau, the delegation leader, refused to sign away the honor of his country and resigned his position, but a warning from Marshal Ferdinand Foch that the Allied armies were poised on the Rhine ready to occupy the entire fatherland left the Germans no choice. A new commission was appointed and signed the treaty under solemn protest.

The Struggle over Ratification

Early in July Woodrow Wilson hurried back to the United Staes to submit the document to the Senate for approval. Keenly aware of the injustices done and brokenhearted that his Fourteen Points had been disregarded, he clung to the hope that in the long run the League of Nations and time itself would eventually heal the inequities of the Paris settlements.

The Wilson-Lodge Feud. At the hands of the Senate, however, Wilson was to meet a final and shattering defeat when he attempted to have the treaty approved. Henry Cabot Lodge, now chairman of the Senate Foreign Relations Committee, would prove to be as wily and tough an opponent as Clemenceau.

The origins of the Lodge-Wilson feud are obscure. On the surface it would appear that the two leaders had much in common. Both were intellectuals; Lodge had been a professor of history while Wilson was teaching political science. Nor was Lodge an isolationist, for he had been a close friend of Theodore Roosevelt and a warm supporter of Roosevelt's policies of internationalism. Yet, like Wilson, Lodge was obstinate and willful, and he shared Roosevelt's bitterness over Wilson's victory in the 1912 election. He also shared Roosevelt's contempt for Wilson's "spineless" idealism and was especially irked that the President had excluded senators from the treaty-making delegation. Wilson, in turn, regarded his Boston Brahmin opponent as a shallow-minded political opportunist.

Stiffening Opposition. Even without Lodge, Wilson had to contend with a hard core of powerful, hostile senators who had been opposed from the beginning to the provisions of the Treaty of Versailles. These isolationists were known as "bitter-enders," "irreconcilables," and "the battalion of death" to the press. Many of them, such as Hiram Johnson of California, "Fighting Bob" La Follette of Wisconsin, and William E. Borah of Idaho, were old progressives who were not without sympathy for Wilson's programs of domestic reform. Yet they regarded Article X of the League Covenant as committing the United States to the solution of problems that were of no conern to the nation. Standing firmly in the Jeffersonian tradition of no entangling alliances, they considered the proposal a surrender of national sovereignty to "mongrelized internationalism," a violation of the Constitution, and a betrayal of the Monroe Doctrine. In their eyes Europe was corrupt and politically and socially ill, as of 1919 with the disease of Bolshevism in particular.

While the Senate Foreign Relations Committee held prolonged hearings on the treaty, listening to opinions from "the man-in-the-street" as well as experts, other rumblings of opposition became more vocal. Irish-Americans viewed the proposed League of Nations as a dastardly British plot against the United States, for Great Britain and her dominions (Canada, Union of South Africa, New Zealand, and Australia) would have five seats in the League Assembly and the United States only one seat. German-Americans considered Wilson a betrayer because he had accepted the injustices that the Treaty of Versailles inflicted on their fatherland. Italian-Americans felt that the treaty cheated Italy of territory rightfully belonging to it.

As the hot summer of 1919 wore on, Wilson recognized that public opinion was turning against the League. Hoping to revive support, the President embarked on a nationwide speaking tour to carry his message directly to the people. In oppressive September weather Wilson delivered thirty-six major addresses before large audiences in twenty-two days. In addition, he spoke on an impromptu basis from the rear of the presidential train and made numerous other personal appearances. At first the reaction of the public was restrained, but as the tour progressed through the West the President's shining idealism and eloquence aroused heartwarming enthusiasm. Traveling right behind Wilson, however, were the irreconcilables Hiram Johnson and William E. Borah. As a self-constituted "truth team," these hard-bitten isolationists followed the President from city to city and, on the day after he had spoken, denounced the League and the Treaty of Versailles.

Wilson's Defeat. By September 25 Wilson had reached the limit of his endurance. He was worn out physically and mentally, for he had never completely recovered from a severe flu attack suffered while he was in Paris. In Pueblo, Colorado, he collapsed. That night, with the shades drawn, the presidential special train sped back toward Washington and all future public appearances were canceled. A few days later Wilson suffered a stroke which temporarily paralyzed portions of his face and body.

In the meantime, Senator Lodge was recommending to the Senate approval of the League of Nations and the Treaty of Versailles—qualified, however, by exactly fourteen reservations, a grim touch of irony on his part. If enacted, the reservations would have seriously limited United States participation in the League.

Wilson, from his sick bed in the White House, denounced Lodge and his reservations, demanding that loyal supporters vote against the Lodge proposals and any other plans to limit United States obligations to the League. When the reservations came to a vote in the Senate on November 19, the Wilsonian Democrats, surprisingly enough, were joined by the bitter-enders in defeating the Lodge compromises. A resolution to ratify the treaty without any reservations was also defeated. The issue came before the Senate again on March 19, 1920, at which time some Wilsonian Democrats, arguing that limited membership in the League based on the Lodge reservations was better than none at all, broke with the President and voted for the treaty with a revised set of reservations. Their votes were not enough. In the end the Senate refused to ratify the Treaty of Versailles and thereby rejected membership in the League of Nations.

The struggle appeared over. The adamant "all or nothing" position of the President and the hostile Republican majority in the Senate had made any compromise impossible and guaranteed the defeat of Wilson's program. But the President still did not give up. He called upon the American people for a final verdict on the League. (Other aspects of the Treaty of Versailles were by now more or less ignored.) The presidential election of 1920, Wilson declared, would be a solemn referendum on the question. He insisted that the Democratic candidates for President and Vice President, Governor James M. Cox of Ohio and Assistant Secretary of the Navy Franklin D. Roosevelt of New York, make League membership the central issue of the campaign. Although Cox and Roosevelt loyally supported Wilson, interest in the League had waned. The campaign tended to focus on such domestic issues as the high cost of living and the fear of radicalism. Senator Warren G. Harding, the Republican nominee and at best a lukewarm internationalist, won a smashing victory over Governor Cox, who received only thirty-four per cent of the vote. The issue of League membership was now dead, and Wilson had been completely defeated. On July 2, 1921 Congress passed a joint resolution officially terminating the war with Germany and Austria-Hungary.

The Historical Controversy. The Treaty of Versailles and the effect that United States membership would have had on the League of Nations have been much debated ever since their rejection by the Senate. Blame for the failure of the treaty and of the League has been placed in varying degrees on Wilson, Lloyd George, Clemenceau, and Lodge. According to many historians, the personality defects of Wilson—his willfulness, messiah complex, and failure to face political realities—were responsible. Others have emphasized the cruel accident of his illness during the nationwide tour. If only his health had held up, this group argues, Wilson could have swayed public opinion to support his position. Still other observers have characterized Clemenceau and Lloyd George as narrow-minded, self-seeking politicians who thwarted Wilson's grand purpose. Enamored with the devil theory, another group of historians has gone so far as to say that Henry Cabot Lodge's reservations, rather than Hitler, brought on the Second World War.

In the opinion of the authors of this textbook, neither the world nor the United States was ready to accept the concept of international cooperation after World War I. Whatever Wilson's political errors and character and the roles played by other leaders, the plan for the League was ahead of its time. Even today the possibility of achieving world order through the United Nations, or any organization, remains nearly as uncertain as it was half a century ago. The horrible weapons now available have not removed the threat of war; the outlook for world peace continues to be grim.

SUGGESTED READINGS

Aaron, D., ed., *America in Crisis* (1958).

*Bailey, T. A., *Woodrow Wilson and the Lost Peace* (1944).

Baker, R. S., *Woodrow Wilson and the World Settlement* (3 vols., 1922).

*Baldwin, H. W., *World War I* (1962).

Barnes, H. E., *The Genesis of the World War* (3rd ed., 1929).

Baruch, B., *American Industry in the War* (1941).

*Bass, H. J., ed., *America's Entry into World War I* (1964).

Borchard, E. M. and W. P. Lage, *Neutrality for the United States* (1937).

*Bourne, R. S., *War and the Intellectuals* (1964).

Buehrig, E., *Woodrow Wilson and the Balance of Power* (1955).

*Falls, C., *The Great War* (1959).

Fay, S. B., *The Origins of the World War* (2 vols., 2nd ed., 1930).
Fite, G. C., *Opponents of the War, 1917–1918* (1957).
Grattan, C. H., *Why We Fought* (1929).
Johnson, D., *Challenge to American Freedoms* (1963).
Kennan, G., *The Decision to Intervene* (1958).
Kennan, G., *Soviet American Relations, Russia Leaves the War* (1956).
Lansing, R., *The Peace Negotiations* (1921).
*Leuchtenberg, W., *The Perils of Prosperity* (1958).
*Link, A. S., *Wilson the Diplomatist* (1957).
*Marshall, S. L. A., *World War I* (1964).
*May, E. R., *The World War and American Isolation, 1914–1917* (1959).
*Mayer, A. J., *The Political Origins of the New Diplomacy* (1959).
Millis, W., *Road to War* (1935).
Morrissey, A. M., *Defense of Neutral Rights* (1939).
Notter, H., *The Origins of the Foreign Policy of Woodrow Wilson* (1937).
*Osgood, R. E., *Ideals and Self-Interest in America's Foreign Relations* (1953).
Peterson, H. C., *Propaganda for War* (1939).
*Pitt, B., *1918: The Last Act* (1962).
Preston, W., *Aliens and Dissenters: Federal Suppression of Radicals, 1903–1933* (1963).
Schmitt, B. E., *The Coming of the War* (2 vols., 1930).
Seymour, C., *American Diplomacy during the World War* (1934).
Seymour, C., *American Neutrality, 1914–1917* (1935).
Slosson, P. W., *The Great Crusade and After, 1914–1928* (1930).
Smith, D. M., *Robert Lansing and American Neutrality, 1914–1917* (1958).
*Stallings, L., *The Doughboys, The Story of the AEF, 1917–1918* (1963).
Tansill, C. C., *America Goes to War* (1938).
*Tuchman, B. W., *The Guns of August* (1962).
Wittke, C., *German-Americans and the World War* (1936).

CHAPTER 26

The Era of Complacency, 1919–1929

America's present need is not heroics but healing; not nostrums but normalcy; not revolution but restoration; . . . not surgery but serenity.
                                    WARREN G. HARDING, 1920

UNITED PRESS INTERNATIONAL

IN 1920 AMERICAN CITIZENS WERE ENTERING a new era of comfort and convenience. Myra Babbitt, the wife of Sinclair Lewis's prosperous real estate broker, cleaned rugs with a vacuum cleaner and stored food in an electric refrigerator. Her husband, George, drove the family automobile each day to his downtown office. By 1939 a greater number of housewives used a better-designed vacuum cleaner and the refrigerator was a fixture in most American homes, but the appliances of 1920 lightened housework just about as much as would those bought nineteen years later. The large, open black touring car, which George Babbitt started with a handcrank, was replaced by a sportier, streamlined sedan whose greatest improvement was a self-starter.

Suburban homes with neatly clipped lawns were as familiar in 1920 as in 1939. Downtown and Main Street looked much the same as they would nineteen years later. In both years churches in middle-class neighborhoods were filled to overflowing on Sundays. Babbitt went to a shoddy speakeasy to drink his highballs, the middle-aged businessman of 1939 to an elegant cocktail lounge or restaurant-bar. When Babbitt drank at home, he surreptitiously bought from the local bootlegger a bottle "just off the boat." In 1939 well-stocked liquor stores openly provided excellent brands for the discriminating customer. But in both years Americans consumed liquor in similar quantities. In 1920 rural areas were pocketed with grinding poverty and city slums were squalid and degrading. In 1939 too, in the Ozarks of Arkansas and the San Joaquin Valley of California, in Harlem and South Chicago, millions of Americans lived in appalling want.

Yet between the two dates the jazz age had flourished and spent itself. The Great Depression had shaken America's faith in capitalism and its future and was receding into the past. The New Deal, instituted with a flourish in 1933, was losing its momentum six years later. A few distinct changes had been wrought in American life. The basic social unit, the family, was noticeably weaker; regional and ethnic differences were disappearing, and each American was more like every other. An urban culture was vying with conservative, small-town

The Era of Complacency, 1919–1929

America. By 1939 government had intruded itself into many aspects of everyday life to a degree undreamed of in 1920. Finally and almost unbelievably, world peace had come and gone. In 1919 the doughboys were still returning home victorious from World War I. In 1939 the new generation nervously braced itself for another world conflict, wondering whether the United States could possibly stay out of the second holocaust in a quarter of a century.

COMPLACENCY, ILLUSION, AND DISILLUSIONMENT

Escapism

At the end of World War I, Americans withdrew swiftly from Europe, physically and mentally.[1] Wilson's Great Crusade to "save the world" had only momentarily held them in thrall. With their brief adventure in internationalism over, they became primarily preoccupied with their own nation and individual destinies.

But in 1920 Americans were finished with progressivism. Reform had lost its savor and pristine freshness; muckraking was too wearying; the term "social justice" aroused contempt and suspicion. The efforts of progressivism in the Roosevelt-Wilson era had not removed grim social injustices, and abroad postwar Europe and Asia obviously had serious problems, but Americans preferred to ignore ugly realities in a frantic determination to have fun.

Normalcy, the word aptly coined by candidate Harding, was the order for the day. Throughout the twenties there prevailed a mood of complacent certainty that America was the best of all possible worlds. Most Americans lived in a colorful, often tawdry dream world which has been variously called the roaring twenties, the mad decade, and the jazz age.

The Golden Age of Sports. Spectator sports offered one outlet for the thirst for good times and excitement. Across the nation millions of Americans jammed newly built stadiums to watch their favorite teams perform. By the end of the decade, millions more were able to follow the action of various sports events on their home radios. Because of the upsurge in interest, verging on mania, the press significantly increased its coverage of athletic events. The sports section became a very important feature of all daily newspapers. Sportswriters and radio sports announcers were only slightly less renowned than the performing athletes.

The image of professional baseball, popular for decades, was badly damaged in 1920 by the disclosure of the "Black Sox" scandal. Eight members of the Chicago White Sox were found guilty of accepting bribes to lose the 1919 World Series to the Cincinnati Reds. But almost immediately Judge Kennesaw Mountain Landis, the "rabbit ball," and Mr. George Herman Ruth came upon the scene and rescued the sport. The tough-minded Judge Landis, appointed baseball commissioner by the clubowners, was given dictatorial powers over organized baseball. Under his stern direction the sport recovered from its shady past and achieved respectability. The ball itself was redesigned, making it easier for batters to hit "the long ball." In the same years Babe Ruth, a successful pitcher with the Boston Red Sox, was converted into an outfielder and purchased by the New York Yankees. Almost overnight Babe Ruth made the homerun the most thrilling aspect of the game. In 1927 he hit 60 homers and eventually achieved a lifetime total of 714, a record that will probably never be surpassed.

---

[1] The 2,500,000 soldiers sent to Europe were brought home in a few months except for token occupation forces stationed in the Rhineland section of Germany. Small contingents of United States troops were stationed in Archangel and Murmansk, Russian ports in the Arctic, from September 1918 to June 1919, to protect United States military supplies originally shipped there to aid the Russian war effort but never used. The Americans around Archangel became involved in fighting with local Bolshevik forces and suffered some 2,000 casualties before they were withdrawn. Americans were also landed at Vladivostok, ostensibly to restrain Japanese forces in the area from seizing Russia's Pacific maritime provinces.

Ruth's antics, his colorful invective, his heroic capacity for beer and hot dogs, as well as his extraordinary ability to "knock the apple out of the park," made him the most legendary sports idol of the times.

Assembled around Ruth in the Yankee line-up were other players only slightly less notable. "Iron Horse" Lou Gehrig, the slugging first baseman, played in 2,130 consecutive major league games. The lordly Yankees, who dominated baseball, were endowed with superhuman qualities by sportswriters and the adoring public. As Yankee power waned in the late 1920's, other teams—the Philadelphia Athletics and the colorful St. Louis Cardinals ("the Gashouse Gang") in the next decade—won a portion of the limelight.

Other sports experienced an equally meteoric surge of interest. College football was big business, and gridiron heroes gained immortality in the public eye. It was commonplace for crowds of 60,000 or more to watch a football game on a fall Saturday afternoon.[2] For a time Harold "Red" Grange of the University of Illinois became to football what Babe Ruth was to baseball. On one notable afternoon the brilliant halfback, nicknamed "the Galloping Ghost," scored five touchdowns against the University of Michigan, four of them in twelve minutes.

Jack Dempsey, who was both hated and revered, made the heavyweight boxing match a vivid sports spectacle. Attendance records were broken again and again by the multitudes who came to see the scowling "Manassa Mauler" crush some hapless opponent with a rock-fisted "haymaker." In 1927 the gate for the second Dempsey-Tunney fight was $2,658,660, a record that stands to this day.

Tennis was revolutionized and popularized by "Big Bill" Tilden and his "cannonball serve."

---

[2]Until 1920 the record was 50,000, set in 1915 at the Yale-Harvard game. The all-time attendance record was established in 1925 when more than 120,000 saw Princeton's "Team of Destiny" play a powerful University of Chicago eleven in a postseason game. During the 1920's professional football was still in its infancy.

The Sultan of Swat. BROWN BROTHERS

Golf also became big-time with the advent of Walter Hagen and Bobby Jones. In 1926 when Jones return from England after his first victory in the British Open tournament, he was given a great ticker tape parade up Broadway in New York City, an honor normally reserved for top-ranking heroes and public figures. He was given another such parade in 1930 when he returned from winning the British Amateur and Open championships and was well on his way to becoming the only golfer ever to place first in all four major British and United States tournaments in one year.

Movies and Radio. The ideal diversion for restless, escapist-minded citizens was provided by

The Era of Complacency, 1919–1929

the movies. In the darkened theater millions could submerge their anxieties and frustrations as they laughed at the touching comedy of Charles Chaplin, thrilled to the acrobatic exploits of Douglas Fairbanks, and wept over the romantic misfortunes of Janet Gaynor and Charles Farrell. The magnetism and excitement that Rudolph Valentino, the Great Lover, generated from the screen in his role as *The Sheik* made women in the audience swoon.

By the end of the decade, movie theaters were selling more than 80,000,000 tickets every week. The adulation for Hollywood heroes and heroines on and off the screen indicated the extent of American disaffection with reality and ordinary existence. Gossip columnists and fan magazines kept the avid public informed of the most minute details of the garish lives of the gods and goddesses of the silver screen. Clara Bow, "the It Girl" and Hollywood sex symbol, was more widely known than the Secretary of State. When Valentino died, more than 100,000 gathered in a driving rainstorm to pay their final respects.

Radio was the most accessible form of escape. In 1920 KDKA, the first voice radio station licensed by the Department of Commerce, went on the air in Pittsburgh. Almost overnight the new industry boomed. By the end of 1922 there were more than five hundred stations in the United States. In 1930 radio was a billion-dollar industry, and radio stars competed with Hollywood idols for public adulation. The music of bandleader Paul Whiteman and the songs of Rudy Vallee, the crooner, reached untold households. In the early 1930's families hurried through their dinners and evening church services were suspended or postponed in order that all might hear "Amos 'n' Andy." Soap opera took up many housewives' empty daytime hours. The radio was also a wonderfully flexible means of dispensing culture, education, and information. No other medium of communication did more to increase the homogeneity of American culture. And no other medium furnished Americans with as cheap and quick an avenue to temporary oblivion.

Fads and Sensationalism. The twenties was an era of unusual and, at times, morbid interest in fads, crime, and the bizarre. The thirst for vapid and often vulgar amusements seemed unquenchable. In 1923 a game called Mah-Jongg, which was imported from China, took the country by storm. For a time manufacturers of Mah-Jongg sets had great difficulty keeping up with the demand. A Mah-Jongg League of America was organized. The sets of colored tiles could be purchased for as little as ten cents or for as much as five hundred dollars. Eventually, interest diminished because the rules of the games were complex and conflicting.

Mah-Jongg had departed from the scene by 1924, and the crossword puzzle craze was in full swing. The fad started when Simon and Schuster, a small publishing firm, came out with a limited printing—only 3,600 copies—of a crossword puzzle book. By the end of the year almost a million copies had been sold. Crossword puzzles became a standard item in the daily newspaper. The passenger with furrowed brow and pencil poised was a familiar sight aboard the commuter trains. But two years later, in 1926, the crossword puzzle fad had passed its peak.

Couéism, which depended on autosuggestion ("Every day in every way I'm getting better and better"), marathon dancing, and miniature golf all flowered briefly in the twenties and faded. Perhaps the most curious fad was flagpole sitting. An unemployed sailor, Alvin "Shipwreck" Kelly, was the first to demonstrate his hardihood in protracted stays atop flagpoles in various cities. Avon Foreman, a fifteen-year-old boy from Baltimore, set the juvenile record by remaining aloft for ten days. When Foreman returned to earth, he was solemnly congratulated by the mayor for his "grit and stamina." Kelly himself claimed the world's record by sitting on a pole in Cleveland for twenty-three days and seven hours. Cities issued ordinances

First in War, First in Peace

"How—how do you—go to the toilet?"
"I've got a can up here."
John Steinbeck, Cannery Row

BROWN BROTHERS

laying down rules for the use of public poles and charged license fees for flagpole sitting.

The craving for vicarious excitement found another outlet in the gangland wars of the twenties. The public interest accorded gangsters—such as Dutch Schultz, the beer baron of the Bronx; Johnny Torrio, who for a time dominated all bootlegging in Chicago; Al Capone, who eventually bought out Torrio; and Bugs Moran, Capone's most successful rival—was that usually reserved for folk heroes. Terms such as "lead poisoning," "taken for a ride," "gat," and "cement suit" enlivened the American lexicon. Movies, radio, and the press eagerly exploited the theme of gangsterism. The savage killing of Dion O'Bannion as he stretched

The Era of Complacency, 1919–1929 239

The gangster ethic: fame, fortune, and a fine funeral. UNITED PRESS INTERNATIONAL

out his hand in greeting to those who murdered him, the shooting up of Al Capone's headquarters in a Chicago suburb by eleven cars of gunmen, and the St. Valentine's Day massacre, when six of Moran's men and a bystander were lined up against a garage wall and killed with a burst of machine gun fire—all claimed greater public attention than the Washington Disarmament Conference and the signing of the Kellogg-Briand Pact.

Grusome murders, especially those flavored with sex, have always had a strong appeal to the newspaper reader. In 1924 he followed the trial of two precocious teenagers, Richard Loeb and Nathan Leopold, Jr., who had confessed to killing young Bobby Franks for the thrill of committing a perfect crime. Two years later Mrs. Frances Stevens Hall's trial, in which she was acquitted of the 1922 murders of her husband, the Reverend Edward Hall, and his mistress, Mrs. James Mills, filled the newspapers for twenty days. Despite its apparently uncomplicated details, the Synder-Gray case of 1927 received particularly complete coverage by press and radio. Ruth Snyder and a traveling salesman named Gray had decided that her husband was an inconvenience and bludgeoned him to death with a sash weight. There were no complications and no expert sleuthing; the culprits were easily caught. Yet to satisfy the morbid curiosity of the reading and listening public about this case, gallons of ink, tons of newsprint, and millions of words were expended.

Of a different nature was the Charles Lindbergh adventure. An engaging young man and a daring aviator somewhat down on his luck, Lindbergh sought a prize of $25,000 offered by a New York hotelowner to the first person, or persons, to fly nonstop from New York to Paris. Two other pilots, the veteran Clarence Chamberlain and the renowned Commander Richard E. Byrd, also hoped to make the flight. On the evening of May 19, 1927, Lindbergh decided to beat his rivals to the punch. The following morning, in a drizzling rain, he took off from Roosevelt Field on Long Island. Once Lindbergh was in flight over the Atlantic

"We (that's my ship and I) took off rather suddenly. We had a report somewhere around 4 o'clock in the afternoon before that the weather would be fine, so we thought we would try it"
(Charles A. Lindbergh).

THE BETTMANN ARCHIVE

Ocean, millions of Americans across the whole nation were seized with a mass hysteria and spent the anxious hours praying for his safe journey. When he arrived in Paris, a mob of 100,000 Frenchmen greeted him at the airport. His countrymen went almost out of their minds with relief and joy. President Coolidge dispatched a cruiser to bring Lindbergh home, but he was criticized for not sending a battleship. On his return Lindbergh was given a monstrous ticker tape parade on Broadway (called the Great Blizzard of June 1927) by vast throngs of enthusiastic New Yorkers. Even the taciturn Calvin Coolidge was moved to temporary eloquence, describing Lindbergh as "our ambassador without portfolio" and "a messenger of peace and good will."

The country's continuing interest in Lindbergh can be attributed partly to his good looks, modest comportment, and his romantic marriage to the lovely, talented, and wealthy Anne Morrow. But the reasons for the initial wild and emotional outburst over the young aviator and his immediate elevation to the status of a national idol are several and more complicated. The difference between the motivation of Lindbergh and, say, that of Shipwreck Kelly was really paper-thin. Lindbergh

The Era of Complacency, 1919–1929

was not furthering the welfare of the American people, nor did he risk his life for the salvation of mankind. The prize money he won was not regarded as a great amount. The great gambler Arnold Rothstein could make many times more on a good night. A Wall Street speculator could amass a fortune in a few hours.

In part, the Lindbergh story was another demonstration of the power of the press and radio. Their sensationalism had left the American people spiritually starved and hungry for relief from the steady diet of scandal and crime. Making his flight only four days after the conclusion of the Snyder-Gray trial, Lindbergh achieved his fame in a manner that appealed to the American public. Through personal effort and pluck he had succeeded—a refreshing triumph of old-fashioned, pioneer individualism in an increasingly dehumanized, modern world. The aviator's background was also in the American tradition. He had lived in rural Minnesota, born of Swedish immigrant stock; his father had been a congressman, and his mother was a school teacher. Then too the airplane in the twenties represented breathtaking progress in man's effort to break down, as President Coolidge put it, "the barriers of time and space." Daredevil flyers and test pilots of the twenties, such as Jimmy Doolittle and Wiley Post, were achieving the kind of renown won in the 1960's by Edmund Hillary and the astronauts. The flight of Lindbergh's tiny plane across the vast expanse of the Atlantic forced Americans to recognize the range and possibilities of air transportation; the dimensions of their world were suddenly much smaller.

Disillusionment and Intolerance

Many Americans were shocked and disillusioned by the cheapness and rampant materialism of the age, and thousands of intellectuals fled to Europe. Through the medium of fiction and verse, angry young writers of the "Lost Generation"—primarily those living in Paris—attacked a "decadent" America. F. Scott Fitzgerald declared that all the old gods were dead. To Ezra Pound America was "a botched civilization," to T. S. Eliot *The Waste Land*. Other writers, Sinclair Lewis, Sherwood Anderson, and Henry L. Mencken, chose to stay home and hammer at society from within. But the literary assault on "normalcy" and on a new and frightening wave of intolerance which had swept the country just after the war had little impact.

Embers of Progressivism. Of the old-time leading progressives, Theodore Roosevelt was dead, Wilson was dying, and Hiram Johnson, Roosevelt's running mate in 1912, was preoccupied with keeping the United States out of the League of Nations. The old muckrakers had lost both their enthusiasm and their audiences. In 1924 Senator La Follette made one final, despairing attempt to revive the reformist spirit. A new Progressive party, backed by the Farm Labor and Socialist parties and the American Federation of Labor, nominated him as its candidate for President. Two interesting planks in the party's platform advocated government ownership of railroads and a constitutional amendment to limit the Supreme Court's power to invalidate laws passed by Congress. La Follette received more popular support than any previous third-party candidate, but he won only the electoral votes of his own home state of Wisconsin. A few more than half of the eligible voters went to the polls.

The majority of the American people had probably opposed from the outset the prohibition so recently inflicted upon them by progressivism. Enforcement of the Volstead Act was never more than spotty and ineffective, for congressmen who virtuously supported prohibition became backsliders and refused to appropriate the funds necessary for proper enforcement. In the meantime, the liquor industry quickly went underground, and the era of bathtub gin, the speakeasy, bootleggers, rumrunners, and racketeers confronted the American conscience. Openly violating the law, usually with the connivance of the police, gangsters took over the operation of the liquor industry in the cities. Prohibition bred lawlessness and hypocrisy, and the federal government was denied a valuable source of revenue. Because the law focused attention on drinking, but was unenforced, it actually led to increased consumption of liquor. Moreover, with no government supervision of production, bootleggers often sold bottles of "mountain dew" or "white lightning" whose contents sometimes caused serious illness or death when consumed.

Women who had just won their seventy-two-year battle for the cherished right to vote frittered away their advantage, contenting themselves with fighting inconsequential, often frivolous battles against the double standard. Before the war the traditional saloon had always been regarded as a male sanctuary. In the twenties women pushed their way into the speakeasy and demanded service at the bar. They took up cigarettes, smoking openly everywhere, and wanted to be dealt into their husbands' poker games. To set off their newly bobbed hair, women chose looser, more comfortable clothing and considerably less of it. The average woman of 1913 is estimated to have swathed in nineteen yards of cloth. By 1928 she wore only seven yards.

Here and there across the country, women were occasionally elected to city councils and local school boards. One of the first, Elizabeth Bates, was elected to the Cranford, New Jersey, school board back in 1913. When her sister-in-law, Frances Miller, an aggressive feminist, aspired to a position of the same board, a whispering campaign was started. It was rumored that Mrs. Miller smoked (true) and that she drank (also true). She was soundly defeated. Obviously, men were not giving up the struggle easily. In the twenties a scattering of women were elected to the House of Representatives and two women, "Ma" Ferguson of Texas and Nellie Taylor Ross of Wyoming, were elected state governors. But the first woman senator, Hattie Caraway of Arkansas, did not take office until 1932.

Antiradicalism. During the last years of the Wilson administration, there was an outburst of feeling against radicalism, occasioned by the unsettling aftereffects of the war, high prices, unemployment, and fear of the Bolshevik tide threatening to engulf Europe. In a still deeper sense, this antiradicalism stemmed from the old nativist hostility of Americans toward foreigners and foreign influences. The resurgence of provincialism struck out in many directions. Bolsheviks, Socialists, pacifists, labor unions, Negroes, immigrants, and nonconformists were all subject to persecution.

In 1919 a wave of strikes swept the country, 3,630 in all involving over 4,000,000 workers. The presence of labor agitators among the strikers fostered the suspicion that these walkouts were part of a Marxist plot to take over the nation. One of the earliest strikes, against the shipyards in Seattle, expanded into a general shutdown which threatened to deprive the city of essential services. Such cooperation among unions was a new phenomenon in America. Mayor Ole Hanson charged that "Reds" had organized the shutdown. Backed by the National Guard, he broke the general strike and became, for a time, the favorite of the conservatives.

In September came the great steel strike, in which the workers were airing genuine grievances—low wages, poor working conditions, and an average workweek of sixty-eight hours—and demanding recognition of their union. The man who was attempting to organize the steel industry for the American Federation of Labor and who called the strike was William Z. Foster, soon to become a Communist. The long walkout was punctuated by acts of violence on both sides; federal and state troops were called in to prevent picketing. The steel companies hired "goons" by the thousands to act as strikebreakers. In November an even more awesome menace diverted public attention. At the order of their pugnacious leader, John L. Lewis, the 425,000 United Mine Workers threw down their picks and walked out of

The Era of Complacency, 1919–1929

the bituminous coal mines. In addition to the familiar demands for better wages and shorter hours, the union demanded nationalization of the industry. When the coal strike threatened to paralyze the economy of the whole country, President Wilson declared that the shutdown was unjustifiable and unlawful and sent in federal troops to end it. In January 1920 the steel strike also collapsed.

A series of bomb outrages added to the antiradical hysteria. In April 1919 a package delivered to the home of Senator Thomas Hardwick of Georgia blew off the hands of a servant while she was unwrapping it. Investigations in various post offices uncovered similar packages addressed to some thirty leading citizens, including John D. Rockefeller, Mayor Ole Hanson, J. P. Morgan, Justice Oliver Wendell Holmes, and Postmaster General Albert Burleson. Two months later a bomb shattered the front porch of Attorney General A. Mitchell Palmer. In September a tremendous explosion was set off near the offices of the J. P. Morgan Company in New York City, killing thirty-eight persons.

The extent of antiradical feeling was frightening, and the reaction to the strikes and bombs was often drastic and shocking. In 1919 Victor Berger, a duly elected congressman who had served an earlier term before the war, was denied his seat in the House of Representatives because he was a Socialist. The next January the New York State legislature expelled five Socialist members because of their party affiliation. Preachers and teachers who espoused unpopular causes were accused of being Reds and dismissed from their jobs. Loyalty oaths for teachers eventually became the law in twenty-two states. The oath in the state of Georgia required the teacher to "refrain from directly or indirectly subscribing to or teaching any theory of government or economics or of social relations which is inconsistent with the fundamental principles of patriotism and high ideals of Americanism."

Attorney General Palmer, once a reformer, launched a series of raids, in November 1919 and early 1920, on "nests" of radicals in immigrant neighborhoods of thirty-three American cities. Over 6,000 persons were arrested by federal agents. Many were beaten, and others were held in custody for weeks without writs of *habeas corpus.* Over five hundred of the aliens seized were deported, but the vast majority were found innocent.

Shortly after the Palmer raids, on May 5, 1920, two Italians anarchists, Nicola Sacco and Bartolomeo Vanzetti, were arrested for two murders in connection with a payroll robbery in South Braintree, Massachusetts. The two immigrants were convicted on very slight evidence and sentenced to death. The belief was widespread that Sacco and Vanzetti had been condemned primarily for their radical views as philosophical anarchists and for their ancestry. Judge Webster Thayer, who presided at the trial, referred to them privately as "dagoes," "sons of bitches," and "anarchistic bastards." Billy Sunday, the Protestant evangelist preacher, chanted, "Give 'em the juice. Burn them. We've had enough of foreign radicals."

From the world of letters came outcries of protest, stimulated by the quiet eloquence of Vanzetti. Poetess Edna St. Vincent Millay, novelist John Dos Passos, and essayist Walter Lippmann joined with Congressman Fiorello La Guardia of New York in seeking pardons or stays of execution. Appeals arrived from across the seas from such disparate individuals as British novelist H. G. Wells and dictator Benito Mussolini. For seven years the two men were kept alive by pleas for a retrial, advanced by men and women from all walks of life and received from almost every country of the world. And when on August 23, 1927 Sacco and Vanzetti were finally electrocuted, the protest was again worldwide.

The Scopes Case. Intolerance threatened education in the South during the twenties. In 1925 the Tennessee legislature had passed a law banning the teaching of evolution by "any theory that denies the story of the divine creation

First in War, First in Peace

of man as taught in the Bible." Friends of John T. Scopes, a young biology teacher in Dayton, Tennessee who had already lectured students on Darwin's theory, persuaded him to test the law. A complaint was filed, and Scopes was soon indicted.

The court trial was an immediate sensation, and Scopes himself was lost in the uproar as giants on both sides seized the limelight. William Jennings Bryan, former Secretary of State and a three-time presidential candidate, was an associate counsel for the prosecution. Clarence Darrow, the most famous criminal lawyer of the age, led the defense. The top-ranking attorney of the American Civil Liberties Union, Arthur Garfield Hays, was one of Darrow's assistants. The scathing on-the-spot press commentary of H. L. Mencken and direct radio coverage imbued the proceedings with the glare of publicity.

The trial dramatized the controversy between the fundamentalists, who defended the biblical story of creation, and the modernists, who accepted Darwin's scientific theory of evolution. Toward the end of the proceedings the defense maneuvered Bryan onto the witness stand as an expert on the Bible. In a sweltering courtroom, with both men in shirt sleeves, Darrow savagely cross-examined Bryan, forcing him to reveal humiliating confusion and ignorance before the whole world. Although Scopes was convicted and fined a hundred dollars, Bryan was shattered physically and mentally and ridiculed even by his own supporters. He died a few days later. Old-fashioned Protestant fundamentalism was badly shaken by the event, even though the state had won its case.[3]

Ku Klux Klan. No phenomenon indicated the social malaise and hostility of the 1920's more sharply than did the Ku Klux Klan. Founded by an evangelist in Georgia in 1915, the Klan was supposedly modeled on its reconstruction predecessor. During the war years the organization languished, but then a pair of shabby promoters, Edward Clark and Elizabeth Tyler, former fund-raisers for the Anti-Saloon League, made the KKK a national organization almost overnight. The purposes of the Klan resembled the Know-Nothing program of nativism—to promote Protestant, white, "100 per cent Americanism" and to repress immigrants, foreigners, Catholics, Jews, and, incidentally, Negroes. Blacks did not live in many of the areas where the Klan flourished. Operating as a secret organization with ceremonies that consisted of weird mumbo jumbo, the Klan was in some ways remarkably similar to Mussolini's *Fasci di combattimento* and Hitler's Nazi party. Through political pressure, economic boycotts, and crude terror, the Klan imposed its will on large portions of the nation.

By 1925 fiery crosses glowed in the night from California to Maine, announcing the presence of robed, hooded, and masked Klansmen. Membership, which was greatest in the small towns of the South, Midwest, and Pacific coast, approached the five million mark; governors of seven states were politically dependent on Klan support. Klan action had blocked the nomination of Governor Al Smith of New York, a Catholic, in the 1924 Democratic convention. Senators sympathetic to the KKK aided the passage of quota laws severely restricting European immigration. According to one reliable source, the Klan was involved in four killings, two mutilations, twenty-seven tar-and-feather parties, forty-one floggings, and five kidnappings in little more than a year.

In 1925 the Klan suffered a serious setback. "Grand Dragon" David C. Stephenson of Indiana raped a girl in the lower berth of a Pullman coach, and she committed suicide. Despite his enormous political power, Stephenson was convicted and sentenced to life imprisonment. When refused a pardon by Governor Ed Jackson, a fellow Klansman, Stephenson revealed to the world the Klan chicaneries of

---

[3]Ironically, the law prohibiting the teaching of evolution remained on the books for many years. In 1967 Gary L. Scott, a teacher in Jacksboro, Tennessee, was convicted under the same statute. The law was finally declared unconstitutional in 1968.

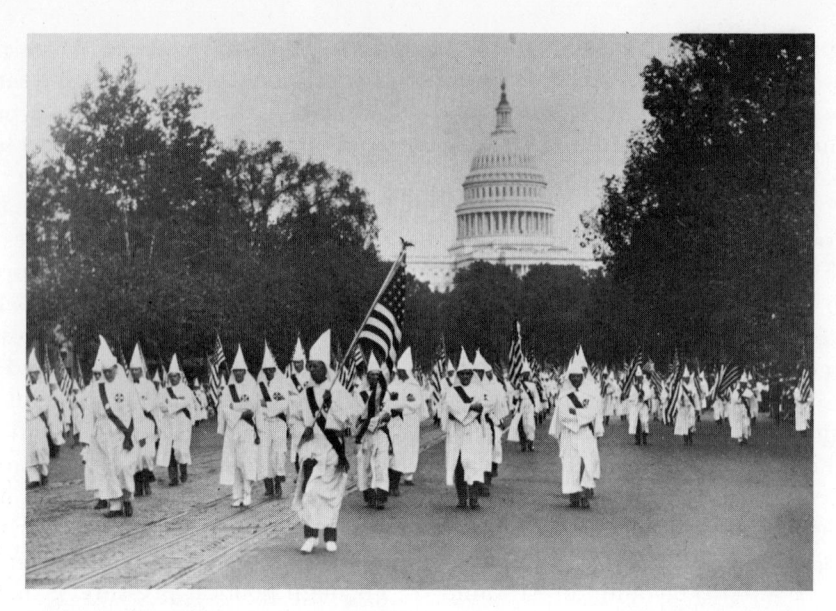

Vigilantes of the twenties. CULVER PICTURES

state officials connected with him. A congressman, the mayor of Indianapolis, and a host of minor state officials were sent to prison. Governor Jackson escaped a similar fate only because of the statute of limitations. But the damage was done, and the Klan went into eclipse. It lives on to this day with a total membership estimated at about 20,000, but its organization is now fragmented.

ECONOMICS—CATALYST OF CHANGE

Never before or since have changes in technology had such an immediate and far-reaching effect on society as did those of the twenties. New manufacturing methods, the introduction of a host of new products, and development of more refined techniques in selling goods to the public brought about an economic revolution.

The Automobile. Even before the First World War Henry Ford recognized the practicality of mass-producing an automobile for the public. Previously, the automobile had been regarded only as a rich man's toy, but Ford introduced the Model T in 1909 and placed a retail tag on it of only $950. In 1914 the Ford Company opened its revolutionary plant at Highland Park, Michigan, with the first large-scale, moving assembly line. An electric conveyor belt carried the gradually assembled automobile past stationary workers, each of whom performed one simple mechanical task. Ford then lowered the price of his car to $490 and achieved fabulous profits. The automobile was now within the price range of the average wage earner. Ford called upon his salesmen to use high-pressure techniques and push the installment plan in order to entice the public into buying cars. Other companies, notably General Motors, adopted and improved upon Ford's methods. In 1920 there were 9,000,000 registered cars in the United States; in 1929 there were 26,000,000.

Automobile companies became the biggest single users of steel, and car sales stimulated a host of derivative industries. Plate glass and rubber corporations became industrial giants. The already mammoth oil companies underwent staggering expansion. Construction of concrete highways accelerated to make the 1920's the greatest road-building era in history.

First in War, First in Peace

In 1921 there were 387,000 miles of paved roads and 662,000 miles in 1929. Along the highways and in the towns, filling stations, restaurants, diners, tourist courts, garages, and parking lots mushroomed and flourished. Railroads suffered from the competition of trucks and buses.

The impact of the automobile on daily life was profound. Recreational horizons of the family were extended as mountain resorts, campsites in the wilds, and bathing beaches became more accessible. The automobile was a major factor in the expansion of spectator sports. In addition, the average wage earner could hunt, fish, and play golf because he could easily drive to woods, streams, and golf courses. The automobile eroded away Victorian morals, and the tightly knit family unit unraveled a bit. Boys and girls in their teens thought nothing of driving twenty miles from home for unchaperoned movie dates. The flapper had to learn to fend for herself alone with an amorous male. The "hip-flask," the "rumble seat," "necking," and "petting" characterized the courtship of the less-inhibited, mobile, younger generation.

New Industries. The twenties spawned a multitude of new industries. Electric appliances — power tools and electric irons as well as refrigerators and vacuum cleaners — were standard conveniences in middle-class homes. Neon signs glowed on Main Street almost as profusely as on Broadway or Sunset Boulevard. A variety of synthetics were introduced, and man-made fibers cut deeply into the sale of natural fibers. Women's legs were sheathed in inexpensive rayon hose instead of dowdy cotton or costly silk stockings. Bakelite, developed from the soya bean, was made into automobile dashboards, telephones, and parts for the burgeoning radio industry. Du Pont cellophane became the added protective covering for almost every nondurable product. Cosmetic face creams were developed from byproducts of oil refining.

Advertising. For many years advertising had been looked upon as a business, but during the 1920's experts in the field began to consider their occupation a profession or even an art — and already some irreverent souls were calling it a racket. Whatever it was, advertising throve mightily. By 1930 it was another billion-dollar industry.

The techniques and goals of advertising shifted markedly during the decade. Admen began to practice what they called "consumption engineering." As they visualized their role, they had the vital responsibility of persuading people to be "healthily dissatisfied with what they now have in favor of something better." The public must learn to use up goods rapidly and get rid of last year's models. Consumers were admonished to "Keep up with the times" and "Keep up with the Joneses." Advertisements had formerly extolled the quality of products, but in the twenties the focus was on the consumer's ego and his desires. The automobile was no longer merely an efficient means of transportation but a goal in life. Every family man was urged to own a fine car in keeping with his high or improving status. The glamor and adventure potential in the automobile were extolled to an escapist-minded America. Magazine and newspaper advertisements displayed flashy automobiles parked before lavish homes with gorgeous females swathed in furs and dripping jewels posed somewhere near the front fender.

Although the "hidden persuader" method of advertising was still somewhat in the future, executives in the field were already convinced that the most important thoroughfare in American life was no longer Pennsylvania Avenue or Wall Street but Madison Avenue, New York, where the offices of the major ad agencies were located. They saw themselves as indispensable to a capitalist society, as vastly increasing consumption by persuading people to keep on buying. And why should the housewife deny herself the best of household appliances until her husband had saved the price when she could buy now through that glorious instrument, the installment plan? The new concept

The Era of Complacency, 1919–1929

of conspicuous consumption was at loggerheads with traditional puritanical thrift.

Consolidation. In the decade following the First World War, business consolidation, which had slowed considerably during the progressive era, resumed once again, creating giant oligopolies. Three companies came to control about seventy per cent of the tobacco industry. By the end of the decade, General Electric and Westinghouse produced more than half of the nation's electrical equipment. The mergers of banks and the "pyramiding" of public utilities corporations were also significant. In spite of the economy's expansion, the 30,000 banks in operation in 1921 had shrunk to 22,000 by 1930, largely as a result of consolidations.

The chain stores, a related form of consolidation, spread quickly during these years, particularly in the fields of drugs and groceries. The A & P Company, which had fewer than 5,000 stores in 1920, had expanded to 18,000 by 1929. Chains of banks, motion picture theaters, and multipurpose retail stores, such as Woolworth's and Penney's, extended throughout large areas. Worried proponents of laissez faire and small businessmen warned of the dangers of such concentration of wealth and economic power into fewer and fewer hands.

Soft Spots in the Economy. In these expansive years of the twenties, industrial production doubled, and the productivity per worker increased to the same extent. National income rose by more than $20,000,000,000, and the real wages of workers increased in spite of inflation. The building boom which persisted throughout much of this decade was tangible evidence of great economic growth. Homes were built at a record rate in sprawling suburbia, skyscrapers proliferated in major cities, and real estate values skyrocketed. A golden glow of prosperity infused the American land.

But all was not well, for there were many dangerous fever spots on the body economic. Certain industries, notably coal mining, textiles, and shipbuilding, did not share in the general prosperity. Even more serious was the deepening distress felt by farmers, hit hard by a general slump in the prices commanded by agricultural goods.

Unemployment, which fluctuated from one to two million annually, was disturbingly high, the displacement of large numbers of workers by new machines (technological unemployment) chronic. Labor organizations suffered from their reputation of radicalism. William L. Green, the head of the American Federation of Labor after 1924, symbolized the inept trade union leadership of the times. Pot-bellied, bespectacled, timid "little Bill" Green accepted the semiskilled and unskilled worker's status as a second-class citizen in the great American capitalistic enterprise, making little effort to unionize the new automobile, chemical, and electrical equipment industries. With management pushing the "American plan" or open shop and the company unions, the one growing area of labor organization, authentic union membership fell from its peak of 5,000,000 in 1921 to less than 3,500,000 in 1929—from twelve per cent of the labor force to less than seven. Many segments of labor, particularly the unskilled workers, employees in the service industries, and minority groups, shared very little in the general prosperity.

A series of "blue-sky" real estate booms, followed by sudden and frightening collapses of prices, left in their wake a horde of ruined speculators. The most spectacular and disastrous was the Florida boom of 1924 and 1925. For a time people poured into the Sunshine State to play the real estate game. Fortunes were made overnight, and profits were fantastically high. Many lots in the town of Miami Beach which had sold for $800 in 1920 were resold for $150,000 in 1925. Swamplands and pine barrens far out in the country suddenly attained great value. The inevitable break in prices, which came in 1926, was hastened by two devastating hurricanes which roared in from the West Indies.

Maldistribution of wealth was another factor of concern to farsighted observers of the economy. The enormous profits of the great corporations went for the most part to the limited numbers of stockholders as dividends. The workers' share in the profits was not compensative. In all too many industries the real wages of workers began to decline. Yet wage earners, stimulated by advertising and the rapid expansion of installment buying, continued to spend at an increasing rate. The percentage of Americans in debt through the extension of credit plans reached a dangerous level. But, as the Big Bull Market gained momentum in 1928, the nation seemed generally mesmerized by its visions of a rosy future. The economy seemed to have achieved a permanent plateau of prosperity. Warnings of a few perceptive economists were brushed aside as "sour grapes."

POLITICS—THE MIRROR OF THE TWENTIES

Election of 1920. In late spring of 1920, the Republicans sensed victory, for the Democratic party had been badly discredited. Wilson's League of Nations had been rejected by the Senate for the second time, and Wilson himself was tired and ill. Attorney General Palmer wanted the Democratic nomination, but his attacks on radicals had shocked liberals. The continued failure of his raids to disclose significant communist activity eventually sobered conservatives as well. Then on May Day the terrorist demonstrations that he had predicted would take place in several large cities never materialized, further discrediting the Attorney General and damaging his chances for the Democratic nomination.

The Republican party that met June 8 in Chicago abounded with prominent, competent, and seemingly acceptable candidates. Leading the pack of contenders was General Leonard Wood of Spanish-American War fame. Almost neck and neck with him in numbers of pledged delegates was Governor Frank O. Lowden of Illinois. The powerful Senator Hiram Johnson of California was ranked third. Charles Evans Hughes, the 1916 candidate, was a possibility, and so was the distinguished Senator Henry Cabot Lodge, who had been Wilson's masterful antagonist in the battles over the League. In addition, there was young Herbert Hoover, Wilson's brilliant food administrator during the war, as well as other prospects. Rated far down the list was Senator Warren Gamaliel Harding of Ohio.

When the convention balloting started, a deadlock quickly developed between Lowden and Wood. Neither could obtain a majority, but each was grimly determined to block the other. Hiram Johnson proved an unacceptable substitute, tainted as he was with a progressivism now out of style and with his former associations with Teddy Roosevelt. Hughes was discredited on two counts: he had been the loser in 1916, and he was a "cold fish." Lodge was of arrogant disposition and had acquired many enemies during his long service in the Senate. Hoover, considered too young and relatively unknown, had no political base, for no state and no state delegates were pledged to him. Only Senator Harding was left.

Warren Harding, formerly a small-town newspaper editor, was completing his first term in the Senate, and his record was competent if not outstanding. His position on issues was balanced. Both conservatives and liberals could approve of stands that he had taken. Blessed with an affable personality, he was also still too new in national politics to have made many enemies. Harding's physical appearance was strikingly impressive, for his handsome features and dignified bearing gave him the august mien of a Roman senator. After some wrangling, Harding won a majority of the convention delegates on the tenth ballot. Calvin Coolidge, the undistinguished Governor of Massachusetts, was designated the vice-presidential candidate.

Governor James Cox of Ohio, chosen the Democratic nominee for President a few weeks later, was a colorless administrator with an undistinguished record. His running mate, Frank-

The Era of Complacency, 1919–1929 249

lin Delano Roosevelt, with his engaging personality and a philosophy derived from the policies of his cousin Theodore Roosevelt and Woodrow Wilson, was the only promising leader among the Democrats. Roosevelt's political career was in the ascendant, much as that of his cousin had been two decades earlier. Would history repeat itself? The parallels were startling. Conservatives of both parties recoiled at the prospects of another "mad" Roosevelt in the national political arena.

While Cox and Roosevelt, the Democratic running mates, traveled throughout the country on frenzied "whistle stop" tours, advocating acceptance of the League of Nations, Harding stayed home at Marion, Ohio, calmly conducting a front porch campaign. Coolidge said nothing. There was no need to, for the election was a shoo-in for the Republicans. Reading any significant meaning into the results of national elections is a risky business, but it seems safe to say that Harding's election was a victory for isolationism over Wilsonian internationalism. Harding was also clearly friendlier to big-business interests than any Democrat. In general, there was a reassuring air about the comfortable, warm Harding. People had had their fill of Wilsonian dogmatism and high-mindedness. No one disliked Cox or even gave him much consideration. Citizens, or the less than half of the potential electorate who bothered to go to the polls, voted against Woodrow Wilson and possibly the name of Roosevelt. Eugene Debs, the most intellectual of the candidates, received more votes than he had in 1912, although he was in a federal penitentiary serving time for sedition.

Harding's Ill-Starred Administration. Warren Harding has been widely characterized as one of the poorest presidents in American history, and his administration is primarily remembered for the scandals attached to it. Allegations about his personal incompetence and questionable morals may be unfair, but they were not entirely untrue. Harding was a man of limited qualifications, of which he was keenly aware. In a revealing outburst to one of his secretaries, Harding exclaimed

"John, I can't make a damn thing out of this tax problem. I listen to one side and they seem right, and then—God!—I talk to the other side and they seem just as right. . . . I know somewhere there is a book that will give me the truth, but, hell, I couldn't read the book. I know somewhere there is an economist who knows the truth, but I don't know where to find him and haven't the sense to know him and trust him when I find him. God! What a job."

Many of Harding's appointments were disastrous. One of the most notorious was the designation of Charles Forbes as head of the Veterans Bureau. Forbes defrauded the government of millions of dollars appropriated for the building and supplying of hospitals. When he was exposed early in 1923, he fled to Europe before resigning. His closest adviser, Charles F. Kramer, committed suicide. Forbes later returned, stood trial, and received a two-year sentence. Harry M. Daugherty, Harding's pal from Ohio politics who was appointed Attorney General, became deeply involved with Thomas W. Miller, the alien property custodian,[4] in the fradulent return of German assets to their original owners. Miller was jailed in 1927, but Daugherty's two trials ended with hung juries. Jesse Smith, Daugherty's sidekick and a scheming "influence peddler," committed suicide in May 1923 before he could be brought to justice.

The most shocking scandal, which will forever characterize the Harding administration even though it was not revealed until late in 1923, after the President's death, was the Teapot Dome affair. Albert B. Fall, Secretary of the Interior, had in 1921 persuaded the President and Secretary of the Navy Denby to transfer to

---

[4]This post was created by Congress in 1917 to manage and dispose of assets of the Central Powers in the United States that had been seized by the government during the war.

First in War, First in Peace

his administration tracts of oil-rich government lands that had been set aside since 1909 for the future needs of the navy. Then quietly, within a year and without competitive bidding, Fall leased the reserves at Teapot Dome, Wyoming, to Harry F. Sinclair and those at Elk Hill, California, to Edward F. Doheny. Both of these private promoters were multimillionaires. A Senate investigating committee untangled the sordid arrangements and discovered that the two oil operators had paid enormous bribes to Fall. Sinclair was ultimately convicted of contempt of the Senate for refusal to testify about the Teapot Dome leases and contempt of court for jury tampering. But he, Fall, and Doheny were all acquitted of the major charge of conspiracy to defraud the government. In 1929 Fall was convicted of accepting a bribe, fined $100,000, and sentenced to a year in prison. He was the only Cabinet official in American history to be accorded such a dubious distinction. The Supreme Court declared the leases invalid in civil suits in 1927, and the two large oil reserves were returned to the government.

Yet some of Harding's appointments were excellent. The distinguished Charles Evans Hughes served as Secretary of State, Henry C. Wallace as Secretary of Agriculture, and Herbert C. Hoover was Secretary of Commerce. Although the achievements of the Washington Disarmament Conference, which convened in November 1921, proved ephemeral, Hughes's formula for scrapping ships and halting construction of capital ships (page 645) was imaginative and regained for the United States some of the moral leadership it had lost by not joining the League of Nations. On Christmas Day, 1921, Harding pardoned Socialist Eugene V. Debs, in prison since 1918. The next year the President courageously vetoed a veterans' bonus bill in the face of angry opposition from his own party in Congress.

More harmful by far than all the scandals, but usually forgotten, were Harding's economic policies. Harding was deeply influenced by the philosophy of Andrew W. Mellon, his Secretary of the Treasury. This billioniare banker and aluminum king from Pittsburgh, who was to retain his post until 1932, was a man of remarkably limited vision and experience. His aims were simple: cut government spending, cut the national debt, and cut taxes on the rich. Under Mellon's direction the debt was reduced sharply, and the federal budget was balanced through the elimination of many jobs and needed government services. Mellon was hard-fisted in demanding that war debts be paid in full and then, with wonderful illogic, he supported high tariffs which deprived European nations of the means of meeting their obligations.

Mellon believed sincerely that high income taxes discouraged business enterprise. He proposed eliminating inheritance taxes and reducing the tax on high incomes by two-thirds to stimulate investment. Taxes for those earning less than $66,000 would not be lowered, however. These suggestions were too extreme for Congress, but in 1921 it did lower the highest income tax rate from seventy-three to fifty per cent, then in 1924 to forty per cent, and in 1926 to twenty per cent. In 1924 Congress also raised exemptions for lower incomes and reduced the general rate of taxation.

Infected with Mellonism, President Harding let antitrust laws go unenforced. To head the federal agencies charged with regulating business, he appointed conservative businessmen and mediocre politicians. "Stock market rigging," "price fixing," "union busting," and dozens of other shoddy business practices again became the order of the day. The nation would someday pay a high price for this era of unrestrained business libertinism.

Harding was gradually becoming aware of the patent dishonesty of his cronies of the "Ohio gang" when in 1923 he exploded in hurt frustration to a newspaperman, "My God, this is a hell of a job. I have no trouble with my enemies. . . . But my damned friends, my God-damned friends, . . . they're the ones that keep me walking the floors nights." That sum-

The Era of Complacency, 1919–1929

Mr. Coolidge refuses point-blank to leave the White House until his other rubber is found.
CULVER PICTURES

mer the distraught and weary Harding left Washington for a Western speaking tour and then took a vacation trip to Alaska. On his return in late July, he suffered a heart attack, rallied for a few days, and then died in San Francisco on August 2. In the end Harding was even betrayed by his incompetent physician, a crony from Marion named "Old Doc" Sawyer, who incorrectly diagnosed Harding's illness as an attack of ptomaine poisoning.[5]

Babbitt in the White House. Calvin Coolidge, the new President, was sharp-nosed, dour, and cold in appearance. Nor were his meager looks deceiving; no great mind inhabited the unprepossessing frame. Petulant, unsmiling, and of-

[5] It was widely rumored that Harding's shrewish wife, Florence, exacting revenge for his extramarital love affairs, deliberately poisoned him. Harding did have two known romances, one with a Nan Britton and another with a Mrs. Carrie Phillips.

ten downright rude, his personality prompted a Washington wiseacre to remark that he must have been weaned on a pickle. Stories about Coolidge's taciturnity and parsimony are legion. One gushing Washington hostess exclaimed, "Mr. Coolidge, I made a bet today that I could get more than two words out of you."

"You lose," Coolidge retorted.

He was as stingy with household expenses at the White House as he was with the federal budget. Austere and silent in public, within the White House he released storms of abuse on the servants. His tantrums were a trial to his wife. A markedly commonplace man of mediocre mind and middle-class virtues was President of the United States.

In the mounting scandal that emerged after Harding's death, Coolidge did little and said less, which proved to be the best course of action. The new President indicated that he would continue Harding's laissez-faire policies toward big business, and he permitted Mellon to remain as economic mentor. Hoover was kept in the cabinet, but Secretary of State Hughes was dropped. Coolidge was ill at ease with the frosty, imperious, and talented statesman. In his place the President chose Frank B. Kellogg, a man of limited ability but easily domineered by the testy Coolidge.

The Democrats in 1924 were unable to make political capital of the Harding scandals. Coolidge had kept his own skirts clean while those of several Democrats had been stained with the oil of the Teapot Dome affair. The Democrats were also burdened by the strong Klan influence within their ranks. John W. Davis, a competent but uninspiring corporation lawyer closely allied with the Morgan interests and as conservative as Coolidge, was nominated by the Democrats. His campaign never had a chance. Coolidge was riding the crest of a wave of economic prosperity for which he was given undeserved credit.

Coolidge's second term was notable for its lack of achievement. Like Harding, Coolidge vetoed a veterans' bonus, but he was unable to

"No matter how thin you slice it, it's still baloney"
(Alfred E. Smith).

THE GRANGER COLLECTION

prevent Congress from overriding his veto. The President did, however, successfully twice veto a bill that would have provided aid for distressed farmers. He believed that farmers had never made money and that there was little to be done about it. He also blocked a measure to develop water resources and a public electric power project in the Tennessee Valley. By opposing new programs and cutting government expenditures ruthlessly, Coolidge reduced the national debt still further.

Election of 1928. Coolidge was as negative a man as ever became President, yet he was also one of the most popular. To the public he personified the prosperity it was enjoying. Many believed that his continued presence in the White House was vital to the welfare of the nation. But in August 1927 he called a number of newspapermen into his vacation headquarters in the Black Hills. They were handed little slips of paper on which were the words "I do not choose to run for President in nineteen twenty-eight." The reporters were promptly dismissed without comment or explanation. For a time Coolidge smugly believed that the Republicans would draft him despite his announcement. But the convention took him at his word and nominated Herbert Hoover. It is reported that Coolidge wept uncontrollably like a child when he received the news. In any case, he detested his competent Secretary of Commerce. On one occasion Coolidge snorted, "That man [Hoover] has offered me unsolicited advice for six years, all of it bad."

To oppose Hoover the Democrats nominated Alfred E. Smith, one of the ablest gov-

The Era of Complacency, 1919–1929 253

ernors the state of New York had ever had. Brought up in New York slums, he had a fine record of support for social welfare legislation and administrative reform. Smith had a number of serious disadvantages. As a Catholic, he faced the hostility of the fundamentalist Protestants of the Bible Belt in the Midwest and the South. Smith was also an avowed "wet," favoring repeal of prohibition. Hoover was a cautious "dry" at a time when prohibition was still popular in many quarters. Above all, Hoover represented a continuation of Republican prosperity.

It was a dirty and exciting campaign. Radio speeches were for the first time a significant device, being substituted for lengthy speaking tours. Both parties raised enormous campaign funds. But small-town, middle-class, and rural America distrusted Smith's breezy manner, his urban liberalism, his criticism of prohibition, and his former associations with the Tammany Hall political machine of New York City. A whispering campaign intimating that Smith's election would put the Pope in the White House frightened many of those Protestants who tended to support the Ku Klux Klan. Hoover, solid and dignified, told the voters that "we shall soon with the help of God be in sight of the day when poverty shall be banished from this nation."

When the votes were counted, Hoover had won a landslide victory. He even carried several states in the formerly Solid South. Outside the South Smith won only the two strongly Catholic states of Massachusetts and Rhode Island. Hoover's victory seemed a mandate for continuing the complacent, pro-business policies of the Harding-Coolidge years.

SUGGESTED READINGS

*Adams, S. H., *The Life and Times of Warren Gamaliel Harding* (1939).

*Allen, F. L., *Only Yesterday* (1931).

*Bernstein, I., *The Lean Years, A History of the American Worker, 1920–1933* (1960).

*Brody, D., *The Steel Strike of 1919* (1965).

Chandler, A. D., Jr., *Strategy and Structure, Chapters in the History of Industrial Enterprise* (1962).

*Churchill, A., *The Improper Bohemians* (1959).

Clark, J. P., *Deportation of Aliens from the United States* (1931).

Coben, S. A., *Mitchell Palmer, Politican* (1963).

*Cochran, T. C., *The American Business System, A Historical Perspective, 1900–1955* (1957).

*Cowley, M., *Exile's Return* (2nd ed., 1951).

Curti, M., *The History of American Thought* (1943).

*Dulles, F. R., *America Learns to Play* (1940).

Fraenkel, O. K., *The Sacco-Vanzetti Case* (1931).

Furniss, N. F., *The Fundamentalist Controversy, 1918–1931* (1954).

*Galbraith, J. K., *The Big Crash* (1955).

*Ginger, R., *Six Days or Forever?* (1958).

Green, L., *The Era of Wonderful Nonsense* (1939).

*Handlin, O., *Al Smith and His America* (1958).

*Hicks, J. D., *Agricultural Discontent in the Middle West, 1900–1939* (1951).

*Hicks, J. D., *The Republican Ascendency* (1960).
*Higham, J., *Strangers in the Land* (1955).
Jacobs, L., *The Rise of the American Film, A Critical History* (1939).
Kazin, A., *On Native Grounds* (1942).
*Leuchtenburg, W. E., *The Perils of Prosperity, 1914–1932* (1958).
Lindsey, B. B. and W. Evans, *The Revolt of Modern Youth* (1925).
Lippmann, W., *A Preface to Morals* (1929).
Lynd, R. and H. Lynd, *Middletown* (1929).
McConnell, G., *The Decline of Agrarian Democracy* (1953).
Moos, M., *The Republicans* (1956).
*Mowrey, G. E., *The Twenties, Ford, Flappers, and Fanatics* (1963).
*Murray, R. K., *Red Scare: A Study in National Hysteria, 1919–1920* (1955).
Nevins, A. and F. E. Hill, *Ford* (2 vols., 1954).
Newton, W. H., *The Memoirs of Herbert Hoover* (1952).
*Noggle, B., *Teapot Dome* (1962).
*Osofsky, G., *Harlem* (1966).
Prothro, J. W., *The Dollar Decade, Business Ideas in the 1920s* (1954).
Rice, A. S., *The Ku Klux Klan in American Politics* (1961).
Sann, P., *The Lawless Decade* (1957).
*Schlesinger, A. M., Jr., *The Crisis of the Old Order, 1919–1933* (1957).
Seldes, G., *The Years of the Locust* (1933).
*Shannon, D. A., *The Great Depression* (1960).
*Sinclair, A., *The Era of Excess (Prohibition)* (1962).
*Sloan, A. P., Jr., *My Years with General Motors* (1964).
*Soule, G., *Prosperity Decade: From War to Depression, 1917–1929* (1947).
Weaver, R., *The Negro Ghetto* (1948).
*White, W. A., *Puritan in Babylon* (1938).
Wilson, E., *Shores of Right* (1952).

CHAPTER 27

The Depression Decade, 1929–1939

Prosperity is just around the corner.
　　　　　　　　　　　　HERBERT HOOVER, 1931

CULVER PICTURES

STOCK MARKET CRASH

In late September 1929 prices of stocks traded on the New York exchanges began to slide downward at a rapid rate. Even the best stocks or "blue chips," such as General Motors, Westinghouse, RCA (Radio Corporation of America), and AT & T (American Telephone and Telegraph), declined significantly. United States Steel, which was selling at $261 a share on September 3, was down to $204 by October 4. General Electric dropped from $396\frac{1}{4}$ to 345.

Few observers were seriously concerned about the "temporary" sag. Most market analysts blamed the situation on technical conditions and a general "staleness." Little attention was paid to Roger Babson, a self-styled expert and notorious prophet of doom, when he predicted that a crash was in the offing. His remarks were more than counterbalanced by the buoyant statements of Professor Irving Fisher, renowned economist at Yale University. Fisher declared that stocks were not overpriced; a crash was out of the question; and, in fact, even higher values were to be expected.

During the first weeks of October, prices of stocks resumed their upward advance. Again the financial vista appeared promising, and investors recovered from their temporary fright. Those with the most gumption, and many small investors with limited savings, bought more stocks than they had cash to pay for. In the last year especially, many speculators had grown accustomed to accepting credit from their brokers—buying on margin, in stock market parlance—and depositing with the brokerage firm only a small percentage of the total price of the securities bought.

In the third week of October, however, prices slid downward again. On Black Thursday, October 24, even the most reputable stocks plummeted in an uproar of feverish selling. The floor of the New York Stock Exchange was a bedlam of brokers clamoring to unload their clients' stocks. United States Steel lost 12 points. General Motors sank 32 points. Montgomery Ward dove from $83\frac{1}{4}$ to 50. Nearly 13,000,000 shares changed hands.

Through the intervention of powerful financial interests, including the House of

The Depression Decade, 1929–1939

Morgan, prices recovered somewhat on the following day. Then came Black Tuesday, October 29. Again the stockholders panicked. Jittery investors who had already lived through a month of erratic fluctuations were frightened by the first drop in prices and began to sell their holdings. Overextended speculators, required by their brokers to put up more margin[1] to hold a particular security, could acquire the needed money only by selling other stock at distress prices. The wave of selling mounted, overwhelming the tickers until they were hours behind current prices. On that awful day a record 16,400,000 shares were traded on the Exchange as "the bottom dropped out of the market." In New York and all through the country, families that had started October 29 in comfortable circumstances ended it in debt.

Nor did the downward spiral halt, for it continued until November 13. During these disastrous days wizards of finance and the federal government issued platitudinous statements to soothe frayed nerves. President Hoover declared that "the fundamental business of the country . . . is on a sound and prosperous basis." John D. Rockefeller announced "that the fundamental conditions of the country are sound . . . and I have for some days been purchasing sound common stocks." Thomas Lamont, a senior Morgan partner, discounted the disaster as "merely a little distress selling." But thousands of ruined investors were forced into bankruptcy. Newspapers carried stories of suicides. A macabre joke along Wall Street was the query of the hotel clerk to a customer seeking to reserve a room on an upper floor: "Sir, do you wish to use the room for sleeping or for jumping?"[2]

The Speculating Society. During the twenties the stock market had become a topic of conversation in every household and meeting place. Millions of Americans achieved real or vicarious pleasure in "following" the rising market, which was to them an extension of the American dream. Waiters and barbers, plumbers and poets, and farmers and foremen picked up the lingo of the financial circles and talked knowingly of "bear raids," "selling short," "corners," and "buying on margin." Market listings were a wonderworld for the amateur statisticians. Americans have long been fascinated with numbers, as evidenced by their eagerness to cite the voluminous baseball statistics—box scores, batting averages, and pitching performances—reported in sports pages of daily newspapers and by the play-by-play sportscasters of radio and television. The stock market section of newspapers, with its neatly arranged columns of figures, some prefixed and suffixed with special symbols, was sheer delight once the reader had been initiated into its mysteries. Persons from almost every walk of life could readily quote the price per share of International Harvester or AT&T on a given day. "Playing the market" seemed to be an easy road, open to anyone who sought wealth. As the millionaire promoter of the Empire State Building, John J. Raskob, put it,

"If a man saves $15 a week and invests in good common stocks, and allows the dividends and rights to accumulate, at the end of twenty years he will have at least $80,000 and an income from investments of around $400 a month. . . . I am firm in my belief that anyone not only can be rich, but ought to be rich."

In the spring of 1928, after nearly a decade

---

[1] When the speculators bought on margin and put up only a percentage of the purchase price for a security, the broker loaned him the rest. But the broker in turn borrowed the money from a bank, giving the shares purchased by the speculator as collateral for the loan. If the prices of the security dropped sufficiently, the shares were no longer valuable enough to secure the loan. The broker then had to ask the speculator for more money to give to the bank, or he had to sell the security to pay off the loan.

[2] It has since been proved that few ruined investors leaped from office windows those first few days after the crash. In fact, the suicide rate was higher for the few months before the market collapse than in those just after it.

First in War, First in Peace

of mounting expectations, the New York Stock Exchange electrified an already fascinated America. Stock prices which had by that time reached historic highs began to surge upward at an even faster rate. That year Wright Aeronautics rose from 69 to 289, Montgomery Ward from 117 to 440. In March a share of RCA was worth less than 100, in November 400. The country was seized with a paroxysm of speculation. Thousands of individuals who had followed the market but never before risked their small savings started pouring them into common stocks. Then after Hoover's election and well into 1929, prices kept on climbing, with only occasional sharp breaks. The small-scale speculators, often buying on margin, continued to enter the market in increasing numbers. In small towns bank executives and trust executors shifted funds from government bonds and business loans to stocks. But even so, Americans who participated in the stock-buying spree of 1928 and 1929 probably numbered only 1,550,000. Of these, 950,000 are estimated to have had cash accounts with brokerage firms, 600,000 margin accounts.

Economic Indicators. When the stock market fell so suddenly in October, the country suffered a psychological shock, for Americans great and small, investors and noninvestors, had come to believe that Wall Street was the financial heart of the nation and the market the core of the economy. They assumed that stock prices were an accurate barometer of the nation's economic climate. Actually, the rising stock prices revealed only limited facets of the financial state of the country. In the late 1920's a variety of conditions—slowdowns in building, widespread unemployment, a decline in world trade, and a depression in agriculture—indicated economic sickness, but prices of stocks climbed rapidly on the exchanges. In other words, the market had reflected how people felt about the economy but not necessarily its true state. Investors had lacked an understanding of economic relationships. Moreover, because taxes in the 1920's were low both for corporations and for the wealthy, savings were out of all proportion to the opportunities for legitimate investments. Enormous cash surpluses had been available for speculation, helping to push up the spiraling stock prices.

Widespread and endemic unemployment had indeed long antedated the Great Crash. New England suffered from the increasing shift of the textile industry to the South. During the 1920's the coal industry languished. "Technological unemployment" (the displacement of workers by labor-saving machines), always a problem in an industrial society, had become more acute after the First World War. In 1928 there were already 2,080,000 unemployed. The jobless transient and the rootless worker adrift in a sea of unemployment, with only occasional jobs to sustain them, were a characteristic segment of the society. Existing conditions simply became worse after October 1929. The Southern Pacific Railroad, which removed 60,000 hoboes attempting to travel illegally or "ride the rails" in 1927, reported the ejection of nearly 700,000 in 1932. Unemployment climbed to a peak of about 13,000,000 in 1933, or nearly twenty-five per cent of the working population.

THE DEEPENING DEPRESSION

Economic and Social Dislocation

The panic created by the collapse of the Big Bull Market led Americans generally to stop any kind of financial transactions. Banks moved to collect overdue mortgage payments. Corporations delayed plans for expansion and sought to reduce inventories. Depositors withdrew savings from banks and buried them in tin cans in the backyard. With many workers either unemployed or restricted by cuts in salaries and wages, purchases declined.

In the large cities soup kitchens appeared and breadlines stretched far down the block. Apple salesmen, some clad in dignified chesterfield overcoats and homburgs, competed on street corners. Beggars in large numbers chanted the litany, "Brother, can you spare a dime?" As the depression deepened, however, even these few outward signs of social catastrophe disappeared. The breadlines, the traditional means of distributing food along skid row, proved ineffective and were no longer seen. On the surface the cities seemed little changed. Only occasionally did the discerning eye observe social erosion—streets a little dingier, here and there factories with smokeless chimneys, and shops that were boarded up. The homeless drifted to the shantytowns (sardonically called Hoovervilles) on the outskirts of cities. Here they improvised shelters of rusted automobile bodies, packing boxes, and scrap tin. In town garbage dumps children scrabbled for rotting melon rinds and grapefruit peelings or anything that seemed the least bit edible.

In desperation, millions abandoned the city to return to the family farm and eke out a bare subsistence, but inhabitants of the countryside were beset with troubles as bad as or worse than those of the cities. Farm products sold at rock-bottom prices. Faltering rural banks sought to survive by seizing the property of mortgagees. Desperate, farmers sometimes gathered in mobs and attempted to block foreclosure sales with force; or they would intimidate prospective buyers, acquire the property with a very low bid, and return it to the original owner. In the Mississippi Valley rural populations lived in abject poverty, their soil first eroded by floods in 1927 and then parched by drought in 1930. Some rural areas, especially in the South, had no local agencies to offer even minimal relief. In the hill country people were reduced to eating weeds, roots, and even clay. Malnutrition in country and city was commonplace, although actual starvation was rare. It was particularly tragic that so many went hungry, for during the depression years there was an overabundance of food in some sections of the country. Crops were left in the fields unharvested, and farmers poured milk on the ground when the price dropped below the cost of producing it.

The Hoover Administration

Something was clearly rotten in the economic state of the nation. As the depression became progressively worse, the United States faced its greatest crisis since the Civil War. In an atmosphere of increasing apathy and despair, many Americans began to lose faith in democracy and the free-enterprise system. By the millions the nation's citizens turned their eyes and hopes toward Washington, D.C., for in these desperate times the man in the White House seemed the only one who might be able to lift the country out of its immense doldrum and relieve the enormous destitution of a stricken population.

Herbert Hoover—the "Great Engineer." In a laudatory review of his first six months in office, the *New York Times* on September 1, 1929 referred to President Hoover as "a practical idealist who is applying his engineering efficiency to increasing the sum of human happiness." The *Times* editorial expressed a point of view shared by the great majority of the American people at that moment. It is ironic that a few weeks later Herbert Clark Hoover was to face the greatest economic setback in the country's history and be cruelly blamed for the Great Depression, for which he was not responsible and had even made some effort to prevent. As Secretary of Commerce Hoover had urged Coolidge to act to curb stock speculation, but the President had consented only to raising Federal Reserve rediscount rates. As soon as Hoover was inaugurated, he urged the Federal Reserve Board to raise the rediscount rates even higher and to refuse loans to banks that were in turn loaning money to brokers.

Hoover appeared eminently qualified for the crushing burdens of the presidency. His early life seemed a prototype for the American success story. Born on an Iowa farm in 1874, Hoover worked his way through Stanford University, graduating with an engineering degree. He spent long years abroad—living many of them in the Orient—where he attained great wealth as a developer of successful mining interests. Hoover achieved international renown as a humanitarian for his selfless relief work in Belgium during the German military occupation after 1914. His reputation was enhanced by his efforts as President Wilson's wartime food administrator in 1917 and 1918 and by his very competent service as Secretary of Commerce under Presidents Harding and Coolidge.

Hoover had the sober and upright mien of a professional man. Shy and solemn, he was like most meticulous persons a born worrier. He had no gift for oratory. His most serious weakness was a lack of political experience, for he had had no direct contact with rough-and-tumble partisan politics until the presidential campaign of 1928. In this one exposure he failed to develop any political flair, and he tended to be unduly thin-skinned to criticism. In his personal philosophy Hoover upheld industry, thrift, and self-reliance; he spoke of "progressive individualism," convinced that American capitalists had lost their self-interest and now devoted themselves to public service and to achieving equal opportunity for all. Favoring the Jeffersonian principle of a federal government of severely restricted powers, he believed that individuals and communities must be allowed to work out their own solutions without outside help.

Hoover's Policies—First Phase. The new President's initial reaction was to do little or nothing about the depression. Agreeing with millions of other thoughtful Americans that the economy would soon reverse the downward trend without federal interference, he tried to allay fears and restore confidence. Even though hordes of jobless tramped the streets, Hoover placed his faith on the personal generosity of family, neighbors, landlords, and employers to help the destitute. If their most immediate associates failed them, then local relief and charity organizations should step in. Any program of federal relief, he declared, would destroy "character . . . and initiative, which are the very foundations of democracy."

As the months wore on, it became evident that some action must be taken. Hoover held a series of conferences at the White House to elicit voluntary cooperation. He urged business leaders not to cut wages, prices, or employment and to go ahead with plans for expansion. He recommended that the first effect of the depression "fall on profits and not on wages." Governors and mayors were called upon to help the economy by initiating public works programs. The President set the example by requesting monies for federal projects. Early in 1930 Congress appropriated $700,000,000 to erect public buildings, improve rivers and harbors, and build public roads. Plans for the giant Boulder or Hoover Dam on the Colorado River, to provide water and hydroelectric power in the Southwest, had been approved in Coolidge's administration. Now construction was begun. The Federal Reserve rediscount rate and both corporate and individual income tax rates had already been reduced, in December 1929. Believing that the nation's economic woes were largely European in origin, in June 1930 Hoover readily signed the Hawley-Smoot Bill, a measure designed to reduce American economic dependence on Europe by establishing prohibitively high tariff rates. Then to help the stricken farmers he directed the Federal Farm Board, established in June 1929, to create stabilization corporations with the power to buy grain and cotton on the open market, in the hope of raising prices. By 1932 the corporations had accumulated such large surpluses that they had to suspend operation. Farmers had increased production faster than the corporations could buy up the excess.

Hoover's Policies—Second Phase. In the early fall of 1931, there was a special drive urging all Americans who could afford it to increase their contributions to private charities, but this campaign, like Hoover's other efforts to gain volun-

The Depression Decade, 1929–1939

tary cooperation, proved woefully ineffective. Many industrialists had for a time been able to avoid cutting wages and employment, but they could not keep men at work producing goods for which there was no market. Prices of agricultural products continued to decline; a bushel of wheat that brought more than a dollar before the depression sold for as little as thirty-eight cents in 1932. The shaky structures of municipal and private relief organizations were collapsing under the weight of increasing numbers of needy families. In addition, the Hawley-Smoot Tariff had failed to accomplish its purpose. This attempt to promote United States economic self-sufficiency merely intensified the depression. European nations retaliated with high tariffs of their own, thereby seriously damaging American businessess involved in foreign trade. In three years trade with other countries fell from nine billion dollars to three.

With the depression worsening every day, Hoover realized that businesses whose deterioration would further damage the economy must receive federal aid. Late in 1931 he backed a bill to charter the Reconstruction Finance Corporation (RFC), with assets of two billion dollars, to negotiate loans to banking institutions, insurance companies, railroads, and large industries on the verge of bankruptcy and forced liquidation. The Glass-Steagall Banking Act of February 1932, passed with administration blessing a few weeks after the RCA law was enacted, liberalized credit and expanded the national currency by allowing Federal Reserve Banks to accept a wider variety of commercial paper as security for loans. In March 1932 the Red Cross was allowed to distribute flour and cloth made from surpluses held by the Federal Farm Board. Then in July Congress created federal home loan banks to help banks and other mortgage holders cut down on foreclosures and promote new construction. But Hoover still regarded the use of federal funds for the direct relief of the needy as an invasion of the responsibilities of the individual to his neighbor, of the private institution to the public, and of local and state governments to their constituencies. He also feared the huge federal bureaucracy and the "regimentation of man under government" that federal care of the unemployed would entail. Thus, lacking the President's support, Senator La Follette's bill to make a direct grant of $375,000,000 to the states, to be used either for public works or for relief, was defeated in February. In July 1932, however, the Congress of Democrats and progressive Republicans insisted that the RCA be empowered to lend $1,500,000,000 to state and local governments for public works and to furnish $300,000,000 in temporary loans to hard-pressed state relief agencies.

The various programs enacted toward the end of the Hoover administration laid the foundation for the later and more extensive New Deal of Franklin Roosevelt. In backing projects such as the RFC, the first measure ever passed by Congress to maintain the economic system, Hoover exhibited what was for him considerable flexibility of thinking. Not only did he accept the principle of federal intervention, but he also gave up, at least temporarily, his cherished belief in the "balanced budget." The national debt increased appreciably, from sixteen billion dollars in 1930 to twenty-one in 1932.

The Bonus War and the Election of 1932. In 1924 Congress had voted the doughboys of the First World War a special remuneration for their wartime services. This money was to be paid out in small amounts until 1945. Hoping to persuade Congress to grant the entire bonus immediately, thousands of impoverished veterans descended upon the capital in the summer of 1932. After their appeal had been rejected, most returned home, but about 2,000 of the "Bonus Expeditionary Force" and their families camped in a shantytown on the edge of Washington. When the Washington police tried to evict them, two veterans and two policemen were killed. President Hoover then ordered the army to drive out the veterans and destroy their unsanitary encampments. His instructions were carried out by General Douglas MacArthur with tanks, cavalry, infantry, tear gas, and bayonets.

The incident hurt Hoover's already sagging reputation rather badly. It was like killing a sick mosquito with a hammer. Despite his belated and precedent-shattering efforts, Hoover was eventually hated for his apparent callousness to human suffering. The great "human engineer," who had fed the war-ravaged Belgians but not his desperate countrymen, was subjected to abusive criticism and deliberate misinterpretation of his statements and actions. When Mrs. Hoover suggested that people should try to "be friendly and neighborly with all those who just happened to have bad luck," she became the butt of derisive jokes. Scarred by corrosive comments, the President retreated to glum silence within the walls of the White House.

In 1932 Hoover was easily defeated by Franklin D. Roosevelt, the popular governor of New York. Hoover waged a listless campaign for reelection, reaffirming his faith in the American system and defending his efforts to stem the depression. His speeches were carping and bitter, and he warned that "grass will grow in the streets of a hundred cities . . . weeds will overrun the fields of millions of farms" if Roosevelt was elected. Although Roosevelt made few firm and some contradictory commitments as he traveled back and forth across the country, speaking everywhere to responsive audiences, he radiated confidence and good cheer and pledged himself to develop "a new deal for the American people."

When the election returns were counted, Roosevelt had won the largest majority in the Electoral College since 1864. He carried every state west and south of Pennsylvania. His margin over Hoover in popular votes was seven million. Countless Republicans crossed party lines—something they would never forgive themselves for in later years—to vote for FDR. The American people were clearly ready for a change.

THE ROOSEVELT YEARS

The New Deal

By March 4, 1933 banks in four-fifths of the states across the nation had closed their doors, many of them giving the impression they would never open again. Throughout the depression bank failures had mounted, but in the early months of the new year banks had closed up at an alarming rate. In a nationwide panic depositors rushed even to sound banks to draw out their savings. Long lines reaching around the block moved with glacial slowness as frantic depositors waited. When they finally arrived at the cashier's window, they often found that money was rationed out to them in small quantities. Cold fear gripped the nation. First in Michigan in mid-February and then in state after state, governors proclaimed long bank holidays to halt the disastrous runs on bank deposits. On the morning of March 4 the New York Stock Exchange closed. Americans in all walks of life felt a direct shock as the entire economy ground to a halt.

On that cold March day the citizenry listened on their radios to one of the most memorable inaugural addresses ever delivered by a president. In his mellow, Harvardian voice Franklin Roosevelt reassured the American people: "The only thing we have to fear is fear itself." He promised to propose effective measures, and if Congress did not act, he said that he was prepared to ask for emergency powers "as great as the power that would be given to me if we were in fact invaded by a foreign foe" to deal with the immediate financial crisis and the lengthening depression.

After the ceremonies of inauguration day, Roosevelt moved swiftly. Congress was called to meet in special session on March 9. The lights of the White House and government offices burned all night during the ensuing weeks as the President and his advisers began to hammer into shape proposals to alleviate the depression. The Capitol building also remained

The Depression Decade, 1929–1939

alive through twenty-four-hour days as the members of Congress considered the profusion of executive measures streaming out of the White House. Cots were hastily set up in corridors so that congressmen could catnap during rare lulls in the proceedings. In the famous "hundred days" from March until June, fifteen important pieces of legislation constituting the most extraordinary reforms in the history of Congress were enacted. After June and in the ensuing years, the pace slowed somewhat, but Roosevelt maintained considerable momentum until 1939.

The various laws affecting the nation's basic social and economic structure that were enacted by Congress at Roosevelt's initiative are generally referred to as the "New Deal." Characterized as a program that created a social revolution, it shattered traditional concepts of limited federal government and seriously eroded the system of checks and balances. New ideas about the relationship of the government to the people, considered revolutionary and even dangerous at the time, were conceived. The President was pragmatic in devising laws to solve particular problems, but the thrust of New Dealism was consistently in the direction of greater social control and organization under federal auspices. For better or for worse, the government of the nation still proceeds along the course that Congress and President Roosevelt blazed for it in the 1930's.

Origins and Philosophy of the New Deal. When FDR took office on that bleak March day in 1933, he entertained only vague and contradictory notions of what should be done about the depression. Roosevelt has been described as a second-rate intellect but a first-rate politician. Unlike his heroes, "Uncle Teddy" and Woodrow Wilson, FDR was not a brilliant student in college, nor had he written and published books during his early career. Roosevelt was not even a profound reader, for his mind was too active and restless to be applied to books of an abstruse and philosophic nature. He had only a vague knowledge of economic theory.

Yet the new, hard-working President had been deeply impressed with the progressive leadership of the Republican Roosevelt and the Democrat Wilson. During his convalescence from a crippling attack of polio in 1921, FDR spent considerable time studying progressivism and its possibilities.

Whatever his other weaknesses, Roosevelt received splendid training in the art of politics and techniques of public administration as a legislator in New York State, as Wilson's Assistant Secretary of the Navy, as the unsuccessful vice-presidential candidate in 1920, and especially as Governor of New York from 1929 to 1933. The statewide relief agency that he set up in New York was the first comprehensive system in the nation. Rather than merely doling out food and clothing, the agency tried to create jobs for the unemployed. During his administration impressive laws establishing old-age assistance, unemployment insurance, a state power authority, and conservation projects were enacted by the New York State legislature. In these years Roosevelt also developed political charm and poise. He cultivated his resonant voice and learned to speak simply and effectively. He discovered the importance of good press relations and understood the value of a good public image. Although his intellect was probably inferior to that of his predecessor, Roosevelt possessed attributes of personality and a readiness to use the powers of government that Hoover had lacked.

The new President's willingness to experiment with new ideas was one of his greatest strengths. If an idea failed, he was quick to abandon it and try another. Although Roosevelt's severest critics accused him of being Marxist in approach and of leading the United States down the road to socialism, such charges were unfair. Roosevelt's experimentation was in the purely American tradition of nineteenth-century Populism and twentieth-century progressivism. But Roosevelt was not even a doctrinaire progressive or dyed-in-the-wool liberal. His "brain trust," a group of college professors

First in War, First in Peace

headed by Raymond Morley, a Columbia political scientist, and including economists Rexford G. Tugwell and Adolf A. Berle, Jr., and Felix Frankfurter of the Harvard Law School, had been recruited to help him draft his speeches during the campaign and to inform him on technical matters. They did indeed give the administration a liberal *élan* and attracted a great deal of attention, but they were not his only advisers. The variety of views represented by the men who surrounded Roosevelt covered a broad political spectrum and illustrated Roosevelt's readiness to listen to conservative counsel as well as liberal.

First Steps. Roosevelt's initial move on March 5 was a proclamation ordering all banks to remain closed for four days. Individual banks could be reopened only after federal auditors had determined that they were solvent. An embargo was also placed on the exportation of gold. On March 9 President Roosevelt sent the hastily convened Congress the Emergency Banking Relief Bill to authorize the emergency steps already taken and to provide for bank reorganization. Within eight hours it was approved by an overwhelming majority. In their haste to conform to the wishes of the President, congressmen passed the measure in thirty-eight minutes after listening to the explanation of Chairman Henry Steagall of the Banking and Currency Committee. They had no printed copies of the bill.

Under the Emergency Banking Act, sound banks in the Federal Reserve System could reopen under licenses from the Treasury Department. The Comptroller of the Currency was to appoint conservators to take care of the assets of insolvent national banks. In addition, the Hoover-created RFC was directed to assist banks that were solvent but in a shaky condition. A few months later the Glass-Steagall Banking Act of June 1933 would force the separation of commercial and investment banking, expanding the Federal Reserve System to include both, and would severely restrict the use of bank credit for speculation.

The act would also create the Federal Deposit Insurance Corporation to insure individual deposits up to $5,000 (later $10,000).

In the first of a series of radio "fireside chats," the President declared on March 12 that the banking crisis was over. "I can assure you," he declared, "that it is safer to keep your money in a reopened bank than under the mattress." An estimated audience of thirty-five million listened to the broadcast. The response was returning confidence, and it took the form of depositors' money flowing back to the banks, many of which had reopened within a week. Only about five per cent stayed closed permanently. Conservatives generally applauded President Roosevelt's decisive action. Even liberals were impressed, although some of the old-fashioned progressives worried about concessions to "Wall Street monopolists."

The next day the President suggested that Congress amend the Volstead Act—which defined as intoxicating any beverage containing 0.5 per cent alcohol—to allow the sale of beer and wine containing 3.2 per cent alcohol. Congress accepted his advice; on April 7 beer was sold legally in the United States for the first time in thirteen years. The lame-duck Congress meeting earlier that year had already passed the Twenty-first Amendment,[3] for the election of Roosevelt, who had campaigned as a "wet," was considered a clear mandate to repeal prohibition. By the end of the year all the states would ratify the amendment. The legalization of the liquor industry took away the livelihood of thousands of gangsters and bootleggers, but it provided as many legitimate jobs and created new revenues for the government through excise taxes. Some former bootleggers became respectable storekeepers; the "numbers racket" and gambling attracted the money-making talents of others.

With Great Britain and many other coun-

---

[3]The Twentieth Amendment, ratified January 23, 1933, changed inauguration day from March 4 to January 20 and moved up the day for convening new Congresses from the first Monday in December to January 3.

The Depression Decade, 1929–1939

A fireside chat.   BROWN BROTHERS

tries of the world off the gold standard (page 644) and the banks just reopening, President Roosevelt moved to protect the vanishing gold reserve and to prevent gold hoarding. On April 5 he ordered all private holdings of gold surrendered to the Treasury in exchange for paper currency, and then on April 19 the nation officially abandoned the gold standard. By inflating the American dollar and permitting its value to sink in terms of foreign currencies, the administration hoped to raise commodity prices at home and to encourage exports.

President Roosevelt moved almost immediately to fulfill his campaign promise that no one should starve. To help the state and local governments whose resources had long since been exhausted, he recommended to Congress on March 21 that it enact measures "aimed at unemployment relief." On May 12 Congress passed the Federal Emergency Relief Act, which at last recognized that relief was a national problem and that the federal government must make outright grants. Of the $500,000,000 appropriated, half was allotted for direct emergency relief to the states and the balance for distribution on the basis of one federal dollar for every three dollars spent by state and local relief agencies.

Relief and Recovery. One of the legends growing out of the early New Deal era is the story of an all-night meeting that Roosevelt held with his advisers at the White House. According to the tale, FDR called upon the men to "brainstorm" solutions to the depression. The more outlandish, the better. Anything could be proposed to stimulate thinking. Coffee and sandwiches were served, and ties were loosened as

268   *First in War, First in Peace*

conferees suggested endless wild ideas. One proposal—possibly it was Rexford Tugwell's—was to take the country off the gold standard. The Bureau of Printing and Engraving was to produce enormous quantities of paper money of all denominations, including ones, fives, and tens. Then all the army bombers were to be assembled at Washington National Airport, loaded with the bales of money, and directed to fly out over different sections of the nation. The pilots were to open the bomb bays and let the paper money flutter down over the countryside.

This procedure would produce pandemonium at first, it was admitted, but people would quickly gather up the money and undoubtedly spend it on necessities that they had long been denied. The local grocery store and the corner drugstore, the department store and the gas station would all be deluged with purchasers. The shops would have to hire additional clerks to handle the increased volume of business. Shelves would be quickly depleted of goods. Managers would have to order additional stocks from warehouses and factories. The factories, in turn, would be obliged to hire workers to produce goods needed to supply the sudden demand. Factories and shops would now have funds to pay their employees, who would in turn be able to buy things that *they* needed. Thus the whole economy, stagnated by the lack of money, would begin to move in an upward spiral.

The story is false, and the proposal dangerously inflationary, but it does illustrate the theoretical basis for the New Deal. The problem as the brain trust conceived it was to build up purchasing power. In other words, money had to reach the hands of the people to "prime the economic pump." The New Deal program employed more practical means to achieve a result similar to the one just described. Credit and cash were poured into the economy through a variety of mechanisms.

During "the hundred days" a giant government corporation called the Public Works Administration was instituted under the National Industrial Recovery Act of June 1933 to create work in the heavy industries. Directed by Secretary of the Interior Harold L. Ickes, the PWA joined with cities and states to finance public works projects. Contracts were made with private companies, which were not obliged to select their workers from the pool of the unemployed. The PWA built power and sewage disposal plants, municipal buildings, schools, hospitals, libraries, bridges, and highways. Military airports, naval vessels, a municipal auditorium for Kansas City, and a water supply system for Denver were also constructed. The giant agency assumed responsibility for the rapid completion of the Hoover Dam. Over a span of four years the PWA spent more than four billion dollars. The construction projects sponsored by the PWA supplied laborers, foremen, engineers, architects, and draftsmen with much-needed work and stimulated the economy of their depressed communities. Industries, especially cement, steel, and lumber companies, benefited from large orders for materials.

A somewhat similar agency, the Works Progress Administration, was established in 1935 under the direction of brain-truster Harry L. Hopkins, a frail, chain-smoking social worker. The WPA was supposed to supply employment in sectors untouched by the PWA. A high proportion of funds was to be spent on wages and salaries rather than on materials. The "security wage" paid on all projects, which were not to compete with private industry and which were to be completed within a year, would be less than that paid in private employment but more than the sums paid for direct relief. The tough "old curmudgeon" Ickes viewed the expansion of WPA in competition with his own agency with alarm and bitterness. He regarded Hopkins as a spendthrift and noted with exasperation the similarity of the title of Hopkins's agency to his own. Certain that Hopkins chose the title deliberately to confuse

"*Come along. We're going to the Trans-Lux to hiss Roosevelt.*"
PETER ARNO, THE NEW YORKER CARTOON ALBUM, COURTESY HARPER AND ROW

the public, the irritable Ickes tried to resign, but FDR turned on his charm and persuaded Ickes to remain at his post. The President seemed to revel in displays of competitiveness among his subordinates.

The WPA built municipal airports, playgrounds, thousands of public buildings, both federal and local, half a million miles of highways, and flood control projects in the Tennessee River area. To achieve its goal of providing the unemployed with the kind of work they were best fitted for, the wide-ranging WPA engaged in activities traditionally outside the scope of the federal government, such as establishing medical and dental clinics to provide free care for the needy. It developed adult education classes and hired unemployed teachers to teach them. Even the suffering world of the arts received attention. The WPA hired musicians, who formed symphony orchestras and bands and gave free public concerts. Threadbare painters and impoverished commercial artists were summoned to decorate local post offices (built by the WPA or PWA) with colorful murals. The Federal Theater Project, an arm of WPA, produced plays and documentary movies.

During this era the WPA was sharply criticized by conservatives. Its projects were condemned as useless and extravagant. A WPA worker leaning on his shovel was a favorite subject for newspaper cartoons. But the WPA spent eleven billion dollars and employed nine million people during its eight-year life-span.

One agency created by the Roosevelt administration that received universal approval was the Civilian Conservation Corps. Organized to maintain a work force of sometimes as many as half a million young men between the ages of eighteen and twenty-five, the CCC quartered them in barracks in camps in the country and appointed army officers to direct them. The young recruits received subsistence and wages of thirty dollars per month, twenty-two of which were sent to their families. Their most extensive program was planting trees as windbreaks and to reforest lands ruined by overlumbering, but they also worked on flood control projects, drained swamps, cleared beaches and camping grounds, fed wildlife, and fought plant and animal diseases and forest fires. By the end of 1941 nearly three million youths had spent a part of their lives in CCC camps.

Much less effective was the National Recovery Administration, also created by the National Industrial Recovery Act of June 1933. Under the command of tough, conservative General Hugh Johnson, the NRA was designed to revive industrial activity and to increase employment. Nearly bankrupt firms, in the effort to keep in business, had fired workers, reduced wages, slashed prices, and sometimes overpro-

270   *First in War, First in Peace*

duced, reducing the market to chaos in many industries. Now business firms were urged to negotiate their own industrywide codes of fair competition. With antitrust laws suspended for the duration of the act, each industry was permitted to raise prices somewhat and to set production quotas. In return, the industry was to shorten hours, so that more workers could be employed, and to raise wages.

The NRA was launched with great fanfare. Its emblem was a blue eagle, and its slogan, "We do our part." Huge parades were held in various cities to publicize the NRA program. In New York City 150,000 people marched down Fifth Avenue in a parade that began early in the morning and did not end until ten o'clock at night. Businesses subscribing to NRA codes displayed the blue eagle prominently on store windows, in offices, and on their products.

Yet problems quickly developed. Companies that refused to accept the NRA codes were subjected to harassment and coercion, and many enterprises paid only lip service to the codes. Some firms raised prices but failed to grant appropriate wage increases to their workers. Industries were especially outraged over the labor provisions of NRA, which guaranteed the right of employees to organize and bargain collectively through representatives of their own choosing in annual negotiations with their companies. A review board headed by Clarence Darrow issued a scathing denunciation of the NRA codes, claiming that they were controlled by the larger firms and fostered monopolies. In 1935 the Supreme Court ended the unwieldy scheme by ruling the NRA unconstitutional.

The Labor Movement. A few weeks after the Court decision, however, the labor section of the NRA was salvaged by passage of the Wagner Act. This new law guaranteed organized labor's right to collective bargaining and prohibited employers from coercing workers to join company unions and from firing them for union membership. A National Labor Relations Board of three members was established to supervise elections among employees when there was a dispute over which union should represent them. The NLRB could also investigate charges of unfair employer practices and issue cease and desist orders when it uncovered them. Union leaders hailed the Wagner Act as a "declaration of independence" for organized labor. The Roosevelt administration, believing that strong unions able to negotiate for better wages would increase consumer purchasing power, strongly endorsed the law as an important step in economic recovery.

With the blessing of the New Deal and the Wagner Act, the labor movement became more militant. Under the leadership of bushy-browed, scowling John L. Lewis, eight AF of L unions defied the parent body in 1935 and formed the Committee for Industrial Organization. Its goal was to organize the mass production steel and automobile industries, which heretofore had had no unions because industry leaders had refused to recognize them and because the AF of L, dominated by craft unions, was officially opposed to organizing all the

THE NATIONAL ARCHIVES

The Depression Decade, 1929–1939

John L. Lewis—father of the CIO. BROWN BROTHERS

workers in an industry, skilled and unskilled, into a single union.

Against General Motors the CIO used a new weapon, the "sit-down strike," in late 1936. Instead of walking off the job, workers simply remained in the factories and refused to produce. This technique frustrated any hope by the company of hiring "scab" (non-union) labor. By February 1937 General Motors capitulated to the powerful United Automobile Workers Union of the CIO. Chrysler and Packard followed suit, but Ford was a tougher foe. It was in this organizing effort that Walter Reuther won his spurs as a top union leader, for he and another unionist were badly beaten by Ford hirelings in 1938. Even the stubborn Henry Ford finally gave in, however, accepting the UAW in 1941.

In March 1937 the United States Steel Corporation voluntarily granted the CIO full bargaining authority for its employees, but the smaller steel companies fought back hard. A clash between Chicago police, who had been called out by Republic Steel Corporation, and employees of the company led to the 1937 Memorial Day massacre. Ten picketers and two policemen were killed. Across the nation that year there were 4,740 strikes involving nearly 2,000,000 workers. By early 1938 another industry had been organized; Philco, Radio Corporation of America, and General Electric had all come to terms with the United Electrical and Radio Workers. Suspended by the AF of L in 1936, the CIO broke with the older organization in 1938 and renamed itself the Congress of Industrial Organizations; Lewis was elected president. Union membership began to spurt upward. In 1936 that of the AF of L was 3,800,000. By 1940 the CIO and the AF of L together had 9,000,000 members.

Farm Relief. Roosevelt's program for agriculture, the most depressed sector of the American economy, illustrated well his willingness to try new ideas. Agriculture was in desperate need of a remedy to cure the chronic overproduction that had kept farm prices down. Accepting a measure drafted by Secretary of Agriculture Henry A. Wallace, Congress established another "alphabet agency," the Agricultural Adjustment Administration, in May 1933. The goal of the AAA was to create a condition that Wallace called "planned scarcity." Production of basic commodities was to be limited in order to increase agricultural prices to "parity" (equal purchasing power) with industrial prices, the ratio being based on price levels just before World War I when farmers had been reasonably prosperous. The Secretary of Agriculture was authorized to negotiate agreements with farmers that would pay them cash subsidies for voluntarily reducing livestock and acreage under cultivation. The money for the subsidies was to be collected through a tax levied on processors of farm produce, who would in turn charge the consumer a higher price. The first commodities to be controlled were corn, wheat, cotton, rice, dairy goods, hogs, and tobacco. Since the 1933 plants were already growing by the time the law was passed, acreage restrictions had to be supplemented with destruction of produce. Cotton planters were paid to plow up one-fourth of their year's crop. Wheat was burned, and six million pigs and pregnant sows were slaughtered and either distributed to persons on relief or simply buried.

The success of these drastic measures was uncertain, although prices began to rise and farm income improved generally. When farmers in the South cut down their cotton acreage, thousands of tenant farmers, most of them blacks, were put out of work. After the extended drought of 1933 on the Great Plains, the terrible Black Blizzards of 1933 through 1935 created an "unplanned" scarcity of wheat, corn, and cattle. Sulfurous clouds of swirling dust made agriculture impossible from the Texas Panhandle to the Dakotas. Hundreds of thousands of "Okies" and "Arkies" were forced to abandon their lands and to migrate. The harrowing story of the refugees from the Dust Bowl is poignantly described in John Steinbeck's *The Grapes of Wrath*, a novel published in 1939.

Criticism of the AAA was scathing. It was denounced as a "left-wing scheme staffed by collectivists." Crop reductions at a time when drought threatened the country with actual shortages were difficult for the public to accept. In 1936 the AAA was declared unconstitutional by the Supreme Court. Later, however, many portions of the program were rescued through the Soil Conservation Act. To replenish soil depleted by the great staple crops, farmers received benefit payments to plant soil-conserving crops or to let the acres remain fallow. The new AAA program passed in 1938, which won the approval of the Court, retained the soil-conservation program and introduced the "ever-normal granary" concept. Farmers were paid to restrict their plantings to acreage allotments that would fill only normal demands. If they produced surpluses, the government lent the farmers money on the produce and stored it for them. When shortages developed and prices rose, the farmer could pay back the loan, reclaim the produce, and sell it on the open market.

Another controversial New Deal agency was the Tennessee Valley Authority. In part, the TVA was created through the unflagging efforts of Senator George Norris of Nebraska, an aging progressive. Far back in the 1920's he had become concerned over the widespread poverty of farmers in the Upper South, an area drained by the Tennessee River. The land had been improperly used and was badly eroded by floods. Moreover, the lack of electric power made the region unattractive to industry.

Financed with billions of dollars appropriated by Congress and directed by a three-man board, the TVA bought or constructed more than thirty dams on the Tennessee River and its tributaries. The hydroelectric power generated by the dams was sold by the TVA directly to individuals and communities throughout the region. Nitrate factories produced abundant nitrates and new forms of fertilizers for farming were developed. In addition, the board was authorized to undertake reforestation, soil conservation, and flood control projects, improve the navigation of the Tennessee River, withdraw marginal lands from cultivation, and promote the economic and social well-being of the seven states in the Tennessee Valley region.

By 1940 the agency had accomplished an astounding rehabilitation of this poverty-scarred area. It continues to operate today, basking in the warm support of the inhabitants of the region. In FDR's time, however, the TVA was bitterly attacked as a form of "creeping socialism," an invasion by government into areas of economic activity rightfully belonging to private enterprise. The President shrugged off such outcries and began planning similar programs for the Columbia and Missouri river valleys, but the growing power of conservatives

Dust storm approaching. BROWN BROTHERS

in the late 1930's forced him to postpone and finally abandon further attempts at regional rehabilitation of river valleys.

Social Welfare Legislation. The scope and variety of New Deal measures were well nigh endless, but the social security program was possibly the most revolutionary of all New Deal undertakings. One of the most tragic aspects of the depression was the plight of millions of the aged. The growing number of senior citizens was a social phenomenon dating from the turn of the century. In 1900 the average life-span of an American was forty-nine years. By 1933, however, it was sixty-one. The decline in the infant mortality rate and the conquest of childhood diseases by medical technology had helped to increase the number of people surviving childhood. Then other medical advances, proper diet, and better understanding of health needs had helped those who survived childhood to live longer. During the depression the ever-increasing number of older people swelled the ranks of the unemployed, for they tended to be the first laid off or fired from their jobs as factories reduced production. The continuing population shift from countryside to city increased the problems of the aged. In 1900 more than three-fifths of the population still lived in a rural environment, but by 1930 the ratio had been reversed. Nearly three-fifths of the nation's citizens were living in or around the cities. On the farm even the elderly could still perform many essential functions. Grandfather chopped wood, mended tools, and assisted his son with planting and harvesting. Grandmother milked cows, cleaned chicken coops, and helped her daughter (or daughter-in-law) with household chores. When young

First in War, First in Peace

"Okie use' ta mean you was from Oklahoma. Now it means you're scum. Don't mean nothing itself, it's the way they say it"
(John Steinbeck, *The Grapes of Wrath*).

THE BETTMANN ARCHIVE

married couples moved to the city to be close to the husband's place of work, however, the older family members were often left behind. Tract houses and apartments were usually too small for the younger people to share with their parents.

The Social Security Act of 1935 was designed to help alleviate this crisis. The federal government would pay pensions of up to fifteen dollars a month to needy persons over sixty-five, with the understanding that cooperating states would contribute an equal amount and administer the pensions. Old-age insurance, or monthly payments to workers who retired at sixty-five years of age, was to be administered directly by the federal government. Equal sums collected through a tax on employee wages and a tax on employer payrolls would fund these social security pensions. To persuade states to legislate unemployment insurance, the law established a federal-state system to be financed by another federal tax on employer payrolls and to be administered by the states. Federal grants-in-aid for the care of needy and delinquent children, for public health work and medical programs for the poverty-stricken, and for vocational training of the physically handicapped were provided on a dollar-matching basis to states that would set up and administer such programs.

The original social security system was woefully inadequate, for far too many occupations were excluded from coverage. Payments were based on the amount earned and barely provided subsistence. But the measure passed in 1935 was a beginning. Over the years the social

The Depression Decade, 1929–1939

security program has been broadened and improved. Today nearly nine out of ten employed persons pay social security taxes and are eligible for benefits.

Other New Deal Measures. To touch on all New Deal creations would be impossible, but the function of a few other agencies should be mentioned in passing: the Securities and Exchange Commission, to regulate the stock market; the Rural Electrification Agency, to provide cheap power to farms; the Home Owners Loan Corporation, to refinance mortgages on low-cost homes; and the Federal Housing Administration, to make loans for home improvements.

Election of 1936. The United States had moved a long way toward economic recovery by 1936. By almost every measurable index, the economy was on the upswing. Unemployment had declined by nearly 4,000,000 since 1933, average weekly earnings of workers had risen from $17 to $22, the annual national income had increased by $23,000,000,000, and a dramatic rise in farm prices had nearly tripled the net income of farmers. But there were still 9,030,000 unemployed.

In 1936 the Republicans selected wealthy oil man Alfred M. Landon, then the respected and able but colorless governor of Kansas, to run against Roosevelt. Landon was himself reasonably liberal, but he was a poor speaker and made little impression in spite of a vigorous Republican campaign. In an overwhelming display of confidence in the New Deal, Roosevelt received nearly 28,000,000 votes, Landon fewer than 17,000,000. Roosevelt won the electoral votes of every state except Vermont and Maine, and the Democratic majorities in both houses of Congress were embarrassingly large.

New Deal in Retreat

Franklin Roosevelt interpreted his sweeping victory in the election as a mandate for him to continue the New Deal's social revolution. With public acclaim for him at its peak, the President announced in his inaugural address on January 20, 1937 his intention to solve the continuing problems of the "one-third of a nation ill-housed, ill-clad, ill-nourished." Yet in the next two years, after this great demonstration of his popularity at the polls, Roosevelt was to suffer a number of stinging setbacks. Moreover, world developments toward the end of FDR's second term in office were destined to overshadow and eclipse the New Deal.

"Packing the Court." Two weeks after his second inauguration President Roosevelt proposed a measure to enlarge the Supreme Court drastically and to reform the lower federal courts. The essential provision would allow the President to appoint one additional justice, up to a maximum of six, for each member of the Court who had reached the age of seventy and chose not to retire within six months. Under this arrangement the Court might be increased to fifteen members. Although Roosevelt's specious contention was that the Supreme Court was overworked and behind in its case schedule, his real concern was that the existing Court, with six justices over seventy, had stood opposed to increasing the scope of federal authority and had ruled against a number of his pet schemes, among them the NRA and the AAA. From Roosevelt's point of view, "fossilized old timers" in the judiciary were blocking the will of the people, and the proposed increase in the number of justices would allow him to appoint to the Court men who were sympathetic to the New Deal program.

An irritated Congress and astounded public reacted against the slick proposal, accusing Roosevelt of trying to pack the Court with "New Dealish sycophants." Many feared that the President was seeking dictatorial powers. Some of his inveterate supporters spoke against the measure. The Republicans wisely kept silent and watched the Democrats split their party on this issue. Finally on July 22, after months of bitter controversy, the Senate recommitted the bill to the Judicial Committee by the overwhelming vote of seventy to twenty. In August

276   *First in War, First in Peace:*

they passed a law that reformed the procedures of the lower courts but did not mention new justices. Roosevelt had lost prestige that would be difficult to regain.

Yet although the President lost the battle, he won the war. Even while the measure was being considered, the Court itself weakened the case for its enlargement. The formerly conservative Justice Owen Roberts, perhaps stung by the charges of ultraconservatism leveled against the Court, started to vote on the liberal side. Some of the Court's earlier decisions were reversed, and during these months the Wagner Act and the social security legislation of 1935 were upheld. On May 18 the impending retirement of one of the oldest conservative justices was announced. By 1941 six more justices had retired and the Court had been largely reconstituted.

The Recession. Worse setbacks lay yet in store for the New Deal. In early 1937 Roosevelt was encouraged by signs that indicated business was recovering. Anxious to halt the criticism leveled at him about the unbalanced budget, he cut back sharply on the spending of the WPA and other relief agencies. High tax rates on large individual and corporate incomes, enacted in 1935 and 1936, probably cut into private investment and business expansion at this time. Moreover, the funds accumulating in the Treasury for social security pensions, which would not begin to be paid until January 1942, cut purchasing power. Between August and October the economy went into a sharp decline. Unemployment rose by two million, stocks plummeted, bankruptcies increased, and farm prices began slipping. The attitude of New Dealers was "Now, let's not get excited. It's just a temporary setback, a kind of recession." In answer, the Republicans roared back, "Let's call a spade a spade! We're still in the depression. The New Deal has failed!"

But business continued to decline, and by January 1938 there were ten million persons out of work. Once again, Roosevelt was obliged to ask Congress for heavy appropriations for relief programs. In February the second AAA law was passed to halt the skid in farm prices, and two months later outlays for the WPA and the lending activities of the RFC were again stepped up. Plans for many of the immense PWA projects were finally completed during this recession and brought aid to the heavy industries. But not until 1940 was the business volume to equal that of July 1937.

Errors in political judgment, defections from voting for Roosevelt's policies within his own party, the labor strife of 1937, the 1937–1938 recession, and the millions of workers still unemployed damaged FDR's image. In the 1938 congressional elections the Republicans came alive again and registered solid gains, although they were still very much a minority in Congress.

Last Acts of the New Deal. Although Roosevelt's second term was somewhat a study in frustration, two additional and significant New Deal measures were passed. The United States Housing Authority was created in 1937 to help state and local public housing agencies finance slum clearance and the construction of low-income housing projects.[4] The second major reform legislation was the Fair Labor Standards Act (popularly called the Wages and Hours Law) of June 1938. This measure fixed the minimum wage of workers engaged in interstate commerce at twenty-five cents an hour (to be raised to forty cents by 1945) and defined the maximum work week as forty-four hours (to be lowered to forty hours by 1941). The law also prohibited labor by children under sixteen in most industries, under eighteen when the occupation was dangerous. The Fair Labor Standards Act fell considerably short of achieving the hopes of its proponents for many of the poorest-paid workers were excluded from its

---

[4] Roosevelt was the first Democrat to win the Negro vote away from the Republicans, but the USHA was the only substantial help extended to Negroes by the New Deal, for FDR depended on white Southern support. Blacks, however, sensed that the man in the White House was sympathetic and continued to vote Democratic in large numbers.

The Depression Decade, 1929–1939

provisions, and the minimum wage established was unrealistically low. But the Fair Labor Standards Act was a start toward the provision of greater protection of workers by the federal government. Since 1938 the law has been expanded to cover almost all classes of wage earners involved in interstate commerce, and the minimum wage has been gradually increased to $1.75 an hour.

By 1939 the New Deal was losing momentum. The increasing power of conservatives in both parties made the enactment of social welfare legislation almost impossible. Moreover, Americans were already preoccupied with momentous events in Europe and Asia. The growing stridency of Fascism in Italy and Germany and the rise of Japanese militarism turned the attention away from domestic social problems. Recognizing the need for bipartisan support on foreign policy in a world rushing toward another war, President Roosevelt was willing to put the New Deal aside. His massive program was halted by war just as Wilsonian progressivism had ended in 1916 with America's preparation to enter the First World War.

SUGGESTED READINGS

*Aaron, D., *Writers on the Left* (1961).
Abbott, G., *From Relief to Social Security* (1941).
*Adams, S. A., *Incredible Era* (1939).
Allen, F. L., *Since Yesterday* (1940).
Alsop, J. and T. Catledge, *The 168 Days* (1938).
Benedict, M. R., *Can We Solve the Farm Problem?* (1955).
Bernstein, I., *The New Deal Collective Bargaining Policy* (1950).
Bingham, A. M., *Challenge to the New Deal* (1934).
Black, J. D., *Parity, Parity, Parity* (1942).
Blum, J. M., *Years of Urgency, 1938–1941* (1964).
*Burns, J. M., *Roosevelt: The Lion and the Fox* (1956).
Conkin, P. K., *Tomorrow a New World* (1959).
*Freidel, F., *The New Deal and the American People* (1964).
*Galbraith, J. K., *The Great Crash* (1955).
*Hofstadter, R., *The American Political Tradition* (1948).
Hoover, H., *Challenge to Liberty* (1934).
Hoover, H., *The Memoirs of Herbert Hoover* (2 vols., 1951).
Ickes, H., *The Secret Diary of Harold L. Ickes* (3 vols., 1953–54).
*Jackson, R. H., *The Struggle for Judicial Supremacy* (1941).
Johnson, H. S., *The Blue Eagle from Egg to Earth* (1935).
Johnson, V., *Heaven's Tableland: The Dust Bowl Story* (1947).
Jones, J., *My Thirteen Years with the R.F.C., 1932–1945* (1951).
*Keynes, J. M., *General Theory of Employment, Interest and Money* (1936).
Latham, E., *The Communist Controversy in Washington* (1966).
*Leuchtenburg, W. E., *Franklin D. Roosevelt and the New Deal* (1963).
Lyon, L. S., *The National Recovery Administration* (1935).
*Mitchell, B., *Depression Decade* (1947).

Peel, R. V. and T. C. Donnelly, *The Campaign of 1932* (1935).
*Perkins, D., *The New Age of Franklin Roosevelt, 1932–1945* (1957).
Perlman, S., *Labor in the New Deal Decade* (1945).
*Rauch, B., *The History of the New Deal* (1944).
Robinson, E. E., *The Roosevelt Leadership, 1933–1945* (1955).
*Roosevelt, E., *This I Remember* (1949).
*Rozwenc, E. C., ed., *The New Deal, Revolution or Evolution?* (1959).
*Schlesinger, A. M., Jr., *The Age of Roosevelt (The Crisis of the Old Order)* (1957).
*Schlesinger, A. M., Jr., *The Coming of the New Deal* (1959).
*Schlesinger, A. M., Jr., *The Politics of Upheaval* (1960).
*Shannon, D. A., *The Great Depression* (1960).
Sherwood, R., *Roosevelt and Hopkins* (1948).
*Swados, H., ed., *The American Writer and the Great Depression* (1966).
*Tugwell, R. G., *The Democratic Roosevelt* (1957).
*Warren, H. G., *Herbert Hoover and the Great Depression* (1959).
*White, E. E., *The Development of the Social Security Act* (1962).
Wolfskill, G., *The Revolt of the Conservatives* (1962).

CHAPTER 28

Internationalism in Retreat, 1921–1939

Only a peace between equals lasts.
WOODROW WILSON, 1917

BROWN BROTHERS

HARDING HAD ACCURATELY READ THE FEELINGS of millions of Americans when he declared in his inaugural address that "Confident of our ability to work out our own destiny, we seek no part in directing the destinies of the Old World. We do not mean to be entangled. We will accept no responsibility except as our own conscience and judgment may determine." In effect, Harding was announcing that the United States was abandoning the Wilsonian ideal of commitment to world association for the more comfortable policy of limited internationalism, in keeping with national tradition. The government would follow a policy of noninvolvement, except when American interests were directly affected. Some observers expressed alarm at the course set by President Harding, yet the same policy was adopted by the subsequent administrations of Coolidge and Hoover and by Franklin Roosevelt in his early years as President. Only in the late 1930's, when the world was menaced by the aggressions of Japan and the rearmed Germany of Adolf Hitler, did President Roosevelt's foreign policy begin to shift toward a course of positive international cooperation.

POSTWAR WITHDRAWAL AND DRIFT

The disillusionment of Americans with their participation in World War I and their dissatisfaction with the peace settlement inevitably induced a new mood of withdrawal and isolationism. Wilson had led his countrymen to believe that their war effort would help bring about a new world order, but it had not. For their unrewarding sacrifice Americans blamed not only their former President but their "noble" wartime allies, whose selfish goals they had unknowingly served, and all the other contentious people of Europe, whose quarrels seemed unending. The continent had never before been viewed so unfavorably by Americans or with such suspicion and hostility. Government policies relating to immigration, tariffs, and European debts reflected this distrust.

Immigration. The reversal of government policies on immigration from Europe was drastic.

Until the 1920's the federal government had permitted European nationals almost completely unrestricted entry into the United States. Attracted by the seemingly bountiful opportunities of America, European immigrants poured into the country throughout the nineteenth century in ever-increasing numbers, their entries reaching the greatest proportions in the early twentieth century. The climax came in 1913 when more than two million Europeans passed through the gates of the immigration inspection post at Ellis Island, New York, on their way to a new life. Then during World War I European immigration fell off sharply.

Native and old-stock Americans had viewed the tide of immigration with increasing restiveness. They saw the traditional American way of life threatened by the hordes of aliens who spoke strange languages and observed markedly different customs. The spread of Bolshevism across Europe in the wake of the 1918 armistice aroused additional apprehension among native Americans, who noted with concern the radicalism of Russian and other eastern European immigrants who began to arrive again in large numbers.

In response to this surge of public anxiety, Congress in 1921 passed an emergency quota bill. This law assigned each European country a quota equal to three per cent of its nationals living in the United States in 1910, when the foreign-born population had still been predominantly northern and western European in origin. Through this system immigration was restricted to about 350,000 persons annually. The Emergency Quota Act of 1921 was replaced by still more restrictive legislation. In 1924 Representative Albert Johnson of Washington proposed a bill to cut quotas to two per cent, based on the census of 1890. By substituting 1890 for 1910 as the base year, the Johnson measure would favor immigration from northwestern Europe to an even greater extent and sharply reduce the influx from southern and eastern Europe. Thus Protestant Nordics from Britain, Germany, and Scandinavia, more akin to the "basic strain of our population," would be permitted to immigrate in relatively large numbers, while the Latin and Slavic peoples, predominantly Roman Catholic and Greek Orthodox, as well as Jews, would be largely excluded.

The 1924 law also provided specifically for the total exclusion of Asians, a particular affront to the sensitive Japanese who considered the measure a violation of the gentlemen's agreement concluded during Theodore Roosevelt's administration. Anti-American mass meetings were held throughout Japan after an official protest lodged by the Japanese ambassador against the proposed bill was ignored. The government of China was also irked. Premier Benito Mussolini reacted angrily to the law as a slur on Italy's national honor.

Congress, supported by business and organized labor, was not to be deterred by such hostile reactions. By 1930 they had amended the law to admit only a maximum of 150,000 immigrants to the United States annually. Although some kind of limitation on immigration may have been necessary and reasonable, the application of biased restrictions was certain to hurt the sensibilities of those nations whose peoples were discriminated against. In their existing mood of withdrawal, however, Americans seemed not to care about world opinion. As far as they were concerned, the less alien "contamination," the better off the nation would be.[1]

Tariffs. During the 1920's the federal government resumed its traditional policy, interrupted during the Wilson administration, of hiking tariffs. In spite of Wilson's admonition in 1921 that "this is no time for the erection of high

---

[1] The quota restrictions remained in effect for decades, with the exception of occasional admission of refugee groups during World War II, the lowering of barriers following the failure of the Hungarian revolt in 1956, and the admittance of refugees from Castro's Cuba during the 1960's. The quota laws were stiffened in 1952 by the passage of the McCarran-Walter Act, but the ban against immigration of Asians was finally removed. Only during Lyndon Johnson's second term, in 1966, were quota restrictions finally eased somewhat and inequities corrected.

trade barriers," Congress enacted an emergency tariff law imposing heavy duties on a number of agricultural goods. Then in 1922 the Fordney-McCumber Tariff established record-high duties for a broad spectrum of agricultural and manufactured products.

The Fordney-McCumber Tariff was a crude, bumbling attempt to provide more protection for Western farmers against their foreign competition. In a deeper sense, however, it reflected the nation's traditional craving for economic self-sufficiency, which extended back to its very early days. To the citizens of the United States this law seemed as appropriate as the crackdown on foreign radicalism and the heavy restrictions on European immigration.

In practice, the Fordney-McCumber Tariff probably hurt rather than helped the farmer. Europeans, quite naturally, were outraged by a policy that sharply decreased the sale of their products to American markets; European statesmen complained that such protectionism hampered Europe's ability to earn American dollars and to pay war debts to the United States. When Congress refused to relent, European governments retaliated by raising the tariffs on American imports, particularly farm products.

The climax of protectionism came in 1930 with the passage of the Hawley-Smoot Tariff, which has been called, with some justification, "the stupidest piece of legislation ever enacted in the history of Congress." It was signed by President Hoover in the depths of the Great Depression, even though a petition bearing the signatures of over a thousand economists urged him to veto the measure. Under the impact of the Hawley-Smoot Tariff, international trade, which was already slipping, declined to disaster levels. The deepening American depression spread until it became worldwide, heightening the bitterness between the United States and Europe.

War Debt Questions. Probably the most disturbing aspect of the increasingly intense mood of isolationism exhibited during the 1920's was the government's policy toward war debts. As indicated in Chapter 25, the government had granted extensive credit to the European Allies during the First World War to purchase war materials in the United States. By November 11, 1918 the Allies had, in effect, borrowed more than $7,000,000,000. After the end of hostilities, the United States continued to grant credit to European countries for relief and reconstruction. These additional sums brought the grand total to more than $10,000,000,000.

The United States had readily offered and the Allies had gladly accepted these extensive loans. By 1920, however, icy financial considerations had replaced the warm glow of wartime cooperation. The United States wanted repayment of all debts, with interest. Americans argued that this demand was simply sound business practice, but Europeans regarded their attitude as callous. They pointed to their war-battered economies and their war dead and to the prosperity that their heavy purchasing had brought to the United States. As the Allied man in the street saw it, his people had bled for democracy while Americans had merely provided the money. Europeans contended that the spilled blood of French, British, and Italian soldiers was more than adequate compensation.

The repayment of war debts to the United States was complicated by three factors, the interallied war debts, the protectionist policy of the United States toward its domestic industries, and the connection that the Allies made between their debts and war reparations owed by Germany. Besides securing loans from the United States, the Allies had borrowed from and loaned to one another during the war. France and Italy were both debtors, for they had borrowed more than they had loaned, but Britain was a creditor, owing $4,000,000,000 to the United States but being owed $10,500,000,000. As early as December 1918 the British offered to cancel debts due them from France and Italy if the Americans would cancel the British debt to the United States. Later, in 1922, Britain proposed canceling all the interallied war debts and offered to abandon claims to reparations as part of a general settlement to end "the economic injury inflicted on the world by the present state of things."

The United States refused to consider either of the British proposals. The Allies would also have been willing to ship goods and foodstuffs to the United States in payment for their debts, or to engage in trade to earn American dollars, but the Fordney-McCumber Tariff prevented the sale of their products on the American market. Finally, the Allies had avowed from the beginning that payment of their debts would depend on their collecting reparations from Germany, but the United States insisted that the interallied debts were not related to reparations.

Continued pressure by the United States forced the Allies to use harsh measures to collect reparations. When the German government defaulted on coal deliveries in 1923, French and Belgian troops occupied the Ruhr industrial district in western Germany and placed business enterprises under military supervision. The German government urged the populace to resist passively in thr Franco-Belgian attempt to collect reparations by force. Miners did not go into the pits, and factory workers performed only perfunctorily or left their jobs. Paper money, printed by the government to support the idle workers and compensate their employers, wildly inflated the currency until the mark fell to one-trillionth its prewar value. In the ensuing chaos the German republic nearly collapsed, creating a receptive audience among the people for the extremist views of Adolf Hitler.

The economic and financial structure of the world was in danger of collapse. In April 1924 an international committee of experts, headed by a Chicago banker, Charles Gates Dawes, worked out a less burdensome scale for reparations payments, arranged for foreign loans to stabilize the German monetary system, and recommended the withdrawal of the French and Belgians from the Ruhr. Germany's economy began to revive with the assistance of extensive loans from banks in the United States and Europe. This policy led to a unique cycle, in which the Germans paid reparations to the French, the French paid the British, the British paid the Americans, who in turn returned the money to the Germans as additional loans. The peculiar but workable process was interrupted by the Great Depression in the United States. With no American funds available for loans, the German government was obligated to default on the payment of war reparations, and in due course the Allies suspended payment of war debts to the United States. By this time too the economic depression had become worldwide and was debilitating Europe. In May 1931 the Austrian Credit-Anstalt failed, and by mid-July all German banks had closed. Then in September Great Britain was forced to abandon the gold standard, and many other countries of the world were soon compelled to take the same measure. President Hoover, persuaded by expert opinion that the burden of paying intergovernmental debts was one of the greatest obstacles to world trade and world recovery, proposed a one-year moratorioum (suspension of payments) on war debts in June 1931. But the next year Congress refused either to permit the continuation of the moratorium or to cancel the debts.

Inflammatory words traveled back and forth across the Atlantic. Americans accused the Allies of reneging, and Europeans angrily denounced the United States for demanding "blood money" during this period of economic distress. When Adolf Hitler came to power in 1933, he solved the problem in his own way by repudiating Germany's war reparations. That year only a few countries made token payments on the war debts, and after that no payments were received, estranging the United States and its wartime partners in the 1930's when unity might have helped to stop Hitler's early aggressions.

CONTINUED INTERNATIONALISM

Even though the United States behaved like an ostrich in conducting international affairs during the 1920's, its citizens did not sever all ties with other countries. When populaces, not governments, were in need, Americans indicated their abiding humanitarianism. Aid from private citizens flowed overseas throughout the 1920's to relieve the stricken in many corners of the globe. The American Relief Association, headed by Secretary of Commerce Herbert Hoover and supported by public and private sources, provided food and medical care for millions of starving people during the famine of 1921 and 1922 in war-wrecked Russia. In 1922, during the Greek-Turkish War, the Near East Relief Committee helped millions of refugees in a similar manner. Massive American aid was supplied to the grateful Japanese following the terrible Tokyo earthquake in 1923.

American charity found less urgent outlets in financing hospitals, educational institutions, and roving medical missions in foreign lands. Particularly active in the Middle East (then called the Near East) was the American Friends Service Committee, a Quaker organization which provided medical aid. American donations and staff continued to help operate Robert College at Istanbul and the American University of Beirut, both founded in the 1860's. The Rockefeller family contributed funds to restore Reims cathedral, a crowning achievement of medieval civilization which had been seriously damaged by artillery fire during the First World War.

In the 1920's American travelers created a bond between the New World and the Old. Tourists in ever-increasing numbers became a familiar sight in European cities during the summer months. No longer was the Continent merely a playground for the rich. Middle-class Americans, college students, school teachers, and businessmen appeased their restless urge for adventure with tours of the Old World. Richard Halliburton called this "horizon chasing" in his lighthearted, entertaining book of travels, *The Royal Road to Romance.* Paris became a mecca for tourists, aspiring American artists, and the literary set. London, Heidelberg, Rome, Florence, and the Riviera were only slightly less popular. The economies of many European countries became dependent on the influx of American tourist dollars.

The Washington Arms Conference, 1921–1922. The United States did on occasion attempt some leadership in world affairs. The situation in the Pacific and the Far East first aroused the United States to action. Japan's policy of expansionism on the Asiatic mainland had not abated, for Japanese forces still occupied eastern Siberia and the Shantung province of China, seized from Germany during the war. The continuation of the Anglo-Japanese alliance of 1902 also worried Americans, who believed it would oblige the British to fight against them should Japan and the United States clash. Moreover, all three of the great naval powers in the Pacific—Great Britain, the United States, and Japan—had developed amibitious programs of naval expansion during the war, programs which were now threatening to engulf them in a dangerous and costly naval arms race. Such a threat to peace, less than two years after the most dreadful war in history, and such expense to the American taxpayer were viewed with grave concern in Washington.

In December 1920 Senator William E. Borah introduced a resolution requesting the President to call a three-power disarmament conference. Winning wide public approval, the resolution had passed both houses of Congress by the following June. Secretary of State Hughes proceeded to invite representatives of eight other nations—Great Britain, Japan, China, France, Italy, Portugal, Belgium, and the Netherlands—to meet in Washington, D.C., on Armistice Day, 1921.

Secretary Hughes opened the conclave with the dramatic proposal that the major naval powers scrap large portions of their existing fleets, halt present construction of battleships, and agree to build no more for ten years. After much discussion the major powers accepted Hughes's rates of 5:5:3 for limiting their navies. The United States and Great Britain would restrict the tonnage of capital ships (battleships and cruisers weighing more than 10,000 tons) to a total of 525,000 tons, and Japan would be limited to 315,000 tons. The two Mediterranean powers, Italy and France, accepted a limit of 175,000 tons. Although a similar ratio but less tonnage was established for aircraft carriers, no limitation was placed on smaller naval craft, such as destroyers and submarines. It was stipulated that before the ten-year period for this Five-Power Pact ended, there should be another meeting to reconsider the limitation of naval forces.

The United States, France, Great Britain, and Japan also signed the Four-Power Pact, aimed at preserving the status quo in the Pacific. In this forceless agreement, they pledged to keep the peace in the Pacific by respecting one another's rights in that area and merely declared an intention to confer if these rights should be threatened by aggression. The Four-Power Pact did specifically terminate the Anglo-Japanese alliance, however.

A third important agreement reached at the Washington meeting, called the Nine-Power Pact, concerned the status of China. The other eight governments agreed to respect its territorial integrity and to recognize the Open Door principle (page 550) guaranteeing the right of all nations to participate freely in the commercial development of China. Another treaty between China and Japan provided for the withdrawal of Japan from Shantung province and the return of its sovereignty to China.

In retrospect, the Washington Conference was well-meaning in its attempt to reduce international tensions, but its accomplishments were dubious. The three principal agreements were all to be nullified by Japan in the 1930's. The only one of any substance was the 5:5:3 pact, but an attempt to include limitations on smaller craft at the Geneva Conference in 1927 failed after fruitless discussions. At the London Naval Conference in 1930, however, some limitations were imposed on the building of auxiliary ships, the 5:5:3 ratios were revised slightly, and the moratorium on naval construction was extended to 1936. The unwieldy arrangement began to collapse in the early 1930's, partly because of France's increasing reluctance to restrict itself to a smaller navy without additional compensations. At this time Japan was already secretly violating the treaty. The end came in 1934 when the Japanese government denounced the agreement that was to bind it until 1936 and openly declared its intention to build capital ships without international restriction.

The conferees had felt that it was inappropriate to invite two important countries to the conference table; Russia was excluded because they feared its Bolshevism, Germany because it was blamed for the war.[2] This failure and the unwillingness of the major powers to make any significant sacrifice of their narrow national interests kept the participants from achieving lasting results.

The Kellogg-Briand Pact. In 1928 the United States made substantial effort to provide world leadership for peace. A year earlier, on the

---

[2]Germany and Russia, acting partly out of pique for their exclusion from the Washington deliberations, held a conference of their own at Rapallo, a resort town in northern Italy, in 1922. Under the provisions of the Rapallo Treaty, the two governments contracted a number of commercial agreements. By secret clauses of the treaty, Russia hired German military experts to help build up the Red army, which in effect allowed Germans to establish deep inside the Soviet Union officer training camps denied them by the Versailles Treaty. Germany also agreed to construct factories for the manufacture of tanks and poison gas.

The Rapallo Conference demonstrated that, conflicting ideologies notwithstanding, the aristocratic Prussian militarists of the Weimar Republic could do business with hard-line Marxists. The agreement they reached foreshadowed the momentous Hitler-Stalin pact of 1939 which led to the outbreak of World War II.

tenth anniversary of the American declaration of war against Germany, Aristide Briand, the French foreign minister, had addressed a message to the United States proposing that it make an agreement with France to outlaw war between the two nations.

Secretary of State Frank B. Kellogg, to whom Briand's plan was eventually submitted, was one of the less inspiring holders of the high office of Secretary of State. The querulous but honest Midwestern lawyer lived in awe and fear of three men—his cranky chief, President Coolidge; his able predecessor, Charles Evans Hughes; and the isolationist chairman of the Senate Foreign Relations Committee, William E. Borah. At first, Kellogg was cool to Briand's idea, but he changed his mind when Borah, Hughes, and eventually Coolidge, and indeed peace advocates and isolationists throughout the country, supported it. Then, with the tenacity of a bull terrier, Kellogg went to work to broaden the proposal by inviting other governments to join in the deliberations.

He succeeded in persuading representatives of fourteen nations to meet in Paris in June 1928, where they signed an agreement to "condemn recourse to war . . . and renounce it as an instrument of national policy." After the ceremony the delegates drank a toast to "eternal peace." When the news of the signing was announced to the multitudes in Paris and across the world, there was great jubilation. Ultimately, more than sixty nations signed the Kellogg-Briand Peace Pact. The Senate ratified it by a vote of eighty-five to one.

Yet the treaty was an exercise in futility and illustrated the unrealistic reasoning of the 1920's. People actually believed that, whatever the economic, social, and psychological tensions in the world, aggressive war could be abolished by merely declaring it an international crime. By implication, the pact exempted "defensive wars." This fact alone guaranteed its ineffectiveness. In fewer than fourteen years most of the signatory nations would be at war.

THE EMERGENCE OF FASCISM

For the failure of the great democracies to establish a lasting peace during the 1920's, the American people must share a heavy responsibility. Turning their backs on Europe, they rejected international cooperation and the leadership that the war had revealed to be their immediate and necessary role in world affairs. By 1929 time was already running out. Across Europe the galaxy of apparently democratic governments created after World War I had already begun to flicker out as dictatorships were established in Poland (1926), Portugal (1926), Yugoslavia (1929), and Bulgaria (1931). With the onset of the Great Depression, the process accelerated and less firmly entrenched democracies became prisoners of events. Poverty and social dislocation bred fear and hatred. Mobs and armies led by political extremists toppled governments. Amidst confusion and despair, the surviving European democracies felt the grim ideology of Fascism spreading its shadow toward them.

The Great Crash of 1929 had shocked the American people from the unreality of their roaring twenties, but, transfixed by their own misfortunes of the next decade, they were even more intent on avoiding involvement in world affairs. With the deprivation suffered during the depression to block their vision, they did not discern the threat of Fascism as it gathered power and momentum in the 1930's.

The Fascist Challenge to World Order

The Philosophy of Fascism. In the 1920's a young Italian political agitator, Benito Mussolini, adopted the word *fascismo*[3] (Fascism) and built an ideology around it. Possibly the only ideational word ever chosen first and then endowed with a gobbet of ideas to give it meaning, Fascism has been erroneously identified in the

---
[3] The Italian word *fascio*, from which it derives, means "bundle." The *fasces*, a bundle of rods bound about an ax, was a symbol of authority in ancient Rome.

Il Duce. CULVER PICTURES

Der Führer. BROWN BROTHERS

political spectrum as the persuasion farthest removed from Communism. In recent years the term has become an epithet flung by left-wingers at those who disagree with their point of view. Mussolini originally attached to the word Fascism a strange amalgam of musty, contradictory ideas. Compounding his philosophy of discarded notions of nineteenth-century Romantic philosophers, vague fragments of medieval thought, and ideas gleaned from Marxist socialism, he garnished it all with the pseudo-scientific ideas of racial Darwinism.

Amidst the mystical nonsense of Fascism — the elevation of the state above the individual, rule by the elite, the pursuit of a life of action, and the vaunting of violence — two ideas stand out clearly, the nobility of war and the "fruitful" inequality of races. Both concepts defy rational comprehension. According to Mussolini, war was good, and peace only an unfortunate interlude between two wars. As he put it,

"War alone brings up to its highest tension all human energy and puts the stamp of nobility upon the peoples who have the courage to meet it. All other trials are substitutes, which never really put men into the position where they have to make the great decision — the alternative of life or death. Thus a doctrine which is founded upon this harmful [*sic*] postulate of peace is hostile to Fascism."

The concept of racial difference was developed in its most precise and irrational form by the philosophers of Nazism, the German counterpart of Fascism. The Nazis established a gradation of races, from very superior to very

First in War, First in Peace

inferior, bestowing upon Germans the title "the master race." Other racial groups—English, Dutch, and Scandinavians, with their strong infusion of Germanic (Teutonic) blood—were considered to possess many of the attributes of the master race. Although the Latin races had traces of Germanism, they were ranked much lower because their stock has been "diluted" and "corrupted" by darker-skinned, "inferior" Mediterranean strains.[4] Slavic peoples, such as the Russians, Poles, and Yugoslavs, were delegated to a much lower status and were to serve as slaves in the Nazi "new order." The darker-skinned peoples of Asia and Africa were even below the Slavs, their rankings to depend on the pigmentation of their skins. Although white, the Jews were placed at the bottom of the scale as a "racially tainted" people. Millions of people believed fervently and tragically in the Fascist-Nazi principles.

First Fascist Government. In October 1922 the black-shirted followers of Benito Mussolini "marched" on Rome. In fear of increased civil violence—which Mussolini and his *fasci* had already helped to foment through their street fighting with Red agitators and attacks against strikers—King Victor Emmanual III capitulated and appointed Mussolini premier of Italy. He was given broad authority to resolve the nation's economic crisis and to restore national pride. Yet many Italians were already concerned about the would-be Caesar's strident talk of war and Italy's imperial destiny.

In his early years of office, Mussolini converted Italy into a dictatorship and ruthlessly stamped out opposition, but he exchanged his uniform for civilian clothes and toned down his speeches. The premier also brought about civil order, embarked on an extensive program of social reform, and built bridges, hospitals, and highways. The Pontine Marshes, where mosquitoes bearing malaria bred, were drained and developed, and the long-standing controversy about the relationship of the Vatican to the state was settled. In addition, the dictator made the Italian trains run on time, widely regarded as a heroic feat.

Many observers began to believe that Mussolini was not such a meance after all. The responsibility of power had apparently sobered the noisy Fascist leader, and perhaps the Italian people needed his kind of dictatorship to achieve progress. Admiration for Mussolini as an able statesman and constructive example for his people soon dispelled earlier fear and doubt, and Fascism for the time being achieved a measure of respectability.

Japanese Militarism. The first serious challenge to global peace in the post-World War I era came not from Italy but from Japan. Through the centuries the Japanese had developed an ideology that had many of the earmarks of Fascism, such as the *samurai* tradition which exalted war and the belief that Japanese are culturally superior. Although the state was deified and the emperor worshiped as the Son of Heaven, there was a two-house Diet similar to the English Parliament, and a cabinet advised the emperor. But a few fantastically rich families controlled all the wealth, and the branches of the military were very powerful. The effects of the Great Depression on Japan's economy played into the hands of the military cliques, which were bent on Japanese expansion, and by 1930 they dominated the government.

Sabotage of a Japanese-controlled railroad outside the Chinese city of Mukden during September 1931 gave the Japanese militarists an excuse to overrun the rich province of Manchuria. This invasion caught the government of China at a particularly weak moment, for Generalissimo Chiang Kai-shek, the chief of state, was attempting to suppress the many semi-independent warlords as well as the Chinese Communists. Ill-equipped to resist Japan with force, the Chinese called upon the League of Nations and the United States for diplomatic

---

[4] The Nazi revised this thesis to mollify Italian pride when Hitler and Mussolini formed their Rome-Berlin Axis partnership in October 1936. The next month the Germans concluded the Anti-Comintern Pact with the Japanese, and a year later Italy adhered to this anti-Communist agreement.

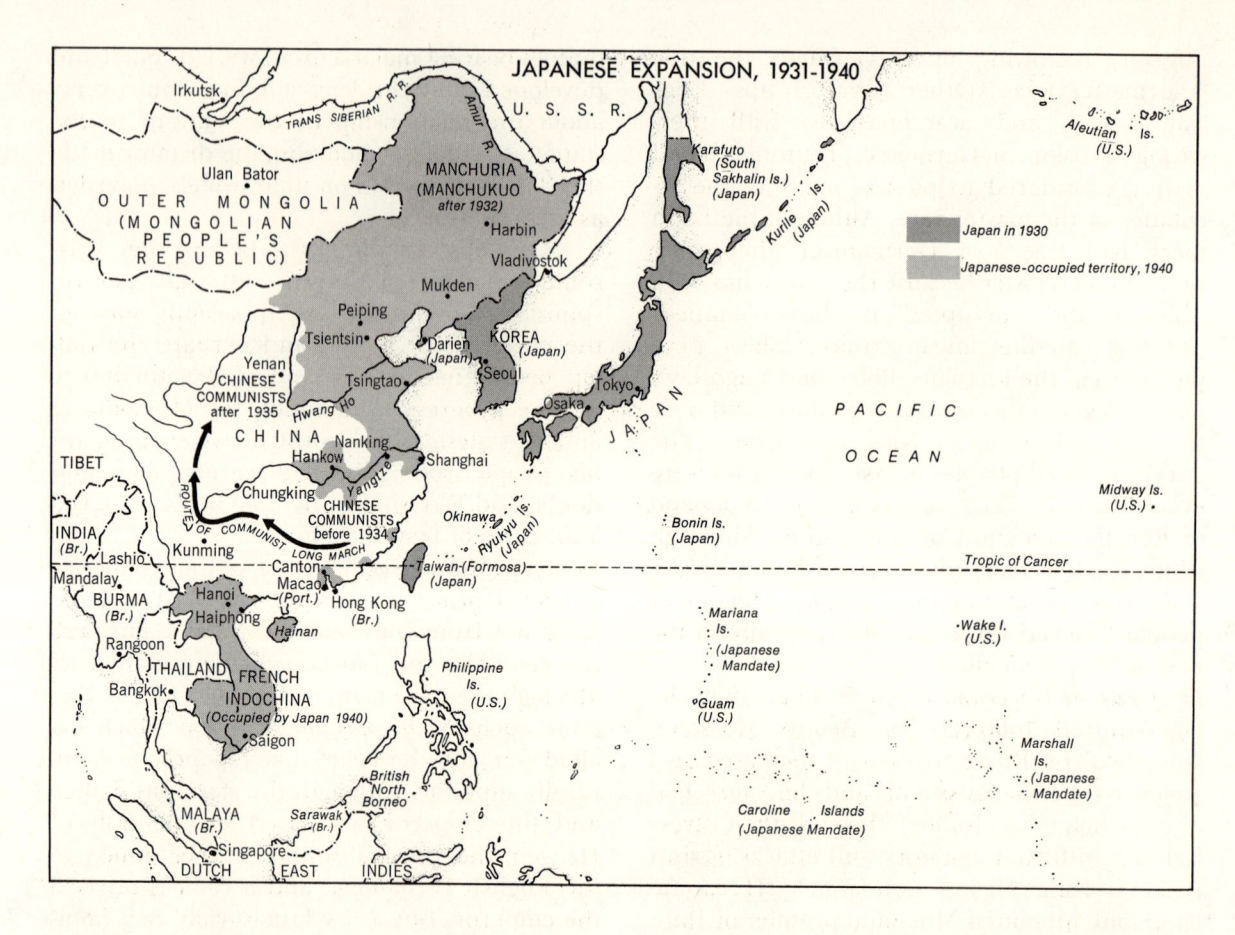

help. The League hesitated and, as Secretary of State Henry L. Stimson put it, became "yellow bellied." The United States promptly protested to the Japanese that they were violating their treaty obligations, but it was also unwilling to act, even though the Open Door policy had acquired a prestige similar to that of the Monroe Doctrine. Secretary Stimson suggested the possibility of economic sanctions (economic blockade) against Japan to Hoover, but the President, feeling that sanctions might lead to war, firmly opposed them. In December the League of Nations appointed the Lytton Commission to investigate the Manchurian crisis. Early the next month Stimson addressed identical notes to Japan and China, and to other signatories of the Nine-Power Pact, stating that the United States could not recognize territorial conquest through armed force in violation of the Kellogg-Briand Pact. Undeterred by mere words, the Japanese military and naval forces subjected Shanghai, China's largest city, to furious attack and fastened their hold on Manchuria, which by February had been organized into the satellite state of Manchukuo.

Japan's conquest of Manchuria was devastating to world stability, for the first overt challenge to the authority of the League of Nations had demonstrated its weakness as a force for peace. When the Lytton Report condemning Japan's action, but acknowledging its special interests in Manchuria, was adopted by the League in February 1933, Japan promptly gave notice of withdrawal from the organization. The Japanese had also discovered that they could defy United States authority in the Far

First in War, First in Peace

East without danger of retaliation. President Hoover, preoccupied with the Great Depression and unwilling to act with firmness in an area that was of secondary concern to United States security, had clearly set a course of short-sighted isolationism. In fairness to Hoover, however, it must be acknowledged that Americans would probably not have supported the use of force, or even a show of force, at that time. In any event, the naval power of the United States in 1931 was extremely limited.

Acceleration of Fascist Aggression

Italy's Invasion of Ethiopia. Having noted Japan's successful seizure of Manchuria, Mussolini started planning in 1933 and was ready by 1935 for his own war of conquest. He chose Ethiopia, the only important independent state left in Africa. Italian and Ethiopian troops clashed in December 1934 and then the following October Mussolini ordered an invasion of the landlocked Ethiopia. Large Italian armies had been massed in the meantime in the adjacent Italian colonies of Eritrea and Somaliland and were able to penetrate the country without much resistance. Ethiopia was an impoverished, technologically backward nation, most of those peoples lived in a primitive tribal society. Haile Selassie, the emperor, appealed to the League of Nations to halt Italy's flagrant aggression, warning that the League was doomed as an international organization if it failed to intervene.

The League declared Italy the aggressor and voted to apply economic sanctions. Credit was denied Italy, and arms and other goods were embargoed—but not oil, the product Mussolini needed most, for he threatened war against any nation that applied the oil sanction. French Premier Pierre Laval had already assented to Mussolini's interest in Ethiopia earlier that year. Without France's military support and with a navy and air force ill-prepared for war, Britain was unwilling to risk provocative action. Moreover, France and Great Britain feared driving Italy into an alliance with Germany. The United States imposed an arms embargo on both belligerents under the Neutrality Act of 1935 (page 660), and Secretary of State Cordell Hull appealed to American business leaders to impose a voluntary embargo on strategic goods to Italy. His plea was ignored, however, and neither he nor President Roosevelt was willing to take any further steps as American trade with Italy increased.

The valiant soldiers of Ethiopia, fighting with rifles and spears against tanks, bombs, and mustard gas, were soon overcome. Mussolini's forces entered Addis Ababa, the capital of Ethiopia, on May 5, 1936, and the nation became a colony of the "New Roman Empire." Haile Selassie went to live in England. The failure of the League to act effectively in this crisis marked the end of its power to influence international affairs, but the League was rendered impotent, not by Mussolini but by the timidity of the British government and the unwillingness of the United States to take positive action.

Hitler's Repudiation of Treaties. While in prison in 1924 for leading his National Socialist German Workers' party in an early and unsuccessful revolt against the Weimar Republic, Adolf Hitler started to write his book *Mein Kampf*, in which he revealed his intentions of destroying the Treaty of Versailles and conquering the world. Nine years later as chancellor of Germany under the same Weimar Republic, whose democratic institutions he was fast destroying, he directed his first insult against the international community by withdrawing Germany from membership in the League of Nations.

In the intervening years the republic had faltered badly, hindered by the humiliation and social demoralization of the German people—stung by defeat in war, the hated terms of the Versailles Treaty, and the demands for reparations—and by their inexperience in making the machinery of a democratic government work. They had formed innumerable political parties, which meant that delegates of many persuasions were elected to the Reichstag; laws were passed only when the factions could agree enough to form coalitions. In addition, the ambitious military was so eager to find means of circumventing the Versailles restrictions on German troops that it allowed the political parties and other groups their own irregular paramilitary forces. Then the catastrophic currency inflation after the Ruhr occupation had wiped out middle-class savings and destroyed political moderacy. Finally, the German people suffered desperate unemployment in the wake of worldwide depression and the cancellation of foreign loans. Beginning in 1929 the hungry and frightened masses turned both left and right politically, but Hitler seized the opportunity and won the greatest allegiance. His spellbinding voice preaching defiance of the Treaty of Versailles and blaming all Germany's woes on the scapegoat Jews; the huge Nazi rallies, staged with stirring martial music, parading storm troopers, and mesmerizing ritual; the decision of conservative industrialists, fearful of a Communist revolution, to support the Nazi party; the constant disruptions of Communist and Socialist meetings by Hitler's storm troops, their ranks now swelled by thousands of unemployed young men — all served to make the National Socialist party the most formidable political force in Germany. Even though Hitler could not win the presidency from Paul von Hindenburg in 1932, by the next February Hindenburg was obliged to make him his chancellor. Then in August 1934, when Hindenburg died, Hitler abolished the office of president by combining its powers with those of the chancellor. Hitler designated himself *der Führer*, his dictatorship the Third Reich.

On March 16, 1935 Hitler took a second step toward world conquest; he denounced the clauses of the Versailles Treaty providing for German disarmament and declared his intention of reintroducing compulsory military training and rebuilding Germany's armed might. As opposed to the Versailles limitation of only 100,000 men, Hitler proclaimed an army of 550,000 to be his goal. The next month Britain, France, and Italy held a conference at Stresa to align themselves against Germany's rearmament, and the League formally denounced Hitler's statement, but no action was taken. A few months later Britain and Germany signed a naval agreement recognizing Germany's right to build a navy one-third the size of the royal navy and to have submarine tonnage equal to sixty per cent of British tonnage. Since the United States had not ratified the Treaty of Versailles, it ignored the affair.

Sensing division and indecision in this testing of the will of Germany's former enemies, Hitler took the next step in his program to reestablish his nation as a world power. In March 1936 he ordered German troops to reoccupy the Rhineland, an area of Germany between the Rhine River and the Franco-Belgian frontier which the Treaty of Versailles had designated as a permanently demilitarized buffer zone. The allies had left the Rhineland ahead of schedule, in 1930. France quickly mobilized 150,000 soldiers, but Great Britain did not want to resort to military action in defense of the treaty. The German Führer had correctly judged the vacillating temper of the democracies. Later he admitted that if "the French had then marched into the Rhineland we would have had to withdraw with our tails between our legs." With these dramatic diplomatic successes to his credit, Hitler prepared for even greater accomplishments.

Civil War in Spain. In July 1936 a junta of army officers headed by General Francisco Franco raised the standard of revolt against the Popular Front government of the Spanish republic. Franco and his insurgents had the support of most of the regular army troops and the air force. The Fascist governments, eager to ensure his victory, almost immediately came to his aid with money, supplies, and military advisers. Mussolini ultimately sent 100,000 Italian "volunteers," and Hitler provided the crack Condor Legion, units of the *Luftwaffe* (German air force).

The Spanish people throughout much of the country united to fight for the republic. They appealed to Great Britain, France, and the United States for aid against Franco and his allies, but these nations sought only to contain the war. When the Loyalists asked to purchase munitions, they were coldly rebuffed by the British and the French, who forbade the export of war materials to both sides and tried to unite all powers on a policy of nonintervention. Later the French wanted to open their borders to pass supplies to the Spanish republicans but were persuaded not to by the British. At first, President Roosevelt and Secretary of State Hull unofficially discouraged businesses in the United States from selling munitions to either side; then on January 6, 1937 the President secured a resolution (page 660) from Congress placing an official embargo on arms shipments to the opposing forces in a civil war.

Only one nation, the Soviet Union, responded to Loyalist Spain's plea for help. The Russians supplied large quantities of equipment as well as technicians and specialized combat units. In return, however, they demanded greater Communist participation in the government. By 1938 the republic had become a virtual prisoner of the Spanish Communists, backed by their Russian allies. Franco learned that Hitler also expected a high price for his assistance. Although Franco protested that the town of Guérnica had no strategic value, the *Luftwaffe* devastated the city in order to test new "terror" and dive-bombing tactics. When a German freighter bringing supplies to Franco was bombed by planes of the Loyalist air force, Hitler retaliated drastically by ordering four German battleships to shell the undefended port of Almería.

For three years the civil war in Spain continued. Although the United States remained neutral and scrupulously gave no aid to either side, many Americans—liberals and members of the intellectual left—volunteered to serve in the Loyalist army. Thousands of them, as well as English and French volunteers, joined the International Brigade of the Spanish republic, and many lost their lives. But the nonintervention policies of their governments condemned the Spanish republic to defeat. By early 1939 Franco's forces had captured Madrid and Barcelona, the two principal centers of Loyalist resistance, and the struggle ended in another triumph of Fascism over the retreating democracies.

The Sino-Japanese War. After having digested Manchuria, Japan was ready in July 1937 to extend its "Greater East Asia Co-prosperity Sphere" by invading China itself. By this time the Chinese people had achieved a degree of unity under the leadership of Chiang Kai-shek. Yet, despite valiant Chinese resistance, the larger and better-equipped Japanese forces proved their superiority and occupied several important industrial areas within the first few months. Chinese cities were mercilessly bombed by the Japanese, outraging world opinion. Initially, Chiang was advised by a staff of German military specialists headed by General Erich von Falkenhausen. In 1938, however, because of increasingly friendly ties between Japan and the Axis powers (Germany and Italy), Hitler ordered the military mission to return home.

In desperation, Chiang Kai-shek inaugurated a "scorched earth" policy and exhorted the Chinese people to resort to guerrilla fighting. He was forced to move his capital from Nanking to Hankow and, finally, to the remote city of Chungking on the upper Yangtze River in October 1938. In the meantime, Chiang again appealed to the Western powers for help, and the Soviet Union responded with equipment, credits, and military specialists. The British allowed a trickle of aid to reach China over the Burma Road, a highway constructed across difficult mountainous terrain from British-held Burma, but eventually increasing preoccupation with Hitler in Europe made the British unwilling to risk conflict with the Japanese. Although sympathetic toward China, the United States was also unwilling to antagonize Japan. Because war was never formally declared by either China or Japan, Roosevelt was not obliged to invoke the Neutrality Act (page 660), and he did not, thus allowing the Chinese to purchase munitions. But in September 1937 he forbade the transport of munitions to either Japan or China on government ships and announced that private shippers acted at their own risk. Japan, with its extensive merchant marine, benefited from his ruling. From 1937 to 1939, American businesses supplied massive quantities of oil, aviation gasoline, machinery, and scrap iron needed by Japan's industries and war machine. Some of this scrap iron was later delivered back to the Americans at considerable velocity, for it was converted into munitions for bombardment of United States forces. In 1941 the war in China became part of the Second World War and fighting continued across the ravaged country until 1945.

The Rape of Czechoslovakia. By 1938 Hitler, a latecomer to the game of aggression, was ready for his first conquest. In March the Nazis marched into Austria and eliminated it as a separate nation. The Austrian government collapsed almost immediately, having been undermined for several years by the activities of Austrian Nazis, Hitler's "fifth column," inside the small, nearly defenseless country. On July 25, 1934 the Austrian Nazis had raided the chancellery and assassinated Chancellor Engelbert Dollfuss. But the Austrian authorities, backed up by Mussolini's troops in the Brenner Pass, were able to rout the conspirators, forcing Hitler to reconsider sending help to the Austrian Nazis and to disavow the *putsch*. Hitler had at that time promised Kurt von Schuschnigg, Dollfuss's successor, that he would respect Austrian independence. Now, four years later, Mussolini was Hitler's ally and von Schuschnigg

First in War, First in Peace

was hustled off to a German concentration camp. In the Western democracies the newspapers headlined the destruction of Austria, but Britain and France were too deeply involved in other problems to consider action.

About this time Americans began to read the English translation of Hitler's *Mein Kampf*, which had first been published in 1927. To a large extent Hitler had borrowed geopolitical concepts developed by Dr. Karl Haushofer, a professor of geography at the University of Munich. According to the Haushofer-Hitler thesis, the heartland of the world was the area encompassing southern Russia, the Balkans, and the Middle East. Here lay the strategic waterways—the Suez Canal and the Straits of the Dardanelles and the Bosporus—the belt of the rich black soil in the Ukraine, and the vast oil deposits around the Persian Gulf. According to Hitler and Haushofer, the nation that controlled the heartland would be able to control the "world island" (the Eurasian and African continents), and whoever controlled the world island would rule the globe. To achieve world domination, Germany must expand eastward.

By seizing Austria, Hitler had taken the first step toward this goal; and it was likely, if not obvious, that Czechoslovakia would be his next victim. In April 1938 Hitler stepped up his incitement of the German-speaking people in the Sudetenland, the fringe area afixed to Czechoslovakia by the Paris Peace Conference of 1919. The Sudeten German party, Nazi in origin, had for several years been active in the area. On April 24, the Sudeten leader Konrad Henlein presented the government with an eight-point program for demanding full autonomy for the Sudetenlanders and a revision of Czech foreign policy. The Sudeten leaders and the government negotiated throughout the spring and summer, but little progress was made. In a series of inflammatory speeches, Hitler indicated that Germany would attack Czechoslovakia on October 1 if the issue was not resolved to his satisfaction. Then in August massive military maneuvers were conducted in many parts of Germany for the benefit of the Czechs and other outsiders. Foreign newspaper correspondents, military experts, and diplomats had an opportunity to see for themselves the huge siege guns, swarms of warplanes, new and highly mechanized equipment, and endless columns of coldly efficient German infantry that composed the armed might of the Nazis.

The Czechoslovakian government was concerned but not dismayed by Hitler's threats. It quietly ordered partial mobilization of its armed forces and moved them into powerful mountain fortifications along the German frontier. This small nation had been a source of pride to Woodrow Wilson before he died, for it was the one creation of the Paris Peace Conference that functioned as a successful democracy with a viable economy. Under the leadership of the founder of their government and their first president, Thomas Masaryk, the Czechs had become a tough, independent-minded people. In addition to a strong army, Czechoslovakia had an excellent munitions industry, the giant Skoda works in the city of Pilsen. The Czechs also had firm treaties of mutual assistance with France and the Soviet Union and believed that they could rely on the support of Great Britain.

The other nations of Europe also quickly prepared for what appeared certain to be the outbreak of World War II. The French ordered partial mobilization and began to move troops into the Maginot Line, a massive series of defensive fortifications along the German border, constructed years earlier at tremendous cost. The British placed their fleet on "standby orders" and began to dig slit trenches as hastily improvised shelters against air raids.

On September 12, in a particularly vitriolic speech at Nuremberg, Hitler reiterated his demand for settlement by October 1 and again threatened that Germany must otherwise use force. Disorders were by then widespread in the Sudetenland, and the Czech government imposed martial law. On September 15 Prime Minister Neville Chamberlain flew to Germany to meet with Hitler at Berchtesgaden in a desperate attempt to avert war. He assured Hitler that he did not oppose the right of the Sudetenland to become an autonomous district within the Czech state. Much to Chamberlain's astonishment, however, Hitler promptly increased his price for peace by demanding the outright cession of the Sudetenland to Germany.

Chamberlain returned to London to meet with French officials, and together they decided to inform Czechoslovakia that it should agree to the cession of the Sudetenland. The Russian government, which was not represented, announced publicly that it would back up Czechoslovakia if France would, but the French were clearly unwilling to oppose Germany unless the British stood with her. The Prague government was forced to agree to cession; Chamberlain at once arranged another meeting with Hitler to work out the details of the transfer.

At Godesberg, as at Berchtesgaden, Hitler stepped up his demands. The Sudetenland must be surrendered at once, without removal or destruction of military and economic establishments. Although his demands were not so bluntly stated, Hitler wanted his troops to enter and occupy the Sudetenland immediately, with a great display of military force. Plebiscites could be held later. Chamberlain considered these terms quite unacceptable and the conference broke down.

The British and French, meeting again in London, agreed that they must support the Czechs against the latest demands. With war so imminent, Czechoslovakia ordered full mobilization of its forces. Chamberlain appealed again to Hitler for a conference to arrange the cession by discussion rather than by force; Mussolini, President Roosevelt, and his own generals helped persuade Hitler to invite the British and French to Munich. The terms accepted by the appeasing Chamberlain and the French premier, Édouard Daladier, with Czechoslovakia and Russia unrepresented at the meeting, were those demanded by Hitler at Godesberg, with only a few face-saving clauses added by Mussolini. Thus on October 1, the date designated earlier by Hitler, German tanks and motorized infantry rolled into the Sudetenland. Not a shot was fired as the area passed under German rule. Czechoslovakia was stripped of her defenses, valuable industrial resources, and nearly five million people, and the promised plebiscites were never held.

On his return to London, Neville Chamberlain was greeted with wild enthusiasm as he announced "it is peace for our time." Because the tall, aristocratic-looking prime minister had supposedly rescued western Europe from the brink of war, people throughout the world regarded him as the apostle of peace and breathed a sigh of relief. To those in England and the United States who criticized Neville Chamberlain, the *New York Times* thundered:

"Let no man say that the statesmen of Britain and France were out-traded in the bargain they have struck, until he has attempted to add the total price they might have had to pay for any other settlement than the one which they have taken — the price in death and destruction spread across the face of Europe; in whole cities laid waste by high explosives and seared with poison gas; in broken and mangled bodies of women and their children. . . ."

The *Kansas City Star* echoed the sentiments of the *Times*:

"Europe not only has been saved from imminent catastrophe of war. It has been definitely set on the road toward a more stable peace. The announcement of the Anglo-German understanding should prove a forerunner to a general settlement that will bring the world out from the nightmare that has been haunting it for years."

In a much more realistic vein, the *New York Tribune* declared:

"To rescue a few million Sudetens, at least partially protected by treaty of their civil rights, the Allies have surrendered many more mil-

298 *First in War, First in Peace*

"Peace for our time."   PHOTOWORLD

lions to the tender mercies of a Hitler who has pursued his own minorities with a savagery for which modern Europe holds no parallel."

During the Munich conference Hitler told Chamberlain that he would respect the integrity of what remained of Czechoslovakia and that he had "no further territorial designs in Europe." The German dictator managed to keep his word for almost six months. But on March 15, 1939 Hitler put an end to Czech independence by ordering German tanks to enter Prague, the nation's capital. The western portion of Czechoslovakia (Bohemia and Moravia) were converted into a German protectorate. Slovakia, the eastern rump of the small country, became a satellite of Greater Germany. Without an opportunity to resist, Czechoslovakia had ceased to exist, and Hitler had taken a long step eastward toward the heartland whose possession he regarded as necessary for his conquest of the world. Three weeks later the

Internationalism in Retreat, 1921–1939   299

Italians bombarded the coast towns of Albania, landed an army, and soon overran the whole country.

THE BEGINNING OF THE RECKONING

American Isolationism, 1932–1938

While the Fascist nations moved from triumph to greater triumph, the American people and their government remained largely in the grip of isolationism, for the most part oblivious to the threats posed to the national security of the United States. In the face of ominous change in Europe and the Far East, President Franklin Roosevelt refused to alter significantly the policies of previous administrations when he took office in 1933.

Isolationist Policies of Franklin Roosevelt. The presidential election campaign of 1932 focused primarily on the great domestic crisis created by the deepening depression; foreign affairs were rarely mentioned in the speeches of the candidates, President Hoover and Governor Roosevelt of New York. Sensing the isolationist sentiment of the American people, the New York governor felt he must alter the impression that he, an ardent Wilsonian advocating United States membership in the League of Nations, had conveyed in his 1928 campaign for the vice presidency. As early as February 1932 he gave assurances to the press lord William Randolph Hearst that he was opposed to the United States joining the League as it was then constituted. During the election campaign Roosevelt indicated further that he took the hard line of Calvin Coolidge—that the debts owed to the United States by European nations from World War I were "debts of honor" which must be paid.

Early in Roosevelt's administration an international conference was scheduled to meet in London to consider world economic problems. Hoover had committed the United States to participation, in line with his belief that the causes of the American depression were as much external as internal. Roosevelt accepted the commitment, and Secretary of State Cordell Hull, a crusader for free trade, had great hopes that much would be accomplished. But even while the delegates were convening, Roosevelt had second thoughts about an international approach to halting the depression. He sent Secretary Hull, en route to the conference, instructions to limit his participation to the negotiation of bilateral tariff treaties. A principal reason for assembling was to effect a general lowering of tariffs to improve languishing world trade. Then on July 2, in a radio message, Roosevelt rebuked the conference for concentrating on the international stabilization of currencies. The delegates assembled in London had hoped to work out some kind of currency standardization to ease the international depression. Roosevelt's message to the conference, which he later admitted "fell upon it like a bombshell," brought the deliberations to a grinding halt. Since the United States would not cooperate, the delegates from other nations felt that there was no point in further discussions, and they packed their bags and went home.

Although President Roosevelt watched with increasing concern the rise of Fascism in Germany during his first term, he was grappling with grave domestic problems and was unwilling to divide public opinion on foreign affairs, thereby risking perhaps the rejection of his New Deal programs. He avoided taking any stand in support of League action against Mussolini's invasion of Ethiopia. In 1936 the German government protested when Fiorello La Guardia, major of New York, referred to Hitler as "that brown-shirted fanatic." To the stunned surprise of many observers, Secretary of State Hull expressed to Germany the official regrets of the United States for the mayor's remark. In 1938 Roosevelt accepted Hitler's seizure of Austria by converting the United States legation in Vienna to a consulate.

Other acts demonstrated Roosevelt's isolationist policies. In the Sudeten crisis, for example, the President appealed to the major powers to resolve the problem by peaceful means. Unlike Theodore Roosevelt in 1905, the President was unwilling to bring the power and prestige of the United States to the conference table. After the Munich agreement was concluded, Roosevelt professed to be satisfied with the results. Yet FDR could actually have done little to influence the outcome, for his domestic political position at the time was precarious, and any threat to Hitler would have had little effect.

Isolationism in Congress. Although the President was isolationist in his attitude toward developments in Europe and Asia, his position was mild compared to the far more extreme isolationism maintained by Congress during the 1930's. The aversion of this body to involvement in world affairs was reason enough to explain Roosevelt's unwillingness to take a more active internationalist role. From 1934 through 1938, members of Congress were dedicated to avoiding a repetition of the events that led the United States to enter World War I. They were convinced, and public opinion backed them in their suppositions, that a conspiracy of anglophiles, softheaded internationalists, and munitions makers had maneuvered the nation's intervention in 1917; British propaganda has persuaded Americans that they were helping noble democracies defend themselves against brutal German militarism. Journalists had for some time been accusing arms manufactureres, international bankers, and Jews of involving the United States in World War I for profit. In the late 1920's and early 1930's, in newspapers, magazine articles, and books, the argument was advanced that the Allies were at best as guilty of causing the war as Germany was. Leading the assault to "revise" the verdict of Germany's "guilt" were such publicists as Harry Elmer Barnes, C. Hartley Grattan, and Walter Millis. Revisionism became as much a fad as muckraking was at the beginning of the century. A spate of war novels depicting the ugliness and horror of war, most notably Humphrey Cobb's *Paths of Glory* and Erich Maria Remarque's *All Quiet on the Western Front*, intensified emotional isolationism during this era.

In April 1934 a special committee of the Senate was created under the chairmanship of Gerald P. Nye of North Dakota, to study the relationship of the munitions industry to foreign policy and to determine whether the United States had gone to war to protect and advance the interests of the "moneymen" and the "merchants of death." The investigative assistants to Senator Nye, who was an inflexible isolationist, uncovered sensational facts about the lobbying and profits of various concerns and their hostility to disarmament, but they failed to prove these interests responsible for American entry into the war. The public, however, was overwhelmed by the profits disclosed. The revelations of the Nye committee, whose activities continued until 1936, strengthened the isolationist cause and hampered Franklin Roosevelt's efforts in later years to develop effective opposition to the dictators of Europe.

Earlier that same month Congress had passed the Johnson Debt Default Act, which prohibited American citizens and corporations from lending money to or buying securities from any government in default of payment of war debts to the United States. The law was named for Senator Hiram Johnson of California, one of the "irreconcilables" who had helped defeat the Treaty of Versailles and League of Nations in 1919. Johnson regarded the Default Act as a means by which the United States could revenge itself against the British and the French.

After fifteen years of intermittent consideration, the Senate in 1935 rejected United States membership in the World Court, which had been established to arbitrate international disputes. Claiming that Court membership would endanger the sovereignty of the United States, isolationists Johnson and William K. Borah of Idaho engineered the defeat of the proposal. They were aided by two Democrats, Huey P. Long of Louisiana and Robert Reynolds of

North Carolina. Concerned with domestic affairs, President Roosevelt had delayed risking debate on the issue until January 1935, but then he urged ratification.

The climax of congressional isolationism came in 1935 through 1937 with the passage of a series of Neutrality Acts. These laws, the first of which was passed when Mussolini was threatening invasion of Ethiopia, required the federal government to place an embargo on shipments of munitions and to prohibit private or public loans to both opposing forces during any international or civil conflict. Americans were forbidden to travel on belligerent vessels or enter war zones. These policies indirectly helped Fascist and aggressor nations, which had usually piled up armaments before they attacked; the victim nations could not obtain aid from the United States when they were forced to arm. The Loyalist government of Spain, as indicated earlier, was unable to buy munitions from the United States, although the insurgent leader, Franco, was supplied with all he needed by Mussolini and Hitler.

The reaction to the sinking of the U.S.S. *Panay* also revealed the deep isolationist mood of the times. The Japanese air force deliberately destroyed this gunboat on December 12, 1937, while its crew was evacuating Americans from war-torn China. Instead of expressing anger toward Japan, however, some members of Congress demanded withdrawal of United States ships from Chinese waters to avoid provoking the Japanese.

Reviving International Leadership

Good Neighborism. During the isolationist years of the 1930's, the United States did make some efforts to establish sound foreign relations. Its policies toward Latin America were an about-face to the "big stick" principle and the Roosevelt corollary. In 1930 President Hoover ordered publication of the Clark Memorandum, prepared by Undersecretary of State J. Reuben Clark, which denied that enforcement of the Monroe Doctrine extended to United States intervention in Latin America, thus repudiating the Roosevelt corollary. The right to keep other nations out of Latin America did not give the United States the authority to intervene there itself. Putting words into action, Hoover had withdrawn the last marines from Nicaragua by January 1933. A year earlier he had begun to remove United States forces from Haiti, a process that was completed during Franklin Roosevelt's first term. Even earlier, during President Coolidge's first year in office, complete self-government had been restored to Haiti's neighbor, the Dominican Republic, by an agreement initiated by Wilson.

The new policy toward Latin America that had been stated in the Clark Memorandum and put into effect by Hoover was broadened and given a name by Franklin Roosevelt. In his inaugural address on March 4, 1933, the new President notified the world that henceforth he would follow "the policy of the good neighbor." Roosevelt moved swiftly to implement this statement. During the Seventh Pan-American Conference held in 1933 at Montevideo, Uruguay, Secretary of State Cordell Hull, himself a strong advocate of good neighborism, urged that the American republics sign a resolution that "no state has the right to intervene in the internal or external affairs of another." Unanimously approved, this resolution made the policy of nonintervention a part of international law.

Subsequent developments also reflected the new attitude toward Latin America. In 1934 the Cuban government negotiated a treaty with the United States abrogating the Platt Amendment of 1901 and thereby making Cuba a truly independent nation. Two years later, in a similar move, the United States renounced by treaty (ratified 1939) its right to intervene in the affairs of the Republic of Panama and increased its annual payments for canal rights.

Mexico tested Roosevelt's determination to maintain the Good Neighbor Policy in 1938 when the government expropriated extensive oil properties owned by American companies. Strong public pressure was exerted on the President to retaliate, either with troops or by imposing an embargo. Roosevelt, however, admitted Mexico's right to expropriate property, but urged that American owners be compensated; late in 1941 a treaty was concluded to the satisfaction of both governments.

As a result of the Good Neighbor Policy, Latin-American nations were generally cooperative with the United States during World War II. After the United States entered the conflict, all the Latin-American states declared war or severed diplomatic relations with the Axis powers. They worked willingly with the United States on a hemispheric policy to protect the colonies of European nations that had been conquered by Hitler and sent the United States the raw materials it needed in return for economic aid. Brazil even provided troops, which served with United States forces during the Italian campaign from 1943 to 1945. Only the Argentinians, preserving a long-standing coolness toward the "Colossus of the North," were reluctant to break diplomatic relations with the Axis powers but in April 1945 they finally did.

Reciprocal Trade Agreements. The United States exerted powerful international leadership through its tariff reforms. Secretary of State Cordell Hull, a Wilsonian progressive, had long been an advocate of low tariff schedules. With his prodding the cautious Roosevelt and a reluctant Congress passed the Trade Agreements Act in 1934. This law authorized the President to negotiate reciprocity agreements with specific nations on certain imports—for the mutual lowering of tariff rates. For example, without referring the matter to Congress, the administration might lower the tariff on coffee from Brazil, by as much as fifty per cent below the Hawley-Smoot rates, in return for Brazil's reduction of duties on automobiles and appliances from the United States. During the 1930's Secretary Hull, who exercised the authority of the act, negotiated reciprocal agreements with twenty-one nations, and American foreign trade expanded significantly. Some of the bitterness abroad stemming from the harsh Hawley-Smoot Act of 1930 was eased, and the United States moved away from economic isolationism toward a policy of free trade. Reciprocity was of particular value in improving relations between the United States and the countries of Latin America.

Recognition of the Soviet Union. For sixteen long years, formal diplomatic relations between the United States and Russia had been suspended, and trade was discouraged. This policy of nonrecognition was strongly supported by American public opinion, for the Soviets had refused to pay international debts incurred by the previous tsarist government. Moreover, long after the Red scare of the 1920's had subsided, many citizens continued to be fearful of the subversive tactics of international Communism. Marxist ideology, especially in its Russian form, was heartily detested by the vast majority of Americans.

In 1933, however, Franklin Roosevelt decided that it was time to reestablish diplomatic relations with the Soviet Union, for it had already won recognition from many of the other powers. The Soviets formally promised to refrain from "agitation or propaganda within the United States" and to negotiate a settlement of outstanding claims. The President for his part was anxious to promote trade as another means of reducing the effects of the depression.

Diplomatic recognition did not produce the results that the President had in mind. The repudiated debts were never negotiated, and trade between the United States and the U.S.S.R. did not materialize. By 1935 it was clear that, despite Russian assurances, subversive Communist activities in the United States continued. In the late 1930's the American people were also annoyed by Soviet interference in China and Spain.

The Quarantine Speech. At Chicago in October 1937, several months after Japan had invaded China, Roosevelt delivered a speech in which he called upon the "peace-loving nations" to establish "a quarantine" against international lawlessness. The President's address seemed at the time a clarion call for collective action against the Fascist aggressors, but he was quickly to mute his position. In the speech Roosevelt mentioned no names and proposed no program, but even the veiled assertion produced adverse reactions in both political parties and even among members of the President's staff. Ever the politician with his ear to the ground, Roosevelt promptly abandoned the theme.

Feeble though it was, the "quarantine speech" served as the first official recognition of the fact that the United States might have to abandon isolationism. The aftermath of Munich, Hitler's seizure of Czechoslovakia, and Japanese aggression in China contributed measureably to a shift in public opinion. By May 1938 Congress had yielded to President Roosevelt's request for funds to build a truly "two-ocean navy." Yet in the months between Hitler's seizure of Prague and the Nazi attack on Poland in September 1939, the United States did little to avert the impending conflict. Only after the Second World War was well under way did Americans realize that the nation could not remain aloof from the great battles of the Old World. And even then isolationist sentiment continued vigorous and diminished only when bombs fell on Pearl Harbor.

SUGGESTED READINGS

*Adams, S. H., *Incredible Era* (1939).
*Adler, S., *The Isolationist Impulse, Its Twentieth Century Reaction* (1957).
*Bagby, W., *The Road to Normalcy* (1962).
*Bailey, T. A., *Woodrow Wilson and the Great Betrayal* (1945).
*Bailey, T. A., *Woodrow Wilson and the Lost Peace* (1944).
*Bemis, S. F., *The Latin American Policy of the United States* (1943).
Bidwell, P. W., *Tariff Policy of the United States* (1933).
Birdsall, P., *Versailles Twenty Years After* (1941).
Borchard, E. W. and W. P. Lage, *Neutrality for the United States* (1940).
Borg, D., *American Policy and the Chinese Revolution, 1925–1928* (1947).
Browder, R. P., *Origins of American-Soviet Diplomacy* (1953).
Buell, R. L., *The Washington Conference* (1922).
*Carr, E. H., *The Twenty-Year Crisis, 1919–1939* (1942).
DeConde, A., ed., *Isolation and Security* (1957).
*Divine, R. A., *The Illusion of Neutrality* (1962).
*Divine, R. A., *The Reluctant Belligerent* (1965).
Ebenstein, W., *Fascist Italy* (1939).
Ellis, L. E., *Frank B. Kellogg and American Foreign Relations, 1925–1929* (1961).
*Ferrell, R. F., *American Diplomacy in the Great Depression Era* (1957).
*Ferrell, R. F., *Peace in Their Time* (1952).
Garraty, J., *Henry Cabot Lodge* (1953).
Grew, J. C., *Ten Years in Japan* (1944).
Grew, J. C., *The Turbulent Era* (1952).
Griswold, A. W., *The Far Eastern Policy of the United States* (1938).

*Guttman, A., ed., *American Neutrality and the Spanish Civil War* (1963).

Harris, B., Jr., ed., *The United States and the Italo-Ethiopian Crisis* (1965).

*Hicks, J. D., *Republican Ascendancy, 1921–1933* (1960).

Hollborn, J., *The Political Collapse of Europe* (1951).

*Hoover, H., *The Ordeal of Woodrow Wilson* (1958).

Langer, W. L. and S. E. Gleason, *Challenge to Isolation, 1937–1940* (1952).

Lattimore, O., *Manchuria, Cradle of Conflict* (2nd. ed., 1935).

Lodge, H. C., *The Senate and the League of Nations* (1925).

McKenna, M. C., *Borah* (1961).

Meyers, W. S., *The Foreign Policy of Herbert Hoover* (1940).

Moos, M., *The Republicans* (1965).

*Morison, E. E., *Turmoil and Tradition* (1960).

Nevins, A., *The United States in a Chaotic World* (1950).

Perkins, D., *America in Crisis* (1952).

*Sinclair, A., *The Available Man: Warren G. Harding* (1965).

*Soule, G., *Prosperity Decade: From War to Depression, 1917–1929* (1947).

Taylor, F. J., *The United States and the Spanish Civil War, 1936–1939* (1956).

*Thomas, H., *The Spanish Civil War* (1961).

Unterberger, B. M., *America's Siberian Expedition, 1918–1920* (1956).

Wheeler, G. E., *Prelude to Pearl Harbor: The United States Navy and the Far East, 1921–1931* (1963).

UNIT VII

Time of Trial, Time of Hope:

WHAT STEPS ON THE EDGE OF EXTINCTION?

Why is the nation plagued by continuing crisis? For the second time American men found themselves fighting in a world war far from home, but this time Asia as well as Europe was involved, and for four years the world was consumed by total war. With total victory came the sobering realization that peace was not created on the battlefield or even in a world organization. Although Russia and the United States had been allied against the Axis, confrontation followed and soon turned to cold war. The monolith of Communism seemed to threaten the free world, yet differences soon began to divide the Communist nations. At the same time a new wave of nationalism swept the globe and emerging nations multiplied, weakening old alliances. At home, minorities who had tasted progress lost their patience and violence increased. Some Americans began to fear that the future held nothing but decline and decay. Others, looking out into space and planning for a better life on earth, have hope for tomorrow.

308

UNITED PRESS INTERNATIONAL

LONDON DAILY EXPRESS — PICTORIAL PARADE

309

STATE OF FLORIDA DEVELOPMENT COMMISSION

PARIS MATCH — PICTORIAL PARADE

NASA

	National		*International*
1941	LEND-LEASE ACT; ATTACK ON PEARL HARBOR UNITED STATES ENTERS WORLD WAR II	1941	GERMANY INVADES U.S.S.R.; ATLANTIC CHARTER
1942	CESSATION OF AUTO MAKING; RATIONING	1942	INVASION OF AFRICA; STALINGRAD
		1943	INVASION OF ITALY; TEHERAN CONFERENCE
1944	G.I. BILL OF RIGHTS	1944	D-DAY; LIBERATION OF FRANCE; "ISLAND HOPPING" IN THE PACIFIC
1945	TRUMAN TAKES OFFICE	1945	ATOMIC BOMB DROPPED; JAPAN SURRENDERS; UNITED NATIONS CHARTER
1947	TAFT-HARTLEY ACT; TRUMAN DOCTRINE; MARSHALL PLAN		
1948	TRUMAN DEFEATS DEWEY	1948	BERLIN AIRLIFT; ISRAELI INDEPENDENCE
		1949	NATO FORMED
		1950	WAR IN KOREA
1952	UNITED STATES EXPLODES FIRST H-BOMB		
1954	MC CARTHY CONDEMNED BY SENATE; DESEGREGATION CASE—*Brown v. Board of Education of Topeka*	1954	SEATO PACT
1955	AF OF L—CIO MERGER	1955	WARSAW PACT
1956	EISENHOWER REELECTED	1956	SUEZ CRISIS; HUNGARIAN REVOLT
1957	LITTLE ROCK INCIDENT	1957	SPUTNIK—SPACE AGE BEGINS; COMMON MARKET
		1960	U-2 INCIDENT; CONGO CRISIS
1961	UNITED STATES SENDS FIRST AMERICAN INTO SPACE; UNITED STATES SENDS ADVISORY GROUP TO SOUTH VIETNAM	1961	BERLIN WALL; BAY OF PIGS INVASION; GUERRILLA WAR IN LAOS AND VIETNAM
1962	CUBAN MISSILE CRISIS		
1963	FREEDOM MARCH; KENNEDY ASSASSINATED	1963	TEST-BAN TREATY
1964	CIVIL RIGHTS ACT; TONKIN GULF RESOLUTION	1964	WIDENING SPLIT BETWEEN CHINA AND U.S.S.R.
1965	ESCALATION IN VIETNAM; MEDICARE; WAR ON POVERTY	1965	RHODESIAN INDEPENDENCE FROM BRITAIN
1967	RACE RIOTS	1967	SIX-DAY WAR IN THE MIDDLE EAST
		1968	SOVIET OCCUPATION OF CZECHOSLOVAKIA
1969	UNITED STATES MANNED MOON LANDING		

CHAPTER 29

From Isolation to World Leadership, 1939–1946

We must be the great arsenal of democracy.
FRANKLIN DELANO ROOSEVELT, 1940

WORLD WAR II COLLECTION OF SEIZED ARMY RECORDS, NATIONAL ARCHIVES

MONSTROUS NAZI AND JAPANESE AGGRESSIONS IN 1939 and the years that followed, coupled with vast changes in military technology, shattered isolationism in the United States and made Americans realize the futility of trying to live apart from other nations on the globe. First they watched for years from the sidelines, increasingly anxious as friendly nations were overwhelmed or threatened with destruction by boldly aggressive powers. Then suddenly they were the ones attacked by the Japanese at Pearl Harbor in 1941.

For many Americans the Second World War began on December 7, 1941, but some of the crucial phases of the war had actually ended before American military power was engaged in the intensive struggle. As in the First World War, the nation entered the conflict late, almost too late. In 1945, after the Allied victory in Europe, General Eisenhower remarked "We won this war and we won it just in time." The Germans were by the end of the war making such fantastic advances in weaponry that further delay would have rendered victory doubtful if not impossible.

PROLOGUE TO WAR IN EUROPE

Hitler's diplomatic triumph in the Sudeten crisis of September 1938 and the absorption of the rest of Czechoslovakia in March 1939 left the democracies of western Europe confused and shaken. Within a few weeks after the Munich agreement, the false glow of hope for "peace for our time" dissipated, and Prime Minister Chamberlain recognized the probable failure of his appeasement policy. Hitler's appetite for power had only been whetted by the acquisition of the Sudetenland. Throughout England reappraisal was agonizing as protest against Chamberlain's policy intensified. Dominating the uproar was the stentorian voice of Winston Churchill, ceaselessly denouncing the bankruptcy of appeasement. The English soon accepted the probability of a new war with Germany and speeded up production of armaments, particularly of aircraft; in April 1939 they started conscripting young men of twenty and twenty-one.

Across the Straits of Dover, Premier Edouard Daladier, in despair that despite the promises made at the Munich conference all of Czechoslovakia was seized, asked for and received power to govern by decree. He stepped up rearmament and partially mobilized French forces. Around the perimeter of Hitler's Third Reich, smaller nations cringed before the cyclonic winds of war blowing out of Germany.

Hitler's Preparations to Invade Poland. Poland was clearly the next country marked for conquest. Almost immediately after absorbing Czechoslovakia, Hitler mounted a propaganda offensive against the Polish government. As with the country just seized, he found his excuse in the alleged mistreatment of a German minority of three million living in the Polish Corridor, the strip of land taken from Germany by the peacemakers of Versailles to provide Poland with access to the Baltic Sea. The Führer's stated demands were the return of the port city of Danzig[1] and rights to a wide zone across the Polish Corridor, in which to build a German highway and railroad. The Poles rejected such exactions and with fatalistic determination prepared for war, recognizing that they had little chance of survival against German military might but, unlike the Czechs, determined to go down fighting. Belatedly, the British and French offered Poland a pact of mutual military assistance. Keenly aware of the Franco-British sellout of Czechoslovakia the year before, the Polish government placed little faith in Western support but accepted the agreement. Now that the inordinate ambitions of Hitler were obvious, Europe had little hope for peace that summer.

America on the Eve of War. During the same spring and summer very little was happening in the United States. Franklin Roosevelt had no further controversial reforms to propose, for he was still licking his wounds after the election of Republicans to Congress in November 1938. There was desultory interest in the coming presidential election of 1940. In the Republican ranks Senator Robert A. Taft of Ohio, a spokesman for conservative causes, and Thomas E. Dewey, the young rackets-busting attorney from New York, were the leading contenders of the moment. A few Democrats were engineering a boomlet for Paul V. McNutt, the affable and handsome chief of the Federal Security Administration. But the white-haired Indianan had two grievous disadvantages—his unfortunate resemblance to Warren Harding and the nonendorsement of Franklin Roosevelt, his political boss, which reinforced speculation that FDR would seek an unprecedented third term.

Increasingly aware of the cataclysmic march of events abroad, however, Americans were very much preoccupied with the Polish crisis. Since Roosevelt's quarantine speech of October 1937, Americans had undergone a change of heart. According to the Gallup poll of April 1939, fifty-seven per cent of all Americans favored revision of the Neutrality Acts in order to allow the United States to sell war supplies to England and France. Almost two-thirds wanted some kind of boycott against Germany. (Three years earlier sentiment had favored embargoes on munitions applied against *all* belligerents.) Fifty-one per cent of the people expected a European war within the year, and fifty-eight per cent believed that the United States would be involved. Only forty-four per cent had held this opinion two years earlier.

By 1939 the amount of space in the press devoted to foreign affairs had increased significantly, and *Time* magazine had inaugurated a regular feature entitled "Background to War." Radio foreign correspondents and commentators such as H. V. Kaltenborn, Quincy Howe, and Quentin Reynolds spoke to millions of confused Americans anxious to grasp the sig-

---

[1] Danzig was technically under the administration of the League of Nations, another minor decision made by the treaty makers at Versailles. Both Poland and Germany had been granted free use of Danzig's harbor facilities, but German control of the city would give Hitler a stranglehold over Poland's economy. Hitler did have a good case for demanding Danzig, for ninety-five per cent of its inhabitants were Germans. The enfeebled League of Nations seemed almost willing to give up Danzig to Hitler, but the Polish government was naturally alarmed at the prospect.

nificance of the latest diplomatic moves. Newspapers featured syndicated columns by such military experts as Hanson Baldwin and Major George Fielding Eliot.

The Nazi-Soviet Pact. As they anticipated impending war with Hitler, the British and the French finally realized their serious error in snubbing the Soviet Union during the Sudeten crisis. Whatever their repugnance for Communism, the British and French governments wanted Russian military help in the coming conflict. In early August an Anglo-French military mission traveled posthaste to Moscow to negotiate an alliance with the rulers of the Kremlin.[2] Although the British and French were politely received by Russian diplomats and military chiefs, it became obvious as negotiations got underway that the Russian hosts were dragging their feet. They had not forgotten that the Soviet Union had been ignored a year earlier. Vyacheslav Molotov, the new foreign minister, was a tough old Bolshevik with an ingrained contempt for the Western democracies. He noted with scorn that the British and French representatives in Moscow were "second-raters" lacking the authority to make binding decisions. Molotov demanded ironclad guarantees of a full alliance and mutual military assistance plus a free hand in dealing with the Baltic states; later he demanded the right to send troops through Poland in the event of war. Now it was the turn of the British and French to drag their feet.

While the British and French stalled, Hitler did not. Much earlier in *Mein Kampf* he had attributed Germany's defeat in the First World War to the error of fighting on two fronts at the same time. As the Polish crisis grew in intensity, Hitler was aware that this time the Western powers might not back down. Fearful that Russia would join Britain and France and thus create the dreaded threats on two fronts, the Nazi dictator moved to neutralize Russia.

As early as May, Hitler had made secret overtures to dictator Stalin. After some diplomatic maneuvering, Joachim von Ribbentrop, Germany's foreign minister, was invited to Moscow. On the evening of August 23, 1939, Ribbentrop and Molotov signed a treaty by which the Soviet Union and Germany agreed not to attack each other or to form an alliance with powers hostile to either party for a period of ten years. This agreement also contained secret provisions for the division of Poland and eastern Europe between the two superpowers.

News of the Nazi-Soviet nonaggression pact fell on an unsuspecting world like a thunderclap on a clear, sunny day. World opinion had fondly taken the position that Communism and Fascism were so diametrically opposed to one another that an agreement between the Soviet Union and Germany was unthinkable. In the United States liberals and left-wingers, who had long viewed the Soviet experiment favorably, were shocked and disillusioned. Yet more sober and farsighted students of world affairs were not surprised, for Communist Russia and the Weimar Republic had contracted agreements at Rapallo in 1922 (page 646 n.). Like their Nazi counterparts, the Russian rulers were masters of expediency and never allowed their particular brand of ideology to becloud practical political considerations.

THE NAZI BLITZKRIEG

With the signing of the Nazi-Soviet nonaggression pact, the British and French military chiefs who were still in Moscow recognized the failure of their mission and left quietly for home. The last diplomatic move had been made. The German army stood posed on the Polish frontier. In the west Hitler hastened the completion of the Siegfried Line, designed to protect the Reich against French attack. Prime Minister

---

[2]The Kremlin, built in the heart of Moscow during the Renaissance, was once a great fortress. Within its walls are now housed the central offices of the Soviet government. The term Kremlin commonly identifies the Russian government just as White House and Ten Downing Street are synonymous with the executive authority of the United States and Great Britain.

From Isolation to World Leadership, 1939–1946

Blitzkrieg in the east—by traditional cavalry UNITED PRESS INTERNATIONAL

Chamberlain declared in the last days of August that a German attack on Poland would bring war with Britain and France. The sands of peace were running out. The twenty-one-year truce was about over.

Poland Falls

Early the morning of September 1, 1939 the Nazi army smashed into Poland from three directions. German bombers pulverized the Polish air force before it even left the ground. In the next two weeks Poland's armies were quickly encircled by fast-moving panzer (armored) divisions and destroyed piecemeal by follow-up German infantry units. Then on September 17, as German armored columns reached across the San River, Russian troops poured into eastern Poland, in accordance with a secret clause of the pact signed less than a month earlier. Except in Warsaw, organized Polish resistance to these assaults lasted only a few days. But the citizens of the capital city, fighting with a courage born of despair, put up a fierce defense after the collapse of the Polish army. Warsaw withstood seventeen days of shattering artillery bombardment and savage street fighting before it was captured by the Germans September 27 and Polish resistance ended.

During this campaign Hitler revealed to the world a new method of waging war—the *Blitzkrieg*, or "lightning war." In this brief conflict the German military machine proved even more awesome than anticipated.

The "Phony War"

Shortly after the news of the invasion reached England, Chamberlain addressed an ultimatum to Hitler, demanding that the Germans get out of Poland or face war with Great Britain. A similar message went out from France. Hitler did not even bother to reply. On September 3, 1939 both Great Britain and France declared war against Germany. In the next few days

. . . and modern panzer division.

various British dominions—Australia, Canada, and New Zealand—also issued declarations of war. The Union of South Africa, where there was strong anti-British feeling as well as some pro-Nazi sentiment, hesitated but finally joined the Allies some weeks later.

At the outbreak of the conflict, President Roosevelt proclaimed the neutrality of the United States but strongly implied that American sympathies lay with the anti-Nazi nations. Moreover, he called Congress into special session to revise the Neutrality Acts, which required that an embargo on arms apply equally to all belligerents. The revised law, ready for Roosevelt's signature November 4, was not all that the President had hoped for, but it did allow belligerents to purchase arms on a "cash and carry" basis. Now the British and French could obtain much-needed materials, even though they were not permitted to negotiate loans and were required to carry the purchases on their own ships. The British control of the seas obviously made it impossible for the Germans to obtain any war materials in America on any basis. Yet this problem would not worry Hitler, for he had all the resources that he needed.

By the time that Congress had enacted the cash and carry law, the Polish compaign was over, and the pace of the war had slowed down. Great Britain and France seemed in no immediate danger of attack by German forces. But in eastern Europe Russia moved quickly. On September 25, October 5, and October 10, Estonia, Latvia, and Lithuania signed treaties allowing the Russians to occupy valuable naval and air bases in these countries. Within the year the Baltic states would be incorporated as republics within the Soviet Union. Then the Russians made similar demands of Finland, but this small nation was prepared to fight. Rarely in history had the odds been more disproportionate, for Russia's population was forty times that of Finland. Americans remembered with sympathy that Finland had been the only nation to pay its war debts in full. Now they experienced

From Isolation to World Leadership, 1939–1946

a great, nationwide surge of admiration for the tiny Finnish forces which were initially able to trounce the invading Russian armies. The daring exploits of Finnish ski troopers became legendary; Field Marshal Carl Gustaf von Mannerheim, Finland's soldier-president, was a national hero in the American press. Robert Sherwood would write within the year *There Shall Be No Night*, a popular Broadway play about the Soviet invasion of Finland.

In the end, however, the Soviet Union's massive military might crushed the Finns. On March 12, 1940 the "Winter War" came to an end when Finland sued for peace. Although the U.S.S.R. stripped the small country of valuable territories, it was allowed to remain intact and independent.

On the western front (along the border of France and Germany) the winter of 1939–1940 was a period of extended inaction. After declaring war on Germany, the French army had moved into the Maginot Line, and British expeditionary forces crossed the English Channel to take up positions in one sector. While the Siegfried Line facing them was still undermanned during the attack on Poland, the French ventured only a cautious advance into the Saar basin. Then as the German divisions in the western front built up, both sides were unwilling to undertake a major offensive before the onset of winter.

The United States wire services and major newspapers mobilized their battalions of correspondents and sent them to Europe to cover the "Second World War," but there was little to report. Occasionally, a French patrol would encounter a German patrol in "no man's land," but after a brisk skirmish both units would retire quickly to the safety of their own lines. A German reconnaissance plane might be seen over northern France or England, or a British plane might fly over German cities, "bombing" them with propaganda leaflets. This continued inactivity moved Senator Borah to remark that the conflict was not a Second World War after all but merely a "phony war." One American correspondent observed that in Poland there had been the *Blitzkrieg* and now there was a *Sitzkrieg*, or "sitting-down war."

Hitler Moves West

The illusion of the phony war did not last long. On April 9, 1940 Hitler's troops struck Denmark and Norway with paralyzing suddenness and overwhelming power. The populations of these two small nations had naively believed that their obscurity and careful neutrality would provide them the same protection as in World War I. Denmark was crushed in only four hours, Norway, except for the very far north, in seventeen days. The British and the French landed forces in Norway, but they got there too late with too few and were compelled to withdraw after two weeks.

With the conclusion of the Scandinavian campaigns, an uneasy quiet settled once again over western Europe, but now no one called it a phony war. The only question was when and where Hitler would strike next, and the answer was not long in coming. On May 10, 1940 Hitler attacked both Holland and Belgium. In four days Holland was conquered. The Dutch had foolishly believed that their dikes provided an impregnable defense against any invader. Mined with explosives years earlier, the dikes could be destroyed by means of electric detonating devices located in control towers, thereby halting an invasion force. German paratroopers captured the control points and thus quickly neutralized Holland's only effective defense. Hitler demonstrated to the world another example of German *Schrecklichkeit* (frightfulness) by ordering the *Luftwaffe* to bomb undefended Rotterdam. The center of the Dutch city was reduced to ashes, and thousands of civilians perished.

The German forces sweeping through Holland and Belgium outflanked the Maginot Line and caught the Western Allies off guard. Despite the experience of World War I, the defense system through Belgium and northern

Blizkreig in the west—France falls. MAURITUIS FROM BLACK STAR

France was inadequate. In desperation, the Allies improvised a new makeshift arrangement. British and Belgian forces took up positions on the left flank, and the French moved over to cover the sector between them and the Maginot Line while continuing to hold the latter. At best, the new defense system was a feeble, leaky affair, unable to halt the hard-charging German panzer units. British forces moving forward were hampered by hordes of terrified refugees fleeing southward in a futile attempt to escape the Nazi fury. The *Luftwaffe* compounded the confusion by bombing and strafing the highways, slaughtering civilians and soldiers alike.

After eighteen days of fighting, King Leopold of Belgium suddenly surrendered his entire army without bothering to inform his allies. German armored divisions poured into northern France through the gaping hole thus created. As the British and French sought to revise their defenses to meet this newest onslaught, an additional German army, a mighty host of nearly a million men and thousands of tanks, smashed through the Ardennes forest in eastern Belgium and dashed around the left end of the Maginot Line. In the face of these combined assaults, coordinated Allied resistance came to an end. What was left of the British army and some French units were penned up in a perimeter around the port of Dunkirk. Yet, through the extraordinary efforts of the British people, these troops were rescued. Between May 28 and June 4, in every type of craft imaginable—ocean liner, merchant vessel, private yacht, and yawl—345,000 soldiers were evacuated to safety in England.

While the French in other sectors were reeling before successive advances of the Nazi armies, Mussolini declared war on their country and invaded from the south on June 10, in what has been described as "the most cowardly attack in history." Italian intervention did not make any difference. The various French armies, encircled and disheartened, began to surrender. On June 22, 1940 an armistice was

From Isolation to World Leadership, 1939–1946 321

signed, and France withdrew from the war. The Germans occupied the northern half of the country, and the remainder became a satellite, with its capital in the resort town of Vichy. Hitler allowed the Vichy government to retain control of the French overseas territories in Africa and Asia. The new head of Vichy France was Marshal Henri Philippe Pétain, an aged military hero who was believed to be compliant with Hitler's wishes. At the time of France's capitulation, however, a significant number of French soldiers escaped to continue the war against Germany under General Charles de Gaulle, who organized a Free French government in London.

Reaction in the United States

As the seemingly invincible Nazi columns rolled toward Paris in the early days of June, many Americans had comforted themselves in the belief that there would be another last-ditch Battle of the Marne, as in World War I. Surely the retreating French would turn on their pursuers and force them to halt as they had in 1914. In the American mind France had always existed and would continue to exist. Millions of Americans subscribed to FDR's remark of two years earlier that their nation's frontier was on the Rhine River. But now that frontier was gone. France, the "great bulwark of democracy" on the European continent, lay prostrate at the booted feet of the Nazi conquerors. Shock, anguish, and anger were the immediate emotional responses of Americans to the stunning German victories in western Europe.

On June 10 President Roosevelt had entrained for Charlottesville to deliver a commencement address at the University of Virginia. Deeply concerned over the pacifist and isolationist sentiment rife on college campuses across the nation, the President had decided that the time had come to speak plainly to the American people. In his speech Mr. Roosevelt warned against "the now obvious delusion that the United States can become a lone island in a world dominated by the philosophy of force." He said

"Let us not hesitate—all of us—to proclaim certain truths. Overwhelmingly we, as a nation . . . are convinced that military and moral victory for the gods of force and hate would endanger the institutions of democracy in the Western World, and that equally, therefore, the whole of our sympathies lies with those nations that are giving their life blood in combat against these forces."

After denouncing Mussolini's stab "into the back of its neighbor" (Italy had declared war on France and Great Britain a few hours earlier), the President proposed a dual policy of extending "to the opponents of force the material recources of this nation" and preparing the Americas for "any emergency and every defense."

The Charlottesville address marked a turning point in the position of the United States toward the conflict, for it was a declaration of open commitment to help in the struggle against Nazism. In general, the message was well received by the American people.[3] The long era of withdrawal and isolationism was drawing to a close. Roosevelt's decision to speak out and then to act was speeded by the formation in May of a powerful pressure group, the Committee to Defend America by Aiding the Allies. Headed by William Allen White, a Kansas newspaper publisher, this well-financed group campaigned in Congress and through the press to grant all material aid to the Allies short of war. The Century Group, a smaller

---

[3]Despite developments in Europe, there was still strong opposition to intervention, led by the America First Committee. Its chairman was Robert Wood, head of Sears Roebuck, and its chief spokesman was Charles A. Lindbergh. Associated with the America Firsters were such powerful senators as Bennett Champ Clark of Missouri, Gerald P. Nye of South Dakota, and Burton K. Wheeler of Montana, as well as General Hugh Johnson, former head of the NRA. The America First Committee hurt its own cause, however, with its strident anti-British and anti-Semitic declarations.

lobby composed of influential Easterners, called for direct military intervention.

A few days before Roosevelt's statements at Charlottesville, the Burke-Wadsworth Bill had been introduced in Congress. This measure sought to establish peacetime compulsory military service, and after considerable opposition this precedent-shattering proposal would become law in September 1940. In May and June Congress voted immense sums for tens of thousands of planes and for the construction of the giant two-ocean navy. After the British had left military equipment strewn across northern France in the evacuation from Dunkirk, the War Department released huge amounts of surplus and outdated arms and ammunition to private American concerns so that the munitions could be resold to Great Britain. Roosevelt also ordered the freezing of the economic assets of the conquered nations that were held in the United States to keep them out of German hands. In addition, on July 26 and September 24, he placed an embargo on the shipment of three strategic materials—high-octane gasoline and scrap iron and steel—to Japan, Germany's Far Eastern partner. A provision of the new National Defense Act, which established a National Defense Research Committee, allowed the President to prohibit the export of any materials deemed essential to the national defense. With France and the Netherlands defeated and Britain threatened, Japan had just obtained from the helpless Vichy government permission to build airfields in French Indochina and was now eying British Malaya and the Dutch East Indies (now Indonesia).

During this summer of 1940 the United States moved toward a coordinated hemisphere defense policy as well. In a conference at Havana, the United States and the Latin-American republics agreed to act in concert in preventing the American colonies of Nazi-conquered European nations from falling into Hitler's hands. The Act of Havana stipulated that the American republics might, collectively if possible but individually in an emergency, take over and administer any European possession in the New World endangered by aggression. As another step toward solidarity, President Roosevelt and Prime Minister William Lyon Mackenzie King of Canada, which was now at war with Germany and Italy, conferred in August at Ogdensburg, New York. They set up a Permanent Board on Defense to study the problem of defending the "north half of the Western Hemisphere."

The most dramatic step toward commitment, however, marking the end of American neutrality, was the "destroyers-for-bases" deal concluded with the British on September 2, 1940. At the urging of the Century Group and White's committee, the President by executive agreement handed over to Great Britain fifty overage destroyers dating back to World War I. The British, with half of the destroyers stationed in their home waters already lost, needed the American warships for convoy duty against the German submarines. In return, the United States was granted ninety-nine-year leases for naval and air bases in Newfoundland, Bermuda, the West Indies, and British Guiana. Prime Minister Churchill also pledged never to scuttle or surrender the British navy to the Nazis.

In the midst of world crisis, the American public was faced with a presidential election. The Republicans, meeting in late June, just a few days after the surrender of France, passed by their front-runners, Senator Robert A. Taft of Ohio, Senator Arthur Vandenburg of Michigan, and Thomas E. Dewey of New York, all isolationists, although to varying degrees. On the sixth ballot the delegates nominated instead an internationalist utilities executive, Wendell L. Willkie, who had led the private power companies in their earlier fight against the TVA. Willkie, energetic, homespun, and openhearted and possessing a personal magnetism comparable to Roosevelt's own, had been maneuvered to the forefront by a group of amateur politicians.

The Democrats, convening on July 15, had

From Isolation to World Leadership, 1939–1946

no other candidate comparable to the incumbent. Roosevelt had undoubtedly hoped earlier in the year to relinquish the burden of the presidency, but eventually the war changed his mind. He sent a message to the convention on July 16 stating that he had no desire for the nomination, probably a necessary gesture, for the tradition against a third term was not to be lightly dismissed. Two days later the delegates chose to draft him on their first ballot with an all but unanimous vote.

Because Willkie approved of many of the New Deal reforms and also favored aid to Britain, he could attack only Roosevelt's methods, not his policies. He conducted a vigorous and generally high-level speaking campaign, and he was greeted everywhere with great enthusiasm. The advantage, however, was clearly with the President. Busy at his desk, Roosevelt hardly campaigned at all, but when the voters went to the polls in November in unprecedented numbers, nearly five million more of them voted for him than for Willkie. Roosevelt's majority, although less than in the two earlier elections, was still an impressive 54.3 per cent. The American public, threatened by the war abroad, had decided that retaining an experienced hand was more important than maintaining the two-term tradition.

The Battle of Britain

After the fall of France, Americans awaited tensely the imminent German invasion of Britain. Its chances for survival seemed tragically reduced. Although the British army had been saved by the "miracle of Dunkirk," the Nazis stood supreme from the equator to the Arctic Circle. The Nazi supermen were expected to cross some thirty miles of open water to the beaches of England and quickly conquer the island. But in any event, the British had at last found a leader. The haggard and feckless Neville Chamberlain had resigned as prime minister in favor of the valiant Winston Churchill. Through his air of confidence and determination and with his words as well as by his deeds, Churchill instilled new hope in the dispirited British people. He warned them that all he could promise was "blood, toil, sweat, and tears" in the moment of trial now at hand. In rousing oratory and unforgettable words Winston Churchill called upon the British people to hurl back the Nazi barbarians in the cause of civilization: "Let us therefore brace ourselves to our duties and so bear ourselves that if the British Empire and its Commonwealth last for a thousand years, men will say, 'This was their finest hour.'"

With Churchill's words ringing in their ears, the Royal Air Force (RAF) took up the battle against the hundreds of German planes that winged in over the island. The German air assault was believed the preliminary step to invasion. Around the clock the *Luftwaffe* hammered hard at British cities, factories, ports, and landing fields. Tens of thousands of civilians were killed and wounded. But the British fought back hard. Throughout August and September 1940 the air battle kept up with unrelenting fury.

Before many weeks had passed, it was apparent that the numerical advantage of the *Luftwaffe* over the RAF would not defeat them. The British fighter planes, particularly the famed Spitfire, were superior to the German planes, and British pilots were better trained than their *Luftwaffe* counterparts. By the end of September even Hitler could not stand the heavy losses. Daylight attacks were abandoned, but nightly the Nazis continued their bombing runs over British population centers. The destruction of cities, especially of London, could be measured in square miles.

The British continued to improve their techniques of air warfare. New methods of detection, especially radar, made it possible to identify German planes long before they arrived. High-powered antiaircraft batteries shot down the German bombers from altitudes of 30,000 feet and more. Barrage balloons with nets hanging between them hampered bombing by low-flying German planes. With the coming of shorter days and stormy weather, and with the Germans clearly unable to provide an effective air cover, the threat of immediate invasion passed.

All through the winter of 1940 and 1941 the air battle raged on. In November the city of Coventry was devastated. On December 29 came the terrible fire bomb raid on London. But after a shattering assault on London May 10, 1941, when the houses of Parliament and the British Museum were damaged, the intensity of German bombing attacks distinctly lessened. As the raids became less frequent, however, few British were deceived into believing they had crushed or even defeated the *Luftwaffe*. Hitler had only temporarily suspended the Battle of Britain in order to deal with problems and plans elsewhere.

Campaigns in the Balkans and Africa

Hitler's junior partner had gotten himself into trouble and needed help. Benito Mussolini had watched with growing envy as Nazi armies marched from triumph to greater triumph, for he too wanted glory. In October 1940, from the Italian protectorate of Albania, his Fascist army invaded Greece, a tiny country with a population of only seven million people. The Italian troops had advanced only a few miles before they were halted by determined Greek resistance. Then came a counterattack, throwing the Italians back across the mountains into Albania. On December 3 the Greeks turned the tables on the Italians and invaded Albania. Mussolini's humiliation was great, but much worse was to happen in another sector beginning that same December.

A few weeks before the attack on Greece, Mussolini had ordered a large army in Libya, then an Italian colony, to conquer Egypt and seize the strategic Suez Canal. At the time, Egypt was under British protection and military occupation. Beyond this country lay the vast wealth and oil resources of the Middle East, the southern sector of Hitler's "heartland." The Italian army in Libya was large, 250,000 soldiers backed up with 1,500 first-line planes. Opposing the Italians initially was a small British force of only 30,000 men and a tiny air force of 250 obsolete planes. One British model, the Gloster Gladiator, had a top speed of only 120 miles per hour.

When the Fascist forces entered Egypt, the British retreated across the desert about sixty miles eastward and then halted. There they stopped the Italians, and for two months each side built up its forces for an offensive. On December 8 the British suddenly counterattacked. In a campaign that has few equals in military annals, the British army raced westward. Before it the Fascist forces simply collapsed. The British took 130,000 prisoners and, amazingly, shot the Italian air force out of the skies. Even though the British sweep was slowed by the problem of supplying guards and facilities for the enormous number of captured enemy troops, they had seized half of Libya by March 1941. In extreme mortification Mussolini turned to Hitler to bail him out of his debacles.

Hitler decided to help his fallen ally, first in Greece and then in Africa. In order to attack Greece, control of the other Balkan nations was necessary. Hungary, Rumania, and Bulgaria had already accepted Nazi overlordship, but Hitler was particularly anxious to bring Yugoslavia into the German orbit as well, since it had a common frontier with Greece. In March he therefore addressed a brusque ultimatum to the Yugoslav government, in which it was instructed to cooperate and accept German occupation or face war. When the Yugoslavs hesitated, Hitler's troops struck and struck hard. On Easter Sunday the *Luftwaffe* bombed Belgrade, and armored columns raced through the country. Despite the difficulties caused for the invaders by the mountainous terrain, Yugoslav resistance came to an end after only eleven days.

Without pausing the Nazi forces pushed on into Greece. In response to a call for help,

Germans March on Yugoslavia and Greece; Attacks in Thrace and Macedonia Resisted; Moscow and Belgrade Sign Friendship Pact

Churchill ordered 60,000 men of the victorious British army in Africa to move across the Mediterranean and bolster the Greeks' sagging defenses. The British, however, could do nothing to stem the German tide, and Greece was subjugated in seventeen days. In a minor "Dunkirk" the British army barely managed to escape from Athens. Their forces were removed to the island of Crete where, guarded by the navy, it was believed the exhausted men could recuperate. But the British were not to have that much time. On May 20 thousands of German paratroopers came down out of the skies and overran the island, and superior German air power sank or damaged many of the British destroyers and cruisers. The British were forced to flee again, all the way back to their point of origin in Africa. Nor would they there be safe from the German fury. General Erwin Rommel had in the meantime landed in Libya with his legendary *Afrika Korps*, consisting of two divisions of crack German troops; and by the end of May Rommel, known as the Desert Fox, had driven the British forces entirely out of Libya.

The Invasion of Russia

To Americans in the late spring of 1941, the international situation looked very grim indeed. Hitler was now master of southeastern Europe. The British had been badly mauled in Africa by numerically inferior forces under Rommel. Again they questioned, "What will Hitler do next?" In May there were rumors of massive German troop concentrations along the long border between the Nazi Empire and the Soviet Union, although the pact between Hitler and Stalin had seemed workable. While the Nazi dictator gorged himself with conquests in the west and south, Stalin had busily helped himself to Finland, parts of Rumania, and the Baltic states. On June 22, 1941 the blow fell. Without warning the Nazi armies suddenly smashed into Russia. The most tremendous war in history had begun. Across a front of nearly two thousand miles, the gigantic German military machine lunged forward.

With the news of this German aggression against the Soviet Union, Americans were generally jubilant. In the eyes of many, the prospect of the two aggressive dictators locked in deadly combat was most welcome, for the pressure was temporarily off Great Britain. Some Americans even conceded a grudging admiration for "Uncle Joe" Stalin. There was considerable talk about the might of the Red army and the dogged courage of the Russian soldier.

In the ensuing weeks, however, the enthusiasm in the United States turned to dismay, for the German war machine seemed in perfect working order. Large Russian armies were encircled and destroyed during the first days of the conflict. In subsequent weeks three great

German armies drove deep into Russia, and Americans heard reports of incredible Russian losses and endless defeats. By early November one German army besieging the great city of Leningrad had almost completely surrounded it. Another German thrust overran the Ukraine, capturing Kiev, third largest city in the Soviet Union, and then Kharkov farther east and Kerch in the Crimea. In late October a third principal drive exploded directly toward Moscow. By mid-November Germans were penetrating the suburbs of the Russian capital, and the collapse of Soviet Russia appeared likely.

In spite of stunning defeats, the Soviet people fought back with stubborn ferocity. Ordered by Stalin to utilize the scorched-earth policy, they destroyed all property of possible use to the invaders before withdrawing from a region, sector, town, or village. In areas occupied by the Nazis, the people were instructed to wage guerrilla warfare. Entire factories in the Ukraine were dismantled, loaded on railroad box cars, and shipped to regions beyond the Ural Mountains, where they would be safe from the invaders.

The Germans countered obstinate resistance with unspeakable cruelty, and massacres were commonplace. Millions of Russians were shipped off to slave labor camps where many were worked to death. At last, however, the terrible Russian winter came to the rescue of the struggling Red armies. Heavy snow and record low temperatures helped the Soviet forces in halting the Nazi hosts, who were not equipped for winter fighting. Final victory had eluded Hitler by a narrow margin.

THE UNITED STATES IN THE SECOND WORLD WAR

"Yesterday, December 7, 1941—a date which will live in infamy—the United States of America was suddenly and deliberately attacked by the naval and air forces of the Empire of Japan."

So spoke President Roosevelt as he called upon Congress to declare war on Japan. A few days later Congress also declared war on Germany and Italy. All that had transpired since the fall of France had led inevitably to the entry of the United States into the worldwide conflict. After the commitment to aid the British in the summer of 1940, the United States had taken an increasingly hard line toward the Axis nations.

Quasi-belligerency in Europe, 1940–1941

After the destroyers-for-bases agreement with Britain was concluded, the United States edged reluctantly but almost unavoidably toward an open break with Germany. A dramatic step in this direction was taken in January 1941 when Roosevelt asked Congress for an initial appropriation of seven billion dollars to purchase war materials, which he would then "sell, . . . lease, lend, or otherwise dispose of" to any country whose defense he deemed vital to United States security. Churchill had informed Roosevelt that by June Britain's financial reserves would be exhausted and it would no longer be able to pay cash for badly needed war materials. Instead of lending the British money, Roosevelt proposed lending them arms, to be paid back by them in goods and services after the war was over.

Isolationist opposition voiced against the Lend-Lease Bill was shrill. Senator Wheeler declared that this measure "will plough under every fourth American boy." Roosevelt replied that Wheeler's statement was "dastardly" and "the rottenest thing that has been said in public life in my generation." Passage of the bill in March made the United States, in Roosevelt's words, "the arsenal of democracy."[4]

---

[4] By allowing the President to "lease" war materials, the government avoided the problem created in World War I by loans to the Allies. After World War II there was no war debt issue to trouble relations between the United States and its former Allies.

From Isolation to World Leadership, 1939–1946

In April, to protect lend-lease shipments, American naval vessels were patrolling far out into the Atlantic. United States warships assisted convoys out of American waters and shadowed German U-boats, radioing their locations to the British. That month Greenland was occupied by American forces, to prevent the Germans from using it as a supply depot for submarines; then in July American troops replaced the British garrison in Iceland. Roosevelt announced that the United States navy would keep convoy lines open as far as that island. On June 24, immediately after Hitler's invasion of Russia, President Roosevelt promised American aid to the Soviet government.

In September, after several American merchant ships had already been sunk, the American destroyer *Greer* was attacked by a German submarine—described by President Roosevelt as an "unprovoked aggression." Thereafter American warships were instructed to "shoot on sight" any German craft in the North Atlantic. By October 1941 a small-scale naval war had developed between Germany and the United States; there were losses on both sides. In November Congress responded by repealing a section of the Neutrality Acts. American merchantmen could now arm and carry lend-lease supplies all the way to England.

Crisis in the Pacific

A Year of Building Tension. In the Far East the United States also moved toward a position of quasi-belligerency. In November 1940, a few months after the United States had stopped selling aviation fuel and scrap iron and steel to Japan, Chiang Kai-shek appealed to the United States for military and financial aid. At the end of the month the White House announced a loan of $100,000,000 to China; privately Chiang was also promised fifty pursuit planes. Moreover, the administration began formulating a plan that would allow army, navy, and marine corps pilots to resign their commissions and join Colonel Claire L. Chennault's "Flying Tigers," a group of American volunteers[5] in the Chinese air force.

Then in December the United States added iron ore, pig iron, and many forms of finished steel to the list of items prohibited Japan. Each month thereafter and then almost weekly additional goods were embargoed. Japanese industries began to feel the restrictions. The most critical supplies, however, petroleum products other than high-octane gasoline, were not banned, for Secretary Hull feared that an oil embargo would bring on war with Japan.

A new Japanese ambassador, Admiral Kichisaburo Nomura, arrived in Washington in February to discuss the issues causing friction between the two countries. Within the next few months he and Secretary Hull met some forty times and tragically misunderstood each other. By July the Japanese had decided that to resist American economic pressure it must move south in Asia and gain access to needed supplies.

As their first full step southward, the Japanese invaded southern French Indochina on July 24, 1941 and proclaimed a joint protectorate with Vichy France over the whole country. Two days later President Roosevelt impounded Japanese funds in the United States, bringing Japanese-American trade to a full halt and cutting off a country that had been at war for four years from the source of eighty per cent of its oil. Although Japan had carefully conserved petroleum products during the 1930's, it now

---

[5] A number of other American volunteer units were also formed to aid the Allied nations before the United States entered the war. In early 1941 Colonel Charles Sweeney organized a group of American pilots as the Eagle Squadron to serve with the RAF. The American Field Service, which had participated in World War I, was revived. It provided ambulances and volunteer drivers to serve with the British and the French in Europe, the Middle East, and Burma.

had less than two years' supply on hand.

Although the militarists occupied most ministries in Japan, the prime minister, Prince Fumimaro Konoye, did not want war with the United States. In August he proposed a personal meeting with President Roosevelt to seek a peaceful settlement of the current crisis. The President was receptive, but Secretary Hull feared that the proposal was a trap; on October 2 his rigid statement of American policy precluded such a meeting. Within days Konoye resigned and General Hideki Tojo, an aggressive expansionist, became premier. A special envoy, Saburo Kurusu, joined Nomura in Washington on November 15. The Japanese proposals offered at that time, as well as earlier, seemed to Americans a demand that the United States approve a Japanese-dominated Asia. On November 26 the State Department as unrealistically insisted, as it had in the past, that Japan must withdraw all its forces from China and Indochina. On that same day the Japanese carrier force set out from its base in the Kurile Islands, bound for a fatal mission against Pearl Harbor should negotiations fail. Early the morning of December 7 it would virtually erase United States air power in Hawaii and destroy enough ships to paralyze the Pacific fleet for many crucial weeks.

The Axis at Peak Strength. After Pearl Harbor the Allies were victims of a series of additional disasters. Simultaneous with the attack on Hawaii came Japanese air and naval assaults on American bases in Manila and on Guam and Wake Island and against British forces in Hong Kong and Malaya. Guam fell without resistance. After a brief, desperate fight the Marines on Wake Island were forced to surrender. British forces at Hong Kong turned the city over to the Japanese on Christmas Day.

Having destroyed the American air force, Japanese forces swiftly invaded the Philippines. The unprepared American and Philippine troops under General Douglas MacArthur were quickly hemmed in on Bataan Peninsula, across the bay from Manila. By early April the forces on Bataan, suffering from serious shortages of food and other supplies, were obliged to give up. On May 6, 1942 the last resistance to the Japanese was extinguished with the surrender of the island fortress of Corregidor. President Roosevelt had arranged for General MacArthur to escape secretly from the Philippines by PT boat in March.

In the meantime Japanese power rolled across Southeast Asia. Japanese military forces invaded the Dutch in the East Indies in January and had easily engulfed the islands by March, gaining for Japan the vital natural resources oil, tin, and rubber. Other Japanese troops, having landed on the coast of Malaya December 8, advanced toward the great British naval base at Singapore. The British had arrogantly boasted that Singapore was "impregnable," but it took the Japanese only the first two weeks in February to capture it. Reaching out still further, Japanese armies rolled through Thailand—which had almost immediately agreed to a Japanese overlordship—into Burma and began an invasion of British India. Crossing the Pacific in another direction, Japanese forces overran the Solomon Islands and portions of New Guinea.

News from the Atlantic theater of war was almost as disheartening. Long-range German U-boats sped through the ocean to sink American merchant vessels at a frightful rate. By January 1942 nearly 200,000 tons of shipping had been sent to the bottom. In February the total had grown to 384,000 tons. Destruction of ships was particularly heavy in the Caribbean, but losses began to taper off in May after the United States perfected submarine detection devices and employed more destroyer escorts for convoys.

1942, the Year of Decision

In 1942 an Axis victory appeared likely, but during this year the Allies won three great battles with the enemy, each victory achieved through the individual effort of a particular Ally. If the Axis nations had won any of these three key engagements, an Allied victory would have been long postponed or perhaps have become virtually impossible.

Turning Point in the Pacific. In the spring of 1942, the Japanese launched two naval assaults, one aimed at Australia and the other at Hawaii. Off the northeastern coast of Australia, in the Coral Sea, the Americans and units of the Australian navy managed to turn back a larger Japanese fleet on its way to attack Port Moresby on New Guinea, whose airfields were important to the American-Australian supply lines. It was victory by a narrow margin. Another principal Japanese thrust across the Central Pacific was intercepted by an American fleet near Midway Island during early June. Dive bomber pilots managed to destroy four Japanese aircraft carriers and nearly three hundred planes, whereas the United States lost only one carrier and retained most of its aircraft. Discouraged by its tremendous losses, the Japanese withdrew, giving the Americans their first clear victory of the war and ending the threat to Hawaii and the West coast of the continental United States. After Midway the Japanese were on the defensive. For the remainder of the Pacific war, they sought to fend off, along steadily contracting lines, a crescendo of American naval and military pressure.

In August 1942 the United States forces launched their first major offensive; marines made a daring landing and seized the airport on Guadalcanal, an island in the Solomon Archipelago. After a half-year of intense jungle and mountain, air and sea fighting, the Japanese abandoned the island in February 1943. During the same period American and Australian forces, which had been holding the southeastern tip of New Guinea, began to reconquer Japanese-held portions of the island.

Crisis in Africa. In June 1942 General Rommel's forces hit the British hard in Libya and Egypt.[6] Within a few weeks the vaunted *Afrika Korps* had driven close to the key British naval base at Alexandria, but the offensive was finally brought to a halt at El Alamein, a tiny oasis in the desert less than sixty miles from the rich Nile Valley. After several months of careful preparation, the British Eighth Army, commanded by General Sir Bernard Montgomery, launched an overpowering counterassault. By November 1 the British had achieved a clean breakthrough. Now it was the turn of the Germans along with their Italian allies to flee and for the British to pursue. During the next several weeks the British army pushed westward, close on the heels of Rommel's shattered forces.

While the German troops retired before the British onslaught, an attack from another direction was being mounted. On November 8, 1942 American and additional British forces under the command of General Dwight D. Eisenhower made a number of successful landings in French North Africa. These armies pushed rapidly eastward, catching Rommel's troops in a giant pincer movement in February 1943. The *Afrika Korps*, accompanied by the hapless Italians, was squeezed into Tunisia by Eisenhower from the west and by Montgomery from the east. In the skies and on the Mediterranean, Allied air and naval forces gained supremacy. In May 1943 the German and Italian forces in Africa, numbering some 250,000 men, laid down their arms. Just before the final collapse, Hitler ordered Rommel away from the debacle to be used elsewhere by the German high command.

El Alamein was the beginning and Tunisia the end of a two-thousand-mile-long journey that eliminated the German threat to the Middle East. The struggle in Africa was a successful testing ground for Anglo-American collaboration. Field Marshal Montgomery emerged

---

[6]In November 1941 British forces had managed to regain control of Cyrenaica, the eastern section of Libya.

ALLIED STRATEGY IN EUROPE AND AFRICA, 1942-1945

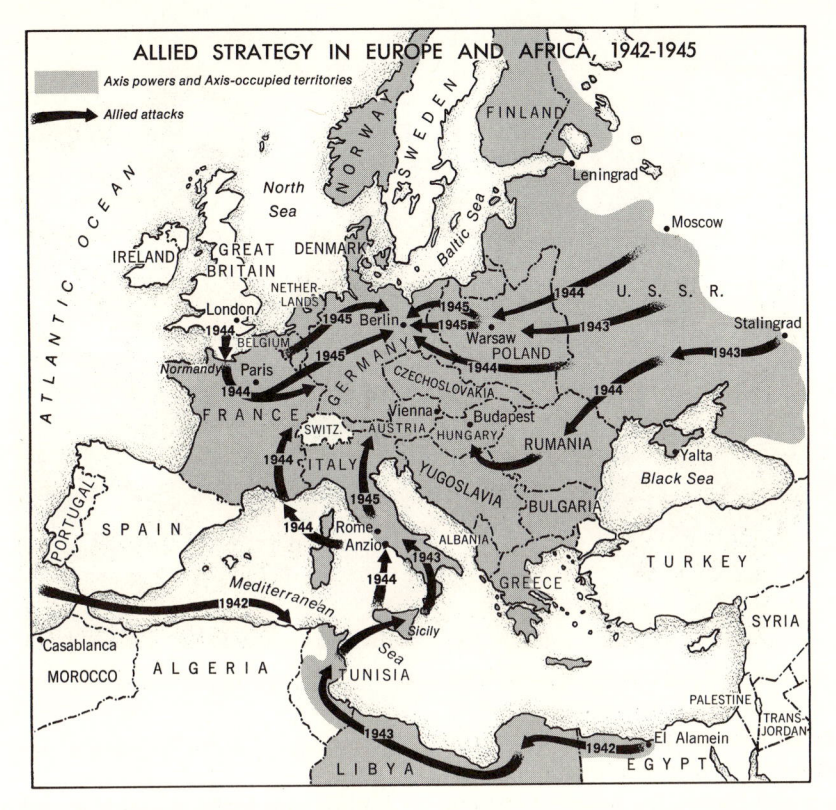

from the African campaign as Britain's leading military hero, and General Eisenhower demonstrated his skill in coordinating the vast Allied military machine. The combat experience gained in Africa was to prove valuable to the Allies later on.

Decision in Russia. In the spring of 1942, the German armies that had been halted in Russia during midwinter gradually thawed with the coming of warmer days. Reequipped and reinforced, they resumed their offensive in late June, driving powerfully southward from Kursk to Rostov and on along the eastern rim of the Black Sea. They captured important Russian oil fields and by August 9 had reached Maikop and the foothills of the Caucasus Mountains. The principal effort, however, was aimed directly eastward toward the Urals. Gathering momentum as it moved, the German army reached the Volga River August 22. At this point the Germans halted to besiege the Russian bastion and industrial city of Stalingrad. This assault proved a slow, ceaseless, hand-to-hand struggle through burning, smoke- and rubble-choked streets. The German advance was measured by house and factory and block rather than in miles as the retreating defenders fought with tenacious fury. At one point the Russians retained only a few acres of the city, but they hung on grimly. During this great struggle the roles gradually became reversed, and the besiegers became the besieged. Fresh army units allowed the Reds to surround the Stalingrad Germans, and now it was their turn to fight with fanatic courage against overwhelming odds. Cornered and starved, the surviving 90,000 invaders (from an original army of 600,000) surrendered in February 1943.

Stalingrad was the deepest point of Nazi

From Isolation to World Leadership, 1939–1946

Stalingrad—high water mark for the Wehrmacht.   IMPERIAL WAR MUSEUM, LONDON

penetration. After the military disaster at the Volga city, the Germans began a long period of withdrawal from the Soviet Union. As German power waned, Soviet power grew. The constantly growing Russian armies, equipped with weapons manufactured in the Soviet Union rather than in America, harried the Nazis ceaselessly during their long retreat.[7] Heavily outnumbered and often outgeneraled, the Germans nevertheless fought with immense courage. But after their defeat at Stalingrad there was little doubt about the eventual outcome.

[7] It must be recognized, however, that American equipment played a significant role in the Soviet offensives. Supplies reached the Soviet Union by way of the Persian Gulf, across the Iranian plateau, and around the North Cape of Norway into the Russian port of Murmansk. American and British losses in the Murmansk convoys were tremendous. In one convoy twenty-two of thirty-three ships were sunk by German naval and air attacks. Nonetheless, many shipments reached their destination; 400,000 vehicles alone arrived in the Soviet Union under lend-lease between 1941 and 1945.

Diplomacy of the Grand Alliance

Unlike the First World War, which was termed "a generals' war," the new global conflict was "a politicians' war." Military commanders had dictated the strategy in the earlier struggle, and planning for peace was belated and haphazard. In the Second World War, on the other hand, the heads of state of the three great Allied nations made the crucial decisions; planning for peace began at an early stage. Even before the United States entered the war, President Roosevelt had established personal liaison with Prime Minister Churchill. In August 1941 the two leaders met aboard the warships U.S.S. *Augusta* and H.M.S. *Prince of Wales* off the coast of Newfoundland. At this conference the Atlantic Charter, a statement of broad common principles—a pledge of nonaggression, self-determination in territorial changes, the right of self-government, access of all states to the raw materials of the world, freedom of the seas, and freedom from war, fear, and want

Time of Trial, Time of Hope

—was formulated. This charter, which was essentially a restatement of Wilson's Fourteen Points, was issued to the world over the joint signatures of Roosevelt and Churchill on August 14, 1941. After Pearl Harbor the United States and its Allies began intensive strategy planning for the war and for the structuring of the postwar world. In late December 1941 Churchill came to the White House for a second meeting with Roosevelt, and the broad outline of the shape of things to come began to emerge. The decisions made by FDR and Churchill, and later with Stalin, were to affect vitally the conduct of the war and the order of the world as it exists today.

"Hitler First" and "Unconditional Surrender." In the first few months after the United States entered the conflict, the junior partner in the Anglo-American alliance accepted direction from the more experienced British. As the war progressed and as United States military power grew, the roles were gradually reversed. By the end of the war, the United States had taken the lead in making crucial decisions. The British were obliged to accept, often very reluctantly, an increasingly minor role in world affairs.

Although Japan had attacked the United States, Churchill argued successfully that Hitler, not Tojo, was the real threat to the Allies. Admiral Ernest J. King, the Chief of Naval Operations, vigorously opposed this decision, but FDR and the Army Chief of Staff, General George C. Marshall, concurred with Churchill. According to the "Hitler first" strategy, the major portion of United States power would be devoted to crushing the German *Wehrmacht*, and only limited forces would be diverted to the Pacific for what were intended to be merely holding operations against the Japanese. Limited military aid would also be sent to Chiang Kai-shek to keep the faltering Chinese in the war. After Hitler was beaten, the United States and Britain—hopefully with the help of Russia—would concentrate on conquering Japan. Despite his earlier commitment to Churchill's plan, FDR began to change his mind somewhat as the war progressed, under pressure from Admiral King and General MacArthur. Even while United States attacks against Germany were being undertaken, the President diverted more and more men and matériel for offensives in the Pacific theater.

At Casablanca, Morocco, FDR and Churchill met again in January 1943 to make one of the most controversial decisions of the war—that of demanding "unconditional surrender" by the Axis nations. Adoption of this policy closed the door to any negotiated peace. Borrowed from General Grant, who used it in the Civil War, the term "unconditional surrender" made it clear to all Allied peoples, especially the suspicious Russians, that Britain and the United States intended to wage war until victory was complete. The Soviet leaders had been quite fearful that the United States and Great Britain might negotiate another "Munich" and leave Russia in the lurch. Historians have since debated whether Roosevelt and Churchill's policy of unconditional surrender prolonged the war by making the Axis peoples fight with great desperation in the face of such a hopeless alternative.

The seeming ruthlessness of this policy appeared reinforced by the Morgenthau Plan, devised by Secretary of the Treasury Henry L. Morgenthau. Although President Roosevelt eventually rejected the plan, it was leaked to the press in 1944. Its intent was to strip Germany of industrial resources and to convert the country into a group of small, semi-independent agricultural states incapable of ever again waging an aggressive war. The broadcasts and writings of Lord Robert Vansittart, an intimate adviser to Churchill, on the "black record" of Germany further convinced the Germans that the Allies intended nothing less than extinction of their nation.

Teheran and Yalta Conferences. At Teheran, the capital of Iran, Roosevelt and Churchill met Joseph Stalin in the first "Big Three"

From Isolation to World Leadership, 1939–1946

The Big Three at Yalta.   CULVER PICTURES

summit conference of the war. At this meeting, held from November 28 to December 1, 1943, the three leaders made momentous decisions. Stalin approved wholeheartedly of the Anglo-American plans, formulated earlier, to open a "second front" by a cross-Channel invasion of western Europe in the spring of 1944. Stalin promised a mighty Soviet offensive in the east at the same time so that Hitler could not shift troops to combat the western invasion. The Big Three also accepted an American proposal to establish a new international organization to replace the defunct League of Nations. A conference would be held during the following year at Dumbarton Oaks in the District of Columbia to draft specific proposals for the United Nations Charter. At Teheran Stalin reaffirmed Russia's intention to enter the war against Japan after hostilities ended in Europe, and the three powers agreed that Germany would in some way be partitioned.

The Teheran conference was the high point in the grand coalition against the Axis. At its conclusion Roosevelt declared, "We came here with hope and determination. We leave here, friends in fact, in spirit, and in purpose." But even at Teheran principles of the Atlantic Charter were violated. It was decided that parts of eastern Poland would be given to Russia, and that Poland would be compensated with territory taken from Germany. Nor did the aura of friendship last. By late summer 1944 Great Britain and the Soviet Union were locked in a bitter dispute over Poland, partly because the British had sponsored a Polish government-in-exile in London. The Russians insisted that the Communist-dominated provisional government in Lublin, a city in by then Russian-held eastern Poland, be recognized as the legal authority. The future of other Nazi-conquered countries in eastern Europe was a further source of friction.

To resolve these and other problems, a second Big Three meeting was convened at Yalta, a resort town on the Crimean Peninsula, in February 1945. Held while Hitler's power was fast declining, this conference was by far the most critical and controversial of the wartime meetings of top-level Allied leaders. During this session they did achieve a solution of sorts

Time of Trial, Time of Hope

on the Polish question. At the insistence of Stalin, the so-called Curzon line of 1919 was fixed as the eastern boundary of Poland, but the country's western boundary, to be extended by annexation of German territory, was not decided on. Roosevelt and Churchill would have preferred a completely reorganized interim government for Poland and, as soon as possible, free elections under effective supervision to form a permanent government. But Stalin would agree only to enlarging the existing Lublin government to include democratic leaders from the London group;[8] he rejected supervision of the elections as an insult to Polish independence. Elsewhere in liberated Europe, Stalin agreed, there should be "free elections of governments responsive to the will of the people."[9]

At this conference the three leaders decided that defeated Germany would be divided into four zones of military occupation, one of them to be administered by the French, and that Germany would pay reparations from current production rather than in cash. They also announced to the world that a conference would be convened in San Francisco on April 25 to formulate the United Nations Charter. A crucial topic was the voting procedure in the Security Council of the proposed United Nations. Roosevelt insisted that the big powers (the five nations to be permanent members of the Council) each have veto power, but Churchill was dubious, and Stalin seemed uninterested in the proposal. Roosevelt was very anxious to avoid the opposition that plagued Wilson after World War I. Therefore he offered the veto clause to be certain of Senate ratification of United States membership in the United Nations, believing that the Senate, ever jealous of yielding any sovereignty, would demand such a guarantee. Churchill and Stalin finally agreed, and the veto power was granted to the so-called "big five nations" (China, France, the United Kingdom, the United States, and the U.S.S.R.). In years to come, the Russians would use the veto power to nullify actions by the Security Council. As a result, this presumed executive branch of the United Nations has atrophied and lost its effectiveness.

Yet the most critical discussions at Yalta related to the Far East. Reaffirming an earlier agreement, Stalin promised to declare war on Japan approximately three months after the surrender of Germany. As a reward the Soviet dictator wanted the Kurile Islands and the return of southern Sakhalin (taken from Russia by the Treaty of Portsmouth). He also demanded recognition of the Monogolian People's Republic, which had severed its connections with China and had accepted Russian influence, as well as "pre-eminent interests" in the railroads and principal seaports of Manchuria.

Strongly anti-Roosevelt critics over the years have characterized the outcome of the Yalta conference as a "betrayal." They have hinted that Communist sympathizers in the State Department influenced the sick and dying President (Roosevelt was to die a few weeks later) to make unnecessary concessions to Stalin. The United States, so the story goes, abandoned eastern Europe to the Communists. By insisting that Russia enter the war against Japan, the United States unnecessarily provided Russia with an excuse to intervene in the Far East and to aid the Communists in China.

The accusation is not without some foundation yet is in its entirety false. About eastern Europe, which was controlled by Soviet military power, the United States and Britain could do little more than extract Stalin's promise—which was not kept—to establish democratic governments. Although the Russians would probably have intervened in the Far East anyway, Roo-

---

[8] By July 1945, when Allied leaders met at Potsdam, the Russians had already turned over to the Polish provisional government all German territory east of the Oder and Neisse rivers. Eventually, the Lubliners, supported by the Soviet Union, seized complete control of the Polish government, liquidating or exiling the London representatives. By 1946 Poland had become a Communist dictatorship.

[9] As Nazi power receded and Russian armies advanced, this promise was not kept. Communist governments were soon imposed in Bulgaria, Hungary, and Rumania.

sevelt certainly made it easier by asking Stalin for help in the war with Japan. But FDR had based his request on inaccurate information. As it turned out, United States military intelligence greatly overestimated Japan's will and ability to resist, and Soviet help was not needed. The argument that Roosevelt was influenced by Communists or "pinks" in the State Department is baseless. At the most the President erred in an egotistical belief that he could make friends with and influence the tough, suspicious Soviet dictator. The controversy over Yalta continues but has measurably abated.

FINAL CAMPAIGNS, 1943–1945

Collapse of Axis Europe

Although the year 1943 was primarily one of preparation and testing, the coordinated military-industrial power of the Allies was already being applied with telling effect against the Axis nations. Hitler refused to recognize the fact, however, and the endurance of the Nazis in the face of overwhelming odds was astounding.

Surrender of Italy. After driving Rommel from Africa, the British and American forces under Eisenhower quickly moved across the Mediterranean Sea to Sicily on July 10; in five weeks they had easily conquered the island. A new military hero emerged in the person of General George S. Patton, commander of the U.S. Seventh Army. Patton's brilliant use of armored units rivaled that of the German panzer generals at their greatest. During the course of the campaign, the Italians decided to surrender. Mussolini was overthrown and placed in temporary custody on top of a mountain, and the new Italian government started negotiating with the Allies. Italian naval units yielded to the British, and the new government even suggested that it was willing to join the Allies against Hitler.

While the "unconditional surrender" terms were being negotiated, however, Nazi troops streamed over the Alps and in a few days overran most of the Italian peninsula. On September 15 Mussolini was rescued from his mountain jail by a small group of daredevil German paratroopers. *Stuka* divebombers sank Italian warships trying to escape across the Mediterranean.

The armistice was signed September 3. The American public, elated at the course of events, had a popular saying, "One down and two to go." Mussolini was gone, and soon it would be the turn of Hitler and Tojo. But Italy was still not won. A day before the armistice was signed the British crossed the Straits of Messina, and on September 9 the Americans landed at Salerno. By the end of the month the two forces had reached Naples, and there the advance slowed. The difficult terrain of the peninsula provided the scene for a dreary, frustrating struggle as the Germans held each successive line with great skill and tenacity. Not until June 1944 did the Allies reach Rome. The fighting ended only when Germany collapsed in May 1945.

Operation Overlord. The basic plans for the great amphibious invasion of western Europe, identified by the code name "Overlord," were completed in the summer of 1943. In January 1944 General Eisenhower arrived in London to take charge as supreme commander of the projected invasion armies. Throughout the early months of that year troops and equipment poured into England in preparation for the cross-Channel invasion.

In the meantime, British and American air forces weakened Nazi defenses by relentless, round-the-clock bombing of transportation networks and industrial centers. The Americans concentrated on pinpoint daylight bombing of specific targets, such as factories, bridges, storage areas, and railroad-marshaling yards. The RAF used the "saturation" technique, devastating by night great sections of cities with incendiaries and "blockbusters" (twelve-ton bombs). Entire urban centers were reduced to rubble and ruin. The bomb tonnage

Time of Trial, Time of Hope

Lafayette we are here—again. OFFICIAL COAST GUARD PHOTO

dropped during the Anglo-American assault of 1944 was two hundred times that of the German air blitz on Britain in 1940 and 1941. Nearly 500,000 German civilians were killed in the holocaust.

The bombing of Dresden was a spectacular example of the ferocity of these attacks. A city of limited industrial importance, crowded with refugees fleeing from the advancing Russians, it was savagely attacked by the RAF on two successive nights. Incendiary bombs were dropped, and storm-fires of cyclonic velocity gutted the city. At great distances from the actual bombing strikes, persons were found dead without a mark of their bodies, asphyxiated because the fires had consumed all the oxygen in the air. On the morning after the second RAF attack, while Dresdeners were digging themselves out of debris and putting out the fires, American planes caught the population by surprise with a third bombing raid, this last one brief but again furious.

Invasion of Normandy. On June 6, 1944 (D-Day) American and British forces successfully stormed ashore at five points along a forty-mile strip of beach on the coast of Normandy, a province on the northwestern coast of France. For months the island they had crossed from bulged with troops and equipment, but the Germans proved unprepared for a major assault in this particular area. Yet the German forces under Field Marshal Rommel resisted with skill and courage after recovering from their initial surprise. The Allied forces, within a month a million men strong, were contained for several weeks by Rommel's troops, who used the Norman hedgerow countryside to great advantage in fighting the invaders.

The breakthrough came in late July when General Patton's U.S. Third Army thrust out of Normandy and slashed across northern France. British armies under Field Marshal Montgomery then pushed northward along the coast toward Belgium. In mid-August other American forces, assisted by General de Gaulle's Free French troops, made surprise landings near Toulon on the Mediterranean coast of France and moved northward against meager resistance.

A special French division dashed toward Paris to rescue it from the imminent destruction ordered by Hitler. An unexpected uprising by the Parisians themselves helped save the capital city. By August 25 the last Germans had

From Isolation to World Leadership, 1939–1946

either been captured or had fled, and Paris was free. Two days later General Charles de Gaulle entered the city and established the French provisional government.

In the east Stalin launched overpowering offensives to keep the Germans off balance. Massive Soviet armies had in the spring swept the Germans from the Ukraine. Now in July and August they burst into Poland and Rumania; Bulgaria was conquered in three days in early September. The Greeks, again aided by the British, rebelled against their German oppressors in October. That same month Marshal Tito and his partisans were also busy clearing Yugoslavia of Nazi control. The Russians helped them seize Belgrade on October 20.

Battle of the Bulge. In September the Nazi empire appeared already tottering. Patton's hard-driving armored divisions crossed the German frontier north of Trier, and the U.S. First Army, under General Courtney Hodges, pushed through the Ardennes Forest into the fringes of Rhineland Germany, both on September 12. Farther north Brussels and Antwerp had already been liberated by British and Canadian forces. The end seemed in sight; once again the popular cry in America was "The boys will be out of the trenches by Christmas."

Hitler's military power had indeed been badly shaken, but it was not crushed. He collected sufficient resources for one last thrust at his tormentors, and he aimed it directly at the Americans. Under the cover of a rolling fog, giant Royal Tiger tanks, accompanied by battle-hardened German infantry, moved forward into Belgium early in the morning of December 17, 1944. Now it was the turn of the overconfident allies to be caught off balance. Along an eighty-mile front, the German panzer units burst through the paper-thin American lines in the Ardennes Forest, advancing fifty miles in ten days. This counteroffensive, which became known as the Battle of the Bulge, momentarily imperiled the Allied armies. Apprehension approaching panic spread through the American ranks as entire divisions collapsed.[10] But the German strength was broken by the stubborn and courageous resistance of the U.S. 101st Airborne Division, rushed from a hundred miles behind the lines to reinforce the troops at Bastogne, just before the Germans encircled it. The Americans suffered heavy casualties, however, before they could regroup to counterattack. In the first half of January 1945, aided by complete air superiority in clearing skies, the American forces quickly deflated the German bulge in Belgium. Hitler had lost his final gamble.

Final Battles. The end came swiftly. Hitler had hoped that the Rhine River would be an effective barrier to the advance of the Americans and British. The U.S. First Army managed, however, to seize the bridge at Remagen while it was still intact. Happening upon it just before the first demolition charge went off, they were able to prevent the Germans from exploding others. Farther south General Patton's Third Army slipped across the Rhine without resistance. To the north British forces and still additional American troops under Montgomery crossed the river after a gigantic artillery bombardment. They encircled the Ruhr, Germany's industrial core. To the east a giant Russian assault crossed the Oder and drove on toward Berlin.

In these waning moments of the conflict, American and British forces were poised for a race against the Russians into Berlin, but Eisenhower called off the contest. Over the vigorous objections of Churchill, Eisenhower declared that Berlin was "no longer militarily significant." He ordered the American and British troops to stop when they reached the Elbe

---

[10]The confusion was compounded by stories of thousands of Germans, dressed in American uniforms, filtering through the American lines. According to the rumors, these Germans chewed gum and quoted baseball statistics in Brooklyn or Midwestern accents. Although the rumors were vastly exaggerated, a few dozen Germans trained by Colonel Otto Skorzeny, the Nazi war hero, did slip through in G.I. garb to commit acts of sabotage.

River, April 11; there the Russians joined them fourteen days later, after entering Berlin. Marshal Georgy Zhukov, commander of the Russian army on the Oder, had been grimly determined to take Berlin himself. He claimed that had the Americans arrived in Berlin first, he would have ordered his men to "throw them out." If Zhukov's statement can be believed, Eisenhower's controversial decision avoided a serious collision with Soviet troops.

After a devastating bombardment and vicious street fighting, Russian forces completed the occupation of Berlin on May 2. Two days earlier Hitler had committed suicide in his underground bunker, which was located in the heart of the city. Everywhere across Europe German forces began to lay down their arms. By May 8, 1945 the war in Europe had come to an end.

As Americans and British troops moved ever deeper into Germany during the final months, they encountered increasing hordes of the uprooted—millions of Germans who were without homes because they had been destroyed by bombing raids or in Russian attacks to the east. Far more heartrending were the millions of "displaced persons," peoples of many nationalities who were refugees from Hitler's slave labor camps. Then when troops of General Patton's Third Army overran Nordhausen and the British took Belsen, the revelations sickened the world. The "concentration camps" had long been rumored places of ultimate horror, but their reality proved beyond comprehension. When General Patton visited the barbed fence enclosure of the Nordhausen camp, the tough general quietly vomited. In rage over the barbarity that he saw, Patton ordered all the Germans living in the nearby town to be paraded through the camp. Later, Eisenhower came to see for himself the mounds of decaying corpses and the emaciated, skeletal bodies of those who somehow still lived. Dozens of other such death camps were liberated. The Russians had already seen even larger concentration camps in Poland, the bales of human hair and the mounds of gold fillings at Maidenek, and the "showers" and ovens of Auschwitz. The horrifying "medical" and "survival" experiments that had reportedly taken place at Buchenwald and Ravensbruck were confirmed.

Down through history conquerors and dictators, from the Assyrian kings and Genghis Khan to Stalin and Chiang Kai-shek, have achieved notoriety for their cold-blooded slaughter of millions of victims. But the impersonal and long-range atrocities of the Nazis stand alone. Hitler may well have been the most brutal ruler in the record of man. The ultimate in man's inhumanity took place among a civilized Western people of Christian heritage, in the "progressive" twentieth century.

Victory over Japan

Even during the large-scale campaigns against Nazi Germany, an increasing amount of American—and British—military strength was diverted to the Far East. In China, United States equipment and military forces under the command of General Joseph ("Vinegar Joe") Stilwell increased the fighting capacity of Chiang Kai-shek's armies. Strong American air units under brilliant General Chennault, formerly the commander of the Flying Tigers, harried the Japanese in the skies over China. In Burma, British-Indian forces launched a counteroffensive against the Japanese.

The principal theater of operations, however, was in the Pacific. Here the United States developed a massive, two-pronged pincer movement against Japan. The plan was simple, spectacular, and amazingly successful. Under Admiral Chester Nimitz United States naval forces were to thrust across the Central Pacific, clearing out Japanese-held islands. This campaign was completed without a hitch, although there were hard-fought battles against stubborn Japanese defenders. The marines added to their remarkable combat record in the fighting on such islands as Tarawa, Kwajelein, and

AMERICAN STRATEGY IN THE PACIFIC, 1942-1945

Iwo Jima. In June 1944 American carrier-based planes destroyed a considerable portion of Japan's naval air arm in the Battle of the Philippine Sea, near the Marianas (more popularly known as "the Mariana Turkey Shoot"). In three days United States pilots shot down 365 Japanese planes and sank three of their carriers; American losses were insignificant.

General MacArthur directed operations in the southern prong of the pincer movement. His strategy in New Guinea consisted of leapfrogging along the northern coast, isolating Japanese garrisons and leaving them "to wither on the vine." After New Guinea MacArthur's forces invaded the Philippines. During the ensuing battles the Japanese navy made one last, despairing effort to retain the archipelago by destroying MacArthur's transports and supply ships. In the Battle of Leyte Gulf, the Japanese on three successive days in October 1944 sent out the bulk of their remaining surface fleet in a coordinated maneuver. The Americans won engagements with each armada, completing the destruction of Japan's sea power.

On April 1, 1945 the United States navy and marines joined army units in a vast amphibious assault on Okinawa, which was to be the staging area for the final assault on Japan's home islands. During the conflict on Okinawa, the navy was harassed by *kamikazes* (suicide pilots) who crashed their dynamite-loaded planes into American ships. American losses were extensive—thirty-two ships sunk and sixty-one others badly damaged. By June, however, Okinawa was securely in American hands. The final scene of the final act of the Second World War was about to begin.

While the battles for the Philippines and Okinawa were in progress, the Japanese homeland was being rained with air and naval bom-

Time of Trial, Time of Hope:

"I shall return"
(General Douglas MacArthur).

PARIS MATCH—PICTORIAL PARADE

bardment. Long-range bombers (B-29 Superfortresses) hit Japan day and night from the Marianas (Guam, Saipan, and Tinian). As the campaigns for the various Japanese island bases across the Pacific were won, more and more aircraft carriers were released for the bombardment of Japan. Giant American battleships raked Japanese coastal cities with artillery fire. By June significant numbers of British battlewagons and carriers from European waters pounded industrial centers. In the meantime, United States submarines had virtually destroyed the Japanese merchant marine.

Although Japan was beaten and the end was near, most Americans were unaware of this fact. They had been deeply impressed with Japanese ferocity and were convinced that a bloody invasion of Japan was necessary. United States intelligence erred badly in overestimating Japan's will to resist. On July 18 Premier Tojo resigned and was replaced by General Kuniaki Koiso, a moderate, who chose a cabinet of peace-minded men. But on August 6 an American Superfortress dropped the first atomic bomb on Hiroshima. On August 8 Stalin kept his promise; Russia declared war on Japan, and Soviet troops poured into Manchuria and Korea with whirlwind speed. On August 9 the United States dropped a second atomic bomb on Nagasaki. Two days later the Japanese made an offer of surrender. It was unconditional except for one reservation—that the Emperor Hirohito retain his throne. On August 14 the Allies accepted the terms of surrender, including the reservation, and the war came to an end. General MacArthur presided at the formal surrender ceremony, which took place September 2 aboard the battleship U.S.S. *Missouri* in Tokyo Bay.

The Russians participated in the war only six to eight days. Yet in that brief time they managed to overrun Manchuria and northern Korea. In the process they engulfed a stunned Japanese army and seized enormous stockpiles of military equipment, which they turned over to the Chinese Communist forces of Mao Tsetung. As the Soviet forces withdrew, they allowed the Chinese Communists, not the Nation-

From Isolation to World Leadership, 1939–1946

alists of Chiang Kai-shek, to occupy Manchuria. The captured Japanese equipment and the base of operations in Manchuria were vital resources in the ultimate victory of the Communists over Chiang some four years later. Russian occupation of Korea divided that land and set in motion events that were to lead to the Korean War in June 1950.

If the Japanese had surrendered even as late as August 4, Russia would not have intervened in the Far East. Korea would have been unified, and perhaps Chiang Kai-shek, not Mao, would be master of China today. The basic reason for Japan's delay in offering to surrender was the demand that it be unconditional. The atomic bombings of Hiroshima and Nagasaki, proved unnecessary by subsequent events and cast a dark shadow on the reputation of the United States.

Military Settlements

Under the surrender terms Japan was stripped of its overseas territories. Southern Sakhalin and the Kurile Islands were ceded to Russia. Korea was placed under temporary military occupation of the United States and the Soviet Union. American forces occupied the area south of the 38th parallel, and Russians held the north. It had been agreed that American and Russian troops would withdraw from Korea as soon as a permanent democratic government could be constituted. Taiwan (Formosa) was turned over to the Nationalist Chinese under the leadership of Chiang Kai-shek. Troops of Chiang and Mao Tse-tung scrambled to occupy other areas of China evacuated by the Japanese. Pending the signing of a peace treaty, the Japanese home islands were placed under United States military occupation, directed by General MacArthur.

Arrangements for the occupation of Germany had been completed at the last wartime conference of the Big Three in July 1945. The meeting took place at Potsdam in the suburbs of Berlin, site of the palace of former Prussian kings and German emperors.[11]

Leaders of the three Allied nations had decided that all Germany—and Austria as well—should be placed under Allied military occupation until the signing of a peace treaty. The United States and Great Britain were assigned the western portions of Germany, and the Soviet Union was to be responsible for the large eastern sector. To satisfy the sensitive Charles de Gaulle, the Rhineland was carved out of the American and British areas as a zone for French occupation. Austria was divided in a similar manner. Deep inside the Russian zones Berlin and Vienna were cut up as smaller pieces of pie, and a sector in each city was awarded to one of the four occupying powers.

Unlike Germany and Austria, Italy faced relatively few difficulties in regaining independence. After a treaty was approved by the major powers in 1947, American and British troops were removed. Italy was stripped of her colonial empire, however, Libya and Italian Somaliland becoming United Nations trust territories. Long before the end of the war, in 1941, British military forces had restored Haile Selassie to his throne in Ethiopia.

In the aftermath of the Second World War, only two major world powers emerged. The shattering effects of the conflict had removed five other nations from pretensions to this status. Although the French were numbered among the victors, they had not recovered physically or psychologically from the crushing defeat by Germany in 1940. With an economy crippled by the protracted struggle, Great Britain began to abandon its role of world leadership. The three defeated Axis nations were also

---

[11]At Potsdam President Truman represented the United States, for Roosevelt had died three months earlier. Churchill represented Great Britain at the beginning of the conference; but during the proceedings he was defeated in a British general election, to the astonishment of people throughout the world. Clement Attlee of the Labour party became Prime Minister, replacing Churchill in the final sessions at Potsdam. Thus of the wartime Big Three leaders only Stalin remained.

Normandy plus two years.

It is eighteen years, I cried. "You must come no more."
"We know your names. We know that you are the dead.
Must you march forever from France and the last, blind war?"
"Fool! From the next!" they said.
    Stephen Vincent Benét, "1936"*

of course eliminated from the list of great powers. Only the Soviet Union and the United States remained in this category. The Soviet Union had suffered enormous losses in the war, but its recuperative abilities were extraordinary. By 1945 Russia's military power was greater than ever before. The United States emerged largely unscathed from the war, its colossal military establishment and monopoly of atomic weapons making it the greatest power in the world.

The United States had occupied such a preeminent position once before, in 1918, and had abandoned it for more comfortable, less costly isolationism. In 1945, however, the nation recognized and assumed the role of world leadership. Reluctantly but dutifully Americans accepted the fact that survival depends on a relatively peaceful world and that such a world can be achieved only through the unqualified participation of the United States in international affairs.

*From *Burning City*. Published by Holt, Rinehart and Winston. Copyright 1936 by Stephen Vincent Benét. Copyright renewed © 1964 by Thomas C. Benét, Stephanie B. Mahin, and Rachel Benét Lewis.

SUGGESTED READINGS

Arnold, H. H., *Global Mission* (1949).

Brunner, J. S., *Mandate from the People* (1944).

*Buchanan, A. R., *The United States and World War II* (vol. 1, 1964).

Bundy, M., *On Active Service in Peace and War* (1948).

Butow, R. J. C., *Japan's Decision to Surrender* (1954).

*Churchill, W., *The Second World War* (6 vols., 1948–1953).
*Cline, H. F., *The United States and Mexico* (1953).
Cole, W. S., *Senator Gerald P. Nye and American Foreign Relations* (1962).
*Divine, R. A., *The Reluctant Belligerent* (1965).
Drummond, D., *The Passing of American Neutrality* (1955).
Dulles, F. R., *Forty Years of American-Japanese Relations* (1937).
*Eisenhower, D. D., *Crusade in Europe* (1948).
Feis, H., *Between War and Peace* (1960).
*Feis, H., *The China Tangle* (1953).
Feis, H., *Churchill, Roosevelt, Stalin* (1957).
Feis, H., *Japan Subdued, the Atomic Bomb and the End of the War in the Pacific* (1961).
Fenno, R. F., Jr., ed., *The Yalta Conference* (1955).
Grodzins, M., *American Betrayed: Politics and Japanese Evacuation* (1949).
Hewlett, R. G. and O. E. Anderson, Jr., *The New World* (1926).
Janeway, E., *The Struggle for Survival* (1951).
Knebel, F. and C. Bailey, *No High Ground* (1960).
Langer, W. L., *Our Vichy Gamble* (1947).
Langer, W. L. and S. E. Gleason, *Undeclared War, 1940–1941* (1953).
*Lord, W., *Day of Infamy* (1957).
*Mauldin, B., *Up Front* (1945).
Millis, W., *This Is Pearl* (1947).
*Morison, E. E., *Turmoil and Tradition, A Study of the Life and Times of Henry L. Stimson* (1960).
Morison, S. E., *The Two-Ocean War* (1963).
Nelson, D. M., *Arsenal for Democracy* (1944).
Ogburn, W. F., ed., *American Society in Wartime* (1943).
*Perkins, D., *The New Age of Franklin Roosevelt* (1957).
Rauch, B., *Roosevelt: From Munich to Pearl Harbor* (1950).
Schroeder, P. W., *The Axis Alliance and Japanese American Relations, 1941* (1958).
Schuman, F. L., *Europe on the Eve* (1939).
*Sherwood, R. E., *Roosevelt and Hopkins* (1950).
Smith, B., *Seven Great Decisions* (1956).
*Smith, G., *American Diplomacy during the Second World War* (1964).
*Snell, J. L., *Illusion and Necessity: The Diplomacy of Global War, 1939–1945* (1963).
Snell, J. L., ed., *The Meaning of Yalta* (1956).
*Taylor, A. J. P., *The Origins of the Second World War* (1961).
Thomas, D. S. et al., *Japanese American Evacuation and Resettlement* (3 vols., 1946–1954).
Trefousse, H. L., *Germany and American Neutrality* (1951).
Vinson, J. C., *The Parchment Peace* (1950).

Viorst, M., *Hostile Allies* (1965).
Welles, S., *Time for Decision* (1944).
Welles, S., *Where Are We Heading?* (1946)
*Wheeler-Bennett, J. W., *Munich: Prologue to Tragedy* (1948).
*Wilmot, C., *The Struggle for Europe* (1952).
*Wohlstetter, R., *Pearl Harbor, Warning and Decision* (1962).

CHAPTER 30

Competitive Coexistence, 1946–1961

There are at the present time two great nations in the world, which started from different points, but seem to tend toward the same end. I refer to Russians and the Americans. Their starting point is different, and their courses are not the same; yet each of them seems to be marked out by the will of Heaven to sway the destinies of half the globe.

ALEXIS DE TOCQUEVILLE, 1835

PICTORIAL PARADE

President Roosevelt had hoped that the United States and the Soviet Union would be able to cooperate in establishing a stable and peaceful world; but Roosevelt's dream was to be shattered in the following years. Even before the end of hostilities, there was evidence that the Soviet government and the United States were pursuing increasingly divergent policies. In fact, the outstanding phenomenon in international affairs after 1945 was the bitter antagonism between the two powers, which was to affect, and in turn be affected by, all of the many other problems of the postwar world.

POSTWAR SETTLEMENTS, 1945—1946

Creation of the United Nations

Long before the war ended, President Roosevelt and his advisers had developed ideas for a new international organization for maintaining peace in the world. Plans for such an organization, which would serve to replace the defunct League of Nations, were discussed in 1943 at Big Three conferences in Moscow and Teheran. In the following year at Dumbarton Oaks (in Washington, D.C.) representatives of the major Allied nations drafted blueprints for the proposed United Nations, which would include a General Assembly, or world parliament, and a Security Council, which, it was hoped, could be used to enforce peace. Crucial decisions on membership and voting procedures were agreed upon during the Yalta conference in February 1945. At Roosevelt's insistence the permanent nations on the Security Council (United States, Soviet Union, Great Britain, France, China) were granted the power of absolute veto over any actions that were proposed. As a concession to Stalin, Roosevelt and Churchill agreed that the Soviet Union would have three seats in the General Assembly and that each of the other nations would have only one. On the basis of this apparently illogical principle, one seat each was granted to Byelorussia, the Ukraine, and the Soviet Union as a whole.[1] In June 1945 the representatives of fifty nations signed the Charter, which officially established the United Nations.

By May Congress had already given unanimous approval of United States membership in the new world organization. The strong bipartisan support was partially the result of President Roosevelt's skill in working with congressional leaders of both major parties in developing plans for the United Nations. In this way Roosevelt avoided the pitfalls that confronted Wilson when he sought support for the League of Nations in 1919. Roosevelt was especially fortunate in having the able assistance of Senator Arthur Vandenberg of Michigan, a prominent Republican and one-time isolationist.

The United Nations, like the former League, was largely the result of American experience and planning. Its advocates strongly believed that one of its primary functions was the provision of a forum for conciliatory discussion of international questions. The essential task of preventing aggression and maintaining the peace was assigned to the Security Council, while commissions and special agencies were created as part of the organization's effort to improve the general welfare of mankind. Among these were the World Health Organization, the Human Rights Commission, the Food and Agricultural Organization, UNESCO (United Nations Educational, Scientific and Cultural Organization), and the International Labor Organization. An International Court of Justice also was constituted to arbitrate disputes between nations.

After more than a quarter-century the world organization has still not realized the hopes of its founders. All too often the General Assembly has been the scene of acrimonious debate or the platform for propaganda statements. At first the Security Council achieved some limited success, such as a cease-fire agreement between Israel and the Arab nations in 1948. A year later the Council also persuaded India and Pakistan to end the fighting over Kashmir. Yet both settlements failed to last; the bitter warfare has broken out again and again in both rivalries. The only significant and permanent achievement of the Security Council was to persuade the Dutch to give independence to the Indonesian peoples in 1949. Since that time it has been unable to solve other major questions; and, hampered by the Soviet Union's frequent use of the veto power, the Council has therefore declined in importance.

Operating without sufficient funds and the confidence of some member nations, the special agencies and commissions have been handicapped in performing their functions. In addition, the International Court of Justice has lacked the authority to make decisions of major importance. Thus, although not as feeble as the old League, the United Nations has diminished in prestige since it was established, and its prospects for the future are not bright. As though to dramatize this fact, while high-ranking representatives of member states were gathering at the organization's New York headquarters to celebrate its twenty-fifth anniversary, the People's Republic of China, the Soviet Union, and the United States set off nuclear explosions.

Establishing Peace in Europe

The Partition of Germany. After the close of the Second World War, the victorious Allied leaders placed Germany under the total military occupation decided upon earlier. At the Potsdam summit conference in July 1945, Prime Minister Churchill and President Truman had agreed reluctantly to the Soviet Union's demand that Poland "temporarily" control certain eastern provinces of Germany (East Prussia,

---

[1] The President and the British prime minister felt that such a concession was appropriate since the Soviet Union, especially the two Soviet republics of Byelorussia and the Ukraine, had absorbed the brunt of the war against Germany. In addition, the Americans and the British were still fearful that the Soviet government might sign a separate peace treaty with Germany.

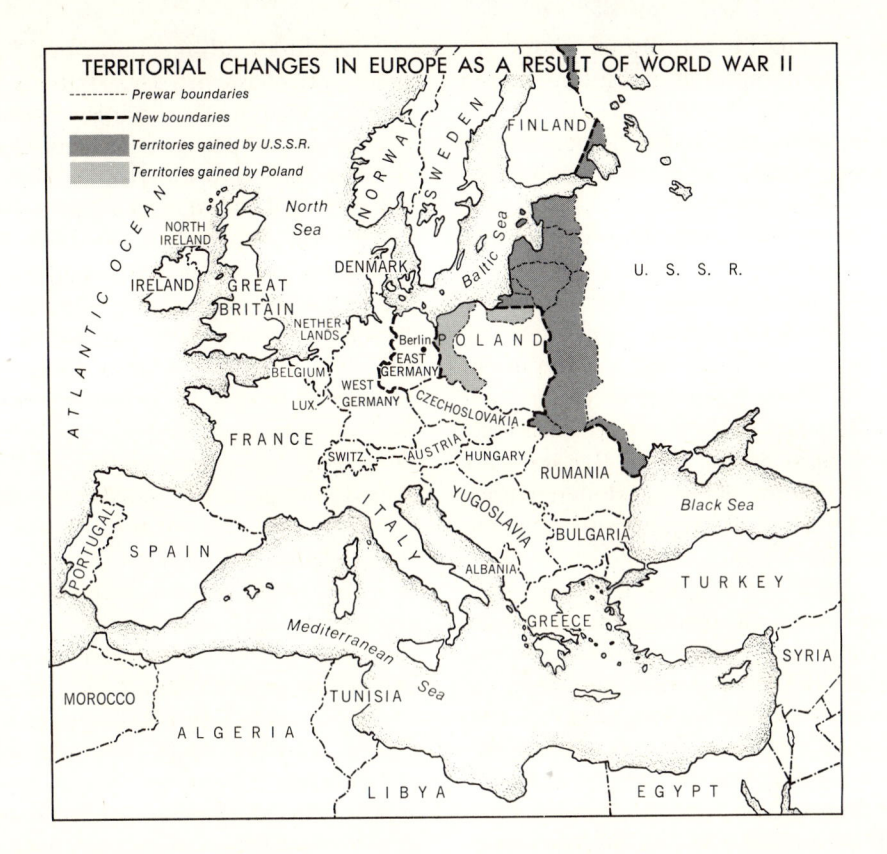

TERRITORIAL CHANGES IN EUROPE AS A RESULT OF WORLD WAR II

Pomerania, and Silesia). The new boundary between Poland and Germany was set along the Oder and Neisse rivers.[2]

Because Berlin within the Soviet zone was divided among the four occupying powers, an Autobahn (highway) and one railroad, stretching from Berlin to the British zone, were designated as routes to be used by the Western nations for moving supplies and personnel in and out of their sectors. Special air corridors also were established to connect Berlin with the West.

An Allied Control Council, composed of representatives of the four occupying powers, was established to supervise the disarmament and democratization of Germany. The defeated nation's armaments industries were to be dismantled or converted to the production of nonmilitary goods, and its giant cartels, or trusts, were to be dissolved. In order to prepare the German people for the implementation of a democratic form of government, the Council was determined to rid Germany of Nazi influences and punish war criminals. Both the Allied Control Council and the occupation zones were regarded as interim arrangements pending the signing of a peace treaty, following which the Western powers expected that occu-

---

[2] Poland, with the approval of Stalin, took prompt steps to make the temporary occupation permanent. Millions of Germans were driven from their homes, and the land was resettled by Poles. The refugees fled to other parts of Germany, where they have nursed their bitterness toward Poland to this day. To eradicate vestiges of German culture in the former eastern provinces, the Poles renamed cities and even streets. Thus the Polish government made it clear that it would never allow Germany to regain these lands. In late 1970 the established boundary was recognized by a treaty between West Germany and Poland.

Competitive Coexistence, 1946–1961

pation troops would be withdrawn and Germany would become reunited and independent once again.

As differences between the Soviet Union and the Western nations grew during the late 1940's, however, hope that a peace treaty would ever be signed faded. Faced with this impasse, the three Western powers consolidated their zones and agreed to allow the West Germans to establish a republic, which emerged in 1949 as the German Federal Republic. Konrad Adenauer was named as its chancellor, and Bonn designated as the temporary capital. In 1955 the United States, Great Britain, and France signed treaties with the Adenauer government, granting it full recognition as an independent nation.

In 1954 the Soviet Union gave an East German Communist government control over its internal affairs and in the following year granted the new German Democratic Republic (East Germany) political independence. The Western powers, however, have consistently refused to recognize the sovereign status of the East German regime, and the Soviets have until recently refused to grant diplomatic recognition to West Germany.

The Nuremberg Trials. During the Second World War the Allies made it known that they intended to indict Nazi leaders for "crimes against humanity," violations of international law, and conspiracy to wage aggressive war. For this purpose an International Military Tribunal was constituted as a war crimes court in Nuremberg, the site of the former Nazi party headquarters.

Twenty-two Nazi leaders were brought to trial before judges and prosecutors representing the four major occupation powers. Despite the hideous record of Nazi barbarism revealed in the proceedings, Hermann Goering, the principal defendant and formerly Hitler's right-hand man, sought to turn the trial into a circus by his antics and used the courtroom as a forum to denounce "the criminal acts" of the victorious Allies. The trial had other grotesque aspects and leading characters, including the prim and roosterish Dr. Hjalmar Schacht, the former Nazi finance minister; the apparently insane Rudolf Hess, once ranked as second in the line of succession from Hitler; and the arrogant Field Marshal Wilhelm Keitel, who acted the role of a ruthless Prussian general.

Nineteen of the Nazi leaders were found guilty, and twelve were sentenced to death (Goering cheated the hangman by committing suicide); others were sentenced to prison terms of various length. Hess was imprisoned for life and still remains in Spandau Prison in Berlin, completely alone except for the contingents of Allied soldiers who guard him night and day.

Although the purpose of the war crimes trials was to establish an international code of morality, they did not achieve this goal. For one thing, the judges readily excluded evidence of war crimes that might have implicated leaders of the victorious nations. To many observers the Nuremberg trials appear to have been merely another means of exacting vengeance on defeated Germany, for, in the opinion of many, war crimes have not ceased with the conclusion of the war in 1945; rather, they contend, it is merely a question whether the war criminal ends up on his feet or vanquished.

Other European Settlements. Following the close of the war Austria was also carved into occupation zones controlled by the Allies. This little nation, however, escaped the fate of a permanent partition: in 1955, after much wrangling between the Soviet Union and the West, it was unified and granted independence.

In December 1946 treaties were concluded with Italy, Bulgaria, Hungary, Finland, and Rumania. Finland and Italy gained complete independence, but the former Nazi satellite nations of eastern Europe were forced to accept Soviet-dominated governments. Although this represented a violation of Stalin's pledge at Yalta that democracies would be established, President Truman accepted, and the Senate approved, the treaties. It was their hope that over the years these inequities would be re-

Requiem for the Third Reich — trial of the Nazi leaders at Nuremberg. WIDE WORLD PHOTOS

solved by United Nations actions or by voluntary withdrawal of Soviet control. Today it is evident that this optimism was not altogether unfounded. In all the countries of eastern Europe there has been an increasing tendency by the governments, although still Communist, to pursue an independent course from that of the Soviet Union.

There were also a number of territorial adjustments in eastern Europe at the conclusion of the war. Large portions of eastern Poland containing mainly Byelorussians and Ukrainians were turned over to the Soviet Union. The U.S.S.R. also gained valuable land from Finland and Bessarabia, a region north of the Danube formerly belonging to Rumania. In addition, the eastern tip of Czechoslovakia and half of East Prussia were annexed by the Soviet government, which continued to hold the former Baltic republics of Latvia, Lithuania, and Estonia, seized in 1940. In all, the Soviet Union gained some 90,000 square miles and approximately 18,000,000 people as a result of the Second World War.

Asian Settlements

Japan. The difficulties created by the rivalry between the East and the West in postwar Germany were avoided in Japan since the United States was the sole occupying power. Under the direction of General Douglas MacArthur policies of democratization and demilitarization were quickly instituted. Although the emperor

Competitive Coexistence, 1946–1961   353

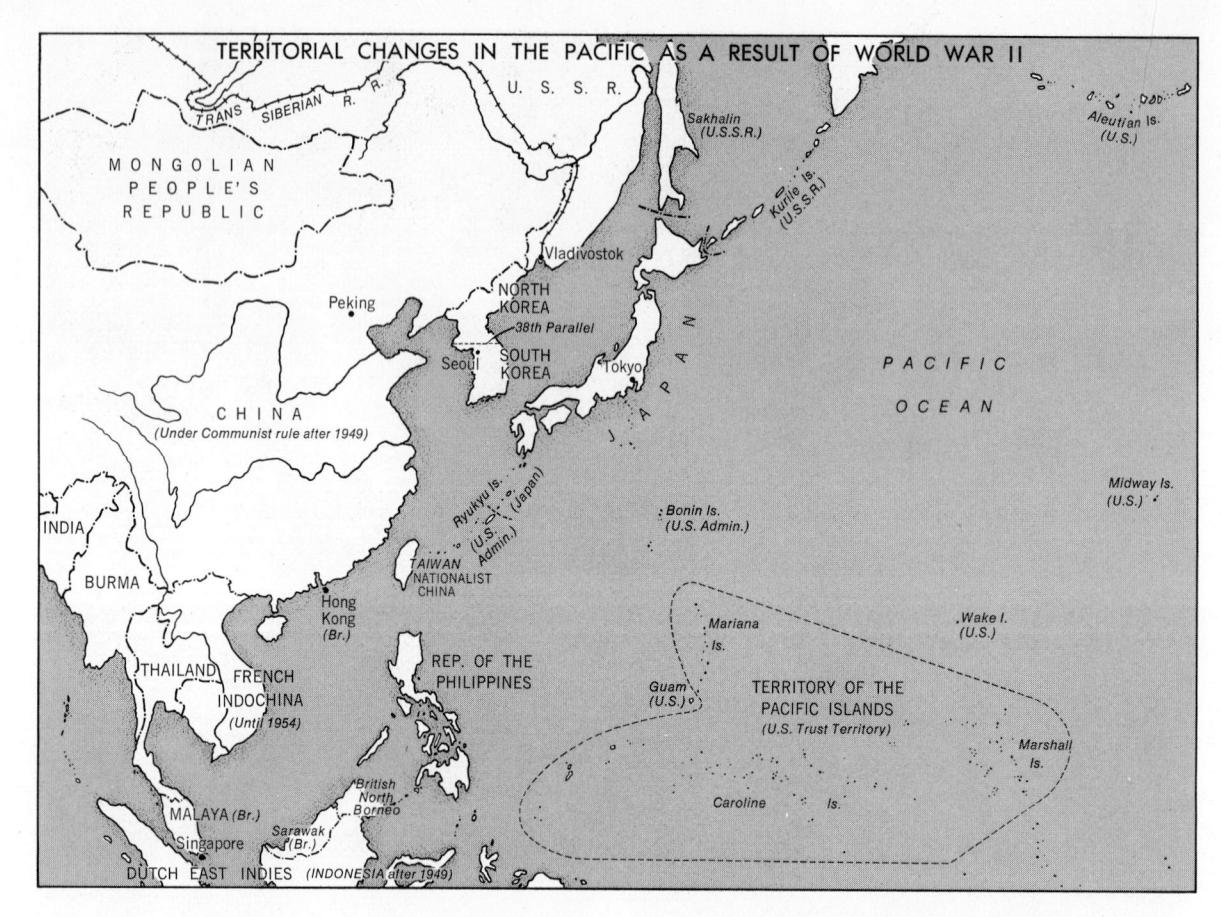

TERRITORIAL CHANGES IN THE PACIFIC AS A RESULT OF WORLD WAR II

remained on his throne, he had become only a figurehead with little real power. In 1946 a new constitution was adopted by which Japan was converted into a democracy. Under American guidance trade unionism was encouraged, women received the right to vote, and the educational system was reformed. An international tribunal punished former Japanese officials for war crimes, and Japan's armies were brought home from overseas and disbanded.

To create a bastion against Communism in Asia, the United States and Great Britain concluded a peace treaty with Japan in 1951. In a separate security treaty Japan agreed to permit American troops to be stationed on its soil for the protection both of that country and of other areas in the Far East.

Korea and Southeast Asia. In 1945 the United States and the Soviet Union placed Korea under joint military occupation, pending a general settlement of peace negotiations in the Far East. Korea was divided in half at the 38th parallel, with Soviet troops north of the line and American forces in the south. As in Germany, the division became rigid since the expected settlement never came. The U.S.S.R. established a Communist dictatorship in the north. In South Korea a democratic type of government was formed under United States supervision. Dr. Syngman Rhee, who became the country's first president, hoped to use military force to unite all of Korea, but he was left little military power when the United States withdrew its troops in 1949. The Soviets also with-

Time of Trial, Time of Hope

drew from their sector in the north at about the same time, but they left Dictator Kim Il Sung ample military equipment and a well-trained army.

In Southeast Asia the former European rulers resumed control of their colonies with one exception—Great Britain granted independence to Burma in 1946. (At the same time the United States fulfilled a pledge made ten years earlier and gave the Philippines their independence.) Meanwhile the British reoccupied Malaya and aided the Dutch in regaining control of the East Indies (Indonesia). As we have already seen, however, in 1949 the Dutch were expelled by the Indonesians, who were supported by the United Nations. With assistance from the British and the Nationalist Chinese, the French resumed control of Indochina (Laos, Cambodia, and Vietnam). But, as elsewhere in Southeast Asia, the native Vietnamese were determined to free themselves from European colonial rule. In 1946, under the leadership of Ho Chi-Minh, they revolted against the French, who were forced to withdraw from Indochina after a long and bloody war that lasted until 1954.

The China Question. While the political situation in Korea and Southeast Asia remained uncertain, the hostility of China grew to such proportions that it soon was regarded as a menace to the interests of the United States. As the Second World War ended in the Far East, United States forces hastily assisted the Chinese Nationalists in disarming Japanese armies in China and in turning over political control of most of the country to the Nationalist leader, Generalissimo Chiang Kai-shek. The Chinese Communist forces of Mao Tse-tung, however, already held large areas in the north. In addition, the Soviets had helped Mao by securing for him Manchuria and large quantities of captured Japanese military equipment.

To help avert a serious civil war, President Truman sent General George C. Marshall as a special envoy to China in December 1945, with an assignment to serve as mediator between the opposing factions; but the mission failed. In 1947 full-scale civil war broke out, at which point the United States dropped all pretense of impartiality and supported the Chiang government. Despite enormous quantities of American aid, the inept Nationalists were unable to prevent the southward advance of the Communists. Thus Chiang and the remnants of the Nationalist army were forced to abandon the mainland and seek refuge on the island of Formosa late in 1949.

There was probably nothing that the United States could have done to strengthen the Chiang government sufficiently to prevent the Communist victory. Nevertheless, the policies of the Truman administration toward China became the subject of a hot controversy on the American political scene during the late 1940's and 1950's.

THE COLD WAR DURING THE TRUMAN ERA

By 1946 it had become clear to all Americans that the United States and the U.S.S.R., although formerly allies, were moving into positions of hostile confrontation in many parts of the world. The facade of wartime cooperation fell away, revealing the two great powers in pursuit of goals clearly antagonistic. The moves and countermoves of the two nations on the world's diplomatic chessboard in the years after 1945 were aptly described as a "cold war" rather than a "hot," or shooting, war. During the cold war each nation maneuvered to gain advantages for itself and followed policies aimed at weakening its adversary. Again and again the two superpowers appeared to be on the brink of war; but in each crisis one or the other gave way, and the threat of total war receded for the moment.

As a result of this long and bitter rivalry, the government and the American people were forced to face the harsh reality that peace had not been achieved even after a victory in the bloodiest war in history. By 1946 the Truman administration was groping for policies to meet the challenge created by the hostile Soviet Union.

Containment

Surprisingly, former Prime Minister Winston Churchill accepted an invitation in 1946 to address the students of tiny Westminster College in Fulton, Missouri; the importance of Churchill's visit was enhanced when it became known that President Truman would also be present. In one of his most renowned speeches, the famous guest grimly warned the people of the Western world that "From Stettin in the Baltic to Trieste in the Adriatic, an iron curtain has descended across the Continent [of Europe]." In condemning the police governments under Soviet control, Churchill called for Anglo-American cooperation in opposing what he felt was the Stalin government's implacable pursuit of world domination. The former prime minister's "iron curtain speech" was only one of many warnings voiced in 1946 concerning Soviet antagonism. Despite the tepid reception of the speech by the public, the Truman administration began to formulate new policies to check Soviet expansion in Europe.

In the July 1947 issue of *Foreign Affairs*, George F. Kennan, a State Department expert of Soviet affairs, proposed a policy of containment. Kennan argued that the leaders in the Kremlin still subscribed to the Marxist-Leninist doctrine that capitalism was doomed. Since, as they saw it, history was on their side, the Soviet leaders would move with caution, retreating "in the face of superior force" on occasion, but maintaining their strength in readiness to exploit weaknesses in the capitalist nations. As Kennan put it, "the main element of any United States policy toward the Soviet Union must be that of a long-term, patient but firm and vigilant containment of Russian expansive tendencies." Kennan reasoned that such a policy would lead to the frustration and possible disruption of the international Communist movement, and the Soviet leaders would sooner or later be obliged to moderate their policies. Kennan concluded that it was fortunate that the challenge had come, for it compelled the American people to unite and accept "the responsibilities of moral and political leadership that history plainly intended them to bear."

The Truman Doctrine. Even before Kennan's proposal was explicitly formulated, containment had been a government policy. It was first used significantly in the Mediterranean in 1946 when the Soviets were applying heavy pressure on the unstable Greek and Turkish governments. Communist guerrilla forces in Greece received aid from the Soviet Union and the Communist governments of Yugoslavia and Bulgaria. At the same time, the Soviet government was demanding that Turkey grant it effective control of the strategic straits of the Dardanelles and the Bosporus.

A crisis developed in February 1947 when the British government notified the United States that it could not give further military assistance to the feeble royalist government of Greece in its struggle with the Communist rebels. Faced with a possible Communist coup in Greece and the equally possible collapse of an economically weak Turkey, President Truman acted decisively: in March he asked Congress for an emergency appropriation of $400,000,000 to help the two countries. In defending his request, the President declared, in what has become known as the Truman Doctrine, that "it must be the policy of the United States to support free peoples who are resisting attempted subjugation by armed minorities or by outside pressure."

With military advice and large quantities of American armaments, the Greeks were able to take the offensive against the Communist guerrillas, and as a result the insurrection was crushed by 1949. The United States was equally successful in relieving Soviet pressure on Turkey, whose military and naval forces were

THE IRON CURTAIN DIVIDING EUROPE

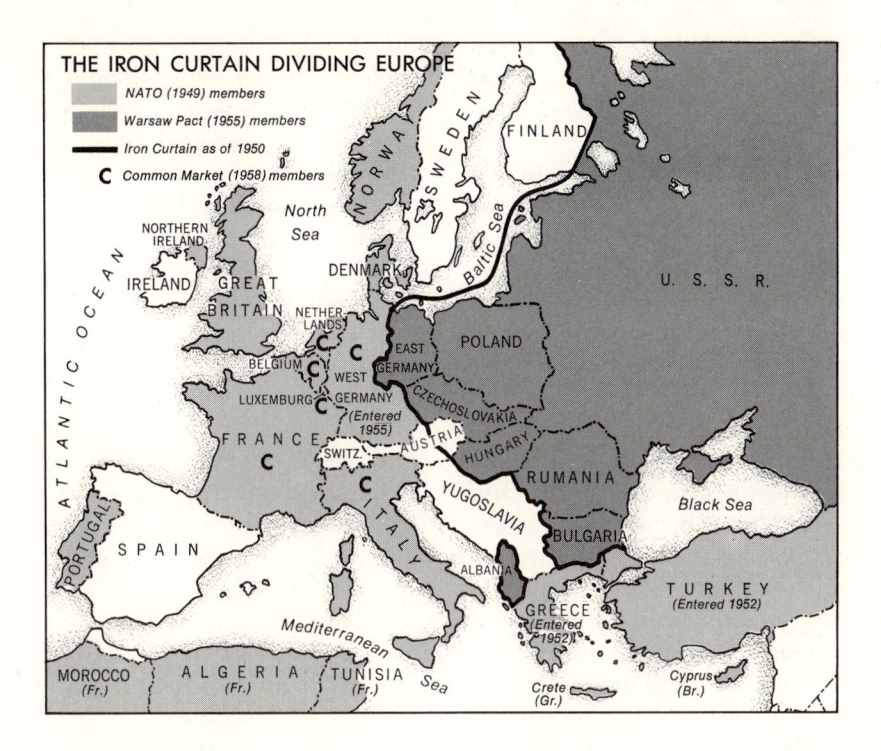

modernized; American funds and financial advice also were used to stabilize Turkey's faltering economy.

The implications of the Truman Doctrine were far reaching. Historically, the doctrine represented a departure from United States foreign policy of the nineteenth century. In 1823 President Monroe had said, in effect, that America should stay out of Greece. Now in 1947 Truman was urging that the United States intervene in this country. The policy of aiding "free peoples" everywhere had the obvious disadvantage of overextending American strength by commitments in too many places on the globe at the same time. An additional complication in Greece was that the United States was placed in the embarrassing position of aiding the reactionary and authoritarian royal government, which did not have the support of the people. Critics also denounced Truman's action in Greece and Turkey as a unilateral policy, in which the United Nations was bypassed and consequently weakened.

The Marshall Plan. There were alarming signs in 1947 that Greece and Turkey were not the only nations too weak to resist Communism. In varying degrees all the countries of western Europe were staggering under the crushing burdens of reconstruction. Since the end of the war the United States had provided huge quantities of food, clothing, and shelter for the war-stricken peoples of Europe through emergency services administered by such agenices as UNRRA (United Nations Relief and Rehabilitation Administration). But relief was not enough. Recovery programs would also be needed to restore the European economy. The distress of western Europe was underscored by the rapid expansion of national Communist parties, particularly in France and Italy.

In a speech at Harvard in June 1947, Secretary of State George C. Marshall proposed a solution. He called upon the European nations to cooperate in a massive economic recovery program in which the cost would be underwritten by the United States government in the

Competitive Coexistence, 1946–1961   357

form of loans and grants. The Communist-bloc nations were invited to participate; but, as had been expected, they followed orders from Moscow and spurned the invitation.

The European Recovery Program cost the United States twelve billion dollars during its first three years, but it was a success. By 1951, with the completion of the most extensive phase of the Marshall Plan, western Europe was on the road to economic health; and by the end of that year industrial production was forty-one per cent above the prewar level and sixty-four per cent ahead of the level reached in 1947. During the same period Communist parties in western Europe dwindled in size and effectiveness. Later, Marshall Plan aid was extended to Japan, Formosa, and South Korea, also with strikingly successful results.

NATO. Economic containment of Communism was vital, but, as government policymakers saw it, additional measures were essential to counter extensive Soviet military forces in eastern Europe and possible aggression in the west. In 1948 there were 175 Soviet divisions on occupation duty in eastern Europe, backed by an additional 60 divisions from Soviet-bloc countries.[3]

In response to what seemed a threat to western Europe, the North Atlantic Treaty was concluded at Washington, D.C., in April 1949. Twelve "Atlantic" nations, including the United States, joined in this defensive agreement. The other signatories were Canada, Iceland, the United Kingdom, France, Belgium, the Netherlands, Luxembourg, Denmark, Norway, Portugal, and Italy. (In 1952 Greece and Turkey joined the North Atlantic Treaty Organization—NATO—and West Germany became a member in 1955.) In 1951 NATO's forces were unified under one commander, General Dwight Eisenhower, and the military headquarters were established outside Paris. NATO's strategic purpose was to create a military force of units from member nations that would have sufficient strength to check a Soviet invasion until the strategic air power of the United States could be fully utilized. In supplementary agreements to NATO, the United States supplied nearly six billion dollars' worth of military equipment to its European allies. By 1953 NATO had at its disposal about 60 divisions and more than 5,000 planes. It was further strengthened when Yugoslavia became an affiliate through a common defense treaty with Greece and Turkey. In geographic area the NATO nations extended in a great arc from the North Cape of Norway almost to the Caspian Sea. Thus most of the major industrial centers of the Soviet Union would be vulnerable to strikes by long-range United States bombers operating from bases in Turkey, Norway, and western Europe.

In the years after 1953, however, NATO declined steadily in strength. During the temporary thaw in the cold war in 1955, western European nations were reluctant to maintain NATO military strength up to what the United States regarded as adequate levels; and the tendency after 1954 to rely on nuclear weapons made the nations less willing to maintain conventional armies. The strength of NATO was further reduced by France's withdrawal of NATO divisions to fight in Vietnam and Algeria, and internal discord within the alliance was intensified after 1955 by the bitter quarrels of Greece, Turkey, and Great Britain over Cyprus. In addition, the censure of Great Britain and France by the United States during the 1956 Suez crisis led to further bitterness.

As a result of the gradual withdrawal of France, NATO since 1966 has declined almost to the level of a mere paper organization. Even the United States, which was long the most ardent advocate of the defense agreement, is

---

[3]This threat was more apparent than real. Although large in numbers, Soviet forces were not prepared for offensive war: veterans of the Second World War had been largely replaced by untried troops, and Soviet industry in 1948 had hardly begun to recover from the shattering effects of the war. In recent years it has become evident that Soviet policy was not as potentially aggressive as Kennan and others considered it at the time.

beginning to lose interest in it. NATO, however, may have fulfilled its purpose in its earlier years by acting as a restraint upon Soviet military power while western Europe was still recovering from the Second World War.

Like the Truman Doctrine, the Marshall Plan and NATO were significant departures from traditional American foreign policies. In conceiving and executing the Marshall Plan, the United States made it clear that it was abandoning to a large degree its earlier isolationist attitude toward the economic problems of other nations. In joining the NATO pact, the Truman administration sought to bury the nation's traditional antipathy to entangling alliances.

Containment Challenged

While the United States was erecting its containment structure in Europe, the Soviet Union was busily consolidating power over its satellite nations. In 1948 the Communists seized control of Czechoslovakia, and Jan Masaryk, son of the founder and leader of the anti-Communist opposition, jumped or was pushed to his death from a second-story window in Prague. At Warsaw in 1955, the Soviet Union organized the Communist bloc into a military league, or "NATO of Eastern Europe." Finally, two major challenges were issued to the policy of containment, one in Europe and the other in Asia.

The Berlin Crisis. In early 1948 the Soviet government issued a strong protest against the plans of the three Western occupying powers for the unification and independence of their zones of Germany. When this objection was rejected, the Soviets applied massive pressure: on June 24, 1948 the Soviet forces in East Germany closed the Autobahn and other surface accesses from the British zone to West Berlin. Ultimately this action would have ruptured the economy and starved the people of West Berlin, since the highway was essentially the lifeline of the city.

The Soviet move thus created the most serious international crisis since the Second World War. The United States and its allies had a number of alternative courses of action, none of which was attractive. For example, Western nations could abandon plans for unification of Germany, which undoubtedly would placate the Kremlin and end the blockade. But this would be yielding to blackmail and would allow the Soviets to use Berlin as a pawn in the future. Alternatively, the Western countries could withdraw their forces from Berlin and continue to seek unification, but this would mean abandoning the people in Berlin, to whom the West had promised protection. In any case, withdrawal would be a sign of weakness and would damage the prestige of the United States as well as that of Great Britain and France. A third alternative was the use of force in breaking the Soviet blockade. This course also had a serious disadvantage: it could lead to a third world war. The military posture of the West at the time was weak, for both the United States and Great Britain had demobilized rapidly after the Second World War. In 1948 there were fewer than a million men in the United States army, scattered in various outposts around the world, many of them only half-trained recruits. Nevertheless, President Truman stated flatly that "we will stay in Berlin."[4]

There was still another alternative, proposed by General Lucius Clay, the United States member of the four-power Allied Control Council. Clay urged that a huge airlift be mounted to supply the industries and more than two million people of West Berlin. This plan would shift the burden to the Soviets: any attempt to violate or block the air corridors to Berlin would place them in the position of committing the final act leading to war, a conflict that the United States and its allies were certain they did not want.

On paper the idea appeared fantastic, yet the operation was launched; and by July 5

---

[4] At the time, the Western allies had only 6,500 military personnel and dependents in Berlin. The Soviets had 18,000 troops in their sector of the city and 300,000 in East Germany.

Soviet-American confrontation in Berlin. United States relief plane over Templehof Airport.

United States and British planes were transporting 3,000 tons of supplies daily; but this was not enough: fuel, especially coal, would have to be stockpiled for the coming winter. By the end of September, a plane was landing every three minutes. Even so, Berliners were having a difficult time. As winter approached, there was no heat for homes and barely enough to supply industries and electric power plants; and the people, although not starving, were on short rations.

In the meantime the Soviets were busy trying to frustrate the airlift and break the will of the West Berliners: fighter planes buzzed the corridor and the airfields, hampering landing operations; the electric power supplied by East Berlin to the Western sector was cut; Soviet antiaircraft batteries ringing Berlin occasionally held practice maneuvers using live ammunition; landing signals for United States and British aricraft were deliberately scrambled by East Berlin radio; and East Berlin police and organized mobs raided the Western sector, beating up, kidnapping, and generally terrorizing West Berliners. In addition, fog and extreme cold during the winter aided the Soviets. Nevertheless, by December the average daily tonnage provided by the airlift climbed to 4,500 tons.

The Western powers, however, countered Soviet pressure with political maneuvers. Plans for West German unification and the formation of NATO were hastened, and the dismantling of German industrial equipment for shipment to the Soviet Union as war reparations was halted. The Western allies also imposed a counterblockade on shipments to the Soviet zone of Germany, which needed goods and raw materials from the West. To reinforce the challenge to the Kremlin President Truman ordered two additional squadrons of B-29 bombers moved from the United States to Great Britain.

Time of Trial, Time of Hope

Cold war becomes hot in Korea. SOVFOTO

With the coming of spring, the success of the airlift was assured. On a single day in April almost 13,000 tons were landed by 1,400 planes that arrived every 62 seconds. As Kennan had predicted in 1947, Soviet resolve crumbled in face of this show of strength. On May 12, 1949, after more than 300 days, the blockade ended: the Autobahn was reopened, and trains were again permitted to pass through the Soviet zone. During the period in which the blockade had been in force, the Western powers had flown 1,600,000 tons of fuel and food to Berlin, but at the cost of the lives of forty-five American and British airmen. It was a tactical victory, but other Soviet challenges were bound to come in Berlin and elsewhere.

The Korean War. On January 12, 1950 Secretary of State Dean Acheson declared that the American defensive perimeter in the Pacific stretched from the Aleutian Islands to Japan and the Philippines. Within this arc the United States would provide immediate military assistance to nations attacked from the outside, while those beyond this perimeter would have to rely on their individual resources to resist aggression until ultimately the United Nations came to their assistance. This policy of containment in Asia notably excluded Korea as well as Formosa and Southeast Asia.

The significance of Acheson's statement was not lost on leaders in the Communist world. On June 25, 1950 the North Korean Communist forces suddenly attacked across the 38th parallel. Their goal was the conquest of the south and unification of Korea under Communist rule. During the next few days the North Korean troops pushed rapidly southward, and within one week—the first of the war—Seoul, the capital of South Korea, fell. The small South Korean army, ill trained and poorly equipped, was easily brushed aside by the Communist invaders.

For all this the United States found itself unprepared, but President Truman acted resolutely. He ordered American forces in Japan under General MacArthur to intervene and

Competitive Coexistence, 1946–1961

drive the invaders out of South Korea. Despite insufficient troops MacArthur moved swiftly, and American units were able to arrive in Korea just in time to prevent North Korean seizure of the entire peninsula. Nevertheless, by the end of July the last remaining stronghold of the South Koreans and the Americans consisted of only a very small area around the port of Pusan.

This struggle to halt the North Korean invasion was soon joined by the United Nations. When news of the attack reached the United Nations, the Security Council promptly declared the North Korean action as a "breach of the peace." Member nations were called upon "to render every assistance to the United Nations" to expel the North Koreans. Paradoxically, although the Soviet delegate to the Security Council could have cast a crippling veto, he was absent in the course of temporarily boycotting Security Council sessions in order to protest the continued presence of Nationalist China on the Council.

As a result of United Nations assistance, the armies commanded by General MacArthur soon became internationalized. In addition to the United States and ROK (Republic of Korea) forces, there were troops from fifteen other nations.[5] The tide of battle turned in September 1950, when General MacArthur's troops executed a brilliant flanking assault on the enemy's rear by an amphibious attack at Inchon. Now it was the turn of the North Koreans to be surprised, and they abandoned South Korea in panic.

Within two weeks South Korea was liberated. After hesitating briefly at the 38th parallel MacArthur's forces advanced into North Korea in accordance with the United Nations resolution of October 7 calling for "stability" and the "unification" of Korea. At first the United Nations armies encountered little resistance; Pyongyang, the capital of North Korea, was captured on October 19. But as American troops dashed northward toward the Yalu River—the border between Korea and Manchuria—there were hints of trouble: Chinese troops were said to be crossing the Yalu from Manchuria. On November 26, 1950 the Chinese forces crashed the United Nations lines, which wavered and then buckled under the assault. Once again the tide of battle flowed southward. In the freezing, subzero weather the United Nations forces barely escaped disaster; but after the loss of Seoul to the enemy, they regrouped and halted the Communist forces, although well below the 38th parallel.

In March 1951 the complexion of the war changed again. On March 14 Seoul was recaptured by United Nations forces for the second and last time; and on April 3 American troops recrossed the 38th parallel.

During this series of almost bewildering advances and reversals of the fortunes of war a crisis was developing between MacArthur and President Truman over the containment policy of the government. The problem was intensified by the conflict of personalities: the proud and flamboyant general and the irascible, outspoken President.

For some years the administration in Washington had been critical of MacArthur's public statements; now Truman was deeply disturbed over the error, as he saw it, of MacArthur's decision to go to the Yalu despite the threat of Chinese intervention. Matters came to a head when MacArthur demanded that his forces be allowed to attack the "privileged sanctuary" of the Chinese in Manchuria. In a letter to Congressman Joseph W. Martin, Jr., made public on April 5, 1951, MacArthur openly criticized the policy of the Truman administration in waging a limited war, having as its objective a

---

[5]The fifteen were Great Britain, Canada, Turkey, Australia, Thailand, the Philippines, France, Greece, New Zealand, the Netherlands, Colombia, Belgium, Ethiopia, the Union of South Africa, and Luxembourg. Most of the military assistance, however, consisted of token forces of battalion size. The largest forces of the fifteen were from Great Britain and Canada.

settlement by negotiation. Instead, he declared, "We must win. . . . There is no substitute for victory."

On April 10 the angry President reacted sternly to what was felt by many to be an act of "insubordination": MacArthur was relieved of his post as Supreme Commander in the Far East and replaced by General Matthew B. Ridgway, field commander of the United Nations forces in Korea.

A bitter political controversy surrounded MacArthur's removal. Republicans in Congress sharply denounced Truman's policies—even his personal character—and loudly supported MacArthur's proposal to enlarge the conflict. Nevertheless, administration leaders stiffly defended the policy of limiting the war and seeking peace by negotiation. George C. Marshall, the Secretary of Defense, expressed the intent of the government "to confine the conflict to Korea and to prevent its spreading into a third World War," and General Omar Bradley, Chairman of the Joint Chiefs of Staff, flatly declared that an attack on China would be "the wrong war, at the wrong place, at the wrong time, and with the wrong enemy." Despite the intensive criticism of its position, therefore, the Truman administration continued the policy of Asiatic containment and the search for a settlement of the Korean War by negotiation.

After stabilizing the Korean front in early 1951 at a location slightly north of the 38th parallel, United Nations forces inflicted heavy losses on the Chinese, which in turn helped induce in the Communist leaders a willingness to negotiate. In response to a suggestion from Moscow, Chinese and North Korean officials opened negotiations with General Ridgway's representatives in July. But the discussions were acrimonious; frequently one negotiating team or the other walked out during the proceedings. Meanwhile, Communist and United Nations forces continued to fight limited, but often bloody, actions along the Korean front.

The Communists broke off discussions in October 1952 over problems concerning the exchange of prisoners.[6] President Eisenhower, who had been inaugurated early in 1953, was determined to break this deadlock, however, and Secretary of State John Foster Dulles strongly hinted that hostilities would be resumed on a large scale unless peace could be achieved. Eisenhower's tough stance was assisted by the death of Stalin in March 1953 and the desire of the new Soviet rulers to achieve at least a temporary accommodation with the Western powers.

Thus an armistice was finally concluded at Panmunjom on July 27, 1953, and a new demarcation line was established between the two Koreas, generally along the battle lines that had been slightly north of the 38th parallel. Under the truce supervisory leadership of India, prisoners were exchanged and a demilitarized zone was designated between South and North Korea. No steps were taken to unify the peninsula politically, however, and the two Koreas continue to this day to maintain strong armies on both sides of the DMZ (demilitarized zone). Under United Nations authority the United States also continues to station troops along the border to supplement South Korea's army.

In 1954 the Eisenhower administration moved to include South Korea in the United States defense perimeter in the Far East when it concluded a mutual defense treaty with the South Korean government. Since 1953, however, the cease-fire agreement has been punctuated by occasionally sharp clashes between the hostile forces, the land remaining a breeding ground for future conflict.

Thus containment of Soviet power was achieved in Asia, but the task was extremely difficult and costly: more than 33,000 Americans were killed in the Korean War, and the

---

[6]This was the third suspension of negotiations, the Americans being the first to have walked out of the armistice conference (August 5).

cost of the war in dollars and cents has been put at $80,000,000,000.

The Balance Sheet

During the Truman years both the Soviet Union and the United States won victories and suffered setbacks in their competition for world leadership. On the one hand, the Soviet threat to Greece and Turkey in 1947 was repulsed. By means of the Marshall Plan, introduced in that same year, western Europe achieved economic recovery, and through the creation of NATO, in 1949, the United States was able to establish a coordinated defense for western Europe against possible Soviet invasion. The unification of West Germany and the Berlin airlift in 1948 and 1949 were also solid achievements of United States foreign policy. On the other hand, the Soviet Union tightened the hold on its satellite countries in eastern Europe. Two ways in which this manifested itself were the elimination in Czechoslovakia of all traces of democratic and pro-Western elements and the prohibition, exerted on all Communist regimes, from participating in the Marshall Plan.

The Soviets, however, suffered a serious setback in Yugoslavia. In 1948 Marshal Tito defied Stalin and embarked upon an independent course in domestic and foreign policies. This defection destroyed the image of solidarity and strength in the Communist movement, and directly contributed to the United States and the Greek royalist victory over Communist guerrillas in northern Greece. The United States exploited this breach in Communist ranks by cautiously extending limited economic and military aid to the Yugoslav government. In 1949 this blow to Soviet prestige was diminished somewhat when Russian scientists announced that they had developed an atomic bomb, thereby ending American monopoly of the weapon.

Developments in Asia also strengthened Soviet power. In 1949 the Chinese Communists defeated the Nationalists. Furthermore, the position of the United States in Southeast Asia was threatened by the increasingly pro-Soviet policy of the Sukarno government of Indonesia and the bitter war in Indochina between the French and the Vietminh (Vietnamese nationalists under Ho Chi-Minh).

The outstanding triumph of the United States in the Asian cold war was the postwar reconstruction of the Japanese economy and the 1951 peace treaty, which yielded Japanese independence and friendly relations with the West. And, as we have seen, the United States also achieved a limited success by its action in saving South Korea from conquest. The repression of the Huk (Communist) uprising by the Philippine government and the defeat of Communist guerrillas in Malaya by the British in 1953 also aided in strengthening the position of the United States in Asia. But the cold war was destined to continue, and other confrontations were bound to occur as Truman left the White House in 1953.

THE COLD WAR DURING THE EISENHOWER YEARS

In 1953 momentous changes of leadership occurred in the United States and the Soviet Union. On January 20 Eisenhower became President of the United States, and on March 5 the death of Stalin was announced. The resulting changes were accompanied by significant shifts in the philosophies and foreign policies of both nations.

The principal spokesman for the "new look" foreign policies of the Eisenhower administration was Secretary of State John Foster Dulles. As an experienced diplomat and international lawyer, Dulles was eminently qualified for his new post. A man of high intelligence, abundant energy, and profound self-assurance, he was to be one of the most forceful and controversial secretaries of state in American history.

In personality and philosophy Dulles was strikingly similar to Woodrow Wilson: both were Presbyterians, graduates of Princeton, and men of domineering will. And both were convinced of the righteousness of their convictions. Like Wilson, Dulles injected morality into foreign policy, maintaining that there were "good" and "bad" governments and that Communism was inherently evil. It was the duty of the United States as the leader of the "Free World," Dulles contended, to oppose Communism manfully and to bring about its destruction. Speaking in this vein, Dulles called for the liberation of the peoples of eastern Europe and denounced the Truman policy of containment as static, asserting that it left the initiative to the Soviet Union to instigate crises wherever and whenever it wished. In Dulles's eyes, it was an error for the United States to be drawn into "brush fire" engagements, such as the Korean conflict, fought along the periphery of Soviet power. He believed that the appropriate response to such Russian-made crises was "massive retaliation" — implying nuclear assault, by United States strategic bombers, on the citadels of Communism in the industrial heart of the Soviet Union. Although President Eisenhower was a man of considerable experience in international affairs, he tended to accept the crude formulas devised by his strong-willed Secretary of State.

The death of Joseph Stalin led to a struggle for power within the Soviet Union. As a result, Lavrenti Beria, the powerful chief of the Soviet secret police, was put to death at the hands of a junta, and a caretaker regime was established with Georgy Malenkov as the new titular ruler. In 1955 Malenkov was demoted and replaced by Nikolai Bulganin, but the new premier served as a figurehead. By this time it was apparent that the real power lay largely in the grasp of Nikita Khrushchev.

In the following year Khrushchev removed Bulganin and assumed the premiership for himself and charted new directions in the Soviet domestic and foreign policies. At home, Khrushchev sought to stimulate the production of consumer goods and to improve the standard of living. In foreign affairs the new leader pursued a bewildering, shifting, vacillating, and often contradictory set of policies. On occasion Khrushchev seemed to be bent on a policy of "accommodation" toward the United States, stating that there was no reason why Communism could not coexist with capitalism; but on other occasions he made blunt assertions easily construed as threats, such as his well-known utterance, "We will bury you." Although Khrushchev seemed willing to relax the iron grip of Soviet power on the satellite nations of eastern Europe, he reversed himself in 1956 and ruthlessly crushed the Hungarian uprising.

The international position of the Soviet Union was complicated by the emergence of Mao Tse-tung's China as a competitor for leadership in the Communist world. This rivalry was one reason why Khrushchev looked hopefully to the United States as a possible friend, or at least a neutral, in the event of a struggle between the Soviet Union and China.

Nevertheless, the cold war persisted, the two major powers continuing in their attempts to weaken each other's international position. In Southeast Asia, the Middle East, Africa, and Latin America, Khrushchev exploited opportunities of embarrassing the United States. Dulles responded to the various Soviet moves by seeking to forge a chain of steel around the Communist world.

Containment in Southeast Asia

In Europe the line of containment had been firmly drawn by the Truman Doctrine and the North Atlantic Treaty Organization. In the Far East the line was also clear: American forces guarded Japan and South Korea, and the United States Seventh Fleet protected Chiang Kai-shek's regime on Formosa. But the situation in Southeast Asia during 1953 was uncertain. Dulles and the Eisenhower administration therefore took a number of vigorous steps to extend containment formally to that portion of the globe.

The War in Indochina. Since 1946 the French

had been fighting the guerrillas of Ho Chi-Minh in Indochina. After the Communist victory in China in 1949, however, the conflict became increasingly bitter. Large quantities of equipment that were sent by the Peking government to the Vietminh forces were matched by the growing French military effort. The Truman administration had already provided the French in Indochina (Vietnam, Laos, and Cambodia) with large quantities of arms, and the Eisenhower government continued this policy on an even larger scale.

Despite the massive American aid, the French forces were unsuccessful in suppressing the Vietminh rebellion, and by March 1954 their position was becoming increasingly desperate. Dulles and Admiral Arthur W. Radford, Chairman of the Joint Chiefs of Staff, proposed United States military intervention in the form of air strikes against the Vietminh army surrounding a French paratroop division at Dienbienphu; but leaders in Congress, including Senator Lyndon Johnson, objected to enlarging the war. When Dulles later approached the British for aid against the Vietminh, Prime Minister Anthony Eden flatly declined. The possibility of United States intervention ended when the French surrendered at Dienbienphu on May 7, 1954.

The French defeat in Indochina revealed the ineffectiveness of Dulles's policy of massive retaliation, for the American people were clearly unwilling to approve an all-out assault on China as punishment for aiding Ho Chi-Minh in Indochina. The budget-cutting Eisenhower administration was equally unwilling to ask Congress for the enormous expenditures necessary to wage a large-scale war in Southeast Asia. In any event, neither Eisenhower nor Congress wanted the United States to become involved in "another Korea."

The Geneva Accords and SEATO. Even before the decisive French defeat at Dienbienphu, a foreign ministers conference at Geneva sought to bring about a settlement of the war. Represented at the conference were the United States, Great Britain, the Soviet Union, France, and the People's Republic of China. In July an armistice was signed, under the terms of which France agreed to withdraw from Indochina, and Cambodia and Laos became independent states. Vietnam was divided at the 17th parallel, with the Communists under Ho Chi-Minh to control the north and a United States–supported government under Ngo Dinh Diem to rule the south. Included in the accords was a provision for free elections in 1956, to be supervised by an international control commission. According to the terms of this proposal, all the Vietnamese people were to have the right to choose unification either under Ho Chi-Minh or under Ngo Dinh Diem, but the elections were never held. With the support of Secretary Dulles, President Ngo refused to accept the plan, arguing that free elections would be impossible in Communist-controlled North Vietnam. Although the United States was represented at the Geneva Conference, Dulles refused to approve, or be bound by, its agreements.

While the Geneva discussions were in progress, Dulles moved to plug the hole in the dam of containment in Southeast Asia that had been created by the expulsion of the French. As a result of his efforts, eight nations formed the Southeast Asia Treaty Organization (SEATO) at Manila in September 1954. Members were the United States, Great Britain, France, Australia, New Zealand, Thailand, the Philippines, and Pakistan. Bangkok became the SEATO headquarters.

SEATO, however, bore only a remote resemblance to NATO: it lacked military forces and any clearly defined purpose. France was a reluctant participant, having already suffered defeat in that part of the world, and Pakistan had very little interest in Indochina. The organization was further weakened by the refusal of three important nations in Southeast Asia (India, Indonesia, and Burma) to become members. From its inception SEATO has thus been only a paper organization and of little value as a deterrent to Communism. The "burden" of protecting Southeast Asia—and the new states carved out of French Indochina—from Communism fell almost entirely on the United States.

Containment in the Middle East

The Middle East was already seething with political rivalries, unrest, and economic problems before it became still another front in the cold war. Since the creation of the new Jewish nation of Israel in 1948 tension had existed, and when, in the same year, the Arab countries attacked Israel, a bitter war ensued in which the greatly outnumbered Israelis were nevertheless able to prevail. The United Nations with difficulty managed to achieve a cease-fire agreement in 1949, but Arab-Israeli hostility continued to simmer, leading to occasional open conflicts in subsequent years.

During the Truman era the United States sought to avoid involvement in the complex politics of the Middle East. Although the United States had sponsored the creation of Israel, it also desired to maintain friendly relations with the unstable, oil-rich Arab states by giving them economic and military aid. There matters stood at the time when Eisenhower and Dulles assumed the leadership of American foreign policy.

The Baghdad Pact and Gamal Nasser. In 1955 Dulles added the last link in his chain around the Communist world by erecting a regional defense system in the "northern tier" of Mideastern nations. This new alliance was composed of Turkey, Great Britain, Iraq, Pakistan, and Iran. Much to the astonishment of the signatories of the pact at Baghdad, the United States refused to join the organization that it had sponsored.[7] The Baghdad Pact was the last of the defensive agreements created to contain Communism and the first to disintegrate. It is ironic that Dulles, who had denounced the policy of containment in 1952, had become its most assiduous practitioner.

In addition to being ineffective as a defense agreement the Baghdad Pact aroused the ire of Gamal Abdel Nasser, the new strong man of Egypt, who had seized power in 1954. He had announced that his goals were to (1) strengthen Egypt's economy; (2) unify the Arab nations under his leadership; (3) destroy Israel; and (4) eliminate the vestiges of British imperialism in the Middle East. The Egyptian dictator was clever, tough, and charming, and he was capable of rousing the masses to his support. Nasser considered the Baghdad Pact a personal affront and a resurgence of Western imperialism in the Middle East.

To placate the new Egyptian leader, the British and United States governments made tentative offers to assist him in building the proposed "high dam" at Aswan on the Nile River. But Nasser spurned the offer after accepting an agreement with the Communist bloc that called for the exchange of Czechoslovakian military equipment for Egyptian rice and cotton. Nasser also negotiated a series of alliances among the Arab nations to counter the Baghdad Pact. To embarrass the French, he sent military aid to Algerian rebels, and in 1956 the French and the British were both indignant when Nasser nationalized the Suez Canal Company, the majority of whose stockholders were British.

Dulles again proposed that the United States help build the Aswan dam, but, irked by Egypt's flirtation with the Communist nations, he then withdrew the offer, which offended the Egyptian leader. Later in the same year the Western world was shocked by the announcement that the Soviet government had underwritten the huge cost of building the dam and that Soviet technicians and equipment would be provided to do the job. As this very concrete dam rose from the ground, the paper dam of containment was coming apart in the Middle East.

---

[7]Secretary Dulles took the position that the United States should remain aloof from the alliance and thereby discourage accusations of American domination of the pact.

Frontier of hatred in the Middle East. Sunken ships in the Suez Canal after the second Arab-Israeli war, 1956.

The Suez War. Although Nasser had promised to preserve the Suez Canal as an international waterway open to all nations, he nevertheless barred Israeli shipping from it in addition to blockading Israel's only port on the Red Sea. Israel had previously been alarmed by Egypt's military buildup, and the British and French had become irate both over Nasser's refusal to compensate canal company stockholders and by his use of the canal as a pawn in international politics. More and more, in American as well as European eyes, Gamal Nasser appeared to be "the Hitler of the Nile."

On October 29, 1956 the Israeli forces launched a sudden and powerful offensive against Egypt. As Israeli armored units were overrunning the Sinai Peninsula, Great Britain and France launched air attacks on Egyptian bases along the Suez Canal and around Cairo on October 31. Within a few hours the Anglo-French bombardment had annihilated Nasser's air force, and within a few days British and French troops captured Port Said on the Mediterranean end of the Suez Canal.

Nasser retaliated by sinking ships in the canal, thus effectively blocking it; and pro-Nasser saboteurs in Syria destroyed British oil pipelines from Iraq to the Mediterranean. Although an American resolution in the Security Council to halt the war was blocked by British and French vetoes, the General Assembly, by an overwhelming majority, called for an immediate cease-fire and a return of Israeli troops to the 1949 armistice line. The Soviet Union trumpeted threats of intervention "to crush the aggressors," but President Eisenhower, who had already put American global forces on an alert, nevertheless firmly refused any support for the two Western powers or Israel. In the face of general world hostility, Great Britain and France halted their attack on Egypt, and the arrival of a United Nations Emergency Force composed of volunteer units from several nations enabled the invaders to withdraw without complete humiliation.

The war had lasted only eight days, but the repercussions and losses from the brief conflict were widespread. Nasser lost most of his new military equipment provided by the Communist bloc. The prestige of France and Great Britain was badly damaged by their ill-timed, inept, and dilatory intervention. The United

States lost prestige through its sporadic handling of negotiations with the infuriated Egyptian government; and Great Britain and France were angered by the refusal of their great ally to back them. The Israelis were hurt by being forced to abdicate their conquest of Sinai without achieving any permanent settlement of their differences with the Arab states.

Despite Egypt's material defeat, Nasser emerged from the affair with enhanced prestige in the Arab world, bitter toward the United States, and as determined as ever to destroy Israel. For the Soviet Union the Suez affair was a victory: through its friendly association with Nasser's Egypt it now had a foothold in the Arab world beyond the containment line. The Middle East was to continue to be a trouble spot and a source of worry to the United States.

The Lebanese-Iraq Crisis. Anticipating further trouble in the Middle East, Congress declared in March 1957 that the stability of that area was vital to the national interest and so granted President Eisenhower the authority "to use armed forces to assist any such nation or group of nations requesting assistance against armed aggression from any country controlled by international Communism." Technically the resolution was meaningless, since the President already had such powers. In addition, it did not define the term "Middle East" or indicate clearly whether Nasser was covered by the phrase "any country controlled by international Communism." The so-called "Eisenhower Doctrine" accomplished two purposes, however. Friendly Mideastern nations living under the shadow of Nasser and Soviet power were strengthened and encouraged to maintain their independence. In addition, Eisenhower believed that the pronouncement strengthened his hand and would avoid the criticism that had been leveled at President Truman for not consulting Congress before acting in the Korean crisis. The Eisenhower Doctrine was denounced by Nasser and Khrushchev as part of an imperialist conspiracy.

Throughout 1957 the political atmosphere of the Middle East was poisoned by intrigues, vitriolic threats, and minor crises. On February 1, 1958 Egypt and Syria formed the United Arab Republic. From the southern tip of the Arabian Peninsula to the Caucasus Mountains, Nasserite subversive groups intensified their activites to overthrow pro-Western Arab governments. By the spring of 1958, Lebanon was torn with internal dissension and harassed from without by border clashes. Pro-Nasser elements also were threatening to topple King Hussein of Jordan from his throne. Finally, on July 14 the king of Iraq was assassinated, his naked body tied to the back bumper of a station wagon and dragged through the streets of Baghdad. General Abdul Kassim al-Kassem then seized control of the Iraqi government. On July 19 the new ruler withdrew his nation from the Baghdad Pact and signed a mutual defense agreement with Nasser.

In the meantime the despairing Lebanese and Jordan governments appealed to the West for help. On July 15 American troops landed at Beirut to bolster the tottering Lebanese government, and British paratroopers poured into Jordan. The world teetered once again on the edge of global conflict as Nasser appealed to Moscow. Faced again by an American show of strength, the Soviet government backed away. It restrained Nasser, and the situation was temporarily cooled. Serious bloodshed was avoided in Lebanon, and King Hussein of Jordan was able to remain on his uneasy throne, but the United States lost further ground in the Middle East: the Baghdad defensive pact was largely undone by the withdrawal of Iraq. Meanwhile Nasser remained quiescent but ready for future adventures in the curiously ambivalent role of Arab firebrand and behind-the-scenes conciliator that ended only with his sudden death in 1970.

Shifts in Soviet–United States Relations

During the Eisenhower years cold war tensions occasionally eased. There were moments of

Russian tanks destroyed during 1956 Budapest insurrection. WIDE WORLD PHOTOS

hope that the Soviet Union and the United States might achieve a condition of mutual accommodation or even friendship. Although the two superpowers continued to remain generally antagonistic, Khrushchev abandoned the Stalinist policy of relentless hostility. The United States under Eisenhower suffered disturbing setbacks in the cold war, but so did the Soviet Union. It was these defeats that partly caused Soviet policy to be sometimes less hostile.

Soviet Problems. After the death of Stalin a series of spasmodic uprisings against Soviet control occurred in the Iron Curtain countries of eastern Europe. In June 1953 a peaceful, unorganized, and spontaneous strike spread among construction workers in East Berlin; however, it soon reached the proportions of a huge riot and spread to other sections of East Germany and to Czechoslovakia, and eventually Russian troops and tanks were used to restore order. This blow to Soviet prestige and the myth of Communist solidarity was enormous, but even worse events were in store.

In October 1956 there were armed insurrections in Poland and Hungary. The result in Poland was new, independent Communist leadership under Premier Wladyslaw Gomulka; but the Hungarians carried their revolt too far.

A provisional government sought to break all ties with the Soviet Union. Thus at the same time that the guns were roaring along the Suez Canal in the Middle East, Soviet troops poured into Hungary. By November 4 Soviet military forces had crushed the uprising after bitter street fighting in Budapest. The Soviet Union promptly installed a new puppet government with János Kádár as premier.

Geneva 1955 and After. Although the Soviet Union lost additional prestige by its action, the reputations of the United States and the United Nations were also damaged in the Hungarian affair. Many people felt that Eisenhower, by failing to aid the Hungarian "freedom fighters," had broken his 1952 campaign promise to liberate the enslaved nations of eastern Europe. But Eisenhower was distracted by his campaign for reelection and by the second Arab-Israeli war. Even if Eisenhower's hands had been free, it is doubtful whether he would have risked military action in Hungary and the certainty of war with the Soviet Union. And many Americans were forced to conclude that their own nation could not expect to be the only one with a "Monroe Doctrine."

The simultaneous Hungarian and Suez crises dissipated what little remained of "the spirit

Time of Trial, Time of Hope

of Geneva," where the leaders of Great Britain, France, and the United States had met with Bulganin and Khrushchev in July 1955 in what was described as "a summit conference." The conversations were conciliatory, but little was accomplished in lessening cold war tensions. Khrushchev, who dominated the Soviet delegation, declared bluntly that the Soviet Union would abandon its Marxist-Leninist goals only "when shrimps learn to whistle."

Camp David and the U-2 Incident. In 1958 the Lebanese crisis and new tension in Berlin soured Sovet-American relations once more. Yet in 1959 the skies again began to clear. President Eisenhower invited Premier Khrushchev to tour the United States and meet with him at Washington, D.C., for another summit conference. For the American people it was an opportunity to look at the rambunctious Soviet leader at close hand and under less formal conditions. Khrushchev lived up to his advance billing. He was alternately prim, caustic, and effusive.

The most bizarre part of Khrushchev's tour was his visit to Los Angeles, where he was denounced to his face by the mayor, whom he in turn characterized as an ignoramus, and with heavy-handed humor he criticized the United States Secret Service for refusing to allow him to visit Disneyland. During a trip to a Hollywood movie set, Khrushchev professed to be shocked by the scanty garments worn by rehearsing can-can dancers. But the smiling and motherly Madam Khrushchev won the hearts of Americans wherever she went. In her personality and simple, peasantlike appearance she seemed the embodiment of the friendly Soviet people.

But Khrushchev's conferences with Eisenhower at Camp David (a presidential retreat near Washington) achieved little more than agreement on cultural exchanges between the Soviet Union and the United States. Nevertheless, there was again an atmosphere of cordiality, and newspaper writers referred to the warm "spirit of Camp David." Eisenhower and Khrushchev agreed to meet again in Paris, and Eisenhower accepted an invitation to visit the Soviet Union. The Paris meeting, which was held in May 1960, was a disaster: a few days before it convened a U-2 reconnaissance plane was brought down over Soviet territory, and the American pilot, Francis Gary Powers, was captured. Caught by surprise, the United States government issued a number of contradictory statements—the plane was off course; it was only a "weather plane" checking atmospheric concitions; and, finally, the truth: the U-2 was in fact a spy plane.

This "act of aggression" was denounced by the angry Khrushchev, who demanded that Eisenhower apologize. When the President refused, Khrushchev canceled Eisenhower's scheduled visit to the Soviet Union in June, and the Paris summit conference broke down.

The Soviet government exploited this episode for its propaganda value. Powers was put on public trial, where he acknowledged his "guilt." After being sentenced to hard labor, Powers was exchanged for a Soviet agent who had been captured in New York by the FBI.

Balance Sheet

Despite the many crises in the continuing cold war, the sharp lines of rivalry between the Soviet Union and the United States began to soften during the Eisenhower years. For one thing, both powers found their leadership challenged within their own spheres.

Although it was not immediately evident, Charles de Gaulle, President of France as of 1958, was preparing to dispute United States leadership in the non-Communist world. During the late 1950's France experienced remarkable economic growth and was aided by the establishment of the Common Market (European Economic Community, or EEC) in 1958. The principal objective of the market, which included France, Italy, West Germany, and the Benelux countries, was the gradual abolition of tariffs between the member nations.

Under De Gaulle, France, which was never an enthusiastic member of NATO, began a policy of deliberately undermining that organization. And through financial aid programs to emergent nations of Africa and Asia, as well as to underdeveloped Latin-American states, France began to compete with United States leadership in those areas.

The Soviet Union also found itself challenged in the Communist world by the People's Republic of China. By 1959 a gap between Khrushchev's inconsistent, improvised policies and the hard Stalinist line of China's Mao Tse-tung was evident. And in Europe tiny Albania broke with the Soviet Union and aligned itself with China.

Although the policy of containment was weakening, Khrushchev's clumsy attempts to meddle in the confused politics of the new African countries far beyond the line of containment were unsuccessful. He also tried to woo the West African states of Ghana and Guinea into Moscow's orbit; but in 1966 the pro-Soviet dictator of Ghana, Kwame Nkrumah, was overthrown. The Marxist leader of Guinea, Sekou Touré, meanwhile steered a neutral course, at the same time accepting Soviet aid. In 1963 this former French colony began to drift into the French orbit after signing an agreement to accept French aid and commercial ties. Following Belgium's withdrawal from the Congo in 1960, Khrushchev attempted to take advantage of the civil war, but bad luck and ineptitude resulted in the defeat of the Soviet-supported leaders. Although the Congo is not pro-Western, it is less likely at the present time to be a potential base for Soviet machinations in Africa. Soviet and Czech arms, along with Egyptian volunteers, meanwhile aided Algeria in becoming independent in 1962; yet the Algerian government has rejected domination by either Moscow or the United Arab Republic, partly because of generous economic aid from France, Algeria's former enemy.

Still, the revelations of the Soviet Union's scientific achievements during the 1950's enormously enhanced its prestige and power, whereas belief in the technological superiority of the United States and the free enterprise system as opposed to the "collectivist" system was thoroughly shaken. In addition, rapid advances of the Soviet Union's military technology alarmed Western observers: although the Soviet Union had not tested an atomic bomb until 1949—four years after the United States had first done so—the Russians nevertheless developed the hydrogen bomb only a few months behind the schedule of the United States.

Although America maintained a considerable lead in number and quality of sophisticated armaments, by 1958 the Soviet Union had acquired long-range bombers and intercontinental ballistics missiles sufficient to devastate American cities in time of war. Thus the atomic bombs and strategic bombers of the United States were regarded as less effective deterrents to possible Soviet aggression. Foreign policy experts and pundits began to talk about the "balance of terror" rather than the "balance of power," and by the end of the 1950's Dulles's theory of the threat of massive retaliation as a restraint on Soviet leaders was totally meaningless. Equally disturbing to Washington was the expansion of the Soviet navy after the Suez crisis: by 1960 it had replaced that of Great Britain as the second most powerful in the world.

During the middle of the 1950's the Soviets also achieved impressive results in such varied fields as oceanography and medical technology. The most exciting and, for some, disturbing news of the decade was the launching of Soviet space vehicles ("Sputniks") in the fall of 1957. The Soviet Union was far ahead of the United States in the space race and was to maintain this lead for many years to come.

In the wake of the Soviet achievements, the weakening of the containment policy, and the failure of Dulles's policies of liberation and massive retaliation, the foreign policies of the

Eisenhower administration dragged on wearily until their end in 1961.[8] Dulles's programs had all too often been idealistic and rigid, and his tendency to treat all nations and statesmen who were neutralist, or who disagreed with him, as members of a hostile camp chilled relations between the United States and the rest of the world. Moreover, his conduct of foreign policy was further weakened by his willingness to accede to the Communist-baiting antics of Senator Joseph McCarthy of Wisconsin in the early 1950's.

But the mistakes of the United States did not always result in gains for the Soviet Union during the years between 1946 and 1961. The implacable hostility and overt ruthlessness of the Soviet government under Stalin's leadership generated counterhostility and fear leading to containment and gains for the United States. The blundering, dilatory adventurism of Khrushchev generally kept the Soviet Union from deriving significant advantage from the mistakes of the Eisenhower administration. To be sure, the cold war would continue in the 1960's—but its character would be altered. In addition, still other regions of the world would become arenas of this struggle.

[8] Dulles died in 1959, and Christian A. Herter, a former Governor of Massachusetts and an experienced foreign service officer, became Secretary of State. In his last two years in office, Eisenhower assumed more direct control of foreign affairs and followed policies less harsh and unyielding than those of Dulles.

SUGGESTED READINGS

*Agar, H., *The Price of Power, America since 1945* (1957).
Brooks, J., *The Great Leap, the Past Twenty-Five Years in America* (1960).
Brown, S. G., *Conscience in Politics: Adlai E. Stevenson in the 1950s* (1961).
Campbell, J. C., *Defense of the Middle East* (1957).
*Carleton, W. G., *The Revolution in American Foreign Policy* (1964).
Clay, L. D., *Decision in Germany* (1950).
Cohen, J. B., *Japan's Economy in War and Reconstruction* (1949).
Crabb, C. V., Jr., *American Foreign Policy in the Nuclear Age* (1965).
Davison, W. P., *The Berlin Blockade, A Study in Post-War Politics* (1956).
DeConde, A., ed., *Isolation and Security* (1957).
Douglas, P. H., *Ethics in Government* (1952).
Dulles, J. F., *War or Peace* (1950).
*Eisenhower, D. D., *The White House Years, Mandate for Change, 1953–1956* (1963).
Eisenhower, M. S., *The Wine is Bitter: The United States and Latin America* (1963).
Fehrenbach, T. R., *This Kind of Peace* (1966).
*Feis, H., *The China Tangle* (1963).
Feis, H., *Foreign Aid and Foreign Policy* (1964).
Fifield, R. H., *The Diplomacy of Southeast Asia, 1945–1958* (1960).
Finer, H., *Dulles over Suez* (1964).
Gerson, L. L., *The Hyphenate in Recent American Politics and Diplomacy* (1964).

*Goldman, E. F., *The Crucial Decade and After, America 1945–1960* (1960).
*Graebner, N. A., *Cold War Diplomacy, 1945–1960* (1962).
Graebner, N. A., *The New Isolationism* (1956).
Gunther, J., *Eisenhower, the Man and the Symbol* (1957).
Hertz, M. F., *Beginnings of the Cold War* (1966).
*Hofstadter, R., *The Paranoid Style in American Politics and Other Essays* (1965).
*Hughes, E. J., *The Ordeal of Power, a Political Memoir of the Eisenhower Years* (1963).
Jackson, R. H., *The Case Against Nazi War Criminals* (1946).
Kennan, G., *Realities of Foreign Policy* (1954).
*Kennan, G., *Russia and the West under Lenin and Stalin* (1961).
*Latham, E., *The Communist Controversy in Washington* (1966).
Latourette, K. S., *The American Record in the Far East* (1952).
Mills, C. W., *The Causes of World War Three* (1958).
Mitchell, J. C., *Second Failure in Asia* (1951).
Moore, B. T., *NATO and the Future of Europe* (1958).
*Nicholas, H. G., *The United Nations as a Political Institution* (2nd ed., 1963).
O'Brian, J. L., *National Security and Individual Freedom* (1955).
Phillips, C., *The Truman Presidency* (1966).
Price, H. B., *The Marshall Plan and Its Meaning* (1955).
Rees, D., *Korea, the Limited War* (1964).
Reischauer, E. O., *Wanted: An Asian Policy* (1955).
Roberts, H. L., *Russia and America, Dangers and Prospects* (1956).
Safran, N., *The United States and Israel* (1963).
Schmidt, K. M., *Henry Wallace: Quixotic Crusader* (1960).
Shannon, D. A., *The Decline of American Communism* (1959).
*Spanier, J. W., *American Foreign Policy since World War II* (1962).
*Spanier, J. W., *The Truman-MacArthur Controversy and the Korean War* (1959).
*Truman, H. S., *Memoirs* (2 vols., 1955).
Vandenberg, A. H., Jr., *The Private Papers of Senator Vandenbert* (1952).
Wedemeyer, A., *Wedemeyer Reports* (1958).
Wise, D. and T. Ross, *The U-2 Affair* (1962).

CHAPTER 31

The Truman and Eisenhower Years, 1945–1961

Whatever America hopes to bring to pass in the world must first come to pass in the heart of America.
DWIGHT D. EISENHOWER, 1953

WIDE WORLD PHOTOS

WHEN THE SECOND WORLD WAR ENDED, television was still regarded as a thing of the future; frozen foods and shopping centers were novelties; the "new look" of long skirts was soon to be the fashion, while the two-piece bathing suit was still considered daring. Detergents, DDT, and the automatic dishwasher had not yet deluged the market, or produced a problem of pollution; "smog" was a rarely used term applied mainly to Los Angeles. Automobiles were scarce, and for some years demand exceeded Detroit's ability to supply. With the jet engine in its infancy and the sonic boom unheard of, bus and train were the means for long-distance travel. What would result from war-spawned technology was unclear, but people marveled at the wonders of penicillin and sulfa drugs, which had gained wide use on the battlefield.

In 1946 Notre Dame resumed its winning ways in football and by 1947 the Yankees had reestablished themselves as lords of baseball. Clark Gable was still king of Hollywood (though Van Johnson had become the heartthrob of the younger set), and the drive-in theater gained popularity with families and young lovers. Benny Goodman was the "king of swing" and Frank Sinatra was tops with the bobby-soxers.

Equal rights for Negroes (it would be more than two decades before the term "black" came into currency) were considered idealistic, unworkable, impossible, or unlikely, and Jim Crow laws and school segregation were enforced in the South and practiced extensively in other states. Mexican-Americans in the Southwest suffered from severe social discrimination, while Japanese-Americans were still reeling from the effects of wartime persecution.

The end of the war brought fears of depression, labor strife, Communism, and the atom bomb. As the hordes of servicemen returned to civilian life, severe social problems and dislocations were anticipated.

By 1961 the television set had joined the refrigerator and the living room sofa as a fixture in the home and had begun to replace the popular magazines — *Collier's* was gone and the *Saturday Evening Post* was dying. The movie industry too had suffered fearful setbacks with the growth of television. In fashion, the bikini

The Truman and Eisenhower Years, 1945–1961   377

had arrived and skirts were still below the knee, but not by much.

Trailers and campers were beginning to clutter highways and jam resort areas. The jet airliner was starting to dominate commercial travel, while the Pullman was becoming a relic of the past. Smog and other pollutants were becoming major sources of anxiety. The word "gap" expressed a multitude of concerns—there were missile gaps, culture gaps, generation gaps, and education gaps. In 1961 the space race with Russia was on. The United States, striving to overcome the early Soviet lead, was hurling quantities of celestial hardware into the void. The American people, however, found grounds for satisfaction in medical technology: the Salk vaccine virtually eliminated poliomyelitis as a disease, and a new crop of miracle drugs such as aureomycin flourished.

People continued to worry about Communism but with less intensity, and China had replaced Russia as the principal external Red menace. The standard of living rose significantly, but so did the divorce rate, the incidence of mental illness, and the amount of juvenile delinquency. Yet even while the population zoomed upward (from 142,000,000 in 1946 to nearly 184,000,000 in 1961), as President Kennedy was to point out, one-fifth of the people were still ill housed, ill clad, and ill fed, deprived of educational opportunities and essential medical care. As always the burden of poverty fell most heavily on ethnic minorities—Indians, Mexican-Americans, Puerto Ricans, and Negroes. But legal segregation was gone in states outside the South, while freedom riders, "sit-inners," and Martin Luther King were challenging the bastions of white supremacy in Alabama and Mississippi. In the fifteen-year period after World War II, America had undergone many changes. A good number of them were merely matters of fashion and technology, but as old social and political problems were dwindling in significance, new problems appeared in their place. Even so, the changes in American society had been relatively mild.

Despite occasional tremors in the form of recessions, there had been no economic earthquake comparable to the Great Depression of the 1930's. And in spite of the great cost in American lives and materials, the Korean War had not produced significant social strains.

PRELUDE—THE TRANSITION FROM WAR TO PEACE

The American people were involved in the Second World War for three years and ten months, the longest and most costly armed conflict since the Civil War. Such a prolonged struggle inevitably brought about domestic social change, and the transition to peace resulted in further tensions. The war and the period of postwar adjustment, however, produced much less social shock than the two previous major conflicts, the Civil War and the First World War.

Social and Economic Change during the War

Within a few months following the attack on Pearl Harbor, the nation converted rapidly to a wartime economy. Price and rent controls were established to halt inflationary pressures created by shortages of consumer goods and housing. Rationing was instituted for goods in short supply (because of the diversion of raw materials to war production) such as rubber tires, automobiles, gasoline, sugar, shoes, and coffee. Although these restrictions were accepted good naturedly, black markets, inevitable features of wartime controls, sprang into existence.

Since the armed forces drained the existing industrial manpower reservoir of some 16,000,000 persons, the labor force had to be supplemented from other, previously untapped sources. One source was rural Negroes, especially from the South, who were attracted to high-paying jobs in industrial cities of the North and Far West. On the eve of World War II, the black population in Northern cities was 2,800,000 but by 1945 it had increased to

4,300,000. Another source was women, who took jobs in industry, accepting even heavy labor tasks. Rosie the riveter, the woman in coveralls on the assembly line, became a symbol of the American female contributing to the war effort. Women also donned police uniforms, delivered the mail, punched train tickets, and drove the city buses. Large numbers of Mexicans who worked in the agricultural enterprises in the Southwest further supplemented the still-depleted labor force.

Because of the voracious demand for war materials, factories in the older industrial cities expanded or multiplied. Areas and cities where industry had formerly been insignificant or nonexistent became major production centers. Cities on the West coast especially boomed, as aircraft production gravitated to San Diego, Los Angeles, and Seattle, and shipyards proliferated in the San Francisco Bay area. The first steel mill west of the Mississippi was erected by the Kaiser Company in Fontana, California, and a large steel fabricating plant was built by United States Steel Corporation near Ogden, Utah.

In the increasingly overcrowded cities, racial tensions between the newly arrived black ghetto dwellers and the whites reached the flash point. In Detroit thirty-three people were killed in riots between blacks and whites. Race hatred also led to unrest in Chicago and Harlem. Clashes between Mexican-Americans and servicemen resulted in riots in Los Angeles. The most serious racial discrimination, however, was leveled at the Japanese-Americans on the West coast. In early 1942, 117,000 of these people were herded into concentration camps located in desolate regions on California, Arizona, and Utah. In the process, they lost most of their property. The ostensible motive for this action was security, yet there was no proven case of espionage or sabotage by a Japanese-American and despite the harsh treatment, thousands of Nisei (American-born Japanese) served with the armed forces in Europe with distinction. Indeed, the Nisei 442nd Regimental Combat Team became the most decorated unit in the United States army in Europe during the war.

With the significant exception just mentioned, there was little of the hysterical hatred that had been directed in World War I against enemy aliens or people of German or Italian descent. And in contrast to 1917–1918, there was only limited censorship and government propaganda for the war was low-keyed.

Problems of Conversion to Peace

As the war ended, a serious problem was the demobilization of some twelve million men and women in the armed forces. Heavy pressure was exerted on the President and Congress —"I-want-my-daddy-to-come-home" letters soon formed a considerable bulk of a congressman's daily mail—to discharge servicemen as rapidly as possible. The government responded by making a prodigious effort "to bring the boys home." President Truman declared that his aim was to muster our servicemen at the rate of 25,000 a day throughout 1946. Truman made this pledge despite warnings from his advisers that such rapid demobilization might threaten the national security. But by August 1946 the army was down to 1,500,000, and the navy to 700,000.

In order to ease the return to civilian life, Congress in 1944 had foresightedly passed the Servicemen's Readjustment Act, one of the most significant pieces of social legislation ever enacted. Known as the "G.I. Bill of Rights" this act provided aid for veterans' hospitals, low-cost life insurance, vocational rehabilitation, low-interest loans for purchases of homes and businesses, and four years of college education (including payment for tuition, books, and living expenses). In addition, the G.I. Bill allowed for a year of unemployment compensation at the rate of twenty dollars a week. Hundreds of thousands of veterans took advantage of this opportunity and joined the "52-20" club. Even greater numbers elected to attend college and obtain an education that before the war they could not have afforded. As a result, the Quonset hut and the converted gymnasium stuffed with army bunks became common features on college campuses trying to accomodate the great influx of ex-G.I.'s.

One area in which readjustment was less easy was marriage. Some 90,000 soldiers and sailors had married or were engaged to foreign girls primarily from Germany, Japan, and France. A majority of the marriages ended in divorce. Men in uniform at bases within the United States had also been inclined during the war to contract "quickie" marriages with local girls. As a consequence, the marriage rate zoomed upward and the average age at which American males married dropped sharply from twenty-five to twenty-one. When the men returned home, inevitably there was a baby boom. The divorce rate, however, rose even more rapidly than the birthrate.

The reconversion of the economy to peace was unexpectedly smooth even though the government canceled some thirty-five billion dollars' worth of war contracts. By November 1945 ninety-three per cent of the plants formerly involved in the manufacture of war materials had converted to the production of peacetime and consumer goods. The transition sometimes involved considerable losses, however. For example, in 1946 the Grumman Aircraft Corporation, which had grown to giant size during the war, was obliged to turn to the less lucrative manufacture of aluminum canoes and kitchen hardware. Yet the unemployment problem was generally minimal, partly because of the G.I. Bill of Rights.

The smoothness of reconversion was darkened somewhat by bitter tensions over the continuation of wartime price and rent controls and especially by postwar inflation. The terrific inflationary pressure was intensified by swollen savings accumulated during the war when there was little to buy. The desire for radios and cars gave rise to black markets, "tie-in" sales, and queues. When a store was rumored to have nylon stockings or men's shirts in stock, a line of people reaching around a city block would quickly form.

Another shadow on the period was sporadic labor unrest from November 1945 to the end of 1946. Strikes, often of long duration, occurred in key industries, particularly in autos, steel, and coal. The especially bitter coal strike ended only after a federal judge fined the United Mine Workers $3,500,000 and threatened the union chief, John L. Lewis, with imprisonment. And a railroad strike was halted when President Truman seized the railroads and operated them with army personnel. During 1946 a total of 4,500,000 workers were out on strike at one time or another.

Yet despite the turmoil in industry, inflation, and rancor over prices and rents, the conversion to peace was accomplished with far less dissension than in previous wars. The numerous strikes of 1946, for example, were far less destructive of life and property than the strikes after the First World War. Nevertheless, problems developing out of wartime social and economic change were to generate future tensions.

THE TRUMAN YEARS

In the spring of 1944, a major topic of conversation between President Franklin Roosevelt and Democratic leaders was the question of who should be the party nominee for Vice President. Roosevelt had already decided to run for an unprecedented fourth term. Although it seemed likely that he would win, the Democratic party leadership did not want to take any chances. Henry A. Wallace, the current Vice President, was considered a liability. Notorious for his obstreperousness, his forays into mystical cults, and his espousal of left-wing causes, he had alienated the party regulars. When Roosevelt proposed to substitute James F. Byrnes of South Carolina, a former Supreme Court Justice and an able wartime administrator, labor leaders and Northern political bosses opposed the notion. They considered the segregationist Southerner with a poor labor record to be a significant vote loser. But Harry S. Truman, a relatively unknown senator from Missouri, proved to be generally acceptable. Although not a Southerner, he was from a border state with some sympathy for Southern causes; he was noted for his loyalty to the Democratic party; and his liberal voting record would help the Democratic cause in the big cities, with organized labor, and among the Negroes. Truman had gained favorable national attention by his effective chairmanship of a Senate committee investigating frauds and inefficiencies in the wartime defense program.

Both during the campaign and afterward — FDR's victory over Thomas E. Dewey of New York was decisive, although his popular vote was somewhat less than in previous elections — Roosevelt took little notice of Truman, regarding him with genial contempt. As Vice President, Truman was rarely invited to participate in top-level wartime conferences on strategy or politics. The Missourian, however, modestly accepted his obscure role with apparent good humor. The obscurity was of short duration for, worn out by his exertions and responsibilities, especially after the Yalta meeting with Churchill and Stalin, Franklin Roosevelt died of a massive cerebral hemorrhage on April 12, 1945. He had served less than three months of his fourth term.

As President, Harry Truman, the man from the small city of Independence, Missouri, was called upon to assume immense responsibilities for which he was poorly prepared. He had to follow in the giant footsteps of a man already considered one of the greatest presidents in history. Truman was fully aware of his own shortcomings, his unprepossessing personality, his flat Missouri twang, and his lack of knowledge and executive experience. Nevertheless, he assumed his difficult role with commendable determination and confidence. In his new position he was obliged to make crucial decisions despite the lack of time to study the problems and the failure of high officials to acquaint him earlier with the necessary facts. Not the least of these was the decision to use the atom bomb on Japan.

But the new President learned quickly. He participated in the important Potsdam conference in July 1945, earning the respect of both Stalin and Churchill for his efficient conduct at the council tables. With the end of the war, Truman guided the nation through the painful readjustment to peace. He recognized his difficult situation, vividly aware of the failures of two earlier postwar presidents, Andrew Johnson and Warren G. Harding. Nevertheless, Truman was determined to lead the nation, and his self-confidence, humor, and common sense never deserted him in times of great trial.

The Fair Deal, First Phase

As President Turman saw it, his job was to continue and consolidate the social programs launched by the New Deal and halted by the war. In September 1945, only a few days after the Japanese surrender ceremonies in Tokyo Bay, the President outlined for Congress a far-reaching twenty-one point domestic program. (Truman's policies became known later as the "Fair Deal," a name evoking the memory and spirit of Roosevelt's New Deal of the 1930's, from his use of the phrase in his State of the Union message in 1949.) In his 1945 speech to Congress, President Truman declared that it was the responsibility of the federal government to provide full employment for everyone willing and able to work. He requested that the Fair Employment Practices Commission (FEPC), established during the war to prevent job discrimination by race, be continued on a permanent basis. He further called for expansion of social security, an increase in the minimum wage, enactment of public housing and slum clearance programs, additional protection of

"The buck stops here." WIDE WORLD PHOTOS

natural resources, and extension of existing public works programs. In subsequent months and into 1946, the President continued to bombard Congress with requests for social legislation—federal aid to education, nationally sponsored medical care and health insurance programs, development of the St. Lawrence Seaway project, and expansion of the national atomic energy program.

Truman's ambitious proposals were received with lukewarm enthusiasm by cautious congressmen. Nineteen forty-six was an election year; moreover, the storm of public protest over prolonged strikes made them reluctant to pass legislation that would favor organized labor. Southerners were hostile to the civil rights aspects of the President's programs. As in other postwar eras, there was a tendency to look for conservative solutions and a desire to "return to normalcy." As a result of that trend and the new President's lack of vigorous leadership, only his least controversial schemes were put into law.

Republican Revival—1946

In November 1946 voters trooped to the polls in impressive numbers to register through the ballot their feelings on the state of the nation and particularly Harry S. Truman, even though this was not a presidential election year. When the election was over, the Republicans had won control of Congress for the first time in sixteen years.

During the campaign Republicans skillfully exploited the frustrations of the people with the provocative slogan, "Had enough?" Discontent was fueled by rampant inflation, strikes, and an uncertain foreign policy. Bitter quarrels between Truman and his Cabinet officials added to the discomfiture of the Democrats. Harold L. Ickes, the crusty Secretary of the Interi-

382 *Time of Trial, Time of Hope*

or, had resigned after an angry exchange with the President over conservation. Henry A. Wallace, Secretary of Commerce, was forced to resign after crossing swords with Truman over foreign policy.[1] His tendency to "cronyism" —especially the appointment of an old poker-playing, bourbon-drinking friend, Harry Vaughan, as presidential military adviser with the rank of brigadier general—produced an outburst of criticism. Truman's "gift for the gaffe" made him the butt of innumerable jokes (perhaps his most notorious remark was his offer to poke a certain music critic in the nose for daring to criticize his daughter Margaret's singing). After the election Truman's stock had sunk so low that a Democratic senator even proposed that the President resign, having obviously and completely lost the support of the people.

Harry Truman was undismayed by the election and his poor showing in the public opinion polls. He even seemed to gain confidence in this period of adversity. With the new Republican-controlled Congress, the President continued to press for enactment of his proposals for social legislation. In addition, he called for revision of the income tax to ease the burden on the poor and recommended amendments to immigration statutes to lessen restrictions on persons entering the United States from southern and eastern Europe.

Congress, with Senator Robert A. Taft of Ohio firmly in command, moved to frustrate Truman's schemes and to implement its own "Old Guard" policies. Most of the President's proposals were either pigeonholed by congressional committees or tossed into the wastebasket. Tough old John Taber of New York, chairman of the powerful House Appropriations Committee, bellowed that he would "cut expenditures to the bone" and apply the "meat-axe to government frills."

During 1947 and the early months of 1948, Congress did enact tax revisions, but it substantially reduced taxes on *large*, not small, incomes, cut government aid to the farmers, and slashed appropriations for conservation and public power projects. The principal handiwork of the conservative Eightieth Congress was the passage of the Taft-Hartley Labor-Management Relations Act in 1947, a most controversial piece of legislation. In the view of its opponents, this law was designed to penalize organized labor which the Eightieth Congress considered its enemy, but the Republicans were convinced that the public mood called for curbs on the unions.

Under the Taft-Hartley Act a number of standard labor practices were prohibited such as the "closed shop," "secondary boycott," "jurisdictional strike," "featherbedding," "checkoff." In addition, union leaders were required to file affidavits that they were not Communists. Furthermore, a union could be prohibited from calling a strike until it had waited for at least sixty days (called "the cooling-off period") after declaring its intent to do so. These and other provisions of the Taft-Hartley Act were denounced by labor as discriminatory. The more extravagant critics declared it a "slave labor law."

President Truman stingingly vetoed the measure along with sixty-one other bills of the Eightieth Congress; however, most of his vetoes were overridden by the necessary two-thirds majority. In the case of the Taft-Hartley Bill, the House overrode the President's veto 331 to 83 and the Senate by the vote of 68 to 25.

Despite the conservative temper of Congress, Truman was mildly successful in obtaining passage of some of his measures. A diluted public housing bill was enacted, with the unexpected support of Senator Taft, providing government credit for veterans to purchase homes and for low-cost cooperative housing projects. In 1947 Congress approved the National Secu-

---

[1] Wallace had been given the post in the Commerce Department by FDR in 1945 as a consolation prize after yielding the vice presidency.

rity Act, which overhauled the defense structure. This law created the post of Secretary of Defense, an officer with cabinet rank to coordinate the three branches of the armed forces. This act also created new bodies such as the Central Intelligence Agency and the National Security Council. The President's recommendations for reorganization of the executive branch were accepted by Congress. Passage of this act was facilitated because the chairman of the commission that prepared the proposals was former President Hoover, whose reputation with Republicans and Congress remained high despite the many years he had been out of office.

Congress also cooperated, sometimes grudgingly, with President Truman on foreign policy. It advanced the necessary sums for military aid to Greece and Turkey under the Truman Doctrine. It also underwrote the gigantic outlays called for in the Marshall Plan for the economic reconstruction of western Europe. In matters of foreign policy, President Truman was fortunate in having the staunch support of Senator Arthur H. Vandenberg of Michigan, whose prestige in Congress was only slightly less than that of Taft.

Truman's hopes for civil rights laws were, however, completely dashed by Congress. He had been galvanized to action following a report on the deplorable condition of civil rights, especially for Negroes, prepared by a special commission in 1947, headed by Charles E. Wilson of the General Electric Corporation. Despite the glaring inequities in civil rights dispassionately presented by the commission, Congress ignored the report and the President's recommendations.

Nevertheless, a significant breakthrough in equality came about in the sports world in 1947. Organized sports, except for boxing, had traditionally excluded blacks unless they participated in all-Negro organizations. One of the first Negroes to achieve fame outside of boxing was track star Jesse Owens, who became a gold medal winner at the Berlin Olympics in 1936. Signs of coming change began to appear in the early 1940's as Negroes were introduced to the lineups of college football teams. Elsewhere, however, the doors of organized sports remained closed until Branch Rickey, the astute general manager of the Brooklyn Dodgers, signed Jackie Robinson to play second base. Rickey was subjected to bitter recrimination, and it was wildly predicted that Robinson's presence in various cities would lead to race riots and boycotts. Much to everyone's surprise, the first Negro in major league baseball produced no disaster or disorder. The quick acceptance of Robinson led other major league teams to begin tapping the large reservoir of black talent, and by 1949 the race barrier was gone in baseball and was crumbling in other major spectator sports, notably football and basketball. But the walls did not come down in other areas of American life so easily. The 1950's were to see the beginning of a long and bitter struggle by black citizens for full citizenship.

The Incredible Upset of 1948

As the summer of 1948 approached, Harry S. Truman appeared to be floundering in a morass of political discontent and public rejection. A cross-country tour by the President during the spring was labeled a disaster. Bad planning of speaking engagements and Truman's own errors fortified the impression. His offhand remark in Spokane, Washington, that he "liked old Joe Stalin" brought a storm of criticism. His earthy prose was seized upon by editorial writers as evidence of his crassness and poor taste. A news photo of the President speaking to a mere 1,000 supporters in the cavernous Ak-Sar-Ben auditorium in Omaha, with a seating capacity of 12,000, underscored Truman's unpopularity. He seemed to have split his party as well. As early as 1947, the militant Henry A. Wallace had broken with the Democrats openly, taking out of the party with him assorted leftists and liberals who were disenchanted by

Truman's domestic failures and dismayed by his hard-line policies toward the Soviet Union. On the right flank the President was facing smoldering revolt by Southern conservatives angered by his civil rights schemes.

In an atomosphere of bubbling optimism, the Republican national convention met in Philadelphia in June. They passed over Senator Taft and the brilliant young Harold Stassen of Minnesota in order to nominate for President once again the statesmanlike Governor of New York, Thomas E. Dewey. The popular Governor of California, Earl Warren, was nominated as Dewey's running mate.

A few weeks later, despairing Democrats gathered in the same hall to nominate their candidates. At the beginning of the convention, a liberal faction made an abortive move to persuade the popular but nonpolitical General Eisenhower to accept nomination in order to save the party from what seemed to be certain defeat, but this notion was effectively squelched by Eisenhower's firm refusal to run. Left with no other choice, the convention listlessly nominated Truman. An old political warhorse, Senator Alben Barkley of Kentucky, was nominated for Vice President. As expected, Southern Democrats, incensed over the civil rights planks in the party platform, walked out of the convention to organize a new party, the States' Rights Democratic party, and were soon dubbed by the press "the Dixiecrats." The Dixiecrats nominated Governor J. Strom Thurmond of South Carolina as their candidate for President. And Henry A. Wallace was nominated by his own newly organized Progressive party. It was predicted that Wallace would garner over five million votes, mostly from dissident Democrats, and that the Dixiecrats would siphon off millions of Southern votes normally guaranteed to the Democratic column. Thus the Democratic party was in shambles, split three ways. As one prominent Republican remarked, "Truman is a gone goose."

The spunky Missourian was fighting mad. As he put it, "I'm going to give 'em hell. I shall

Black breakthrough in baseball. Jackie Robinson of the Brooklyn Dodgers. PICTORIAL PARADE

expose the record of the do-nothing, good-for-nothing Eightieth Congress." He then embarked upon a strenuous speaking campaign across the nation, lambasting Congress and selling the Fair Deal, as he was to call it, to the people. Nevertheless, Truman's political fortunes continued to decline, and Governor Dewey was speaking almost as if he was already President. By mid-October the scrappy Truman seemed headed for certain defeat. A *Newsweek* magazine poll of fifty experts unanimously and flatly predicted a Republican victory. On election eve a news magazine published a feature article on what "Dewey will do" as President.

Only twenty-four hours after the polling booths closed, it was clear that Truman had won. He received 24,106,000 popular votes to 21,970,000 for Dewey. Thurmond and Wallace trailed far behind with only 1,169,000 and

The Truman and Eisenhower Years, 1945–1961

"The fickle finger of fate." Governor Dewey, November 2, 1948.
WIDE WORLD PHOTOS

1,157,000 votes respectively. In the Electoral college the count was more lopsided, with Truman gaining 303 to 189 for Dewey. Thurmond received 39 votes, carrying only four Southern states, and Wallace got no electoral votes. Truman had pulled off the greatest upset in the history of presidential elections. Almost incidently, the Democrats regained control of both houses of Congress.

How did it happen? Obviously, the explanations are many and complex, but a few general observations can be safely made. Inaccurate forecasts by pollsters bred smugness in the Republican camp. Confident of victory, Dewey conducted what one historian called "a gentlemanly canvass," disdaining the rough-and-tumble tactics of his hard-bitten opponent. Dewey's polish, his elegant toothbrush mustache, and his lack of personal warmth worked against him. In sharp contrast, Truman's off-the-cuff remarks, his common-man approach, his direct personal references to his prissy opponent were appreciated by audiences, who would roar back, "Pour it on, Harry. Mow 'em down." Organized labor, despite its differences with Truman, was so alienated by the Taft-Hartley Act that it remained firmly in the Democratic column. Farmers, normally Republicans, were fearful that a Republican victory would lose them the federal subsidies on which so many of them depended. The administration's vigorous foreign policy, the Truman Doctrine, the Marshall Plan, and the Berlin airlift all gained voter respect. In contrast, Wallace scared away many of his early supporters by his flirtation with left-wing extremists and his espousal of the "soft line" toward the Soviet Union. Negroes in the North and the West ignored him and were won over by Democratic promises of more civil rights. Finally, millions of Southern voters were alienated by the arid, turn-back-the-clock proposals of the Dixiecrats.

Ultimately, the election results were a vindication of the much-criticized Harry S. Truman. His cocky personality in spite of his underdog position, his refusal to quit in the face of overwhelming odds, won him extensive public acclaim, even among those who disliked him or his views.

Foul Weather for the Fair Deal

With Democratic majorities in both houses of Congress, Truman considered the election as a mandate for social reform legislation. The acceptance of the President's Fair Deal proposals in his State of the Union address of January 1949 was limited, however. The minimum wage under the 1938 Fair Labor Standards Act was increased from forty to seventy-five cents per hour. Social security was extended to cover an additional ten million persons and benefits were increased to pensioners. There were larger appropriations for public works such as TVA, and federal aid was granted for the construction of more housing for low-income families.

The temper of Congress remained conservative, however. A move to repeal the Taft-Hartley Act was defeated. A plan devised by Secretary of Agriculture Charles Brannan to establish a guaranteed annual income for farmers (while maintaining low prices for the public) was shelved. Truman's proposals for civil rights, federal aid to education, and government-sponsored health insurance were sidetracked. Congress in its turn enacted over a presidential veto the Internal Security Act of 1950 requiring the registration of all Communist and Communist-front organizations. Congress also passed the McCarran-Walter Act in 1952, again over the President's veto, endorsing the discriminatory quotas for immigrants enacted during the 1920's.

The reputation of the Truman administration was undermined by charges of scandal. The gifts of a deep freezer to General Vaughan, the President's military aide, and an expensive mink coat to the wife of an official of the Reconstruction Finance Corporation became popular symbols of corruption. Even more serious were the attacks leveled against the administration for "the failure" of its China policies, accusations of extensive disloyalty in the government, and the President's dismissal of General MacArthur in 1951, all matters to be discussed below. Despite his momentary resurgence in popularity in 1948, Truman's political stock continued to slide downhill. By 1952 he had become one of the most unpopular presidents in history.

As early as 1946, President Truman had instituted loyalty commissions and review boards to check on subversives and ferret communists out of the government. After extensive investigation, more than 2,000 persons had resigned and 212 had been dismissed. The President's drive to eliminate disloyal personnel was so rigorous that some persons were dismissed or obliged to resign through practices of questionable constitutionality and in violation of their civil liberties. Yet, in spite of the President's vigorous actions, the issue of loyalty and Communism in government became a source of discontent and political dissension contributing powerfully to the decline of Truman and the Democratic party.

Fear of Communism had its roots in the 1920's, beginning with the Palmer "Red hunts" at the end of the Wilson era. This fear subsided in the 1930's as Americans became increasingly preoccupied with Fascism and Japanese militarism. During the Second World War, with the United States and the Soviet Union allied, worries over internal Communism remained quiescent.

In 1946, however, worry over domestic Communism revived as the people became alarmed over the aggressive foreign policies of the Soviet government in Europe. Concern became dismay as Chiang Kai-shek's forces were defeated and expelled from mainland China by Mao Tse-tung and his Communist troops. The failure of Chiang in China, despite extensive aid from the United States, was interpreted in certain quarters as evidence of the bankruptcy of Truman's foreign policy. Some Americans even charged that Chiang's downfall was deliberately arranged by Communists and "pinks" inside the United States government.

As the Communist tide flowed outward, engulfing large portions of the Eurasian continent, fears of Communist infiltration within the United States increased proportionately. These apprehensions were nurtured by the uncovering of a Communist spy ring within the Canadian government in 1946, making it seem likely that a similar ring existed within our own government. The fear of traitors in the government was given a tangible basis in 1948 by the charge that Alger Hiss, a former State Department employee, had been a Communist; the worst fears were confirmed when Hiss was eventually convicted in 1950 of perjury for denying any Communist affiliations. More evidence of Communist infiltration came in 1949 when Judith Coplon, a clerk in the Justice Department, was charged by the FBI of delivering confidential information to a Soviet

The Truman and Eisenhower Years, 1945–1961

agent in New York City. Even more startling was the revelation of a spy ring among scientists working on the atom bomb during the war; the group and their cohorts apparently kept the Soviet government informed about the development of that weapon. A gauge of the severity of the national response was the conviction of Julius and Ethel Rosenberg for complicity in the plot and their execution in 1953, an unprecedented peacetime penalty for espionage.

McCarthyism and MacArthurism

In the turmoil over Reds in the government, Senator Joseph R. McCarthy of Wisconsin saw an opportunity to restore his own declining political fortunes. He launched his campaign in February 1950, a month after the conviction of Alger Hiss. In an address before a women's club in Wheeling, West Virginia, McCarthy accused the State Department of being "thoroughly infested" with Communists. He claimed that he held in his hand a list of 205 State Department employees who were or had been Reds. In the weeks following his Wheeling speech, McCarthy delivered a volley of contradictory and confusing charges at the administration, changing his figures with bewildering rapidity to 57 and later to 81 "card-carrying Communists in the State Department." He denounced Secretary of State Dean Acheson as a "pompous diplomat in striped pants with a phony British accent."

As critics sought to pin him down on his wild oratorical forays, McCarthy employed what has been called "the multiple un-truth." In other words, while opponents were seeking to disprove one statement as a lie, McCarthy would fire verbal buckshot full of innuendo and half-truths in other directions, thus diverting public attention from the original issue. When the senator was called upon to turn his list of names over to the FBI, he blandly refused, declaring that it was the responsibility of Congress as a whole to force the executive branch to open its personnel files.

A Senate committee, chaired by Millard Tydings of Maryland, attempted to expose the rambunctious Red-baiter, but McCarthy turned the hearings into a circus performance. He hinted that Senator Tydings was himself a pink and in league with the administration in "the task of protecting the traitors, Communists, and fellow travelers in our government." In the end the committee and the Senate approved by a narrow margin a resolution to investigate the senator's activities. The outbreak of the Korean War in late June 1950 deflected public interest, however, and the resolution was quietly pigeonholed.

In the beginning McCarthy waged a lonely struggle, but the press, recognizing the publicity value, gave him front-page coverage. Public acclaim soon followed, and many people rationalized their support by saying, "While I don't approve of his methods, he's doing a job that needs to be done." Powerful newspapers such as the Hearst chain and the Chicago *Tribune* hailed his fight against "subversion in government." Money poured into his coffers from sympathizers, great and small. Other Republican leaders began to see the value of McCarthy in their efforts to discredit further the Truman administration. Senators William F. Knowland of California and Edward Jenner of Indiana, among others, all old hands in Red baiting, joined in the effort to embarrass the presidency. Even Senator Taft, that monument of conservative probity, gave quiet encouragement to the brawling Wisconsinite.

In the 1950 election campaign McCarthy used his newfound popularity to confound those who had the temerity to oppose him. In a nationwide speaking tour, he denounced his enemies with vitriolic effectiveness. Senate Majority Leader Scott Lucas of Illinois went down in defeat. The Wisconsin senator gave special attention to the Maryland campaign where Tydings was making what seemed to be an easy bid for reelection. McCarthy money was poured into the fight. A few days before the election, a McCarthy staff member released a doctored photograph showing Tydings apparently engaged in amiable conversation with Earl Browder, former leader of the Communist party. When the votes were counted, Tydings was badly trounced by an obscure Baltimore lawyer and McCarthy ally, John Marshall Butler. The 1950 elections provided significant gains for the Republicans in Congress, five more seats in the Senate and twenty-eight in the House, for which McCarthy received substantial credit.

To his worshipful followers McCarthy had become a saviour and fearless fighter against perverters of the American way of life such as anglophiles, intellectuals, atheists, Jewish internationalists, and Reds. In the eyes of his detractors, he was a Fascist demagogue, a satanic scaremonger, and an opportunist with the morals of a rattlesnake. In short, McCarthy had become a towering political force, engendering fervid enthusiasm among his supporters and spreading dismay in the ranks of his enemies. As a national symbol of the moment, only General Douglas MacArthur was his equal.

The last half of 1950 and the beginning of 1951 were a time of particular tribulation for President Truman. While trying to parry the thrusts of McCarthy at home, the President became embroiled in policy disputes with General MacArthur, commanding the United States and United Nations forces in the Korean War that had broken out in June. The Commander in Chief and his field general began to disagree sharply on the ultimate goals of the war. Truman's primary objective was to inflict punishing defeats on the North Korean aggressors and drive them out of South Korea. MacArthur considered the limited aims of the administration to be "appeasement." He insisted that Communist aggression could only be resolved by conquest and forcible unification of North and South Korea. At the same time, he urged that Chiang Kai-shek's army in Formosa be "unleashed" for invasion of the Red Chinese mainland.

When the President met with the haughty general in October at Wake Island, MacArthur assured Truman that the war would be over by Thanksgiving. (At the moment United Nations forces were sweeping northward toward the Yalu River and apparently complete victory.) In an atmosphere of relative cordiality and agreement, the conference was concluded. But in the ensuing weeks MacArthur's prediction of a quick end of the war dissipated as the Red Chinese intervened and forced the United Nations forces into a costly retreat. In order to reverse the Korean military situation, General MacArthur made persistent and public demands for permission to extend the war by bombing the Chinese "sanctuary" in Manchuria. His truculent manifesto to the Chinese in March 1951, warning them of possible invasion, brought matters to a head. MacArthur's interference in political affairs by using the press and congressmen as levers to force administrative compliance with his views created a crisis with the hard-headed Chief Executive. "MacArthur left me no choice," Truman declared, "I could no longer tolerate his insubordination."

With the full concurrence of his staff, including Secretary of State Acheson, Secretary of Defense George C. Marshall, and the Joint Chiefs of Staff, on April 11, 1951 the President fired MacArthur. As expected, the dismissal of the most renowned American general in the twentieth century produced a public explosion of anger against Truman. MacArthur's return to the United States was marked by a wave of emotionalism including a tumultuous welcome in San Francisco and a hysterical greeting by supporters at Washington National Airport. On April 19 MacArthur delivered a memorable oration to a joint session of Congress. In his speech the hero harshly indicted the timidity of the administration in waging limited war in

Korea, declaring that "there is no substitute for victory." He concluded his dramatic address with tears in his eyes,

"I still remember the refrain of one of the most popular barracks ballads . . . which proclaimed most proudly that old soldiers never die; they just fade away.

"And like the old soldier of that ballad, I now close my military career and just fade away, an old soldier who tried to do his duty as God gave him the light to see that duty.

"Goodbye."

It was MacArthur's finest hour and Truman's loneliest. When the President went to Griffith Park the next day to throw out the first baseball to inaugurate the new season, he was greeted by a stunning chorus of boos. Yet despite the apparently universal loathing for him, the President was not without his admirers, and it has since been argued that this was the most courageous act of his entire public career.

In hearings conducted by the Senate, MacArthur seized the opportunity to lambast the administration's foreign policies. Republicans capitalized on the proceedings to cast further discredit on the President. Senator Jenner even demanded his impeachment.

After the Senate's inquiry into his dismissal ended inconclusively, MacArthur embarked on an extensive tour of the nation. Crowds always gathered to greet him but with decreasing enthusiasm. As Henry L. Mencken acidly remarked, "The general is fading away satisfactorily." MacArthur, unwilling to involve himself in the political arena, withdrew to a palatial suite in New York's Waldorf-Astoria from which he rarely emerged.

Joe McCarthy, however, was ready to seize the initiative. In June 1951 he denounced General Marshall as part of a "conspiracy so immense and an infamy so black as to dwarf any previous such venture in the history of man." Even McCarthy's most ardent supporters were shaken by his latest foray. Soldier-statesman Marshall occupied a niche in the national pantheon of military heroes as high as MacArthur's. Jolted by the hideousness of the attack on Marshall, the Democrats again lashed back. Senator William Benton of Connecticut became the white knight leading the charge against the obstreperous, battle-hardened McCarthy. Benton demanded the expulsion of the Wisconsin senator on grounds of perjury, fraud, and lack of fitness for office. McCarthy hit back hard, calling Benton a "mental midget" and a "megaphone for Communists." He attacked Guy Gillette, head of the Senate committee investigating his conduct, with such bruising fury that the Iowa senator withdrew from the proceedings. Indeed, the committee generally was so demoralized that it ended up by doing nothing. Senator Benton became another casualty in the struggle against McCarthy when he was defeated for reelection in 1952.

Changing the Guard—Election of 1952

Although Harry Truman would have been the last person to admit it, the Democratic party was in bad shape in 1952. Scandals continued to plague the administration. Particularly disturbing were the exposures of fraud in the Bureau of Internal Revenue. In addition, the President was regarded as irresponsible because of his momentary and unconstitutional seizure of steel mills during a strike in 1951. In the meantime fruitless negotiations with the North Koreans dragged on while American soldiers continued to be killed in the barren Korean hills. The miasma of McCarthyism spread far beyond the federal government to state and local levels. The general feeling that Democrats were "soft on Communism" put candidates and officials wearing the party label on the defensive.

Although Truman could have run for a third term, he took himself out of the race in late March 1952.[2] There were only two serious contenders for the Democratic presidential nomination, Senator Estes Kefauver of Tennessee and Governor Adlai Stevenson of Illinois. Kefauver had achieved national renown for his effective exposure of the extent of organized crime, through lengthy hearings conducted before television cameras. Stevenson, however, had the inside track. He had a background of experience in foreign affairs and had demonstrated competence as Governor of Illinois. Stevenson's most important advantage was Truman's support of his candidacy, and the President, despite his unpopularity, still had considerable control over the Democratic party machinery. Although Stevenson was a liberal and an advocate of equal rights for Negroes, he was less unacceptable to Southern conservatives than other candidates. Stevenson was nominated on the third ballot. Senator John Sparkman of Alabama was selected as his running mate for a conventional "balanced ticket."

A few weeks earlier, the Republicans had nominated General Dwight Eisenhower after a bitter convention struggle with the supporters of Senator Taft. Eisenhower's nomination was achieved to a large extent through the efforts of Eastern liberals such as Governor Dewey and Senator Henry Cabot Lodge of Massachusetts, but the breach between liberals and conservatives in the party was partly closed by the nomination of Senator Richard M. Nixon of California for Vice President. He was young; he was regarded with favor by the Old Guard; and he was known as a vigorous anti-Communist, having achieved fame for his persistence in exposing Alger Hiss.

After his nomination Eisenhower sought to assuage further the embittered right-wing supporters of Taft. On September 12 Eisenhower met Taft in New York and signed what Democrats sneered at as "the articles of surrender." With the nodding approval of Taft, he properly pledged himself to fight "creeping socialism," "the swollen bureaucracy," and the encroachment of the federal government on states' rights. After that the Republicans mounted a powerful and well-financed campaign, focusing on the issue of Communism and "the mess in Washington."

The Democrats remained in bad shape. Stevenson and Truman had deep personal differences. Stevenson toured the country delivering statesmanlike speeches deftly laced with his sparkling wit. He made it clear from the outset that he was going to run his own show. Truman more and more regarded Stevenson's high-level style with contempt. The President still felt the way to win was "to give 'em hell," and so he campaigned, unasked, for Stevenson's election. While Stevenson took the high road, Truman took the low road, hitting hard at Eisenhower and his entourage with personal references.

In September the Democratic National Committee uncovered a slush fund provided to Nixon as senator by wealthy Californians. It was a mere $18,000, but it was enough, Democrats felt, to tar Nixon's reputation. Eisenhower was so upset by the disclosure that he considered dropping the young Californian from the ticket. But Nixon struck back at his enemies masterfully by making an emotional radio and television broadcast on September 23. In his speech Nixon referred to his own humble background, his wife's cloth coat, and his children's little dog, "Checkers." Even hard-boiled television cameramen on the scene had tears in their eyes. Nixon himself broke down and wept after it was over. The reaction was a national wave of sympathy for the courageous underdog, Dick Nixon. The fund was forgotten as Eisenhower forgave his running mate during a brief meeting in West Virginia shortly after, thumping

---

[2] The Twenty-second Amendment, ratified in March 1951, prevented any president from being elected for more than two terms or from serving more than two and a half terms if moved up from the vice presidency. Truman himself, however, was specifically exempted from the provisions of the amendment.

Nixon on the back and saying to the press, "He's my boy."

Eisenhower himself regarded his declaration on October 24 that "I shall go to Korea" as the turning point in the election campaign. This statement evoked significant support, although it was uncertain what Eisenhower would do when he got there. Stevenson briefly considered the same idea but rejected it as "grandstanding."

Despite his elegant style, Stevenson could not overcome Eisenhower's tremendous popularity. Stevenson polled 27,315,000 votes, but it was not enough. Eisenhower won a massive victory with 33,824,000 popular votes, and he carried thirty-nine states with a total electoral vote of 442. Yet the Republicans gained only a slender majority of eight seats in the House and they broke even with the Democrats in the Senate. Other Republican candidates ran far behind their leader. McCarthy was reelected by only a small majority in Wisconsin and Henry Cabot Lodge was unexpectedly beaten in Massachusetts by Congressman John F. Kennedy.

It is difficult to draw great meanings from the 1952 election. The anti-Communist theme, so avidly seized upon by many Republicans, does not seem to have been a significant factor. Certainly the reputed ineptness of Truman and the high-toned intellectualism of Stevenson bothered some people, but less than expected. Some conservative Southerners, worried about the emphasis of Democratic liberals on civil rights, voted Republican. Virginia and Florida, usually members of the Solid South, went into the Republican column. Essentially, though, the only obvious fact of the election was that it was a personal triumph of the homespun and genial war hero, Dwight D. Eisenhower.

THE EISENHOWER YEARS

Eisenhower took office as President in 1953 with a uniquely contradictory set of qualifications for that high position. In many respects, the new Chief Executive was superbly qualified for the job. He was extremely popular. Even his political opponents had difficulty nurturing hatred for the affable general. He seemed to be the epitome of the success story so admired by conservative, rural Americans. His boyhood in Abilene, Kansas, close to the frontier, added to the aura of the Eisenhower legend.

He had been born into a thrifty family of Pennsylvania Dutch ancestry, and as a youngster he had worked hard, had done fairly well in his studies, and had excelled in athletics. At West Point, however, he was an average student, and his early military career was undistinguished. During his long tour of competent military service, promotions came very slowly, although at one time he became the protégé of Douglas MacArthur and served under that renowned soldier in Washington and in the Philippines. His first big break came in 1941 when he caught the eye of General Marshall, who was then the Army Chief of Staff. With his sponsorship, the Eisenhower star rose rapidly. He was appointed commander of the Anglo-American invasion of North Africa in 1942. During the North African campaign, the inherently nonpolitical Eisenhower learned with difficulty to wrestle with labyrinthine French military politics; not the least difficult were his awkward relations with the strong-willed Charles de Gaulle.

Eisenhower's success in the Mediterranean theater led to his appointment in 1943 as Supreme Commander of the Allied forces preparing for the invasion of Hitler's Europe. Again he was obliged to learn, and he gained experience in difficult problems of coordination. In executing the invasion of Europe in 1944, "Ike," as he was already affectionately called, refined his skill in molding the various Allied armies and their officers into a unified, highly motivated team. He had to resolve conflicts among the clashing personalities of colleagues and subordinates such as the domineering Winston Churchill, the hot-headed

General Patton, the imperious Field Marshal Montgomery, and again General de Gaulle. Although there is yet no agreement by historians on Eisenhower's success as Supreme Commander, there is no doubt that public opinion in the United States promoted him to the status of America's greatest general in the war. His service as occupation commander in Germany after the war, as Chief of Staff of the army, and as commander of the newly organized NATO forces in 1950 did nothing to damage his favorable image in the public mind.[3]

Eisenhower's outward composure, his ready smile, his fatherly dignity, and his straightforward approach to complex problems were distinct assets. His proposals and solutions, unadorned by any attempts at eloquent language, served to heighten his popularity in the hearts of millions of Americans who saw Eisenhower as a military man without the tarnish of being militaristic.

On the other hand, the new President was charged with having a commonplace mind and seeking simplistic solutions. His political philosophy was conservative but hazy. Eisenhower often seemed to operate on the assumption that his charm, his honesty, and his competence in coordination were sufficient to surmount all obstacles. As Eisenhower understood it, when a problem arose, it was his presidential function to be supreme coordinator and get people together to talk things out until a solution was found. He saw himself as President of all Americans, and he hoped to preside in a new "era of good feelings." With his innate distaste for the rough-and-tumble aspects of political party activities, he was ill prepared for a number of rude shocks as he came to grips with the harsh realities of politics soon after taking office.

[3] A curious episode in Eisenhower's career was his brief tenure as president of Columbia University from 1948 to 1950. A man who read only military history, Western novels, and detective stories, he had little talent for the job and no passion for scholarly activities.

Climax and Decline of McCarthyism

It was widely assumed that one possible blessing of the new Eisenhower administration would be the lessening of the sting of Senator McCarthy's Red-scare tactics. McCarthy himself ruefully admitted at first that "it will be unnecessary for me to conduct a one-man campaign to expose Communists in government. We have a new President who doesn't want party-line thinkers or fellow travelers. He will conduct the fight."

But the respite from McCarthyism did not last long. After a short honeymoon, the Wisconsin senator resumed shooting venomous barbs at a variety of executive agencies and departments. He attacked the State Department for appointing Charles E. Bohlen as ambassador to the Soveit Union on the grounds that he had been present at the Yalta conference in 1945 (anyone who had been at that conference was held suspect by militant anti-Communists). McCarthy intimated that Bohlen had influenced FDR at Yalta to "sell out" to the Russians. In order to appease McCarthy's wrath, Secretary of State Dulles reached an understanding with the senator that future diplomatic appointments would not be made without his approval. As a further sop to the Wisconsin rabble-rouser, Scott McLeod, a presumed McCarthy disciple, was chosen to be the State Department's chief security officer. When Harold Stassen, head of the Mutual Security Agency, sharply criticized McCarthy's interference in certain foreign policy matters, he was advised to tone down his statements.

Having struck pay dirt again in the form of newspaper headlines, McCarthy's appetite was whetted for more political profit at the expense of the administration's prestige. In the spring of 1953 he sent two young assistants, Roy Cohn and G. David Schine, to investigate alleged Communist literature in the United States Information Agency libraries in various European cities. The antics of Cohn and Schine spread

"Point of order, Mr. Chairman, point of order!" The Wisconsin senator at the army–Joseph McCarthy hearing, 1954.

WIDE WORLD PHOTOS

dismay throughout the foreign service and created sardonic amusement in the European press. Such established works as those of Thoreau and Emerson, along with the detective stories of Dashiell Hammett, were quickly removed from United States Information Agency library shelves after a critical word or two from the two youthful "Commie" hunters. About the same time McCarthy staff members and sympathizers struck out in other directions, charging that American universities and the Protestant clergy were "riddled with subversion." Inspired by McCarthy, agencies of the federal government launched frantic investigations of themselves and each other in order to eliminate all persons who had even the remotest taint of disloyalty. State and local agencies across the nation feverishly increased their search for subversives and left-wingers, aided by service clubs, veterans groups, and self-appointed individual Red hunters. Textbooks in schools and colleges purporting to show the Soviet Union in a favorable light were banned. The stories of Robin Hood, the Girl Scout Handbook, and literature dealing with the United Nations were denounced as Communistic.

Presiding over the uproar he helped create, McCarthy casually promoted an assault on the integrity of the army by denouncing the grant of an honorable discharge to a dentist who had refused to sign a loyalty certificate. The dentist's superior officer, General Ralph Zwicker, was called before McCarthy's committee where he was bullied and humiliated by the senator and Roy Cohn. The reckless attack on the army seemed to enhance McCarthy's prestige. By early 1954 public opinion polls reported that fifty per cent of the people approved of the senator's actions and that another twenty-one per cent were not sure.

President Eisenhower sought to remain aloof from the tumult. His disgust with McCarthy was undoubted, but he was uncertain about how to deal with him. On one occasion the President angrily declared, "I will not get down in the gutter with that guy." But the closest he came to a public attack on McCarthy was a speech at Dartmouth College in June 1953 in which he denounced "book burning" in general

"There is . . . a steady course to be followed between an assertion of strength that is truculent and a concession of helplessness that is cowardly. There is . . . a middle way between untrammeled freedom of the individual and the demands for the welfare of the whole nation."
(Dwight D. Eisenhower). This unusual photograph of three men who served as president was taken at Sam Rayburn's funeral, 1961.

but without specific reference to any individual.

The downfall of McCarthy's reign of terror began when the army in 1954 charged the senator with seeking special favors for Schine, who had been recently inducted. McCarthy's own Senate committee conducted hearings on the charges and countercharges in open session before national television. Although the hearings ended inconclusively, the television record was probably a turning point in McCarthy's career. The doctored photographs, the twisted testimony, and the ham-handed obstructionist tactics of the senator were exposed to millions of shocked and fascinated viewers over a thirty-six-day period.

Sensing the public's change of heart, the timid Senate was finally moved to act. A special committee, headed by Senator Arthur Watkins of Utah, recommended that McCarthy be reprimanded. In December 1954 the Senate formally approved the recommendation by a vote of sixty-seven to twenty-two. Afterward, President Eisenhower publicly complimented Senator Watkins, and McCarthy's name was stricken from the list of approved visitors to the White House.

Although the reprimand was little more than a verbal slap on the wrist, McCarthy was finished. He had lost most of his audience. No longer could senators or other government officials be intimidated by his threats. When he died less than three years later, he was a bitter and largely forgotten man. In the meantime McCarthyism gradually subsided partly because of McCarthy's tarnished image and basic failure—he had never substantiated a single one of his charges—and partly because of a decline in the tensions of the cold war.

Black Revolution—First Phase, 1954–1961

For the distraught Eisenhower May 1954 was a time of unusual anxiety. Throughout the month, concerned with the seemingly endless McCarthy-army hearings, the President was also distracted by the surrender of Dienbienphu, presaging France's ultimate defeat in Indochina. His staff was hard at work preparing for a conference in Geneva which was to arrange for French capitulation and withdrawal from Southeast Asia. During these fretful days he took only momentary notice of the portentous and long-awaited Supreme Court decision of May 17 in the case of *Brown* v. *Topeka* (Kansas) *Board of Education.*

Although the Court order to desegregate schools was recognized as crucial at the time, in the years since it has become ever more evident what a watershed in American history the Court's action was; indeed, this was possibly the most far-reaching judicial decision since *Marbury* v. *Madison* in 1803, for it accelerated significantly the Negro revolution in America.

In declaring unanimously that segregation in public schools by race was unconstitutional under the "equal protection" clause of the Fourteenth Amendment, the Court reversed the traditional "separate but equal" doctrine established in the 1896 case of *Plessy* v. *Ferguson*. In speaking for the Court, recently appointed Chief Justice Earl Warren declared that "separate educational facilities [according to race] are inherently unequal." The Chief Justice presented a wealth of statistical evidence to support his contention, demonstrating that where segregation of schools existed the quality of teachers and facilities for Negro children lagged invariably far behind that of the whites. In the state of Mississippi, the most extreme example, expenditures per pupil favored whites by a ratio of about five dollars to one.

For several years the Supreme Court had been gingerly examining the constitutionality of school segregation as well as of all "Jim Crow" laws. As early as 1946, the Court had issued the pronouncement that race discrimination in interstate transportation was a violation of the commerce authority of Congress. In 1948 the high Court had ruled that restrictive clauses binding white property owners to sell houses only to other whites was unenforceable. In the case of *Sweatt* v. *Painter* (1950), the Court had decided that a separate law school established for Negroes in Texas did not satisfy the standards of equality in eduction.

During the lengthy hearings preceding the Brown decision, Southern legalists, relying on the Tenth Amendment and essays of Jefferson and Calhoun, contended that authority over public school education was the exclusive province of the individual state. These arguments were effectively countered by the evidence of NAACP lawyers such as Thurgood Marshall and Roy Wilkins. The findings of civil rights commissions during the Truman administration and the sympathetic assistance of the Justice Department aided significantly in winning the victory for desegregation. The Supreme Court somewhat diluted its ruling, however, when it declared in 1955 that local school boards should proceed with plans for integration "with all deliberate speed." In states in the Deep South, this phrase was interpreted as an invitation to permanent postponement.

At first, the reaction of Southern opinion was mild. In border states and outside the South the task of integrating schools proceeded rapidly. In 1954, 150 school districts desegregated. The momentum increased to 362 in 1955 but fell off to only 200 in 1956. But in 1957 only 38 school districts desegregated and in 1958 a mere 13 districts became integrated. In the Deep South rejection of the Court order was nearly total.

Whatever President Eisenhower's private

Crisis and change in the South. Central High School in Little Rock, Arkansas, September 1957.

BERN KEATING—BLACK STAR

opinion may have been, publicly he indicated lack of enthusiasm for federally enforced integration. Although a believer in equal rights for the Negro, he maintained that implementation of these rights must be achieved on state and local levels. As a result the President's dilatory attitude encouraged political leaders and demagogues in the South to initiate programs of "massive resistance" or evasion of desegregation, and they were abetted by the threats and terroristic tactics of White Citizens' Councils and the Ku Klux Klan.

Eisenhower was jolted out of his apathy by events in Little Rock, Arkansas, during the late summer of 1957. A district federal judge issued an order at the request of the school board to integrate Central High School. The integration plan was blocked, however, by Arkansas national guardsmen under orders from Governor Orval Faubus. According to the governor, bloodshed would occur if the nine qualified blacks were admitted to the school. Faced by this challenge to federal authority, the President reluctantly ordered a contingent of paratroopers to Little Rock to enforce the Court order and to protect the Negro students attending Central High School. The confrontation between angry whites and the paratroopers produced moments of great tension but serious violence was avoided. Despite continued harassing tactics by the governor, Little Rock schools were completely integrated by 1960. Nevertheless, piecemeal integration continued at a very slow pace throughout the last years of Eisenhower's administration. It was not until Kennedy came into office in 1961 that the rate of school integration again speeded up.

The Supreme Court decision on schools was only the first breach in the segregation dike during the Eisenhower years. In a number of separate rulings, the Court began to strike down the legality of Jim Crow laws. Laws ordering segregation in *intrastate* transportation, public swimming pools, municipal golf courses, restaurants, theaters, and sports arenas were one by one declared unconstitutional.

Inspired perhaps by the Court's leadership, Congress in 1957 passed a civil rights bill, the first of its kind since 1875. In the law Congress established a Civil Rights Commission with power to subpoena witnesses and authority to investigate denial of voting rights to Negroes. Again, however, Eisenhower's lukewarm enthusiasm for the bill and his apparent confusion over its meaning undermined its effectiveness. Without the President's strong support, the proposal was amended and weakened by a conservative coalition in Congress. As a result the new law lacked provisions for effective enforcement and the hoped-for increase in registered Negro voters in the South did not materialize. Another civil rights act passed in 1960 closed some of the loopholes in the 1957 law, but these statutes were at best faltering steps in the march to provide Negroes with political rights. Yet they did serve as precedents for further advances in the 1960's.

In any great social revolution impetus for change can come from above, but for real progress the disaffected people themselves must seize the initiative and through their own efforts achieve their goals. This principle held true in the black revolution as Negroes, given hope by the Supreme Court's decisions, began to develop their own momentum in the struggle for equality.

The battle against white supremacy in the South got under way after an insignificant incident on December 1, 1955 in Montgomery, Alabama. On that evening Mrs. Rosa Parks, a Negro seamstress, boarded a bus and sat down wearily in a section reserved for whites. When instructed by the driver to give up her seat to a white man, she refused. Mrs. Parks was jailed for violating a municipal segregation ordinance.

This apparently minor incident, however, lit the fuse of black activism. Following the arrest of Mrs. Parks, Montgomery Negro leaders, headed by a Baptist minister, Dr. Martin Luther King, Jr., planned a mass protest. The technique was simple in concept, difficult in execution, but in this case very effective. The Montgomery blacks decided en masse to boycott the municipal buses until accorded better treatment. For the next several months they either walked or used car pools to get to their destinations.

When the city government retaliated by indicting Dr. King and others for conspiracy, the Montgomery black population responded with an amazingly disciplined refusal to bow down to white authority. Since the profits for the municipal bus lines were largely derived from Negro patronage, the boycott hurt white Montgomery in the pocketbook. Despite the conviction of King, the boycott went on for more than a year. By late December 1956, prodded by the Supreme Court decision declaring that bus segregation was unconstitutional, the Montgomery city council capitulated. When the newly integrated bus lines resumed full operation, there was little violence or attempted humiliation of Negro passengers.

The victory over segregation in Montgomery propelled Martin Luther King into leadership of the black struggle for equal rights. The youthful minister became both a leading theoretician and an important strategist of the Negro movement for the next decade. During these years Dr. King gradually evolved a philosophy that was primarily an amalgam of the teachings of Jesus, the writings of Henry David Thoreau, and the thought of Mahatma Gandhi. At the core were the concepts of "civil disobedience" and "passive resistance." As King put it, "laws of men are subject to the 'higher laws' of God and Christian morality. Where a law is unjust it may become necessary to refuse to obey it. However, the violater must accept the penalties and consequences cheerfully.... We can never forget that everything Hitler did in Germany was legal and everything the Hungarian freedom fighters [in 1956] did in Hungary was illegal."

Despite the success story in Montgomery and the support of the Supreme Court, the black revolution moved forward sluggishly. Bus boycotts were attempted in other Southern cities with indifferent success. White terrorists struck back. The homes of Negro leaders, including Martin Luther King's, were bombed. Lack of real protection under the civil rights acts made Negroes hesitate to vote in elections. The attempt of Mrs. Autherine Lucy in 1956 to be the first Negro student at Alabama ended twenty-six days later after she had suffered endless vituperation and abuse. Despite orders of the Interstate Commerce Commission and the Supreme Court, interstate transportation in the South remained segregated.

Thus struggle for equality took a different direction with the first "sit-in" in 1960. This technique originated when four Negro college students sat down at a Greensboro, North Carolina, lunch counter and refused to leave after being denied service by the management. The idea spread rapidly to other Southern cities, sponsored in part by CORE (Congress of Racial Equality) and influenced by King's philosophy of nonviolent but direct action. Lunch counter "sit-inners" schooled themselves in the techniques of nonviolent protest. They taught each other to endure humiliation and physical violence passively. They learned to accept ketchup poured on their heads, vicious taunts, and kicks without striking back or showing anger. The success of the sit-ins was remarkable. Throughout the South, especially in the cities, segregation in lunchrooms and restaurants began to fade away.

The battle for equal rights was just beginning, however. After 1961 it was to spread into the North and the Negro revolution was to change in focus and character radically.

Conservatism in Washington

Eisenhower's nomination as the Republican candidate for President in 1952 was interpreted as a victory for moderate "Dewey" Republicans over the conservative forces of Taft. Tired of the contentiousness of Truman and suspicious of the intellect of Adlai Stevenson, many Democrats happily voted for Ike in the fall election. They felt certain that the new President would continue the social and economic programs of the Roosevelt and Truman era. The Democrats and moderate Republicans were not to be entirely disappointed, but the Eisenhower administration proved to be more conservative than anticipated.

Eisenhower's Cabinet appointments provided an early indication of the philosophy of the new administration. John Foster Dulles, the Secretary of State, had been a wealthy corporation lawyer. The new Secretary of the Treasury, George Humphrey, was the former president of a steel company. Charles E. Wilson resigned as president of General Motors to head the Defense Department. Two other Cabinet appointees, Secretary of the Interior Douglas McKay and Postmaster General Arthur Summerfield, were successful automobile distributors. Sinclair Weeks, the Secretary of Commerce, was a New England manufacturer; Ezra Taft Benson, in Agriculture, achieved a reputation as a conservative specialist in farm marketing; and Oveta Culp Hobby, the new Secretary of Health, Education, and Welfare, was the wife of a wealthy Texan. Humphrey became probably the most influential Cabinet official on domestic affairs, and the President listened sympathetically to Humphrey's drumfire remarks in Cabinet meetings on cutting the budget and holding the lid on inflation. Humphrey's key position in the government was succinctly indicated by Eisenhower's remark, "When George speaks, all the rest of us listen."

It would be a mistake, however, to assume that the Eisenhower administration represented a turning back of the clock to the Harding-Coolidge era of the 1920's. On occasion, Secretary Humphrey was a willing participant in New Deal techniques of government regulation of the economy. In 1954, to halt a business recession, Humphrey supported the Federal Reserve Board in lowering the rediscount rate to stimulate credit expansion. Eisenhower also aided in the increase of consumer purchasing power by getting Congress to increase payments for unemployment compensation and to expand the social security program.

Throughout Eisenhower's eight years the administration continued to tinker modestly with the economy. The government sought to take the sting out of a recession in 1957 and 1958 by expansion of public works programs, especially highway construction, and making additional funds available for building schools and public housing projects.

But in other ways the Republican administration reflected its conservative philosophy. A tax reform bill enacted in 1954 granted allowances for corporations for more rapid depreciation. The President, who denounced the TVA as an example of "creeping socialism," preferred wherever possible to promote electric power development by private business rather than public corporations such as TVA. Eisenhower subscribed to the Dulles proposal of massive retaliation (page 723), partly as a means for cutting expenditures for the armed forces. By manufacturing more atom bombs and increasing the carrying capacity of the Strategic Air Command (SAC), the administration felt that it could cut down on the enormous cost of conventional armaments. Secretary of Defense Wilson pithily summed up this policy as "getting more bang out of the buck." The President resisted the Fair Deal proposals for an extensive national health insurance program as "socialized medicine," preferring instead a limited plan of subsidizing private insurance companies issuing health policies.

In agriculture Eisenhower sought to implement the philosophy of Secretary Benson. In Benson's opinion it was high time that the federal government began to get out of the business of buying up farm surpluses and storing them in order to maintain high prices. Therefore Benson opposed the New Deal policy, in operation since the days of Henry A. Wallace in the 1930's, of paying government subsidies to farmers. In order to cut down the "subsidy merry-go-round," Benson proposed the principle of "flexible supports" whereby the Department of Agriculture would be empowered to scale down price parity from ninety per cent to seventy per cent.[4] One of the aims of the program was to discourage overproduction since the price support figure was tied to production (the more produced, the lower the support price). But greater efficiency continued to lead to greater surpluses—and lower prices. Naturally, farmers opposed Benson's program and indicated their resentment by voting against the Republicans in large numbers in the 1954 congressional elections. The program was abandoned and Eisenhower sought to solve the problem of farm surpluses by his "soil bank" plan, which Congress enacted into law in 1956. According to this plan, farmers who reduced their productive acreage would receive government compensation for the smaller crop. Although about 30,000,000,000 acres were taken out of production by 1960, production continued to increase because of continually higher yields per acre. As a result, in 1960 the government owned a staggering billion bushels of wheat alone. Indeed, if all the government-accumulated surpluses of 1960 were stored in one place, they would have covered an area of approximately fifteen square miles to a height of one mile. An average of six billion dollars were spent on price supports annually from 1951 to 1960. The government meanwhile made serious efforts to dent the crop surpluses by making gifts or exchanging these commodities with other nations as well as by using surplus food to stock school lunch programs and to help needy American families through the issuance of stamps redeemable at local stores.

---

[4]Under the price parity principle, in operation in 1954, the government was obliged to purchase certain commodities in quantities sufficient to maintain the price at ninety per cent of the 1948–1949 price level. Because of the efficiency of production by wheat farmers, for example, the government was obliged to buy up such vast amounts that it was hard put to provide storage facilities. Such a policy made little sense since the enormous surpluses were excessive even if the United States should suffer from the threat of prolonged famine. In any case, much of the stored wheat eventually rotted.

Despite numerous and courageous attempts by the Eisenhower administration to resolve the farm dilemma, little progress was made. Agricultural prices declined and surpluses of staple products continued to pile up. But in other areas of the economy there was generally increasing prosperity. Even though there were occasional recessions, business expansion occurred at record rates, and the decade saw a steady rise in living standards and increased purchasing power of the consumer.

ELECTION OF 1960

The choosing of the president has been referred to as "one of the world's most mysterious and complicated transactions in power," and one foreign observer has characterized the process as "America's quadrenniel madness." Whatever the description, the office of president, including the procedure for electing someone to that post, is a uniquely American phenomenon. For one thing, the president is both head of state and chief executive officer, roles that are split up in most other countries. Where the office is ceremonial, as in Switzerland, West Germany, or the Soviet Union, the election or appointment of a president usually involves little fanfare. A further, significant difference lies in the relation of the chief executive—whether called president, premier, prime minister, or chancellor—to the lawmaking branch of government. In many countries his power derives from and is limited by a council of ministers as in Russia or a parliament as in Great Britain. But in the United States the president is elected independently of Congress and is not necessarily beholden to that lawmaking body for support. He possesses enormous powers, granted to him by the Constitution, that allow him a freedom of action and confer on him an authority that would make an ancient Roman emperor envious.

The presidency, ever since Washington, who did so much to dignify the office at the outset, has been of great symbolic significance and the focus of public authority. Even in the nineteenth century when most presidents, Jackson and Lincoln being two notable exceptions, generally chose not to flex their executive muscle, the president was accepted as the living symbol of American nationhood and the most important person in the United States.

In the twentieth century, as the authority of the president became magnified, the office took on greater symbolic and actual significance. Thus presidential elections, always a process that engaged the interest of the people, became matters of increasing concern, particularly as more of the people gained the right to vote. Two additional factors that contributed to the heightened interest were the increasing complexity of issues and the expansion of the mass media of communication. With the growth in population, the advance of industrialism, the incredible breakthroughs in the sciences, the development of knowledge in the social sciences, the increasing role of the United States in world affairs, and the "shrinking" of the world through new means of transportation and communication, Americans in the twentieth century have faced problems that at times have seemed to defy human comprehension. Coping with the issues requires a high degree of sophistication, and even so the answers are not easy. For example, the economic implications of Franklin Roosevelt's decision in 1933 to take the United States off the gold standard were difficult, even boring, for the average citizen to follow. In considering the proposal of the Nixon administration in 1969 to establish an antiballistic missile system, even the experts disagreed sharply, leaving the public in a state of confusion. In such a situation, many a citizen has sought refuge in voting for and supporting the man he trusted most. Through the mass media Americans have had an increasingly better chance to examine the opposing candidates. Lengthy biographies in newspapers, magazines, and books, often replete with pictures, allowed readers to learn intimate details about office seekers and their backgrounds. With the advent of radio and television, candidates in action were brought easily into the family living room for close scrutiny. With the twentieth-century revolution in transportation, millions even had a chance to see their hero or his opponent firsthand as candidates resorted more and more to the "whistle stop campaign." The "front porch style" used by McKinley and Harding became an anachronism. Candidates have found it essential to storm about the nation by plane and train, submitting themselves to ogling spectators and the ordeal of the handshake.[5] But making effective use of the mass media and conducting a modern campaign cost enormous amounts of money. As a result presidential aspirants have found it increasingly necessary to begin planning and building public support years before the nominating conventions.

As 1960 approached, there were already several Democratic hopefuls warming up and building power bases from which to launch their race for nomination: Senator Stuart Symington of Missouri, with administrative experience as a former Secretary of the Air Force and the support of former President Truman; Lyndon B. Johnson of Texas, the skilled majority leader of the Senate with strong support in the South; the articulate Senator Hubert Humphrey of Minnesota, a favorite among liberals, labor leaders, and Negroes in the North; the twice-defeated Adlai Stevenson, still strongly supported by liberal factions; Edmund G. "Pat" Brown, fresh from a smashing victory in the California gubernatorial race; and the personable Governor of New Jersey, Robert Meyner, pinning his hopes on a deadlocked convention. But the obvious front-runner was Senator John F. Kennedy of Massachusetts. He had lost a bid for the vice-presidential candidacy in 1956, but he yielded graciously and fought hard for the Stevenson-Kefauver ticket, and he had scored an overwhelming victory in 1958 in the race to hold on to his Senate seat.

In the Republican camp the situation was much less fluid. With Eisenhower prevented from running by the Twenty-second Amendment, Vice President Richard Nixon virtually had the field to himself. While Eisenhower for eight years had played the role of President of the people, above partisan politics, Nixon had taken to the hustings and cultivated the support of party regulars. Nixon was available to campaign anywhere for Republican candidates for state or national offices. By default, Eisenhower left Nixon with a major share of the job of holding the Republican party organization together. Because of his cautious positions on issues, Nixon was not unacceptable to the party's liberals or conservatives. After 1954 he played down the domestic anti-Communist issue and even spoke circumspectly in opposition to Joe McCarthy. Nixon was the most active Vice President in history. During Eisenhower's illnesses—he had two heart attacks and a bout with ileitis—Nixon assumed temporarily a portion of the President's duties. The Vice President was constantly consulted on foreign policy and national security matters. In the steel strike of 1958 Nixon was instrumental in bringing about a settlement between management and labor. In the same year he achieved national and international renown for his fortitude and cool behavior in the violent anti-Yankee demonstrations that erupted during his tour of South America. The Vice President's reputation was further enhanced by his vigorous interchange with Premier Khrushchev in the famous "kitchen debate" at the 1959 Moscow Exposition.

The only challenge to Nixon's candidacy

---

[5]Senator Kefauver, in his bid for the 1956 Democratic nomination, was finally obliged to shake with his left hand, his right having become puffy, calloused, and bandaged from enduring the iron grips of his many admirers. Vice President Nixon in 1960 managed to make a personal appearance in every state in the Union and in fact visited the more populous states several times. It was estimated that his opponent in that campaign, Senator Kennedy, was seen in person by more than four million people.

came from a belated, poorly organized attempt by Governor Nelson Rockefeller of New York to wrest the nomination from him. It folded before the convention opened and Nixon was nominated unanimously, but he agreed to alterations in the party platform to conciliate Rockefeller. Nixon chose as his running mate Henry Cabot Lodge of Massachusetts, a former senator and then the United States Ambassador to the United Nations.

In contrast with the cut-and-dried Republican situation, the battle for nomination in the Democratic camp was wide open and exciting. Senator Humphrey sought delegate votes by running in states where there were open primaries. Kennedy, carefully selecting states where he would be the apparent underdog, challenged Humphrey, particularly in Wisconsin and West Virginia. Outside of Milwaukee, Wisconsin was considered a Humphrey stronghold; however, Kennedy emerged a narrow victor in the March primary. The *coup de grace* was delivered to Humphrey in West Virginia. It was presumed that in the heavily Protestant mountain state the Catholic Kennedy would be at a fearful disadvantage, yet Kennedy money and organization crushed Humphrey in the May primary and the disconsolate Minnesotan promptly withdrew from the race. In other primary battles the Kennedy machine steamrolled over local or insignificant opposition. Only in California did Kennedy avoid an open primary fight with powerful Governor Pat Brown, who counted himself out of the race and was inclined toward Stevenson. In contrast with Kennedy, Senator Symington campaigned languidly, hoping mainly for support from party bosses and a deadlocked convention which would turn to him in desperation. Lyndon Johnson held on firmly in the South but could not mobilize much support elsewhere. Stevenson garnered little support outside California; even delegates from his own home state of Illinois were already committed to Kennedy.

As the Democratic National Convention opened on July 8, the only three serious contenders were Johnson, Kennedy, and Stevenson. Kennedy won on the first ballot, despite a thunderous last-minute demonstration by thousands of Stevenson supporters in the galleries. The following day Lyndon Johnson accepted Kennedy's invitation to be his running mate.

The 1960 campaign for the presidency began in late August with Nixon in the lead. While Kennedy was pinned down in Washington by a special session of Congress, Nixon invaded Democratic sanctuaries in the South. The reception, particularly in Atlanta, Georgia, on August 26, was stunning and overwhelmingly favorable to the Republican candidate. A Gallup poll issued at the time showed Nixon with a substantial six per cent lead over his rival. A few days later the Kennedy campaign got under way. At first, the organization was ragged, schedules were poorly planned, and the candidate's voice became hoarse as he floundered for themes to develop.

On September 12 Kennedy met head-on the issue of his Catholic faith. The candidate was acutely aware that the American people were predominantly Protestant and that many had a strong bias against Catholics. Kennedy knew, as did millions of Americans, that Al Smith's candidacy in 1928 was badly damaged by a whispering campaign warning that if the New Yorker were elected the Pope would be able to dictate White House decisions. In a talk with Protestant leaders in Houston, Kennedy answered searching and often hostile questions on his attitudes toward religion, the state, and the presidency. In forthright replies Kennedy clearly indicated to the audience that, if elected, he would always act independently of his church and he would sharply admonish as improper any attempt by the hierarchy of his church to influence presidential decisions. He put himself on record strongly favoring the Jeffersonian concept of absolute separation of church and state. At the conclusion of the confrontation, the candidate was rewarded with

The Truman and Eisenhower Years, 1945–1961

applause and the sympathies of most who attended the meeting.[6]

Nixon's initial momentum evaporated when he lost crucial time in September from a knee infection, fever, exhaustion, and loss of weight. Hoping to regain lost ground, Nixon readily accepted the notion of four personal confrontations on television with his opponent.

The television debates were the climax of the campaign. The two doughty candidates were both intent and youthful—Nixon was forty-seven and Kennedy forty-two years old—but the Vice President's face reproduced poorly on the television screen. And although both were tired from campaign exertions, Kennedy seemed to be suffering less from the strain. Appearance and personality were what counted, for what the two men said in the course of the debates was insignificant. No great themes were enunciated. There were no flourishes of oratory. Although both candidates were highly articulate, there was no opportunity for either one to trap the other as Lincoln had done in his debates with Stephen Douglas in 1858. Kennedy devoted himself mainly to criticism of the Eisenhower record, which Nixon, of course, defended. It has been estimated that 65,000,000 people watched each debate. But when the series concluded, the American people knew little more than before about the issues.

Yet Kennedy apparently emerged the victor. Republicans were shocked over the haggard appearance and tense, defensive manner of the Vice President, while Democrats were elated over the vigorous yet mature conduct of their candidate. And most significantly, by appearing on an equal footing with Kennedy, Nixon lost his advantage of experience and notoriety.

During the remainder of the campaign, Nixon continued to lose ground. The pledge he made and kept, to appear personally in every one of the fifty states, added to the drain on his physical powers. He refused to avail himself of the proffered assistance of President Eisenhower until the closing days of the campaign.[7] His running mate, Lodge, proved to be a lazy, ineffectual candidate. On the other hand, Lyndon Johnson performed creditably and campaigned vigorously, helping to hold most of the Southern states in the Democratic column.

The role of black voters turned out to be critical in the election. In late October, when Martin Luther King was sentenced to hard labor following a sit-in demonstration in Georgia, the Kennedy organization acted quickly. Senator Kennedy promptly telephoned Mrs. King assuring her of his concern. His brother Robert petitioned for King's release, which the judge surprisingly granted. King's father, like King himself a Baptist minister with considerable influence in the Negro community, immediately declared he was changing his support from Nixon to Kennedy. Nixon did not hear about the incident immediately, but he neglected to act when he did. Nixon further alienated Negro voters when he had to repudiate a prediction by Henry Cabot Lodge that, if elected, Nixon would appoint a Negro to the cabinet. In the voting black support put Kennedy over the top in three states.

When the results of the November 8 election were in, Kennedy had won in the Electoral College by a comfortable majority of 303 to 219 for Nixon. His percentage over Nixon in popular votes, however, was razor-thin, less than two-tenths of one per cent. It was so narrow that the shift of a few thousands votes in key states would have made Nixon President.

At the time Kennedy's victory was hailed as

---

[6] It was to the credit of Nixon, himself of the Quaker faith, that he adamantly refused to exploit Kennedy's religion and did everything he could to discourage his supporters from injecting the religious issue into the campaign.

[7] At a press conference, early in the campaign, when asked by a reporter for one concrete accomplishment of Nixon as Vice President, Eisenhower replied, "Give me a week to think about it and I might come up with an example."

an upset. Admittedly, the party in power has advantages, and the support of Eisenhower, one of the most popular presidents in history, should have been enough to carry the experienced Nixon to victory. A contrary view, which is gaining credence among students of presidential elections, is that what is amazing is the narrowness of Kennedy's margin over his opponent. The Kennedy machine had money, brains, and know-how. The candidate had a united Democratic party behind him. He was attractive, able, and energetic. The Democrats committed no major errors in the campaign. Kennedy had the general support of the working press and editorial endorsement of newspapers normally in the Republican camp. The union leadership, with the glaring exception of Jimmy Hoffa of the Teamsters, was mainly loyal to the Democratic cause. Negroes who had been shifting to the Republican party (Eisenhower got thirty-nine per cent of the black vote in 1956) came back to the Democrats. Eighty-nine per cent supported Kennedy in 1960. And his themes—"We've got to get moving again" and "We stand today on the edge of a new frontier"—were more appealing than the phrase "peace, prosperity, and progress," a legacy from Eisenhower that Nixon stuck to doggedly throughout the campaign. Therefore a reasonable conclusion can be made that it is surprising that Kennedy did not win by a much larger margin despite his Catholic, "Eastern establishment" background.

SUGGESTED READINGS

Caughey, J. W., *In Clear and Present Danger* (1958).

Chandler, L. V., *Inflation in the United States, 1940–1948* (1951).

*Christman, H. M., ed., *The Public Papers of Chief Justice Earl Warren* (1966).

Clark, K. B., ed., *The American Negro* (1966).

Clark, T. D., *The Emerging South* (1961).

Curtis, C. P., *The Oppenheimer Case, the Trial of a Security System* (1955).

Douglas, P. H., *Ethics in Government* (1952).

*Drucker, P. F., *The New Society: The Anatomy of the Industrial Order* (1950).

Eisenhower, D. D., *The White House Years* (2 vols., 1963–1965).

Eulau, H., *Class and Party in the Eisenhower Years* (1962).

Ferguson, C. C., *Desegregation and the Law* (1957).

*Galbraith, J. K., *The Affluent Society* (1958).

Galbraith, J. K., *American Capitalism* (1952).

*Guttman, A. and B. Ziegler, eds., *Communism, the Courts and the Constitution* (1964).

Hesseltine, W. B., *The Rise and Fall of Third Parties from Anti-Masonry to Wallace* (1948).

Hiss, A., *In the Court of Public Opinion* (1957).

Howe, I. and L. Coser, *The American Communist Party* (1957).

Hughes, E. J., *The Ordeal of Power* (1963).

Kefauver, E., *Crime in America* (1951).

*King, M. L., *Stride toward Freedom* (1958).

*King, M. L., *Why We Can't Wait* (1964).

Lattimore, O., *Ordeal by Slander* (1950).
*Lens, S., *The Crisis of American Labor* (1959).
*Lippman, W., *The Public Philosophy* (1955).
*Lomax, L. E., *The Negro Revolt* (1962).
Lubbell, S., *The Future of American Politics* (1952).
Lubbell, S., *The Revolt of the Moderates* (1956).
*Mason, A. T., *The Supreme Court from Taft to Warren* (1958).
Miller, L., *The Petitioners, the Story of the Supreme Court of the United States and the Negro* (1966).
*Mills, C. W., *White Collar* (1951).
Mills, H. A. and E. C. Brown, *From the Wagner Act to Taft-Hartley* (1950).
*Myrdal, G., *An American Dilemma* (2 vols., 1944).
Nixon, R. M., *Six Crises* (1962).
Prothro, J. W., *Negroes and the New Southern Politics* (1966).
*Riesman, D., *The Lonely Crowd* (1950).
*Rovere, R., *Senator Joe McCarthy* (1959).
Shoemaker, D., ed., *With All Deliberate Speed* (1957).
Sorensen, T. C., *Kennedy* (1965).
Soth, L., *Farm Trouble in an Age of Plenty* (1957).
*Wallace, J. C., ed., *Loyalty in a Democratic State* (1952).
*Warren, R. P., *Who Speaks for the Negro?* (1966).
*White, T. H., *The Making of the President* (1960).
*Whyte, W. H., Jr., *The Organization Man* (1956).

CHAPTER 32

Due to Circumstances . . .

Now the trumpet summons us again . . . to bear the burden of a long twilight struggle . . . against the common enemies of man: tyranny, poverty, disease, and war itself. Can we forge against these enemies a grand and global alliance, north and south, east and west, that can assure a more fruitful life for all mankind? Will you join in that historic effort?

JOHN F. KENNEDY, Inaugural, 1961

WIDE WORLD PHOTOS

ON A CHILLY BUT SUNNY JANUARY DAY, AN elderly but robust gentleman stepped into an open touring car to ride from the executive mansion to the Capitol building. Seated beside him was John F. Kennedy, the youngest elected president in American history. At the inauguration ceremony about to take place, Dwight D. Eisenhower would end his public career and assume the role of gentleman farmer. The brief ritual on the Capitol rotunda would mark more than the transfer of power from one president to the next, however. Later that moment would come to symbolize the end of an era. The relatively placid Eisenhower years were to be succeeded by the most turbulent decade in the United States in a hundred years.

During the sixties accepted behavior patterns and traditional institutions of American democracy were shaken by a social earthquake. Although most of the citadels remained standing at the end of the decade, they had been either sharply altered or badly eroded. Change, which always characterizes history, occurred with a rapidity that left both unwary participants and hardened observers breathless and amazed.

In the arena of foreign affairs, the uncertainty of the early Kennedy-Johnson years was followed by involvement in a conflict from which the nation seemed unable to extricate itself. The Vietnam war became the longest in American history as well as one of the costliest. As the war dragged on, an atmosphere of acrid bitterness was generated at home and abroad. Allies and friendly states became increasingly alarmed. Within the United States criticism mounted to disturbing proportions. In these same years, almost unnoticed, American living standards continued to improve. The gross national product, about $500,000,000,000 in January 1961, had doubled by January 1970. Yet there were dire predictions of environmental or ecological disaster as problems of pollution escalated. During the sixties the United States was able to catch up to and pass the Soviet Union in the "race for space," landing American "earthlings" on the moon twice in 1969. But whether these astounding technical feats were a portent of the conquest of the galaxy by man, or merely a cosmic stunt, still remains to be seen.

Due to Circumstances . . .

CAMELOT AND CATASTROPHE

The presidential inauguration ceremony held on January 20, 1961 set the tone for the incoming Kennedy administration. A reading by the venerable poet Robert Frost was followed by Kennedy's ringing appeal to national idealism:

"The torch has been passed to a new generation of Americans, born in this century, tempered by war, disciplined by a hard and bitter peace, proud of our ancient heritage, and unwilling to witness or permit the slow undoing of those human rights to which this nation has always been committed. . . . And so, my fellow Americans, ask not what your country can do for you; ask what you can do for your country."

Thus began the "New Frontier" administration of this new generation. From its advent, the presidency exuded brilliance and excitement. Innovative approaches to old problems and fresh and daring schemes stirred the public imagination. The Peace Corps, which Kennedy had proposed during the election campaign and which he created by executive order on March 1, 1961, less than two months after his inauguration, became a symbol of the hope and promise of the New Frontier. The Corps became a cadre for thousands of young volunteers, bursting with idealism, who carried American energy and skills to peoples living in over twenty different countries in the underdeveloped regions of the world. Kennedy's bold plan, announced after the first successful orbital flight in space by a Soviet cosmonaut, to initiate a crash program to place an American on the moon before the end of the decade was also indicative of the resolve of the new administration.

Artistic and intellectual achievement was given new status by the President and his gracious wife Jacqueline. Mrs. Kennedy transformed the many public areas of the mansion from cold museum rooms to warm, artistically pleasing salons, furnished with art objects in the best of American tradition. Performances by eminent artists, including a recital by world-renowned cellist Pablo Casals, were arranged in the large East Room of the White House. In a bow to intellectuals, the President invited fifty Nobel prize winners to dinner and, in a brief toast of congratulations, banteringly remarked, "This is the most extraordinary collection of talent . . . that has ever been gathered together at the White House—with the possible exception of when Thomas Jefferson dined alone."

The evening was given added significance when Kennedy congratulated geneticist Linus Pauling, who had been picketing the White House during the day against the testing of atomic weapons, on expressing his views.

The electric spirit of John F. Kennedy transformed disgruntled Democrats and even many Republicans into Kennedy supporters. Some were attracted by his interest in athletics and physical fitness. Kennedy's revival of the fifty-mile walk, advocated for his staff as well as the nation, and his enjoyment of touch football games with family and friends were found invigorating by those grown too dependent on cars and television. Others were attracted by the President's affection for his two young children, whose occasional intrusions into formal meetings were a source of amusement for visitors and Americans everywhere. Then too Kennedy's moments of sadness—the death of his two-day-old son, the crippling stroke suffered by his father—stirred the sympathies of the nation. The media focused much attention on the young President, and people began to speak of "the Kennedy style." The obscure word charisma was revived to describe Kennedy's gracious and seemingly magical public image.

The New Frontier on the Domestic Scene

John F. Kennedy, similar to the Roosevelts in political philosophy, was a strong advocate of the concepts that the government must be an active agent in promoting social justice and that the president, the only nationally elected official, must lead Congress. During the course of his brief term of office Kennedy sent hundreds of legislative requests to Congress, including proposals to provide medical aid for the old and the poor, to promote education and scientific research, to reform taxation, to attack the problems of the cities, and to insure civil rights for all Americans.

Unfortunately, despite the glamour of the Kennedy years and although he had hoped to repeat the great legislative victories of Franklin Roosevelt, Kennedy soon discovered that it is one thing to give orders but quite a different matter to see them carried out. Kennedy had been partially aware of the difficulties that lay ahead. He was, after all, a "minority President." Kennedy also recognized that even though he had served in Congress and had many friends there, his own youthfulness would hamper his effectiveness with the often aged and conservative congressional leaders. Moreover, although there was a Democratic majority in both houses, the President knew that Republicans and Southern Democrats could easily form a conservative coalition. The recalcitrant Congress which Kennedy faced passed only 172 of the 355 measures introduced in his first, and most successful, year as President. Kennedy was willing to accept occasional setbacks, yet he was unprepared for the massive resistance of Congress, which, in cavalier fashion, jettisoned most of his pet New Frontier programs by refusing even to act on such proposals as medicare, tax reform, and civil rights. But like the Roosevelts before him, Kennedy was prepared to circumvent Congress by stretching his executive authority to the limits prescribed by the Constitution, or perhaps a little beyond.

Economic Problems. There had been considerable growth during the Eisenhower years, but the economy was sluggish. The unemployed numbered over five million in 1961, an alarming eight per cent of the total labor force. Rural pockets of poverty, particularly in the Appalachia region where unemployment was much higher than the national average, remained as bad as they had been during the depression, and the plight of migratory farm workers, especially among Mexican-Americans in the Southwest, was acute. The great urban sprawls needed federal assistance to untangle transportation snarls on the ground and in the air and to aid the inner cores of cities which were rotting as slums proliferated. In addition, environmental pollution was becoming a costly economic as well as a serious health problem.

Though plagued by setbacks, Kennedy's efforts with Congress were not totally devoid of achievement. At his instigation the Area Redevelopment Act (1961) was passed to aid such areas as Appalachia by enticing industry into the region through low-interest government loans and grants and through a retraining program to provide the necessary workers for these industries. A bill providing more than one billion dollars in appropriations was pushed through Congress to expand unemployment relief. In addition, with a view to increasing buying power and thereby encouraging expansion of industries, legislation was enacted to increase the minimum wage from $1.00 to $1.25 per hour and to broaden social security benefits. The Housing Act, designed to stimulate construction of moderate-income housing, both rural and urban, and to promote improvement of mass transportation, was adopted in 1961. All these measures served to boost the economy, but when Congress rejected Kennedy's plea for the creation of a new executive Department of Housing and Urban Affairs, substantial aid to the cities was indefinitely postponed.

The President achieved his major successes in revitalizing the economy outside the realm of Congress. Kennedy fought recession by persuading the Federal Reserve Board to lower interest rates in order to encourage business expansion. He also used existing funds to accelerate federal building programs, such as post office and highway construction. Yet while seeking to stimulate economic growth, Kennedy did not ignore the threat of sudden inflation. To combat this possibility, he used the prestige of his office to elicit the voluntary cooperation of organized labor and management in limiting prices and wages. Although generally successful, the President found himself on a collision course with the steel industry and its principal spokesman, Roger Blough, head of the giant United States Steel Corporation. Despite informal agreements reached between Secretary of Labor Arthur Goldberg, the steel union, and United States Steel to keep down wage demands and prices, Blough abruptly announced a sweeping increase by his company of $6 per ton, about 3.5 per cent. On the following day, April 11, 1962, Kennedy convened a White House press conference and in icy tones denounced Blough's action as "a wholly unjustifiable and irresponsible defiance of the public interest." He indicated that future government defense contracts would be awarded only to those companies which held the line on prices, and instructed Attorney General Robert F. Kennedy to consider indictment of major steel companies for "price fixing" in violation of the Sherman Anti-Trust Act. Within forty-eight hours Blough and the other steel chiefs had rescinded their price increases. Despite accusations leveled at Kennedy for "over-reaching," "executive tyranny," and "intemperate retaliation," public reaction was enthusiastic on his behalf. The incident was reminiscent of the executive leadership of Theodore Roosevelt at his best during his struggles with the coal companies and J. P. Morgan.

The New Frontier and Social Justice. Kennedy was acutely aware of the multitude of educational and social problems facing the nation. Although there was a tremendous need for more and better schools, states were finding it more and more difficult to finance educational expansion. Moreover, the enormous "dropout" rate and the task of retraining jobless people suffering from technological displacement made special programs increasingly necessary. In line with Kennedy's view of federal responsibility and the importance of education—"Our progress as a nation can be no swifter than our progress in education. The human mind is our fundamental resource."—various efforts were made by the administration on behalf of schools. A comprehensive education bill was introduced in Congress in 1961 but was defeated by a coalition of Republicans who feared federal aid and of Catholics who objected to the exclusion of parochial schools from the benefits. In 1962 a bill to aid higher education was similarly slaughtered by Congress. Kennedy's efforts to combat the problems of increasing automation met with better success: the Manpower Development and Training Act, authorizing a three-year retraining program, was passed in 1962.

The President also recognized the needs of the more than sixteen million citizens over sixty-five. Health needs of this group were high and incomes generally low. Thus, before Kennedy's first month as President had elapsed, he submitted a medicare bill to provide extensive medical insurance for the elderly through federal financing as part of social security. This proposal was opposed, among others by the powerful American Medical Association, which delivered a vituperative attack on Kennedy. At a news conference afterward, the President remarked with wry humor, "I read their statement, and I gathered they were opposed to it." The AMA held that medicare would lead to socialized medicine; others feared that it would drain the entire social security system. In the end the bill was defeated by a narrow margin, a discouraging setback for Kennedy.

In the area of civil rights the record is somewhat less bleak. Since it was obvious that the Southern Democrats were very strong, the President avoided direct legislative action. Instead Kennedy chose to use executive action to promote equal opportunity. He influenced defense industries in the South and elsewhere to hire blacks for high-paying supervisory positions wherever possible and he appointed Negroes to high posts in government. Thurgood

Marshall, the NAACP's legal counsel, became a judge on the Court of Appeals; Robert Weaver, a prominent urban expert, took over as chief of the New Housing and Home Finance Agency; and a number of Negroes were appointed as ambassadors to European as well as to African nations.

Kennedy's greatest contribution to equal rights lay in his willingness to protect those persons who chose to attack discriminating practices and to support Supreme Court decisions on school desegregation. When in May 1961 white mobs viciously assaulted "freedom riders" traveling in the South in defiance of Jim Crow practices in public transportation, Attorney General Robert F. Kennedy sent 400 armed United States marshals to protect them. Prompted by these freedom riders, Robert Kennedy and the Department of Justice induced the Interstate Commerce Commission to prohibit segregation on interstate bus facilities.

Unlike Eisenhower, President Kennedy left no doubt that he supported the Supreme Court decisions on school desegregation, and during his administration the Justice Department initiated federal court action ordering that public schools in Virginia, closed to prevent integration, be reopened. In October 1962 James H. Meredith, a Negro air force veteran, was denied admission to the University of Mississippi by university authorities assisted by Governor Ross Barnett and the state legislature. This refusal to admit Meredith was in direct violation of a federal court order. Kennedy dispatched several hundred marshals to assure that Meredith was properly registered and when riots ensued on the campus, leaving two dead, Kennedy ordered 3,000 federal troops and federalized national guardsman into the area. Governor George C. Wallace, who in May 1963 attempted to block the admission of two Negro students at the University of Alabama, backed down under the threat of military force by the state militia, which Kennedy had ordered nationalized.

In reaction to the Kennedy brothers' determination to press for equal rights, ugly violence erupted. Medgar Evers, head of the Mississippi NAACP, was murdered by a white racist. In Birmingham, Alabama, civil rights demonstrators headed by Reverend Martin Luther King encountered bullying police, snarling dogs, and high-pressure fire hoses. Again in Birmingham a bomb exploded in a church, killing four Negro children. There were also more demonstrations for civil rights, in the North as well as in the South, and Congress might finally be expected to react favorably to a civil rights bill. Thus President Kennedy on June 19, 1963 called for far-reaching legislation to curb discrimination. He received support from over 200,000 people who participated in "The March on Washington" on August 28 to convince Congress of the urgency of civil rights legislation. But the massive demonstration was to no avail, for balky Congress stalled until the sands of President Kennedy's life ran out.

The New Frontier Abroad

It has been the fate of presidents who were eager to achieve reforms at home to see international problems take precedence long before domestic goals had been achieved. Woodrow Wilson's progressivism was abandoned when the United States was drawn into World War I, and Franklin Roosevelt's New Deal withered as the second global conflict broke out in 1939. Kennedy's New Frontier programs also foundered, partly because of the immediate intrusion of successive foreign crises that diverted his energies away from domestic affairs. Kennedy had extensive knowledge of international affairs but few new approaches to the problem of relieving world tension.

Latin-American Relations. On March 13, 1961 President Kennedy proclaimed in glowing terms a hemispheric extension of the New Frontier. The proposed "Alliance for Progress" called for a ten-year commitment of twenty billion dollars by the United States to aid economic growth and to improve living conditions, education, and public health in Latin-American countries. On its part, it was understood that Latin America would pledge eighty billion dollars and enact extensive social and economic reforms. Yet hopes of solid achievements quickly dwindled, partly through bureaucratic confusion in Washington and partly through the reluctance of major Latin-American nations to undertake anything other than token reforms. By the late sixties the Alliance was all but forgotten, Congress severely cut financial support in 1968, and Latin America was plagued by a reemergence of unstable military juntas and dicatorships having varying degrees of hostility toward the United States.

A particular factor in rendering the alliance both more important and less effective than might otherwise have been the case, was the disastrous Bahía de Cochinas (Bay of Pigs) invasion. Since his seizure of power in 1959, Fidel Castro had become increasingly a source of embarrassment and irritation to the United States. His leftist philosophy and expropriation of American-owned property caused concern, but his attempts to export Castroite revolutions to other Latin-American countries created general alarm in Washington.

Near the end of the Eisenhower administration, the Central Intelligence Agency, in an effort to remove what was by this time seen as a Communist threat within the Western Hemisphere, hatched a plot to overthrow the dictator. In accordance with the plan, the CIA trained Cuban exiles in guerrilla tactics with the intention of putting them back in Cuba to inspire a spontaneous revolt against Castro. The agency was convinced that the Cuban people would eagerly join the invaders and that victory would be an easy as well as a popular one. President Kennedy reluctantly assented to the scheme, which was monumentally mishandled. Supposedly secret training camps were reported extensively in the *New York Times*, of which Premier Castro was an avid reader. The exiles themselves were divided into dissident factions which were infiltrated with Castro's agents.

Castro was therefore ready for the invaders when they landed at the Bay of Pigs on April 17, 1961. Lacking the promised air support and the expected popular uprising, the guerrillas were forced to surrender after a brief but savage fight.

The CIA had badly misjudged the temper of the Cuban people. Castro's prestige, already high, was greatly enhanced in Cuba and elsewhere in Latin America by the defeat of the invaders, while Kennedy was criticized both abroad and at home. In one stroke, the Bay of Pigs disaster did as much damage to the reputation of the United States as had all the diplomatic misjudgments of Eisenhower and Dulles. To President Kennedy it was an embittering experience. Afterward, he remarked sourly, "All my life I've known better than to depend on the experts. How could I have been so stupid to let them go ahead?" It was, however, much to his credit that the President accepted full responsibility for the fiasco.

JFK versus Khrushchev. Although continuing the policy of containment, Kennedy recognized the necessity of a *détente* with the Kremlin and was willing to try to achieve this goal through personal diplomacy. Premier Khrushchev was still angry over the U-2 incident, but Kennedy hoped that the Soviet leader would meet with him, the new American head of state, untainted with the mistakes of the Eisenhower administration. Thus the two leaders agreed to a conference in Vienna during June 1961. They talked about a wide range of topics—the status of Berlin, the space race, atomic testing, Southeast Asia. Despite the superficial cordiality, nothing was accomplished, for Kennedy and the Soviet premier had engaged in a collision of wills on almost every issue. Yet the conference was not without value. Kennedy had failed to reach an agreement on limiting atomic testing; he had also failed to resolve any of the issues which might possibly lead to open hostilities. He did, however, size up the unbending Khrushchev.

Continued Soviet hostility toward Western

nations was evidenced by the building of the Berlin Wall in mid-August of 1961. It encircled all of West Berlin, halted the flow of East German refugees, who numbered over two million since 1949, to West Germany, and sealed the Communist-bloc countries from further Western influences. Hundreds of East Germans were shot trying to escape across the Wall. Khrushchev then resumed nuclear testing and sent planes, tanks, and 50,000 additional soldiers to East Berlin.

Kennedy, realizing that he must meet force with force, announced his firm intention to protect West Berlin, resumed United States nuclear testing, and reported the full extent of America's atomic arsenal. The possibility of nuclear war loomed, and millions of Americans frantically began erecting jerry-built air raid shelters. All over the world, United States military forces were placed in a state of readiness, and reserves were hastily called up. Kennedy had thus far only reacted to Soviet challenges; he now took the offensive and ordered a powerful force of American troops to proceed through East German territory to West Berlin. The convoy moved along the Autobahn, the only surface link between West Berlin and the Western world. Tension was high, but the troops arrived at their destination safely, and the crisis eased as Kennedy rejected proposals that the United States forces smash the Wall. Although West Berlin remained free, Kennedy did experience something of a setback for the Wall still stands.

In the fall of 1962, the United States again approached the brink of war with the U.S.S.R., this time over developments much closer to home. U-2 reconnaissance flights had been carefully observing the increasing number of shipments to Cuba during the summer, and by fall intelligence agents were able to report that Castro had received medium-range missiles and had begun construction of launching platforms on the island. The plan, a nuclear build-up ninety miles from the United States, was audacious; the stakes, destruction of the existing balance of power, high. President Kennedy reacted grimly but firmly. On October 22, 1962 he announced in a televised broadcast that the United States was imposing an immediate quarantine on future arms shipments from the Soviet Union. He further demanded that all missile sites be dismantled and warned that any attack by Cuba would be interpreted as an attack by Russia and reacted to accordingly. The entire world now witnessed the terrifying fact of confrontation. Khrushchev's reaction was tensely awaited by the peoples of all nations. The Soviet leader, facing the determination of a nation resolved to defend its vital interests, backed down. Uncertainly, Khrushchev proposed to withdraw all offensive weapons from the island in return for a promise by the United States that it would not invade Cuba. The President consented; launching pads were dismantled and missiles shipped back to Russia. A second major crisis had been resolved without resort to war.

As a consequence of this incident Khrushchev's prestige within the Kremlin and in the Communist world fell, while Kennedy's rose in international circles. But two confrontations in two years, both of which could have ended in war, transcended in gravity any of the recurring crises between the Soviet Union and the United States during the Truman-Eisenhower years. It was obvious that a nuclear holocaust would become inevitable unless some major preventive measures were taken. With this knowledge in mind, President Kennedy called for a halt to nuclear testing in space, in the atmosphere, and underwater. Premier Khrushchev was amenable, and on July 25, 1963 a limited test ban treaty was signed in Moscow by the United States, Great Britain, and the U.S.S.R. Kennedy described the treaty as "only a faltering half step toward disarmament, but it is a beginning." The pact did not prevent the proliferation of nuclear weapons, and France and Red China, two other members of the nuclear club, ominously refused to participate in the agreement. Yet the treaty was an important recognition of the need for control and for restraint. Kennedy rammed the treaty through the Senate in face of serious opposition and regarded this beginning as the greatest achievement of his administration.

Entanglements in Southeast Asia. One of the most complex and difficult issues that JFK inherited from his predecessor was the increasing tension in Southeast Asia, an area in which the United States had become involved during the Eisenhower administration. At first the situation in Laos appeared to be the most immediately threatening. To stabilize the Royal Laotian government and halt the Communist guerrillas (the Pathet Lao), Eisenhower had poured $400,000,000 into the country. Despite the magnitude of this American aid, which represented $150 for every Laotian, by 1960 the country was divided into pro-Western, neutralist, and pro-Communist camps; and the anti-Communist position was continuing to deteriorate in 1961. Concerned with the strategic location of Laos but unwilling to commit American troops, Kennedy resorted to the negotiating tables and adopted a neutralist position. In a multination conference at Geneva, in which the U.S.S.R. participated, diplomats achieved a solution of sorts, establishing a tripartite regime of Pathet Lao, royalists, and neutralists. This shaky arrangement disintegrated when the Pathet Lao withdrew from the coalition. But at this time the neutralists, who had supported the pro-Communist forces, allied themselves with the pro-Western element in order to preserve Laotian independence. Still, the Pathet Lao had wide support and the situation in Laos remained of serious concern to the United States.

In the meantime, developments in neighboring Vietnam forced a suspension of attempts to resolve the Laotian puzzle. In South Vietnam the Viet Cong, another Communist guerrilla group, was threatening the United States–supported government headed by Ngo Dinh Diem. Opposition to Diem and his program of repression was also developing from the peasants and from within the government itself. However, Vice President Johnson and General Maxwell D. Taylor, the President's personal military adviser, announced after whirlwind visits to South Vietnam that the Diem government was basically sound. Johnson even declared that Diem was "the Winston Churchill of Asia." As a result, the administration poured money and thousands of military "advisers" into the country to stiffen resistance to the Viet Cong. The United States air force began bombing guerrilla hideouts, and as the United States inched toward war, the advisers began taking a more active role in the fighting.

South Vietnamese criticism of the Diem regime mounted simultaneously with the United States commitment to it. Anti-Communist nationalists denounced Diem as a former French puppet and a tyrant. Buddhist monks incinerated themselves in protest against Diem's pro-Catholic policies. After one of these self-immolations, Diem's sister-in-law, the beauteous Madame Nhu, known as "the Dragon Lady," callously remarked "Goody, another Buddhist barbecue." On November 1, 1963 a military junta led by General Duong Van Minh took over the government and murdered Diem and his brother. The United States promptly recognized the new regime, but it failed to make any real progress as it became obvious to some that Kennedy had waded to dangerous depths in the Asian quagmire.

Kennedy versus De Gaulle. Early in his administration the President had called for an Atlantic partnership to establish close economic and political ties between western Europe and North America. Included in this plan would be the admission of Great Britain to the Common Market and a gradual elimination of trade restrictions between the United States and the nations of western Europe. Although apparently sound and hopeful, Kennedy's grand design was to be shattered by the granite intransigence of President Charles de Gaulle of France, who viewed American economic and cultural penetration of western Europe with alarm and scorn. He despised what he referred to as the "gross materialism and barbarism of American culture." Further, De Gaulle regarded Kennedy's proposals as an imperialist scheme to subordinate western Europe to American power and considered Great Britain to be little more than a satellite of the United States.

The French President moved decisively to frustrate Kennedy. France vetoed Britain's request for admission to the Common Market in January 1963, and about a week later De Gaulle managed to dislodge West Germany partially from the American orbit by signing pacts of friendship, designed to help bury ancient Franco-German enmities, with West German Chancellor Konrad Adenauer. De Gaulle also, in June 1963, withdrew his naval forces from the NATO fleet in the North Atlantic as a preliminary step to the complete separation of France from the United States-dominated NATO system. The development of French nuclear and conventional weapons was speeded up so that France might operate as an independent "third force" in world politics. Also with this end in mind, De Gaulle inaugurated an extensive program of economic aid to emerging nations in competition with the United States and the Soviet Union. The tough-minded French leader was aided in his flamboyant anti-American policies by the astounding growth of France's economy and technology and the temper of the French people who generally supported him in his efforts to become independent of the United States. Kennedy and his advisers tended to dismiss De Gaulle as a minor and temporary irritant; however, they badly misjudged that great man's political strength and durability.

Elsewhere in the world there was little evidence of the Kennedy initiative. The United States avoided involvement in the confused politics of the Congo and steered clear of Nasser and his never-ending quest to annihilate Israel. Although Adlai Stevenson, the United States ambassador to the United Nations achieved great popularity among the African states by denouncing South Africa's apartheid policies and calling for an end to Portuguese occupation of Angola, his words were not acted upon. Still, Kennedy's reputation among most African states remained high.

In short, Kennedy's achievements in foreign policy are hard to assess, but he was President for only approximately one thousand days. Given his energy, his finesse, and his ability to learn from mistakes, he might have achieved a notable record had his career not been abruptly ended by an assassin's bullets.

Disaster in Dallas

In late 1963 President Kennedy began a speaking tour in Texas to mend political fences in preparation for his 1964 election campaign. While riding through the streets of Dallas with his wife at his side, the young President was shot and killed. That day, Friday, November 22, will long be remembered by people throughout the world who listened to the somber announcement in shocked disbelief. The following Sunday when millions witnessed the death of the suspected assassin, Lee Harvey Oswald, at the hands of Jack Ruby, the nation was stunned, not only by the fact of death but also by the state of violence that these killings signified. The details of these slayings, despite strenuous efforts to demonstrate the existence of a vague conspiracy, are far less important than their dispiriting effect on the nation and the world.

John F. Kennedy was given a stately funeral. Marching to the burial site at Arlington Cemetery were carefully selected contingents of the armed forces, handsome young men, black and white, symbolizing the finest that America can produce. Following the funeral cortège were eighteen heads of state, including Emperor Haile Selassie of Ethiopia, Prime Minister Harold Macmillan of Britain, and King Baudouin of Belgium. International differences were abandoned: as the casket was lowered into the grave, the aged Charles de Gaulle gave a crisp military salute to his former opponent; and Madam Khrushchev signed the guest register at the American embassy in Moscow in honor of the fallen President. Millions of Americans and people the world over wept openly and unashamed, and even seasoned news reporters struggled for control.

However history judges his success as a President, John F. Kennedy set a tone and style that signified the coming to political maturity of a new generation. His tragedy—and the nation's—is that he was denied the opportunity to fulfill the promise he had manifested.

"ALL THE WAY WITH LBJ"

On with the New Frontier

Vice President Lyndon B. Johnson, riding in the presidential procession in Dallas, suddenly found himself knocked to the floor of his limousine and racing to Parkland Memorial Hospital where Kennedy lay. Johnson waited, as did the world, yet during this period contacts were being made with command centers all over the globe. When Johnson heard the words "He's gone," the former Vice President was prepared to take over Kennedy's duties. He decided that an immediate announcement of Kennedy's death was unwise. Since no one was certain what had prompted the assassination, the action could have involved a plot against the entire government; and all would be more secure if Johnson were first safely aboard the official plane. There he announced his formal acceptance of the presidency and was sworn in, standing next to Mrs. Kennedy, who was still blood-smeared but amazingly brave. The careful, correct transfer of power was consistent with Johnson's plan to maintain "continuity" of leadership and to disturb as little as possible a nation disrupted by fear and shock.

Johnson was well prepared for the responsibilities of the presidency. After attending Southwest Texas State Teachers' College, and teaching school for a short while, Lyndon B. Johnson embarked on his political career as secretary to a newly elected congressman. Johnson lived in the atmosphere of change and excitement generated in Washington during FDR's administration and was an ardent New Dealer. After his two-year experience as state director of the National Youth Administration in Texas, in which capacity he developed his belief that "There ain't nothing government can't fix," Johnson successfully ran for Congress. He served continuously in the House from 1937 to 1948, when he was elected to the Senate. Johnson rose continuously from being one of FDR's favorite young men to Democratic whip in 1951 to Democratic majority leader in 1953.

In view of his vast experience and recognized skill in working with congressmen, it was probably very difficult for Johnson to accept his party's invitation to be the vice-presidential candidate in 1960. He was now bypassed by younger men who treated him with casual disdain. Kennedy did not, however, misjudge Johnson's talents or importance. During his years as Vice President not only was Johnson involved in decision making about national affairs but he was also continually briefed by Cabinet members and Chiefs of Staff, particularly concerning plans in the event of nuclear attack or the sudden death of the President. No one could have been better trained to face the disaster that occurred when President Kennedy was slain.

Still suffering from the shock, Johnson launched into a wide-ranging series of domestic programs and foreign involvements and convinced an equally shocked nation that life must continue. Kennedy's New Frontier legislation had not fared well, and Johnson sought to complete what unfinished business he could. Civil rights measures had been blocked in Congress, and concerns over the budget were adding to the legislative-executive deadlock. Johnson was a congressional veteran, and he had not only has his own vast experience and influence, but also the memory of the martyred President to aid him in realizing Kennedy's

418 *Time of Trial, Time of Hope*

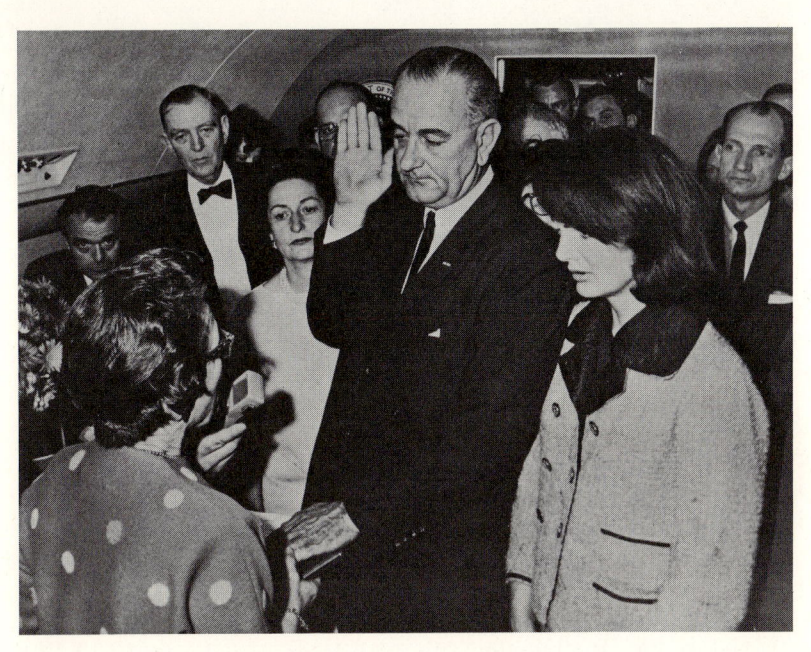

The king is dead—long live the king.   CECIL W. STOUGHTON

dream. By mid-January 1964 Johnson was clearly leading the nation, yet it was equally clear that he had mandated the continuation and expansion of Kennedy's social program.

Johnson's first success was with the Tax Reduction Act, which he pushed through Congress in February 1964. His emphasis, however, was on the Civil Rights Bill, introduced by Kennedy on June 19, 1963. President Johnson rushed the measure through the House, where it was passed in February by a vote of 290 to 130. The Senate, however, proved less amenable, but by June of 1964 this body, too, had approved the bill. This was the most inclusive civil rights legislation ever passed by Congress, but in a way it came too late. About 10 p.m. on Saturday, July 18, rioting broke out in New York City's black Harlem. The immediate cause of this violence was attributed to alleged police brutality. But behind this lay the tension of frustration in the mushrooming urban core areas to which many blacks had come expecting something better. Events in Harlem triggered rioting in other Northern cities causing widespread alarm and fear. Yet no evidence of an organized plan of disruption has been found. Often destruction was heaped by one black on another, but the explosion of naked rage bit into the consciences of all Americans and affected all phases of American life. These events were to become crucial to the political campaigns that followed, particularly in the matter of black-white relationships.

But Johnson was also being pressed to act on his own initiative. Kennedy's advisers had been urged to remain, and although they did so for a while, one by one they left. And there was talk of political chicanery when Bobby Baker, once a Johnson employee, was indicted for influence peddling and Johnson had to explain a gift that he had received from Baker. There was unrest in the cities and increasingly militant activities by civil rights and black nationalist groups. Moreover, although tragedy had buried politics for a while, there was another election coming soon, and by the middle of February Johnson began to sound like a politician once more. He also began to demonstrate

Due to Circumstances... 419

that he had his own program and was not limited to measures already initiated by his predecessor. The Economic Opportunity Act, passed in August 1964, was in keeping with Kennedy's idea of a war on poverty, but was Johnson's proposal. Training programs, community action programs, and a domestic peace corps were included in this act.

Election of 1964

The Republicans selected their presidential candidate at San Francisco in July 1964, and their convention was a fascinating example of the ability of politicians to delude themselves and of defects in the party nominating machinery. Despite a continuing liberal momentum and the availability of several personable and able candidates, including William Scranton of Pennsylvania and Nelson A. Rockefeller of New York, the delegates chose conservative Senator Barry Goldwater of Arizona to head the ticket. Goldwater extolled unlimited individual freedom and basic moral goodness, while more and more it was becoming apparent, particularly to members of racial minorities, that there could be no individual freedom until there was acceptance of the rights of all groups. Goldwater preached against the evils of big government, moderates, liberals, and expedient political compromises, but did not address himself to the question of how to cope with the complex problems of a modern and divergent America. Even some members of the nominating convention shuddered as the candidate ended his acceptance speech with "Extremism in the defense of liberty is no vice. And . . . moderation in the pursuit of justice is no virtue!"

During the summer of 1964, the Democrats were faced with a different kind of problem in selecting a standard-bearer. Johnson was the obvious presidential candidate, but there was a plethora of vice-presidential hopefuls. Robert F. Kennedy, who had been the Attorney General and who carried his magic family name, appealed to the young, the romantic, the Northeastern liberal, and the Catholic. Adlai Stevenson, the party's grand old man, was also available, but he was scarred by two defeats. There were also, among others, the two Senators from Minnesota, Hubert H. Humphrey and Eugene J. McCarthy. The Republicans' selection of Goldwater helped to settle the issue. Since Goldwater had little influence in the Northeast Johnson no longer had to appeal to that area, and he was therefore able to overcome the Kennedy supporters and to gain acceptance of Humphrey as his running mate.

The Democrats, who met in Atlantic City during August, were quite confident. Their programs in Congress had been successful. In addition to the legislation dealing with taxes, civil rights, and poverty, a Mass Transit Act and a Civilian Pay Act, increasing salaries of underpaid civil servants, had been passed; and it appeared that Johnson could count on forty-five major bills being passed by the Eighty-eighth Congress. Already Johnson had made remarkable progress toward achieving what he termed "the Great Society."

Johnson clearly managed the Democratic convention and did so with a minimum of conflict. The only problematic issue developed over the seating of a dissident group of blacks representing "the Freedom party" from Mississippi. For three days a committee attempted to reach a compromise, including issuance of a statement that "At the Convention in 1968, and thereafter, no delegations shall be seated from states where the Party deprived citizens of the right to vote by reason of their race or color." For the time being, however, the regular delegates from Mississippi were seated, on condition that they promised to support the party, and two of the Freedom party representatives were authorized to vote as delegates at large.

The partisan rhetoric of the two candidates did not clarify the issues of the ensuing campaign. Goldwater was denounced by some as wanting to end social security and defoliate all of Vietnam, although he never made such proposals. He was supported by others for "holding down" the Negroes, even though he had largely avoided any statement on that issue. Campaigning for his war against poverty and for the Great Society—ambiguous but widely popular concepts—Johnson was elected in the greatest landslide in American politics. Goldwater's defeat can be attributed to attitudes more than issues, for to the majority of voters he seemed too unbending, too much concerned with his own concepts of what was good for the country, and too extremist. Johnson, on the other hand, was both moderate and willing to compromise. The nation cast 43,126,218 votes, or 61.0 per cent, for the Democrats and only 27,174,898 votes, or 38.5 per cent, for the Republicans; and the Democratic majority in both houses of Congress was over two to one.

The Great Society?

Johnson had begun to formulate his ideas for the task which lay ahead in the spring of 1964. He tried out the phrase "a great society" on April 23, at a University of Michigan commencement. The Great Society, as Johnson then defined it, rested "on abundance and liberty for all" and would end racial injustice, poverty, ignorance, and useless or boring leisure. As the President phrased it,

"It is a place where the city of man serves not only the needs of the body and the demands of commerce, but the desire for beauty and the hunger for community. It is a place where man can renew contact with nature. . . . It is a place where men are more concerned for the quality of their goals than the quantity of their goods. But most of all the Great Society is not a safe harbor, a resting place, a final objective, a finished work. . . ."

Johnson's victory appeared to be a popular endorsement of his program for improvement in "classroom, city, countryside." This widespread support and the President's positive relationship with an overwhelmingly Democratic Congress presaged success for Johnson's Great Society. The Eighty-ninth Congress was, indeed, one of the most productive in history. Medicare was passed to provide health care for the aged. Billions were pumped into education at all levels through the first comprehensive aid-to-education laws. Voting rights were extended, and the poll tax abolished wherever it still existed. Welfare aid was increased, especially to economically depressed Appalachia, and new programs were created to finance job retraining and a Youth Corps. Environmental control laws were passed asserting federal authority to fight air and water pollution and to improve the beauty and safety of highways. During its second session Congress voted more aid to schools and antipoverty projects and continued the beautification program.

But while there was much positive action to relieve the ills of the nation, many saw Johnson's programs as being inadequate. Despair continued to overwhelm parts of American society as evidenced by the riots of summer 1965—worse than those of the year before. Watts, the sprawling ghetto section of Los Angeles, exploded, leaving thirty-five dead and over $46,000,000 in property damage. The tone of the civil rights movement changed from the philosophy of Martin Luther King's "I have a dream" to Stokeley Carmichael's "to hell with the laws of the United States."

Disruption in Foreign Affairs. In addition to domestic problems, Johnson encountered escalating criticism of his foreign policy. Throughout 1964 increasing numbers of United States special forces began to arrive in Vietnam until by midsummer a force of more than 23,000 men were stationed in this small country. Then, in August, alleged attacks by North Vietnamese PT boats on a United States destroyer in the Gulf of Tonkin prompted the *Maddox* and the *C. Turner Joy* to retaliate by firing on enemy bases. President Johnson then ordered air strikes against North Vietnam, and on August 7 Congress approved a resolution supporting Johnson's action in the Vietnamese crisis. This resolution, empowering the President to "repel any armed attack against the force of the United States and to prevent further aggression," set the stage for the kind of involvement which was eventually to lead to Johnson's withdrawal from politics. Between 1964 and 1969, when Johnson left office, the number of Americans in Vietnam rose to more than 500,000 men and the casualty figures were 30,000 killed and 100,000 wounded. But the end of the war was no closer, nor were the long-awaited, long-promised reforms within the United States–supported government of South Vietnam. Moreover, although Johnson had asserted that all civilian and military needs of the nation could be met, it was becoming obvious that the government could no longer buy—because the public could no longer afford—both "guns and butter." As the years dragged on, the war became a major cause of dissent at home and of criticism abroad.

In Latin America Castro continued to be a source of irritation to the United States. His threat to drive Americans out of Guantánamo Bay was short-lived, and he was censured by all his neighbors except Mexico. The United States' attempt to influence the rulers of the Dominican Republic was also short-lived and widely censured. When this tempestuous island country was involved in one of its many revolutions in 1965, it was thought that Communists might be part of the insurgent force. Fearing the establishment of a second pro-Communist regime, the United States landed 405 marines, officially to protect American lives; 24,000 men were eventually deployed before an Inter-American peace force took charge. The damage was extensive, for all the ghosts of "gunboat" diplomacy again haunted the minds of Latin Americans. The image of the United States was once more in question after decades of good-neighborliness.

Nor was there peace in other parts of the world. China developed an atomic bomb and became a serious threat, but the Soviet Union continued to be the major antagonist of the United States. Although direct confrontations were avoided, the Israeli-Arab war of June 1967 caused great international tension. The Russians, who backed the Arabs, and the Americans, who supported the Israelis, waited as lightning struck; and in six days Israel was victorious. The United States had escaped the need to decide whether it should intercede.

In addition to these varied foreign commitments, all of which involved extensive military expenditures, the United States had been engaged in a highly successful and enormously costly space program. "Gemini" became a household word as millions watched the two-man Gemini VII stay aloft thirteen days, eight hours, and thirty-five minutes. By the end of the Gemini series, the total United States time in space was 1,944.2 man hours, and the total United States commitment in its effort to land an American on the moon was twenty billion dollars. The Apollo program was interrupted in 1967 when three astronauts were burned to death during a training session and the new three-man spacecraft had to be redesigned. But by October 1968 the program was once more functioning.

These various financial commitments deflected much-needed funds from Johnson's domestic programs, and conditions at home worsened. Events during the summer of 1967 increased the feeling of crisis. There were riots in one hundred cities, and eighty-six people died—forty-two in Detroit and twenty-six in Newark, New Jersey. The four years of black agony had resulted in 141 deaths, more than 4,000 serious injuries, and 20,000 arrests. And there were many, both black and white, who felt that the endeavor of creating a great society was a sick joke.

College campuses, beginning with the University of California at Berkeley, became centers of dissent rather than "ivory towers" of noninvolved study. Some youths turned to psychedelic drugs, agreeing with Dr. Timothy Leary that they should "Turn on, tune in, drop out." The hippy culture began to make news as

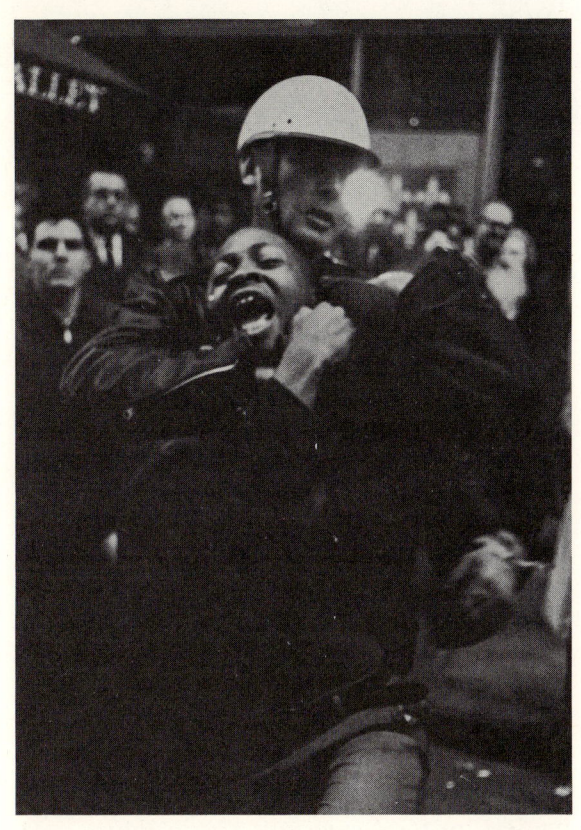

Aspects of dissent. DANNY LYON, © MAGNUM   UNITED PRESS INTERNATIONAL

the *Free Press*, a free-swinging underground newspaper devoted to attacks on the Establishment and to pronouncements of the new sexual freedom, printed its first issue in Los Angeles in 1964. Music became the voice of discontent. Bob Dylan and Joan Baez led the singers of social protest, while the Beatles and the Rolling Stones sang of other yearnings, and Aretha Franklin made "soul" music popular. The new morality and "situation ethics" were being discussed in church as well as out. Some were saying "God is dead," but the trend toward ecumenical convergence continued.

End of Johnson's Consensus—1968

The concept of the Great Society was dying as 1967 wore on, killed by competition with other priorities, by lack of measurable change, by violence, and by a "backlash" against violence. The United States seemed steeped in turmoil. College campuses became battlegrounds. Columbia University was shaken to its foundations as 148 persons were injured and 700 arrested in violent protests. Martin Luther King, who had received the Nobel prize for peace in 1964, was shot by a white escaped convict named James Earl Ray. Rioting continued, and the ghettos of Chicago, Baltimore, Detroit, Pittsburgh, Boston, and Washington, D.C., burned. Other minority groups began to agitate. The Chicanos spoke proudly of their Mexican heritage, and Cesar Chavez took on the great agricultural complex of central California to organize the grape pickers and attack DDT as dangerous to man and beast.

Due to Circumstances . . .

Politics was also a center of excitement and tragedy. The year 1968 had not even begun when the first candidate, Senator Eugene J. McCarthy of Minnesota, decided to challenge the President, a member of his own party, on the issue of withdrawing United States forces from Vietnam. To many such an act was unthinkable. Some observers said that McCarthy was not even a very good senator. Quiet, reserved, and professorial, he seemed to have little appeal to the public, but suddenly his crusade caught fire. McCarthy had a quixotic charm which appealed to youth and, more importantly, he raised the Vietnam issue at a time when more and more young people were becoming disgusted with the war and the draft. Soon, the "McCarthy Kids" became a political symbol. During 1968 they cut their hair and set out to persuade middle-aged and middle-class Americans to vote for the senator, and they succeeded—at least for a time. In the New Hampshire Democratic primary on March 12, for example, McCarthy carried forty-two per cent of the vote against Johnson. This was obviously a disaster for the President.

And then there was Senator Robert Kennedy, former Attorney General and younger brother of the martyred President. He too attracted youth, for he was himself young and committed and possessed the famous Kennedy charisma. At first he refused to run against President Johnson, even after McCarthy had opened the way. But on March 16, a few days after McCarthy's good showing in New Hampshire, Kennedy announced his candidacy and began a hectic campaign tour during which he was mobbed by admirers.

In the meantime, voters had received no word from the White House during this critical period, except that a "really, truly cease fire" was a vital first step to any Vietnamese peace talks and that taxes would have to be raised to pay for the war. In January the President also had to deal with the crisis caused when the U.S.S. *Pueblo*, a navy reconnaissance ship, was seized by North Koreans, and all eighty-three men aboard the United States vessel were held as spies for many months. Despite American protests, North Korea refused to return the *Pueblo*; but, even though there was a mobilization of some reserves in the United States, further hostilities were avoided. Then came the Tet (lunar New Year) offensive in Vietnam when the enemy attacked Saigon and occupied the city stronghold of Hue during February. American casualties increased threefold, making a total of more than 20,000 deaths in that war. Each of these developments, of course, had a negative effect on Johnson's prospects for reelection.

In a nationally televised speech on March 31, the President announced a unilateral plan to de-escalate the war and to stop the bombing of North Vietnam. But, as dramatic as this proposal was, it was topped by his disclosure that "I shall not seek, and I will not accept, the nomination of my party for president." Johnson explained that he would be a more effective peacemaker if he were not fighting for his political life and that the party's position was not secure, even though there were two strong contenders for the Democratic nomination.

As the preconvention campaign continued, first Kennedy, and then McCarthy, seemed to be the front-runner. McCarthy carried Oregon, and then Kennedy took California on June 5. This was a great victory for Kennedy, and his future never looked brighter as he left the celebration of his achievement at a hotel in Los Angeles. Then, as he crossed through a kitchen hallway, eight shots rang out. Next day, Robert Kennedy, aged forty-two, was dead, killed by a Jordanian who resented what he imagined was Kennedy's support for Israel. Once again, the nation was grieved by the assassination of a Kennedy, and many citizens were losing faith in a society in which such a shocking event could be repeated, especially so soon after the murder of Martin Luther King.

McCarthy continued to campaign, but he seemed tired and dispirited. By the time Democrats gathered for their national convention in

American soldiers and Vietnamese villagers, 1968.   P. J. GRIFFITHS, © MAGNUM

Chicago, it was evident that the party leaders had decided to back Vice President Hubert H. Humphrey for the nomination. This choice was not a surprise, but the bitterness and violence of dissent which occurred were unexpected. These feelings were climaxed by fighting in the streets between police and young antiwar groups of all persuasions. Although Humphrey was named as the candidate, the party itself had been torn apart before the eyes of television viewers. The shocking developments in Chicago surely made Humphrey's task more difficult.

On the other hand, the Republicans had had a smooth and well-managed convention in Miami two weeks earlier. Richard Nixon was the obvious candidate, having defeated George Romney in the New Hampshire primary and having achieved impressive successes in his political come-back. At the last minute, Nelson Rockefeller, the Governor of New York, and Ronald Reagan, the Governor of California, made abortive efforts to stop the drive for Nixon's nomination, but they were too late.

Despite all the many events that occurred, however, the most unusual political happening of 1968 was the rise of a third force, the American Independent party. George C. Wallace, former Governor of Alabama, had been campaigning widely and believed the time was ripe to organize those segments of American society opposed to the violent changes that had been shaking the country. Wallace was a "hawk" on Vietnam, a critic of the intellectual liberals who, he charged, were encouraging violence, a de-

Due to Circumstances . . .

fender of Southern traditions in racial matters, and a supporter of "law and order." He organized his campaign on appeals to voters who held the same values.

Although Nixon did not ever seem to excite tremendous enthusiasm in the ensuing campaign, the polls predicted his election from the beginning. Humphrey, limited by his loyalty to Johnson's policies in Southeast Asia, seemed to vacillate between the choice of immediate withdrawal and gradual disengagement in Vietnam. Wallace seemed to have much support at first, but gradually the tide turned. Humphrey gained in popularity as the weeks passed, but he was never able to overcome his slow start. "Middle America" had spoken, although the election was extremely close. Nixon received 31,770,237 votes, Humphrey 31,270,533 votes, and Wallace 9,906,141 votes. What effect the "third man" in the race had is unclear. Nevertheless, Richard Nixon was elected with 43.4 per cent of the votes to 42.7 per cent for Humphrey and 13.5 per cent for Wallace.

"NIXON'S THE ONE"

Richard Milhous Nixon was inaugurated on January 20, 1969, as the thirty-seventh President of a nation which seemed to many of its citizens to be on the verge of collapse. His election was disparaged by many as a fluke, a meaningless victory, since his plurality over his opponents was minute. Yet the election of Nixon marked the end of the New Deal coalition and gave evidence of support for the Republican party that had been lacking since Eisenhower's time. Americans had cast sixty-one per cent of their votes for the Democratic candidate in 1964; yet in 1968 they cast fifty-seven per cent of their votes against the party's choice.

The Democratic party lost in 1968 in part because the problems of social engineering, of urbanism, and of black discontent were not being solved. This is not to say that the dissenting voters could agree on any solution. Rather there was a feeling among the predominantly white middle and working classes that the time had come for them to be heard, that those who were doing all the "right things" and obeying the law were not being rewarded, that, in short, "the right things don't seem to be paying off." This dissatisfaction of middle America evolved in spite of continuing prosperity and increasing affluence.

Richard Nixon's main appeal to the electorate seemed to be his "normalcy"—to borrow a term from the 1920's. He adhered to the old values and virtues which had come under increasing attack during the 1960's. He gave "average" Americans hope that the worst was over, that solutions could be found for their festering ills, and that careful, rational approaches to these problems could be more successful than shouting or phrase making.

But Nixon came into office without legislative support, for the Republicans did not gain a majority in the Ninety-first Congress; at midterm, to the President's disadvantage, the 1970 elections did not shift the partisan balance in his favor. Indeed, in that year the relations between the Senate and the President became increasingly strained because little or no legislation was passed on the big issues.

Foreign Affairs

Vietnam and More Vietnams? In 1969 a vast number of citizens became "doves" on the issue of Vietnam. Americans had become committed in Southeast Asia to deter attacks by Communist China or North Vietnam, or to prevent or limit "wars of national liberation" by local guerrillas. In the 1960's many citizens had supported the "domino theory" then held by American leaders —that a chain reaction of Communist revolts in neighboring nations would follow a Communist victory or a United States military withdrawal. But this position had fallen into disfavor with most Americans by 1969 as the scope of the war became obvious. By the end of 1970 over 53,000 servicemen had died and the cost of the war had exceeded that of World War II. Nixon, having

426   *Time of Trial, Time of Hope*

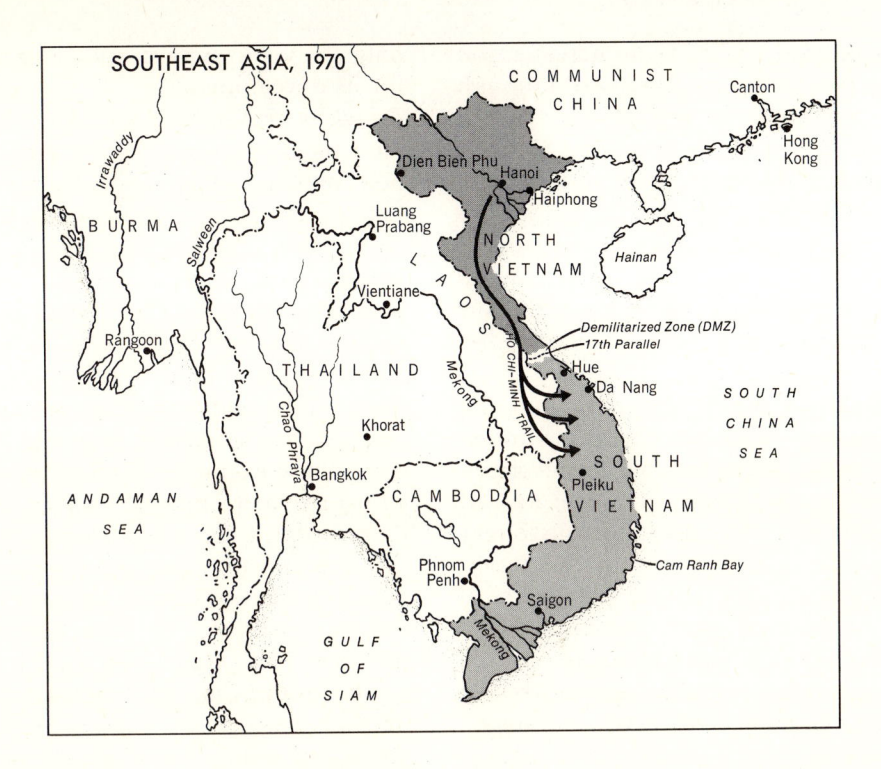

promised to find a way to bring peace or at least to "Vietnamize" the war and bring home American troops, began ordering troop withdrawals during the summer of 1969; and during 1970 well over 140,000 G.I.'s were removed from Vietnam. The administration continued to talk of plans that would "virtually eliminate" American involvement by 1972 (leaving fewer than 40,000 "advisers").

To many Americans Nixon's schedule was much too slow; yet, to others, it was dangerously rapid. Citizens representing many different segments of society demonstrated against the war on the "Moratorium" days during October and November 1969. Thousands paraded, read lists of war dead, and appealed for immediate withdrawal. But the effect of these actions was limited, and plans for continued protest seemed to falter. Apparently rejecting the domino theory, however, the Senate voted in late 1969 to prevent the presence of American troops in Laos and Cambodia. It then passed a foreign aid bill only after funds for the Vietnamization program were guaranteed. Further, there was mounting public conviction that involvement in Vietnam had been a grave error and that additional difficulties—even economic disaster for the nation—would follow unless the war could be ended soon. Yet in the spring of 1970 President Nixon ordered American forces to move against North Vietnamese–held areas in Cambodia. The operation was a military success but a domestic disaster, for most Americans disapproved of this expansion of the war. After a month the United States forces were removed, and Congress later passed legislation preventing their return.

Arab-Israeli Tinderbox? The crackling tension in the Middle East continued. Since the June War in 1967, shots were exchanged nearly every day, and almost every day one side or the other rejected some attempt at peacemaking. In late 1969 the United States announced a peace proposal that suggested Israeli evacuation of certain territories captured in 1967, including the west bank of the Jordan; Israel promptly rejected the plan. Diplomatic tension between the two countries increased although the Arabs continued to regard the United States as their principal foe. In August both the United Arab Republic and Israel accepted the terms of a cease-fire proposed by Nixon. Although the sudden death seven weeks later of Egyptian President Gamal Abdel Nasser caused concern, both combatants later extended the cease-fire; even so, real peace remained remote.

Thaws in the Cold War? Although both the United States and the Soviet Union continued to dominate world affairs and still found themselves adversaries in a cold war, there was increasing feeling that this conflict was no longer all important. Contacts between the two superpowers continued, with a real possibility of some kind of bilateral arms limitation. Time seemed to have proved that having atomic weapons no longer meant world domination, but an equal ability to destroy could create a tenuous—and tense—peace.

As these developments occurred, other nations became less impressed with the need to choose sides in the cold war. De Gaulle's defeat in the French elections of 1969 opened the possibility of greater cooperation in the European community, including the participation of Great Britain. The West Germans grew more powerful because of their booming economy, and throughout Europe fear of the Soviets seemed to be diminishing, although it was revived by Russia's crushing of Czech liberalism in 1968. In Asia, Japan became the world's third most important economic giant. The Chinese Communists continued to pursue a path of isolation, although an increasing number of nations were voicing support for the inclusion of Red China in the United Nations.

Despite the lessening of some tensions, however, Americans continued to be concerned about the need for military preparedness. For example, the 1969 military appropriations bill passed the House 330 to 33, and opponents of the antiballistic missile system could muster only 25 votes against spending $359,500,000 for its development.

Tribalism or New Nations? After World War II the United States committed itself to aiding the new nations which rose from the ashes of nineteenth-century empires, but the number of these new states continued to grow even though most of the imperial structures have long been gone. Local civil wars multiplied, and nations formed from colonial lands divided and subdivided until they became almost tribal units. This trend toward localism was not limited to emerging nations, although African states offer many examples. India was also confronted with violent outbreaks within its boundaries that reflected the same trend, and there was grave pressure to give more local autonomy to culture groups within technologically advanced societies. Such was the case with the Scots and Welsh in Britain and with the French-speaking population in Canada. Even in the more homogeneous nations of Latin America and Asia, American policy faced major dilemmas. Rich and powerful citizens, often with American support, continued to ignore the suffering of the growing numbers of poor people. And yet there seemed to be no way for American aid to go directly to those groups in dire need. Their discontent and unrest seemed likely to continue for years to come, along with the graffiti that appeared on walls clearly denouncing Yankee interference. Perhaps significantly, in Chile Salvador Allende was sworn in as president, the first Marxist to be elected to such high office in open balloting. After twenty-five years of qualified success at best, Americans seemed by 1970 to be losing interest in aiding nations where little progress was evident.

Americans, too, became increasingly concerned with the impact of foreign involvement on problems at home. Maintaining 3,500,000 men under arms required a vast expenditure of doubtful value in a world where the chances of American ground warfare in the future were less likely. Many observers feared that the American economy could not stand another major military buildup unless the government imposed special controls or massive taxes on the nation.

Domestic versus Foreign Affairs. During the post-World War era, each president had to face the dilemma of financing foreign security while at the same time attempting to pay for the solutions to major domestic problems. Johnson promised to do both, but eventually was able to accomplish neither. By the end of his second year in office, Nixon had made no major changes in policy but had tried to "lower the profile" of the United States in both domestic and foreign affairs. He had attempted to reduce the number of American commitments abroad without actually abandoning any specific obligations. His domestic programs, however, had demonstrated neither progress nor innovation, aside from a bold proposal for an overhaul of the welfare system that would double the number of those eligible—and this bill failed to achieve congressional approval. The people themselves were deeply divided over national goals, and as the conflict in Vietnam dragged on, the polarization of opinion deepened. Drafting young men to fight in a war that many considered to be illegal and immoral continued to have an impact on national morale and on individual lives. The massacre at My Lai, for which American G.I.'s were put on trial, was a shocking example of the damage war can do to all participants. It was hoped that the lottery system, initiated in early 1970, would provide a more equitable system of selecting draftees, but the larger problem remained. Expectations of a clear-cut victory were largely abandoned. Although some military men claimed that they were betrayed by civilians inside or outside of the government, most accepted withdrawal as the goal representing the least possible expense to American lives and prestige. On the other hand, certain citizens felt that they had been led into a catastrophic war by what they referred to, in President Eisenhower's phrase, as "the military-industrial complex." Judgments and interpretations of the country's involvement in Vietnam varied widely, but there was no doubt that the division of opinion over Vietnam caused great strains in the fabric of American society. A minor irritation—a modest war seemingly entered into for good, liberal, patriotic reasons—had become a cancer, eating at the nation's soul.

"To Heal a Nation"

Yet the shouting over Vietnam did little more than underscore vast areas of discontent at home. The nation faced the need to diagnose the ills of a pluralistic society before any solutions could be found, if indeed solutions were still possible. Could anyone deal effectively with the passions of the young, the black, or that "forgotten American," the white, lower-middle-class laborer?

The Romantic Young. The youth of the 1960's became increasingly visible as the decade passed. About forty million American were between fourteen and twenty-four, a figure forty-seven per cent above that for 1960. There were so many young people that hereafter they would dominate the nation's population.

Most of those youth who supported Senator Eugene McCarthy or Robert Kennedy did not register their disenchantment with Democratic candidate Humphrey by voting for Nixon. Some, dismayed by the assassination of the Kennedys and Martin Luther King and bitterly disappointed by the defeat of McCarthy, now joined with other young people who, in the tradition of the Romantics of the nineteenth century, turned away from anything they considered to be part of the Establishment, rejecting the "ticky-tacky" values they found in their "hypocritical" parents' world. Some built their own self-image on the shock values of drugs, bizarre dress, obscenity, promiscuity, and violence. Others championed ecological reform or civil liberties, including expanded students' rights, and worked in the Peace Corps, Vista, or other projects to aid the less fortunate. The divergent groups converged in attempting to

© 1968 JULES FEIFFER. REPRINTED BY PERMISSION OF PUBLISHERS-HALL SYNDICATE

live outside the materialistic system which they believed had dehumanized and befouled all it touched. Following the pattern which had turned campuses from Berkeley to Columbia into battlefields, militant students succeeded in temporarily shutting down major universities. Some progress was made in sharing decision making with students; but, in the main, the institution of the university continued as it had in the past, even if police had to enforce the status quo.

In the spring of 1970 a confrontation at Kent State University in Ohio between students aroused by the expansion of the Indochina war into Cambodia and National Guardsmen resulted in sudden death for four students and a time of agony for the nation. Many predicted that chaos would follow, but students vowed instead to work for change within the system. Planned massive involvement in the November elections did not materialize, however. A time of "privatism" seemed to have begun, even though for the first time eighteen-year-olds gained, later in the year, the right to vote in national elections.

Changing Life Styles. Led by youth, many other Americans also found themselves unsure about their values and morals by the early 1970's. Nixon's clear, ringing appeals to the old virtues fell on many deaf ears, although there was certainly a majority of the nation that still accepted them. The "pop" culture, however, continued to draw a large and enthusiastic following. The Beatles were still able to enlist loyalty, even among older citizens, although other more earthy, obvious musical styles found increasing favor. Pop art, which satirized the blatantly materialistic nature of our culture, continued to survive. Op art, minimal sculpture, and other fleeting art movements of the 1960's were elevated virtually to the status of "old masters" as some new artists carved giant "earthworks" on the desert or offered "concepts" of works in place of the works them-

430 *Time of Trial, Time of Hope*

selves. Marshall McLuhan became the prophet of communication above and beyond the written word, claiming that "the medium is the message." The musical *Hair,* described as a tribal rock happening, became a phenomenal success at home and abroad, and was one of the first productions to feature nudity on stage, a device that soon became almost commonplace on stage and screen, whatever the initial shock value.

For large numbers of Americans feelings about sexual morality, about violence, and about religious faith became increasingly ambivalent. With contraceptive pills and devices in wide use, old taboos about pre- and extra-marital sex trembled, and the Women's Lib movement added another dimension of protest. Frankness in the treatment of sex and the extent of public interest were evidenced by the enormous popularity of such books as *Portnoy's Complaint, The Sensuous Woman,* and *Everything You Always Wanted to Know About Sex But Were Too Afraid to Ask.* Violence seemed to become an increasing part of American life. The presentation of violence in television was condemned and efforts were made to lessen its depiction, yet bloody films like *The Wild Bunch* were popular and well reviewed. Conventional religion was going through a period of soul searching and there was much concern about social relevance, though many worried worshipers turned to the mysticism of the East and to astrology and other pseudo-scientific faiths.

The hippie life style was dying by 1970; yet it had in truth become part of a broader culture. Some people continued to drop out, to move to rural communes like those of their utopian predecessors, and to reject the work ethic, but many others of like mind remained in the traditional society, even if their appearance and concerns varied greatly from those of an earlier generation. Yet, despite the widely publicized aberrations in behavior, most Americans lived their accustomed quiet, middle-class, conservative lives—and approved of the statements of Vice President Spiro Agnew as he defended what he and they conceived of as the "old values." Many were, however, not quite so sure that they could, or even should, continue to do so.

The Spread of Dissent. More and more Americans were testing the limits of dissent in the late 1960's. Just how free was free speech? Was civil disobedience or outright violence illegal if laws were unjust or discriminatory? The question of what was legal and what was not legal was tried in the nation's courts, but even more difficult to decide was what was moral. For example, could a political leader be branded as immoral when all the facts were not, or could not be, made available? Surely, citizens had the right to judge the worthiness of any cause, but the point at which civil disobedience became justified was still extremely unclear. Some felt that subjection of law to conscience must lead to anarchy. Others held that blind acceptance of existing standards did nothing but perpetuate injustices. Advocates of the New Left continued to feel justified in deciding just what kinds of dissent were "liberating," in the phrase of their mentor, Marxist philosopher Herbert Marcuse. Naturally, they felt that their own version of truth was sacred.

Is Growth Good or Bad? With the advent of the 1970's the nation also faced frightening problems created by growth, both of the economy and of population. In 1969 a President publicly declared for the first time that overpopulation posed a threat to the nation. In the same year the first international treaty on pollution was signed; it concerned safety requirements to prevent leakage of oil tankers into the world's oceans. Many other crises caused by explosive growth loomed as massive threats. Urban sprawl, smog, use of dangerous pesticides, crowded airways and airports increased the possibilities of disaster for humanity. The delicate balance of man and nature was threatened—rivers burned because of pollution, the ocean was covered with oil because of drilling seepage, and fish were declared unfit for consumption because of DDT and mercury poisoning. These blights were not only physical dangers but also threats to essential human qualities. For it was felt that man needs the serenity and beauty of nature to preserve his own humanity. Psychological research indicated that crowding turns tame animals into snarling, tearing beasts and that it might well affect the ability of human beings to live in peace and dignity.

And still inflation continued. The economy trembled under the impact of aerospace cutbacks as the war in Vietnam slackened. Yet the purchasing power of the dollar declined and the smaller war continued to cost as much as the bigger one had. Unemployment rose above the five per cent level (in some areas geared to the aerospace industry, such as the Pacific Northwest, it reached ten per cent), and those who were hit hardest were not only the usual unskilled and poor but also, and unexpectedly, the educated engineer, the forward-looking scientist, the affluent stockbroker. The dilemma of increasing national production while controlling mounting inflation remained unresolved.

The picture was not all grim, however. In 1969 men walked and worked on the moon, and the whole world watched on television. Transplants of many vital organs became almost commonplace. The Supreme Court finally ordered Southern schools to desegregate "at once." The New York Mets became World Champions after years in the cellar. Never were more persons enrolled in adult education classes. Never were more books sold, nor more concert halls built; and never had more citizens traveled through the world. Americans were better educated; and even much-maligned television helped to keep the public informed, more concerned, and more articulate than ever before.

The Acceleration of Change

The explosive changes initiated in the 1960's were worldwide, and Mr. Nixon probably could have very little influence on the nature or speed of change. But the process itself had become a constant. We all share the same fantasies about the abilities of science and technology to solve our problems, and we were all disappointed when the fast-changing society was still unable to find solutions.

Some of us were dissatisfied because the freedom from drudgery had not provided instant gratification and self-realization. For others the rapid changes in our society served to emphasize the fact that minorities suffer deprivation in the midst of plenty. With the threshold of violence lowered, reaction to poverty in a society in which affluence had become commonplace could be hysteria. There was even talk of revolution, although this too could be a fantasy, for revolutionary youths and blacks mouthed slogans of leaders who did not want to increase the power of a state machine — and taking over that power is usually the goal of revolution.

There *was* a revolution in education, based on the notion that everyone must go to school and should be able to learn anything if he is taught properly. Parents joined the chorus of complainers and somehow expected both public schools and colleges to "provide all the blessings for which they used to pray to God." At any rate, more and more Americans were spending more time in school, whatever its worth. And for most Americans there remained at the beginning of the decade of the 1970's the hope that somehow we as a nation would find satisfaction and freedom.

Even so, change had undermined the more obvious goals of the past. The need to earn a living had receded as the years of protection and support of young people were extended. With this freedom from pressure came increasing emphasis on hedonism—the pursuit of pleasure that rises when no other goals seem worth pursuing. Finally, there was boredom, the most frightening result of all, for when human beings are bored they often create their own excitement through violence, anarchy, or the politics of hysteria.

Time of Trial, Time of Hope

In midmorning motorists inched through the Stygian haze with smarting eyes and headlights ablaze.   THE NEW YORK TIMES

Yet eventually, a social organism is unable to tolerate too much change too fast. A suppressive reaction may set in, for anarchy is the greatest tyranny. Law and order can become, not a code phrase for racism but a necessity for social survival. As the nation approached its two-hundredth anniversary, most Americans clung to the hope that the freedoms we cherish would not be destroyed by some who are too close to them to recognize their real worth.

SUGGESTED READINGS

*American Friends Service Committee, *Peace in Vietnam* (1966).
*Bell, D., ed., *The Radical Right* (1963).
Bell, J., *Mr. Conservative: Barry Goldwater* (1963).
Beloff, M., *The United States and the Unity of Europe* (1963).
Black, C. E., *The Dynamics of Modernization* (1967).
Burns, J. M., *The Deadlock of Democracy: Four Party Politics in America* (1963).

*Campbell, J. C., *Defense of the Middle East* (1960).
*Draper, T., *Castro's Revolution: Myths and Realities* (1962).
Faber, H., ed., *The Road to the White House* (1965).
Fall, B. B., *The Two Viet-Nams* (1963).
*Gardner, J. W., ed., *To Turn the Tide* (1962).
Geyelin, P., *Lyndon B. Johnson and the World* (1966).
Gordon, L., *A New Deal for Latin America: The Alliance for Progress* (1963).
*Gossett, T. F., *Race: The History of an Idea in America* (1963).
Heilbroner, R. L., *The Great Ascent: The Struggle for Economic Development* (1963).
Heller, W. W., *New Dimensions of Political Economy* (1966).
Herter, A., *Toward an Atlantic Community* (1963).
Hilsman, R. and R. C. Goods, eds., *Foreign Policy in the Sixtires* (1965).
Humphrey, H., *The War on Poverty* (1964).
Lane, M., *Rush to Judgment* (1966).
*Lewis, A., *Gideon's Trumpet* (1964).
Lorenz, K., *On Aggression* (1966).
*McLuhan, M., *Understanding the Media* (1964).
Manchester, W., *Death of a President* (1967).
Meyer, K. C. and T. Szulc, *The Cuban Invasion* (1962).
Novak, R. D., *The Agony of the G.O.P., 1964* (1965).
Novak, R. D. and R. Evans, *Lyndon B. Johnson, the Exercise of Power* (1966).
Pettigrew, T. F., *A Profile of the Negro American* (1964).
Platt, J. R., *The Step to Man* (1966).
Rosencranz, R. N., ed., *The Dispersion of Nuclear Weapons* (1964).
*Rostow, W. W., *The United States in the World Arena* (1960).
Sagan, C., *Intelligent Life in the Universe* (1966).
Schelling, T. C., *Arms and Influence* (1966).
Schlesinger, A. M., Jr., *A Thousand Days, John F. Kennedy in the White House* (1965).
Schwarz, U., *American Strategy: A New Perspective, the Growth of Politico Military Thinking in the United States* (1966).
Shaplen, R., *The Lost Revolution* (1965).
Silberman, C. E., *Crisis in Black and White* (1964).
Silver, J. W., *Mississippi: The Closed Society* (1964).
Stillman, E. and W. Pfaff, *Power and Impotence, the Failure of America's Foreign Policy* (1966).
White, W. S., *The Professional: Lyndon B. Johnson* (1964).

THE DECLARATION OF INDEPENDENCE

When, in the course of human events, it becomes necessary for one people to dissolve the political bands which have connected them with another, and to assume, among the powers of the earth, the separate and equal station to which the laws of nature and of nature's God entitle them, a decent respect to the opinions of mankind requires that they should declare the causes which impel them to the separation.

We hold these truths to be self-evident, that all men are created equal; that they are endowed by their Creator with certain unalienable rights; that among these, are life, liberty, and the pursuit of happiness. That, to secure these rights, governments are instituted among men, deriving their just powers from the consent of the governed; that, whenever any form of government becomes destructive of these ends, it is the right of the people to alter or to abolish it, and to institute a new government, laying its foundation on such principles, and organizing its powers in such form, as to them shall seem most likely to effect their safety and happiness. Prudence, indeed, will dictate that governments long established, should not be changed for light and transient causes; and, accordingly, all experience hath shown, that mankind are more disposed to suffer, while evils are sufferable, than to right themselves by abolishing the forms to which they are accustomed. But, when a long train of abuses and usurpations, pursuing invariably the same object, evinces a design to reduce them under absolute despotism, it is their right, it is their duty, to throw off such government and to provide new guards for their future security. Such has been the patient sufferance of these colonies, and such is now the necessity which constrains them to alter their former systems of government. The history of the present King of Great Britain is a history of repeated injuries and usurpations, all having, in direct object, the establishment of an absolute tyranny over these States. To prove this, let facts be submitted to a candid world:—

He has refused his assent to laws the most wholesome and necessary for the public good.

He has forbidden his governors to pass laws of immediate and pressing importance, unless suspended in their operation till his assent should be obtained; and, when so suspended, he has utterly neglected to attend to them.

He has refused to pass other laws for the accommodation of large districts of people, unless those people would relinquish the right of representation in the legislature; a right inestimable to them, and formidable to tyrants only.

He has called together legislative bodies at places unusual, uncomfortable, and distant from the depository of their public records, for the sole purpose of fatiguing them into compliance with his measures.

He has dissolved representative houses repeatedly for opposing, with manly firmness, his invasions on the rights of the people.

He has refused, for a long time after such dissolutions, to cause others to be elected, whereby the legislative powers, incapable of annihilation, have returned to the people at large for their exercise; the state remaining, in the meantime, exposed to all the danger of invasion from without, and convulsions within.

He has endeavored to prevent the population of these States; for that purpose, obstructing the laws for naturalization of foreigners; refusing to pass others to encourage their migration hither, and raising the conditions of new appropriations of lands.

He has obstructed the administration of justice, by refusing his assent to laws for establishing judiciary powers.

He has made judges dependent on his will alone, for the tenure of their offices, and the amount and payment of their salaries.

He has erected a multitude of new offices, and sent hither swarms of officers to harass out people, and eat out their substance.

He has kept among us, in time of peace, standing armies, without the consent of our legislatures.

He has affected to render the military independent of, and superior to, the civil power.

He has combined, with others, to subject us to a jurisdiction foreign to our Constitution, and unacknowledged by our laws; giving his assent to their acts of pretended legislation:

For quartering large bodies of armed troops among us:

For protecting them by a mock trial, from punishment, for any murders which they should commit on the inhabitants of these States:

For cutting off our trade with all parts of the world:

For imposing taxes on us without our consent:

For depriving us, in many cases, of the benefit of trial by jury:

For transporting us beyond seas to be tried for pretended offences:

For abolishing the free system of English laws in a neighboring province, establishing therein an arbitrary government, and enlarging its boundaries, so as to render it at once an example and fit instrument for introducing the same absolute rule into these colonies:

For taking away our charters, abolishing our most valuable laws, and altering, fundamentally, the powers of our governments:

For suspending our own legislatures, and declaring themselves invested with power to legislate for us in all cases whatsoever.

He has abdicated government here, by declaring us out of his protection, and waging war against us.

He has plundered our seas, ravaged our coasts, burnt our towns, and destroyed the lives of our people.

He is, at this time, transporting large armies of foreign mercenaries to complete the works of death, desolation, and tyranny, already begun, with circumstances of cruelty and perfidy scarcely paralleled in the most barbarous ages, and totally unworthy the head of a civilized nation.

He has constrained our fellow citizens, taken captive on the high seas, to bear arms against their country, to become the executioners of their friends, and brethren, or to fall themselves by their hands.

He has excited domestic insurrections amongst us, and has endeavored to bring on the inhabitants of our frontiers, the merciless Indian savages, whose known rule of warfare is an undistinguished destruction of all ages, sexes, and conditions.

In every stage of these oppressions, we have petitioned for redress, in the most humble terms; our repeated petitions have been answered only by repeated injury. A prince, whose character is thus marked by every act which may define a tyrant, is unfit to be the ruler of a free people.

Nor have we been wanting in attention to our British brethren. We have warned them, from time to time, of attempts made by their legislature to extend an unwarrantable jurisdiction over us. We have reminded them of the circumstances of our emigration and settlement here. We have appealed to their native justice and magnanimity, and we have conjured them, by the ties of our common kindred, to disavow these usurpations, which would inevitably interrupt our connections and correspondence. They, too, have been deaf to the voice of justice and consanguinity. We must, therefore, acquiesce in the necessity which denounces our separation, and hold them, as we hold the rest of mankind, enemies in war, in peace, friends.

We, therefore, the representatives of the United States of America, in general Congress assembled, appealing to the Supreme Judge of the world for the rectitude of our intentions, do, in the name, and by the authority of the good people of these colonies, solemnly publish and declare, that these united colonies are, and of right ought to be, free and independent states: that they are absolved from all allegiance to the British Crown, and that all political connection between them and the state of Great Britain is, and ought to be, totally dissolved; and that, as free and independent states, they have full power to levy war, conclude peace, contract alliances, establish commerce, and to do all other acts and things which independent states may of right do. And, for the support of this declaration, with a firm reliance on the protection of Divine Providence, we mutually pledge to each other our lives, our fortunes, and our sacred honor.

THE CONSTITUTION OF THE UNITED STATES OF AMERICA

We the people of the United States, in order to form a more perfect union, establish justice, insure domestic tranquillity, provide for the common defense, promote the general welfare, and secure the blessings of liberty to ourselves and our posterity, do ordain and establish this Constitution for the United States of America.

ARTICLE I

Section 1

All legislative powers herein granted shall be vested in a Congress of the United States, which shall consist of a Senate and House of Representatives.

Section 2

1. The House of Representatives shall be composed of members chosen every second year by the people of the several States, and the electors in each State shall have the qualifications requisite for electors of the most numerous branch of the State legislature.

2. No person shall be a representative who shall not have attained to the age of twenty-five years, and been seven years a citizen of the United States, and who shall not, when elected, be an inhabitant of that State in which he shall be chosen.

3. Representatives and direct taxes* shall be apportioned among the several States which may be included within this Union, according to their respective numbers, which shall be determined by adding to the whole number of free persons, including those bound to service for a term of years, and excluding Indians not taxed, three fifths of all other persons.† The actual enumeration shall be made within three years after the first meeting of the Congress of the United States, and within every subsequent term of ten years, in such manner as they shall by law direct. The number of representatives shall not exceed one for every thirty thousand, but each State shall have at least one representative; and until such enumeration shall be made, the State of New Hampshire shall be entitled to choose three, Massachusetts eight, Rhode Island and Providence Plantations one, Connecticut five, New York six, New Jersey four, Pennsylvania eight, Delaware one, Maryland six, Virginia ten, North Carolina five, South Carolina five, and Georgia three.

4. When vacancies happen in the representation from any State, the executive authority thereof shall issue writs of election to fill such vacancies.

5. The House of Representatives shall choose their speaker and other officers; and shall have the sole power of impeachment.

Section 3

1. The Senate of the United States shall be composed of two senators from each State, chosen by the legislature thereof,* for six years; and each senator shall have one vote.

2. Immediately after they shall be assembled in consequence of the first election, they shall be divided as equally as may be into three classes. The seats of the senators of the first class shall be vacated at the expiration of the second year, of the second class at the expiration of the fourth year, and of the third class at the expiration of the sixth year, so that one third may be chosen every second year; and if vacancies happen by resignation, or otherwise, during the recess of the legislature of any State, the executive thereof may make temporary appointments until the next meeting of the legislature, which shall then fill such vacancies.*

3. No person shall be a senator who shall not have attained to the age of thirty years, and been nine years a citizen of the United States, and who

---

*Revised by the Sixteenth Amendment.
†"Other persons" refers to Negro slaves. Revised by the Fourteenth Amendment, Section 2.

*Revised by the Seventeenth Amendment.

shall not, when elected, be an inhabitant of that State for which he shall be chosen.

4. The Vice President of the United States shall be President of the Senate, but shall have no vote, unless they be equally divided.

5. The Senate shall choose their other officers and also a president pro tempore, in the absence of the Vice President, or when he shall exercise the office of the President of the United States.

6. The Senate shall have the sole power to try all impeachments. When sitting for that purpose, they shall be on oath or affirmation. When the President of the United States is tried, the chief justice shall preside: and no person shall be convicted without the concurrence of two thirds of the members present.

7. Judgment in cases of impeachment shall not extend further than to removal from office, and disqualification to hold and enjoy any office of honor, trust or profit under the United States: but the party convicted shall nevertheless be liable and subject to indictment, trial, judgment and punishment, according to law.

Section 4

1. The times, places, and manner of holding elections for senators and representatives, shall be prescribed in each State by the legislature thereof; but the Congress may at any time by law make or alter such regulations, except as to the places of choosing senators.

2. The Congress shall assemble at least once in every year, and such meeting shall be on the first Monday in December, unless they shall by law appoint a different day.*

Section 5

1. Each House shall be the judge of the elections, returns and qualifications of its own members, and a majority of each shall constitute a quorum to do business; but a smaller number may adjourn from day to day, and may be authorized to compel the attendance of absent members, in such manner, and under such penalties as each House may provide.

2. Each House may determine the rules of its proceedings, punish its members for disorderly behavior, and, with the concurrence of two thirds, expel a member.

3. Each House shall keep a journal of its proceedings, and from time to time publish the same, excepting such parts as may in their judgment require secrecy; and the yeas and nays of the members of either House on any question shall, at the desire of one fifth of those present, be entered on the journal.

4. Neither House, during the session of Congress, shall, without the consent of the other, adjourn for more than three days, nor to any other place than that in which the two Houses shall be sitting.

Section 6

1. The senators and representatives shall receive a compensation for their services, to be ascertained by law, and paid out of the Treasury of the United States. They shall in all cases, except treason, felony, and breach of the peace, be privileged from arrest during their attendance at the session of their respective Houses, and in going to and returning from the same; and for any speech or debate in either House, they shall not be questioned in any other place.

2. No senator or representative shall, during the time for which he was elected, be appointed to any civil office under the authority of the United States, which shall have been created, or the emoluments whereof shall have been increased during such time; and no person holding any office under the United States shall be a member of either House during his continuance in office.

Section 7

1. All bills for raising revenue shall originate in the House of Representatives; but the Senate may propose or concur with amendments as on other bills.

2. Every bill which shall have passed the House of Representatives and the Senate, shall, before it becomes a law, be presented to the President of the United States; if he approves he shall sign it, but if not he shall return it, with his objections to that House in which it shall have originated, who shall enter the objections at large on their journal, and proceed to reconsider it. If after such reconsideration two thirds of that House shall agree to pass the bill, it shall be sent, together with the objections, to the other House, by which it shall likewise be reconsidered, and if approved by two thirds of that House, it shall become a law. But in all such cases the votes of both Houses shall be determined by yeas and nays, and the names of the persons voting for and against the bill shall be entered on the journal of

*Revised by the Twentieth Amendment, Section 2.

each House respectively. If any bill shall not be returned by the President within ten days (Sundays excepted) after it shall have been presented to him, the same shall be a law, in like manner as if he had signed it, unless the Congress by their adjournment prevent its return, in which case it shall not be a law.

3. Every order, resolution, or vote to which the concurrence of the Senate and the House of Representatives may be necessary (except on a question of adjournment) shall be presented to the President of the United States; and before the same shall take effect, shall be approved by him, or being disapproved by him, shall be passed by two thirds of the Senate and House of Representatives, according to the rules and limitations prescribed in the case of a bill.

Section 8

The Congress shall have the power

1. To lay and collect taxes, duties, imposts and excises, to pay the debts and provide for the common defense and general welfare of the United States; but all duties, imposts, and excises shall be uniform throughout the United States;

2. To borrow money on the credit of the United States;

3. To regulate commerce with foreign nations, and among the several States, and with the Indian tribes;

4. To establish a uniform rule of naturalization, and uniform laws on the subject of bankruptcies throughout the United States;

5. To coin money, regulate the value thereof, and of foreign coin, and fix the standard of weights and measures;

6. To provide for the punishment of counterfeiting the securities and current coin of the United States;

7. To establish post offices and post roads;

8. To promote the progress of science and useful arts, by securing for limited times to authors and inventors the exclusive right to their respective writings and discoveries;

9. To constitute tribunals inferior to the Supreme Court;

10. To define and punish piracies and felonies committed on the high seas, and offenses against the law of nations;

11. To declare war, grant letters of marque and reprisal, and make rules concerning captures on land and water;

12. To raise and support armies, but no appropriation of money to that use shall be for a longer term than two years;

13. To provide and maintain a navy;

14. To make rules for the government and regulation of the land and naval forces;

15. To provide for calling forth the militia to execute the laws of the Union, suppress insurrections and repel invasions;

16. To provide for organizing, arming, and disciplining the militia, and for governing such part of them as may be employed in the service of the United States, reserving to the States respectively, the appointment of the officers, and the authority of training the militia according to the discipline prescribed by Congress;

17. To exercise exclusive legislation in all cases whatsoever, over such district (not exceeding ten miles square) as may, by cession of particular States, and the acceptance of Congress, become the seat of the government of the United States, and to exercise like authority over all places purchased by the consent of the legislature of the State in which the same shall be, for the erection of forts, magazines, arsenals, dockyards, and other needful buildings; and

18. To make all laws which shall be necessary and proper for carrying into execution the foregoing powers, and all other powers vested by this Constitution in the government of the United States, or in any department or officer thereof.

Section 9

1. The migration or importation of such persons as any of the States now existing shall think proper to admit, shall not be prohibited by the Congress prior to the year one thousand eight hundred and eight, but a tax or duty may be imposed on such importation, not exceeding ten dollars for each person.

2. The privilege of the writ of habeas corpus shall not be suspended, unless when in cases of rebellion or invasion the public safety may require it.

3. No bill attainder or ex post facto law shall be passed.

4. No capitation, or other direct, tax shall be laid, unless in proportion to the census or enumeration hereinbefore directed to be taken.*

5. No tax or duty shall be laid on articles exported from any State.

6. No preference shall be given by any regulation of commerce or revenue to the ports of one State over those of another: nor shall vessels bound

*Revised by the Sixteenth Amendment.

to, or from, one State be obliged to enter, clear, or pay duties in another.

7. No money shall be drawn from the treasury, but in consequence of appropriations made by law; and a regular statement and account of the receipts and expenditures of all public money shall be published from time to time.

8. No title of nobility shall be granted by the United States: and no person holding any office of profit or trust under them, shall, without the consent of the Congress, accept of any present, emolument, office, or title, of any kind whatever, from any king, prince, or foreign State.

Section 10

1. No State shall enter into any treaty, alliance, or confederation; grant letters of marque and reprisal; coin money; emit bills of credit; make anything but gold and silver coin a tender in payment of debts; pass any bill of attainder, ex post facto law, or law impairing the obligation of contracts, or grant any title of nobility.

2. No State shall, without the consent of the Congress, lay any imposts or duties on imports or exports, except what may be absolutely necessary for executing its inspection laws: and the net produce of all duties and imposts laid by any State on imports or exports, shall be for the use of the treasury of the United States; and all such laws shall be subject to the revision and control of the Congress.

3. No State shall, without the consent of the Congress, lay any duty of tonnage, keep troops, or ships of war in time of peace, enter into any agreement or compact with another State, or with a foreign power, or engage in war, unless actually invaded, or in such imminent danger as will not admit of delay.

ARTICLE II

Section 1

1. The executive power shall be vested in a President of the United States of America. He shall hold his office during the term of four years,* and, together with the Vice President, chosen for the same term, be elected as follows:

2. Each State shall appoint, in such manner as the legislature thereof may direct, a number of electors, equal to the whole number of senators and representatives to which the State may be entitled in the Congress: but no senator or representative, or person holding an office of trust or profit under the United States, shall be appointed an elector.

The electors shall meet in their respective States, and vote by ballot for two persons, of whom one at least shall not be an inhabitant of the same State with themselves. And they shall make a list of all the persons voted for, and of the number of votes for each; which list they shall sign and certify, and transmit sealed to the seat of the government of the United States, directed to the president of the Senate. The president of the Senate shall, in the presence of the Senate and House of Representatives, open all the certificates, and the votes shall then be counted. The person having the greatest number of votes shall be the President, if such number be a majority of the whole number of electors appointed; and if there be more than one who have such majority, and have an equal number of votes, then the House of Representatives shall immediately choose by ballot one of them for President; and if no person have a majority, then from the five highest on the list the said House shall in like manner choose the President. But in choosing the President, the votes shall be taken by States, the representation from each State having one vote; a quorum for this purpose shall consist of a member or members from two thirds of the States, and a majority of all the States shall be necessary to a choice. In every case, after the choice of the President, the person having the greatest number of votes of the electors shall be the Vice President. But if there should remain two or more who have equal votes, the Senate shall choose from them by ballot the Vice President.*

3. The Congress may determine the time of choosing the electors, and the day on which they shall give their votes; which day shall be the same throughout the United States.

4. No person except a natural born citizen, or a citizen of the United States, at the time of the adoption of this Constitution, shall be eligible to the office of President; neither shall any person be eligible to that office who shall not have attained to the age of thirty-five years, and been fourteen years a resident within the United States.

---

*The Twenty-second Amendment limits a President to two terms.

*This paragraph has been superseded by the Twelfth Amendment.

5. In case of the removal of the President from office, or of his death, resignation, or inability to discharge the powers and duties of the said office, the same shall devolve on the Vice President, and the Congress may by law provide for the case of removal, death, resignation, or inability, both of the President and Vice President, declaring what officer shall then act as President, and such officer shall act accordingly, until the disability be removed, or a President shall be elected.*

6. The President shall, at stated times, receive for his services a compensation, which shall neither be increased nor diminished during the period for which he shall have been elected, and he shall not receive within that period any other emolument from the United States, or any of them.

7. Before he enter on the execution of his office, he shall take the following oath or affirmation:—"I do solemnly swear (or affirm) that I will faithfully execute the office of President of the United States, and will to the best of my ability, preserve, protect and defend the Constitution of the United States."

Section 2

1. The President shall be the commander in chief of the army and navy of the United States, and of the militia of the several States, when called into the actual service of the United States; he may require the opinion, in writing, of the principal officer in each of the executive departments, upon any subject relating to the duties of their respective offices, and he shall have power to grant reprieves and pardons for offenses against the United States, except in cases of impeachment.

2. He shall have power, by and with the advice and consent of the Senate, to make treaties, provided two thirds of the senators present concur; and he shall nominate, and by and with the advice and consent of the Senate, shall appoint ambassadors, other public ministers and consuls, judges of the Supreme Court, and all other officers of the United States, whose appointments are not herein otherwise provided for, and which shall be established by law: but the Congress may by law vest the appointment of such inferior officers, as they think proper, in the President alone, in the courts of law, or in the heads of departments.

3. The President shall have power to fill up all vacancies that may happen during the recess of the Senate, by granting commissions which shall expire at the end of their next session.

Section 3

He shall from time to time give to the Congress information of the state of the Union, and recommend to their consideration such measures as he shall judge necessary and expedient; he may, on extraordinary occasions, convene both Houses, or either of them, and in case of disagreement between them with respect to the time of adjournment, he may adjourn them to such time as he shall think proper; he shall receive ambassadors and other public ministers; he shall take care that the laws be faithfully executed, and shall commission all the officers of the United States.

Section 4

The President, Vice President, and all civil officers of the United States, shall be removed from office on impeachment for, and conviction of, treason, bribery, or other high crimes and misdemeanors.

ARTICLE III

Section 1

The judicial power of the United States shall be vested in one Supreme Court, and in such inferior courts as the Congress may from time to time ordain and establish. The judges, both of the Supreme and inferior courts, shall hold their offices during good behavior, and shall, at stated times, receive for their services, a compensation, which shall not be diminished during their continuance in office.

Section 2

1. The judicial power shall extend to all cases, in law and equity, arising under this Constitution, the laws of the United States, and treaties made, or which shall be made, under their authority;— to all cases affecting ambassadors, other public ministers and consuls;—to all cases of admiralty and maritime jurisdiction;—to controversies to which the United States shall be a party;*—to

*Affected by the Twenty-fifth Amendment.

*Revised by the Eleventh Amendment.

controversies between two or more States;—between citizens of different States;—between citizens of the same State claiming lands under grants of different States, and between a State, or the citizens thereof, and foreign States, citizens or subjects.

2. In all cases affecting ambassadors, other public ministers and consuls, and those in which a State shall be party, the Supreme Court shall have original jurisdiction. In all the other cases before mentioned, the Supreme Court shall have appellate jurisdiction, both as to law and to fact, with such exceptions, and under such regulations as the Congress shall make.

3. The trial of all crimes, except in cases of impeachment, shall be by jury; and such trial shall be held in the State where the said crimes shall have been committed; but when not committed within any State, the trial shall be at such place or places as the Congress may by law have directed.

Section 3

1. Treason against the United States shall consist only in levying war against them, or in adhering to their enemies, giving them aid and comfort. No person shall be convicted of treason unless on the testimony of two witnesses to the same overt act, or in confession in open court.

2. The Congress shall have power to declare the punishment of treason, but no attainder of treason shall work corruption of blood, or forfeiture except during the life of the person attainted.

ARTICLE IV

Section 1

Full faith and credit shall be given in each State to the public acts, records, and judicial proceedings of every other State. And the Congress may by general laws prescribe the manner in which such acts, records and proceedings shall be proved, and the effect thereof.

Section 2

1. The citizens of each State shall be entitled to all privileges and immunities of citizens in the several States.*

2. A person charged in any State with treason, felony, or other crime, who shall flee from justice, and be found in another State, shall on demand of the executive authority of the State from which he fled, be delivered up to be removed to the State having jurisdiction of the crime.

3. No person held to service or labor in one State under the laws thereof, escaping into another, shall, in consequence of any law or regulation therein, be discharged from such service or labor, but shall be delivered up on claim of the party to whom such service or labor may be due.*

Section 3

1. New States may be admitted by the Congress into this Union; but no new State shall be formed or erected within the jurisdiction of any other State; nor any State be formed by the junction of two or more States, or parts of States, without the consent of the legislatures of the States concerned as well as of the Congress.

2. The Congress shall have power to dispose of and make all needful rules and regulations respecting the territory or other property belonging to the United States; and nothing in this Constitution shall be so construed as to prejudice any claims of the United States, or of any particular State.

Section 4

The United States shall guarantee to every State in this Union a republican form of government, and shall protect each of them against invasion; and on application of the legislature, or of the executive (when the legislature cannot be convened) against domestic violence.

ARTICLE V

The Congress, whenever two thirds of both Houses shall deem it necessary, shall propose amendments to this Constitution, or, on the application of the legislatures of two thirds of the several States, shall call a convention for proposing amendments, which in either case, shall be valid to all intents and purposes, as part of this Constitution when ratified by the legislatures of three fourths of the several States, or by conventions in three fourths thereof, as the one or the other mode of ratification may be proposed by the Congress; Provided that no amendment which may be made prior to the year one thousand eight hundred and eight shall in any manner affect the first and fourth clauses in the ninth section of the first arti-

---

*Elaborated by the Fourteenth Amendment, Section 1.

*See the Thirteenth Amendment abolishing slavery.

cle; and that no State, without its consent, shall be deprived of its equal suffrage in the Senate.

ARTICLE VI

1. All debts contracted and engagements entered into, before the adoption of this Constitution, shall be as valid against the United States under this Constitution, as under the Confederation.*

2. This Constitution, and the laws of the United States which shall be made in pursuance thereof; and all treaties made, or which shall be made, under the authority of the United States, shall be the supreme law of the land; and the Judges in every State shall be bound thereby, anything in the Constitution or laws of any State to the contrary notwithstanding.

3. The senators and representatives before mentioned, and the members of the several State legislatures, and all executive and judicial officers, both of the United States and of the several States, shall be bound by oath or affirmation to support this Constitution; but no religious test shall ever be required as a qualification to any office or public trust under the United States.

ARTICLE VII

The ratification of the conventions of nine States shall be sufficient for the establishment of this Constitution between the States so ratifying the same.

Done in Convention by the unanimous consent of the States present the seventeenth day of September in the year of our Lord one thousand seven hundred and eighty-seven, and of the independence of the United States of America the twelfth. In witness whereof we have hereunto subscribed our names.

AMENDMENTS

First ten amendments submitted by Congress September 25, 1789. Ratified by three-fourths of the states December 15, 1791.

AMENDMENT I

Congress shall make no law respecting an establishment of religion, or prohibiting the free exercise thereof; or abridging the freedom of speech, or of the press; or the right of the people peaceably to assemble, and to petition the government for a redress of grievances.

AMENDMENT II

A well regulated militia, being necessary to the security of a free State, the right of the people to keep and bear arms, shall not be infringed.

AMENDMENT III

No soldier shall, in time of peace be quartered in any house, without the consent of the owner, nor in time of war, but in a manner to be prescribed by law.

AMENDMENT IV

The right of the people to be secure in their persons, houses, papers, and effects, against unreasonable searches and seizures, shall not be violated, and no warrants shall issue, but upon probable cause, supported by oath or affirmation, and particularly describing the place to be searched, and the persons or things to be seized.

AMENDMENT V

No person shall be held to answer for a capital, or otherwise infamous crime, unless on a presentment or indictment of a grand jury, except in cases arising in the land or naval forces, or in the militia, when in actual service in time of war or public danger; nor shall any person be subject for the same offense to be twice put in jeopardy of life or limb; nor shall be compelled in any criminal case to be a witness against himself, nor be deprived of life, liberty, or property, without due process of law; nor shall private property be taken for public use without just compensation.

AMENDMENT VI

In all criminal prosecutions, the accused shall enjoy the right to a speedy and public trial, by an impartial jury of the State and district wherein the crime shall have been committed, which district shall have been previously ascertained by law, and to be informed of the nature and cause of the accusation; to be confronted with the witnesses against him; to have compulsory process for obtaining witnesses in his favor, and to have the assistance of counsel for his defense.

*See the Fourteenth Amendment, Section 4, for additional provisions.

AMENDMENT VII

In suits at common law, where the value in controversy shall exceed twenty dollars, the right of trial by jury shall be preserved, and no fact tried by a jury shall be otherwise reëxamined in any court of the United States, than according to the rules of the common law.

AMENDMENT VIII

Excessive bail shall not be required, nor excessive fines imposed, nor cruel and unusual punishments inflicted.

AMENDMENT IX

The enumeration in the Constitution of certain rights shall not be construed to deny or disparage others retained by the people.

AMENDMENT X

The powers not delegated to the United States by the Constitution, nor prohibited by it to the States, are reserved to the States respectively, or to the people.

AMENDMENT XI

Submitted by Congress March 5, 1794, declared ratified January 8, 1798.

The judicial power of the United States shall not be construed to extend to any suit in law or equity, commenced or prosecuted against one of the United States by citizens of another state, or by citizens or subjects of any foreign state.

AMENDMENT XII

Submitted by Congress December 12, 1803, declared ratified September 25, 1804.

The electors shall meet in their respective States, and vote by ballot for President and Vice President, one of whom, at least, shall not be an inhabitant of the same State with themselves; they shall name in their ballots the person voted for as President, and in distinct ballots, the person voted for as Vice President, and they shall make distinct lists of all persons voted for as President and of all persons voted for as Vice President, and of the number of votes for each, which lists they shall sign and certify, and transmit sealed to the seat of the government of the United States, directed to the President of the Senate;—The President of the Senate shall, in the presence of the Senate and House of Representatives, open all the certificates and the votes shall then be counted;—The person having the greatest number of votes for President, shall be the President, if such number be a majority of the whole number of electors appointed; and if no person have such majority, then from the persons having the highest numbers not exceeding three on the list of those voted for as President, the House of Representatives shall choose immediately, by ballot the President. But in choosing the President, the votes shall be taken by States, the representation from each State having one vote; a quorum for this purpose shall consist of a member or members from two thirds of the States, and a majority of all the States shall be necessary to a choice. And if the House of Representatives shall not choose a President whenever the right of choice shall devolve upon them, before the fourth day of March next following, then the Vice President shall act as President, as in the case of the death or other constitutional disability of the President.* The person having the greatest number of votes as Vice President shall be the Vice President, if such number be a majority of the whole number of electors appointed, and if no person have a majority, then from the two highest numbers on the list, the Senate shall choose the Vice President; a quorum for the purpose shall consist of two thirds of the whole number of Senators, and a majority of the whole number shall be necessary to a choice. But no person constitutionally ineligible to the office of President shall be eligible to that of Vice President of the United States.

AMENDMENT XIII

Submitted by Congress February 1, 1865, declared ratified December 18, 1865.

Section 1

Neither slavery nor involuntary servitude, except as punishment for crime whereof the party shall have been duly convicted, shall exist within the United States, or any place subject to their jurisdiction.

Section 2

Congress shall have power to enforce this article by appropriate legislation.

*Superseded by the Twentieth Amendment, Section 3.

AMENDMENT XIV

Submitted by Congress June 16, 1866, declared ratified July 28, 1868.

Section 1

All persons born or naturalized in the United States, and subject to the jurisdiction thereof, are citizens of the United States and of the State wherein they reside. No State shall make or enforce any law which shall abridge the privileges or immunities of citizens of the United States; nor shall any State deprive any person of life, liberty, or property, without due process of law; nor deny to any person within its jurisdiction the equal protection of the laws.

Section 2

Representatives shall be apportioned among the several States according to their respective numbers, counting the whole number of persons in each State, excluding Indians not taxed. But when the right to vote at any election for the choice of electors for President and Vice President of the United States, representatives in Congress, the executive and judicial officers of a State, or the members of the legislature thereof, is denied to any of the male inhabitants of such State, being twenty-one years of age, and citizens of the United States, or in any way abridged, except for participation in rebellion, or other crime, the basis of representation therein shall be reduced in the proportion which the number of such male citizens shall bear to the whole number of male citizens twenty-one years of age in such State.

Section 3

No person shall be a senator or representative in Congress, or elector of President and Vice President, or hold any office, civil or military, under the United States, or under any State, who having previously taken an oath, as a member of Congress, or as an officer of the United States, or as a member of any State legislature, or as an executive or judicial officer of any State, to support the Constitution of the United States, shall have engaged in insurrection or rebellion against the same, or given aid or comfort to the enemies thereof. But Congress may by a vote of two thirds of each House, remove such disability.

Section 4

The validity of the public debt of the United States, authorized by law, including debts incurred for payment of pensions and bounties for services in suppressing insurrection or rebellion, shall not be questioned. But neither the United States nor any State shall assume or pay any debt or obligation incurred in aid of insurrection or rebellion against the United States, or any claim for the loss of emancipation of any slave; but all such debts, obligations, and claims shall be held illegal and void.

Section 5

The Congress shall have power to enforce by appropriate legislation, the provisions of this article.

AMENDMENT XV

Submitted by Congress February 27, 1869, declared ratified March 30, 1870.

Section 1

The right of citizens of the United States to vote shall not be denied or abridged by the United States or by any State on account of race, color, or previous condition of servitude.

Section 2

The Congress shall have power to enforce this article by appropriate legislation.

AMENDMENT XVI

Submitted by Congress July 12, 1909, declared ratified February 25, 1913.

The Congress shall have power to lay and collect taxes on incomes, from whatever source derived, without apportionment among the several States, and without regard to any census or enumeration.

AMENDMENT XVII

Submitted by Congress May 16, 1912, declared ratified May 31, 1913.

The Senate of the United States shall be composed of two senators from each state elected by the people thereof, for six years; and each senator shall have one vote. The electors in each State shall have the qualifications requisite for electors of the most numerous branch of the State legislature.

When vacancies happen in the representation of any State in the Senate, the executive authority of such State shall issue writs of election to fill such vacancies: *Provided*, That the legislature of any State may empower the executive thereof to make temporary appointments until the people fill the vacancies by election as the legislature may direct.

This amendment shall not be so construed as to affect the election or term of any senator chosen before it becomes valid as part of the Constitution.

AMENDMENT XVIII*

Submitted by Congress December 18, 1917, declared ratified January 29, 1919.

After one year from the ratification of this article, the manufacture, sale, or transportation of intoxicating liquors within, the importation thereof into, or the exportation thereof from the United States and all territory subject to the jurisdiction thereof for beverage purposes is hereby prohibited.

The Congress and the several States shall have concurrent power to enforce this article by appropriate legislation.

This article shall be inoperative unless it shall have been ratified as an amendment to the Constitution by the legislatures of the several States, as provided in the Constitution, within seven years from the date of the submission hereof to the states by Congress.

AMENDMENT XIX

Submitted by Congress June 5, 1919, declared ratified August 26, 1920.

The right of citizens of the United States to vote shall not be denied or abridged by the United States or by any State on account of sex.

The Congress shall have power by appropriate legislation to enforce the provisions of this article.

AMENDMENT XX

Submitted by Congress March 3, 1932, declared ratified February 6, 1933.

Section 1

The terms of the President and Vice President shall end at noon on the 20th day of January, and the terms of Senators and Representatives at noon on the 3d day of January, of the years in which such terms would have ended if this article had not been ratified; and the terms of their successors shall then begin.

Section 2

The Congress shall assemble at least once in every year, and such meeting shall begin at noon on the 3d day of January, unless they shall by law appoint a different day.

Section 3

If, at the time fixed for the beginning of the term of the President, the President-elect shall have died, the Vice President-elect shall become President. If a President shall not have been chosen before the time fixed for the beginning of his term, or if the President-elect shall have failed to qualify, then the Vice President-elect shall act as President until a President shall have qualified; and the Congress may by law provide for the case wherein neither a President-elect nor a Vice President-elect shall have qualified, declaring who shall then act as President, or the manner in which one who is to act shall be selected, and such person shall act accordingly until a President or Vice President shall have qualified.

Section 4

The Congress may by law provide for the case of the death of any of the persons from whom the House of Representatives may choose a President whenever the right of choice shall have devolved upon them, and for the case of the death of any of the persons from whom the Senate may choose a Vice President whenever the right of choice shall have devolved upon them.

Section 5

Sections 1 and 2 shall take effect on the 15th day of October following the ratification of this article.

Section 6

This article shall be inoperative unless it shall have been ratified as an amendment to the Constitution by the legislatures of three-fourths of the several States within seven years from the date of its submission.

AMENDMENT XXI

Submitted by Congress February 20, 1933, declared ratified December 5, 1933.

Section 1

The Eighteenth Article of amendment to the Constitution of the United States is hereby repealed.

Section 2

The transportation or importation into any State, Territory, or possession of the United States for de-

*Repealed by the Twenty-first Amendment.

livery or use therein of intoxicating liquors in violation of the laws thereof, is hereby prohibited.

Section 3

This article shall be inoperative unless it shall have been ratified as an amendment to the Constitution by conventions in the several States, as provided in the Constitution, within seven years from the date of the submission thereof to the States by the Congress.

AMENDMENT XXII

Submitted by Congress March 24, 1947, declared ratified March 1, 1951.

No person shall be elected to the office of the President more than twice, and no person who has held the office of President, or acted as President, for more than two years of a term to which some other person was elected President shall be elected to the office of the President more than once.

But this article shall not apply to any person holding the office of President when this article was proposed by the Congress, and shall not prevent any person who may be holding the office of President, or acting as President, during the term within which this article becomes operative from holding the office of President or acting as President during the remainder of such term.

This article shall be inoperative unless it shall have been ratified as an amendment to the Constitution by the legislatures of three-fourths of the several states within seven years from the date of its submission to the states by the Congress.

AMENDMENT XXIII

Submitted by Congress June 16, 1960, declared ratified April 3, 1961.

Section 1

The District constituting the seat of Government of the United States shall appoint in such manner as the Congress may direct:

A number of electors of President and Vice-President equal to the whole number of Senators and Representatives in Congress to which the District would be entitled if it were a State, but in no event more than the least populous State; they shall be in addition to those appointed by the States, but they shall be considered, for the purpose of the election of President and Vice-President, to be electors appointed by a State; and they shall meet in the District and perform such duties as provided by the twelfth article of amendment.

Section 2

The Congress shall have power to enforce this article by appropriate legislation.

AMENDMENT XXIV

Submitted by Congress August 27, 1962, declared ratified February 4, 1964.

Section 1

The right of citizens of the United States to vote in any primary or other election for President or Vice President, for electors for President or Vice President, or for Senator or Representative in Congress, shall not be denied or abridged by the United States or any State by reason of failure to pay any poll tax or other tax.

Section 2

The Congress shall have the power to enforce this article by appropriate legislation.

AMENDMENT XXV

Submitted by Congress July 6, 1965, declared ratified February 23, 1967.

Section 1

In case of the removal of the President from office or of his death or resignation, the Vice President shall become President.

Section 2

Whenever there is a vacancy in the office of the Vice President, the President shall nominate a Vice President who shall take office upon confirmation by a majority vote of both houses of Congress.

Section 3

Whenever the President transmits to the President pro tempore of the Senate and the Speaker of the House of Representatives his written declaration that he is unable to discharge the powers and duties of his office, and until he transmits to them a written declaration to the contrary, such powers and duties shall be discharged by the Vice President as Acting President.

Section 4

Whenever the Vice President and a majority of either the principal officers of the executive departments, or of such other body as Congress may by law provide, transmit to the President pro tempore of the Senate and the Speaker of the House of Representatives their written declaration that the President is unable to discharge the powers and duties of his office, the Vice President shall immediately assume the powers and duties of the office as Acting President.

Thereafter, when the President transmits to the President pro tempore of the Senate and the Speaker of the House of Representatives his written declaration that no inability exists, he shall resume the powers and duties of his office unless the Vice President and a majority of either the principal officers of the executive departments, or of such other body as Congress may by law provide, transmit within four days to the President pro tempore of the Senate and the Speaker of the House of Representatives their written declaration that the President is unable to discharge the powers and duties of his office. Thereupon Congress shall decide the issue, assembling within forty-eight hours for that purpose if not in session. If the Congress, within twenty-one days after receipt of the latter written declaration, or, if Congress is not in session, within twenty-one days after Congress is required to assemble, determines by two-thirds vote of both houses that the President is unable to discharge the powers and duties of his office, the Vice President shall continue to discharge the same as Acting President; otherwise, the President shall resume the powers and duties of his office.

ADMISSION OF THE STATES TO THE UNION

Order of Admission	State	Date of Admission
1	Delaware	December 7, 1787
2	Pennsylvania	December 12, 1787
3	New Jersey	December 18, 1787
4	Georgia	January 2, 1788
5	Connecticut	January 9, 1788
6	Massachusetts	February 6, 1788
7	Maryland	April 28, 1788
8	South Carolina	May 23, 1788
9	New Hampshire	June 21, 1788
10	Virginia	June 25, 1788
11	New York	July 26, 1788
12	North Carolina	November 21, 1789
13	Rhode Island	May 29, 1790
14	Vermont	March 4, 1791
15	Kentucky	June 1, 1792
16	Tennessee	June 1, 1796
17	Ohio	March 1, 1803
18	Louisiana	April 30, 1812
19	Indiana	December 11, 1816
20	Mississippi	December 10, 1817
21	Illinois	December 3, 1818
22	Alabama	December 14, 1819
23	Maine	March 15, 1820
24	Missouri	August 10, 1821
25	Arkansas	June 15, 1836
26	Michigan	January 26, 1837
27	Florida	March 3, 1845
28	Texas	December 29, 1845
29	Iowa	December 28, 1846
30	Wisconsin	May 29, 1848
31	California	September 9, 1850
32	Minnesota	May 11, 1858
33	Oregon	February 14, 1859
34	Kansas	January 29, 1861
35	West Virginia	June 19, 1863
36	Nevada	October 31, 1864
37	Nebraska	March 1, 1867
38	Colorado	August 1, 1876
39	North Dakota	November 2, 1889
40	South Dakota	November 2, 1889
41	Montana	November 8, 1889
42	Washington	November 11, 1889
43	Idaho	July 3, 1890
44	Wyoming	July 10, 1890
45	Utah	January 4, 1896
46	Oklahoma	November 16, 1907
47	New Mexico	January 6, 1912
48	Arizona	February 14, 1912
49	Alaska	January 3, 1959
50	Hawaii	August 21, 1959

GROWTH OF UNITED STATES POPULATION AND AREA*

Census	Resident Population of the United States	Increase over the Preceding Census — Number	Per Cent	Land Area, square mile	Population per square mile
1790	3,929,214	...	...	864,746	4.5
1800	5,308,483	1,379,269	35.1	864,746	6.1
1810	7,239,881	1,931,398	36.4	1,681,828	4.3
1820	9,638,453	2,398,572	33.1	1,749,462	5.5
1830	12,866,020	3,227,567	33.5	1,749,462	7.4
1840	17,069,453	4,203,433	32.7	1,749,462	9.8
1850	23,191,876	6,122,423	35.9	2,940,042	7.9
1860	31,443,321	8,251,445	35.6	2,969,640	10.6
1870	39,818,449	8,375,128	26.6	2,969,640	13.4
1880	50,155,783	10,337,334	26.0	2,969,640	16.9
1890	62,947,714	12,791,931	25.5	2,969,640	21.2
1900	75,994,575	13,046,861	20.7	2,969,834	25.6
1910	91,972,266	15,977,691	21.0	2,969,565	31.0
1920	105,710,620	13,738,354	14.9	2,969,451	35.6
1930	122,775,046	17,064,426	16.1	2,977,128	41.2
1940	131,669,275	8,894,229	7.2	2,977,128	44.2
1950	151,325,798	19,161,229	14.5	3,552,206	42.6
1960	179,323,175	27,997,377	18.5	3,540,911	50.5
1970	204,765,770	23,861,597	13.3	3,530,940	58.2

*Adapted from U.S. Bureau of the Census, *Statistical Abstract of the United States, 1970.*

JUSTICES OF THE UNITED STATES SUPREME COURT

Name and Residence	Service Term	Years	Appointed by	Name and Residence	Service Term	Years	Appointed by
John Jay, N.Y.*	1789–1795	5	Washington	Lucius Q. C. Lamar, Miss.	1888–1893	5	Cleveland
John Rutledge, S.C.	1789–1791	1	Washington	*Melville W. Fuller*, Ill.	1888–1910	21	Cleveland
William Cushing, Mass.	1789–1810	20	Washington	David J. Brewer, Kans.	1890–1910	20	B. Harrison
James Wilson, Pa.	1789–1798	8	Washington	Henry B. Brown, Mich.	1891–1906	15	B. Harrison
John Blair, Va.	1789–1796	6	Washington	George Shiras, Jr., Pa.	1892–1903	10	B. Harrison
Robert H. Harrison, Md.	1789–1790	—	Washington	Howell E. Jackson, Tenn.	1893–1895	2	B. Harrison
James Iredell, N.C.	1790–1799	9	Washington	Edward D. White, La.	1894–1910	16	Cleveland
Thomas Johnson, Md.	1791–1793	1	Washington	Rufus W. Peckham, N.Y.	1896–1909	13	Cleveland
William Paterson, N.J.	1793–1806	13	Washington	Joseph McKenna, Calif.	1898–1925	26	McKinley
John Rutledge, S.C.	1795–†	—	Washington	Oliver W. Holmes, Mass.	1902–1932	30	T. Roosevelt
Samuel Chase, Md.	1796–1811	15	Washington	William R. Day, Ohio	1903–1922	19	T. Roosevelt
Oliver Ellsworth, Conn.	1796–1799	4	Washington	William H. Moody, Mass.	1906–1910	3	T. Roosevelt
Bushrod Washington, Va.	1798–1829	31	J. Adams	Horace H. Lurton, Tenn.	1910–1914	4	Taft
Alfred Moore, N.C.	1799–1804	4	J. Adams	Charles E. Hughes, N.Y.	1910–1916	5	Taft
John Marshall, Va.	1801–1835	34	J. Adams	Willis Van Devanter, Wyo.	1911–1937	26	Taft
William Johnson, S.C.	1804–1834	30	Jefferson	Joseph R. Lamar, Ga.	1911–1916	5	Taft
Brockholst Livingston, N.Y.	1806–1823	16	Jefferson	*Edward D. White*, La.	1910–1921	11	Taft
Thomas Todd, Ky.	1807–1826	18	Jefferson	Mahlon Pitney, N.J.	1912–1922	10	Taft
Joseph Story, Mass.	1811–1845	33	Madison	James C. McReynolds, Tenn.	1914–1941	26	Wilson
Gabriel Duvall, Md.	1811–1835	24	Madison	Louis D. Brandeis, Mass.	1916–1939	22	Wilson
Smith Thompson, N.Y.	1823–1843	20	Monroe	John H. Clarke, Ohio	1916–1922	6	Wilson
Robert Trimble, Ky.	1826–1828	2	J. Q. Adams	*William H. Taft*, Conn.	1921–1930	8	Harding
John McLean, Ohio	1829–1861	32	Jackson	George Sutherland, Utah	1922–1938	15	Harding
Henry Baldwin, Pa.	1830–1844	14	Jackson	Pierce Butler, Minn.	1923–1939	16	Harding
James M. Wayne, Ga.	1835–1867	32	Jackson	Edward T. Sanford, Tenn.	1923–1930	7	Harding
Roger B. Taney, Md.	1836–1864	28	Jackson	Harlan F. Stone, N.Y.	1925–1941	16	Coolidge
Philip P. Barbour, Va.	1836–1841	4	Jackson	*Charles E. Hughes*, N.Y.	1930–1941	11	Hoover
John Catron, Tenn.	1837–1865	28	Van Buren	Owen J. Roberts, Pa.	1930–1945	15	Hoover
John McKinley, Ala.	1837–1852	15	Van Buren	Benjamin N. Cardozo, N.Y.	1932–1938	6	Hoover
Peter V. Daniel, Va.	1841–1860	19	Van Buren	Hugo L. Black, Ala.	1937–	—	F. Roosevelt
Samuel Nelson, N.Y.	1845–1872	27	Tyler	Stanley F. Reed, Ky.	1938–1957	19	F. Roosevelt
Levi Woodbury, N.H.	1845–1851	5	Polk	Felix Frankfurter, Mass.	1939–1962	23	F. Roosevelt
Robert C. Grier, Pa.	1846–1870	23	Polk	William O. Douglas, Conn.	1939–	—	F. Roosevelt
Benjamin R. Curtis, Mass.	1851–1857	6	Fillmore	Frank Murphy, Mich.	1940–1949	9	F. Roosevelt
John A. Campbell, Ala.	1853–1861	8	Pierce	*Harlan F. Stone*, N.Y.	1941–1946	5	F. Roosevelt
Nathan Clifford, Maine	1858–1881	23	Buchanan	James F. Byrnes, S.C.	1941–1942	1	F. Roosevelt
Noah H. Swayne, Ohio	1862–1881	18	Lincoln	Robert H. Jackson, N.Y.	1941–1954	13	F. Roosevelt
Samuel F. Miller, Iowa	1862–1890	28	Lincoln	Wiley B. Rutledge, Iowa	1943–1949	6	F. Roosevelt
David Davis, Ill.	1862–1877	14	Lincoln	Harold H. Burton, Ohio	1945–1958	13	Truman
Stephen J. Field, Calif.	1863–1897	34	Lincoln	*Fred M. Vinson*, Ky.	1946–1953	7	Truman
Salmon P. Chase, Ohio	1864–1873	8	Lincoln	Tom C. Clark, Tex.	1949–1967	18	Truman
William Strong, Pa.	1870–1880	10	Grant	Sherman Minton, Ind.	1949–1956	7	Truman
Joseph P. Bradley, N.J.	1870–1892	22	Grant	*Earl Warren*, Calif.	1953–1969	16	Eisenhower
Ward Hunt, N.Y.	1873–1882	9	Grant	John Marshall Harlan, N.Y.	1955–	—	Eisenhower
Morrison R. Waite, Ohio	1874–1888	14	Grant	William J. Brennan, Jr., N.Y.	1956–	—	Eisenhower
John M. Harlan, Ky.	1877–1911	34	Hayes	Charles E. Whittaker, Mo.	1957–1962	5	Eisenhower
William B. Woods, Ga.	1881–1887	6	Hayes	Potter Stewart, Ohio	1958–	—	Eisenhower
Stanley Matthews, Ohio	1881–1889	7	Garfield	Byron R. White, Colo.	1962–	—	Kennedy
Horace Gray, Mass.	1882–1902	20	Arthur	Arthur J. Goldberg, Ill.	1962–1965	3	Kennedy
Samuel Blatchford, N.Y.	1882–1893	1	Arthur	Abe Fortas, Tenn.	1965–1969	4	Johnson
				Thurgood Marshall, N.Y.	1967–	—	Johnson
				Warren E. Burger, Minn.	1969–	—	Nixon
				Harry A. Blackmun, Minn.	1970–	—	Nixon

*Chief justices names are in italics.
†Acting Chief Justice; Senate refused to confirm appointment on December 15, 1795.

451

PRESIDENTS AND VICE PRESIDENTS

Term	President	Vice President
1789–1793	George Washington	John Adams
1793–1797	George Washington	John Adams
1797–1801	John Adams	Thomas Jefferson
1801–1805	Thomas Jefferson	Aaron Burr
1805–1809	Thomas Jefferson	George Clinton
1809–1813	James Madison	George Clinton (d. 1812)
1813–1817	James Madison	Elbridge Gerry (d. 1814)
1817–1821	James Monroe	Daniel D. Tompkins
1821–1825	James Monroe	Daniel D. Tompkins
1825–1829	John Quincy Adams	John C. Calhoun
1829–1833	Andrew Jackson	John C. Calhoun (resigned 1832)
1833–1837	Andrew Jackson	Martin Van Buren
1837–1841	Martin Van Buren	Richard M. Johnson
1841–1845	William H. Harrison (d. 1841) John Tyler	John Tyler
1845–1849	James K. Polk	George M. Dallas
1849–1853	Zachary Taylor (d. 1850) Millard Fillmore	Millard Fillmore
1853–1857	Franklin Pierce	William R. D. King (d. 1853)
1857–1861	James Buchanan	John C. Breckinridge
1861–1865	Abraham Lincoln	Hannibal Hamlin
1865–1869	Abraham Lincoln (d. 1865) Andrew Johnson	Andrew Johnson
1869–1873	Ulysses S. Grant	Schuyler Colfax
1873–1877	Ulysses S. Grant	Henry Wilson (d. 1875)
1877–1881	Rutherford B. Hayes	William A. Wheeler
1881–1885	James A. Garfield (d. 1881) Chester A. Arthur	Chester A. Arthur
1885–1889	Grover Cleveland	Thomas A. Hendricks (d. 1885)
1889–1893	Benjamin Harrison	Levi P. Morton
1893–1897	Grover Cleveland	Adlai E. Stevenson
1897–1901	William McKinley	Garret A. Hobart (d. 1899)
1901–1905	William McKinley (d. 1901) Theodore Roosevelt	Theodore Roosevelt
1905–1909	Theodore Roosevelt	Charles W. Fairbanks
1909–1913	William H. Taft	James S. Sherman (d. 1912)
1913–1917	Woodrow Wilson	Thomas R. Marshall
1917–1921	Woodrow Wilson	Thomas R. Marshall
1921–1925	Warren G. Harding (d. 1923) Calvin Coolidge	Calvin Coolidge
1925–1929	Calvin Coolidge	Charles G. Dawes
1929–1933	Herbert C. Hoover	Charles Curtis
1933–1937	Franklin D. Roosevelt	John N. Garner
1937–1941	Franklin D. Roosevelt	John N. Garner
1941–1945	Franklin D. Roosevelt	Henry A. Wallace
1945–1949	Franklin D. Roosevelt (d. 1945) Harry S. Truman	Harry S. Truman
1949–1953	Harry S. Truman	Alben W. Barkley
1953–1957	Dwight D. Eisenhower	Richard M. Nixon
1957–1961	Dwight D. Eisenhower	Richard M. Nixon
1961–1965	John F. Kennedy (d. 1963) Lyndon B. Johnson	Lyndon B. Johnson
1965–1969	Lyndon B. Johnson	Hubert H. Humphrey, Jr.
1969–	Richard M. Nixon	Spiro T. Agnew

PRESIDENTIAL ELECTIONS

Number of States	Year	Candidates	Party	Electoral Vote	Popular Vote	Percentage of Popular Vote
10	1789	George Washington (P)		69		
		John Adams (VP)		34		
		Other candidates		35		
15	1792	George Washington (P)	Federalist	132		
		John Adams (VP)	Federalist	77		
		George Clinton	Democratic-Republican	50*		
		Other candidates		5		
16	1796	John Adams (P)	Federalist	71		
		Thomas Jefferson (VP)	Democratic-Republican	68		
		Thomas Pinckney	Federalist	59		
		Aaron Burr	Democratic-Republican	30		
		Other candidates		48		
16	1800	Thomas Jefferson (P)	Democratic-Republican	73		
		Aaron Burr (VP)	Democratic-Republican	73		
		John Adams	Federalist	65		
		Charles C. Pinckney	Federalist	64		
		John Jay	Federalist	1		
17	1804	Thomas Jefferson	Democratic-Republican	162		
		Charles C. Pinckney	Federalist	14		
17	1808	James Madison	Democratic-Republican	122		
		Charles C. Pinckney	Federalist	47		
		George Clinton	Independent Republican	6		
18	1812	James Madison	Democratic-Republican	128		
		De Witt Clinton	Republican, Federalist	89		
19	1816	James Monroe	Republican	183		
		Rufus King	Federalist	34		
24	1820	James Monroe	Republican	231		
		John Quincy Adams	Independent	1		
24	1824	John Quincy Adams	No distinct party designations	84†	108,740	30.54
		Andrew Jackson		99†	153,544	43.12
		William H. Crawford		41	46,618	13.09
		Henry Clay		37	47,136	13.23
24	1828	Andrew Jackson	Democratic	178	647,286	56.02
		John Quincy Adams	National Republican	83	508,064	43.97
25	1832	Andrew Jackson	Democratic	219	687,502	54.96
		Henry Clay	National Republican	49	530,189	42.38
		William Wirt	Anti-Masonic	7	33,108	2.64
		John Floyd	Independent Democrat	11		
26	1836	Martin Van Buren	Democratic	170‡	761,549	50.90
		William Henry Harrison	Whig	73	735,651	49.09
		Hugh L. White	Whig	26		
		Daniel Webster	Whig	14		
		Willie P. Mangum	Anti-Jackson	11		

*For Vice President
†Choice submitted to the House of Representatives because no candidate had a majority in the Electoral College.
‡Includes three disputed Michigan votes.

PRESIDENTIAL ELECTIONS (Continued)

Number of States	Year	Candidates	Party	Electoral Vote	Popular Vote	Percentage of Popular Vote
26	1840	William Henry Harrison	Whig	234	1,275,017	52.87
		Martin Van Buren	Democratic	60	1,128,702	46.82
		James G. Birney	Liberty		7,059	0.29
26	1844	James K. Polk	Democratic	170	1,337,243	49.55
		Henry Clay	Whig	105	1,299,068	48.13
		James G. Birney	Liberty		62,300	2.30
30	1848	Zachary Taylor	Whig	163	1,360,101	47.35
		Lewis Cass	Democratic	127	1,220,544	42.49
		Martin Van Buren	Free Soil		291,263	10.14
31	1852	Franklin Pierce	Democratic	254	1,601,474	50.93
		Winfield Scott	Whig	42	1,386,578	44.10
		John P. Hale	Free Soil		156,149	4.95
31	1856	James Buchanan	Democratic	174	1,838,169	45.34
		John C. Frémont	Republican	114	1,335,264	33.08
		Millard Fillmore	American	8	874,534	21.57
33	1860	Abraham Lincoln	Republican	180	1,867,198	39.87
		John C. Breckinridge	Democratic (Southern)	72	854,248	18.20
		Stephen A. Douglas	Democratic	12	1,379,434	29.38
		John Bell	Constitutional Union	39	591,658	12.61
36	1864	Abraham Lincoln	Republican (National Union)	212	2,213,665	55.08
		George B. McClellan	Democratic	21	1,805,237	44.91
		(Not voted)		81		
37	1868	Ulysses S. Grant	Republican	214	3,013,421	52.70
		Horatio Seymour	Democratic	80	2,706,829	47.29
		(Not voted)		23		
37	1872	Ulysses S. Grant	Republican	286	3,597,132	55.63
		Horace Greeley (died)	Democratic, Liberal Republican	66*	2,834,125	43.82
		Thomas A. Hendricks		42		
		B. Gratz Brown		18		
		Charles J. Jenkins		2		
		David Davis		1		
		(Not voted)		17		
38	1876	Rutherford B. Hayes	Republican	185	4,036,298	47.87
		Samuel J. Tilden	Democratic	184	4,300,500	51.01
		Peter Cooper	National Greenback		81,737	0.96
38	1880	James A. Garfield	Republican	214	4,454,416	48.31
		Winfield Scott Hancock	Greenback Labor		308,578	3.34
		James B. Weaver	Democratic	155	4,444,952	48.21
38	1884	Grover Cleveland	Democratic	219	4,874,986	48.49
		James G. Blaine	Republican	182	4,851,981	48.26
		Benjamin F. Butler	Greenback Labor		175,370	1.74

*Greeley died soon after the election. Presidential electors supporting him cast their votes for the four men listed beneath his name.

PRESIDENTIAL ELECTIONS (Continued)

Number of States	Year	Candidates	Party	Electoral Vote	Popular Vote	Percentage of Popular Vote
38	1888	Benjamin Harrison	Republican	233	5,444,337	47.79
		Grover Cleveland	Democratic	168	5,540,050	48.68
		Clinton B. Fisk	Prohibition		250,125	2.19
44	1892	Grover Cleveland	Democratic	277	5,554,414	46.07
		Benjamin Harrison	Republican	145	5,190,802	42.92
		James B. Weaver	People's	22	1,027,329	8.63
		John Bidwell	Prohibition		271,058	2.19
45	1896	William McKinley	Republican	271	7,104,779	51.02
		William Jennings Bryan	Democratic, People's	176	6,502,925	46.70
		John M. Palmer	National Democratic		133,148	0.95
		Joshua Levering	Prohibition		132,007	0.94
45	1900	William McKinley	Republican	292	7,219,530	51.61
		William Jennings Bryan	Democratic, Populist	155	6,358,071	45.53
		John C. Woolley	Prohibition		209,166	1.49
		Eugene V. Debs	Social Democratic		94,768	0.70
		Wharton Barker	People's		50,232	0.36
45	1904	Theodore Roosevelt	Republican	336	7,628,834	56.42
		Alton B. Parker	Democratic	140	5,084,401	37.58
		Eugene V. Debs	Socialist		402,460	2.97
		Silas C. Swallow	Prohibition		259,257	1.91
		Thomas E. Watson	People's		114,753	0.86
46	1908	William H. Taft	Republican	321	7,679,006	51.57
		William Jennings Bryan	Democratic	162	6,409,106	43.04
		Eugene V. Debs	Socialist		420,820	2.82
		Eugene W. Chafin	Prohibition		252,683	1.70
		Thomas L. Hisgen	Independence		83,562	0.55
		Thomas E. Watson	People's		28,131	0.19
48	1912	Woodrow Wilson	Democratic	435	6,286,214	41.86
		Theodore Roosevelt	Progressive	88	4,126,020	27.40
		William H. Taft	Republican	8	3,483,922	23.18
		Eugene V. Debs	Socialist		897,011	5.99
48	1916	Woodrow Wilson	Democratic	277	9,129,606	49.27
		Charles E. Hughes	Republican	254	8,538,221	46.08
		Allen L. Benson	Socialist		585,113	3.15
48	1920	Warren G. Harding	Republican	404	16,152,200	60.36
		James M. Cox	Democratic	127	9,147,353	34.18
		Eugene V. Debs	Socialist		919,799	3.43
48	1924	Calvin Coolidge	Republican	382	15,725,016	54.05
		John W. Davis	Democratic	136	8,385,586	28.82
		Robert M. La Follette	Progressive	13	4,822,856	16.57
48	1928	Herbert C. Hoover	Republican	444	21,392,190	58.21
		Alfred E. Smith	Democratic	87	15,016,443	40.86
48	1932	Franklin Delano Roosevelt	Democratic	472	22,809,638	57.30
		Herbert C. Hoover	Republican	59	15,758,901	39.65
		Norman Thomas	Socialist		881,951	2.21

PRESIDENTIAL ELECTIONS (Continued)

Number of States	Year	Candidates	Party	Electoral Vote	Popular Vote	Percentage of Popular Vote
48	1936	Franklin Delano Roosevelt	Democratic	523	27,751,612	60.83
		Alfred M. Landon	Republican	8	16,681,913	36.56
		William Lemke	Union		891,858	1.93
48	1940	Franklin Delano Roosevelt	Democratic	449	27,244,160	54.30
		Wendell L. Willkie	Republican	82	22,305,198	44.46
48	1944	Franklin Delano Roosevelt	Democratic	432	25,602,505	53.39
		Thomas E. Dewey	Republican	99	22,006,278	45.89
48	1948	Harry S. Truman	Democratic	303	24,105,812	49.51
		Thomas E. Dewey	Republican	189	21,970,065	45.12
		J. Strom Thurmond	States' Rights	39	1,169,063	2.40
		Henry A. Wallace	Progressive		1,157,172	2.37
48	1952	Dwight D. Eisenhower	Republican	442	33,824,351	54.94
		Adlai E. Stevenson	Democratic	89	27,314,987	44.36
48	1956	Dwight D. Eisenhower	Republican	457	35,590,472	57.28
		Adlai E. Stevenson	Democratic	74	26,022,752	41.90
50	1960	John F. Kennedy	Democratic	303	34,226,731	49.7
		Richard M. Nixon	Republican	219	34,108,157	49.5
50	1964	Lyndon B. Johnson	Democratic	486	43,126,218	61.0
		Barry M. Goldwater	Republican	52	27,174,898	38.5
50	1968	Richard M. Nixon	Republican	301	31,770,237	43.4
		Hubert H. Humphrey	Democratic	191	31,270,533	42.7
		George C. Wallace	American Independent	46	9,906,141	13.5

PUBLIC DEBT OF THE UNITED STATES, 1855–1969*

June 30	Gross Debt, 1,000 dollars	Per Capita, dollars	June 30	Gross Debt, 1,000 dollars	Per Capita, dollars
1855	35,588	1.30	1931	16,801,281	135.45
1860	64,844	2.06	1932	19,487,002	156.10
1861	90,582	2.80	1933	22,538,673	179.48
1862	524,178	15.79	1934	27,053,141	214.07
1863	1,119,774	32.91	1935	28,700,893	225.55
1864	1,815,831	52.08	1936	33,778,543	263.79
1865	2,677,929	75.01	1937	36,424,614	282.75
1870	2,436,453	61.06	1938	37,164,740	286.27
1875	2,156,277	47.84	1939	40,439,532	308.98
1880	2,090,909	41.60	1940	42,967,531	325.23
1885	1,578,551	27.86	1941	48,961,444	367.09
1890	1,122,397	17.80	1942	72,422,445	537.13
1895	1,096,913	15.76	1943	136,696,090	999.83
1900	1,263,417	16.60	1944	201,003,387	1,452.44
1905	1,132,357	13.51	1945	258,682,187	1,848.60
1910	1,146,940	12.41	1946	269,422,099	1,905.42
1915	1,191,264	11.85	1947	258,286,383	1,792.05
1916	1,225,146	12.02	1948	252,292,247	1,720.71
1917	2,975,619	28.77	1949	252,770,360	1,694.75
1918	12,455,225	119.13	1950	257,357,352	1,696.68
1919	25,484,506	242.56	1951	255,221,977	1,653.42
1920	24,299,321	228.23	1952	259,105,179	1,650.06
1925	20,516,194	177.12	1953	266,071,062	1,666.74
1930	16,185,310	131.51	1954	271,259,599	1,670.14

June 30	Gross Debt, million dollars	Per Capita, dollars
1955	274,374	1,660
1956	272,751	1,622
1957	270,527	1,580
1958	276,343	1,587
1959	284,706	1,606
1960	286,331	1,585
1961	288,971	1,573
1962	298,201	1,598
1963	305,860	1,615
1964	311,713	1,622
1965	317,274	1,631
1966	319,907	1,625
1967	326,221	1,637
1968	347,578	1,728
1969	353,720	1,741

*Adapted from U.S. Bureau of the Census, *Historical Statistics of the United States, Colonial Times to 1957* and *Statistical Abstract of the United States, 1970*.

EMPLOYEES IN NONAGRICULTURAL ESTABLISHMENTS, 1920–1970*

Year	Total	Mining	Contract Construction	Manufacturing	Transportation and Public Utilities	Wholesale and Retail Trade	Finance, Insurance, and Real Estate	Service and Miscellaneous	Government
1920	27,088	1,230	848	10,534	3,998	4,623	1,110	2,142	2,603
1925	28,505	1,080	1,446	9,786	3,824	5,810	1,166	2,591	2,802
1929	31,041	1,078	1,497	10,534	3,907	6,401	1,431	3,127	3,066
1930	29,143	1,000	1,372	9,401	3,675	6,064	1,398	3,084	3,149
1932	23,377	722	970	6,797	2,804	4,907	1,270	2,682	3,225
1935	26,792	888	912	8,907	2,771	5,692	1,262	2,883	3,477
1940	32,058	916	1,294	10,780	3,013	6,940	1,436	3,477	4,202
1943	42,106	917	1,567	17,381	3,619	7,189	1,435	3,919	6,080
1945	40,037	826	1,132	15,302	3,872	7,522	1,428	4,011	5,944
1950	45,222	901	2,333	15,241	4,034	9,386	1,919	5,382	6,026
1955	50,675	792	2,802	16,882	4,141	10,535	2,335	6,274	6,914
1960	54,234	712	2,885	16,796	4,004	11,391	2,669	7,423	8,353
1965	60,815	632	3,186	18,062	4,036	12,716	3,023	9,087	10,074
1970	70,582	623	3,270	19,564	4,441	14,778	3,667	11,439	12,800

*In thousands of persons. Before 1960 the labor forces of Alaska and Hawaii are excluded. Adapted from U.S. Bureau of the Census, *Historical Statistics of the United States, Colonial Times to 1957* and *Statistical Abstract of the United States, 1970*.

INDEX

Acheson, Dean, 361, 389
Act of Havana, 323
Adams, Charles Francis, 116
Adams, John Quincy, 110
Addams, Jane, 136, 169, 199
Adenauer, Konrad, 352, 417
Advertising, 247
Africa, 372
　World War II campaigns in, 325, 330-331
Agricultural Adjustment Administration, 272-273
Agriculture, see Farmers
Aguinaldo, Emilio, 186
Alaska, 119
Aldrich, Nelson W., 156
Algeciras Conference, 195
Allende, Salvador, 428
Alliance for Progress, 413-414
Allied Control Council, 351
Altgeld, John P., 78-79
American Federation of Labor, 243
American Friends Service Committee, 287
American Protective Association, 30
Amerindians, see Indian nations, end of
Anderson, Sherwood, 242
Antiballistic Missile System, 428
Anti-Imperialist League, 198
Apache War, 49
Arab-Israeli conflict, 367, 422, 427-428

Arapahoe, 47, 49
Area Redevelopment Act, 411
Arizona, 43, 58
Arkansas, 397
Armory Show, 165
Armour, Philip, 69
Arthur, Chester, 96, 98
"Ash Can School," 165
Assembly lines, 246
Atchison, Topeka, and Santa Fe railroad, 65
Atlantic Charter, 332
Automobiles, 246-247

Babcock, Orville E., 91
Baez, Joan, 423
Baghdad Pact, 367
Baker, Bobby, 419
Balkans, 323-324
Ballinger, Richard A., 157
Barnes, Harry Elmer, 301
Baruch, Bernard M., 217
Battle of Britain, 324-325
Battle of the Bulge, 338
Bay of Pigs invasion, 414
Beard, Charles A., 164
Beatles, 423, 430
Beecher, Henry Ward, 128
Belknap, William W., 91
Bell, Alexander G., 31
Bellamy, Edward, 128
Benson, Ezra Taft, 399-400
Benton, Thomas Hart, 45

Benton, William, 390
Berger, Victor, 244
Berle, Adolf A., Jr., 267
Berlin airlift, 359
Berlin Wall, 415
Bessemer system, 68
Beveridge, Albert, 187
Bismarck, Otto von, 204
Black Codes, 14-15, 20
Black Tuesday, 260
Blaine, James G., 91, 98, 100
Bland-Allison Act, 97
Bliss, Tasker H., 223
Blitzkrieg, 317-320
Bohlen, Charles E., 393
Bolshevism, 219, 243, 284, 288
Bonus War, 264-265
Booth, Evangeline C., 136
Borah, William F., 229-230, 287, 289, 301
Boxer Rebellion, 192
Bradley, Omar, 363
"Brain trust," 266-267
Brandeis, Louis, 31, 164
British North America Act, 119
Brooks, Phillips, 128
Brown, Ruth Standish, 169
Bruce, Blanche K., 19
Bryan, William Jennings, 133, 155, 196, 199, 245
Bryan-Chamorro Treaty, 196
Buchannan, James, 110
Buffalo, 49-50

459

Bulganin, Nikolai, 365
Bull Moose Party, 159
Bureau of Indian Affairs, 48
Burke-Wadsworth Bill, 323
Byrnes, James F., 380

California, 41
Cambodia, 427
Canada, 119
Capone, Al, 239
Caraway, Hattie, 243
Cardozo, Francis, 18
Carmichael, Stokeley, 421
Carnegie, Andrew, 68, 70-71, 199
Carpetbaggers, 17-19
Carranza, Venustiano, 197-198
Carver, George Washington, 168
Catholicism, 26, 129
Cattle kingdoms, 51-53
Central Intelligence Agency, 384, 414
Central Pacific railroad, 46, 65
Chamberlain, Neville, 297-299, 318
Chase, Salmon Portland, 17
Château-Thierry, battle of, 219
Chavez, Cesar, 423
Chennault, Claire L., 328, 339
Cheyenne, 47, 49
Chiang Kai-shek, 286, 295, 328, 333, 339, 341, 355, 365, 387
China, 113, 192, 295-296, 355, 372
 immigration to United States, 30, 365
Chinese Exclusion Act, 76
Chisholm Trail, 51
Chivington Massacre, 49
Churchill, Winston, 206, 315, 324, 332, 333-336, 356
Cities, growth of, 24
Civilian Conservation Corps, 270
Civil Rights Act of 1866, 14-15
Civil Rights Act of 1963, 419
Civil Service Commission, 99
Civil War, aftermath of, 9-10, 87-90
 economics in, 65
 moral damage of, 88
Clark Memorandum, 302
Clay, Lucius, 359
Clayton Anti-Trust Act, 161
Clayton-Bulwer Treaty, 189
Clemenceau, Georges, 224
Cleveland, Grover, 79, 93, 96, 102, 105, 132, 180, 198
 election of, 100
 reelection of, 104
Cody, William F., 50, 53
Cohn, Roy, 393-395
Cold War, 355-373
Colfax, Schuyler, 91
Colleges, 163
Colorado, 42, 58
Committee for Industrial Organization, 271-272

Committee on Public Information, 218
Common Market, 371, 386
Communes, 431
Comstock Lode, 43
Concentration camps, 339
Confederate cruiser controversy, 116
Congress of Industrial Organizations (CIO), 272
Congress on Racial Equality (CORE), 399
Conkling, Roscoe, 97-98
Conservation, 143
Constitution, amendments, Thirteenth, 13
 Fourteenth, 14
 Fifteenth, 14
 Sixteenth, 156
 Seventeenth, 138, 156
 Eighteenth, 170
 Nineteenth, 171
 Twenty-First, 267
Cook, James, 112
Coolidge, Calvin, 241, 252-253
Cooper, Peter, 96
Copperheads, 15
Corbin, Abel R., 90
Corporations, 73
Covode Resolution, 16, 17
Cowboys, 53-54
Cox, James M., 231, 249
Coxey's Army, 130
Crane, Stephen, 165, 179
Crazy Horse, 49
Crédit Mobilier affair, 67, 91
Creel, George, 218
Cuba, 110, 185-186
 missile crisis in, 415
Cushing, Caleb, 113
Custer, George A., 49
Czechoslovakia, 227, 296-300, 428

Daladier, Edouard, 315-316
Danzig, 316
Darrow, Clarence, 245, 271
Darwin, Charles, 72, 128
Daugherty, Harry M., 250
Davis, John W., 252
Dawes, Charles Gates, 286
Dawes Severalty Act, 50, 101
D-Day, 337-338
Debs, Eugene V., 79, 155, 159, 218, 250-251
Deere, John, 57
de Gaulle, Charles, 322, 337-338, 342, 371, 416-417, 428
Democratic party, 87, 93, 385
Dempsey, Jack, 237
Dependent Pension Act, 102, 104
Depression (Great), 235, 261-279
Depression of 1893, 129
Dewey, George, 183
Dewey, John, 127, 162, 169

Dewey, Thomas E., 316, 323, 381, 385-386
Diaz Porfirio, 197
Diem, Ngo Dinh, 416
Direct election of senators, 138
Dissent, 431
Distribution-Preemption Act, 55
Dixiecrats, 385
"Dollar diplomacy," 196
Dominican Republic, 190-191, 196-197, 422; *see also* Santo Domingo
Donnelly, Ignatius, 128
Dos Passos, John, 244
Douglas, Stephen A., 45
Draft Riots, 24
Dred Scott Affair, 14
Dreiser, Theodore, 165
Dresden, bombing of, 337
Drew, Charles, 31
DuBois, W. E. B., 126, 169
Dulles, John Foster, 363-364, 367, 373, 393, 399
Dumbarton Oaks Conference, 334, 349
Dunkirk, 321
Duvalier, Francois, 197
Dylan, Bob, 423

East Germany, 352
Economic Opportunity Act, 420
Economy of the United States, in the 1920's, 246-248
Edison, Thomas A., 24
Eisenhower, Dwight D., 330, 338, 358, 363, 364ff, 370, 385, 391-400, 409
 election of, 391-392
Eisenhower Doctrine, 369
El Alamein, battle of, 330
Eliot, Charles W., 163, 198
Eliot, T. S., 242
Elkins Act, 142
Ely, Richard T., 127
Emergency Banking Act, 267
Emergency Quota Act, 284
England, 285-286, 287-288
 disputes with United States after Civil War, 120
 imperialist expansion, 179
 migration from, 28
Espionage Act, 218
Ethiopia, 293
Evers, Medgar, 413
Expansionism, 109ff, 177ff

Fair Deal, 381-382, 385
Fair Employment Practices Commission, 381
Fair Labor Standards Act, 277-278, 386
Fall, Albert B., 250
Farmers, 79-81, 126
Farmers Alliances, 81, 131

460 Index

Farming on the frontier, 54-58
Fascism, 289-299
Faubus, Orval, 397
Federal Deposit Insurance Corporation, 267
Federal Emergency Relief Act, 268
Federal Farm Board, 263
Federal Reserve System, 161, 267, 399, 411
Federal Trade Commission, 161
Fenian Brotherhood, 119
Ferguson, "Ma," 243
Fillmore, Millard, 114
Finland, 319-320
First Reconstruction Act, 15
Fisk, James, 67, 90
Fitzgerald, F. Scott, 242
Florida, 248
Forbes, Charles, 250
Force Act, 20
Ford, Henry, 246
Fordney-McCumber Tariff, 285-286
Foreign affairs of the United States, 115-118, 187-199, 355-373
Forrest, Nathan Bedford, 20
Fourteen Points, 221-223
France, imperialist expansion, 179
 and Morocco, 195
Franco, Francisco, 294-295
Frankfurter, Felix, 267
Franklin, Aretha, 423
Franz, Ferdinand, 203-205
Freedmen's Bureau, 13-14
"Freedon party," 420
Free France, 322
"Free silver," 97, 132-134
Frick, Henry Clay, 79, 104
Frémont, John C., 45
Frontier, 37ff, 58-59

Gadsden Purchase, 111-112
Garfield, Harry, 217
Garfield, James A., 91, 98
Garvey, Marcus, 169
Gauss, Christian, 223
Gehrig, Lou, 237
Geneva Accords, 366
Geneva Award, 120
"Gentlemen's agreement," 31, 194
George, Henry, 128
Georgia, 16
Germans in the United States, 25-26
Germany, 286, 288
 and Morocco, 195
 partition of, 350-352
 and Soviet Union, 317
Ghettos, 23, 29, 419, 421-422
Ghost Dance Uprising, 49
Giannini, Amadeo P., 31
Gibbon, James, 129
Gibbs, Jonathan C., 19
G. I. Bill of Rights, 379

Ginn, Edward, 199
Gladden, Washington, 129
Glass-Owen Federal Reserve Act, 161
Glass-Steagall Banking Act, 264, 267
Glavis, Louis, 157
Goering, Hermann, 352
Gold Conspiracy of 1869, 90
Gold Rush, 40
Gold standard, 268
Goldwater, Barry, 420
Gompers, Samuel, 31, 77, 199
Gould, Jay, 67, 90
Graduation Act, 55
Grand Army of the Republic, 102
Grange, 81
Grant, Ulysses S., 19-20, 22, 88, 90-91, 119
Great Northern railroad, 66
Great Society, 421
Greece, 325-326, 356
Greeley, Horace, 21
Grey, Edward, 207
Guiteau, Charles J., 98

Haile Selassie, 293
Haiti, 197
"Half-breeds," 97
Hall, G. Stanley, 127
Hanna, Marcus A., 134
Hanson, Ole, 243-244
Harding, Warren G., 231, 249-252, 381
Harris, Townsend, 115
Harrison, Benjamin, 104, 132
Harvard University, 163
Haskins, Charles Homer, 223
Hawaii, 112, 184
Hawley-Smoot Bill, 263, 285, 303
Hay, John, 181-182, 189, 192, 199
Hayes, Rutherford B., 22, 77, 88, 89-90, 96
Haymarket Riot, 76-77
Hay-Pauncefote Treaty, 188-189
Haywood, "Big Bill," 218
Hearst, William Randolph, 181
Hemingway, Ernest, 208
Hepburn Act, 142
Hess, Rudolf, 352
High schools, 162
Hill, James J., 31, 66
Hippies, 431
Hiroshima, 341
Hiss, Alger, 387
Hitler, Adolf, 286, 293, 297-299, 315ff, 317, 318, 339
Hoar, George F., 198
Hobby, Oveta Culp, 399
Ho Chi-Minh, 355, 366
Hoffa, Jimmy, 405
Hofstadter, Richard, 125
Holding companies, 73
Holmes, Oliver Wendell, 164, 244
Home Owners Loan Corporation, 276

Homestead Act, 55
Homestead Strike, 78, 104
Hoover Dam, 263, 269
Hoover, Herbert, 217, 249, 251-252, 254, 262-265, 287, 302
Hopkins, Harry L., 269
House, Edward M., 213, 223
Howells, William Dean, 165, 169, 199
Huerta, Victoriano, 197
Hughes, Charles Evans, 137, 214, 249, 251, 287-288, 289
Hull, Cordell, 293, 295, 300, 302, 303, 328
Humphrey, George, 399
Humphrey, Hubert, 402-403, 420, 425-426
Hungary, 370

Ickes, Harold L., 269, 382
Idaho, 43
Immigration to the United States, 25-32, 283-284
 contributions of immigrants, 31
Indian Reorganization Act, 50
Indian nations, end of, 46-51
Indochina, 365-366; *see also* Vietnam
Industrial growth, in the United States, 63ff
Inland Waterways Commission, 143
Internal Security Act, 387
International Court of Justice, 120, 350
International Garment Workers' Union, 137
Internationalism, 281ff
Interstate Commerce Act, 101
Interstate Commerce Commission, 103, 142, 156
Irish in the United States, 26
Iron Curtain, 356
Isolationism in the United States, 300-304
Italy, 207, 224
 and Fascism, 289ff
 invades Ethiopia, 293
 surrender of, 336

Jackson, Andrew, 112
James, Henry, 165
James, William, 127, 162
Japan, 114-115, 188, 208, 287-288, 295-296, 353-354, 428
 immigration to the United States, 30
 imperialist expansion, 179
 militarism in, 291-293
 Russo-Japanese War, 192
 surrender of, 341
Jefferson, Thomas, 110
Jenner, Edward, 388
"Jim Crow," 22
Johns Hopkins University, 163
Johnson, Andrew, 12-13, 15, 381
 impeachment trial of, 16, 17

Index 461

Johnson, Hiram W., 137, 229-230, 249
Johnson, Hugh, 270
Johnson, Lyndon, 191, 366, 402-404, 416, 418-424
Johnson, Tom Loftin, 137
Johnson Debt Default Act, 301
Jones Act, 187
Jones, Samuel M., 137
Jordan, David Starr, 198
Juarez, Benito, 117

Kansas-Nebraska Bill, 110
Kefauver, Estes, 391
Kellogg, Frank B., 252, 289
Kellogg-Briand Pact, 288-289
Kelly, Oliver H., 81
Kennedy, John F., 392, 402-404, 409-418
  assassination of, 417
Kennedy, Robert F., 412-413, 420, 423
  assassination of, 424
Kent State University, 430
Kerensky, Alexander, 219
Khrushchev, Nikita, 365, 370-373, 402, 414-415
King, Martin Luther, 378, 398, 404, 413, 421, 423
King, William Lyon Mackenzie, 323
Knights of Labor, 76
Knowland, William E., 288
"Know-Nothing" Party, 26
Knox, Philander C., 195, 199
Korea, 341, 354-355
Korean War, 361, 363
Ku Klux Klan, 20, 22, 245-246

Labor, 74-79
Lafayette Escadrille, 212
La Follette, Robert, 137, 157, 214, 229, 242
La Guardia, Fiorello, 244, 300
Laissez-faire, 63, 127
Land speculation, 248
Landon, Alfred M., 276
Lansing, Robert, 223
Laos, 416
Lawrence, T. E., 227
Lawson, W., 136
League of Nations, 225-226, 228, 250
Lebanese-Iraq crisis, 369
Lend-Lease Bill, 327
Lenin, N., 219
Leningrad, 327
Leopold of Belgium, 321
Leo XIII, Pope, 129
Lewis, John L., 243, 271
Lewis, Sinclair, 235, 242
Liberal Republicans, 93, 96
"Liberty Loans," 217
Libya, 325
Lincoln, Abraham, 12, 45, 87-88

Lindbergh, Charles, 240-242
Lippmann, Walter, 223, 244
Little Rock, Arkansas, 397
Lloyd George, David, 224
Lodge, Henry Cabot, 179-182, 186, 213, 223, 229, 249
Lodge, Henry Cabot, 402, 404
London, Jack, 165
Long, Huey P., 301
López, Narciso, 110
Lusitania, sinking of, 212-213
Lytton Report, 292

Madero, Francisco, 197
Maginot Line, 297
Mahan, Alfred Thayer, 179, 181, 184
Maine, sinking of, 181
Malenkov, Georgy, 365
Manchuria, 291-292
Manifest Destiny, 109
Mann-Elkings Act, 156
Manpower Development and Training Act, 412
Mao Tse-tung, 341, 355, 365, 372, 387
Marcuse, Herbert, 431
Marne, battle of the, 207
Marshall, George C., 333, 355, 357-358, 363, 389-390
Marshall, Thurgood, 396, 413
Marshall Plan, 357-358, 384
Masaryk, Jan, 359
Masaryk, Thomas, 227, 297
Mason, James, 115
Mason, John Y., 110
Maximilian of Austria, 117
McAdoo, William Gibbs, 217
MacArthur, Douglas, 265, 329, 341, 353, 361-363, 387, 389-390
McCarran-Walter Act, 387
McCarthy, Eugene, 420-423
McCarthy, Joseph, 373, 388-389, 390, 392, 393-395
McDonald, John, 91
McKinley Tariff Act, 104, 130, 181
McKinley, William, 181-182, 184, 186-187, 192
McLuhan, Marshall, 431
Meat Inspection Act, 143
Meat packing industry, 69
Medicare, 412, 421
Mellon, Andrew W., 251
Mencken, Henry L., 242, 246, 390
Mexican War, 109
Mexico, 111, 116-118, 197-198
Midway, battle of, 330
Millay, Edna St. Vincent, 244
Miller, David Hunter, 223
Miller, Thomas W., 250
Millis, Walter, 301
Minimum wage, 277-278, 386
Missionaries, 112, 113
"Molly Maguires," 77

Molotov, Vyacheslav, 317
Monroe Doctrine, 118, 180, 188, 190
Montana, 43
Montgomery, Bernard, 330, 337
Montgomery bus boycott, 398
Morgan, J. P., 70, 71-72, 89, 182, 196, 211, 244
Morgenthau Plan, 333
Morley, Raymond, 267
Morocco, 195
Morrill Act, 56, 163
Movies, 237-238, 431
Muckrakers, 136
Mugwumps, 100
Munich agreement, 297-300, 315
Mussolini, Benito, 289-291, 321, 325, 336
My Lai, massacre at, 429

Nagasaki, bombing of, 341
Napoleon III, 116-117
Nasser, Gamal Abdel, 367-369, 428
National Association for the Advancement of Colored People (NAACP), 169, 396
National Defense Act, 323
National Farmers' Alliance, 81
National Greenback Party, 96
National Labor Reform Party, 96
National Labor Relations Board, 266
National Labor Union, 76
National Recovery Administration (NRA), 270-271
National Security Council, 384
National Socialist German Workers' party, *see* Nazism
National Union Convention, 15
National Urban League, 169
Nazism, 290ff
Nazi-Soviet pact, 317
Negroes, 395-399
  black riots, 419, 421-422
  in cities, 378-379
  after Civil War, 10, 13-15, 18-19, 23
  and progressivism, 167-169
  in sports, 384
Neutrality Acts, 293, 302
Nevada, 43
New Deal, 235, 265-278
New Frontier, 410-417
New Mexico, 43, 58
Newspapers, 181
New York Central, 67
Nez Percé War, 49
Nhu, Madame, 416
Nicaragua, 111, 196
Nimitz, Chester, 339
Nisei, 379
Nixon, Richard M., 391-392, 401, 402, 404, 425-426, 429
Normandy, invasion of, 337
Norris, Frank, 70, 165

Norris, George, 273
North Atlantic Treaty Organization (NATO), 358-359, 393
Northern Pacific railroad, 65
Nuremberg Trials, 352
Nye, Gerald P., 301

Oil industry, 68, 71, 73
Okinawa, battle of, 340
Oliver, James, 57
"Open Door" policy, 192, 288, 292
Operation Overload, 336
Opium War, 113
Oregon Trail, 39
Organic Act, 187
Orlando, Vittorio, 224
Orwell, George, 128
Ostend Manifesto, 110
Oswald, Lee Harvey, 417
O'Sullivan, John L., 110

Pacific Railway Act, 45
Palestine, 227
Palmer, A. Mitchell, 244, 249
Palmer, John M., 133
Palmerston, Lord, 115
Panama Canal, 188-190
Panama Revolution, 189
Panay, sinking of, 302
Panic of 1857, 43, 55
Panic of 1893, 25, 105, 129
Panic of 1873, 25, 55, 94
Paris Conference, 223-229
Parks, Rosa, 398
Patten, Simon Nelson, 127
Patton, George S., 336-337, 339
Payne-Aldrich Bill, 157, 161
Peace Corps, 410
Peace Movements, 198-199, 427, 430
Peace of Paris, 225-229
Pearl Harbor, attack on, 329
Pendleton Act, 99
Perry, Matthew C., 114
Pershing, John J., 198, 219
Pétain, Henry Philippe, 322
Philippine War, 186-187
Pierce, Franklin, 110-111, 112
Pinchott, Gifford, 157
Pingree, Hagen S., 137
Platt Amendment, 185-186
Poland, invasion of, 316, 318
Polk, James K., 110
Pollution, 431-432
Pools, 72
Populist movement, 23, 130-133, 135
Portsmouth Conference, 192-193
Potsdam Conference, 350-351, 381
Pound, Ezra, 242
Powderly, Terence V., 76
Powers, Francis Gary, 371
Progressive Party, 157; *see also* Bull Moose Party

Progressivism, 135-143, 155-172
Prohibition, 169-170
Prohibition National party, 156, 169
Propaganda, 210-211, 218
Public education, 162
Public Works Administration (PWA), 269
Pueblo incident, 423
Pulitzer, Joseph, 31, 181
Pullman Strike, 79
Pure Food and Drug Act, 143

Quarantine Speech, 303-304
Quitman, John, 110

Radical Reconstruction, *see* Reconstruction
Radical Republicans, 12, 13, 15-16, 19, 22, 126
Radio, 237-238, 316
Railroads, 44-46, 51, 55, 65-67, 102-103
Railroads strike of 1877, 77
Raushenbusch, Walter, 129
Recession of 1937, 277
Reclamation Act, 143
Reconstruction, 11-25, 88
  military reconstruction, 16
  white resistance to, 20-21
Reconstruction Finance Corporation, 264
Red River War, 49
Reform Darwinists, 127, 135
Reform movements, 125ff
  state and municipal government, 138
Remarque, Erich Maria, 301
Republican party, 87-88, 100, 156-157, 382; *see also* Radical Republicans
Reuther, Walter, 272
Revels, Hiram, 19
Reynolds, Robert, 301
Rhee, Syngman, 354
Ribbentrop, Joachim von, 317
Ridgway, Matthew B., 363
Riis, Jacob, 31
Roberts, Edmund, 112-113
Roberts, Owen, 277
Robinson, James H., 164
Rockefeller, John D., 67, 69, 71, 244, 260
Rockefeller, Nelson, 402, 425
Rolling Stones, 423
Rommel, Erwin, 326, 330, 337
Roosevelt Corollary, 190-191
Roosevelt, Franklin D., 231, 249-250, 265-278, 295, 300-301, 302, 316, 319, 322, 324, 332, 333-336, 349-350, 401
Roosevelt, Theodore, 31, 139-143, 155, 169, 179, 181, 183-184, 187-195, 213-214

Root, Elihu, 194, 199
Root-Takahira agreement, 195
Rosenberg, Julius and Ethel, 388
Ross, Nellie Taylor, 243
Rural Electrification Agency, 276
Russell, Charles E., 136
Russia, 192, 199, 288; *see also* Soviet Union
Russo-Japanese War, 192
Ruth, Babe, 236

Sacco-Vanzetti case, 244
Salvation Army, 136
Samoan Islands, 180, 184
Santa Anna, Antonio, 110
Santa Fe Trail, 39
Santo Domingo, 90-91, 119; *see also* Dominican Republic
Schine, David, 393-395
Schlieffen Plan, 207
Schurz, Carl, 31, 97
Scopes trial, 244-245
"Scalawags," 18
Sectionalism, decline of, 11
  on the frontier, 38
Securities and Exchange Commission, 276
Sedition Act, 218
Seidel, Emil, 137
Selective Service Act, 216
Seward, William Henry, 116-117, 119-120
Seymour, Horatio, 19
Sheridan, Phillip, 117
Sherman, John, 98
Sherman Anti-Trust Act, 79, 103, 142, 412
Sherman Silver Purchase Act, 104, 130
"Short ballot," 139
Shotwell, James T., 223
Siegfried Line, 317
Sinclair, Upton, 69, 136
Sino-Japanese War, 295-296
Sioux, 47, 49
Sitting Bull, 49
Slidell, John, 115
Slums, 25, 27
Smith, Alfred E., 253-254
Smith-Hughes Act, 164
Smith-Lever Act, 164
Social Darwinists, 72, 127, 205
Social Security system, 275-276, 386
Soil Conservation Act, 273
"Solid South," 92
Somme, battle of the, 207
Soulé, Pierre, 110
South Dakota, 43
Southeast Asia Treaty Organization (SEATO), 366-367
Southern Pacific railroad, 65
Soviet Union, 303, 317, 326-327, 355-373

Index 463

in World War II, 317-343
Spain, 180, 182-184, 294-295
Spanish-American War of 1898, 180, 182-184
Spanish Civil War, 294-295
Specie Resumption Act, 95
Speculation in stocks, 260
Spoils system, 98
Squatters, 55
Stalin, Joseph, 326, 333-336
Stalingrad, 331
"Stalwarts," 97, 100
Standard Oil Company, 69, 71, 73
Stanford, Leland B., 45
Stanton, Henry B., 17
Stassen, Harold, 393
Steagall, Henry, 267
Steel industry, 67-68
Steffens, Lincoln, 136, 199
Steinbeck, John, 273
Stephens, Uriah S., 76
Stevens, Thaddeus, 12, 15
Stevenson, Adlai, 391, 402-403, 417
Stilwell, Joseph, 339
Stimson, Henry L., 292
Stock market crash of 1929, 259-261
Strategic Air Command (SAC), 400
Strikes, 77, 79, 272
Strong, Josiah, 178
Suez War, 368-369
Sullivan, Louis H., 165
Sumner, Charles, 12, 120
Sumner, William Graham, 179
Sunday, Billy, 244
Supreme Court of the United States, 22, 102, 164, 396-397, 432
  "packing of," 276-277
Swift, Gustavus F., 69

Taft, Robert A., 316, 323, 383, 388, 391
Taft, William H., 155, 156-158, 193, 195-196
Taft-Hartley Labor-Management Relations Act, 387
Taft-Katsura Memorandum, 194
Tarbell, Ida M., 136
Tariff Act of 1816, 64
Tariffs, 94-95, 101-102, 104-105, 160-161, 284-285
Tax Reduction Act, 419
Taylor, Maxwell D., 416
Teapot Dome scandal, 251
Teheran Conference, 333-334
Television, 377, 404, 432
Teller, Henry, 185
Tennessee, 15
Tennessee Valley Authority, 273-274, 400
Third Reich, 294
Thurmond, Strom, 385
Tilden, Samuel J., 22, 91-92
Tillman, Benjamin, 198
Tito, Marshall, 364
Tojo, Hideki, 329
Toscanini, Arturo, 31
Trade Agreement Act, 303
Trade unions, 75-77
Treaty of Paris (1898), 184, 186
Treaty of Washington, 120
Trent affair, 115
Triple Alliance, 204-205
Triple Entente, 205
Trujillo, Rafael, 197
Truman Doctrine, 356-357, 384
Truman, Harry S., 350, 355ff, 362-363, 379, 380-390
Trusts, 73, 142
Tugwell, Rexford, 267
Turkey, 208
Tuskegee Institute, 168
Twain, Mark, 165, 199
"Tweed Ring," 92
"Twenties," 235-254
Tydings, Millard, 388
Tyler, John, 113

U-boats, 209, 212-213
U-2 incident, 371
Underwood Tariff Bill, 161
UNESCO, 350
Union Pacific railroad, 46, 65
Unions, 75-77, 271-272
United Arab Republic, 369
United Mine Workers, 137, 141, 243
United Nations, 334, 335, 349-350
United States Steel Corporation, 71
U'ren, William S., 138

Vandenburg, Arthur, 323, 350, 384
Vanderbilt, Cornelius, 66, 68, 89
Veblen, Thorstein, 127
Verdun, battle of, 207
Versailles Treaty, 225-227, 229
Veterans' demands, 102
Vichy France, 322
Viet Cong, 416
Viet Nam, 355, 416
  war in, 409, 421-422, 426-427
Villa, Francisco, 198
Villard, Oswald Garrison, 169
Volstead Act, 267

Wade-Davis Manifesto, 12, 15
Wages and Hours Law, 277
Wagner Acts, 271
Wald, Lillian D., 136
Walker, William, 110
Wallace, George C., 413, 425
Wallace, Henry C., 251, 272, 380, 383-385
War debts, 285-286
War, glorification of, 178
War Industries Board, 217
Ward, Lester F., 127
Warren, Earl, 385, 396
Washington, Booker, T., 31, 167-168
Washington Arms Conference, 251, 287-288
Watson, Thomas E., 156
Weaver, James B., 96, 132
Weaver, Robert, 413
Weimar Republic, 293
West Germany, 352
Weyerhauser, Frederick, 30
"Whiskey Ring," 91
White, Henry L., 223
White, William Allen, 322
Wilhelm II, Kaiser, 188, 205
Wilkie, Wendell L., 323-324
Wilkins, Roy, 396
Wilson-Gorman Tariff Act, 105, 181
Wilson, Woodrow, 139, 159-162, 167, 196-198, 210-231
Women, 243
  education for, 164
  rights for, 170-172
  voting rights for, 171
Wood, Leonard, 249
Workingman's Party, 30
Works Progress Administration (WPA), 269-270
World War I, 203-231
  American neutrality in, 210-214
  cost of, 220-221
  home front, 216-218
  Paris peace conference, 223-229
  propaganda, 210-211, 218
World War II, 315-343
  adjustment to peace, 379-380
  settlements after, 341-343, 350-354
  United States role in, 327ff
Wright, Frank Lloyd, 165-166
Wright, Jonathan J., 18
Wyoming, 43

Yalta Conference, 333-336
Youth, alienation of, 429
Youth Corps, 421
Ypres, battle of, 207
Yugoslavia, 227, 325, 364

Zapata, Emilio, 198
Zimmerman, Alfred, 215

464   Index